Dictionary of
COMPUTING

Dictionary of COMPUTING

Data Communications
Hardware and Software Basics
Digital Electronics

Edited by
FRANK J. GALLAND
Datology Press Ltd, Windsor, England

JOHN WILEY & SONS
Chichester · New York · Brisbane · Toronto · Singapore

Copyright © 1982 by Datology Press Ltd.

Reprinted 1983

All rights reserved.

No part of this book may be reproduced by any means, nor transmitted, nor translated into a machine language without the written permission of the publisher.

British Library Cataloguing in Publication Data:

Galland, Frank J.
    Dictionary of computing.
    1. Computer—Dictionaries
    2. Electronic dataprocessing—Dictionaries
    I. Title
    001.64'03'21   QA76.15

    ISBN 0 471 10468 X (Cloth)
    ISBN 0 471 10469 8 (Paper)

Produced for John Wiley & Sons by Datology Press.

Printed and bound in Great Britain by
Robert Hartnoll Ltd. Bodmin Cornwall

Preface

This dictionary is designed to assist the student of programming, systems analysis, operating, or field engineering to obtain more knowledge from the instruction manuals, books, magazines, and product specifications that he/she will encounter. It is intended to be useful to both beginning and advanced students. The dictionary may also be useful to technical writers, instructors, managers, members of data processing staff, and others who have a need to deal with the terms and technology of modern computing.

The dictionary has been compiled by British and American technical authors with extensive current experience in writing instruction manuals and training manuals in the fields of mainframe and minicomputer software, microprocessor systems, word processing, and data communications hardware and software. Valuable assistance has been provided by British Telecom and the U.K. training departments of International Computers Limited, Digital Equipment Corp., and Honeywell Information Systems in arranging for members of staff to read and comment on relevant portions of the typescript in progress.

Many manufacturers of computers, computer equipment, and supplies have assisted by providing glossaries, product specifications, and instruction manuals. We wish to particularly thank International Business Machines, International Computers, Honeywell Information Systems, Digital Equipment Corp. Racal-Milgo, Hewlett Packard, Data Recording Instruments, Control Data Corp., Texas Instruments, Computer Technology, Ltd., Data General Corp., 3M Data Recording Products, and Motorola Semiconductor Products. Major inputs have been obtained from books/documents produced by the International Organization for Standardization (ISO), the Consultative

Committee on International Telephone and Telegraph (CCITT), the British Standards Institution (BSI), the National Computing Centre (NCC), and the Infotech State-of-the-Art Reports. Many entries have been obtained from the British and American computer press; particular mention is due to Systems International, Datamation, New Electronics, EDN, Computer Weekly, and Computing.

We have attempted to include the 'computer room' and jargonistic usages as well as the terms of more formal application. An illustration is provided where it can be of help in explaining an operation, device, or concept. Extensive cross-referencing is provided to assist in following a topic of interest or in locating supporting entries. Every effort has been made to ensure that definitions are accurate, clearly written, and understandable without prior knowledge of the subject.

Any errors of fact or interpretation are the responsibility of the Editors and Datology Press and not of the sources of information.

Windsor, April 1982

THE EDITORS

General Editor: *Frank J. Galland*

Associate and Contributing Editors:

    Christopher M. Johnson

    Erica W. Holding

    Peter J. Bloxsom

Structure and Use of the Dictionary

The word list - The word list has been obtained from the publications of recognised international organisations, the British and American computer and electronics press, and the product specifications and instruction manuals of the major software development organisations and manufacturers of computers, computer peripherals, data communications equipment, data media, and microelectronic devices. The dictionary contains more than nine thousand definitions.

Definitions - The language of definition is kept as simple as possible, consistent with completeness and precision and the avoidance of repetition of more basic material contained in other entries. Where applicable, cross references are provided to identify the location of more basic information. All specialised or technical terms used in definitions are, themselves, defined elsewhere in the dictionary.

Basics - Often the understanding of a computer or electronic operation requires a degree of familiarity with more basic principles. A number of basic entries are, therefore, provided to improve the utility of the dictionary for persons who may lack this familiarity. For examples of basic entries, see *electricity, magnet,* and *binary.*

Current and historical usage - Unless of significant historical interest, a term that is no longer in current use has been excluded from the word list. Unfortunately, it is not always possible to determine when a technology or practice has been finally abandoned and, where doubt exists, an entry is treated as current. When of historical interest, but no longer in common use, this is indicated in the language of definition. For examples, see *magnetic drum, store and forward,* and *delay line memory.*

Abbreviations - Treatment of abbreviations varies widely among publishers and equipment manufacturers, and between the U.S. and the U.K. For consistency, most abbreviations are in capital letters and without periods (a solidus may be included). If the abbreviation has current acceptance in another form, it is included in parentheses immediately following. The first (or only) parenthetical form is usually the one of widest acceptance. For examples, see *AC, BPS, CL,* and *OPS.*

Substandard usage - No judgements are made as to merit, or relative merit, of terms except that a term that would be considered questionable by many computer practitioners may be so identified by a 'sometimes' or 'has been'. For examples of treatment, see *direct access, graunch, bucket brigade,* and *command (def. 5).*

Terms of narrow application - A term that is used by a single manufacturer (or, possibly, by a small minority of manufacturers) is usually so identified by the term 'in some systems'. For examples, see *index field* and *instruction processor.*

Synonyms and equivalent terms - When two terms are synonyms or identify essentially the same unit of hardware or software, usually only a single definition is provided and this definition identifies the other terms following an 'Also'. The other terms have individual entries with a reference to the 'main' entry. For examples, see *electron tube* and *hesitation.*

Terms with multiple meanings - All known meanings of a term that apply to computing and related fields are included. When the meanings are closely related and/or when second and subsequent meanings are of infrequent application, the definitions are numbered within a single entry. The ordering is by approximate frequency of use. When there are two or more reasonably significant meanings that are not closely related, separate entries are used. For examples, see *array, block, key,* and *filter.*

Examples of context - An example of context is given wherever the correct (common) usage of a term is not obvious from the definition. Such terms are often 'spoken' or jargonistic. Multiple examples are also used to indicate differences in application. For examples, see *active,*
delete, package, and the several *load* entries.

Examples - Examples are provided to show differences between similar meanings, to indicate type or class, and to help explain operations. A 'work-through' example is provided for each mathematical operation. See *automatic, bind, binary arithmetic,* and *Hamming code.*

Cross references - A reference to another entry is provided following a 'See' at the end of a definition. A reference may be to a more basic term, to specific entries included in a generic term, to a synonym that includes a full definition, or to an entry that defines a related item or concept. For examples, see *printer, block parity,* and *clock.*

Illustrations - An attempt has been made to provide an illustration wherever it would be helpful in explaining a device, electronic circuit, operation, or concept. For examples, see *analogue loop test, band, liquid crystal display,* and *operational amplifier.*

Tables - Tables are provided to illustrate number systems, logic operations, and codes. For examples, see *hexadecimal, biquinary code, truth table,* and the *Logic Operation Table.*

Collating sequence - Spaces collate before letters; for example, *answer tone* collates before *answerback.* The solidus and hyphens used to form prefixes do not collate; for example, *de-suspend* collates after *destructive read.* All other hyphens collate after spaces; for example, *high-threshold logic* collates before *highlight.*

Indexing - Each right-hand (odd numbered) page contains a thumb index with the first letters of the first entry on the facing left-hand (even numbered) page and of the last entry on the indexed page. This indexing method permits rapid location of required entries. (Individual entries must be checked to locate an entry in a sequence of pages in which the first letters remain unchanged.)

A

abacus A device for performing addition and subtraction by moving beads (counters) on rods. It is a biquinary device; a bead above a dividing bar is equal to five beads below the bar. Each rod holds the beads that total a decimal digit and, as in conventional representation, the leftmost rod holds the most significant digit. If a decimal point is required, the position can be marked or remembered. A bead is selected (used to form a digit) by moving it towards the bar. Whenever a rod holds '10',

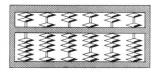 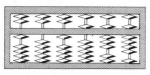

it is cleared (by moving its beads toward the frame) and a single, lower bead is moved towards the bar on the next rod to the left. In the llustration on the left, the bead positions represent 94835. The illustration on the right shows the positions after adding 6754. The device shown is the Chinese 'suan-pan'. The Japanese 'sorobon' has only four beads below the bar and a single bead above it and, thus, eliminates the (unnecessary) facility for holding '10' on a rod.

abandon With respect to an operation; to terminate it before completion; to deallocate resources and leave it in an unfinished state. See *abend; abort.*

abend *ABnormal END of task.* Termination of a task prior to its completion because of an error condition that cannot be resolved by the recovery facilities that operate during execution. See *abort; recovery; error; restart.*

abnormal condition Any condition (hardware or software) that requires correction before processing can continue

abnormal end of task See *abend.*

abnormal ending See *abend.*

abnormal termination With respect to processing; termination before results are produced or before the usual end condition is reached.

abort (1) To discontinue program execution, release allocated main storage, and close files at a point during execution other than a normal exit point. It is usually done because of an error condition that prevents further execution. **(2)** To terminate any operation prematurely. See *abandon.*

ABS *Air Bearing Surface.*

absolute addressing (1) The addressing of main storage locations by their absolute addresses; the method of a control unit after any required address modification has been completed. See *address modification; direct addressing.* **(2)** Addressing in which instructions in object code are absolute addresses. **(3)** The addressing mode of absolute coding.

absolute coding Also *absolute programming; specific coding.* Source coding that makes use of no programming language;

coding in which the programming input consists of absolute addresses and operators in their machine code (bit pattern) form. It may be used to code a patch or to write a (simple) program for a microprocessor.

absolute data In computer graphics; display data in which all display elements are expressed as coordinates (X and Y displacements) from a common origin. See *relative data; vector scan.*

absolute error (1) The algebraic difference between a value that is in error and the true or correct value; the error described by its magnitude and without considering whether the error value is greater or less than the true or correct value. **(2)** An error expressed in the same units as the value to which it relates (and not as a ratio or percentage). See *relative error.*

absolute generation number a generation number in sequence from the first generation number assigned to a file; it is incremented by one each time a new generation is created. See *generation.*

absolute instruction An effective instruction; an instruction in final, executable form.

absolute language Machine language.

absolute operator In an instruction; an operator that is in its executable, machine code form.

absolute program A non-relocatable program; an object program in which the addresses are absolute (hardware) addresses. See *absolute address; relocatable program.*

absolute programming Absolute coding.

absolute term A term whose value is not affected by relocation of the program in which it is contained.

absolute value (1) An absolute term. **(2)** A value considered only with respect to magnitude and not to sign.

absolute vector In computer graphics; a vector (line segment) with end coordinates specified as X and Y displacements from a point designated as the origin.

absolute zero The temperature ($-273°$ C.) at which molecular activity ceases; the temperature just below the boiling point of hydrogen. See *cryogenic memory.*

abstract symbol A symbol without a generally established meaning or significance; a symbol that must be defined for the application in which it is used.

AC (A.C.) *Alternating Current.*

ACC *ACCumulator.*

acceleration time (1) With respect to a magnetic tape access; that part of access time in which the tape speed is increased to the speed required for reading or writing. **(2)** With respect to a magnetic disc drive that has been stopped; the time required for the spindle to reach the speed at which normal read and write operations can be performed.

accept By a task; to receive an input without a detected error.

access (1) With respect to a unit of code or data; to locate it in computer storage and use it in processing. The term may be applied to action by a user, user program, member of DP staff, or system software and the unit of code or data can be anything from a subroutine to a data base. **(2)** To identify a backing storage location and a main storage location and initiate a transfer from the backing storage location to the main storage location. In this sense, the term applies to an action by user program or system software and refers to the transfer of such units as blocks, buckets, pages, and segments. See *direct access.* **(3)** Also *address.* By an instruction during decoding; to produce an address of a storage location to or from which a transfer is to be made. See *address (Data transfers); reference.* **(4)** By a control unit; to receive or derive two addresses and transfer bit patterns between them. Unless otherwise indicated, one address is in main storage and the other is of a control unit or arithmetic unit register. See *store; fetch.* **(5)** With respect to a file; to write records to it or read records from it. See *sequential access; serial access.* **(6)** With respect to a storage medium; the physical operation of writing bits to it or reading bits from it.

access arm Also *seek arm.* The element of a movable-head magnetic disc unit that supports one or more read/write heads and is moved by the servo unit when changing cylinders. See *magnetic disc unit.*

access bits Also *access control bits.* Bits associated with an identifier of a volume or unit of code or data (page; segment) in an index or table to specify the type of access (read; write; execute) permitted. See *access restriction; use bits.*

access control (1) The process of defining and limiting the access rights of individuals or programs to the data in computer storage. See *access right; access restriction; storage protection; access control register.* **(2)** The process of limiting the rights of individuals to enter areas or use equipment.

access control levels See *storage protection; access control register.*

access control register (ACR) In some systems; a register used to hold dynamically changeable values that specify the access rights of concurrent programs during the various phases of their execution. For example, during most of its processing time a program may have a high number that restricts it to its own code and data, while, during certain phases, it may have a lower number that permits it to access certain system routines or shareable segments. (The lowest numbers that permit broad access are reserved for the operating system.) Such numbers may be termed **access control levels**. See *protection rings; storage protection.*

access frequency loading The ordering of records in magnetic disc files in such a way that those most frequently accessed are in storage locations with short access times. Typically, it involves placing such records in home locations on the same track or cylinder to reduce seeks and table lookups.

access method A method by which an item of data is located in storage. See *access mode.*

access mode (1) The type of physical access being performed (read; write; execute). **(2)** The type of file access being performed (serial; sequential; skip sequential). **(3)** Access right (def. 3).

access path A sequence of pointers that can be followed to access items of a certain type in a data structure. See *pointer; chain; net; tree.*

access restriction (1) A limitation on the code or data that can be accessed by a program during execution. **(2)** A limitation on the type of access that can be made to a volume or other unit of storage; the usual ones are 'read' and 'execute'. **(3)** A limitation on the use of computer equipment or presence in computer areas.

access right (1) The right of an individual or group to use the resources of a computer system; for example, to have batch jobs run or to make enquiries via a terminal. **(2)** The right of a user or program to access a particular unit of code or data. See *storage protection.* **(3)** Also *access mode.* The type of access permitted to a program with respect to a unit of code or data; the usual ones are 'execute', 'read', 'write', 'read/write', and 'append'.

access time (1) The time between receipt of an instruction in a control unit register and the completion of transferring a bit pattern between two internal storage locations, at least one of which is identified in the instruction. **(2)** The time between the generation of an address of a location in backing storage by a control unit or peripheral controller and the completion of a data transfer between the location and main storage. **(3)** The time for a read signal to go from the external interface of a storage unit or device to the storage medium and to read the first bit (or first bit pattern, if reading is bit-parallel) back out across the interface. The following are some representative access times: (A single figure indicates that the storage is experimental or no longer in common use.)

BIPOLAR SEMICONDUCTOR
Emitter-Coupled Logic (ECL)	15-30 ns.
Schottky TTL	25-50 ns.
Transistor-Transistor Logic (TTL)	30-90 ns.
Integrated Injection Logic (I^2L)	30-150 ns.
Resistor-Transistor Logic (RTL)	40-100 ns.
Diode-Transistor Logic (DTL)	50-100 ns.
ROM (Mask programmed)	25-50 ns.
PROM (Fusible link)	40-100 ns.
Memory cycle (TTL RAM)	300-500 ns.

UNIPOLAR SEMICONDUCTOR
Gallium arsenide	100 ps.
N-Channel MOS (NMOS) Static RAM	55-500 ns.
N-Channel MOS (NMOS) Dynamic RAM	150-400 ns.
Complementary MOS (CMOS) Static RAM	180-350 ns.
P-Channel MOS (PMOS) Static RAM	300-1000 ns.
ROM (NMOS Mask programmed)	50-80 ns.
PROM (Fusible link)	50-100 ns.
EPROM (FAMOS, U.V. erasable)	300-600 ns.
EAROM (MNOS)	350-2000 ns.
Memory cycle (NMOS Static RAM)	350-650 ns.

MAGNETIC
Plated Wire	125-250 ns
Three-dimensional Core	200-400 ns.
Two-dimensional Core	500-750 ns.
Thin Film	250-400 ns.
Memory cycle (3D Core)	500-1000 ns.

BEAM ACCESSED
Holographic	20 ns.
BEAMOS	50 ns.
Electrostatic	4-10 μs.
Photodigital	1-10 sec.

RECIRCULATING
  Cryogenic   10 ps.
  Charge Coupled Device   400-800 µs.
  Sonic Delay Line   750 µs.
  Bubble   4-20 ms.

MAGNETISABLE SURFACE
  Magnetic Drum   8-10 ms.
  Fixed-head Disc   8.3-12 ms.
  Movable-head Disc   30-75 ms.
  Flexible Disc   100-800 ms.
  Magnetic Card   100-450 ms.
  Magnetic Tape   1-50 sec.

accessor In a mass storage system; the mechanism that transports data cells between their storage locations and the read/write location.

account (1)A record of debits and credits to a particular customer or to some aspect of an organisation's operations; ('the Redfern account'; 'the Vehicle Operations account'). (2)A user; an individual or organisation to which computer services are supplied.

account number In some systems; a customer identification number.

accounting (1)The profession or activity involved in establishing and verifying financial records. (2)The operations by a computer operating system and/or operators relating to recording usage of computer resources for purposes of charging or debiting users.

accounting check digit A self-check digit.

accounting computer See *visible record computer*.

accounting machine A non-computerised, keyboard-actuated office machine used to perform calculations and prepare accounting records; for example, a billing machine or a tabulator.

accumulate (1)To gather together in one place. (2)To form the results of an operation in an accumulator.

accumulator (1)An arithmetic-unit register that has an associated full adder. It is used to hold operands and partial results when performing arithmetic and logic operations. See *register; adder*. (2)In some systems; a main storage location in which the results of arithmetic/logic operations are 'accumulated'.

ACK *ACKnowledge*. A transmission control character indicating that a block or message has been received without a detected error. See *NAK*.

acknowledge (1)By a terminal operator or computer; to send a character or other short message to indicate that the previous message has been received. (2)By a console operator; to press a key or otherwise indicate to an operating system that a message has been received. (3)By receiving hardware in a data link; to send a short message indicating that a message or block has been received without a detected error. See *ACK*.

acoustic Concerning audible sound and its generation, transmission, or use.

acoustic coupler An elementary low-speed modem used with an ordinary telephone to couple an asynchronous terminal (say, a Teletype) to a dialed circuit. When a call is connected, the handset is placed in a cradle on the device to send and receive data.

acoustic delay line A delay line in which signals move at the speed of sound through some medium such as mercury. See *delay line*.

acquisition See *data acquisition*.

ACR *Access Control Register*.

acronym A pronouncable 'word' made up of letters taken from a word or group of words (say, a name or phrase), usually in the order in which they appear. For example, 'COBOL' is an acronym formed from 'Common Business Oriented Language'. See *symbol; mnemonic*.

action paper Carbonless copy paper.

activate (1)To prepare a system or functional unit for use. (2)To place a unit of hardware or software into operation. (3)To execute a module of reentrant code.

active (1)Being used; ('an active line'; 'an active peripheral'). (2)Characterised by frequent use; ('an active file'). (3)Resident in main storage or being processed; ('an active program'; 'an active segment'). (4)Not passive; ('an active element').

active element See *element*.

active element group (a.e.g.) One storage cell or one logic gate (in an integrated circuit).

active job A job that is being processed or in the job queue.

active set See *virtual storage system—processing units*.

activity (1)That which is done or performed; ('a data control activity'). (2)A process. See *process (Processing unit)*.

actual address A real address. See *address*.

actual decimal point A decimal point that is represented by a coded character and thus occupies a byte or character of storage, as contrasted to an assumed decimal point. See *assumed decimal point*.

actual storage Also *real storage; physical storage*. Any hardware addressable storage in a virtual storage system.

A/D *Analogue to Digital*.

Ada A general-purpose, high-level language developed under U.S. military sponsorship and now available on many computers for scientific and industrial applications.

ADC *Analogue to Digital Converter*.

ADCCP *Advanced Data Communications Control Procedure*.

addend See *augend*.

adder (1) An element of an arithmetic unit that can add the contents (binary numbers) held in two registers. It may be a **carry-look-ahead adder** that adds the bits in all bit positions simultaneously or a **ripple-carry adder** (also **serial adder**) that adds the bits in the least-significant bit positions first and outputs the results to the next bit position with the operation performed in successively higher bit positions until the bits in all register positions have been added. Such an adder is shown in Fig. 1, it consists of multiple 'adders' by Def. 2. (2) A combining logic circuit that can input pulses representing bits and output pulses representing their sum. A **full adder** can input two bits and a carry bit (if there is one) and output a bit that represents their total plus a carry bit (if there is one) for the next stage of addition. A one-bit full adder is shown in Fig. 2. If A2 and B2 are both high (both represent 1-bits) then the only output is from AND-1 which is input to OR-1 to cause a high carry digit C3 which is input to the adder of next higher bit position. (Other inputs and results can be traced with the aid of the Truth Table.) A **half adder** is the same as a full adder except that it has no provision for outputting a carry digit.

address (Communications) The part of a message that identifies the intended recipient and/or the sender. See *interchange address; terminal address*.

address (Computer storage) A bit pattern that uniquely identifies a storage location, or a word, symbol, character, or number from which such a bit pattern can be derived. **absolute address** (1) An address in an instruction that is a hardware address (def. 1). (2) A hardware address (def. 1). **actual address** A real address. **base address** The lowest numbered location in a storage area; a value from which other addresses in the area are expressed as displacements. See *relative address*. **direct address** Also *one-level address*. An address in a machine code instruction that is converted to a hardware address in a single step (say, by adding it to a base address or applying an algorithm). **effective address** A hardware address (def. 1) obtained by address modification. See *presumptive address*. **hardware address** (1) Also *absolute address*. A bit pattern (binary number) that is interpretable by logic circuits in a control unit to set up a data transfer path to a location in main storage. (2) As definition 1 but including backing storage. **indirect address** Also *multilevel address*. An address in a machine code instruction that is a pointer to a location in a table or index that holds either an effective address or another pointer. See *address modification*. **physical address** A bit pattern interpretable by logic circuits in a control unit and/or peripheral controller to set up a data transfer path to a location in backing storage. **presumptive address** A symbolic address or an address in a machine code instruction that, when modified, produces an effective address. **real address** Also *actual address*. (1) A hardware address (def.

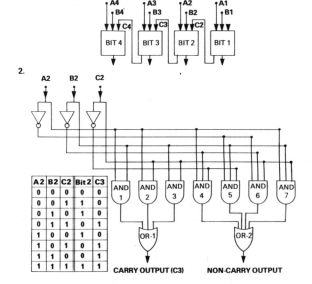

1); particularly in a virtual storage system. See *virtual storage addressing*. (2) An address other than a virtual address; a 'real address' (def. 1) or a physical address. **relative address** (1) In a machine code instruction; an address that is a displacement from another address. See *base address*. (2) In a low-level language; an address expressed as a displacement from another address; ('NAME + 6'). **relocatable address** An address that is intended to be changed to a (new) hardware address by applying a constant; for example, an address in a subroutine that is adjusted to make it relative to the base address of a program in which it is incorporated or an effective address that is changed when the module containing it is moved in main storage. **symbolic address** An address in source language coding; for example, 'TOTAL-A'; it is usually also a mnemonic. **virtual address** In a virtual storage system; any address other than a real or physical address. See *virtual storage addressing*.

address (Data transfers) Also, in some contexts, *access*. To identify a storage location and to initiate or effect a data transfer between it and some other location. The term may be used synonymously with 'access'; when the terms are differentiated, 'address' is location-oriented and 'access' is content-oriented; ('address a block on magnetic disc'; 'access a file').

address (Display) To cause a display element to appear on a display field; an electron beam 'addresses' points on the screen of a cathode ray tube. See *display; addressable point*.

address (Instruction) The place in a fixed-format instruction where an operand can be placed.

address mapping Address modification. See *mapping*.

address mapping table A mapping table.

address modification (1) Also *address computation; address transformation; address mapping*. An operation performed during execution in which an address in a machine code instruction is converted to a hardware address. When performed in a single step (as by adding a constant or applying an algorithm) it is **direct addressing** and when two or more steps are required (usually, table/index look-ups) it is **indirect addressing** (also **indirection**). See *pointer; modifier; index*. (2)Also *indexing*. The process of changing an operand address (usually, by incrementing a count) between successive performances of a loop in order to perform an operation on or with different operands. See *index register; loop*.

address register (1)A register that is used to hold an address; ('a current address register'). **(2)**In a movable-head magnetic disc unit; a register that holds the cylinder number to which the heads are positioned. See *seek*.

address space The range of addresses (virtual, relative, or absolute) used by, or assigned to, a program.

address syllable The part of a source language instruction that contains an operand.

address transformation (1)A control unit and/or peripheral controller operation of producing a backing storage address from an address in an instruction. (2)Address translation. (3)Address modification (def. 1).

address translation (1)A compiler or assembler operation of changing the form of an address, usually from symbolic to relative or virtual. See *bind*. (2)Address modification (def. 1).

addressable cursor A facility of a VDU that allows external (computer) positioning of the cursor by sending X-Y coordinates.

addressable point An element of a raster; the smallest unit of the display surface of a raster-scan VDU screen that can be addressed (made bright or left dark) by the electron beam. See *raster; display*.

addrout file A file produced by an internal sort of a relative record file; a file consisting of relative record numbers (disc addresses) in the new order for file updating or revision.

ADLC *Advanced Data Link Control.*

ADP *Automatic Data Processing.*

ADT (1)*Application-Dedicated Terminal.* **(2)***Active Disc Table.*

advanced data communications control procedure (ADCCP) A term applied to the operation of a data link using an advanced (SDLC; HDLC) protocol.

advanced data link control (ADLC) A link protocol as used in HDLC and SDLC systems.

advice language A language for communicating with a computer in which the system provides sophisticated guidance to a user to assist in locating items in a data base that are determined (directly or inferentially) to be of interest. See *conceptual language*.

AEG (1)*Allgemeine Elektricitats-Gesellschaft (AEG-Telefunken)* (Konstanz) **(2)**(a.e.g.) *Active Element Group.*

AFIPS *American Federation of Information Processing Societies.* (Montvale, New Jersey)

after journal (1) An after-look journal. **(2)**In some systems; a file identifying system resources and their permitted access/utilisation.

after-look journal A backup file to which changes are written for purposes of reconstructing a current master file in event of its corruption. See *before-look journal.*

after-look journalising When a file is updated; to record the new version of the updated parts in a journal file. See *journal; before-look journalising.*

agglomerate A defect in the magnetisable surface coating (say, on magnetic disc) consisting of a raised or thick area.

aggregate (1) A total. **(2)** A data aggregate.

aiming symbol A mark displayed on the screen of a graphics VDU and used in conjunction with a light pen to identify a point of interest.

air bearing surface (ABS) The contoured surface of the slider of a read/write head that supports the head on an air cushion in a hard-disc magnetic disc unit. See *head; fly; load.*

air boundary layer The air adjacent to a moving surface (magnetic disc) that is influenced by the surface texture and tends to move with the surface. See *fly; air cushion.*

air cushion The part of an air boundary layer that is 'trapped' between the rotating surface of a magnetic disc and the air bearing surface of a read/write head to support the head.

air gap The place in a magnet where the magnetic flux passes through air (or other non-ferrous medium). See *magnet.*

algebraic language A programming language in which many statements are constructed to resemble algebraic expressions; for example, FORTRAN and ALGOL.

ALGOL *ALGOrithmic Language.* A common programming language that makes extensive use of algorithms; it is used mainly for mathematical and scientific applications. The basic version is 'ALGOL 60' while 'ALGOL 68' is a more powerful version intended for general-purpose use.

algorithm A set of rules or procedural steps that are intended to be followed in sequence to solve a particular problem or to produce a particular result. In programming, it is usually implemented by a reentrant sequence of instructions.

algorithmic language A programming language with extensive algorithms; for example, FORTRAN or ALGOL.

alias (1) An alternate name or label by which an operating system recognises a data item, a sequence of instructions, or a device. **(2)** In a transmission by pulse code modulation; a spurious signal formed from harmonics of the signal frequency and the sample frequency.

alien (1) Not of the same manufacture as the other equipment; ('an alien computer'). **(2)** Not catered for by the facilities of the particular computer; ('an alien code').

aligned With respect to a data item in coordinate-addressable storage; placed so that its first or last bit is on an access-significant boundary. See *synchronised.*

allocatable space Also *free space.* Storage space available to an operating system for any purpose required.

allocation (1) The assignment of storage locations to programs. Unless otherwise indicated, the term, by this definition, refers to the assignment of main storage locations to user programs. The assignment of storage locations by their absolute (hardware) addresses is **absolute allocation**. A compiler function of assigning storage locations in relation to a common 'base address' is **relative allocation**. If the main storage assigned to a program remains unchanged during execution, it is **static allocation**. Allocation by an operating system to meet changing needs of programs in a multiprogramming system is **dynamic allocation**. **(2)** The assignment of any resource; for example, a peripheral, a communications line, or processing time.

allocation algorithm (1) An algorithm used to allocate space in primary storage to segments in a segmented virtual storage system. One such algorithm is **first fit** in which a new segment is placed in the first location (found in a free-space table) that is large enough to hold it. A **best fit** algorithm places a new segment in the smallest available space that is large enough to hold it. A **half-fit** algorithm places a new segment in the space that is closest to twice the size required to hold it. (The assumption is that segments are likely to be of about the same size during a particular phase of processing and the method thus leaves room for another segment of about the same size in the space.) See *partitioning; virtual storage partitioning.* **(2)** An algorithm for placing files on cylinders in magnetic disc storage.

allowance (1) The amount of a resource allocated to a user. **(2)** An unused portion of a budget. See *budget.*

alphabet (1) An ordered set of all the letters required to write a language, including any with diacritical marks (ä, ô) but not including punctuation marks. **(2)** A coded character set; for example, 'International Alphabet No. 2'.

alphabetic Of a group of characters; consisting only of letters or only of letters and spaces. See *numeric; alphanumeric.*

alphabetical order Of items consisting of letters or using letters as keys; arranged in the sequence in which the letters appear in the alphabet. See *numerical order; collating sequence.*

alphameric Alphanumeric.

alphamosaic A term applied to a display that can contain alphanumeric characters and simple graphics elements.

alphanumeric (1) Of a character set or subset; consisting of letters and numbers and, possibly, punctuation marks and symbols. **(2)** Of a character string; consisting of characters from an alphanumeric set or subset. (The term may be applied to such a string that consists only of letters or only of numbers.) See *alphabetic; numeric.*

alphanumeric code A code containing both letters and numbers.

alphanumeric display device An alphanumeric VDU.

alphanumeric VDU Also *character VDU*. A VDU that can display only alphanumeric characters. See *graphics VDU.*

alternate key (1) A secondary key. **(2)** An auxiliary key.

alternate routing In a communications system; the use of a secondary circuit to carry messages when the primary circuit is unavailable.

alternate track On a magnetic disc; an otherwise unused track that is available as a substitute for a primary track that is found defective. See *initialisation.*

alternating current (A.C.) An electrical current that flows first in one direction and then in the other and 'alternates' rapidly between the two. Such a current is generated by an **alternator** that consists, essentially, of a coil of wire that turns in a magnetic field with each end of the coil attached to a 'slipring' by which the current is taken off through brushes. Though the term refers to current, its generation is best illustrated by the voltage generated. (Current is proportional to voltage.) The figure shows basic alternator components and the coil A-B in successive positions during rotation; the dashed vertical lines represent the magnetic flux between the poles of the alternator. At Time 0, no flux is being 'cut' by the coil and, hence, no voltage is being generated and no current flows through the external load. As the coil turns, it begins to cut lines of flux and the voltage rises, as shown at Time 0.5. A current then flows from A, through the external load, and back to B. As the coil continues to turn, the voltage at A reaches a maximum positive with respect to B at Time 1. At this time, the coil is cutting flux at the maximum rate. (At the same time, the voltage at B is maximum negative with respect to A; it is customary to assume that one side of the coil is at constant zero voltage and that all changes take place at the other end, in this case, at A.) Further rotation of the coil to Time 2 again brings it to a position in which no voltage is generated. As the coil continues to rotate, it starts cutting flux in the opposite direction and reaches Time 3 at which the voltage at A is maximum negative with respect to B. Further rotation to Time 4 brings the coil back to

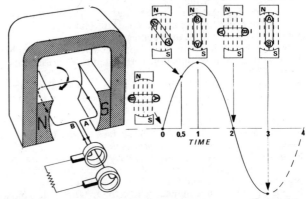

its starting point and one **cycle** of alternating current has been generated. The number of cycles generated per second is the **frequency** which is expressed in **Hertz** (Hz.) For example, the standard mains frequency in Europe is '50 Hz.' and in the U.S. it is '60 Hz.'. Alternating currents above about 400 Hz. are usually generated by 'oscillators' rather than rotating coils. See *sine wave; electricity; oscillator; direct current.*

alternator A generator that produces alternating current. See *alternating current.*

ALU *Arithmetic Logic Unit.*

AM *Amplitude Modulation.*

AMD *Advanced Micro Devices.* (Sunnyvale)

amend To change (to produce a better or more current version).

amendment A change or addition (to a file).

amendments file Also *changes file; update file; transaction file.* A file that contains changes that are to be used to update a master file. If, for example, the master file contains a parts inventory, the file would, typically, contain details of parts received and shipped during a certain period. Such a file may be prepared from source documents (say, weekly) by a data control department, or, in a transaction processing system, the changes may be written as they occur. See *update*.

American National Standards Institute (ANSI) An organisation that formulates and publishes standards for voluntary acceptance by U.S. industry.

amorphous memory A memory in which the storage cells consist of some material (tellerium alloy; chalcogenide) with two stable states, amorphous and crystalline, with different electrical characteristics. See *ovonic memory*.

ampere (I; amp.) The standard unit of electric current; it is equal to a flow of electrons produced by one volt through a resistance of one ohm. See *electricity; current*.

ampere-turn In an electromagnetic device (motor; electromagnet); a current of one ampere passing through one turn (once around the iron part) of a coil. It is an indicator of the magnetic flux produced; '20 ampere-turns' could, for example, be produced by 1 amp. flowing through 20 turns or 10 amps. flowing through two turns. See *magnet*.

amplifier A device or electronic circuit that is used to increase the strength (voltage; amplitude) of weak signals; for example, a repeater in a telephone line or a **read amplifier** used to increase the strength of the weak signals obtained when reading cores in core memory. In its simplest form, it consists of a transistor with the weak signal applied to the base and the stronger signal obtained at the collector or emitter. See *transistor*.

amplitude The strength (voltage) of a signal or pulse or the amount by which a generated wave exceeds its average value. Amplitude is usually expressed relatively in 'decibels'. When signals or waves are converted to sound (as by a radio or telephone) 'amplitude' is synonymous with 'volume'; the greater the amplitude the louder the sound. See *decibel*.

amplitude equalizer A circuit in a modem transmitter or receiver that compensates for line-induced amplitude distortion of signals. See *equalizer; statistical equalizer*.

amplitude modulation (AM) A common system of modulation in which speech or data is transmitted as changes in amplitude of a carrier wave; it is the usual system of radio transmission. Where used in data transmission, AM is usually used in conjunction with frequency modulation. See *modulation*.

AN *AlphaNumeric*.

A/N *AlphaNumeric*.

analogue A term applied to a system or device in which the output at a particular time is directly proportional to the input(s) at that time. (It is a system that provides little if any storage.) The output scale or representation need not be the same as that of the input(s). In analogue, the outputs and inputs can have any values between limits as contrasted to the situation in digital devices and systems in which all values within limits can be represented only by a finite number of discrete values. Consider, for example, an analogue voltmeter and a digital voltmeter, both of which register 15 V. If the voltage increases by 0.1 V., the needle of the analogue will make a small corresponding (analogue) movement (if the device is sensitive enough) and will then record 15.1 V. If the digital meter can register only in 0.5 V. increments it will, by contrast, remain unchanged. If the digital voltmeter can register 0.1 V. increments, it will, like the analogue meter, register 15.1 V. but no matter how small the increment it can measure, there will always be some value (say, 15.11 V.) that can be registered by the analogue meter, if it is sensitive enough, that cannot be registered on the digital. Representation by analogue means can, then, be as fine as the sensitivity and calibration of the device permits whereas, in digital, it can be no finer than that represented by a change of one digit in the least-significant digit position. In addition to a 'needle' voltmeter, some other common analogue devices are a gear train, a thermometer, and a light meter. See *digital; quantising; analogue to digital; computer*.

analogue channel A communications channel used to carry speech; a channel in which signals can have any values within established limits. (As contrasted to a telegraph channel or a narrowband data channel.)

analogue computer A computer with continuously variable inputs and outputs (often voltage or gear movement).

analogue loop test A test of modem internal circuits and a telephone link by which an operator at one modem causes carrier wave or a test pattern to be transmitted to the other modem

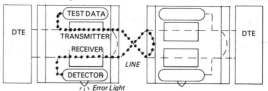

which, in turn, retransmits it back to the testing modem. (It is used only in four-wire systems.) The modem test facilities usually provide for the testing modem to send a distinctive command (tone or data group) which, when received, causes the other modem to assume the test mode. It is often used in conjunction with an error detection circuit that causes an error light to flash if an incorrect bit (say, a 0-bit in a sequence of 1-bits) is detected. See *digital loop test; end-to-end test*.

analogue to digital (AD; A/D) The process of converting an analogue input (voltage, most commonly) into digital form. The usual method involves a 'sample and hold' circuit in which instantaneous values are obtained at short intervals (say, every twenty milliseconds) and imposed on a capacitor. The capacitor is then discharged at a constant rate (through a fixed resistance) with a digital counter enabled during the discharge. At the end of discharge, the counter holds a digital word (commonly 6, 8, or 12 bits) that represents the time of discharge and, thus, the voltage that was imposed upon the capacitor. Other methods of conversion are 'successive approximation' in which known voltages are successively tested for equality with the voltage on the capacitor and 'flash' in which the sample voltage is applied directly to a number of parallel circuits, only one of which responds to any particular level. Analogue to digital conversion is a common operation in telemetry, process control, digital production effects, speech recognition, and in high-speed modems. See *digital to analogue*.

analogue to digital converter Also *digitiser*. A device that receives and measures an analogue input, divides it into levels or bands, and represents each level or band with a distinctive digital output. See *pulse code modulation*.

ancillary (1) A term applied to an operation or device that provides a supporting or additional function. **(2)** Auxiliary.

AND Also *conjunction*. A logic operation with an output that is 'true' if all of its inputs are 'true' and an output that is 'false' if any input is 'false'. See *logic operation*.

AND-NOT Exclusion (logic operation).

angstrom (Å) A unit of measurement of the wave length (and colour) of light; it is equal to 1×10^{-8} cm. (one-tenth of a nanometer; one ten thousandth of a micron). The visible spectrum extends from about 4000 Å (violet) to 7500 Å (red).

anisochronous transmission Data transmission in which there can be variable time intervals between characters and also between the bits that constitute a character. The common method of indicating when a character begins and ends is to use 'framing bits' and when these are used, it is a form of start-stop transmission. See *asynchronous transmission; isochronous*.

annotation (1) Notes made on a document for such purposes as providing references or explaining use. **(2)** Comment; source coding that does not result in executable code. See *comment*.

anode The part of a diode or similar device toward which electrons flow from a **cathode**; the element that is connected to positive in its most common use in circuits. See *diode*.

ANSI *American National Standards Institute*.

answer (1) To respond to an incoming telephone call by placing a telephone device in the 'off-hook' state. **(2)** To send a message in response to a received message.

answer mode Of a modem in a dial-up communications system; the condition in which it receives a telephone call and prepares to send or receive data. See *automatic answer; originate mode*.

answer tone In data communications on PSTN lines; a tone (2100 Hz. in Europe and 2025 Hz. in the U.S.) that can be sent by answering equipment to disable echo suppressors and to notify an operator or equipment at the other (originating) end to connect data to the line.

answerback (1) The action of providing data station or terminal identification when requested. **(2)** An action of a central site modem in providing a training sequence when requested by a (the) remote site modem. The request is, typically, made by either squelching carrier (point-to-point system) or sending a distinctive tone (multipoint system) when the remote site modem experiences degraded signal quality.

answerback memory A read-only memory in a unit of data terminal equipment that holds characters that identify the device or data station and which is automatically read for transmission when it is called.

anticipatory A term applied to an operation that is performed before it is needed.

anti-stream timer In a modem in a multipoint system; a timer that squelches main carrier after it has been high for some preset time (say, 3 minutes). See *stream*.

anvil A hammer; an element of an impact printer.

aperture (1) A hole. See *aperture card*. **(2)** A 1-bit or group of 1-bits in a mask; that which causes characters in the input to (selectively) appear in the output. See *mask*. **(3)** A timed period in which a state is enabled (in which an event can occur).

aperture card A card (often of standard punch card size and material) with an aperture in which a frame (or several frames) of microfilm can be mounted for reading without removal from the card. Such cards are typically printed and/or punched to identify the microfilm; their most common use is to hold engineering drawings. See *COM*.

aperture time In a sample and hold circuit, the time after sampling that a stable 'hold' condition begins.

APL *A Programming Language*. A language designed primarily for mathematical applications, particularly ones using arrays.

apparent storage Storage in a virtual storage system as it appears to a user or user program; any storage other than real or physical storage. See *virtual storage terms*.

append To add at the end; particularly to add records at the end of a file. **append mode** An access mode in which additional records are written to a file following the last record currently in the file. See *access mode*.

application (1)A business or other operation that is performed by a computer (or with the aid of a computer) or an operation in which it appears practical to use a computer. By this definition, the term is applied to such things as preparing payrolls, maintaining inventory records, and reserving seats on aircraft. See *application package*. (2)The type of processing for which a computer is used. Examples by this definition include batch processing, transaction processing, and communications interfacing. (3)A common short form used for 'application program' and, less commonly, for 'application system', mainly in the plural; ('transfer applications to a new machine'; 'develop applications for. . .').

application data base See *subject data base*.

application-dedicated terminal (ADT) A terminal that can be used only for a specified purpose; a terminal with access limited to a particular application program or group of programs.

application package A set of programs sold as a group (package) to enable users of a particular model of computer to implement an application (def. 1) without the need to write all the necessary programs.

application program Also *application* (def. 3) and, in most cases, *user program*. A program that has been written or adapted for use in the processing required in an application (def. 1). See *user program*.

application programmer Also *programmer; problem programmer*. A person who is employed to write and/or maintain application (user) programs. See *system programmer; application program; programmer; coder*.

application suite An application system.

application system Also, often, *application package; application suite*. A group of related programs; particularly a group used to implement a large or complex application (def. 1).

APT *Automatically Programmed Tools*. A programming language used in numerical control systems for machine tools. See *numerical control*.

ARABSAT *ARAB SATellite*. A COMSAT project to provide a regional satellite communications service for the twenty-one countries of the Arab League.

architecture With respect to a computer system; a general term for the type, functions, and interconnections of the various units and devices; ('an architecture designed for batch processing'; 'new applictions requiring a changed architecture'; 'an architecture providing high resiliance').

archive Also *archives*. (1)A storage location for documents, magnetic tapes, etc. that are maintained for record purposes but seldom used. (2)Magnetic tapes (wherever located) that contain infrequently required data, files that have been temporarily deleted from direct access media, or data that must be retained for legal or other purposes. (3)A group of related documents or magnetic tapes in an 'archive' (def. 1). (4)To move data from magnetic disc storage to magnetic tape.

archive file A file in an archive (def. 1 or 2).

archiving (1)The process of writing data to an 'archive' (def. 2). (2)The process of making backup copies (for example, of disc files onto magnetic tape) regardless of purpose or the length of time the copies will be retained.

area (1)A group of contiguous locations in main storage; ('a work area'; 'an operating system area'). (2) Also *realm*. A unit of storage named in a schema. See *realm*.

argument (1)A value used to make a table lookup; for example, 'angle in degrees' is the 'argument' used to find the sine of an angle in a table of trigonometric functions. (2)An independent variable; in the expression 'a = b + c', both the 'b' and the 'c' are 'arguments'.

arithmetic The technique or operation of performing calculations. The term is usually understood to apply to addition, subtraction, multiplication, and division. See *compute*.

arithmetic check Also *mathematical check*. A programmed check in which some arithmetic operation is performed to verify that processing/transcription has been performed correctly. The term usually refers to a check performed on a control total. See *control total*.

arithmetic fault A size error.

arithmetic instruction An instruction that specifies an arithmetic operation; an instruction with an arithmetic operator.

arithmetic logic unit (ALU) Also *arithmetic unit; mill*. That part of a central processor in which arithmetic, logic, and shift operations are performed. See *control unit; execution*.

arithmetic operation An operation with numeric inputs and outputs.

arithmetic operator An operator that specifies an arithmetic operation; for example, ADD, DIVIDE, or COMPUTE.

arithmetic overflow (1)An overflow of digits produced in an arithmetic operation. (2)The number of digits that overflow.

arithmetic register An accumulator; an arithmetic-unit register used to hold operands and intermediate results of arithmetic operations.

arithmetic scan A compilation step in which arithmetic expressions are examined to determine the order of dealing with the operators; typically, it consists of converting arithmetic expressions from infix notation to a Polish form. See *Polish notation*.

arithmetic shift See *shift*.

arithmetic unit See *arithmetic logic unit*.

ARQ *Automatic ReQuest for repetition*. A designation of a data communications system in which error control and recovery is by sending an ACK or a NAK after each block or message is received, and by the sending station retransmitting any block or message when a NAK is returned.

arrange To place items in some specified order; to make a new groupiing. See *series; sequence; sort; merge; collate*.

array (1)Also *table; dimensioned variable;* and other terms. A storage structure of one or more dimensions in which individual locations are addressed by an identifier of the structure plus one or more **subscripts** that identify particular locations or groups of locations; as many subscripts are required as there are dimensions in the array. A one-dimensional array may be termed a **string, list, row**, or **vector**, a two-dimensional array a **flat file, table** or **relation** (mainly data base usage), and an array of two or more dimensions a **matrix**. See *dimension; subscript*. (2)A unit of code or data in an 'array' (def. 1). (3)A unit of coordinate-addressable storage (core; semiconductor). (4)An integrated circuit or an assembly of integrated circuits used to accomplish a particular function; ('a programmable logic array'; 'a storage array').

array computer (1)A computer with multiple control and/or data streams. See *SIMD; MIMD*. (2)An array processor.

array processor Also *parallel processor; multiprocessor*. A small, specialised computer that is designed to perform arithmetic operations at high speed for another (mainframe) computer. Typically, such a processor consists of a number of individual microprocessors (often bit-slice devices) and their directly associated registers and microcode storage arranged in parallel 'lines', each of which performs floating-point arithmetic. All lines may perform the same operations simultaneously by multiple executions of a single set of instructions, or each line may be (microcode) programmed to perform a separate sequence of operations, each of which contributes to producing a final result. Array processors are particularly suited to performing fast Fourier transforms and other high-speed arithmetic operations as required in real-time image enhancement and manipulation of video signals and in seismic analysis and Xray tomography. Such a processor is normally dedicated to a particular function.

arrival An entrant in a queue. See *queue*.

artificial intelligence A term applied to the capability of a machine to learn (to remember what result was produced on a previous trial and to modify the operation accordingly in a subsequent trial) or to reason (to analyse the results produced in similar operations and select the most favourable).

artificial language A language that is created rather than a product of natural development; a language with a set of rules established by directive rather than determined from usage. See *language; natural language*.

ARU *Audio Response Unit*. An audio response terminal.

ASCII *American Standard Code for Information Interchange*. A standard 7-bit code (often 8-bit including parity) for data communications. The full code has 128 characters including upper and lower case letters, digits, symbols, and control characters. Most terminals use a 96-character subset that excludes the communications control characters; this subset is also a common internal storage code for minicomputers and microcomputers. Many word processors use a 64-character subset containing upper and lower case letters, numbers, and common symbols and punctuation. The code, with certain allocatable national characters, has been adopted by the International Standards Organization as ISO-7. See *code; EBCDIC*.

ASCII keyboard A keyboard (of a VDU or teletypewriter) for inputting the ASCII characters. The keyboard illustrated is for the 128-character set. (Similar versions are available for the 64-character and 96-character sets.) See *ASCII; QWERTY*.

ASR (1)*Automatic Send and Receive*. A designation of a teletypewriter or other device that combines a printer, a keyboard, and paper tape reading and punching facilities. It can receive messages by printing and/or punching and send messages either as keyed in at the keyboard or as read from paper tape. See *KSR*. (2)*Automatic Speech Recognition*.

assemble (1) To produce a machine code version of a program or routine from source coding in a low-level or intermediate language. See *compiler; assembler*. (2)To join individual units to form a larger unit.

assemble-and-go Load-and-go. (A term sometimes used when the object code was produced by an assembler rather than by a compiler.)

assembler (1)A program that produces machine code from source code in a low-level language. See *low-level language; compiler*. (2)An assembly language. See *language*.

assembly language Also *assembler*. A low-level language for a particular computer model or range of computer models. See *language*.

assign To allocate one thing for use by or with another. See *assignment*.

assignment (1) The programming operation of designating a resource (peripheral; file; area of storage) that will be used by a program during execution and providing its identifier in the source coding. An assignment may be made by writing a declaration or, if the resource is a file or area of storage, by writing a data description. See *declaration; data description*. (2)The programming operation of providing a numeric value that will be used during processing or designating a relationship that will apply. In several programming languages, assignments are indicated by the symbol ':=' meaning 'becomes' or 'takes the value', for example, 'X := 30'. (3)A function of system software in allocating a resource to a job.

assignment statement A source-language statement that makes an assignment (def. 1 or 2). The term includes data descriptions and is synonymous with 'declaration' with respect to those declarations that designate resources. See *assignment; data description*.

associative addressing Also *content addressing*. The method of addressing (access) used in an associative storage system. See *associative storage*.

associative processor A computer or other device in which the primary method of accessing data in storage is by reading keys and comparing their values with a value that identifies the item sought. The term 'associative' is used because of this comparison which is the essential part of its operation; the storage of such a system (typically high-capacity disc) may be termed **associative storage**. The keys may be values assigned for access purposes (for example, normal record keys) or they may be values in particular fields (say, customer names) used as auxiliary keys. Because the access can be by keys formed from record contents, the storage used may be termed **content-addressable storage**.

associative register A look-aside register.

associative storage Also *content-addressable storage; parallel search storage*. Storage that is accessed by contents rather than by location. There are two forms in use, the first is on **look-aside registers** that are used in some virtual storage systems to hold the real and virtual addresses of recently rolled in pages/segments. These are searched in parallel with the normal address transformation when a new page/segment is referenced by an active process and the normal transformation is discontinued if it is located and, thus, determined to be in primary storage. The second form is in large movable-head magnetic disc storage that is read cylinder by cylinder with heads reading in parallel. See *look-aside registers; content access; content-addressable filestore; associative processor*.

assumed decimal point A place in a register holding a decimal number that is treated by system software as separating the integral and fractional parts; the position may have been indicated in source coding (say, by a PICTURE clause) or it may be the default position which is, conventionally, to the right of the least-significant digit position. See *actual decimal point*.

asymmetric duplex A full-duplex circuit with a high-speed **message channel** (also **forward channel**) that carries messages (user data) in both directions (but not simultaneously) and a slower **supervisory channel** (also **backward channel**) that carries acknowledgements, repetition requests, and any other control or supervisory messages in the direction opposite to the message channel. Asymmetric duplex is usually used on two-wire telephone circuits with modems that provide frequency separation of the channels. For example, the message channel may use a 550-3000 Hz. band while the supervisory channel uses 250-450 Hz. Speeds are from 300 to 2400 bps. on the message channel and 50-75 bps. on the supervisory channel. Asymmetric duplex has an advantage over half-duplex in that it eliminates the modem turnaround time that is inherent in sending user data and supervisory messages (ACK's and NAK's) on the same channel. The figure shows Modem A transmitting and

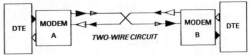

B receiving; when the message channel is reversed (for Modem B to transmit), the supervisory channel is also reversed.

asymmetric half-duplex A half-duplex circuit in which transfers in one direction are at a higher speed than those in the other. See *half-duplex.*

asynchronous (1)Of a device or operation; with independent timing; without a timing signal input that controls its operation in relation to other devices or operations. (2)Of a device or operation; with the completion of one operation or event used to initiate the next one. See *synchronous.*

asynchronous execution Execution in which the instructions of a program execute in a timed sequence without regard to whether or not the action specified by the previous instruction has been successfully completed.

asynchronous operation An operation conducted concurrently with another operation but with independent timing; a parallel operation that does not interact with the other operation. See *autonomous; synchronous.*

asynchronous system trap (ast) The address of the entry point in a routine that is always executed; for example, whenever a communications link is set up or whenever a particular error condition occurs.

asynchronous transfer A peripheral transfer that is performed while the central processor continues to execute program instructions. See *parallel; cycle stealing; autonomous transfer; peripheral transfer.*

asynchronous transmission Data transmission in which there can be variable time intervals between characters with the bits of each character sent synchronously (with fixed time intervals). The common method of indicating when a character begins and ends is to use 'framing bits' and when these are used, asynchronous transmission is also start-stop transmission. See *start-stop transmission; synchronous transmission; anisochronous transmission.*

AT&T *American Telephone & Telegraph Co.*

ATE *Automatic Test Equipment.* A term applied to computer-based devices and techniques for production line testing, particularly of integrated circuits and printed circuit boards.

attach (1)To connect one device or element to another. (2)To assign a peripheral to a job for the duration of the job.

attended operation A term used to indicate that a device (say, a terminal) requires the presence of an operator in order to function.

attention Also *attention signal; attention interrupt.* (1)An interrupt caused by a terminal operator pressing an attention key (or equivalent). (2)A signal from a peripheral or peripheral controller indicating condition; for example, that a seek has been completed and data is ready to transfer.

attention line A circuit from a peripheral device to a computer or peripheral controller on which signals are sent indicating change of status of the device.

attention signal Also *attention.* A signal from a peripheral to the central processor indicating a change in status; for example, the completion of a seek or data transfer.

attenuation Also *line loss.* A reduction in the amplitude of signals caused by losses during transmission; it is usually expressed in decibels. See *decibel.*

attenuation constant The loss in signal strength per unit distance over which the signals are transmitted in a particular medium; it is usually expressed in decibels per mile or kilometer. The following are some representative values in dB per mile:

Separated wires	0.1	Coaxial cable, 2000 kHz.	6
Twisted pairs	2—8	Coaxial cable, 8000 kHz.	10
Coaxial cable, 300 kHz.	2		

attenuator Also *pad*. A resistance introduced in a telephone circuit in order to selectively reduce certain components of the frequency envelope to improve performance.

atto- A combining form indicating 10^{-18}.

attribute (1) That which characterises an entity or provides identification; for example, the age of an employee, the price of a part, or the address of a customer. **(2)** A capability or supported function; for example, sequential access as an 'attribute' of an indexed file.

attribute record An entity record.

ATU *Autonomous Transfer Unit.*

audio disc A magnetic disc used to hold speech; for example, to hold (digitised) words/phrases that are selected to form 'spoken' messages. See *audio response terminal*.

audio response terminal A terminal that receives responses from a computer in spoken rather than printed or displayed form. At the computer, digitised speech in the form of words/phrases on magnetic disc or phonemes in ROM are accessed in the desired order by a program and then converted from digital to analogue for transmission. The terminal for receiving can be an ordinary telephone, speaker, or headset. When used in a multifrequency signalling system, enquiries can be sent by means of pushbuttons on the telephone. See *multifrequency signalling*.

audit (1) An operation to check the accuracy of accounting work. **(2)** A check on the accuracy and completeness of the results of computer processing. **(3)** A check on how efficiently a computer is being used.

audit program (1) A program designed to cross-check inputs and results of processing and/or to compare inputs or results with preset values in order to reveal errors or inconsistencies of the type that could be caused by an attempt to use the system for dishonest purposes. **(2)** Also *data audit program*. A program designed to run independently (not in conjunction with an application program) to check the validity of stored data, particularly data subject to frequent updating with, inherently, a high risk of corruption. Such a program might, for example, check record keys, check table addresses against physical addresses, and follow the pointers on each access path to ensure that no links have been broken.

audit trail (1) A journal of all attempted accesses to a restricted file. **(2)** A journal of the sequence of programs used to process a restricted file and the results of validations performed at each phase of processing.

augend A number to which another number (an **addend**) is added. In the expression '6 + 4 = 10' the 6 is the augend and the 4 the addend. (If their order is reversed to '4 + 6 = 10', the 4 becomes the augend and the 6 the addend.)

auto-abstract The use of a program to produce an elementary abstract of stored text material by locating and printing out key words and their locations in the text.

auto-answer Automatic answering.

auto-call Automatic calling.

auto-decrement The facility or operation of automatically decrementing a count.

auto-increment The facility or operation of automatically incrementing a count.

auto-load The (minicomputer) facility by which pressing a single button or console typewriter key activates a program in read-only memory to load the operating system (from magnetic disc).

auto-poll A capability of a communications control unit that deals with negative poll responses without producing interrupts to the computer.

autocode (1) A term once used synonymously with 'programming language'; for example, the 'Manchester Autocode'. **(2)** An assembly language in a form resembling mathematical notation (as used in programming early computers).

autocoder An 'assembler' for an autocode.

automatic A term applied to the mechanical, electrical, or electronic accomplishment of a task that has been done manually (or could be done manually). **(1)** An action initiated by sensing a physical condition or change in a physical condition. An action termed 'automatic' by this definition is usually simple (say, turning on a circuit) though the sensing may be complicated. Examples include 'automatic channel selection' and 'automatic load transfer'. **(2)** A sequence of autonomous operations with external initiation (possibly by a person). An action termed 'automatic' by this definition is usually complex and often involves feedback. Examples by this definition include 'automatic data processing', 'automatic error recovery', and an 'automatic telephone exchange'. See *manual*.

automatic answering A facility of a modem or line access unit by which it can receive a dialed telephone call in order to set up a data transfer on a PSTN line. When a ring is detected, it goes 'off-hook' and sends a ring indicator (RI) signal to the DTE. If the DTE is in condition to receive, it returns DTR and the modem or line access unit sends an answer tone and switches to 'data'. When the operator or equipment at the other end detects the answer tone, it also switches to 'data' and the transfer can begin. The equipment also releases the line when the local DTE drops DTR or the modem drops DCD (indicating that the other end has stopped transmitting). See *answer tone*.

automatic calling Also *auto-call; automatic origination*. A facility of modem-associated equipment (line access unit; automatic dialer) that can initiate a data transfer over a dialed, PSTN line. Upon initiation from the DTE, it dials the number of equipment at another data station and, when the called station returns an 'answer tone', it connects data to the line. When the transfer is completed, it drops carrier and goes back 'on hook'. See *manual originate; automatic answering*.

automatic carriage A term sometimes applied to the facilities of an electric typewriter that enable it to perform paper feeds, tabulation, and carriage returns with external initiation; for example, from paper tape.

automatic coding A term sometimes applied to the production of source code by a computer or with computer assistance.

automatic control The machine sensing of physical conditions and their interpretation and use to modify an operation.

automatic data processing (ADP) The technology, industry, or functions involved in the use of computers to process data. (The abbreviation ADP is still in use though the term 'data processing' has largely replaced 'automatic data processing'.)

automatic dialer A modem-associated device that can initiate an unattended data transfer. See *automatic calling*.

automatic exchange A term applied to a (private) telephone exchange that can route incoming and outgoing calls without the intervention of an operator. See *PABX*.

automatic field duplication A utility that can copy fields from one record to another to reduce data entry keyboarding.

automatic file rotation An operating system facility by which a preset number of generations of a file are retained with automatic deletion of the oldest when a new version is created.

automatic interrupt An interrupt that is not programmed; an interrupt that is initiated by hardware or monitor program.

automatic origination Automatic calling.

automatic overlaying A term sometimes applied to the paging facilities of a virtual storage system.

automatic polling See *auto-poll*.

automatic programming See *automatic coding*.

automatic request for repetition See *ARQ*.

automatic restart A restart that is performed without resubmitting the job in which the error occurred. See *restart*.

automatic send and receive See *ASR*.

automatic test equipment See *ATE*.

automatic volume recognition (AVR) A facility for identifying operator-replaceable volumes (usually disc packs) to the operating system as they are mounted on their drives.

automation The performance of relatively complex operations with little if any human intervention. The term is most often used with respect to manufacturing operations.

autonomous operation An independent operation; particularly an operation (locating and transferring data; printing results) that is carried out independently by a peripheral device with no involvement of the central processor except in its initiation. See *auxiliary operation*.

autonomous transfer A peripheral transfer that is made concurrently with instruction execution.

autonomous transfer unit (ATU) An intelligent device that is capable of performing autonomous data transfers when initiation and addresses are supplied by the central processor.

autotransformer A transformer with a single coil that is tapped to derive secondary voltages. See *transformer*.

auxiliary(1)Also *ancillary*. A term applied to a separate but supporting operation; for example, decollating as an 'auxiliary' operation of printing. (2)Used in place of, or in addition to, the main unit; ('auxiliary storage'; 'an auxiliary power supply').

auxiliary key All or part of the contents of a field (other than primary key field) used to locate a record. Such a key typically identifies some attribute of the entity such as the discount classification of a customer or the date of purchase of a vehicle. See *key(File organisation); secondary key; inverted file*.

auxiliary key field A field that holds a value used as an auxiliary key. See *control field*.

auxiliary operation Any operation in a computer system not under the control of the central processor. Typically, such operations consist of preparing code or data for placement in storage and handling the results of processing; examples include sorting documents, punching and verifying cards or tape, and decollating continuous stationary.

auxiliary storage Any storage in a computer system other than main storage. The term is used to include backing storage and such internal storage as bulk, cache, and slave. See *storage*.

availability (1) The time a computer or functional unit is capable of being operated as a percentage of the total time it is required or scheduled to be used; ('availability exceeding ninety-five percent'; 'a design that ensures high availability'). (2) The status of being in use or available for use.

availability control The use of fault detection and correction facilities and system reconfiguration in order to provide high availability.

avalanche A term applied to an uncontrolled (and, in some cases, destructive) flow of electrons that begins with the breakdown of a barrier (say, a biased junction) that normally prevents their flow.

avalanche diode A zener diode with high heat dissipation characteristics. It is used as a circuit protection device to 'clip' any transients over a certain voltage.

avalanche injection See *FAMOS*.

AVR *Automatic Volume Recognition*.

axis crossing A zero crossing; a place where a changing voltage passes through zero.

azerty A term sometimes applied to a keyboard in which the alphabetical keys are arranged in the same way as they are in the standard typewriters of continental Europe. (The term consists of the first six letters in the first alphabetical row of keys of such a typewriter.) See *qwerty*.

Azerty Keyboard

B

Bachman notation A method of representing complex data structures such as hierarchies and nets. The method distinguishes between **entity types** (for example, 'departments' and 'employees') and **entity occurrences** (for example, 'accounting department' and 'truck driver').

back end A term used with respect to add-on devices that provide a computer with additional processing or control facilities (as contrasted to 'front end' units that perform interface functions). For example, a special data base or numerical processor may run 'back end' to a mainframe. See *front end*.

back-strike printer See *impact printer*.

background (1) A term applied to low-priority work performed when computer resources are not otherwise required. Examples include batch work in a system that also handles transaction processing and such operations as spooling and making backup copies of files. See *foreground; priority*. (2) In some systems; a part of main storage that is allocated to background jobs. See *foreground*. (3) In optical reading systems (OMR; OCR); the recording surface (paper) considered with respect to its contrast to the characters or marks to be read. (4) Continuously present; ('background illumination'; 'background noise').

background ink Ink of a colour (often magenta) that will not be detected by an optical reader; it is the ink used for grids, instructions, etc. in preprinted forms for OCR and OMR.

background job A job of relatively low priority to which computer resources are allocated when not required for higher priority work.

background noise Also, usually, *white noise*. A continuous low-level noise present on a communications circuit. See *noise*.

backing storage Also *external storage*. That part of the storage of a computer system that can be accessed by the central processor by means of input/output channels; the main types are magnetic disc, magnetic drum, magnetic tape, and mass. See *auxiliary storage; peripheral storage; secondary storage; filestore; storage*.

backplane The reverse side of a control panel, display panel, or the like; the side with the interconnecting wiring.

backspace (1) In a printing device; to move the printing element one space to the left (as with a golfball typewriter) or to move the printing medium one space to the right (as with an ordinary typewriter). (2) With a VDU; to move the cursor one space to the left. (3) In magnetic tape access; to reverse the tape to the beginning of the previous block.

backup Also *standby*. A term applied to an item (file; line; electronic circuit; peripheral) that duplicates the function of a primary unit and is available for use in its place to prevent an interruption of work or the occurrence of a hazardous condition that could otherwise result from its failure.

backup file A copy of a master file retained for use or reference if data in the master file becomes corrupted or is otherwise unavailable. In a critical transaction processing system, a backup file may be maintained concurrently with the master file and on the same type of storage to ensure continuity of service. For other purposes, copies on magnetic tape may be made of disc files at specified intervals or before or after each updating. (A backup file is essential when master files are updated in situ because previous versions of changed records are overwritten.) See *update*.

Backus normal form Also *Backus-Naur form*. A metalanguage structure as used in syntax parsing in ALGOL and related languages.

backward channel A supervisory channel.

backward recovery De-updating.

badge A machine-readable identification card issued to individuals to define their access rights.

badge reader A security device (often part of a terminal) that reads information (often from a magnetic stripe or punched holes) on a badge inserted in a slot.

balance (1) In accounting; the amount owed by a customer or due to a supplier at the end of some period. **(2)** In accounting; to make debits equal to credits; ('balance the books'). **(3)** In electronics; to adjust circuit variables to obtain satisfactory performance.

balanced error An indicated no-error condition that results (by chance) from errors cancelling each other.

balanced line A conditioned line.

ballistic A term used to indicate a mechanism in which movement (say, of a print wire) is obtained by striking with a hammer.

band (1) A portion of a frequency spectrum that has individual significance for some purpose; ('a radio band'; 'the ultraviolet band'). **(2)** A group of contiguous frequencies as used in carrier wave communications (radio; data transfer). It is identified by its included frequencies and/or its upper and lower frequencies; ('a 5 kHz. band'; 'a 65—70 kHz. band'). A band that can

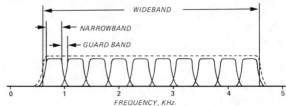

be subdivided for some purpose is termed a **wideband** (also **broadband**) and the smaller bands created are **narrowbands**. A group of unused frequencies of high attenuation between bands is a **guardband** which is used to prevent energy transfer between adjacent bands. See *frequency; group; frequency division multiplexing; voice-grade; subvoice-grade*. **(3)** In a magnetic disc system; a group of contiguous tracks that have a common attribute or function; for example, all the tracks that are accessed by a single read/write head or a 'guardband' at the end of the recordable surface. See *magnetic disc unit*. **(4)** The type-carrying element of a band printer.

band printer A printer that is functionally similar to a chain printer except that the type font is carried as embossed characters in a thin, steel band. It is an impact character printer in which the font moves along the line as it is being printed. Speeds range from about 250 lines per minute to 3000 lines per minute (with a 48-character font). The illustration is of a section of a steel band. The sample of printing was produced at 3000 lines per minute.

band splitting A term sometimes applied to multiplexing in which a few multiplexed channels are provided; for example, to a modem system in which a single 9600 bit per second channel is divided by time division multiplexing into two, three, or four channels of lower speed.

bandoliered With respect to resistors, diodes, and, possibly, other electronic components with axial leads; arranged in parallel (for shipping and handling) with the ends of the leads attached to paper tape.

bandwidth (1) The inclusive frequencies of a 'band', particularly as a limiting factor in data communications. In a carrier system, the bandwidth must be equal to at least the modulation rate (the Baud rate). **(2)** The data transfer capacity (in bits per second) of a bit-parallel computer bus.

bank (1) A side-by-side arrangement of like hardware units; ('a bank of modems'; 'a switch bank'). **(2)** A data bank.

bar code An arrangement of bars and spaces designed to be read by an optical scanner; they are used for such purposes as product identification and, in some countries, for identifying freight cars as trains pass checkpoints.

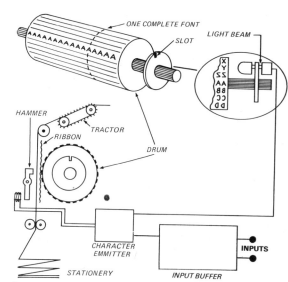

An interactive VAX-11 PSI utility program

bar printer A printer, such as an ordinary typewriter, in which the characters of the type font are embossed on separately movable type bars. See *printer*.

barrel printer Also *drum printer*. An impact line printer that uses shaped characters embossed on a drum. The drum has a complete font of characters in each printing position. A printer with a 64-character set would then have the set embossed in as many positions as there are printing positions (typically, 120, 132, or 160). Each printing position has a print hammer which, when actuated, strikes paper and inked ribbon against a character as it rotates by on the drum. In operation, a full line of characters is read into the buffer and a synchronising disc on the drum shaft and a character emitter constantly output the bit pattern of the character that is approaching the printing position (the line of print hammers). This bit pattern is used to scan the buffer and wherever an identity is found, the print hammer in that position is actuated to print the character. For example, as the letter 'A' approaches the printing position, the scan locates all the A's in the buffer and causes them to be printed simultaneously. Because all the characters of the font pass each printing position during each revolution, a complete line is printed with each revolution of the drum. Printing speeds are from 300 to 1300 lines per minute. See *printer*.

base (1) Also *radix*. In a positional representation numeration system; the amount by which a digit is multiplied or divided when moved to an adjacent digit position. In the decimal system, for example, a '3' becomes '30' if moved one digit position to the left and '0.3' if moved a digit position to the right. It is, thus, multiplied or divided by '10' when moved to an adjacent digit position and the 'base' of the system is 10. See *number*. **(2)** In a logarithm or in floating point representation; the value (usually not expressed) that is exponentiated. See *logarithm; floating point*. **(3)** A value from which other values are expressed or calculated. See *base address*. **(4)** In a bipolar transistor; the control area or the electrical connection to the control area. See *transistor*.

base address. The lowest numbered location in an area of storage; a value that is added to a displacement (or relative address) to produce a hardware address. See *address; instruction; address modification.*

base and displacement A common addressing method in which a displacement (which may be a relative address) is added to a base address to produce a required address.

base and limit See *storage protection.*

base register A register that is used to hold a base address. See *address; instruction; stack.*

base segment A control segment.

baseband signalling The transmission of unmodulated signals on a communications channel, usually by direct current and over short distances as between a terminal and a modem or between a telephone and a local exchange.

BASIC *Beginners' All-purpose Symbolic Instruction Code.* A high-level language originally designed for use in computer instruction but now used more widely. Latest versions have facilities similar to those of FORTRAN, including matrix and string handling. It is commonly used interactively.

basic access A method of access in which data transfers through input/output channels are made only as and when called for in a user program.

basic peripherals Those peripherals that were once considered essential to a small batch processing system; the term is usually considered to include card and paper tape readers and punches, line printers, and magnetic tape units.

batch (1) A collection of related items (documents; punched cards; records on magnetic tape) that are processed together or intended to be processed together. (2) The records constituting the inputs to an application program for a particular run.

batch header A record that identifies a batch and holds common data.

batch processing A mode of computer operation in which application programs and their data are processed individually with, normally, one being completed before the next is started. It is, in effect, planned processing as contrasted to transaction processing or multi-access in which processing is performed to meet needs as they arise. Batch processing is, typically, used for such purposes as preparing payrolls, maintaining inventory records, and producing reports. The normal flow is for a user to provide source documents to a data control department where their data is extracted and placed in computer readable form (say, on punched cards) which are read into computer storage (say, onto magnetic tape). When the user has processing time scheduled, the necessary programs (typically, belonging to the user) are read into storage and used to process this 'batch' of data with the results (payroll checks; printout of a new inventory) returned to the user upon completion. See *on-line; transaction processing; remote batch processing; batch.*

batch stream In mixed-mode computing; the batch jobs that are being processed or are in the (low-priority) job queue.

batch total A control total for a batch of records; the sum of the occurrences or of the contents of a specified field in each of all the records in the batch. The values are derived by the data control department prior to data preparation; typically, the system designer specifies the field(s) to be used and whether the total to be obtained for each is to be a count of occurrences or a sum of contents. The totals are checked by a data vet program and during each run in which the batch is processed; if a different total is obtained than the one input with the batch, the batch is rejected and returned to the data control department for resolution. See *validation; control total.*

batch trailer The final record of a batch; it usually contains the control totals.

battery A device that produces electric current from a chemical reaction. The current produced is **direct current**. The most common batteries are **dry cells** and **storage batteries**. In a dry cell, the chemical reaction is irreversable; when the active materials (zinc and manganese dioxide) are exhausted, the battery is discarded. In a storage battery, the active materials (lead-lead oxide; nickel-cadmium) can be returned to their original condition by a **charge** which consists of applying direct current to a battery from an external source. The process of removing current from a battery is **discharge**. See *electricity.*

Baud (rhymes with 'code') The standard unit for expressing the data transmission capability of lines, terminals, and interface equipment; it is equal to the number of data-significant line transitions that can be made per second. (A line transition is a change of voltage or frequency.) When applied with respect to a two-level system (say, one in which a 0-bit is represented by +6 V. and a 1-bit by —6 V.), the term is synonymous with **data signalling rate**; a 1200 Baud line can transmit 1200 bits per second because one bit is transmitted with each line transition. In a system that uses **multilevel signalling**, each line transition represents multiple bits and speed in Baud is, then, less than the data signalling rate. For example, in a common system of phase shift modulation, each transition represents two bits (one dibit) and a 1200 Baud line can, then, carry 2400 bits per second. See *modulation; phase shift modulation; multilevel signalling.*

Baud clock A clock with one pulse or transition per Baud.

Baudot code A 5-level code that was formerly the European standard for telegraph; it has been supplanted by IA-2. (The term is sometimes applied to any 5-level code.) See *code.*

BCC *Block Check Character.*

BCD *Binary Coded Decimal.*

BCS *British Computer Society.* (London)

BDN *Bell Data Network.*

bead A term used in some multiprogramming systems to denote a system routine that handles one of a sequence of steps (validation; input; formatting) required in a particular type of processing; for example, in handling enquiries in a transaction processing system. A sequence of beads used in pipeline mode may be termed a **thread**. See *thread; multithreading.*

beam-accessed Also *beam addressed.* A term applied to a storage system in which a beam (electron; light; laser) is used to read and write bits representing data; it includes photo-digital, electrostatic, holographic, and BEAMOS.

beam lead A term applied to an integrated circuit or other semiconductor device with leads that are flat bars or 'beams'. The purpose of the construction is to permit the leads to act as heat sinks.

BEAMOS *BEam-Addressed MOS.* A type of memory in which bits are held as electron-beam implanted areas of electron surplus on an MOS semiconductor chip. A beam of electrons from gun A is precisely aligned and directed by grids and deflectors B toward the memory plane C. To write a 1-bit, the memory plane is made positive with respect to gun A and to write a 0-bit (remove a 1-bit) it is made negative. In reading, no bias voltage is applied and bits are detected by the voltage on the memory plane as it is scanned by the beam; the voltage varies slightly depending on whether the beam is directed on a place of electron surplus or deficit. As some of the electron charge is depleted during the reading operation, the memory must be refreshed every five to twenty reads. Packing on the order of 30 megabits per square inch have been obtained with access times of about 30 ns. and transfer rates of up to 20 megabits per second.

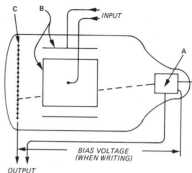

bearer channel A communications channel that is divided (by frequency division multiplexing) into multiple channels.

bed in Of a computer or other system; to achieve a level of reliability at which few failures occur and little unplanned maintenance is required.

bed of nails A term applied to automatic testing equipment (for integrated circuits) that attempts to reveal faults by applying 'worst case' conditions (overspeed clocking; overvoltage).

before journal A before-look journal.

before-look journal A backup file holding data in its previous condition of update which is maintained for purposes of reconstructing a current master file in event of its corruption. See *after-look journal.*

before-look journalising When a file is updated; to record the records that are to be changed in a journal file.

beginning-of-tape (BOT) A marker (reflective strip; transparent section) that indicates the beginning of the recording area of a reel of magnetic tape.

bel (B) Ten decibels.

BEL *BELl.* A character in a data transmission code that is used to cause an electronically generated tone to sound at a terminal in order to attract the attention of the operator; for example, when an error in input is detected.

bell (1) A device that produces an audible sound; for example, in a telephone. **(2)(Bell)** An identifier of a product or service of the American Telephone & Telegraph Co.

Bell Data Network (BDN) An American Telephone & Telegraph Co. system intended to provide subscribers with an extensive range of data-base access and communications facilities, comparable in scope to those provided by the Satellite Business System. See *Satellite Business System*.

belt printer (1) A band printer. **(2)** A printer in which embossed characters on short type bars attached to a belt move along the line to be printed and are selectively struck from behind by a solenoid as they pass the printing position.

benchmark (1) To compare the relative performance of different computer systems or subsystems. Examples of use include determining whether or not additional main storage would be cost effective, comparing competetive computers and/or peripherals, and determining which available operating system would be most effective for a particular workload. It normally consists of running specially designed **benchmark programs** on or with each item to be compared and recording performance. **(2)** With new system software; to compare actual performance with expected performance to determine if tuning is required.

benchmark package A set of programs and data designed to test relative performance. See *benchmark*.

benchmark program See *benchmark*.

bespoke A term sometimes applied to software that has been particularly designed and written for an application (as contrasted, for example, to a program from an application package or provided on ROM).

best fit See *allocation algorithm*.

bias (1) A uniform deviation of values from a reference or correct value; for example, a plus 5 V. error in all the readings of a voltmeter. **(2)** A voltage applied continuously at some point in an electronic circuit for purposes of stabilisation or control. **(3)** An induced inequality; ('biased partitioning').

biased partitioning Partitioning in which concurrent programs are allocated different amounts of main storage. See *partitioning; virtual storage partitioning*.

bidirectional (1) Of a character printer; capable of printing lines from right to left as well as left to right (and, thus, eliminating 'flyback' when beginning a new line). **(2)** Of a data bus; capable of handling transfers in both directions.

bill of materials (BOM) An application package used by a manufacturer to organise and reference records of parts and products. It can, typically, be used to identify the parts and subassemblies in products or larger assemblies, the quantity of each required, unit costs, and production and purchasing details.

binary A number system with a radix of 2; the usual number system of computers and related equipment. It has just two digits, '0' and '1'; the '0' serves the same function as the '0' in decimal in indicating the weight (positional value) of other digits. In the binary system, the '1' is the only non-zero digit; it has no direct relation to '1' in decimal. In decimal, shifting a digit one place to the left multiplies it by 10 (300 is ten times 30) while in binary it multiplies by 2 (100 is two times 10). The decimal equivalents of the first seven binary digit positions are as follows:

64 32 16 4 2 1

(Others can be added by successively multiplying by 2; the next two are, then, 128 and 256. To convert a number in binary to decimal, simply add the positional values of all the 1's. For example, to convert 1001010 to decimal, add 64 (the positional value of the first '1'), 8 (the positional value of the next '1') and 2 (the positional value of the remaining '1'). The result is, then, 74. Conversion from decimal to binary is done by finding the combination of binary positional values required to equal the decimal number and placing ones in the digit positions where the positional values are required and zeros in the other digit positions. For example, to convert decimal 237 to binary requires the values 128, 64, 32, 8, 4, and 1 because this is the combination with a total of 237. To construct the binary number, place a 1 in the seventh digit position (for 128), followed by 1's in all the other digit positions except the fourth where a 0 is placed (positional value 16 is not used). The resulting binary number is, then, 1110111. Following are some other decimal numbers and their binary equivalents:

Decimal	*Binary*	*Decimal*	*Binary*
1	1	10	1010
2	10	22	10110
3	11	65	1000001
7	111	117	1101011

For storage and manipulation by machine, binary has a major advantage over decimal because only two digits are required and these can be readily represented physically by an electric current on or off, North-South magnetisation, and the presence or absence of capacitive charges. See *bit; number; numeration system; character; storage; binary arithmetic.*

binary arithmetic Arithmetic performed with binary numbers, typically, by an arithmetic logic unit of a computer. Addition is fundamental and is performed directly by electronic circuits; subtraction may be performed directly or by means of addition after negative numbers have been complemented. Multiplication is performed by addition and shifting (moving digits to higher or lower digit positions) and division is performed by subtraction and shifting. Operations are performed on only two numbers at a time, The following are the four possible additions of binary digits:

First digit	0	0	1	1
Second digit	0	1	0	1
Total	0	1	1	10

Note that a carry to the next digit position occurs only when a one is added to a one and that '1' is the only possible carry in the system. The following are some examples of binary addition together with their decimal equivalents:

$1+1=2$	$2+2=4$	$6+3=9$	$10+5=15$	$37+22=59$
1	10	110	1010	100101
1	10	11	101	10110
10	100	1001	1111	111011

The following are the four possible subtractions of binary digits; a borrow digit is shown in parentheses where it is required:

First digit	0	(1)0	1	1
Second digit	0	1	0	1
Total	0	1	1	0

Note that a borrow digit is required only when a one is subtracted from a zero. The following are some examples of binary subtraction together with their decimal equivalents:

$2-1=1$	$5-3=2$	$10-2=8$	$15-9=6$	$43-18=25$
10	101	1010	1111	101011
1	11	10	1001	10010
1	10	1000	110	11001

binary cell A storage cell; a basic unit of computer storage capable of holding either a '1' or a '0'.
binary check digit A check bit.
binary chop A binary search.
binary code A code in which each element is a '1' or a '0'.
binary coded decimal (BCD) (1)A method of representing decimal numbers in binary notation in which each decimal digit is held in four binary digits (a 'numeric') between 0000 (zero) and 1001 (nine). Decimal 2 would then be 0010 and 6 would be 0110. Note the difference between BCD and pure binary; for example, in '87' which is 1000 0111 in BCD and 1010111 in binary. See *hexadecimal; EBCDIC.* (2)A 6-level, 64-character code as used in some telegraphy and word processing systems.
binary coded notation The use of binary numbers to represent digits in a non-binary numeration system; for example, 'binary coded decimal'.
binary coded octal See *octal.*
binary data Data in binary representation. See *digital data.*
binary digit Also *bit.* Either a '0' or a '1'.
binary dump A dump in binary form (as contrasted to one in decimal or one in characters). The term may be applied to a dump of the actual bit patterns held in storage/registers or to the (more usual) system in which the bit patterns are expressed in octal or hexadecimal. See *dump.*
binary element A representation of either of the two values in a binary system; for example a bit or a voltage that represents a bit in data transfer.
binary format (1)A term that is sometimes applied to data as represented by bit patterns. (2)A computational format in which numeric data is represented as fixed-point binary numbers. See *computational format.*
binary image See *image.*
binary loader An absolute loader.
binary notation Any representation by means of binary digits; for example, by encoded characters, binary numbers, or the reflected binary code.
binary number A number consisting only of binary digits.
binary numeral (1)A binary digit; a '0' or a '1'. (2)A binary number.
binary numeration system See *numeration system.*
binary operation A dyadic operation.
binary search See *search.*
binary storage The type of storage of a computer system; storage

in which data is held as combinations of 0-bits and 1-bits. The bits may be physically represented in various ways; for example, as direction of magnetisation of cores or surface particles, as a transistor in a flip-flop circuit turned on or off, and as presence or absence of a capacitive charge. See *storage; storage cell.*

binary symmetric A term applied to a data channel in which the chances of 0-bits being changed to 1-bits (by interference; circuit failures) are the same as the chances of 1-bits being changed to 0-bits.

binary synchronous communications (BSC; bisync) A method of data transmission in which synchronisation between a sending and receiving station is established before a message is sent and checked and adjusted during transmission. The bit patterns constituting characters are transmitted in a continuous stream and are separated by receiving hardware by using the synchronising information. It is the common method of medium and high-speed data communications. See *start-stop; synchronous; asynchronous; handshaking.*

bind (1) A compilation step of assigning storage-related (relative; virtual) addresses to the symbolic addresses of a source program. **(2)** To assign an attribute to a variable or a value to a parameter; for example, a variable PERCENT may be bound when declared to be an integer and bound for a particular run when declared to be, say, '10'. **(3)** To join object modules, library routines, and/or other units of code to form a load module.

binding time During compilation; the time when symbolic addresses are converted to storage-related addresses. See *bind* (def. 1).

bionics The study of the structural and functional similarities between machine systems and controls and biological systems and controls; for example, between computer memory and the brain and between thermostats and regulators of body temperature.

biplexor A two-channel multiplexor.

bipolar signalling Signalling (data transmission) consisting of both positive and negative pulses. See *NRZ.*

bipolar transistor An NPN transistor or a PNP transistor; a transistor in which an external circuit is used to control operation by controlling the flow of electrons between the gate and emitter. See *transistor; field effect transistor; unipolar.*

bipolar signalling Polar signalling.

bipolar transmission Polar transmission.

biquinary code A mixed-base code sometimes used to represent decimal digits in a binary form. The three least significant digit positions are used to hold a binary value in the range 0-4 and the fourth digit position holds either a '0' or a '1' which represents '5'. The code is as follows:

Decimal	Binary	Biquinary
0	0000	0000
1	0001	0001
2	0010	0010
3	0011	0011
4	0100	0100
5	0101	1000
6	0110	1001
7	0111	1010
8	1000	1011
9	1001	1100

When the representation form is changed to 'tally', it is the system used with the abacus. See *abacus.*

bistable Having two maintainable states or conditions.

bistable circuit A flip-flop; a trigger circuit with two stable states. See *monostable circuit; flip-flop.*

bistable trigger circuit A bistable circuit.

BISYNC *BInary SYNChronous communications.*

bit *BInary digiT.* **(1)** A digit in the binary numeration system; either a '1' (1-bit) or a '0' (0-bit). **(2)** A physical representation of a 'bit' in transmission or storage; for example a pulse on a data transfer circuit or a magnetised core in core memory. See *binary cell; storage.*

bit cell (1) The time frame for writing a bit to a track (magnetic disc; magnetic tape). **(2)** A length of track with magnetisation interpretable as a bit. **(3)** A storage cell.

bit density Of a storage medium; the number of bits that can be recorded per unit length, area, or volume.

bit interleaved A term applied with respect to time division multiplexing to indicate that the single multiplexed channel receives one bit in turn from each active terminal when sending and supplies one bit in turn to each active terminal when receiving. See *character interleaved; time division multiplexing.*

bit line In coordinate-addressable memory; a conductor that connects to the same numbered storage cell of each location (word;

byte) of a storage module (say, an integrated circuit or core plane). A computer with 32-bit words would, then, have 32 bit lines in each storage module. See *word line; coincident current selection.*

bit manipulation The facility or activity involved in reading and writing single bit positions (of registers); for example, in setting and clearing flags.

bit map A table in which the elements are identifiers (say, of peripheral devices) and single bits associated with each; for example, a 0-bit to indicate that a peripheral is free and a 1-bit to indicate that it is in use.

bit multiplexed Bit interleaved.

bit parallel A term used to denote the simultaneous and multi-channel transfer of bit patterns; for example, those that constitute words, bytes, or characters. It is the method of transfer used within a computer. See *bit serial.*

bit pattern (1) An arrangement or sequence of bits in computer storage; for example, the bits of a word or those that form the dot matrix representation of the letter 'A'. **(2)** A bit sequence that constitutes a binary number or represents a character in some code; for example, 11011 (binary 27) or 10011 (the character 'B' in the IA-2 code.).

bit period (1) A data bit period. See *data bit.* **(2)** The time taken to read, write, or transmit a bit.

bit position (1) An identified bit cell in a storage location; for example, 'bit position 12' in a word. **(2)** A digit position in a binary number.

bit rate Data signalling rate; the speed of data transfer (in bits per second).

bit/s *BITs per Second.*

bit serial A term used to denote the sequential and single-channel transfer of bit patterns; for example, those that constitute words, bytes, or characters. It is the usual method of data transmission over lines and, in a computer system, to and from terminals as well as peripherals. See *bit parallel.*

bit shift Also *peak shift.* A characteristic of high-density magnetisable surface recording in which flux reversals move slightly from the positions in which they were intended to be placed by the head when writing. The movements are in complex but predictable patterns from areas of closely spaced reversals toward more 'open' sections of track. The problem can be overcome by 'write compensation' in which patterns to be written are first analysed in a shift register to determine if each bit is

to be written early, late, or on-time. Further compensation can be obtained by using 'phase-locked loop' read timing.

bit slice A microprocessor 'building block' consisting of an arithmetic logic unit of a certain number of bits ('a 4-bit slice') and associated circuitry. A bit slice is so constructed that it can be interfaced with others to form a larger ALU. For example, a 16-bit ALU for a 16-bit microprocessor could be implemented with four '4-bit slices'.

bit string See *string.*

bit stuffing A provision of SDLC, HDLC and X.25 (packet switching) protocols by which a transmitting DTE adds and a receiving DTE deletes a 0-bit after any sequence of five 1-bits. The purpose is to ensure that no sequence in user data will constitute a 'flag' (the group 01111110).

bit synchronised In bit serial transmission; with the bits of each bit pattern sent in fixed time relationship to each other. The bit patterns (say those that encode characters) need not be synchronised. See *asynchronous transmission; character synchronised; synchronisation.*

bits per inch (BPI; bpi). The number of bits recorded per inch of track on a magnetisable surface storage medium.

bits per second (BPS; bps.; bit/s) The number of bits transferred per second on a data communications channel. See *Baud.*

black box A term sometimes applied to a device (or, possibly a unit of software) that performs some function by a method that is unknown to the user or observer. See *open box.*

black noise Impulse noise; a noise (on a communications line) other than 'white noise'. See *noise.*

blank (1) Not containing bit patterns or hole patterns; ('a blank magnetic tape'; 'a blank punch card'). **(2)** Of a print or display surface or area of such a surface; not containing data or display elements; ('a blank screen'; 'a blank form'; 'a blank line'). **(3)** To remove display elements from a screen or to prevent them from appearing.

blank character A null character or, possibly, a space character.

blank coil A term that has been applied to a roll of paper tape in which no data holes have been punched.

blending A term sometimes applied to the function of a linkage editor or linkage loader in combining two or more modules of code to produce a single load module.

blink Of display elements on a VDU (say, a cursor or an error message); to remove and replace at short intervals (in order to draw the attention of an operator).

blip Also *image count; document mark*. A mark (clear spot on film) placed below frames on roll microfilm in some systems; they are photoelectrically sensed and counted as an aid in locating particular frames. See *COM*.

block (1)In most systems; the standard unit of storage allocation and transfer for data on magnetic disc, drum, or tape; a group of records treated as an entity for access purposes. (2)An area (group of contiguous locations) in main storage or other coordinate-addressable storage as considered for allocation or access. (3)To place two or more units of code or data (record; page; segment) in a single 'block' (def. 1 or 2). (4)A major program unit in a block-structured language; a sequence of statements between BEGIN and END. (5)Also *module*. A standard-size unit of (add-on) coordinate-addressable storage; ('an 8K block of core'). (6)Also *segment*. In some systems; a fixed-length part of a track on magnetic disc. See *magnetic disc unit*. (7)In data communications; the number (or maximum number) of characters sent consecutively (as established by the link protocol); the message unit to which error detection and control are applied. See *block length*. (8)On a communications line; to mask signals with noise. See *noise*. (9)To prevent the flow of current; for example, with a 'blocking diode'. (10)An outline form as in a 'block diagram'.

block binding time During compilation; the point at which the blocks of a block-structured source program are assigned numbers within the address space of the program. See *binding time*.

block cancel character In some systems; a transmission control character that cancels the previous block or portion of an uncompleted block.

block character Also *end of transmission block character*. A transmission control character marking the end of a block in a data transmission.

block check character (BCC) In data communications; a final character of a message or block that is constructed in accordance with some algorithm to assist in detecting errors. See *parity; cyclic check character*.

block diagram A diagram of a device, circuit, or system in which the functional elements are represented by (labelled) outline forms with the outline forms connected by lines that indicate control or sequencing relationships.

block gap An interblock gap.

block ignore character A block cancel character.

block interleaved In transfers of blocks to or from multiple peripheral devices; a method of organising transfers in which one block is read from (or written to) each device in turn until all blocks have been transferred. See *bit interleaved; character interleaved*.

block length (1)In data communications; the maximum number of characters that can be transmitted consecutively (as established by the link protocol). A message shorter than 'block length' constitutes a block and a longer message must be divided into blocks for transmission. (2)The maximum number of bytes, words, or records in a block (def. 1) as specified for a storage device or file on a storage device. (3)The actual number of data units (bits; bytes; characters; words; fixed-length records) in a block.

block loading The placement of a load module in contiguous main storage locations. See *scatter loading*.

block multiplexed Block interleaved.

block multiplexing A peripheral transfer facility in which blocks from different devices are interleaved on the transfer channel.

block parity A parity check made on a block; the use of a block check character. See *parity*.

block sort A two-level sort in which the items to be sorted are first sorted into groups according to the highest-level digit(s) of their keys; the groups are then sorted separately and joined.

block-structured Also *modular*. Organised into discrete sections that can be dealt with individually and linked to form a larger unit.

block transfer The transfer of one or more blocks between storage units or devices with initiation by a single action.

blocked (1)Formed into blocks ('blocked records'). (2)Prevented from occurring; ('blocked access'; 'blocked interrupts').

blocked job A suspended job. See *suspend*.

blocked record One of two or more records held in a single block (def. 1).

blocking diode A diode placed in a circuit to prevent a reverse current flow that could damage other circuit elements or degrade performance. See *diode; wired-OR*.

blocking factor (1)The number of records in a block (def. 1 or 6). (2)The number of units present as a percentage of the number a block can hold.

BNC A designation of a bayonet-type connector for joining coaxial cables in the size range from 0.1 to 0.25 inches in diameter.

BNF *Backus Normal Form; Backus Naur Form.*
board A printed circuit board.
boilerplate A term sometimes applied to a copy intended for use in making other copies; for example, to a macro definition table or a subroutine that is incorporated in different places in a program.
boldface A term applied to type that is **heavier or darker** than the 'medium' face of a type font.
BOM *Bill Of Materials.*
Boolean algebra Also, usually, *symbolic logic.* The statement of logical relationships or the solution of logical problems by the use of expressions in which each element can have only one of two possible values. The values are usually expressed as 'true' and 'false' and are represented in computer operations by '1' (true) and '0' (false). See *logic.*
Boolean expression An expression, such as 'P AND Q' that, when evaluated for a particular set of inputs, produces a result that is either 'True' or 'False'. See *logic; truth table.*
Boolean function A switching function in which each variable is limited to one of two possible values. See *function.*
Boolean operator A logic operator; AND, OR, NOT or a combination.
Boolean test A logical test.
Boolean valued expression A Boolean expression.
boot (1) The operation of loading an operating system and, possibly, other system software (from magnetic tape or disc). It is assumed to be for start-up rather than for recovery. See *cold boot; warm boot.* **(2)** Also *bootstrap.* To load a program or set of programs with a bootstrap loader; for example, to 'boot in' an operating system.
boot up To perform a bootstrap operation; particularly to load an operating system.
bootstrap (1) The technique of bringing a large program or a group of programs into main storage by first inputting a few instructions (usually from a read-only memory) that can bring in other instructions that can, in turn, bring in others until the entire unit (say, an operating system) is loaded. See *auto-load.* **(2)** A sequence of instructions used to load others. **(3)** To write a compiler in the programming language that it will be used to compile.
bootstrap loader A loader that uses simple, preset instructions to load other sequences of instructions.
bootstrap routine A bootstrap loader.

borrow A basic operation in performing subtraction in a positional representation number system such as binary or decimal; it consists of taking a '1' from the digit position of next higher weight when the subtrahend is larger than the minuend in a particular digit position. See *carry; binary arithmetic.*
BOT (1) *Beginning Of Tape.* **(2)** *Beginning Of Transfer.*
both-way communications The communications mode of a full-duplex circuit; communications in which data transfers can occur simultaneously in both directions.
bottom address A base address.
bottom-of-stack pointer Also *frame pointer.* The address of the lowest numbered location in a stack. See *stack; top-of-stack pointer.*
bound (1) Assigned or allocated. See *bind.* **(2)** Of an active program; limited in speed of execution due to restricted availability of a resource; ('processor bound'; 'peripheral bound'). **(3)** Also *boundary.* The highest or lowest numbered location in an area of storage. **bound check** A check by supervisory software to determine that a decoded instruction address is within an area of storage permitted to the program or that it is not outside the limits of an area of storage or data structure (say, an array) that it is accessing at that time. **bound limits** Also *bounds.* The highest and lowest numbered locations in an area of storage or data structure. **bound violation** A flag event resulting from the failure of a bound check.
boundary (1) Also *bound.* The highest or lowest numbered location in an area of storage. **(2)** The end of a storage location and (usually) the beginning of another; ('a block boundary'; 'a word boundary').
boundary layer See *air boundary layer.*
box An outline form; for example, in a flowchart.
BPI (bpi.) *Bits Per Inch.*
BPMM (bpmm.) *Bits Per MilliMeter.*
BPO *British Post Office.*
BPS (bps.) *Bits Per Second.*
branch (1) In a program; one of two or more sequences of instructions that may be followed during execution depending upon the result of a test applied to data ; in a flowchart, it is one path from a decision box. Whether a particular sequence of instructions is to be considered a 'branch' or the 'main sequence' depends upon how the decision instruction is formed; the branch is usually the sequence (or one of the sequences) executed less frequently. See *branchpoint; decision instruction.*

(2) To commence the execution of the instructions of a 'branch' (def. 1). See *call; jump*. **(3)** In a tree structure; all the entities accessible by a single owner (other than the root). See *tree*. **(4)** A fanned-out circuit, for example, from a terminal control unit to one terminal. **(5)** A circuit connecting two nodes of a network.

branch instruction Also *jump instruction*. An instruction that, when decoded during execution, can cause execution to shift to another sequence of instructions. The term includes both conditional and unconditional branch instructions; unless otherwise indicated, it is understood to be 'conditional'. See *conditional statement; branch; sequence control statement*.

branchpoint Also *decision point; switch; switchpoint*. **(1)** A place in a flowchart where a decision box or connector is placed; a place indicating that the sequence of instructions can (or must be) changed during execution. **(2)** A place in source language coding where a branch instruction is written. **(3)** A point during the execution of a program at which the sequence of instructions being executed can (or must be) changed; a place at which an object code branch instruction is decoded. See *instruction; branch; branch instruction*.

breadboard To lay electronic components out on a surface (notionally a 'breadboard') and make wiring interconnections; it is the usual first step in developing an electronic circuit after a circuit diagram has been prepared.

break (1) To discontinue transmitting or receiving a message without completing it. **(2)** A programmed interrupt.

breakout box A unit that can be placed in a multiconductor circuit (say, between a computer and a modem) to provide terminal connections for circuit testing.

breakpoint A place where the execution of a program is to be halted (temporarily) during execution; for example, to permit the operator to make some check. See *interrupt; checkpoint; breakpoint instruction*.

breakpoint instruction An instruction that causes a breakpoint halt; typically, it is an instruction that calls itself thus creating a one-instruction closed loop that is detected by a monitor program to cause an interrupt.

bridgeware Software (and, possibly, hardware) used to convert programs and data so that they can be used with a different type of computer than the one for which they were written and formatted. See *emulation; conversion*.

British Telecom (BT) The telecommunications branch of the British Post Office.

brittle Of a program or type of program; specific to a particular computer or installation; not easily moved or adapted for use in another system. See *portable*.

broadband See *band; wideband*.

brother A twin. See *tree*.

brought-forward file A master file input to a program that updates by copying. See *carried-forward file; update*.

brownout proof A term applied to a power supply that protects against low voltage by either disconnecting the load or switching to a standby if it is unable to maintain a minimum voltage.

brush (1) A spring-loaded element (usually of carbon) that completes an electric circuit to a rotating slipring or commutator (as in a generator). **(2)** In earlier punch card and paper tape readers; wires that electrically detect holes; as a hole passes in a particular punching position, a wire that was previously insulated by the paper makes contact with a metal backing surface and thus 'reads' the hole.

BS (1) *Back Space*. A format effector used to move a printing position or VDU cursor back one character space. **(2)** *British Standard*. Promulgated or approved by the British Standards Institution. **(3)** (b/s) *Bits per Second*.

BSC *Binary Synchronous Communications*.

BSI *British Standards Institution*. (London)

BT *British Telecom*.

bubble memory Also *magnetic bubble memory*. A memory in which bits are represented by small (3-6 micron) magnetised areas (bubbles; domains) in a thin, planar, orthoferrite material (crystalline yttrium-iron garnet). In its unwritten form the orthoferrite material has a random and 'serpentine' magnetisation with some areas weakly North and others weakly South. When a magnetic field is applied to the surface by conductors, a bubble is created and its field repels the weak magnetisation immediately surrounding it. Once created, a bubble can be moved along the surface by applying appropriate magnetic fields and this is done by currents in small 'bars' and 'T's or, alternatively, 'V's in a chevron arrangement, that are deposited on the orthoferrite material by the same techniques used to form conductors in integrated circuits. If the TI bars or chevrons are arranged in interconnected rows with the last joined to the first, the entire crystal area (a square of from 5 to 7 mm. on each side) can be used as a recirculating memory with a capacity of up to about 64K bits and an access time in the range of 4-40 ms. Another construction uses short (say, 1K) loops that are individually addressable with output to a common read channel. Such devices have a capacity of up to 256K bits and an average access time as low as 7 ms. At any given place along the loop, a bubble represents a 1-bit and no bubble a 0-bit; the memory is read by a sensor along the loop that detects the magnetic field of bubbles. In another (experimental) system, bubble spacing is decreased by using bubbles of opposite polarity for 1-bits and 0-bits and these are arranged in 32 × 32 bit matrices with reading accomplished by shifting an entire 32-bit row to a read channel. Bubble memories are used in portable terminals and as VDU buffers and as fast-access backing storage for limited quantities of data. The memory is static and non-volatile.

bubble sort An exchange sort.

bucket The standard unit of transfer in some magnetic disc systems; it may consist of one or more blocks. See *block*.

bucket number A number that identifies a bucket for access.

bucket brigade A term sometimes applied to recirculating memory. See *recirculating memory*.

budget The amount of computer time (and, possibly, other resources) that a user or job (say, the payroll) is allowed to have during a particular period. The operating system and/or the operator keep a record of the amount used in each run for each user and job. See *allowance; accounting*.

buffer (1) An area of storage where data is held temporarily to facilitate transfer between devices operating at different speeds or on different time cycles; for example, an area of main storage that holds incoming messages and outgoing replies in a transaction processing system or a memory in a line printer that holds one line of characters to be printed. **(2)** In a VDU or supporting unit of terminal control equipment; an area of storage that can hold all the characters that appear on the screen at one time; it is scanned to refresh the display. (It may also be termed 'refresh memory'.) **(3)** A circuit isolator; elements between two interrelated circuits that restrict the type of signals or current that can be passed from one to the other. Examples include an optical coupler and a gated D (tri-state) flip-flop.

bug (1) An error in a program or system software. See *debug; fault*. **(2)** In a functional unit; an unidentified fault that causes a degradation of performance. See *fault*.

bulk data A term sometimes applied to data held in large magnetic disc storage.

bulk information Bulk data.

bulk storage (1) Also *large core storage; extended core storage*. An auxiliary core storage that provides an access speed between that of main storage and that of drum or fixed-head disc. Typically, it is slow-speed (say, 5 μs.) core and can be accessed directly by the control unit (without I/O channels). **(2)** Also *mass storage*. Large magnetic disc storage.

bundled A term applied to software (possibly to other items) that are available from a manufacturer or supplier only as part of a package (say, of a new computer) and cannot be purchased separately. See *unbundle*.

bundled cable Round, multi-conductor cable (as contrasted to ribbon cable).

bureau An organisation (usually with a computer) that sells data processing services.

burner A PROM burner.

burst (1) In data transmission; a short sequence of signals with separate identity for some purpose; for example, the signals constituting an address or error message. **(2)** In data transmission, a number of line events that occur more or less consecutively; ('a burst of errors'; 'a burst of noise'). **(3)** Also *decollate*. To separate multi-part continuous stationary after printing.

burst transmission (2) The short, high-speed transmission of a message or group of messages to one addressee. **(2)** Data transmission in buffer-size increments from a high-speed source to a low-speed, buffered receiver (say, a printing terminal) with send initiation from the receiver.

burster A decollator.

bus (1) Also *highway; trunk*. A major path for data transfer within a computer or other functional unit. **(2)** A tube or bar used as a high-capacity electrical conductor.

bus-organised A term applied to a computer system in which all inputs and outputs to and from the central processor are made in standard format and at standard speed over a single bus. The system provides intelligent (often microprocessor-based) interface units (peripheral controllers; communications adapters) to perform code conversion, format changing, and buffering as required between the bus and the various devices and lines of the system.

business machine A machine used to facilitate business clerical or accounting operations; for example, an electric typewriter, a calculator, or a comptometer. (As commonly used, the term does not include computers.)

business system (1) A system (methods; forms; equipment) that performs some business function; ('an accounting system'; 'a payroll system'; 'an inventory control system'). **(2)** A computer system designed to meet business needs. See *small business system*.

business systems analysis See *systems analysis*.

byte (1) A standard-length binary string that is the smallest unit of access in many computers; it is, typically, eight bits in length. **(2)** An accessible unit of coordinate-addressable storage that can hold one byte; it is, typically, a division of a computer word. See *word*. **(3)** Eight bits as a unit of storage capacity or speed of data transfer; ('a 20-byte buffer'; 'a throughput of 20,000 bytes per second'). See *character; word; numeric; kilobyte second*.

byte machine A computer or other intelligent device in which the byte (eight bits) is a standard unit of data access and manipulation. See *word machine*.

byte multiplexor A multiplexor in which the byte is the interleaved unit of data transfer. See *multiplexing*.

C

C (1) *Capacitance*. **(2)** *Combination*.
C-record *Complementary-record*.
cable (1) A flexible wire or group of wires with insulating and damage-protecting external cover as used to carry signals or electric current between locations or between functional units. See *bundled cable; ribbon cable*. **(2)** A large 'cable' (def. 1) as laid on the ocean floor to carry intercontinental messages. **(3)** A transocean telegram.
cache A unit of fast coordinate-addressable storage used in some systems to hold data with high access probability. See *slave store*.
CAD *Computer-Aided Design*.
CAF *Content-Addressable Filestore*.
cage A group of slots with electrical connectors used to hold replaceable printed circuit boards in a functional unit.
CAI *Computer-Aided Instruction*.
CAL *Computer-Aided Learning*.
calc record *CALCulated record*. A record located in storage by an algorithm applied to its key; a record in a random file.

calculator An elementary data processor for performing arithmetic operations; it may have a memory and limited programmability. All functions are, typically, performed by a single MOSFET integrated circuit. The elements of the IC are, typically, user memory to hold keyed inputs, microprogram memory with one program for each function, accumulator registers to hold parameters, counts, and partial results, an adder/subtractor, a clock and scan generator, and a segment decoder to control the display.

call (1) By an executing program (the **calling routine**); to transfer control (use of the central processor) to another sequence of instructions (the **called routine**) with provision for storing the address in the calling routine to which control will be returned when the called routine has finished executing. An **external call** is a call to a separately compiled sequence (say, to a library routine) and it is programmed by writing a **CALL statement**. A unit of system software that performs an external call is a **call routine** which, in some systems, is termed a **procedure call mechanism**. In addition to passing control, it, typically, stores the return address (in a stack or general-purpose register), passes parameters from the calling to the called routine, stores the results produced by the called routine in a register or work area where they can be retrieved by the calling routine when required for further steps of processing, and uses the return address to return control to the calling routine. A return address is often termed a **link** and the instruction that provides it a **linkage instruction**. Called routines may themselves call other routines and such secondary calls are **nested calls**. An **internal call** is a reference by an executing instruction to a sequence of instructions that has been compiled with the program in which it is called. Its purpose is to make use of a single copy of the sequence in two or more locations where it is required and thus to save coding effort and storage space. In the common high-level languages, an internal call is programmed by writing a PERFORM or DO statement. The term 'call' in lower case can refer to either an internal or external call while 'CALL' always indicates an external call. See *invoke; branch; reference*; **(2)** Also *reference*. By an active process in a virtual storage system, to produce an address in a page or segment that is not in primary storage and, thus, to request the operating system to locate the page/segment in secondary storage and bring it into primary storage. See *virtual storage transfers*. **(3)** In a telephone system; to initiate an interchange (by dialing a number). **(4)**An interchange between two users of a telephone system as initiated by a 'call' (def. 3). **(5)**Also *address*. By a data station or data terminal equipment in a data network; to transmit the address of another data station or DTE to initiate a data transfer. See *polling; selection*.

called routine See *call* (def. 1).

called sequence A called routine.

calligraphic See *vector scan*.

calling routine See *call* (def. 1).

calling sequence (1) See *call routine* (def. 1, 2). **(2)**A polling list.

CAM (1)*Computer Aided Manufacturing*. **(2)***Content Addressable Memory*.

CAMAC *Computer Automated Measurement And Control (Association)*.

camp-on To reserve 'next use' rights to a (telephone) line that is in use.

CAN *CANcel*. A transmission control character used to indicate that all previous characters in a message or block are to be disregarded.

cancel character Also *ignore character*. A control character used to indicate that previous characters are to be disregarded. Depending on the system, 'previous characters' may be a word, a line, or the previous part of a message or block. See *CAN*.

canister A metal container (as used to store magnetic tape).

canonical Of data; in standard code and format for the particular computer or computer system. The term is used to indicate that any device or media related variations have been eliminated by preprocessing steps.

CAP *Computer Analysts & Programmers Ltd.* (London)

capability (1) The quality of being able to perform a task or function. **(2)**A reference passed by a compiler and accessed by storage protection software during execution in some systems. It is used to establish the access right of a program to a particular unit of data on the basis that if it can produce a correct reference it has the right to use it. See *storage protection*.

capacitance (C) The amount of static electricity that is stored on conductors of different electrical potential when they are in proximity and separated by a dielectric. The effect is to delay the change of potential when their input potentials change. The usual units of measurement are the microfarad and picofarad.

capacitor A circuit element that stores electrons, typically, as a charge on insulated, adjacent layers of aluminium foil. A capacitor can maintain a (small) current flow after the supply is turned off (to provide a time delay), it can hold a charge and release it when a circuit is closed (to provide timing or control pulses) and it can 'absorb' electrons (to reduce peak voltages or voltage fluctuations).

capacity (1) Maximum volume, say, of a storage device or of a data transfer channel. **(2)**Capacitance.

capacity-activated transducer A proximity sensing device that operates by change of capacitance; for example, an element of a switch that turns on or off when a finger is placed against it.

capstan A motor-driven roller that moves the tape in a magnetic tape unit. See *magnetic tape unit*.

capture See *data capture*.

carbonless copy A term applied to paper used in multipart forms that produce copies by chemical transfer from the back of one piece of paper to the front of another (and, thus, eliminates the need for carbon paper).

card (1)A punched card. **(2)**A removable printed circuit board. **(3)**A magnetic card. **(4)**A ledger card.

card-based A term applied to a computer system in which the main or only input is by means of punched cards.

card code A code used to represent the characters of a character set as patterns of holes in punched cards. See *punched card; code; Hollerith*.

card column A line parallel to the short edges of a punched card along which the hole pattern of a character can be punched. See *punched card; card row*.

card copier A card reproducer.

card deck Also *card pack*. A set of punched cards intended to be read consecutively. A card deck typically contains the source code for a program or module or the data for a run.

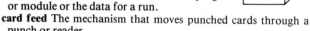

card feed The mechanism that moves punched cards through a punch or reader.

card field On a punched card; a group of adjacent punching positions for a particular item or group; for example, the columns that are used to hold an employee's name and address.

card file (1)A storage location for cards. **(2)**An ordered collection of related data (a computer file) as held on punched cards. See *card deck*.

card image A representation of the hole patterns of a punched card as held in uninterpreted form on the magnetic media of computer storage. (As contrasted to the usual inputs in which the patterns are converted from the card code to the internal storage code of the computer.)

card jam Folded or twisted punched cards in the card path of a punch or reader; a blockage of card flow.

card pack A card deck.

card path The route that punched cards follow through a punch or reader.

card punch A device used to punch data-related hole patterns in punched cards; the term may be applied to a computer-output peripheral, a data preparation keypunch, or a hand punch.

card rate The number of cards punched or read per unit time (usually per minute).

card reader A computer input device that reads hole patterns in punched cards. A roller moves the cards between a light source and a line of photocells in which there is one photocell for each

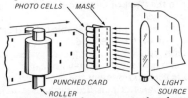

card row. As each card column passes the photocells, those at positions where holes are punched receive light and turn on (change resistance) thus providing an input to electronic circuits that identify the character represented by the pattern.

card reproducer Also *card copier*. A device that reads the hole patterns in a punched card and punches the same patterns in another card.

card row A line parallel to the long edges of a punched card along which holes can be punched; cards typically have ten or twelve rows. See *punched card; card column*.

card sorter A device that locates and separates all the cards of a group with identical punching in specified punching positions.

card verifier A device (in a data preparation department) to check the accuracy of card punching and source document interpretation. After a card has been punched by one operator, it is placed in the verifier where another operator reads the same data from the source document and repeats the key strokes required to punch it. A keystroke in verification that does not duplicate the punching causes rejection of the card.

carriage The part of a printer (such as an ordinary typewriter) that carries a platen roll and moves the print medium horizontally as when printing a line or changing to print a new line. (In some contexts, the term may be used for the part that holds the paper during printing, whether or not it moves.)

carriage return (1) In a printer or VDU; a movement of the printing position or cursor to the beginning of the next line to be printed or displayed. See *CR*. **(2)** A key that causes a 'carriage return' (def. 1). **(3)** A movement to the beginning of the current line. See *newline*. **(4)** Return.

carried-forward file A master file output from an update program. See *brought-forward file*.

carrier (1) A carrier wave. **(2)** The smallest unit that supports electron flow in a semiconductor material; a hole in P-type silicon or a free electron in N-type silicon. See *semiconductor*. **(3)** In a golfball printer or typewriter; the horizontally movable element that carries the golfball.

carrier system A communications system in which data or speech is transmitted by means of a carrier wave. Such systems include radio, multiplexed telephone links, and most data communications systems. See *carrier wave; baseband signalling*.

carrier wave Also *carrier*. A wave generated by an oscillator and transmitted on a communications channel; it is modulated to carry speech or data. See *modulation; band; multiplexing; sideband; baseband signalling; CW*.

carry A basic operation in performing addition in a positional representation numeration system such as binary or decimal; it consists of placing a digit in the digit position of next higher weight when a sum of the digits in one digit position is greater than can be represented in a single digit position. The digit placed in the digit position of next higher weight is the **carry digit**. See *borrow; adder; standing on nines*.

carry-look-ahead adder See *adder*.

cartridge (1) A term applied to a module of magnetisable surface storage medium that is designed to be stored separately from the device on which it is read and written. See *disc cartridge; data cartridge; tape cartridge; volume*. **(2)** A set of slugs for a train printer. See *train printer*.

cartridge tape A data cartridge.

cartridge tape drive A data cartridge drive.

cascade A method of information or energy transfer in which the completion of an event in one of several sequential stages initiates events in the next stage that, in turn, initiates events in the following stage.

cascaded carry A method of addition in which any carry digit resulting from adding two digits is used as the addend in a further step of addition with the process being repeated until there are no more carry digits. For example:

```
  0111   Augend
+  10    Addend
  0101   Sum without carry
+ 100    Next addend (the carry digit)
  0001   New sum without carry
+1000    Next addend (the carry digit)
  1001   Final sum (no carry digit remaining)
```

cassette Also *magnetic tape cassette*. A length of magnetic tape on reels in a protective enclosure. See *digital cassette*.

CAT *Capacity Activated Transducer*.

catalogue Also, depending on the system, *dictionary; directory*. (1) A table of entities as recognised by an operating system; for example, of devices, users, or files. (2) An operating-system maintained table of data units (files; pages; segments) together with their storage locations and, possibly, other information such as access rights.

catenation Concatenation.

cathode A source of electrons or ions; the negative element of a tube/valve or semiconductor. See *anode; diode*.

cathode ray tube (CRT) A vacuum tube with a phosphor-coated screen for the display of characters and/or other images. It is the display element of visual display terminals (VDU's).

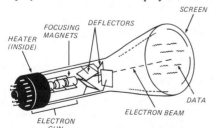

television sets, and oscilloscopes. It contains an electrically heated resistance element (the **cathode**) in the base of the tube to supply electrons, **focusing magnets** to concentrate the electrons into a narrow **electron beam**, a phosphor-coated screen, and means to control the on-off state and position of the electron beam to cause it to scan the screen to produce images. Oscilloscopes and VDU's commonly control the electron beam position with **deflector plates** that attract and repel the beam according to the impressed electrostatic charge. Television and raster scan VDU's have electromagnets ('yoke coils') for beam control. To write or refresh the screen display, the beam is turned on and off as it scans and the screen phosphors luminesce where the beam is on. See *raster scan; vector scan*.

CATV *CAble TeleVision*.
CAW *Channel Address Word*.
CBX *Computerised Branch eXchange*.
CCD *Charge-Coupled Device*.
CCITT *Consultative Committee on International Telephone and Telegraph*. (Geneva)
CCW *Channel Command Word*.
CD *Carrier Detect* (DCD).
CDC *Control Data Corporation*. (S. Minneapolis)
CDV *Check Digit Verification*.
CE *Customer Engineering*.

cell (1) A storage cell; an element of data storage that can hold one bit. (2) In some systems; an automatically loadable unit of storage. See *data cell*. (3) In some systems; any discrete unit of storage (byte; word; block; bucket; cylinder; sector). A **cell boundary** is the beginning or end of a cell's data-recordable area. The term **cellular** may be applied to a unit of code or data that is completely contained within a 'cell'; ('a cellular file').

central office In some countries; a telephone exchange.

central processor Also *central processor unit; CPU; processor* and, in some systems, *order code processor; internal processing unit*. That part of a computer that decodes instructions and controls the hardware (electronic circuits) used to execute them. It consists of the control unit and arithmetic unit (or a single unit that performs both functions) and, in most systems, main storage. A central processor that includes main storage may be termed the **mainframe** of a computer installation. The primary functions of a central processor usually include holding and accessing the order code of the computer and the microcode used to control electronic circuits, providing timing for internal (and often external) operations, decoding instructions, performing arithmetic and logic operations, monitoring the performance of circuits and initiating recovery procedures where required, and performing the physical operations of communicating between the operating system and the console operator. In most systems, functions also include fetching operands and storing results, initiating and controlling peripheral transfers, and performing main storage management functions for the operating system; in a few newer and larger systems, these functions are performed by separate intelligent units. The term 'central processor' is used mainly with respect to medium and large general-purpose computers of 'conventional' architecture. Other terms in use for the unit that performs some or all of the functions of a central processor include, 'control processor', 'main intelligence', 'central intelligence', 'processor unit', 'order code processor', 'instruction processor', and, in a microprocessor system, 'microprocessor'.

central site In a data communications system, the location from which link control is exercised. In most systems, it is the location where the computer (or the main computer) is installed. See *remote site; data network*.

central station A central site or a master station.

centralised Located in one place (rather than dispersed or distributed); ('centralised processing'; 'centralised control').

centralised procedure A procedure that can access public pages/segments. See *procedure; public*.

CEPT *Conference of European Posts and Telecommunications*.

certification That part of magnetic disc initialisation in which each track is checked for defects and appropriately identified. It is performed by writing and reading a repeating test pattern; a track that is found defective is usually retested two or more times to determine if an incorrect read (the presence of a drop in or drop out) was caused by a transient or an actual defect on the track. See *initialisation; formatting*.

chad Also *chip*. The small piece of paper or card that is removed during the punching of paper tape or a punched card.

chadded tape Paper tape with 'clean' holes (with chads removed).

chadless tape Paper tape punched by a process that leaves the chads attached to the edges of holes.

chain (1) A sequence of operations, each of which (except the first) uses the output of the previous operation as input. **(2)** Also *access path* in some contexts. A group of related items in non-contiguous storage locations, each of which (except the last) holds a pointer to the next entity. See *chained file*. **(3)** Any link between entities; ('a screen format that chains to another format'; 'three chained disc units'). See *daisy chain*. **(4)** A sequence of events in which the completion of one causes the start of the next.

chain code A code consisting of bit patterns that are formed by shifting all bits (to the left) one bit position and adding a new bit at the right to form a pattern from the previous pattern. The new bit added at the right (in the least significant bit position) must be such that no previous bit pattern is repeated. For example, the bit patterns of a 3-bit chain code would be as follows: 000 001 010 101 011 111 110 100.

chain printer A line printer that is functionally similar to a train printer except that the slugs are joined to each other as links in an endless chain. See *printer; train printer; band printer*.

chained file A file in which each record contains a pointer to the next record in some sequence (or multiple pointers if there is more than one sequence of which a record is a part). A personnel file could, for example, be organised with records in sequence by personnel number and chained by department, salary scale, and qualifications. See *pointer*.

chained list A list in which a data item or group of data items is located in storage by following pointers associated with other data items. For example, the records of a chained file in which each 'Type A' record holds the address of the next 'Type A' record. See *chain; chained file; key*.

chained record A record in a chained file; a record that can be accessed by following a chain.

chaining The linking of items to form a chain.

chaining overflow On magnetic disc storage; the writing of overflow records on the next higher numbered available track; each track containing a record that holds the address of the overflow track used. See *progressive overflow*.

chaining search A search made by following pointers; a search to locate an item in a chained list.

change bit A bit (in a descriptor) that is set to '1' whenever a change access (write; append; delete) is made to a page or segment in primary storage. When the page/segment is selected for discard, the bit is checked; if it is '0', no change has been made and the page/segment can be overwritten because there is an exact copy in secondary storage. If the bit is '1', the page/segment is rolled out to backing storage to overwrite the unchanged version.

change character A font change character. See *FC*.

change dump A selective dump of storage locations with contents that have been changed during a particular phase of processing or program testing.

changes file An amendments file.

channel (1)In data transmission; a means (line; frequency band) for carrying data in one preassigned direction between two locations. A single channel (at least notionally, two wires) can be used for simplex or half-duplex systems. A duplex circuit consists of two channels between two locations; data is sent in one direction on one channel and in the other direction on the other channel. If it is an asymmetric duplex circuit, it consists of a **message channel** (also **forward channel**) on which user data is sent in both directions (but not simultaneously) and a slower **supervisory channel** (also **backward channel**) that is used to carry acknowledgements, requests for repetition, and any other link-related messages. In a symmetric duplex circuit, a **down channel** (also **go channel**) is used to carry outgoing messages and an **up channel** (also **return channel**) carries incoming messages. If data terminal equipment with the necessary facilities are used at both ends, sending and receiving can be simultaneous. (In symmetric duplex systems, supervisory messages are sent as ordinary messages at full channel speed.) See *duplex; half-duplex; circuit*. (2)Also *bus; highway; path; link; circuit*. A route (wires) used for control or data transfers within a functional unit or between functional units. (3)A port; a connector or location where data enters or leaves a functional unit. (4)An internal conductor in an integrated circuit or other semiconductor device. (5)Also *level*. Any of the (six or eight) lines parallel to the edge of paper tape along which holes have been punched or can be punched. See *paper tape*.

channel activation command A command from a control unit to a peripheral controller or data channel initiating a data transfer. Typically, it identifies the device to or from which the transfer is to be made and the location on the device, the access mode, and the area of main storage involved.

channel address word (CAW) See *channel program*.

channel command (1)A channel activation command. (2)An instruction in a channel program.

channel command word (CCW) See *channel program*.

channel group See *group*.

channel indicator An element of a channel status table; a bit position that holds a 0-bit when a particular channel is not in use and a 1-bit when it is in use.

channel latency See *latency*.

channel program A sequence of instructions that are fetched and executed by a data channel (peripheral controller) and used to perform an autonomous data transfer. The instructions of the program are **channel commands** and their main storage locations are **channel command words**. A channel program is invoked by a single I/O instruction from the control unit which references a **channel address word** that holds the main storage location of a channel program. The usage status of the various channels is held in a **channel status table** that has a **channel status word** for each channel. A **channel indicator** is a bit in a channel status word that indicates the status of a particular channel.

channel status table See *channel program*.

channel status word (CSW) See *channel program*.

channel width The number of bits that can be transferred simultaneously on a channel.

chapter A program segment.

character (1)Also *graphic character; printable character*. An arrangement of elements (lines; dots) of agreed meaning that is visually interpretable; for example, as printed, handwritten, or displayed on the screen of a VDU. (2)A bit pattern of agreed meaning according to some code, for example, 0000110 that represents ACK in the ISO-7 code. The bit pattern may represent an **unprintable character** (such as 'ACK') which has no discrete graphic form, or a **printable character** such as 'A' or '+'. (3)The amount of storage required to hold one 'character' (def. 2) in the internal storage code of a particular computer or other intelligent device. The usual lengths are six, seven, or eight bits. See *word; byte; numeric*.

character assembly See *character disassembly*.

character cell An element of a character generator; a matrix of bit cells that holds a graphic representation of a character as it will appear in dot-matrix form on the screen of a VDU or as printed by a matrix printer.

character density The number of characters per unit (usually one inch) of line length.

character descriptor A character cell.

character disassembly In bit-interleaved time-division multiplexing; the operation of taking a bit at a time from each sending device and transmitting it. The reverse operation at the receiving end is **character assembly**. See *multiplexing*.

character emitter A read-only memory that holds the bit patterns of the characters of a character set and has facilities for outputting them individually as required.

character fill To write repeating bit patterns of some character to a storage location thus overwriting the existing contents. See *spacefill; zerofill.*

character format (1) A term that is applied to data that is input, stored, or output as bit patterns representing alphanumeric characters. Typically, data is input in character format from keyboards, card and tape readers, and communications links, and output in character format to VDU's, printers, communications links, and card and tape punches. With respect to data in computer storage, the term indicates that it is in the storage code of the computer (say, in EBCDIC) and that numeric data is in this non-computational format. See *external decimal; computational format.* (2) A term that, when applied to printed or displayed data, indicates that it is in graphic characters rather than in bit patterns.

character framing See *framing; start-stop.*

character generator (1) In a VDU or matrix printer; a section of read-only memory that holds each character in a matrix of storage cells (say, 7 × 9) as it will be displayed or printed; such a matrix is a **character cell**. The position of 1-bits in a cell controls the on-off condition of the electron beam in a VDU and of print solenoid actuation in a matrix printer. (2) A decoder and driver circuit to energise discrete elements (LED's; filament lights) to provide a matrix display of characters, say on a sign or notice board. (3) A segment decoder; the circuit elements that form characters for an LED or LCD display.

character handling The manipulation of individual encoded characters and strings of encoded characters. To perform this efficiently, a computer requires the ability to access individual characters in main atorage as well as words that contain several characters. Computers with good character handling facilities are, thus, usually byte machines rather than word machines.

character interleaved A term applied to a time division multiplexing system in which the character is the interleaved unit of data transfer. See *bit interleaved; block interleaved; time division multiplexing.*

character machine A character-oriented machine.

character multiplexed Character interleaved.

character-oriented machine A term applied to a computer that can access individually storage locations that contain characters in the storage code; the term is usually synonymous with 'byte machine'.

character parity Horizontal parity. See *parity.*

character printer Also *serial printer.* A printer that constructs a line of characters by printing them one after the other in the order in which they will appear in the finished line; such a printer may be either unidirectional or bidirectional. See *line printer; printer.*

character reader An optical character reader.

character recognition The facilities or operation involved in the machine interpretation of graphic characters. See *magnetic ink character recognition; optical character recognition.*

character set (1) A group of characters that can be distinctively represented and that are suitable for transmitting, storing, or manipulating some type of data. Common examples include the English alphabet, the decimal digits, and a set including the English alphabet, punctuation, and the decimal digits. (The term may be applied to either their graphic or bit-pattern representations.) See *character; character subset.* (2) The group of characters that can be printed or displayed by a particular device. See *font.*

character string (1) A group of characters (bit patterns) in contiguous storage locations. (2) A word, number, or other sequence of graphic characters.

character subset A portion of a character set; a group of characters selected and extracted to meet a particular requirement. See *character set.*

character synchronised A term applied to data transmission in which characters are sent in fixed time relation to each other. In order for character timing to be fixed, the times of sending the bits that comprise the characters must also be fixed so any transmission that is 'character synchronised' must also be 'bit synchronised'. See *synchronisation; start-stop; asynchronous transmission; anisochronous.*

character variable A variable of the size to hold one character. See *variable (Data handling).*

character VDU Also *alphanumeric VDU.* A VDU that only has the facilities to receive and display printable characters and such lines and figures as may be constructed with repeating characters. See *graphics VDU.*

character view A feature of a moving-head printer that causes the most recently printed characters to come into the operator's view when there is a pause between keystrokes of, say, half a second. The purpose is to reveal those characters that are hidden by the print head when it is in its normal printing position. It is accomplished either by moving the print head to one of the margins or by a line feed; depressing a key causes the print head or paper to return to the correct position for continuing the line.

characteristic (1) The part of a logarithm that indicates where the radix point is to be placed; for example, in the logarithm 2.19866, the '2' is the characteristic. See *logarithm; mantissa*. (2) The part of the binary representation of a floating point number that encodes the exponent. See *floating point*.

characters per second (CPS; c.p.s; cps.) The number of characters that are handled or transmitted per second. It is a measure of the speed of data transmission and of the operation of slow devices such as paper tape and card punches and readers and teletypewriters.

charge (1) A surplus of electrons, as on a plate of a capacitor. See *capacitor; electrostatic*. (2) To increase the potential difference between the positive and negative sides of a capacitor or storage battery.

charge-coupled device (CCD) A semiconductor (MOS) recirculating memory. In operation, electrons representing a 1-bit are injected into a linear depletion zone and these are moved along the zone by means of magnetic fields in electrodes that are formed on the surface of the chip. In the figure, electrons are injected at A and are moved by three-phase clock pulses

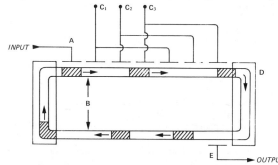

applied at C_1, C_2, and C_3. (Two-phase clocking methods are also used.) The linear depletion layers are connected in series so the entire chip is, in effect, a continuous shift register in which bits are kept in constant, recirculating movement. Because a certain amount of charge is lost each time a bit is moved, a refresh (reading and rewriting) step is performed at the end of each channel as shown at D. Bits are written and read at input and output diffusion areas that are analogous to the source and drain in a field effect transistor.

charge packed memory An experimental high-density memory in which data is held as voltage levels of capacitive charge.

check (1) To examine an item and determine whether or not it meets predefined criteria; ('check a document'; 'check parity'). (2) A term sometimes applied to an error condition; particularly one caused by a hardware fault.

check bit Also *binary check digit*. A bit that indicates the result of some processing operation or step; examples include a flag, a use bit, and a parity bit. See *check digit; parity*.

check character An algorithm-generated character included in a data transfer or transmission to enable receiving hardware to check the data for corruption introduced in transit. See *block check character; polynomial code; check digit*.

check digit A digit calculated from a value and added or appended to the value to make the value conform to some standard pattern; it is used (usually by duplicating the calculation) to detect (and possibly correct) errors introduced in construction, storage, or transmission. Various algorithms are used to calculate check digits; one of the most common is used in a parity system in which an additional 1-bit is added to character bit patterns as necessary to make the number of 1-bits an odd or even number (depending on the system). See *parity*. An algorithm used in calculating check digits for data validation consists of multiplying the value in each digit position of a field by a different **weighting factor**, taking the total, dividing by a constant, and using the remainder as the check digit. The term 'check digit' is used when discussing the concept or calculation; the group of digits used in checking is a **check total** (also **check sum**) regardless of how derived. In data transmission, the group is a **check character**. See *check sum; parity; control total*.

check read A read performed on data immediately after it has been written to magnetisable surface storage in order to compare it with the data in buffer and, thus, to detect errors.

check sum Also *check total* and, often, *control total*. A value obtained by applying an algorithm to an item of data and transmitted or stored with the data for use in checking for corruption in a subsequent step. See *check digit; control total; parity; parity sum.*

check total A check sum.

checkerboarding External fragmentation. See *fragmentation.*

checkpoint (1)A point in the execution of a program where an instruction calls a **checkpoint routine** that performs the operation of writing the contents of specified registers and/or main storage locations to backing storage. (2)The operation of writing data to backing storage at a 'checkpoint' (def. 1). (3)The data that is written to backing storage at a 'checkpoint' (def. 1).

checkpoint dump A dump of the contents of main storage and registers as they existed at a checkpoint.

checkpoint record A record that contains the status of a job and the computer system at a checkpoint; it provides the information required by the operating system to restart a job at a position other than the beginning.

checkpoint restart The resumption of processing from a checkpoint within a job that was running when an abnormal termination occurred. See *restart; automatic restart; deferred restart.*

cheque protection A process to increase the difficulty of altering computer-printed cheques; typically, it consists of filling places where additional numbers could be placed in the 'amount' line with asterisks or other fill characters.

Chinese binary Column binary.

chip (1)A thin, square or rectangular piece of silicon (say, with sides of 5 mm.) on which the circuit elements of a semiconductor device have been formed. See *wafer; semiconductor.* (2)An integrated circuit device; a 'chip' (def. 1) including its encapsulating package and circuit terminations. (3)A chad.

chip count The number of integrated circuits required to perform a particular function or the number on a particular printed circuit board. See *package count.*

chip tray A tray or bin that receives the chads in a card or paper tape punch.

CHPS (chps.) *CHaracters Per Second.*

CHS (chs.) *CHaracterS.*

CIA *Communications Interface Adapter.*

CII-HB *Compagnie Internationale pour l'Informatique* combined with *Honeywell-Bull.* (Toulouse)

CIM *Computer Input from Microfilm.* A term applied to the equipment and techniques used to interpret microfilm images and convert them to a form suitable for input to a computer system. See *COM.*

cinching A movement between layers of reeled magnetic tape (as caused by insufficient or varying winding tension) that causes back-folding of the tape in places. A reel of tape that has had this occur is said to be **cinched**.

cine-mode Also *IA orientation*. With respect to roll microfilm; a term used to indicate that images are oriented across the film as if taken by a cine camera. See *comic mode.*

CIR *Current Instruction Register.*

circuit (1)An arrangement of electrical and/or electronic components and interconnections designed to accomplish a particular function; for example, signal amplification or a logic function. (2)A path for two-way transmission of data; the lines and equipment required for duplex operation. Properly, a circuit is four-wire (or the multiplexed equivalent) and a channel is two-wire or equivalent; the terms are sometimes used interchangeably. See *channel; path; link.* (3)Two wires, or one wire and ground, as used to carry signals or electric current.

circuit board See *printed circuit board.*

circuit breaker A thermal and/or electromagnetic device that turns off electric power (say, of a motor or computer) in event of a short circuit or overload.

circuit grade A term used to indicate the information-carrying capability of (telephone) circuits (which is determined by bandwidth). The commonly recognised grades are broadband, voice, subvoice, and telegraph.

circuit isolation The division of a circuit into parts that are not connected by conductors; for example, to couple two circuits of different voltages or to protect one circuit from transients in the other. It is usually accomplished by a transformer, a capacitor, or an optical coupler.

circuit noise Line noise.

circuit switching A method of operating a data network in which circuits are set up between data stations (as by automatic dialing) only when there are messages to be sent. See *message switching.*

circuit transient A brief and unintended change of energy in a circuit; typically, a 'spike' of higher voltage. With respect to a communications circuit, the term is usually synonymous with 'impulse noise'. See *noise.*

circuit transition A line transition.

circular file A file in which the addition of a new record causes the deletion of the oldest record in the file.

circular process See *recursive*.

circular shift See *shift*.

circulating memory A recirculating memory.

CL (1)*CLear*. (2)(c.l.) *Current Loop*.

clamp (1)With respect to a circuit; to make a connection to another circuit that is maintained until released; ('clamp to —5 V.'). (2)To cause the continuous transmission of a particular digit or line condition; ('clamp to mark').

clamp-on Camp-on.

classic stack A push-down stack with top access only. See *stack*.

CLC *Communications Link Controller*.

clean (1)Of a program or other sequence of instructions; thoroughly tested and known to be free of errors. (2)Of a circuit transition (say, a signal or clock pulse); fast and without bounce or flutter.

clear (1)With respect to a storage location; to overwrite the contents with zeros or spaces. (2)To remove display images from a VDU screen or from an area of the screen. (3)With respect to a fault in equipment; to correct it. (4)With respect to a call in a telephone system; to terminate it and release the circuits.

clerical flowchart Also, sometimes, *system flowchart*. A flowchart showing the flow of paperwork through an office or accounting system. Its construction is often the first step in designing and specifying a computer system.

clipping Scissoring.

CLK *CLocK*.

clock (1)In a computer or other device that performs synchronised operations; an oscillator that generates high-frequency pulses and registers that count the pulses and output accurately spaced **clock pulses** for control purposes. See *time base*. (2)To move bits or data under the control of clock pulses. See *strobe*.

clock cycle (1)The time between successive clock pulses. (2)A cycle with timing supplied by clock pulses.

clock pulse One of a sequence of accurately formed and spaced signals (circuit transitions; changes in voltage) used to initiate or control operations in electronic circuits. See *clock*.

clock ratio The number of clock pulses per timing pulse. See *time base*.

clock sequence (1)A fixed number of clock pulses that has timing significance for some purpose. (2)Also *clocked sequence*. A sequence of operations or steps with timing by clock pulses.

clock signal A clock pulse.

clock track A track (magnetisable surface recording) on which clock pulses are written for read timing. A clock track is required for magnetic tape encoding using PE, NRZI, or GCR.

closed loop A loop for which there is no programmed provision for exit; once entered, it is performed repeatedly until it is externally interrupted (say, by a monitor routine).

closed shop See *open shop*.

closed subprogram See *subprogram*.

closed subroutine See *subroutine*.

closed system A term applied to a data network or information system in which an interface is provided for only certain items or types of equipment (often supplied by the common carrier or PTT). See *open system*.

cluster A group of terminals or peripherals that are in physical proximity and interface to the same device (computer; peripheral controller; terminal control unit). The term is most often applied to units at a data station rather than at a computer installation.

cluster controller A terminal control unit.

CMOS *Complementary Metal Oxide Silicon*. A semiconductor, integrated circuit logic system in which P-channel and N-channel transistors are combined and used in flip-flops. Each gate uses two 'complementary' transistors and an input turns one off and the other on. Virtually no current flows except

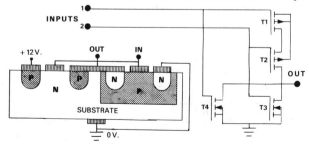

when an output is switched from one state to the other. Because of their low power requirement (say, 5 nA per gate), CMOS devices are commonly used in digital watches and quality

CODE TABLE

CODES

The common storage and transmission codes are shown on this page and the one opposite. The encoded forms are in hexadecimal:

```
0 = 0000    8 = 1000
1 = 0001    9 = 1001
2 = 0010    A = 1010
3 = 0011    B = 1011
4 = 0100    C = 1100
5 = 0101    D = 1101
6 = 0110    E = 1110
7 = 0111    F = 1111
```

The character lengths of the codes (not counting parity) are:

```
IA-2            5-Bit
Baudot          5-Bit
ISO-7 (IA-5)    7-Bit
EBCDIC          8-Bit
ASCII-8         8-Bit
Hollerith      12-Bit
```

HOLLERITH: Represented by three hexadecimal digits:

```
1st Hex. Digit 12-11-0-1
2nd Hex. Digit 2-3-4-5
3rd Hex. Digit 6-7-8-9
```

For example, the letter 'S' is encoded '280'; the '2' indicates a punch in the '0' row and the '8' a punch in the '2' row.

EBCDIC and ASCII-8: Standard hexadecimal representation; D9 indicates 11011001.

ISO-7; BAUDOT; IA-5: The bits in the code are to the right; ignore excess '0's. In ISO-7, '06' indicates 0000110 and in IA-2 '1A' indicates 11010.

(In all codes used for transmission, the right-most bit is in the 'B0' position—the first bit to be transmitted.)

In IA-2 and Baudot, italics indicates 'figure shift'.

	IA-2	BAUDOT	ASCII (ISO-7, IA-5)	EBCDIC	ASCII-8	HOLLERITH		IA-2	BAUDOT	ASCII (ISO-7, IA-5)	EBCDIC	ASCII-8	HOLLERITH		IA-2	BAUDOT	ASCII (ISO-7, IA-5)	EBCDIC	ASCII-8	HOLLERITH
A	03	10	41	C1	A1	900	k			6B	92	EB		V	1E	1D	56	E5	B6	210
a			61	81	E1		L	12	1B	4C	D3	AC	440	v			76	A5	F6	
B	19	06	42	C2	A2	880	l			6C	93	EC		W	13	0D	57	E6	B7	208
b			62	82	E2		M	1C	0B	4D	D4	AD	420	w			77	A6	F7	
C	0E	16	43	C3	A3	840	m			6D	94	ED		X	1D	09	58	E7	B8	204
c			63	83	E3		N	0C	0F	4E	D5	AE	410	x			78	A7	F8	
D	09	1E	44	C4	A4	820	n			6E	95	EE		Y	15	04	59	E8	B9	202
d			64	84	E4		O	18	1C	4F	D6	AF	408	y			79	A8	F9	
E	01	08	45	C5	A5	810	o			6F	96	EF		Z	11	19	5A	E9	BA	201
e			65	85	E5		P	16	1F	50	D7	B0	404	z			7A	A9	FA	
F	0D	0E	46	C6	A6	808	p			70	97	F0		0	*16*	*1E*	30	F0	50	200
f			66	86	E6		Q	17	17	51	D8	B1	402	1	*17*	*10*	31	F1	51	100
G	1A	0A	47	C7	A7	804	q			71	98	F1		2	*13*	*08*	32	F2	52	080
g			67	87	E7		R	0A	07	52	D9	B2	401	3	*10*	*04*	33	F3	53	040
H	14	1A	48	C8	A8	802	r			72	99	F2		4	*0A*	*14*	34	F4	54	020
h			68	88	E8		S	05	05	53	E2	B3	280	5	*10*	*1C*	35	F5	55	010
I	06	0C	49	C9	A9	801	s			73	A2	F3		6	*15*	*12*	36	F6	56	008
i			69	89	E9		T	10	15	54	E3	B4	240	7	*07*	*0A*	37	F7	57	004
J	0B	12	4A	D1	AA	500	t			74	A3	F4		8	*0C*	*06*	38	F8	58	002
j			6A	91	EA		U	07	14	55	E4	B5	220	9	*0D*	*16*	39	F9	59	001
K	0F	13	4B	D2	AB	480	u			75	A4	F5								

CODE TABLE 41

		IA-2	BAUDOT	ASCII (ISO-7, IA-5)	EBCDIC	ASCII-8	HOLLERITH
.	Period	1C	05	2E	4B	4E	842
,	Comma	0C	09	2C	6B	4C	242
;	Semicolon	1E		3B	5E	5B	40A
:	Colon	0E	19	3A	7A	5A	082
'	Apostrophe	05	1D	27	70	47	012
"	Quotation	11		22	7F	42	006
!	Exclamation	0D		21	4F	41	806
?	Question	19	0D	3F	6F	5F	206
*	Asterisk			2A	5C	4A	422
(	Parentheses	0F	13	28	4D	48	812
)	Parentheses	12	0B	29	5D	49	412
-	Hyphen (minus)	03	07	2D	60	4D	400
+	Plus	11	1A	2B	4E	4B	80A
=	Equals	1E	1B	3D	7E	5D	00A
/	Slant	1D	17	2F	61	4F	300
_	Underline			5F	6D	BF	212
#	Number	14		(23)	(7B)	43	(042)
&	Ampersand	1A		26	50	46	800
%	Percent	0D	1F	25	6C	45	222
@	Commercial at	1A		40	7C	A0	022
£	Pounds	14		23	7B	(43)	042
$	Dollars	09		24	5B	44	442
>	Greater than			3E	6E	5E	20A
<	Less than			3C	4C	5C	822
[	Bracket			5B	4A	BB	882
]	Bracket			5D	5A	BD	482

		IA-2	BAUDOT	ASCII (ISO-7, IA-5)	EBCDIC	ASCII-8	HOLLERITH
\	Rev. Slant			5C	E0	BC	282
|	Vertical line			7C	6A	FC	C00
^	Circumflex			5E	5F	BE	406
`	Accent grave			60	79	E0	102
~	Tilde			7E	A1	FE	700
{	Braces			7B	C0	FB	A00
}	Braces			7D	DC	FD	600

CONTROL CHARACTERS, FORMAT EFFECTORS, AND DELIMITERS

		IA-2	BAUDOT	ASCII (ISO-7, IA-5)	EBCDIC	ASCII-8	HOLLERITH	TYPE
ACK	Acknowledge			06	2E	06		TC
BEL	Bell		0B	07	27	07		DC
BL	Blank		00					FE
BS	Backspace			08	16	08		FE
CAN	Cancel			18	18	18		ED
CR	Carriage Return	08	18	0D	0D	0D		DC,FE
DC1	Device No. 1 Control			11	11	11		DC
DC2	Device No. 2 Control			12	12	12		DC
DC3	Device No. 3 Control			13		13		DC
DC4	Device No. 4 Control			14	3C	14		DC
DEL	Delete			7F	07	FF		ED
DLE	Data Link Escape			10	10	10		ES
EM	End of Medium			19	19	19		TC
ENQ	Enquiry			05	2D	05		TC
EOT	End of Transmission			04	37	04		TC
ER	Error				03			ED

		IA-2	BAUDOT	ASCII (ISO-7, IA-5)	EBCDIC	ASCII-8	TYPE
ESC	Escape			1B	27	1B	TC,ES
ETB	End Transmission Block			17	26	17	TC
ETX	End of Text			03	03	03	TC
FF	Form Feed			0C	0C	0C	FE
FS	Figures Shift	1B	02				ES
FS	File Separator			1C	1C	1C	DE
GS	Group Separator			1D	1D	1D	DE
HT	Horizontal Tab			09	05	09	FE
LF	Line Feed	08	11	0A	25	0A	FE
LS	Letters Shift	1F	01				ES
MS	Multiple Space				20		FE
MNL	Multiple New Line				21		FE
NAK	Negative Acknowledge			15	3D	15	TC
NUL	Null			00	00	00	TC,FE
RS	Record Separator			1E	1E	1E	DE
SI	Shift In			0F	0F	0F	ES
SO	Shift Out			0E	0E	0E	ES
SOH	Start Of Heading			01	01	01	TC
SP	Space	04		20	40	40	FE
STX	Start Of Text			02	02	02	TC
SUB	Substitute			1A	3F	1A	ED
SYN	Synchronous Idle			16	32	16	TC
US	Unit Separator			1F	1F	1F	DE
VP	Vertical Position				22		FE
VT	Vertical Tabulator			0B	0B	0B	FE
Who are you?			09				TC

TYPE:

DC *Device Control.* **ES** *EScape*
DE *DElimiter* **FE** *Format Effector*
ED *EDiting* **TC** *Transmission Control*

calculators. Packing density is low and costs have been relatively high because of processing complexity. The figure is of a positive NOR gate. When both inputs are low, the P-channel transistors T1 and T2 conduct and, since they are in series, the output is high. If either or both of the inputs are low, there is no conduction through the P-channel transistors and either or both N-channel transistors T3/T4 conduct and connect the output to ground (low).

CNC *Computerised Numerical Control.* See *numerical control.*

CNP *Communications Network Processor.*

CNS *Communications Network Simulator.*

coalesce To combine two or more sets of items into one set in any form. See *merge; collate.*

COAM *Customer Owned And Maintained.*

coax *COAXial cable.*

coaxial cable A two-conductor cable consisting of a centre conductor of copper wire and outer 'tubular' conductor of braided wire or copper tubing. The two are separated by a dielectric which is usually polyethylene or polyvinylchloride. In larger sizes when the outer conductor is tubing, the dielectric may be gas or air with spaced disc insulators supporting the centre conductor. Common uses include connecting video equipment and in multiplexed trunk lines of a telephone system.

COBOL *COmmon Business-Oriented Language.* A high-level programming language widely used in commerce and industry.

CODASYL *COnference on DAta SYstems Languages.* The group that developed COBOL (1959) and has since provided many additions, extensions, and special-purpose subsets. Other work includes developing machine-independent and applications-independent data base facilities and the associated languages DML and DDL.

code (1) An established relationship consisting of a character set and the signals or bit patterns by which each character is represented for such purposes as transmitting, storing, or manipulating data. Examples include ISO-7 code and Morse code. **(2)** One or more bit patterns from a coded character set. **(3)** A sequence of line transitions that represent characters in accordance with some 'code' (def.1). **(4)** Also *encode.* To read graphic characters and produce their equivalent signals or bit patterns. **(5)** Instructions as written by a programmer in a programming language or such instructions converted to machine language. See *source code; machine code; program.* **(6)** Instructions as contrasted to 'data'; the term may be used to refer to units of any size or type. **(7)** To write instructions in a programming language. **(8)** A privacy code. **(9)** Also *encode.* To convert from some other form to a representation in a privacy code.

code conversion The process of reading bit-pattern characters in one code and producing bit patterns to represent the characters in another code.

code descriptor See *descriptor.*

code extension (1) The process of assigning alternative meanings to the bit patterns (or some of the bit patterns) of a coded character set. See *shift; escape; code extension character.* **(2)** The process of adding new characters and their bit patterns to a code.

code extension character An escape character; a bit pattern that indicates that the bit pattern following it has two meanings in the code and that it is to be interpreted with its second meaning. See *shift; escape.*

code extension key Also, depending upon the system, *code shift key; escape key.* On a keyboard device that generates encoded characters; a key that, when depressed, changes the functions of some or all of the other keys, causing them to generate alternative bit patterns. An appropriately programmed terminal could, for example, produce ASCII bit-pattern characters in the normal or unshifted position and BCD characters when the code extension key is pressed. The facility is commonly used to permit certain keys to have two functions; for example, the N key, when pressed with the code extension key, could generate a bit pattern that would cause a printer to turn off. See *escape.*

code-independent A term applied to a link protocol or communications system that can handle messages in any code without risk of bit patterns in the code being interpreted as transmission control characters or otherwise interfering with correct transmission and interpretation.

code-sensitive (1) Of communications equipment or a link protocol; dependent upon certain bit patterns for control purposes and thus likely to malfunction when such 'reserved' bit patterns occur in transmitted messages. **(2)** Program sensitive.

code shift A change in the meaning of following bit patterns; either a figures shift or a letters shift. See *shift; code; shift in; shift out.*

code shift key See *code extension key*.

code transparent (1)Code-independent. (2)A term that may be applied to a device or system in which the user need have no knowledge of the code being used.

codec A device or circuit used to convert speech or other audio signals into bit patterns for transmission and to reconvert the bit patterns to reproduce the original audio form. See *digitiser; pulse code modulation; quantising*.

coded Also *encoded*. (1)Of characters; in bit-pattern form. (2) Of text; in a privacy code; encrypted. (3)Of a program or other sequence; in source-language form.

coded character set A character set in which the characters are bit patterns rather than graphic representations. See *character; character set*.

coded halt A programmed halt.

coded image A bit-pattern representation of an image as held in computer storage to control a display or plot. The term is more often applied to stored vectors than raster-scan arrays.

coded point An addressable point.

Codeline A system to assist in locating required frames on roll microfilm; it consists of bars placed adjacent to each frame so that the position of the bar in relation to the bottom of the frame relates to the position of the frame in its sequence. As the film passes rapidly in searching, the bar is seen to rise (or fall) and the search is stopped when it reaches the (previously determined) position for the frame required. See *COM*.

coder (1)An encoder. (2)A person who writes source code (but does not design programs). (3)A keyboard terminal and a paper tape punch; a station for preparing punched tapes.

coding (1)Code (def. 5; 6). (2)The process of writing instructions in a programming language. (3)The process of converting characters to their bit-pattern form.

coding sheet A form designed to assist a programmer in writing instructions in a particular programming language (and, often, for a particular computer).

coercive force The counter (opposite polarity) magnetic field that would be required to neutralise existing magnetisation. See *magnet*.

coexist To be in main storage at the same time. A term used with respect to programs in a multiprogramming (often, virtual storage) system. See *exist; concurrency*.

COGO COordinate GeOmetry. A programming language designed for use in engineering applications.

coil A number of turns of wire, usually wound around a laminated iron core; it is a basic element of devices that convert electrical energy to magnetic flux and the reverse; for example, of read/write heads and print magnets.

coincidence (1)The condition of intersection or simultaneous presence in the same location. (2)Identity (def. 2).

coincident current selection Also *coordinate addressing*. The reading and writing process used with core and semiconductor memory; it consists of making electrical connections to two intersecting word lines and bit lines and sending a pulse on at least one of them to set or test the bit cell at their place of intersection. In writing, pulses are sent on both lines; in core memory, this sets the direction of magnetisation of the core where they intersect and in semiconductor memory, this sets one of the transistors at the intersecting flip-flop to conducting and the other to non-conducting. In reading core memory, pulses of opposite polarity are sent on both lines and the status of the core (whether it holds a 1-bit or a 0-bit) is determined by means of a read wire that also goes through the core; a pulse appears on it if there is a flux reversal (change in direction of magnetism). In reading semiconductor memory, a pulse is sent on the word line and the status of the flip-flop is tested by bit lines to each of the two transistors, one of which passes the pulse if it holds a 1-bit and the other if it holds a 0-bit. See *core memory; semiconductor memory; dynamic memory; static random access memory*.

cold boot A term sometimes applied to the sequence of steps required to place a computer system in operation when no part of its system software is presumed to be operational. See *boot; warm boot*.

cold restart Initial program load.

collate (1)To form a new set of items in a specified sequence by combining two or more other sets. The sequence of the items in the new set need not be the same as that of any of the sets being combined and the new set need not include all the items in the other sets. Typically, the operation is performed by sequencing the items of the sets to be combined in accordance with the rules that apply to the new set, checking for duplications between sets, deleting items that are not to be included in the new set, and merging. See *sort; merge*. (2)To place items in a collating sequence. (3) To place printed sheets in the order in which they will be bound or otherwise assembled for use.

collating sequence (1) A set of rules establishing the order in which items will be arranged in a set. Common collating sequences are 'alphabetical order' and 'numerical order' with, often, additional rules for dealing with symbols, punctuation, and spaces. If, for example, spaces collate before letters, then 'digit position' is placed before 'digital'. **(2)** The sequence in which bit patterns appear in a binary code.

collator A machine that sorts and merges sets of punched cards.

collector (1) A language processor that 'collects' modules for loading and assigns their relative positions in storage; in a virtual storage system, a collector attempts to place object code in pages/segments in such a way as to minimise virtual storage interrupts during processing. **(2)** An N-P junction of a bipolar transistor or the external connection to this junction. See *transistor; base; emitter*.

collector journal A transaction file; a journal for recording input and output messages in a transaction processing system.

column A linear, vertical arrangement of items or of locations where items can be placed, for example; on a punched card. See *row*.

column binary Also *Chinese binary*. A vertical arrangement of a binary number in which (typically) the most significant digit is at the top. It is sometimes used to hold binary numbers on punched cards in which each column can hold a binary number of up to twelve digits.

COM *Computer Output on Microfilm*. The equipment and processes involved in using microfilm as the output medium for computers. The recording operations are performed by a **recorder**. It receives characters as bit patterns from the computer (or magnetic disc or tape) and holds them in a buffer with a typical capacity of 64 lines of 132 characters. A character generator converts these to graphic, dot matrix form for display on a small (4-inch by 6-inch) high-resolution cathode ray tube. An automatic camera using 16, 35, or 105 mm. special black-and-white film then photographs the screen, producing one frame of microfilm per exposure. (One frame, typically, corresponds to one sheet of print-out.) When 16 mm. or 35 mm. film is used, the resulting unit for storage and handling is usually a roll of negative film. A recorder that uses 105 mm. film usually operates the camera by a **step-and-repeat** method in which frames are 'scanned' on the film in horizontal and vertical rows. The output from such a recorder is a **microfiche** with, typically, 208 frames. Most recorders have a **form flash** feature for adding grids, headings or other standard elements to each frame as it is exposed. Some recorders employ **laser beam recording** (LBR) in which a laser beam writes directly to the film. Another method is **electron beam recording** (EBR) in which the film (in a vacuum chamber) is written to directly by the electron beam. Still another method uses optical fibres to conduct patterns to the film from an array of light-emitting diodes. Filming speeds vary with the process and equipment; 200 frames per minute is typical for CRT recorders. Copies of microfilm originals can be produced by a **duplicator** onto diazo, vesicular, or silver-halide film. Microfilm can be referenced by the use of a **reader** that enlarges and projects one frame at a time. A **reader-printer** can also make enlarged, paper copies of frames. Because of high recording speeds, low materials costs, and minimum storage requirements, COM is increasingly being used for holding copies of computer-printed documents, as the masters from which documents (such as parts lists) are printed, and as the sole output wherever immediate reference to print-out is not required. See *microfilm; microfiche; reduction; aperture card; CIM; reader; duplicator; form flash*.

comb Of a multiple-disc magnetic disc unit; the element moved by the servo; the assembly of arms on which the read/write heads are mounted. See *magnetic disc unit*.

combination (1) A particular arrangement or grouping; ('a combination of letters'; 'a combination of peripherals'). **(2)(C)** A group of items that has a separate identity only because of the items included (without considering their arrangement). For example, 5-7-3 is one 'combination' of the decimal digits and it is considered to be the same as other arrangements of the same digits such as 3-5-7 or 7-5-3. The formula for finding the number of combinations of a particular size that can be formed from the items of a set is:

$$nCr = \frac{n!}{(n-r)! \times r!}$$

The 'n' is the number of items in the set, 'r' is the number of items in the combination, and '!' denotes 'factorial'. The expression for finding the number of 3-digit combinations in a 10-digit set is then:

$$10C3 = 10! \div (7! \times 3!)$$

It is solved by finding factorial 10:

$10! = 10 \times 9 \times 8 \times 7 \times 6 \times 5 \times 4 \times 3 \times 2 \times 1 = 3{,}628{,}800$
and dividing by factorial 7 times factorial 3:
$7! = 7 \times 6 \times 5 \times 4 \times 3 \times 2 \times 1 = 5{,}040$
$3! = 3 \times 2 \times 1 = 6$
$5040 \times 6 = 30{,}240$
$3{,}628{,}800 \div 30{,}240 = 120$
There are, then, 120 such combinations. See *permutation*.

combinational circuit A logic circuit that receives two or more inputs, evaluates them, and produces a single output. See *logic circuit*.

comic mode Also *IB orientation*. A term applied to microfilm in which the images are arranged lengthwise on the film (in the manner of the frames of a comic strip). See *cine mode*.

command (1) A job control statement. **(2)** A message from a terminal to a computer that requests or initiates some action. **(3)** A bit pattern interpretable by computer hardware to cause an operation to be commenced, modified, or terminated; ('a read command'; 'a stop command'). **(4)** An operator in source coding; a character, symbol, or group that specifies the performance of a pre-defined operation. **(5)** With respect to a low-level language; a term sometimes used synonymously with 'instruction'.

command chaining The sequencing of channel commands; the resulting sequence may be termed a 'channel program'. See *channel program*.

command interpreter A system routine that recognises and acts upon a limited range of commands (LOGON; OPEN; EDIT) as input from a terminal to change program or terminal status.

command language A job control language.

command processing The reading, interpretation, and performance of commands (def. 1; 2).

comment Also *annotation; note.* Material written on a flowchart for purposes of explaining or clarifying the program or indicating some exception condition. **(2)** Non-compilable material inserted in a source program and so identified.

comment statement A source language statement that has no effect on object code and is copied in the output listing.

common (1) Usable by different devices, programs, or users; ('a common buffer'; 'a common line'). See *public*. **(2)** In identical form in different entities; ('a common circuit'; 'a common sequence'). **(3)** A common area.

common area (1) A storage area used to interface separately compiled/assembled routines; for example, to hold assembly language subroutines to be called by different high-level language programs. **(2)** A location for shareable pages/segments.

common carrier A company or government department that provides a telecommunications service for public (subscriber) use. See *PSTN; PTT*.

common mode Occurring in both signal paths of a differential mode system. See *differential mode system*.

common-mode rejection The ability of a differential receiver to discriminate against ('reject') common-mode noise and thus to pass only signals. See *differential mode system*.

common rail A power supply cable (possibly with different voltages) that supplies multiple functional units.

common trunk A term sometimes applied to the 'bus' of a bus-organised computer. See *bus-organised*.

commonality The condition of having the same function or using the same components; ('a range of printers with high mechanical commonality').

comms *COMMunicationS.*

communicate With respect to two programs; to pass parameters or partial results from one to the other.

communications (1) The transmission of information or data between entities. **(2)** Data communications.

communications adapter A line adapter.

communications area A communications region.

communications control character A transmission control character.

communications controller Also *communications control unit* and other names. An intelligent device (typically, incorporating a microprocessor) that performs interface functions between a computer and one or more modems. See *interface computer; front-end processor; communications interface adapter; data terminal equipment*.

communications interface A term applied to the connectors and cable by which a computer or other unit of data terminal equipment is connected to a modem. The most common designations and uses of circuits are those defined in CCITT Recommendation V.24.

communications interface adapter (CIA) In a bus-organised computer system; an intelligent device (often in a single integrated circuit) that provides interface functions between the bus and a modem. Typical functions include bit-serial/bit-parallel conversion, the addition of error-detection and control characters to outgoing messages and appropriate deletions of non-data characters from incoming messages, error detection, and handling interrupts. See *peripheral interface adapter; bus-organised; UART.*

communications link Also *line: circuit.* The equipment and transmission medium used to carry data and/or speech between two geographically separated locations. See *line; circuit; channel.*

communications link controller (CLC) In some systems; an intelligent functional unit used to provide line-oriented interface functions (synchronisation; error detection; acknowledgements) between a group of modems and a computer or communications network processor.

communications network processor (CNP) In some systems; an intelligent functional unit used to perform computer-oriented interface functions (buffering; queue management; code conversion) between a computer and one or more communications link controllers.

communications region A mailbox; an area of main storage in which parameters and partial results can be written by one program to be read by another.

communications satellite A receiver, amplifier, and transmitter in stationary (synchronous) orbit above the equator as used for long-distance and intercontinental telecommunications. The height (22,300 miles) is selected so that it will make a complete orbit in 24 hours and, thus, to remain stationary over some point on the equator. See *satellite communications.*

compact (1) Occupying little space; ('compact code'; 'a compact computer'). **(2)** To reduce the amount of space occupied. See *compaction.*

compaction A storage management operation to eliminate or reduce external fragmentation; it consists of writing segments in primary storage to contiguous storage locations in order to eliminate small unallocatable spaces between them and thus to consolidate the free space so that it can be allocated. See *fragmentation; virtual storage allocation.*

compandor *COMpressor-exPANDOR.* In an amplitude-modulated communications link (typically, a trunk line in a telephone system); a selective amplifier that raises the amplitude of weak signals and lowers the amplitude of strong signals as they are sent to the line. It is done to narrow the range of amplitudes the system must deal with and to improve the signal-to-noise ratio of weak signals. At the receiving end, another compandor performs the reverse operation and restores the signals to their original amplitudes.

comparator (1) A device that compares two items of data and outputs or indicates the result; for example, a verifier or a circuit that performs modulo-2 arithmetic. **(2)** A linear circuit that compares two voltages and indicates whether or not they are equal.

compare To examine two or more items to determine their condition of identity, their relative values, or their position in a sequence.

comparison operator A relational operator.

compatible (1) A term applied to a program written for one type of a computer that can be run (with few if any modifications) on a computer of another type or manufacture. A program that is **forward compatible** can be used with a forthcoming range of computers that will be produced by a manufacturer. One that is **upward compatible** can be used with a manufacturer's larger or enhanced computers. **(2)** A term applied to a functional unit that can be used with computers of different types or of different manufacture. A device that is **plug compatible** is one that is intended to be operated when joined by a standard interface 'plug'. One that is **range compatible** can be used with computers of two (possibly more) ranges.

compile To translate a program in a high-level source language into object code. See *assemble; compiler.*

compile-and-go Compilation followed immediately by loading and execution. See *load-and-go; assemble-and-go.*

compile time (1) The time at which compilation begins. **(2)** The length of time required for compilation.

compiler A language processor that translates source coding in a particular (high-level) programming language into object code that can be executed by a particular make and model computer. Typically, it accomplishes the following: 1. It performs a **lexical scan** to eliminate redundancies, condense statements, and delimit phrases to produce a condensed source text. 2. It analyses the condensed source text to identify the various grammatical items with respect to the syntax of the language and produces a parsed version of the text plus a **symbol table** of the recognised items. 3. It performs an arithmetic scan to convert any arithmetic expressions to a form suitable for computations. 4. It optimises and simplifies the text to produce an improved parsed version. 5. It inserts default options. 6. It causes error messages to be printed or displayed where required. 7. It generates object code in the machine language of the particular computer. 8. It may optimise the object code with respect to the particular type of computer or installation. 9. It lists the source code and the equivalent object code. The output of the compiler is a module of object code that is, usually, an input to a linkage editor.

compiler control statement A compiler directive.
compiler directing statement A compiler directive.
compiler directive An instruction to a compiler that is included in the source coding but does not usually result in executable object code; for example, a declaration or the identification of a symbol used to make a macro call.
compiler generator A program that is intended to assist in writing compilers.
compiling program A compiler.
compiling time Compile time.
complement (1) A number that has been produced by subtracting another number from a constant; for example, the 'tens complement' of 7 is 3. **(2)** To derive the complement of a number. **complement representation** A method of representing a number so that it can be subtracted from another number by addition. The complement representation of a binary number is formed by changing all 1's to 0's and all 0's to 1's and adding 1 in the least significant digit position. If, for example, a computation requires 3 to be subtracted from 9, the 3 can first be complemented. In binary, 3 is 0011 so changing 1's to 0's and 0's to 1's gives 1100 and adding 1 in the least significant digit position produces 1101. When adding with complement numbers, the circuitry drops any carry from the most significant digit position, for example:

Decimal:	By bit carry:	By complement addition:
9	1001	1001
−3	−0011	+1101
6	0110	10110

The following are complements of some other binary numbers:

4	0100	1100 (1011 + 0001)
9	1001	0111 (0110 + 0001)
15	1111	0001
36	100100	11100

See *binary arithmetic; diminished radix complement.*
complementary circuit See *CMOS.*
complementary metal oxide silicon See *CMOS.*
complementary operation With respect to a particular logic operation; another operation that, with the same inputs, produces the opposite result. For example, NAND is the 'complementary operation' of AND.
complementary operator A logic operator that is the NOT of another logic operator. See *complementary operation.*
complementary record (C-record) In an indexed file; a record that does not have an index entry but is pointed to by a primary record. It can, thus, be accessed only via the primary record. See *primary record.*
complex (1) Not simple; consisting of many interrelated elements; ('a complex program'; 'a complex circuit'). **(2)** In relation to an integrated circuit; a term that indicates small element size and high packing density.
complex number See *number.*
complex stack See *stack.*
component (1) That which is part of something else; for example, a scheduler as a 'component' of an operating system or a servo as a 'component' of a magnetic disc unit. **(2)** An electronic device; a circuit element. See *element.*
compose-edit processor A component of a text editor used to locate particular places in text material in computer storage (by string matching) and to perform insertions and deletions. See *text editor.*
composer (1) A typesetter with facilities for justifying and varying margins. **(2)** In some systems; a linkage editor.
composite number See *number.*
composite operator A relational operator that specifies two conditions; for example, GREATER THAN OR EQUAL TO.
composite terminal A terminal consisting of two operationally distinct devices; for example, a VDU that comprises a keyboard and a cathode ray tube.
composited circuit A carrier system that is also used for base band signalling.
compound number A mixed-base number; for example, the time of day in hours and minutes.
compound statement A statement that combines two or more simple statements; for example, IF GREATER THAN 6 AND LESS THAN 20...
compress format A term applied to the output of a printer in

which the characters and/or lines are more closely spaced than usual.

compression See *data compression*.

compressor A circuit that decreases the difference between the strongest and the weakest signals in a particular range. See *compandor; expandor*.

computational format A representation of numeric data for which a computer provides hardware arithmetic facilities; the most common are fixed-point binary, packed decimal, and floating point binary.

computational stability The degree to which computational accuracy is maintained in the presence of hardware or software malfunctions.

compute (1)To perform a mathematical operation, particularly one that is complex or multi-step. (2)To perform an operation by means of a computer.

compute bound Processor bound.

computer A device that can perform a sequence of arithmetic and/or logic operations and produce useful results without human intervention except in preparing the device and, possibly, in initiating the operations. Unless otherwise indicated, a computer is understood to be a **digital computer** in which data is stored and manipulated as binary digits. An **analogue computer** is a device in which data is represented and manipulated as continuously variable quantities, often voltage, cam position, shaft rotation, or a combination; an analogue computer, typically, has little if any storage. A **hybrid computer** is a computer that incorporates both digital and analogue elements; for example, a process control computer in which inputs and first processing steps are analogue and further processing steps and, possibly, outputs are digital. See *general-purpose computer; minicomputer; microcomputer*.

computer aided design (CAD) The use of computers in solving mechanical engineering design problems; for example, plotting the shape of a cam or determining the contours of car bodies.

computer aided instruction (CAI) The use of computers as teaching aids in schools; for example, in designing and grading examinations. See *computer aided learning*.

computer aided learning (CAL) The use of computers as aids to students in their studies; for example, to test progress or to help in research. The term usually implies the use of interactive terminals. See *computer aided instruction*.

computer aided manufacturing (CAM) The use of computers to help make manufacturing decisions and/or to control manufacturing (production line) operations.

computer-dependent language An assembly language.

computer graphics A term applied to the equipment or techniques involved in manipulating, displaying, and plotting graphic images with the aid of a computer. (The term is also applied to the reverse process in which graphic images are analysed and digitised for computer input.) See *raster scan; vector scan; plotter*.

computer input on microfilm See *CIM*.

computer instruction See *instruction*.

computer language Machine code.

computer-oriented language An assembly language.

computer output on microfilm See *COM*.

computer program See *program*.

computer-readable A term applied to data in a form that can be read by machine for input to computer storage. Though the term can be applied to punched cards and paper tape, it usually denotes a form for optical reading (OCR; OMR) or magnetic ink character recognition.

computer system (1)A computer and associated peripherals and interfacing equipment. (2)A 'computer system' (def. 1) plus staff and software.

computer users' association (CUA) Also *user group*. An organisation of the users of computers of a particular manufacture, of a manufacturer's particular model or range, or of a major unit of software (application package; operating system). The purposes are, typically, to exchange methods and techniques, to coordinate work of mutual benefit, and to present user viewpoints and requirements to the manufacturer.

computer word See *word*.

computerised (1)Implemented on a computer; ('a computerised accounting system'). (2)Controlled by a computer; ('a computerised telephone exchange'; 'a computerised manufacturing operation').

computerised branch exchange (CBX) An intelligent, private 'switchboard' that may provide a variety of services (facsimile; data base interrogation) in addition to routing incoming and outgoing telephone calls.

computing (1)A manual or machine-assisted operation of manipulating numbers; ('computing an azimuth'; 'computing third-order intercepts'). (2)The activity, profession, or science of using computers.

COMSAT *COMmunications SATellite Corp.* (Clarksburg, Maryland)

concatenated Joined to form a string.

concatenated key A secondary key.

concentration The process of combining multiple messages into a single message for transmission.

concentrator In a data communications system; a unit that performs a fan-in and/or fan-out function. Typically, it is used to permit a number of terminals to share a single communications line or to permit a single DTE to send and receive over multiple telephone lines (in a star network). Common functions are buffering, speed changing, controlling modem interface circuits, and resolving contention.

conceptual language A language for communicating with a computer and data base that permits a terminal user to make tentative, postulating, and exploratory enquiries of the sort that one might make to a colleague in a particular field. See *expert system; advice language*.

concurrency (1)The condition of multiprogramming; the condition in which a processor is simultaneously executing several or many programs. (The term is most often applied with respect to a virtual storage system.) (2)An indication of the number of programs being executed; ('high concurrency'; 'optimum concurrency of about 20'). (3)The condition of mixed-mode operation. See *mixed mode (def. 2)*.

concurrent (1)Happening at the same time; ('concurrent data transfers'; 'a concurrent search'). (2)Of user programs; with elements simultaneously in main storage. See *concurrency*. (3) Interleaved. See *simultaneous*.

concurrent access The condition in which two or more programs are accessing the same file (or, possibly, the same volume) during the same time period.

concurrent peripheral operation Spooling.

condensed (1)Of type; with minimum character width and inter-character spacing (a variation of a particular type face); for example, '12 pt. Univers condensed'. (2)Compressed.

condition code An error/completion code; a group returned to indicate whether or not a synchronous command has executed successfully and, if not, the reason for failure.

conditional assembly An assembler facility for altering the content and sequence of source statements before assembly.

conditional branch Also *conditional jump*. A change from executing one sequence of instructions to executing another sequence of instructions made as the result of a test applied to data. See *conditional branch instruction; unconditional branch*.

conditional branch instruction Also *conditional jump instruction*. An instruction that specifies a test to be made on data and provides a different address for the next instruction to be fetched for each possible result of the test. When used with respect to a low-level language, the term may apply to an instruction that follows the one in which a test is made and, if so, it holds one of the addresses from which the next instruction can be fetched. When applied to a high-level language, it is a type of **conditional statement** and also a type of **sequence control statement**. See *conditional statement; sequence control statement; branch; unconditional branch instruction*.

conditional jump A conditional branch.

conditional statement In a high-level language; an instruction that specifies a test to be made on data and an action (or alternative actions) to be taken depending upon the result. The term includes conditional branch instructions and instructions of the type: 'ON SIZE ERROR...' and 'IF SWITCHON-12...'. See *conditional branch instruction; sequence control statement*.

conditioned line A leased telephone line to which 'conditioning' has been applied; a line that has been balanced to improve its data handling characteristics.

conditioning Also *equalization*. The operation of testing and compensating a leased telephone line to improve its data-handling characteristics. See *equalization*.

conductor A path for electric current; for example, a wire or a strip of copper on a printed circuit board. See *electricity*.

confidence test A test performed on a new or modified system or functional unit to determine whether or not it is operable.

configuration A particular group of interconnected functional units that forms a computer system or subsystem. See *architecture*.

configuration state With respect to the functional units of a computer system; the condition of being available or unavailable for use. The term **configured in** may be applied to those that are available and **configured out** to those that are not.

configuration table A table showing the configuration state of the various functional units of a computer system.

configure To obtain and interconnect functional units to form a computer system or subsystem.

conjunction AND (logic operation).

connect (1)To join entities. (2)In some systems; an instruction that is written to cause an interrupt.

connect time The time during which an on-line terminal is connected to a computer; it is often a basis for accounting/charging for computing services.

connective A term or symbol that indicates the relation between two items in a source-language instruction.

connectivity A term sometimes used to indicate the ease or practicality of connecting functional units; ('high connectivity making for fast reconfiguration') or to the facility with which software can be used together; ('applications with good connectivity').

connector (1)Also *terminal connector*. A flowcharting symbol (a circle) that is used to break a flowline or instruction sequence and to indicate where it is continued. An **outconnector** (such as the one with the '8') indicates that the sequence is continued elsewhere and an **inconnector** (such as the one with the '9') shows where another instruction sequence joins. See *flowchart*. (2)Also *relationship*. A link between two entities in a data structure established by a pointer in one of them; a part of an access path. See *net; tree; pointer*. (3)An electrical conducting path or device; for example, a jumper, a patch cord, or a termination of a multi-conductor cable. See *terminal; plug; strap*. (4)A channel; conducting metalisation of a semiconductor chip.

consecutive access A term sometimes applied to the serial access of physically separate items, particularly to the serial reading of punched cards.

console The operating station of a computer, usually with a keyboard for entering messages and responses and a screen and/or printer on which messages are received. It may also include switches for controlling certain operations and lights to indicate status.

console log A log maintained of communications between the operator and the operating system of a computer. See *log*.

console operator. An operator who operates a computer from a console. See *operator*.

console typewriter A 'two-way' typewriter at a console that is used by an operator to send messages to and receive messages from a computer.

consolidation (1)Concatenation; the formation of a single string from two or more strings. (2)An operation of a language processor (usually of a linkage editor) in which modules are linked and library routines and external calls are incorporated. See *linkage editor*.

consolidator A linkage editor.

constant (1)A number that represents a fixed relationship that has some significance in a calculation, series of calculations, or type of calculation; for example, a conversion factor or 'pi'. (2)A parameter that remains unchanged for the duration of a run.

constant-carrier system A data communications system in which the carrier wave is transmitted continuously. It is usually understood to be a full-duplex, point-to-point system in which the carrier wave is transmitted continuously on both channels of the link. See *switched-carrier system*.

constant-ratio code An M-out-of-N code.

constraint That which limits or restricts.

contact A conductor termination in a switch or relay; a metal element (usually of special alloy or plating) through which current flows when the device is closed and which separates from another contact to open the circuit. See *relay*.

contact printer A device for making duplicate photographs by placing the negative on (in contact with) unexposed film and exposing to light. See *microfilm; duplicator*.

contaminate With respect to a magnetic disc or tape; to allow dust or other foreign material to be deposited on the recording surface.

content access An access in which the content of the same field in a group of records is read and compared with an input value in order to attempt to match them and thus to locate a particular record or all records holding a certain value or having a certain attribute. It is a keyed access in which the contents of any field may be used as the key. The method is often used in searches that are 'one-off' or required only infrequently. The same technique is used in parallel search of look-aside registers. See *key; search; associative storage, look-aside registers*.

content-addressable filestore (CAF) A disc-based associative processor for use in organising and accessing large files; for example, a file containing all the entries of a metropolitan telephone directory. The file is distributed on a large multi-disc magnetic disc unit that is arranged for all heads to read simultaneously as they move from cylinder to cylinder in a search. In the telephone directory example, the particulars of each subscriber constitute a record, any field of which can be used as a key. It can make straightforward searches in which a telephone number for a particular subscriber is required and more complex ones in which only the street address is known, or, perhaps, in which only a name or initials and a street are known. The system is based upon a minicomputer and is intended to run as a back end to a mainframe computer. See *associative processor*.

content-addressable storage Associative storage.

content addressing Associative addressing; the location of items in computer storage by reading the items rather than their addresses. See *look-aside registers: associative storage; content addressable filestore*.

contention (1) The condition in which two entities attempt to use simultaneously a facility or resource that can be used by only one entity at a time. Examples include an attempt by two programs to access the same file or an attempt by two terminals to send messages on the same circuit. **(1)** A method of operating a (small) data network or multi-terminal data station in which a terminal with a message to send initiates a transfer on a common (shared) channel unless the channel is already being used by another terminal.

context editing In a word processor or computer; the facility for locating words or other character groups by means of 'pattern matching' (in order to make corrections or insertions); for example, the location of all occurrences of a particular word in a block of copy on magnetic disc.

context switching The operation of changing execution from one task or routine to another while saving register and memory contents so that control can be returned to the first task or routine when the second has finished executing. The term includes programmed branching as well as transfers to and from system routines, for example, to deal with interrupts and to transfer control between concurrent tasks. See *branch*.

contiguous Without separation; occupying adjacent positions or storage locations.

contiguous file A file that is not divided in storage by elements of any other file.

continuation line In source coding on a coding sheet; a second or subsequent line that is used to hold part of an instruction or a comment that is too long for a single line.

continuous-form cards Punched cards supplied in fan-fold stacks, joined at their short edges. They are usually edge-punched and remain joined during punching and reading.

continuous stationery A fan-fold web; paper (often multipart) divided into pages by perforations and fan folded. It is the usual paper for a line printer. See *printer; barrel printer; web*.

continuous wave See *CW*.

contrast In optical document reading; the difference in opacity or light reflectivity between the paper and the marks, characters, or punched holes that are intended to be read.

control (1) To specify operations and/or the sequence in which they are to be performed. **(2)** Use of the central processor; that which a program or other sequence of instructions is said to have when its instructions are being executed; ('transfer control'; 'return control to the main sequence').

control area See *control memory*.

control ball Also *track ball*. On a graphics VDU; an operator control that can be used to move a display or elements of a display.

control bit pattern The bit pattern of a microinstruction; a bit pattern that has no individual data meaning but is required to set control points in order to perform some (small) step of execution. See *microcode; control point; microinstruction*.

control block (1) On magnetic disc or tape; a block used to hold control information such as an index of volume contents, access restrictions, size, and file generation numbers. **(2)** An area of main storage used to hold control programs.

control character Also *function character*. A character that is interpreted by hardware to cause a functional unit to take some action; for example, to turn on or off, to change the interpretation of following bit patterns, to change a display on a VDU, or to change a printing format. See *device control character; transmission control character; format effector; print control character*.

control cycle The sequence of operations performed by a control unit between successive instruction fetches. See *execution*.

control data (1) Data used in the monitoring or control of processing; for example, a control total or a block check character. See *system data*. **(2)** A term sometimes applied to field contents that are used as keys in performing searches or sorts. **(3)** Data that is required in order to access other data; for example, the contents of headers, tables, and indexes.

control field In a record; a field that holds a value that is used as a key for access purposes. The term is more often applied to a field that holds a value used for a special-purpose search or sort than one that is used in regular access. A **major control field** holds a value by which a file is first searched to locate a group of required records; for example, if an alphabetical list of customers for each county of a sales area was required, 'county' would be the 'major control field'. A **minor control field** holds a value by which sorted records are further sorted; in the previous example, 'customer name' would be the 'minor control field'. (Depending upon the operation; several minor control fields may be used.) See *primary key field; auxiliary key field; control value.*

control function A control operation.

control hole A designation hole.

control language A job control language.

control loop A format loop.

control memory Also *control area; control storage.* (1)The part of main storage reserved for a supervisor or operating system. (2)Control-unit memory; read-only memory that holds the order code and microcode. (3)A save area. (4)In an intelligent device; the memory that holds the control program(s).

control message A supervisory message.

control module A control segment.

control number A record number.

control operation (1)Also *control function.* An operation (by hardware, software, or a person) that affects the way data is transferred, manipulated, or formatted. (2)An operation by a functional unit that is initiated by a control character. See *control character.*

control panel An element of a console or other operating station; a group of switches and (usually) lights by which an operator can monitor and control certain functions of a system. See *display panel.*

control point A place in an electronic circuit of a central processor (or intelligent device) where the application of a pulse will cause the transfer of one or more bits within a register or between registers. It is a place where an input is made to an AND gate that (typically) has two other inputs, one of which is a timing pulse and the other is the output voltage of a bit cell (transistor flip-flop). An **independent control point** is one that connects to several or many AND gates and, thus, a pulse applied to it causes the transfer of multiple bits. See *register; shift register.*

control processor (1)Also *master processor.* In a multiprocessor system; the processor that holds the programs used to make system decisions and to control the work of other processors. (2)A central processor.

control program (1)A program used to schedule or supervise the execution of other programs; a unit of system software. See *system software; supervisory software.* (2)In an intelligent device (automatic washing machine; traffic light controller); the contents of a read-only memory that is used to control its operation.

control punch A designation hole.

control read-only memory (CROM) A memory of a microprocessor-based device that holds one or more control programs. See *control program.*

control register (1)An instruction register. (2)In some systems; a current address register. (3)Any register in a control unit.

control section (1)A control segment. (2)A separately loadable program segment that cannot be further divided into separately loadable segments.

control segment Also *control section; control module; nucleus.* That part of an overlay program that must be in main storage at all times during the execution of the program.

control station (1)A console or other location from which some operation is controlled. (2)A master station.

control storage Control memory.

control total Also *check total; check sum.* A total of the occurrences or numeric contents of certain fields (usually, in records of a batch) that are reconstructed at various stages of processing and checked against the original to determine whether or not corruption has occurred. See *batch total; hash total; check sum.*

control unit (1)Also *instruction control unit.* That part of a central processor that holds the instruction code of a computer and related microcode and performs such functions as fetching instructions and operands, decoding instructions, allocating operations to the arithmetic logic unit, storing results, initiating peripheral transfers, and monitoring system operation. See *central processor; arithmetic logic unit; execution.*

control value (1)A value that is used to perform a loss or corruption check on data; for example, a batch total, a check sum, or a block check character. (2)The contents of a control field; a value that is used to perform a search or sort.

control variable A variable that is used to hold a value required to control some aspect of processing; for example, one that holds the amount by which addresses are to be incremented in a loop.

control word A word consisting of the control values used to sort or merge a group of records. See *control field; control value*.

controller (1)A device that performs a control function, particularly with respect to inputs and outputs; ('a communications controller'; 'a peripheral controller'). (2)With respect to a file or volume; a user with full access rights.

controller/formatter See *disc controller*.

conversational A term applied to interactive data communications systems in which terminal operators and a computer carry on 'conversations' similar to those between two people. See *on-line; transaction processing*.

conversational remote job entry (CRJE) The input of job control statements and operands from a remote terminal to permit remote, on-line control of batch processing.

conversion (1)The process of changing from one form of representation to another; for example, changing from binary to decimal or from one code to another. (2)The process of changing programs so that they can be run on a different make or type of computer than the one for which they were written. See *emulation; translate*. (3)The process of changing the scale of numeric values; for example, changing from pounds to kilograms or from yen to dollars.

conversion factor A constant used as a multiplier to make a conversion (def. 3); for example, 2.54 is the 'conversion factor' for inches and centimeters.

converter A device for changing electric current; for example, from 50 Hz. to 60 Hz. or from direct current to alternating current.

coordinate-addressable storage Storage that is read and written by the application of electrical pulses to the storage cells of a matrix. The common types are core and semiconductor memory. A characteristic of such storage is that all locations have the same access time. See *coincident current selection*.

copy (1)Also *duplicate; reproduce*. To make another that is identical to the original; ('copy a microfiche'; 'copy a magnetic tape'). (2)To make a content duplicate (that may or may not be a physical duplicate); ('copy a card file to magnetic tape'; 'copy a disc file to magnetic tape'). (3)Also *read; write; move; roll in; roll out* and other terms. To read data in one location and, without changing the data in that location, to write it to another location. (4)That which is produced by a 'copy' operation (def. 1; 2; 3). (5)Also *text*. Data consisting of words and sentences.

CORAL 66 A general-purpose language based upon ALGOL 60 that is used mainly in transaction processing applications.

core (1)A ferrite core. See *core memory*. (2)A short-form term for 'core store'; ('add another 8K of core'). (3)In some contexts, a synonym for 'nucleus'. (4)In an electromagnetic device (relay; transformer; solenoid); the iron part on which a coil is wound. See *coil; transformer*.

core dump A dump of the contents of main storage. See *dump*.

core image A storage image in a computer in which main storage is 'core'. See *storage image; process image*.

core index An index that is held in (core) main storage.

core memory A type of memory in which bits are represented by the direction of magnetism in small, ferrite (iron oxide) rings which are 'cores'. A typical core is about the size of the head of a pin and, when assembled with others into a **core plane**, it usually has four wires going through the centre as shown in 1.

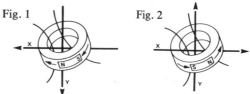

Fig. 1   Fig. 2

To write a 1-bit, currents are sent through the X and Y wires simultaneously in the direction shown. A magnetic field that is strong enough to orient the particles of the core is formed at their point of intersection (in the centre of the core). The particles thus become tiny magnets that point in the same direction. (A wire that carries a current is always surrounded by a magnetic field; the currents and the core characteristics are selected so that a current in one wire only will not 'set' the cores through which it passes; cores are thus set only where two current-carrying wires intersect.) To read a particular core, currents are sent through the wires in the opposite directions as shown in 2; this can be considered as 'writing' a 0-bit. If the core was holding a 0-bit, there is then no change and the particles remain aligned in the same direction as they were in. If the core contained a 1-bit, the read signals cause the particles to reverse direction and become oriented as shown in 2. When they reverse direction, the core acts like a tiny generator and induces a small voltage (pulse; signal) in all the wires that pass through its centre. The only wire that has the circuitry to detect this pulse is the **read wire** which passes through all the cores of the core plane. It carries the pulse to a **read amplifier** where it is amplified and sent to the control unit where it sets a bit in some register. In the process of reading, the 1-bit held by the core has

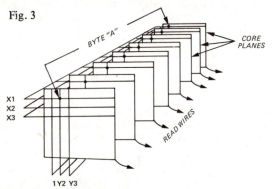

Fig. 3

been 'destroyed' (replaced by a 0-bit), for this reason, the reading of core memory is said to be a **destructive read**. Because a memory is only useful if it can be read repeatedly, it is, then, necessary to restore the 1-bit to the core and this is done by rewriting a 1-bit in the manner previously explained. If, however, the core had previously held a 0-bit, it would also be changed to a 1-bit by the operation. This is prevented by the **inhibit wire**; if the core previously held a 0-bit a current is sent through this wire in a direction to counter some of the magnetic field induced by the X and Y wires and, thus, to prevent the core from changing. Like the read wire, the inhibit wire goes through all the cores of the particular core plane. The fastest core memory is **three-dimensional** (3D) in which there is a core plane for each bit position of the standard-size word or byte, as shown in 3. To read byte A, pulses are sent on X1 and Y2 and all eight bits of the byte are, thus, read simultaneously. See *coincident current selection; random access memory*.

core store Also *core storage*. (1)Any storage that uses ferrite cores as the storage cells. (2)A term sometimes used synonymously with 'main storage' and applied to such storage that is 'core' as well as (incorrectly) to that which is 'semiconductor'.

co-resident (1) Concurrent; in main storage at the same time. **(2)**Installed at the same site; ('a PDP-11 co-resident with a Honeywell 6/43').

correctable error An error that does not result in the loss of data; either a recoverable error or a soft error. See *error; recovery; soft error.*

corrective maintenance Maintenance performed to correct an existing fault. See *preventative maintenance.*

correspondence The degree to which one thing resembles another; ('two order codes with high correspondence').

corrupt To introduce errors in data; to cause data as received or read to differ from the data as transmitted or recorded.

coulomb (Q) A measure of the quantity of electrons passing in a wire in which the current is 1 ampere.

count (1) To note the occurrence of events in a sequence and produce a total. **(2)**A value held in a register and incremented or decremented to control some processing operation.

counter (1)A device or circuit capable of adding and/or subtracting in increments of '1' and producing a total. **(2)**A shift register. **(3)**A program counter.

cover disc A guard disc.

CP (1)*Central Processor.* **(2)***Card Punch.*

CPI (cpi.) *Characters Per Inch.* See *pitch.*

CPM (1)(cpm.) *Cards Per Minute.* **(2)**(CP/M) *Control Program/Microcomputer.* An operating system for Z-80 based microcomputers

CPS (cps.) **(1)***Cycles Per Second.* **(2)***Characters Per Second.*

CPU *Central Processor Unit.*

CR (1)*Carriage Return.* A control character that is sent when the 'Return' key on a terminal is pressed. In most systems, it closes the line buffer and causes the character following it to begin a new line. See *newline.* **(2)***Card Reader.* **(3)***CRedit.*

crash (1)A system breakdown or major loss of capability; ('a hardware crash'; 'a software crash'). See *system crash.* **(2)**A head crash (head-disc interference).

CRC *Cyclic Redundancy Check.*

creation Also *file creation.* The process of opening a file, writing data to it, and closing it for the first time.

credit A term applied to a transaction that reduces the amount a customer owes; for example, to 'credit' his account for a payment received or goods returned. See *debit.*

CRJE *Conversational Remote Job Entry.*
CROM *Control Read-Only Memory.*
cross compiler A compiler used on a computer of one type to produce object code to run on a computer of another type.
crossbar (1)A type of relay used in a telephone exchange to complete telephone calls by connecting any of a number of input circuits to any of a number of output circuits. It is the standard type of connecting device in many countries. See *Strowger relay.* (2)A type of electronic circuit used to make data routing connections of multipath data channels; for example, in a peripheral controller.
crossfire Inter-channel interference in a telegraph system; it is the equivalent of crosstalk in a telephone system.
crosstalk An unwanted transfer of energy (speech or data signals) from one telephone circuit to another as caused by capacitive coupling of wires in a cable or a defective connection in an exchange. The circuit that causes the interference is a **disturbing circuit** and the one experiencing the interference is the **disturbed circuit.**
CRT *Cathode Ray Tube.*
CRT controller A circuit (often a single integrated circuit) that provides control for a VDU. Typical functions include timing of the scan, generating horizontal and vertical synchronisation of the scan, loading and unloading the video buffer, processor interfacing, character generator addressing, and cursor control.
CRT terminal A VDU.
cryogenic memory A memory that operates at a low temperature, typically near the boiling point of helium (—268° C.). The experimental devices that have been constructed are of the recirculating type and take advantage of the very low electrical resistance (superconductivity) that conductors exhibit at low temperatures. Because of the low resistance, charged particles representing bits will continue to circulate indefinitely in a closed loop without the need for refreshment or driving circuitry. Switching times of between 5 and 20 picoseconds have been obtained and packing densities are of the order of half a megabit per square inch. Though energy consumption of the memory itself is very low (possibly 50 mW. for a two-megabyte device), considerable energy and equipment are required to maintain the low temperature.
cryotron A type of cryogenic memory.
cryptography The science or practice of changing the representation of data for security purposes; it consists of placing data in a form (a code) that prevents its correct interpretation without special knowledge or equipment. See *privacy code; encryption.*
CSA *Computer Services Association.* (London)
CSL *Control and Simulation Language.* A high-level language designed for use in linear programming.
CSMA *Carrier Sense Multiple Access.* A method of operating a local area network (Ethernet) by contention. A station with a packet to transmit first checks to see that there is no other packet on the line (that no carrier is being transmitted).
CSW *Channel Status Word.*
CTRL *ConTRoL.* On many terminals; a key that is pressed in conjunction with another key to obtain the attention of the terminal driver and to cause it to perform a control or manipulation function; for example, to start or stop scrolling.
CTS *Clear To Send.* See *modem interchanges.*
cue (1)An audible signal. (2)A term sometimes used synonymously with 'call' or 'invoke'; ('cue a subroutine').
cupping A defect condition of magnetic tape consisting of areas of across-the-tape curvature.
current (1)Being used at the present time; ('a current address'; 'a currently executing program'). See *concurrent.* (2)Of the latest generation; ('a current file'). (3)Of the latest type or issue; ('a current operating system'; 'a current model computer'). (4)In a circuit; a flow of electrons. See *electricity.*
current address register Also *program counter.* A control unit register that holds the address of the next instruction to be obeyed in a particular sequence after the instruction in the instruction register. (If the instruction in the instruction register is a branch instruction, it causes the first address in a new sequence to be placed in the register.) The address in the register is incremented each time an instruction in a sequence is obeyed and thus provides the address for the next instruction fetch. See *fetch; execution; register.*
current drive With a current-loop interface for inputs.
current line In data inputs at a terminal; the most recently entered line as held in the line buffer.
current loop A standard interface for connecting terminals and other equipment in cable (base band signalling) systems. The usual current is 20 milliamps, though some operate on 60 milliamps. Signals are NRZ and are usually received through an optocoupler. Some devices have facilities for receiving both

current loop and V.24 signals; converters are available to change from one to the other.

current range A term applied to a computer or other major equipment that is of the type currently being manufactured. See *new range*.

cursor A movable mark (an underline; two parallel lines) that is used to mark the place on a VDU screen where the next character to be entered will be displayed or, otherwise, to mark a point of interest.

curtate A term applied to a group of adjacent rows on a punched card; the **upper curtate** normally consists of rows 11, 12, and 0 and the **lower curtate** of rows 1—9. See *punched card; zone punch*.

customer A person or company that buys from a particular manufacturer or supplier.

customer engineering (CE) The department of a manufacturer that is responsible for providing field maintenance and repairs to installed equipment. The term may also be applied to facilities for this purpose; ('a customer engineering test'; 'a customer engineering disc').

customer identification number Also *customer number; account number*. A number by which a particular customer is identified in the records of a company and by which transactions relating to the customer are identified for data processing purposes.

customer number A customer identification number.

customise To adapt hardware (possibly software) to meet the needs of a particular user.

cut form A term applied to a form that is a separate piece of paper (as distinguished from one that is joined to others in a roll or fan-fold stack).

cut set A multipart form (say, an invoice or purchase order) that is carbon-paper interleaved or uses carbonless copy paper. See *web; fan fold*.

cutoff frequency The upper or lower frequency passed by a filter. (Unless otherwise indicated, 'upper' is understood.) See *filter; band*.

CW *Continuous Wave*. A term applied to transmissions or a transmission system that employs a constant (unmodulated) carrier wave that is turned on and off in patterns to represent data; for example, to send the dots and dashes of Morse code. See *carrier wave*.

cybernetics The branch of learning concerned with communications systems and control in both living organisms and in man-made systems. See *bionics*.

cycle (1) A clock cycle or fixed number of clock cycles as used to control a sequence of operations or to synchronise two or more sequences of operations. See *clock; clock cycle; time base; synchronisation*. **(2)** An operation or sequence of operations performed with external timing; ('a fetch cycle'; 'a storage cycle.'). **(3)** One pass through a fixed sequence of operations or events; ('a polling cycle'). **(4)** Also *iteration; performance*. One execution of the instructions of a loop. **(5)** The period during which an alternating current passes through each of its possible states of amplitude and polarity; the period between successive zero crossings in the same direction. See *sine wave*.

cycle sharing Cycle stealing.

cycle stealing Also *cycle sharing; hesitation; intervention*. A procedure in which control unit hardware conducts an operation (usually a peripheral transfer) concurrently with processing by 'stealing' small groups of clock cycles from instruction execution; the effect is to allow processing to continue in parallel with a transfer but at slower speed than normal. See *synchronous transfer; asynchronous transfer*.

cycle time (1) Storage cycle time. **(2)** The time required for one performance of any multi-step, repetitive operation; particularly one under external timing control.

cycles per second (cps.) **(1)** Hertz. **(2)** The number of times per second that some multi-step operation is performed.

cyclic access An access made to a rotating storage medium (magnetic disc or drum). See *direct access*.

cyclic check character (CCC) A final character constructed in accordance with a polynomial code and added to a block or other unit of message transfer to facilitate the detection of errors. See *polynomial code; block check character*.

cyclic code A reflected binary code.

cyclic redundancy check (CRC) A check for corruption of data during transfer or transmission as made by using a polynomial code and a cyclic check character. See *polynomial code*.

cyclic shift See *shift*.

cyclic storage Storage in which the data moves in relation to the position in which it is read or written; the characteristic is that access time depends upon where a particular item of data happens to be when it is called for. The term includes recirculating (bucket brigade) memory such as delay line and CCD and direct access memory (magnetic disc and drum).

cylinder In multiple-disc magnetic disc storage; all the tracks of the same number on different disc surfaces; all the tracks that can be accessed by the read/write heads without a seek (without changing radial position). See *seek; magnetic disc unit.*

D

D/A *Digital to Analogue.*
DAA *Data Access Arrangement.*
DAC (1)*Digital to Analogue Converter.* **(2)***Data Acquisition and Control.*
daisy chain (1)A series arrangement of functional units; for example, a 'chain' of disc drives connected together by cables with only the first drive in the chain connected to the peripheral controller. **(2)**A term sometimes applied to a series of backup units arranged so that a failure of one causes the function or control to be passed to the next in succession. **(3)**A term sometimes applied to a pipeline arrangement in which the outputs of one unit constitute the inputs to the next in succession.
daisy wheel A type font in the form of a rotatable wheel with type slugs on the ends of 'spoke' type bars. In operation, the wheel is rotated to bring a particular character to the printing position where the slug is struck from behind by a solenoid to

impact the character against ribbon and paper. The wheel moves along the line as it prints. A printer that uses a 'daisy wheel' may be termed a 'petal printer'.
daisy wheel printer Also *petal printer.* A printer in which the character set is held on a 'daisy wheel'. It is a serial, impact character printer with typical speeds of from 33 to 45 characters per second. The following is an example of the printing:

   All of our Customer Operator Training Centres

dalek voice A term used to indicate a low quality of synthetic speech as characteristic of (Dr. Who) robots.
damping The action of mechanical or electronic elements that introduce delay or establish limits to reduce or eliminate unwanted oscillation or 'hunting'.
dark-trace tube A photochronic tube.
DASD *Direct Access Storage Device.*
data (1) Facts, concepts, or directives in a form that can be communicated and interpreted. Included by the term in this broadest definition are such things as manuscripts, instruction manuals, musical scores, accounting records, and computer programs. It is this definition that is implicit in such terms as 'data processing' and 'data transmission'. See *information and data.* **(2)**Inputs to a computer program or routine that are manipulated by arithmetic/logic operations and determine the results of processing. By this common definition, programs and programming instructions are excluded; 'data' identifies the items on which the programs and instructions work. (The term by this definition can include the data of definition 1 when in a bit pattern form so that it can be manipulated and output under program control). See *code; system data; user data.*
data access arrangement (DAA) A line access unit provided by the PTT or common carrier to permit selective voice/data use of a dialed line; the change is made with an 'exclusion key'.
data acquisition The process of obtaining computer input data from a terminal where it is entered by an operator. It may be solely an entry operation (as with direct data entry) or it may be a programmed operation of obtaining data for file updating as it arises (in a transaction processing system).
data acquisition and control (DAC) The function of receiving, validating, editing, and storing inputs from non-keyboard devices; for example, from sensors or document readers. It is, typically, an automatic operation under program control.
data acquisition, collection, and capture The term 'data acquisition' is usually applied to the process of obtaining data as input from terminals and 'data collection' to the process of extracting data from source documents for entry via punched cards or tape. In some systems, the meanings are reversed with 'data acquisition' being the essentially clerical operation and 'data collection' the terminal operation. In systems where it is used, the term 'data capture' usually relates to the essentially automatic operation of obtaining data by telemetry or machine reading of documents. In many systems, the term 'data acquisition' is broadened to include such methods as well as

entry via terminals. See *data acquisition; data collection; data capture; data control; data preparation.*

data adapter A line adapter. The term is most often used with respect to microprocessor systems, See *communications interface adapter.*

data administration The function of controlling the data of a computer system to ensure its accuracy and protect it from corruption or unauthorised access. The term is most often applied to a data base system and in this context it includes designing the data base, producing a schema to define its structure and contents, and producing subschemas to define the authority and access rights of users and applications. The person in charge of data administration usually has the title **data administrator** or **data base administrator** (DBA).

data aggregate The contents of a group field; related and contiguous data items within a record; for example, a customer's name and address.

data attribute A characteristic of a unit of data; for example, length, access rights, value, or format. See *attribute.*

data bank (1) A large data base or several data bases considered as a unit. **(2)** All of the maintained data of an organisation including data in a computer system as well as data in such forms as microfilm, files in filing cabinets, and manuals and other publications.

data base Also *database.* A pool of shareable data as held in computer storage and controlled by a central authority, the **data base administrator**. It is designed to meet the requirements for maintained (consistent and current) data by many or all of an organisation's application systems. While it is possible for a data base to be a collection of conventional files, the term more often implies the use of such structures as nets and trees. A single item of data is intended to be captured and stored just once and with a single copy in storage and with all applications that require it accessing that copy. The method reduces the requirements for data storage space and eliminates the inconsistencies that can occur when multiple copies of an item (possibly in different update versions) are held in storage. A distinguishing feature of a data base is the interposition of special software (usually a **data base management system** and a **data dictionary**) between users and their applications and the pool of data. This software protects data from unauthorised access and controls the extent of shareability; it locates the particular data required by programs; and it permits the data to be changed in content and organisation without affecting the way it is seen and used by application programs. It, thus, provides **data independence**. A **distributed data base** is one that is divided between geographic locations. A **relational data base** is one that holds data in the form of relations (tables). An **integrated data base** is one that employs structures such as nets and trees to provide a multiplicity of access paths to the data in the pool. See *data bank; schema; subschema; net; tree.*

data base administration Data administration.

data base administrator (DBA) **(1)** A CODASYL defined data base diagnostics system. **(2)** A data administrator. See *data administration.*

data base diagnostics Programs and procedures designed to check the entities and access paths of a data base to detect errors, redundancies, and inconsistencies.

data base key A value in a sequence of system-generated values that is associated with a record in a data base and used to locate it and distinguish it from other records. See *key (File organisation).*

data base management system (DBMS) A set of software for controlling and accessing the data of a data base; it may include a data dictionary or use a separate one.

data base manager (1) A data base management system (software). **(2)** A data administrator (person).

data base processor An auxiliary computer used to handle data base management tasks.

Data Base Task Group (DBTG) The CODASYL committee responsible for producing their data base facilities and associated languages, data description language (DDL) and data manipulation language (DML).

data bit An unchanged signal or line condition that represents a bit or multiple bits. The term is used with reference to data transmission and magnetisable surface recording in which there are fewer line or flux transitions than there are bit cells; for example, in phase shift modulation or NRZI recording.

data bit period The duration of a data bit; the length of time between transitions. See *bit cell; line transition.*

data capture (1) The process of obtaining computer input data from devices that automatically sense conditions or count events; for example, by means of telemetry, process control sensors, or document readers. See *data acquisition, collection, and capture.* **(2)** The process of obtaining computer input data by any means.

data carrier (1) A carrier wave as used for transmitting data. (2) A medium (punched cards; magnetic tape) that can hold data.

data cartridge A plastic, device-replaceable magnetic tape volume consisting of two reels and a belt drive system for winding the tape from one to the other. The '300-A' model contains 300 Ft. of one-quarter inch tape; it is recordable on four tracks and has a capacity of about 3 megabytes with recording at 1600 bpi. The '100-A' model contains 100 Ft. of .15 inch wide tape recordable on two tracks and has a capacity of about 0.7 megabytes. See *digital cassette; magnetic tape*.

data cartridge drive A device for reading and writing data cartridges; the usual transfer rate is 48K bits per second.

data cell (1) In some systems; any individually replaceable unit of storage; for example, a disc pack, a digital cassette, or a magnetic card. (2) A storage cell.

data chain Linked blocks containing related records (including any that have overflowed).

data channel (1) In a telephone system; a channel used to carry data as contrasted to one used to carry speech. (2) A channel; a path for one-way communications in a data network. (3) In some large computer systems; a functional unit (often a minicomputer) that handles peripheral transfers; typical functions include multiplexing, queue management, buffering, code and format conversion, error detection and resolution, and staging. See *peripheral controller*. (4) A channel (def.2); a path for data within or between functional units. (5) In a data transmission or transfer system; a channel used to carry data as contrasted to one that, for example, carries supervisory messages or control signals.

data circuit A term sometimes applied to a duplex circuit suitable for transmitting data.

data circuit equipment Data circuit-terminating equipment.

data circuit-terminating equipment (DCE) A functional unit in a data communications system that performs some or all of the line interfacing functions (connection; signal conversion; synchronisation) between a unit of data terminal equipment (DTE) and a (telephone) data transmission line. As commonly used, the term (or, at least the abbreviation 'DCE') is synonymous with 'modem'. See *modem; data terminal equipment; packet switching system*.

data collection (1) The operations of a data control department in obtaining source documents from users, checking the data, and preparing it for conversion to some computer-readable form, typically, by punching in cards or paper tape. See *data acquisition, collection, and capture; data preparation*. (2) The process of receiving data over communications links (as in a transaction processing system) and holding it in a buffer while it is awaiting processing.

data communications Also *communications; comms; datacomms; DC*. The person-to-program or program-to-program transmission of data between geographically separated locations.

data compaction Data compression.

data compression Also *data compaction*. The removal of unnecessary characters, gaps, or fields in order to reduce the storage space or transmission time of data.

data constant A figurative constant.

data control A term applied to a department with responsibilities for the input and output of data for a batch processing stream of a computer system. Functions, typically, include receiving and checking source documents, sorting and batching the documents, calculating and checking control totals, data preparation, and checking and distributing results. The department also, commonly, has responsibility for maintaining the library of tape and disc volumes and for the physical security of stored data. See *input; data preparation*.

data control block A control block.

data control unit (DCU) A data channel; a small interface computer that handles peripheral transfers.

data control word (DCW) A word that initiates a data transfer.

data declaration See *declaration; assign*.

data description A source language statement that names and provides attributes of an item of data that will be used during processing.

data description language (DDL) A language for describing data, particularly the language defined by CODASYL. Its purpose is to describe the data in a data base, both as it actually is (in a schema) and as it appears to particular applications (in subschemas).

data dictionary A data structure that holds information about the contents of a data base. Typically, it holds a unique identifier for each accessible item, it describes the format of data, it indicates relationships between data items, and it defines access rights to the various items. It provides the data base management system with the inputs needed to service the requirements of application programs and it is the main vehicle by which the data administrator controls and coordinates access to the data base. It can also be interrogated to provide a wide range of reports on the structure and content of the data base. See *data administration; data base.*

data directory (1) A data dictionary. **(2)** An element of a data dictionary.

data division That part of a COBOL program that defines constants and names and reserves areas of storage that will be used during execution. It also describes the files that will be used.

data driven With initiation or control provided by data rather than by instructions. See *dataflow processor*

data element In data base terminology; the smallest unit of data that has individual significance to a user; the term is commonly synonymous with 'field'.

data entry The operation of placing data in on-line computer storage, for example, by means of a card reader or a direct data entry terminal.

data format The way data is represented in storage, processing, or output; ('character format'; 'computational format'; 'page format').

data gathering Data collection (def. 1; 2).

data independence (1) An attribute of a data base in which software provides a flexible interface with data so that data can be changed in structure or content without affecting the application programs that use it. See *data base*. **(2)** The situation in which an operating system may place or structure data in a way different than that specified by a user program; for example, the program could specify a magnetic tape file with numeric data in fixed-point binary and the operating system could 'substitute' a disc file and numeric data in packed decimal. The purpose is to allow the operating system to make the best use of computer resources and to permit changes in hardware or software without necessitating changes in user programs.

data input station Also *data collection station*. A terminal (say, in a warehouse) by which data is entered into a computer system; it may or may not be interactive.

data item (1) A unit of data that can be accessed by name or by name and subscript(s); an item that can be individually referenced during execution. **(2)** Any discrete unit of data; for example, an operand, a record, or the contents of a field.

data library (1) A library. **(2)** A collection of related files.

data link (1) A path (wires; coaxial cable; microwave) and associated equipment by which data can be transmitted between geographically separated locations. See *circuit; channel; data network*. **(2)** A correspondence between data and its representation in a particular code or form. See *DLE*.

data link control (DLC) The implementation of a link protocol; the collection of procedures and non-information interchanges that control the movement and interpretation of data carried on a data link.

data link controller The functional unit or elements of a functional unit (say, of a front-end processor) that implement a link protocol. See *link protocol; data link control*.

data link escape character See *DLE*.

data logger See *logger*.

data logging See *log*.

data management (1) The operating system function of placing and retrieving data in storage and of protecting its security and integrity. **(2)** Data administration.

data management software Those routines of an operating system that perform a data management function.

data manipulation language (DML) A language designed for use in retrieving, storing, and updating data in a data base. Unless otherwise indicated, the language is the one defined by CODASYL and the host language is COBOL.

data matrix (1) Also *observation matrix*. A form for inputting observed or measured data (say, temperature at five-minute intervals) into a computer system; it consists of a column with a row for each observation or measurement. **(2)** A multidimensional array used to hold data.

data medium (1) A physical condition (light; magnetic field; voltage) that can be varied in a way to represent data. **(2)** The material on which or in which the physical condition is varied; for example, a photographic film, a ferric oxide coating, a core, or a transistor. **(3)** A particular type of storage; for example, photo-digital, magnetic disc, core, or semiconductor.

data module A magnetic disc storage volume consisting of two or four magnetic discs and their read/write heads and access arms enclosed in a dust-proof plastic case. The two-disc unit has an unformatted capacity of 35 megabytes and the four-disc unit a capacity of 70 megabytes. The controlled environment permits lower head flying heights (20 microinches), thinner disc

coating (40 microinches), and greater recording density (5636 bpi.) than are practical with open systems. There are two heads per disc surface and, in a module, one head and one-half a disc surface are used for track-following servo. Some versions of the four-disc unit provide for fixed heads to operate on the other half of the servo surface. See *magnetic disc unit; disc pack; disc cartridge.*

data module drive A magnetic disc unit capable of handling data modules; typical operating characteristics are: spindle speed 3000 R.P.M.; average seek time 25 ms.; data transfer rate 1 megabyte per second. See *data module; magnetic disc unit.*

data multiplexor See *multiplexor.*

data name A source-coding identifier of an item of data to which storage will be allocated; it is, typically, a symbolic address.

data network (1) An organisation of terminal equipment and communications facilities for the transmission of data between geographically separated locations. (2) An organisation of terminal equipment, communications facilities, and data processing equipment that provides a data processing service for users at geographically separated locations.

data origination See *origination.*

data preparation Also *data prep.* The function of preparing batch stream computer inputs from source data. It consists of reading the source data as it appears on documents (purchase orders; coding sheets; inventory sheets) and transcribing it by means of a keyboard device into a computer-readable form. The devices generally available for the purpose are card punches, paper tape punches, and direct data entry terminals. The work of the keyboard operator is checked by **verification** which consists of re-reading the source data and keying it in at a keyboard to produce a 'duplicate' of the original; it is usually done by a different operator. In direct data entry, the same terminal (or type of terminal) is used for verification as was used for the original; with punched cards and paper tape, a separate device (a **verifier**) is used for the purpose. If a keystroke made during verification fails to duplicate the original, the device 'locks' while the operator(s) resolve the error. Data preparation is followed by **data entry** in which the bit patterns produced are copied (usually with a code change) onto magnetic tape or disc in the backing storage of the computer. Data preparation is usually the responsibility of the data control department. See *data control; data collection; data capture; data entry; input; direct data entry.*

data processing (DP) The transcription and storing of groups of letters and numbers and their mechanised ordering, selection, form changing, and reproduction.

data processing manager Also *DP manager; DPM.* A person in charge of a computer department. (The usual job title.)

data processing system Also, usually, *computer system.* A group of people, procedures, and devices organised to perform a data processing function.

data processor (1) A device with programmable memory that performs a data processing function; for example, a computer or a calculator. (2) A device that performs a data processing function (in a data processing system); for example, a computer, a peripheral controller, or a card punch.

data pulse An electrical signal that represents one or more bits in reading from or writing to a magnetisable surface storage medium. See *data bit.*

data rate (1) In data communications; the amount of data transferred per unit time on a data link. It is usually expressed in bits per second. (2) The number of words or bytes transferred per unit time between functional units of a computer system.

data receiver An analogue to digital converter used with analogue data received on a communications channel.

data record A record that contains processible data (as contrasted, for example, with a header record).

data recording The process of representing data on a storage medium. Unless otherwise indicated, the medium is assumed to be magnetisable-surface (magnetic disc or tape).

data recording medium A medium suitable for the representation and storage of data; for example, magnetic tape or punched cards.

data reduction The process of sorting and combining data to reduce its volume and place it in a form that is more suitable for some purpose.

data representation (1)An arrangement of observable or detectable elements with an agreed interpretation as one or more letters or digits; for example, a printed character or word, a bit pattern on magnetic tape, or a sequence of signals on a communications channel. (2)The process of representing data.

data retrieval The process of locating and reading data in storage. Unless otherwise indicated, 'backing storage' is assumed.

data selector Also *multiplexor*. A circuit with multiple inputs, any one of which can be selected as the output. It consists of as many AND gates as there are inputs plus an OR output gate and a select matrix. In the figure, if Select A is low and B is

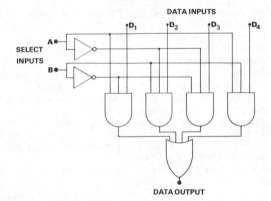

high, Input D_2 will 'pass through' as the output. Data selectors are used in multiplexing, in character generators, in implementing complex logic functions, for making identity checks of bit strings, and in parallel-to-serial converters. See *Karnaugh map*.

data set (1)In some systems; the equivalent of a file; a major unit of storage and retrieval consisting of a collection of data in one of several arrangements for which the system provides access facilities; ('a direct data set'; 'a sequential data set'). (2)A telephone connected to a modem or line interface unit and used by an operator to set up a data transfer (manual originate or answer). (3)A modem.

data signalling rate Also *bit rate*. The rate in bits per second at which data is sent on a communications channel. See *Baud; modulation; data transfer rate*.

data sink Those elements of a DTE (computer; terminal) that receive the information content of messages. (Other elements of the DTE or a separate functional unit implement the link protocol.)

data source Those elements of a DTE (computer; terminal) that provide the information content of messages. (Other elements of the DTE or a separate functional unit implement the link protocol.)

data station (1)A location in a data network that can send and receive messages. Unless otherwise indicated, it is a remote site rather than a central site. (2)A DTE and a connected modem.

data stream (1)A flow of data from a storage unit to an arithmetic logic unit during processing. See *stream; instruction stream*. (2)A continuous flow of data and/or idle patterns that is transmitted on a synchronous, constant-carrier link. (3)The data that passes through an input/output port in a single read or write operation

data structure A unit of data as organised for access purposes; for example, a file, a data set, a net, or a tree.

data terminal equipment (DTE) In a communications system; a functional unit that can originate and/or receive messages; either a computer or a terminal.

data transfer (1)A movement of data within a computer system; a movement that does not make use of a communications (telephone) link. Unless otherwise indicated, the term is synonymous with 'peripheral transfer'. See *data transmission*. (2)A movement of a particular unit of data by any means; ('a data transfer to magnetic tape'; 'a data transfer from a remote terminal').

data transfer rate The average number of data units (characters; bytes; words; blocks) passing between functional units per unit time. The term is used with respect to local transfers as well as transfers over communications links. See *data signalling rate*.

data transmission A movement of data between geographically separated locations or devices by means of a communications channel. See *data transfer*.

data transmission interface (1)A place where data moves between networks or circuits operating under different protocols. (2)A place where the form or representation of data is changed for purposes of transmission; for example, between a modem and a DTE.

data transmission line See *line (Communications)*.

data transmission rate (1)Data signalling rate. (2)Data transfer rate (on a communications channel).

data type The mathematical properties and internal representation of data and functions; the basic types are 'integer', 'real', 'complex', and 'logical'.

data under voice (DUV) A term applied to a telecommunications facility or technique in which a single voice-grade channel is used simultaneously for speech and data.

data unit A bit pattern of standard length used to represent data in storage or transfer; for example, a character, a byte, a word, or a block.

data validation See *validation*.

data vet See *vetting*.

data word An operand that occupies a word of storage.

database See *data base*.

datacomms *DATA COMMunicationS*.

dataflow processor A parallel processor organised so that the data required by a particular (large) program is routed in a 'dataflow' to each of a number of different processors that are set up to handle execution of the instructions of particular segments of the program. As the stream passes, each processor recognises and reads in the data it requires for its particular sequence and when all have been received it executes the sequence and returns the result to the 'flow' where it is available as input for other processors. Such a processor is termed **data driven** as the performance of processing operations depends upon the arrival of the data.

datagram A message of fixed maximum length sent without network-provided facilities for assuring its accuracy, delivery, or correct sequencing with respect to related messages; data sent as a telegram.

Dataplex An extension of the U.K. Post Office 'Datel' service in which British Telecom provides subscribing users with multiplexing equipment.

Datel The data transmission facilities and procedures for data transmission provided by British Telecom. It includes dial-up service to 4800 bits per second and leased line service up to 9600 bps. (voice-grade) and 48,000 bps. (wideband).

datum (1)A base or starting point. (2)An item of data.

datum and limit See *storage protection*.

daughter board A printed circuit board that plugs into (or otherwise connects to) a 'mother board'.

DB (dB) *DeciBel*.

DBA (1)*Data Base Administrator*. (2)(dBa) *DeciBels (Adjusted)*.

DBD *Data Base Diagnostics*

DBM (dBm) *DeciBels (Mean)*. A term that usually denotes levels relative to one milliwatt.

DBMS *Data Base Management System*.

DBTG *Data Base Task Group*.

DC (1)*Device Control*. A character in a data transmission code that is available for controlling a device (typically, for turning it on or off). (2)(D.C.) *Direct Current*. (3)*Data Communications*.

DCB *Device Control Block*. See *control block*.

DCD *Data Carrier Detect*. In a switched-carrier communications system; an interface signal from a modem to a DTE indicating that carrier of adequate quality is being received. See *modem interchanges*.

DCD drop code When a switched carrier onward link is connected to a remote site modem that operates with constant carrier; a distinctive pattern that is transmitted by the remote site modem to the central site modem when carrier drops in the onward link (when RTS drops from the repeater modem). When received by the central site modem, it causes it to drop DCD to the central site DTE. It is used in conjunction with RTS-DCD simulation to permit switched carrier (polling; contention) communications over a constant carrier (point-to-point) link. See *onward link; RTS-DCD simulation*.

DCE (1)*Data Circuit-terminating Equipment*. (2)*Data Communications Equipment*.

DCTL *Direct Coupled Transistor Logic*.

DCU (1)*Device Control Unit*. (2)*Data Control Unit*.

DCW *Data Control Word*.

DDD *Direct Distance Dialing*.

DDE *Direct Data Entry*. (1)The process. See *direct data entry*. (2)A terminal used for direct data entry; ('supports interactive working on both DDE's and VDU's').

DDL *Data Description Language*.

DDP *Distributed Data Processing*.

deactivate (1)Also *delete*. With respect to a program or process; to remove it from main storage and to deallocate resources.

(2) With respect to a system or functional unit; to remove it from operational status. **(3)** To disable.

deadlock Also *deadly embrace*. A term applied to unresolved contention; for example, the situation in which two programs are prevented from processing because each has been allocated a resource required by the other.

deadly embrace Deadlock.

deallocate To withdraw a resource from an entity (user; program; job) to which it has been allocated. See *suspend; discard; delete*.

debit A term applied to a transaction that increases the amount a customer owes; for example, to 'debit' his account for goods or services supplied. See *credit*.

deblock By system software; to read blocked records individually as required for processing.

debug (1) With respect to a program or other software; to detect, locate, and eliminate errors. **(2)** With respect to a system or functional unit; to locate the cause of (minor) malfunctions and to make necessary corrections. See *fault*.

DEC *Digital Equipment Corporation* (Maynard, Mass.)

decade Ten; a term that indicates holding or counting in units of this size; ('a decade counter').

decay Of a signal or voltage; to diminish towards zero amplitude (as when power is interrupted or turned off).

deceleration time (1) In a magnetic tape unit; the time taken to slow the tape from the search or rewind speed to the read/write speed. **(2)** In a magnetic disc unit; the time taken for the spindle to come to a stop after turning off power. See *acceleration time*.

decibel (DB; dB) A measure of relative energy (signal strength; amplitude of sound) between an initial condition and a final condition or between an observed level and a reference level. It is the standard unit of measurement for attenuation of signals on transmission lines and of such things as aircraft noise in relation to background noise; the formula is:

$$dB = 10 \text{ Log } P1/P2$$

Where P1 is the observed or final level and P2 is the reference or initial level. For example, doubling the energy is an increase of 3 dB (the Log of 2 is 0.3010) and an increase of 20 dB is an increase of 100 times (the Log of 100 is 2).

decimal Pertaining to a positional representation number system with a radix of 10; in a computer context, the term differentiates this number system from binary. See *radix; numeration system; binary*.

decimal digit Any of the digits 0 to 9.

decimal notation A notation that uses the decimal digits, whether or not in the decimal numeration system; for example, the biquinary code or a code in which decimal digits represent letters.

decimal numeration system See *numeration system*.

decimal point The radix point in the decimal system; it is usually indicated by a full stop as in .001 or 3.2. It may also be indicated by a comma as in 3,2 or a dot as in 3·2.

decimal system The number system with a radix of 10.

decision By a control unit during program execution; the selection of a processing-relevant value (operand address; program instruction address; address of the first instruction in a utility) depending upon the results of a test applied to data. See *branch; conditional branch instruction; conditional statement; decision table*.

decision box A diamond-shaped flowcharting symbol placed where a 'decision' is to be made during execution. The criteria for the decision is usually written in the box ('Last card?') and the flowlines from the box labeled 'Yes' and 'No'. See *flowchart; decision; decision instruction*.

decision instruction A conditional branch instruction; an instruction that specifies a test to be made on data and indicates the sequence of instructions that is to be followed depending upon the result.

decision point (1) A place in a flowchart where a decision box is placed. **(2)** A place during execution where a decision instruction is decoded.

decision table A table used to represent a problem for purposes of designing a computer program; it may be used as an alternative to constructing a flowchart. It provides an essentially mechanical method of analysing a problem and can be faster and easier than flowcharting for certain types of problems. Suppose, for example, that a numeric value is to be tested as follows to control processing operations: If J is less than 10, perform 1, if equal to 10, perform 2, if greater than 10 and equal to or less than 20, perform 3, if greater than 20 perform 4, if greater than 20 and ODD, perform 5, if less than 10 and EVEN, perform 6. To set up the table, write simple statements to express the conditions and place them in the 'condition stub'. Then write the actions to be taken beneath them in the 'action stub'. (Conditions and actions can be placed

```
J < 10        Y Y Y Y Y Y Y Y N N N N N N N N
J = 10        Y Y Y Y N N N N Y Y Y Y N N N N
J > 10, ≤20   Y Y N N Y Y N N Y Y N N Y Y N N
J ODD         Y N Y N Y N Y N Y N Y N Y N Y N
Perform:
  1                   X X
  2                             X
  3                                X X
  4                                         X X
  5                                            X
  6                      X
```

in any order.) Fill in columns opposite the conditions (the 'condition entry') with Y's (Yes) and N's (No) as shown to represent all possibilities. It will be noted that 2^n columns are required where 'n' denotes the number of conditions. The next step is to examine each column and cross out all entries that represent contradictions. For example, a value of J cannot be both equal to 10 and less than 10. The next step is to put an 'X' in each column of the 'action entry' in which conditions are fulfilled for an action. There should then be at least one 'X' opposite each entry column that has not been crossed out; if there is a column without an 'X', an ELSE statement will be required. See *decision; flowchart*.

decision tree A plot of the different possible sequences of steps that can be taken depending upon the results of tests made upon completion of each step; it is the inherent structure of a trouble shooting procedure.

deck (1) The upper 'user' level of a magnetic disc unit; the part that separates the discs from the drive and circuitry. **(2)** Also *tape deck*. A magnetic tape unit. **(3)** The part of a magnetic tape unit on which the reels mount. **(4)** A card deck.

declaration Also *declarative instruction*. An instruction in source code that identifies a resource or value that a program will use during processing; for example, a file, a peripheral, a work area, a parameter, or a computational format. See *assignment; data description*.

declarative instruction A declaration.

declaratives Compiler-directing sections written at the beginning of the procedure division in a COBOL program.

declare In source coding; to specify a type of data, file structure, initial condition, peripheral device, or other condition or value that affects the way a program will be executed or the resources that will be allocated to it.

decode (1) To change data to a 'final' or 'standard' representation; for example, to change inputs from Hollerith code to EBCDIC. **(2)** To reverse the effect of encoding; for example, to produce an ASCII or English version of data that has been coded for security purposes. **(3)** In addressing coordinate-addressable storage; to convert a numeric address to a pulse on a word line; for example to input address 1001 and to send a pulse on word line No. 9. **(4)** By control-unit circuitry; to interpret the bit patterns of an instruction in the order code of the computer; to perform the first step in executing an instruction. See *instruction; execution*.

decoder An electronic device or circuit that performs a decoding operation. See *decode (def. 1—3); diode matrix*.

decollate Also *burst*. To separate sheets of multipart, continuous stationary after printing (by a line printer).

decollator A device used to separate multipart, continuous stationary. See *decollate*.

deconcatenate Also *unstring*. To separate a chain into discrete elements or into shorter chains. See *concatenate*.

deconcentration In a multiplexed communications system; to separate an incoming data stream into its constituent messages. See *concentrator*.

decrement (1) To decrease a value or quantity by the successive removal of equal-size units; unless otherwise indicated, the unit is assumed to be '1'; ('decrement a count'). See *increment*. **(2)** To perform a subtraction. **(3)** A term sometimes applied to an amount subtracted: ('a decrement of 20').

dedicated (1) Reserved for a particular purpose or user; ('a dedicated line'; 'a dedicated disc'; 'a dedicated terminal'). **(2)** Of an integrated circuit; manufactured to perform a particular function and not programmable for other functions.

DEDS *Dual Exchangeable Disc Storage*.

default A system-provided value or option that is used in processing when no alternative has been specified (by a programmer or operator). Examples might, in a particular system, include setting counts to zero, assigning lowest processing priority, using a disc scratch file, and outputting numeric values in decimal. A programming language or compiler with 'powerful defaults' is one that provides for many such decisions to be taken automatically during compilation.

default option A parameter or processing option that is used in absence of a specific input. See *default*.

default parameter A system-supplied parameter. See *default*.

default value A value used during processing in absence of a specific input. See *default*.

defect A fault; particularly in a hardware unit as received or as manufactured.

deferred addressing Multilevel indirect addressing in which the final (effective) address is determined by specifying the number of levels (number of iterations) to be used.

deferred entry An entry following a deferred exit. See *deferred exit*.

deferred exit With respect to a called routine; the passing of control to another sequence of instructions at a time determined by an external event.

deferred restart A restart performed manually by resubmitting a program to the job queue. See *restart*.

deflection A movement of the beam in a cathode ray tube to a position other than in the centre of the screen. See *cathode ray tube; scan; raster*.

deflector A deflector plate.

deflector plate A metallic plate in a cathode ray tube that can be capacitively charged in a controlled way to attract and repel the electron beam and thus to control the scan. See *cathode ray tube*.

degaussing The process of removing residual magnetisim from electromagnetic devices (such as metallic read/write heads).

degradation A reduction in performance or partial loss of capability due to faults or reallocation of resources. See *fault; failure; reconfiguration; fail soft*.

DEL *DELete*. A control character that causes deletion of the immediately preceding character (as entered, transmitted, or punched). (In some systems, it causes deletion of the current line.) See *CAN; cancel; erase; delete*.

delay (1) To cause to occur or appear at a later time. **(2)** Also *lag*. The amount of time by which an event follows a previous event. **(3)** Also *delay distortion; phase distortion* Of a transmitted signal on a communications link; the condition in which the last part to be received extends beyond the time frame for the signal, it is caused by high-frequency elements of the signal travelling at a lower speed than the low-frequency elements. See *jitter*.

delay circuit See *time delay circuit*.

delay equalizer A phase equalizer. See *equalization*.

delay line (1) A multistage delay circuit. **(2)** The 'delay' element of a delay line memory.

delay line memory A recirculating memory in which signals representing bits move through some part of the circuit at a substantially slower speed than electrical signals move on uninterrupted conductors. The type that was once most common is the **acoustic delay line** memory in which electrical signals are converted to and from pulses of sound (pressure waves) that move at a relatively slow speed through some medium such as mercury. In a simplified system, a stream of input data (possibly as many as 1000 bits) is introduced in an OR gate at A and synchronised by clock pulses in an AND gate. These are supplied to a transducer B where they are changed to sound which travels through the delay medium C to transducer D where they are changed back to electrical signals. These are sent through an amplifier and back through the system; the amplifier has the necessary circuitry for reading. Certain characteristic bit patterns are included with the data to serve as starting points for counting to locate particular items. Delay line memory is 'serial access' and the time taken to locate any particular item depends upon where it happens to be when called for. The storage was once widely used in VDU buffers but has largely been supplanted in this (and other) applications by smaller, faster, and cheaper devices.

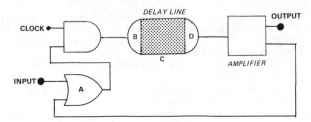

delay unit A device that produces an output signal at some fixed time after receiving an input signal. See *time delay circuit*.

delayed updating Updating performed only when a related sequence of file-affecting events is completed. The purpose is to avoid the possibility of leaving files in a partially updated condition ; for example, if an order entry operation is interrupted before inventory quantities are adjusted.

delete (1) To remove a unit of code or data from a particular storage or type of storage and (often) to write it to another type of storage; ('delete a program from main storage'; 'delete a segment from primary storage'; 'delete a file from disc storage'; 'delete a record from a file'). See *discard; overwrite; deallocate; roll out.* (2) To eliminate a character or line; for example, with a DEL character.

delete character See *DEL*.

deletion record A new record that, when a file is updated, will replace an existing record or cause it to be overwritten or excluded.

delimit (1) To establish bounds; ('delimit an area of storage'). (2) To identify the beginning or end of a group or unit; ('delimit a message address'; 'delimit records on a track'; 'delimit characters with framing bits').

delimiter A character or symbol that separates individual units that would otherwise be 'run together' with certain or possible loss of individual identity. Examples of delimiters include spaces between words, framing bits in asynchronous transmissions, and the control character GS as used to separate groups in transmitted data. See *bound; start-stop bits; FS; GS; US; limit.*

demand paging In a virtual storage system; the roll in of pages as and when required by executing processes.

demand processing Processing in which certain classes of programs are loaded and run immediately upon request; the situation with transaction processing and multi-access.

demand staging Staging under the direct control of the executing program that will use the data. See *staging.*

demarcation The operation of separating or defining limits.

demodulation The receiving operation of reversing the effects of modulation; to reconstruct transmitted data from signal patterns received on a modulated carrier wave. See *modulation; carrier wave.*

demountable device A backing storage device in which the read/write medium is operator replaceable as a volume. See *demountable storage; volume.*

demountable storage Magnetisable surface backing storage in which volumes are operator replaceable on the devices on which they are read and written. The common types are, magnetic tape (open-reel; data cartridge; digital cassette) and magnetic disc (disc pack; disc cartridge; data module).

demultiplexing (1) A receiving operation of converting multiplexed data to its constituent data streams. (2) Bit-serial to bit-parallel conversion.

denary Decimal; with a radix of 10.

density (1) The number of elements per unit length, area, or volume. (2) The contrast between printed images/characters and the background; ('high-density ink').

dependency The condition in which the accuracy of results from one program depend upon the accuracy of results from another; for example, if the first program updates a file and the second uses it.

dependent variable See *variable (Mathematics).*

depletion device An MOS transistor that conducts except when a gate signal is present. See *MOS; enhancement device.*

depletion zone In a semiconductor; an interface that inhibits conduction; an area without carriers (free holes or electrons). See *semiconductor.*

dequeue To remove items from a queue (before they are served). See *queue; enqueue.*

descender In type; the part of a character that extends below the baseline, for example, the lower part of a 'p', or 'y' or the 'tail' of a comma. See *riser.*

description See *data description.*

descriptor Also *keyword* and, in some systems, *pointer*. The contents of a storage location used in address modification; particularly in a virtual storage system. It is an element of a page/segment table, catalogue, directory, or index and consists of an address plus, possibly, other information such as access permitted and use bits. A **vector descriptor** contains the coordinates of an item in an array and, possibly, the bound limits of the array. A **string descriptor** contains the address of an item in a string. A **code descriptor** contains the address of an instruction and is referenced to transfer control from one sequence of instructions to another. A **descriptor descriptor** contains the address of another descriptor. See *pointer; virtual storage addressing; address modification.*

deselect To release or discontinue using an item that has been selected. See *select.*

deserialiser A device that converts data from bit serial to bit parallel, for example, when transferring data from magnetic disc to main storage or magnetic tape. See *serialiser; staticiser.*

design The process of combining available inputs (experience; technology; manipulative aids) to produce a drawing and/or specification of a system or device that is to be produced.

design parameter A function, capability, or structure that is to be provided by (or incorporated in) a system or device.

designation holes Also *control holes*. Holes punched in a punched card for purposes of indicating its type, function, or method of handling.

destage To move data in backing storage from a device of higher speed to one of lower speed. See *staging*.

destination (1)Also, often, *addressee*. In data communications; a location to which data is sent. (2)In data transfers; a register or storage location that receives a data transfer. (3)That which receives or is intended to receive.

destination code In a message in a data network; that part of the heading that identifies a terminal that is to receive the message or (in a message from a terminal to a computer) the application program that is to service the message.

destination field The part of a message that contains the destination code. See *destination code*.

destination file A file that receives the results of processing. See *source file; source-destination file*.

destination station An addressee.

destructive addition Addition in which the new sum overwrites the augend.

destructive cursor On some VDU's; a cursor used to erase; it causes the deletion of any character through which it is moved.

destructive read A term applied to a read operation (core memory) in which the reading destroys the contents of the location that is read. See *core memory; regeneration*.

de-suspend To resume executing a program that has been suspended. See *suspend*.

detach To release a peripheral that has been attached. See *attach*.

detail card A trailer card.

detail file A transaction file.

detail line A single line in a sequence of lines containing related data; for example, in a bank statement, a line that contains details of a particular cheque or deposit.

detail record A record containing the data for a single detail line. See *detail line*.

de-update To reconstruct a file in an earlier version by reversing the effects of updating. See *update*.

device (1)A unit of hardware; for example, a switch, an oscillator, an integrated circuit, a typewriter, or a VDU. (2) Also *functional unit*. A stand-alone element of a computer system; for example, a modem, a card punch, or a magnetic tape unit. Unless otherwise indicated, it is assumed to be a **peripheral device**. (3)Also *element; component*. A unit that performs some function in an electronic circuit; for example, an integrated circuit, a transistor, or a diode.

device adapter An interface unit or circuitry that converts data to and from the representation used by a particular peripheral device or class of peripheral devices; for example, a device that converts between bit serial and bit parallel and resolves differences in transmission speeds.

device address A character or group of characters by which a peripheral device is known to an operating system.

device control character See *DC; control character*.

device control unit (DCU) A peripheral controller; particularly one of several such devices that handles transfers and interface functions for a particular group of the peripherals of an installation.

device-dependent A term applied to a program that requires a particular peripheral device or type of device. See *device independence*.

device driver A unit of hardware or software that performs interfacing functions between an operating system and a peripheral device. Typical functions include passing addresses and interrupts, buffering data, and error detection.

device independence (1)The condition in which an operating system may use a different type of peripheral to service the requirements of a program than the device specified by the programmer. The device is specified in source coding with a **logical device name** or **logical unit number** and a device so specified may be termed a **virtual device**. (2)The condition in a common trunk computer system in which peripheral controllers perform all necessary conversion and reformatting functions in order to permit transfers in standard code and format to and from all peripherals of the installation. The purpose of device independence is to increase the portability of application programs, to permit changes in system architecture without necessitating changes to programs, and to allow the operating system to optimise usage of the available peripheral devices. See *common trunk; data independence*.

device media control language (DMCL) A language defined by CODASYL and used to specify the physical layout and structure of data on storage devices.

device name See *logical device name*.

device number A number that identifies a device to an operating system.

DFC (1)*Disc File Controller*. **(2)***Data Flow Control*.

DG *Data General* Corp. (Southboro, Mass.)

diagnose To identify and locate the cause of software or hardware faults. See *fault; diagnostics*.

diagnostic Pertaining to the identification and location of faults or errors.

diagnostic disc A (flexible) magnetic disc containing one or more diagnostic programs. See *diagnostic program*.

diagnostic function test A program to test overall system reliability.

diagnostic program A program that provides assistance in recognising, locating, analysing, and correcting software errors or hardware faults. See *diagnostic test program; diagnostics*.

diagnostic test program Also *isolation test routine*. A program that is run to identify and localise hardware faults.

diagnostics (1) Built-in hardware facilities of a computer or functional unit that are intended to assist in locating and correcting faults. **(2)**Techniques, results, or tests used in locating and correcting hardware faults or software errors.

diagram A graphic representation; for example, of a system or a procedure.

dial (1) An element of a telephone that is incrementally rotated to select a telephone number as a step in making a telephone call. **(2)**To select a telephone number by means of a 'dial' (def. 1).

dial backup See *switched network backup*.

dial exchange An automatic exchange.

dial pulse A pulse produced on a local loop caused by the opening and closing of contacts in a telephone set as a number is dialed; the number of pulses is equal to the number dialed.

dial tone An audible signal indicating that a number can be dialed.

dial-up A term applied to a data transmission carried on the public switched telephone network and initiated by dialing the telephone number of the receiving station.

dialect Of a programming language; a version used with a particular make or model computer; ('a Sperry Univac 1100 COBOL dialect').

dialogue A term sometimes applied to the interchange that takes place between a terminal operator and a computer in a transaction processing system. See *on-line; conversational mode*.

diazo film See *microfilm*.

dibit (Rhymes with 'try it') Two bits that are represented on a communications channel by a single line transition; the four that are possible are 11, 10, 01, and 00. See *phase shift modulation; Baud*.

dice See *die*.

dichotomise To divide into two parts, classes, or groups.

dichotomising search A binary search; a search in which a group is successively divided into two parts. See *search*.

dictionary (1) Also *table; directory*. A list of contents, of items and attributes, or of items and their relationships; for example, a data dictionary or a symbol dictionary. **(2)**Also, depending upon system and context, *directory; table; index; catalogue*. A list used to locate items in storage; typically, it holds identifiers of all the items in a volume or other unit of storage and their addresses. In an access, the dictionary is searched for the required identifier and the address thus produced is used for a subsequent step which may be the retrieval of the item or a repetition of the process with another dictionary.

die (plural: dice) **(1)**A chip. **(2)**A small chip containing a microcircuit that is assembled on a larger chip as a step in producing a hybrid microelectronic device.

dielectric An insulator; a medium that resists the passage of electricity; for example, air, epoxy, or glass.

difference The result of a subtraction.

differential amplifier An operational amplifier that compares two input signals and amplifies and outputs the difference.

differential analyser An analogue device that uses interconnected integrators to solve differential equations.

differential current-mode system A differential mode system.

differential mode system Also *differential current-mode system*. A communications system in which the line conditions of two paths (twisted pair of wires; two channels of a carrier system) are varied simultaneously and inversely (one goes high while the other goes low) in a data significant way, with a return provided by another path (often ground). A **differential receiver** (also **differential amplifier**) detects the difference between the signals and ignores (rejects) any noise that appears on both paths. Because the two paths are adjacent physically and use the same equipment, any outside electrical events (lightning; cross-talk) that affects one will affect the other and thus be rejected. This ability to discriminate is termed **common-**

mode rejection typically, a receiver in such a system can correctly interpret signals of less than 50 mV. in the presence of **common-mode noise** with peaks of about 3.5 V.

differential modulation A method of modulation in which the significance of a signal (its interpretation as one or more bits) depends upon its relationship (phase or, possibly, amplitude) to the previous signal. See *modulation; phase-shift modulation.*

differential phase shift keying (DPSK) Phase shift modulation. Though the term may be applied to four-phase modulation, it usually denotes an eight-phase method as used to encode tribits (for 7200 bit per second) or quadbits (for 9600 bit per second). In both cases, changes in amplitude as well as phase are used. See *phase shift modulation; quadrature amplitude modulation.*

diffusion A doping process by which an N-type zone is formed in a P-type substrate (or the reverse) by exposing the masked substrate or epitaxial layer to a gaseous concentration of the doping element in a vacuum chamber.

digit A graphic character that represents an integer; for example, any of the characters 0—9 in the decimal system or a 1 or 0 in binary. See *number; numeral; integer.*

digit position In a positional representation numeration system; a place for a digit in relation to other digits of a number that establishes its value (weight) in the number. See *numeration system; weight.*

digit punch On a punched card; a hole punched in any row from 1 to 9. See *curtate; zone punch.*

digital (1) Using (binary) digits to represent data in storage, transfer, or manipulation; ('a digital cassette'; 'a digital modem'; 'a digital computer'). (2) With output displayed as (seven-segment) decimal digits: ('a digital voltmeter'; 'a digital clock'). (3)(DIGITAL) The Digital Equipment Corp.

digital cassette A storage volume that consists of magnetic tape with supply and takeup reels in a plastic enclosure that is unit loadable for reading and writing. One type is dimensionally the same as a standard (say, C—60) entertainment cassette and

contains 282 Ft. of tape that is recorded in bit-serial on two tracks; selection of tracks is made by turning over the cassette in the drive. Capacity is about 500 kilobytes and transfer speeds are about 1200 bytes per second. Other types provide storage of up to 50 megabytes in either special enclosures or as modified versions of video cassettes. See *magnetic tape; data cartridge.*

digital computer Also *computer.* A device that stores, transfers, and performs arithmetic and logic operations on data in digital form. See *computer; data processor; von Neuman machine.*

digital data (1) Data in (binary) digits. (2) Numeric data.

digital loop test A test of the internal circuits of two modems and a telephone link between them by which an operator at one modem causes a test pattern to be transmitted to the other modem which, in turn, decodes it (recovers the bits as with a normal data transmission), re-encodes it, and retransmits it back to the testing modem. (It may be used with four-wire systems or full-duplex, two-wire systems.) the modem test

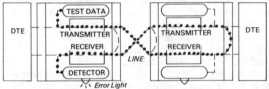

facilities usually provide for the testing modem to send a distinctive command (tone or data group) which, when received, causes the other modem to assume the test mode. It is usually used in conjunction with an error detection circuit that causes a light to flash if an incorrect bit (say, a 0-bit in a sequence of 1-bits) is detected. See *analogue loop test; end-to-end test.*

digital production effects (DPE) The digitisation of video signals and their (microprocessor) manipulation to produce special television effects; for example, zooms and image rotation.

digitise With respect to analogue data; to place it in digital form. See *analogue to digital.*

digitiser An analogue to digital converter.

DIL *Dual In-Line pin.* A designation of a device (integrated circuit; switch) in which the electrical connectors (pins) are in two downward-pointing, parallel rows, one on each side of the device. The configuration is designed to facilitate assembly to printed circuit boards.

DILIC *Dual In-line pin Integrated Circuit.* A designation of an integrated circuit device designed to connect to a printed circuit board by means of two parallel rows of connectors (pins). See *DIL; pinout.*

dimension An actual or notional axis of storage locations in an array. The first three dimensions correspond to 'length', 'height' and 'width' and thus equate to the geometrical use of the term. An array of four dimensions is, in effect, two arrays each of which has three dimensions. An identifier of a location along a dimension is a **subscript** (sometimes an 'index'). See *array; index; subscript.*

dimensioned variable An array.

diminished radix complement A method of complementing numbers in which the number to be complemented is subtracted from a 'number' consisting of that digit which is 1 less than the radix in each digit position. In decimal, it is a **nines complement** ($10 - 1 = 9$) and in binary it is a **ones complement** ($2 - 1 = 1$). For example, the diminished radix complement of 763 is 236 and of 110101 is 001010. See *complement; radix complement.*

DIMS *Distributed Intelligence Microcomputer System.*

diode A semiconductor that inherently conducts current in only one direction. The element towards which electrons flow is the **anode** and that from which they come is the **cathode**. When used in a conducting mode (say, in an OR circuit) the anode is connected to a part of the circuit that is more positive than the cathode; when used in a blocking mode (to prevent a current flow in one direction), this is reversed. Diodes are rated according to the amount of current they can carry (without

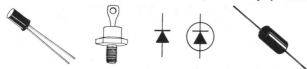

overheating or fusing), to forward voltage drop (the difference between anode and cathode voltage when conducting), and peak inverse voltage (the maximum voltage in the 'wrong' direction that they can resist without breakdown). Diodes are the basic building blocks of semiconductor devices and electronic circuits. In computers, they are used as elements of all logic gates, to 'clip' high-voltage transients, and as elements of rectifiers in power supplies. See *semiconductor; rectifier; wired OR; logic circuits.*

diode clamping The use of diodes to limit the voltage at some point in a circuit (to prevent over voltage). Assuming diodes with a typical 1 V. forward drop, the maximum at A will be 3 V. and at B 1 V.

diode matrix A circuit to perform code or logic conversion. It consists of two major components, a **decoder** as shown in the upper part of the illustration and a **coder** as shown in the lower part. If inputs A and B are both low, then matrix line 1 is held low through diode 1 and line 3 is held low through diode 3. The inverted input from A allows line 2 to go high if it receives a

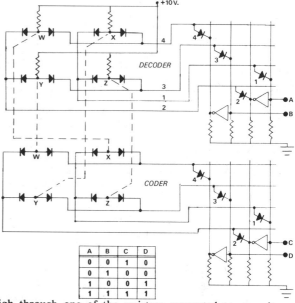

A	B	C	D
0	0	1	0
0	1	0	0
1	0	0	1
1	1	1	1

high through one of the resistors connected to + voltage. Similarly, the inverted B input will allow line 4 to go high. Point W is, then, the only one to be high because it is the only one controlled by both lines 2 and 4. (Points X, Y, and Z are all low because they are held low through either or both diodes 1 and 3.) Each of these decoder points is connected to a similar point in the coder, as indicated by the dotted lines for one of the possible connections. The way the two sets of points are connected determines the conversion function that is performed. If Point W is connected to Point X in the coder, then high is output to coder diodes 1 and 4. The high through diode 4 has no effect upon output D because it cannot pass through the inverter and D, thus, is low. The high through diode 1 raises diode C and this output is high. Such a matrix, then, allows just one decoder point to go high for each of the possible combinations of inputs and the resultant output depends upon which coder point is connected to it. The device is commonly used to perform the conversion in both directions. For example, if low is placed on C and high on D, points X and Z of the coder are pulled low through diode 1 and points X and W are pulled low through diode 4. This leaves only point Y high and this connects to point X of the decoder, making it the only high point in the decoder. The high on X causes lines 1 and 4 to be high. The high through diode 1 causes A to be high and the high through diode 4 is blocked by the inverter causing B to be low. The truth table shows the conversions for the particular interconnections shown by the dotted lines. There are as many decoder and coder points as there are combinations of two inputs, for example, there are 64 points for a matrix that performs an 8-bit conversion.

diode-transistor logic (DTL) A versatile logic circuit in which transistor inputs are through diodes. In the positive NAND circuit shown, the transistor is biased OFF through R1 when any or all of the inputs 'A', 'B', or 'C' are or low. Output 'D' is

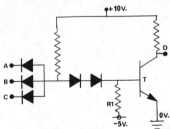

therefore high. When all of the inputs are high, the transistor turns ON and the output goes low. (The diodes between the two resistors are intended to prevent the transistor from saturating.)

DIP *Dual In-line Pin.* See *DIL*.

dipole encoding Also *non-polarised return-to-zero encoding;*

dipole modulation. The representation of data in recording or transmission as signals of one polarity (say + 5 V.) to represent a 1-bit and absence of signal (zero voltage) to represent a 0-bit.

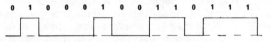

(Or the reverse, depending upon the system.) See *NRZ; NRZI encoding; polar signalling.*

direct access (1)Also, sometimes, *cyclic access.* A term used to denote an access to data on magnetic disc or drum. (2)An access to data on magnetic disc or drum or in main storage or some other form of coordinate-addressable storage; any 'fast' access, as distinguished from a magnetic-tape access. See *random access; serial access.*

direct access device A peripheral storage device that supports direct access; either magnetic disc or magnetic drum.

direct access storage Storage on a direct access device or group of such devices (as contrasted to main storage and magnetic-tape storage).

direct access storage device (DASD) A direct access device.

direct address Also *one-level address.* In an object code instruction; a binary number that is converted to a hardware address by the addition of a single value (usually a base address). See *address; indirect address; absolute address; address modification.*

direct addressing (1)Absolute addressing. (2)Either absolute addressing or a process in which an effective (hardware) address is obtained from a presumptive (instruction) address in a single step. See *indirect addressing; address modification.* (3)A method of storing or retrieving a record in a direct file.

direct current (DC; D.C.) An electric current (as from a battery or rectifier) in which electrons flow in one direction only. See *alternating current; polarity; rectifier.*

direct data entry (DDE) A system for simultaneously performing the operations of data preparation and data entry. Source data is entered by an operator at a **direct data entry terminal** which is, typically, a VDU. The terminal is on-line to the computer and transfers data to magnetic tape (**key-to-tape**) or magnetic disc (**key-to-disc**). The operation is under control of a program that can validate the input with respect to certain types of errors (fields omitted; groups repeated; numbers not recognised) and indicate the location of the error and its type on the screen of the VDU. Complete verification still requires the reentry of the source data (by a different operator). DDE is increasingly replacing punched cards and paper tape as the 'standard' data entry method. See *data entry; verification*.

direct distance dialing (DDD) A telephone system facility that permits users to make long-distance and overseas telephone calls by dialing (and without the need for operator routing).

direct file (1)A random file. (2)A file with direct serial organisation.

direct-insert subroutine An open subroutine.

direct instruction An instruction in which the operands are in the form of either absolute or direct addresses.

direct memory access (DMA) An input/output system in which data is transferred directly between main storage and backing storage devices without going through the control unit. It is the usual system with modern general-purpose computers and minicomputers; microprocessors may use DMA or a system that routes memory transfers through control unit registers. See *common trunk; peripheral controller*.

direct outward dialing (DOD) A facility of a branch exchange that permits external calls to be dialed directly from internal extensions.

direct program interface An interface (provided by a communications processor) between an interactive terminal and an application program.

direct serial Also *direct* (FORTRAN); *relative* (COBOL). A file organisation that provides a numbered record space for each possible record. (Record 20 thus occupies space 20 whether or not records 1—19 are present.) The record numbers are not keys and they need not be held in the records.

direct store transfer Direct memory access.

direct view storage tube (DVST) See *storage tube*.

director Message routing equipment in a telegraph message switching system.

directory See *dictionary; file directory*.

directory device A peripheral storage device that contains a directory of its contents.

disable To prevent an event from taking place or to prevent an action from taking place in response to the event; ('disable a sector mark'; 'disable an interlock'; 'disable interrupts'). See *enable; inhibit*.

disaster dump A dump made to retain storage and register values before a system crash or during a power failure.

disc Also *disk*. A magnetic disc.

disc-based A term applied to a (minicomputer) computer system to indicate that magnetic disc is the main or only backing storage.

disc cartridge A single magnetic disc in a plastic enclosure that is unit-mountable on a magnetic disc drive. The two common types are identified as (IBM No.) 2315 and 5440; both have 14-inch discs that are recorded at 100 or 200 tracks per inch at a density of either 1100 bpi. (FM) or 2200 bpi. (MFM).

Capacities are from 1.2 to 6 megabytes, depending upon track and recording densities. The 2315 is side-loading on a drive with a retractable spindle and operates at 1500 R.P.M.. The 5440 is top-loading and operates at 2400 R.P.M. See *magnetic disc; disc pack; data module*.

disc controller A peripheral controller specifically to handle transfers between main storage and two or more magnetic disc units. Typical functions include bit-serial/bit-parallel conversion, error detection (and, possibly, correction), buffering, controlling transfers, and disc initialisation. A disc controller that handles formatting and transfer functions for a small number of disc drives (say, two or four) may be termed a **controller/formatter** or **formatter**. See *formatter; peripheral controller*.

disc drive (1)The disc-rotating elements of a magnetic disc unit. (2)A magnetic disc unit.

disc file A file on magnetic disc.

disc file controller (DFC) A disc controller.

disc formatter See *formatter; disc controller*.

disc handler A magnetic disc unit.

disc operating system (DOS) (1)An operating system that is stored on, and loaded from, magnetic disc. (2)A standard operating system for 16K and larger IBM System/360 and System/370 computers.

disc pack An assembly of from two to twenty magnetic discs that is unit-replaceable on a magnetic disc drive by an operator; it is the standard volume of an exchangeable disc system. See *mag-*

netic disc; disc cartridge; data module; EDS.
disc storage Magnetic disc storage.
disc transport A magnetic disc unit.
disc unit A magnetic disc unit.
discard Also *delete; deallocate.* To eliminate a page/segment from primary storage by overwriting it or by rolling it out to secondary storage.
discard algorithm See *discard policy.*
discard policy Also, in a paged system, *paging policy.* In a virtual storage system; a policy concerning the retention and discard of pages and/or segments. It is expressed by a **discard algorithm** (in a paged system, a **paging algorithm**) and implemented by the operating system. It attempts to ensure that each active process has the pages/segments it requires in primary storage at each phase of execution and that few if any unneeded pages/segments are in primary storage. Most discard policies are FIFO in which the page/segment that has been longest in primary storage is the first to be discarded when additional space is required. Others are LRU in which the one that has remained unused for the longest time is the first to be discarded and FINUFO in which the first to be discarded is the one that has been in primary storage longest and has not been used for a certain length of time or number of instructions. (There are many variations and combinations.) A **local discard policy** is one that applies to individual processes; when a process has insufficient space for a required page/segment in its allocated space, an existing one is rolled out or overwritten. A **global discard policy** is applied to primary storage space considered as a common 'pool'; when one process requires a new page/segment, space may be made for it by discarding one from the resident set of another process. Discard policy also includes **load control** in which entire resident sets may be discarded in order to maintain some VSI rate or to provide a particular rate of execution for high-priority jobs. See *virtual storage transfers.*
discharge To cause a current flow that reduces the potential of a storage device; ('discharge a battery'; 'discharge a capacitor').
disconnect (1) Of a communications device (telephone; terminal) to go 'on-hook'; to terminate operation in the send/receive mode. **(2)**With respect to a device; to remove it from a system or from a source of electric power.
discrete (1) Capable of being separately identified or treated; having features or delimiters that separate it from others; ('a discrete signal'; 'discrete representation of a character'). **(2)** Assuming one of a limited number of possible values (that can be represented by digits); not analogue. **(3)**Of an electronic component; separately wireable in a circuit; not part of an integrated circuit; ('a discrete transistor').
discrimination instruction A decision instruction.
discriminator Also *comparator.* A circuit or device that receives two inputs and produces an output related to their difference. See *comparator.*
disjunction Inclusive OR (logic operation).
disk A disc.
diskette A flexible disc.
dispatcher See *scheduler.*
dispersed intelligence Distributed intelligence.
dispersed processing Distributed processing.
displacement A numerical difference between two values, one of which is a base or reference value; for example, a relative address is a 'displacement' from a base address when a program using relative addresses is loaded. The term is also used with respect to a form of addressing in a low-level language in which one address is expressed in relation to another; for example, in the address WEIGHT + 6, the '6' is a 'displacement'.
display (1)A meaningful arrangement of visually contrasting elements (light and dark; different colours). Though the term is sometimes applied to filmed images or the output of a plotter, unless otherwise indicated, it denotes an electronic presentation; for example, by LED's, LCD's, a gas-plasma panel or on a screen of a VDU. **(2)**An arrangement of lights as on a 'display panel'. **(3)**With respect to data (in character form or otherwise); to cause it to appear in a 'display' (on a VDU screen). **(4)**In COBOL; a term that identifies data in character format with numeric data in unpacked decimal.
display area (1)A display field. **(2)**A display surface.
display background (1)A reserved field; an area of a VDU screen that cannot be changed by an operator. **(2)**That on which a display appears; the area in visual contrast to the display elements.
display console A computer operator's console at which messages can be displayed on a VDU.
display cycle One pass through all the steps of refreshing a display image; the time between beginning successive scans of the screen by the electron beam.

display device (1) A device with a screen (cathode ray tube; gas plasma panel) on which data from computer storage is displayed for an operator. See *VDU*. (2) Any computer-associated device that presents data in graphic form; for example, a VDU, a plotter, or a microfilm recorder.

VT-52

display driver The elements of a device that contains an LED or LCD display that successively connect segments in each character position to create the display. It, typically, consists of a scan generator and a segment decoder that connects the particular segments required to form each character.

display element The basic visually contrasting unit of which a display is constructed; for example, an addressable point on a screen or a single LED (a segment of an LED display).

display field (1) A part of a display that can be controlled or manipulated as a unit; for example, a 'reserved field' on the screen of a VDU. (2) A display surface.

display file The bit-pattern representation of related display images as held in computer storage.

display foreground An area of a VDU screen that can be changed by an operator. See *display background*.

display format (1) A particular arrangement of display elements or groups. (2) Also *screen*. One of the display arrangements (say, an invoice) that is available in a particular program or which can be presented on a particular terminal.

display frame A frame (microfilm). See *COM*.

display group A number of visually related display elements that can be manipulated as a unit.

display image The elements of a display that appear on a screen at the same time. See *coded image*.

display line One of the horizontal positions along which characters can appear in a display.

display memory Memory that holds the bit-pattern representation of data displayed on the screen of a VDU. See *video buffer; pixel store*.

display panel An arrangement of lights (and, possibly, switches or other indicators) used to show the status of circuits or devices; for example, as part of an operator console.

display point An addressable point.

display processor Hardware and software that accesses a display file and produces a display image.

display space That portion of a display surface that can hold an image. See *raster*.

display subroutine Software or read-only memory that generates some 'standard' element of a display; for example, an AND logic symbol or a graphic character.

display surface The part of a display device on which a display can appear; for example, a screen of a VDU or the plotting surface of a plotter. (Display images may not be able to be placed in all locations on the surface.)

display tube A cathode ray tube.

display writer The part of a display device used to create display elements; for example, an electron beam of a cathode ray tube or a pen of a plotter.

dissuasion tone In a telephone system; a distinctive tone used to indicate to the caller that no connection can be made to the number as dialed (out of service; incorrect dialing code).

distortion In speech or data transmission; an annoying or error-causing change in signals; a difference between the signals as transmitted and as received. See *noise; jitter; delay; attenuation; cross-talk*.

distributed Also, often, *dispersed*. Divided among different locations; not centralised.

distributed array processor A high-speed, intelligent storage device in which each addressable storage location has an associated microprocessor to perform transfers and arithmetic and logic operations.

distributed data base (1) A system in which an entire data base is held in each of two or more geographically separated locations. (2) A data base in which sections are held in geographically separated locations. See *data base*.

distributed function (1) A function, such as order entry, shipment, and invoicing; in which elements are performed at different locations. (2) A term sometimes applied to a function; for example, communications interfacing, that is performed by multiple intelligent devices at the same location. (3) A network function that is performed at both ends of a link.

distributed intelligence (1) A term applied to a data network in which some overall function is accomplished by means of interconnected computers at different locations. (2) A term applied to a data network in which the various data stations have intelligent devices (terminals; computers; terminal control units) to perform communications-related tasks such as error detection, code conversion, and multiplexing. (3) Also, sometimes, *dispersed intelligence*. A term applied to a computer installation in which auxiliary computers and/or other intelligent devices perform some of the processing functions; for example, data base management or communications interfacing. See *network; distributed processing.*

distributed processing Processing in which some of the inputs or outputs of the computer are carried by communications links. The term includes transaction processing, remote job entry, and remote monitor and control systems. See *distributed intelligence; on-line.*

distributing frame A bank of wire-connection terminals used to make circuit interconnections in a telephone system; for example, between telephone circuits and the internal circuits of an office building.

distribution tape A magnetic tape used by a manufacturer or systems house to provide software to customers.

disturb signal In core memory; a read or write pulse that passes through other cores than those being read or written and causes a weakening of their magnetism. The cumulative effect (in defective or badly designed memory) may be to cause neutralisation or reversal of core magnetism with loss of data.

disturbed circuit See *crosstalk.*

disturbing circuit See *crosstalk.*

dither tone A tone (in the region of 400 Hz.) that may be used in a data communications system with PSTN lines in order to keep echo suppressors disabled during times when no data is being transmitted.

dividend A number that is divided by another number (the **divisor**) to produce a **quotient**. In the expression 6/3 = 2, the 6 is the dividend, the 3 the divisor, and the 2 is the quotient.

division (1)The mathematical operation of finding the number that Number A must be multiplied by to equal Number B. The operation is indicated by a solidus ('B/A') or a **division sign** ('B ÷ A'). (2)A part of a larger unit; for example, the 'procedure division' of a COBOL program.

divisor See *dividend.*

DLC *Data Link Control; Data Link Controller.*

DLE *Data Link Escape.* A control character used in binary synchronous communications systems to indicate that the character that follows it is a control character and not a character in the customer code. If the bit pattern of the DLE is used in some other way, it must be 'negated' by preceding it with a DLE character. See *escape.*

DLT *Data Loop Transceiver.*

DM *Data Module.*

DMA *Direct Memory Access.*
DMCL *Device Media Control Language.*
DMD *Data Module Drive.*
DMM *Digital MultiMeter.*
DMOS *Discrete Metal Oxide Silicon.*
do-nothing instruction A no-operation instruction.
document A sheet of paper (or a group of related sheets) on which data is represented by characters or marks. The term usually denotes a **source document**; for example, a purchase order or an invoice, as received in the data control department of a computer system. See *form; set; document reader; data control.*

document mark A blip.

document reader A computer input device capable of interpreting characters or marks on source documents. See *optical character recognition; optical mark recognition; magnetic ink character recognition; cut form.*

documentation A written record or collection of records used to hold information about the software of a computer system. Ideally, each application program and system routine has associated with it (possibly included with the source code) such information as details of changes and updates, test results, standards adhered to, and current status. The overall purpose is to facilitate future maintenance and possible conversion or replacement.

DOD *Direct Outward Dialing.*

domain (1)In a relation; all of the data items of one type considered as a group. See *relation.* (2)A unit of a homogeneous or randomly oriented substrate (ferric oxide; doped silicon; amorphous glass) that has received a physical change representing one bit. In a bubble memory, a bubble is a 'domain'. See *storage cell; bubble memory.*

dongle A hardware element (scrambler-descrambler) that must be in place to permit successful access to a program disc or tape containing proprietary software. Its purpose is to prevent unauthorised copying.

don't care A term applied to an input or output with a value that is irrelevant for a particular operation or consideration.

dopant An element with three or five valence electrons that is diffused in trace quantities into pure silicon to give it semiconductor properties (to make it N-type or P-type). See *semiconductor.*

dope To add a 'dopant' to silicon as a step in making semiconductors. See *dopant; semiconductor*.

dope vector A supplementary descriptor used in accessing some multidimensional arrays; it points to other vectors that describe a subsection of the array.

doping The process of converting undifferentiated silicon into N-type or P-type for semiconductors. It consists of introducing a small amount of another element (phosphorous; boron) to provide **carriers** or conductors of electrons. The introduced elements are termed 'impurities' or 'dopants'. See *diffusion; semiconductor; epitaxial*.

dormant A term sometimes applied to a program that is loaded in main storage but is not being executed. See *inactive*.

DOS *Disc Operating System.* An operating system for IBM System/360 and System/370 computers.

DOS/VS *Disc Operating System/Virtual Storage.*

dot matrix A grid (say, 5 × 7 or 7 × 9) in which marks (dots of light on a screen; inked impression from a stylus) can be placed to construct graphic characters. It is the usual method of character formation in VDU displays and is a common form for computer print-out. A **dot matrix character** is a character formed in this way. See *character generator; shaped character; matrix; matrix printer*.

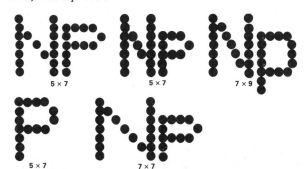

dot printer A matrix printer.

double buffering The use of two buffers as a method of smoothing or speeding an operation; data can be read into one of the buffers while an operation is being performed with data from the other.

double density recording With respect to magnetisable surface recording; a method of doubling the number of bits recorded per unit length of track; the term usually indicates recording by MFM rather than by FM or PE. See *modified frequency modulation*.

double dial-up The establishment of a full-duplex data transmission circuit on two dialed PSTN lines. The usual purpose is to provide a backup for a four-wire leased line.

double diffusion A term applied to a semiconductor manufacturing process in which diffusion doping is used on both the substrate and an epitaxial layer. See *diffusion; epitaxial layer*.

double frequency recording (2FM) Frequency modulation recording. The term is used because in writing 0-bits a flux reversal is made with every clock pulse and when writing 1-bits a reversal also takes place between clock pulses. Writing or reading 1-bits is, then, at 'double the frequency' of writing or reading 0-bits. (A representative figure would be 2.5 MHz. for 0-bits and 5 MHz. for 1-bits.) See *frequency modulation (Data recording)*.

double-length register Two registers that, for some purpose, are treated as a single register; for example, in double precision floating point operations.

double precision See *precision*.

double precision floating point See *floating point*.

double pulse recording Magnetisable surface recording using track trimming. See *track trimming*.

double-sided Of a flexible disc; recordable on both sides.

double word A processing unit available in many computers for use in arithmetic operations when a level of accuracy is required that is higher than can be obtained with a single word. (It provides more digit positions for expressing fractional parts of numbers.) In a word machine, a double word has a main storage address divisible by two and in a byte machine with 4-byte words, one that is divisible by eight. See *word; floating point*.

doublet Also, sometimes, *two-bit byte*. Two contiguous bits or a storage location for two bits.

down Out of service; inoperable because of a fault or during maintenance. See *fault*.

down channel A forward channel; a channel of a four-wire circuit on which a data station transmits. See *channel; up channel*.

down line A down channel.

down-line load See *teleload*.

down-load A term applied to the use of a general-purpose computer to develop and test programs that are to be 'loaded' and run on a computer of lesser capability; for example, a microcomputer or a terminal control unit. See *cross compiler*.

down time The time (as a percentage of the total for a period) that a system or functional unit is inoperable. See *up time; availability*.

downlink The path on which transmissions are sent from a communications satellite to an earth station; the usual frequency (Intelsat 4A) is 4 GHz. See *uplink; satellite*.

downshift To change a typewriter or printer from the 'shifted' position (numbers; symbols; upper-case letters) to the normal or 'unshifted' position. See *shift; upshift*.

DP *Data Processing*.

DPE *Digital Production Effects*.

DPM *Data Processing Manager*.

DPSK *Differential Phase Shift Keying*.

DPX *DataPleX*.

drain The positive terminal or area of silicon in a field-effect transistor; the place towards which electrons flow during conduction. See *source; field-effect transistor*.

DRAM (dRAM) *Dynamic RAM*.

DRI *Data Recording Instrument Co.* (Staines, England)

drift Of signals, to change frequency or move from time frames.

drive (1) The motor and power transmission elements of a moving-medium storage device such as a magnetic disc unit or a magnetic tape unit. **(2)** Also *disc drive*. A magnetic disc unit. **(3)** Also *tape drive*. A magnetic tape unit. **(4)** To provide input signals, control, or electric power of the correct characteristics; ('drive a display'; 'drive an interface circuit'; 'capable of driving up to eight VDU terminals').

drive latency See *latency* (def. 2).

drive line Also *drive wire*. A word line.

driven (1) Provided with electric power or with input signals and control. **(2)** A term used to indicate an initiating input; ('an interrupt-driven operating system').

driver (1) An unintelligent device that provides signals, control, or electric power; ('a line driver'; 'a display driver'). **(2)** Software that performs a control or interfacing function; ('a peripheral driver'; 'a terminal driver').

drop (1) To delete or miss out; ('drop bits'; 'drop significant digits'). **(2)** A subscriber termination of a telephone line. See *local loop; multidrop line*.

drop in A 1-bit that is read from a magnetisable surface storage medium but which was not (intentionally) recorded there; it may be added during transfer or may result from a defect in the recording surface.

drop out A 1-bit that was intended to be recorded on a magnetisable surface storage medium but which cannot be read; it may result from a defect in the recording surface.

drum (1) A magnetic drum unit. **(2)** The rotating, data-storage element of a magnetic drum unit. **(3)** Also *barrel*. The rotating, type-carrying element of a barrel printer.

drum plotter A computer graphics output device in which a pen or stylus moves across the plotting paper and selectively contacts locations on it to form images while the paper advances in relation to the printing position. Earlier models used a drum to which a sheet of paper was fixed while later models use continuous stationary that is moved in increments over a

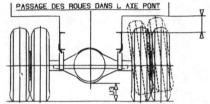

bar or small roller during printing. The illustration is a section of an engineering drawing produced by a drum plotter.

drum printer A barrel printer.

drum storage Storage on a magnetic drum unit.

dry cell See *battery*.

dry contacts Electrical contacts that carry little current.

DS *Data Set*.

DSR *Data Set Ready*. A signal from a modem (data set) to a DTE indicating that it is ready to operate. See *modem interchanges*.

DSU *Disc Storage Unit*. A (large capacity) magnetic disc unit.

DTE *Data Terminal Equipment*.

DTL *Diode Transistor Logic*.

DTR (1) *Data Terminal Ready*. A signal controlled by a data terminal (DTE) that is held high while it is ready to operate. See *modem interchanges*. **(2)** *Distribution Tape Reel*.

dual exchangeable disc storage (DEDS) A magnetic disc unit with two spindles capable of simultaneous access to two volumes (disc packs). See *magnetic disc unit*.

dual-gap head (1)A head for magnetic tape recording that consists of two adjacent but electrically separate heads, one of which is used for writing and the other for reading; such heads are used for normal reading and writing as well as for read-after-write. (2)A head for magnetic disc recording that incorporates tunnel erase. See *track trimming*.

dual in-line See *DIL*.

dual operation Of a logic operation, another operation that, when performed on the opposite (negated) inputs produces the opposite result. For example, XOR is the 'dual operation' of AND. See *logical operation*.

dual-porting The provision of two output ports on a peripheral storage device or, possibly, on a peripheral controller or data input device. The purpose is to provide identical data streams to two higher-level devices one of which is, usually, a back-up for the other.

dumb Unintelligent; without programmable memory; ('a dumb terminal'). See *smart*.

dummy argument A formal parameter.

dummy instruction (1)A no-operation instruction. (2)An instruction identified as comment and, thus, not executed.

dump (1)To write the contents of specified internal storage locations (main storage; control unit or arithmetic unit registers) to backing storage. Unless otherwise indicated, the operation is assumed to be performed for purposes of retaining the contents at a particular stage of processing (for use in the event of a failure and restart) or for debugging. When performed as a step in debugging, the term is commonly used to include **listing** which is the production of a printed copy. A dump is performed by a utility which is a **dump routine** A **binary dump** is a dump in binary form; the term is only used when listing is included as all dumps to backing storage are 'binary'. A **core dump** is a dump of the contents of main storage; the term is sometimes used even when main storage is 'semiconductor'. A **dynamic dump** is a dump performed under the control of an application program during its execution. A **dump point** is a place in a program where a dump is made; it is also a 'checkpoint'. A **postmortem dump** is a dump performed at the end of a run for purposes of checking or debugging. A **selective dump** is a dump of the contents of specified registers or main storage locations. A **snapshot dump** is a selective dump initiated by an operator or supervisory program rather than by an executing application program. See *delete; discard; listing; checkpoint*. (2)The backing storage copy of the location contents that have been dumped. (3)Also *listing*. A printed copy of the location contents that have been dumped and listed.

dump cracking Debugging in which the cause of software errors is determined by analysing dumps.

dump point A place during program execution where a dump is performed; a place where a jump is made to a dump routine.

dump routine A utility that performs dumps. See *dump*.

duodecimal Also *duodenary*. A number system with a radix of twelve; the digits are usually 0-9 plus 't' for 10 and 'e' for 11.

duplex Also *full duplex*. A designation of a circuit, operation, or functional unit that provides simultaneous data transmission in both directions between two points. A circuit that is identified

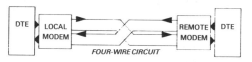

as full-duplex is assumed to be four-wire, or the multiplexed equivalent. See *circuit; channel; half-duplex; simplex; asymmetric duplex*.

duplexed (1)Provided with a circuit suitable for full-duplex operation. (2)Paralleled; provided with a functional equivalent for use in case of unavailability of the primary unit or facility; ('duplexed buffers'; 'duplexed processors').

duplicate (1)To make a copy on the same medium; ('duplicate a punched card'; 'duplicate a magnetic tape file'). (2)To provide a similar or identical facility; ('duplicate a circuit'). (3)To perform the same operation; ('duplicate data punching'). (4)A copy or an identical item; ('a duplicate punched card'; 'a duplicate circuit').

duplicate key A primary key that is assigned to two or more records in the same file. (One such assignment is usually in error unless provision is made for access by secondary keys.) See *key; secondary key*.

duplication check A check on the accuracy of data made by duplicating the operation by which it was captured or transcribed. See *verification*.

duplicator A device that makes copies. In microfilm processing, a **roll-to-roll duplicator** accepts a master film and unexposed film, both on rolls, and passes them together beneath a light in a continuous process; the process usually includes developing in the same device. A **sheet-to-roll duplicator** is used to make multiple copies of a single frame or fiche; unexposed roll film is passed in increments beneath the master and a light that is 'flashed' to make each exposure. A **sheet-to-sheet duplicator** is a 'contact printer' in which a sheet of unexposed film is placed beneath a master and a light and thus exposed. See *COM; microfilm*.

duty cycle (1)The percentage of time that a device is operated or is designed to be operated; for example, a printer that is used an average of 12 minutes per hour could be said to be operating 'on a 20% duty cycle'. (2)Of a circuit or device with two operational states; the percentage of time that it is in the higher level or more active state. For example, a clock circuit in which positive and negative pulses are of equal duration is said to have a '50% duty cycle'. (A tolerance is often given to indicate the allowable variation from the stated duty cycle.)

DUV *Data Under Voice.*

DVM *Digital VoltMeter.*

DVST *Direct-View Storage Tube.*

dyadic Concerning 'two'; with two entities or states.

dyadic Boolean operation Also *dyadic logic operation*. A logic operation performed with two and only two inputs; for example, exclusive OR. See *logic operation*.

dyadic logical operation A dyadic Boolean operation.

dyadic operation A computer operation performed on or with two operands; for example, addition, subtraction, or a logical operation (dyadic or otherwise) with only two inputs.

dyadic operator An operator that specifies a dyadic operation; an arithmetic operator ('ADD'; 'SUBTRACT'; 'MULTIPLY'; 'DIVIDE'), a relational operator ('EQUAL TO'; 'GREATER THAN') or a logic operator ('AND'; 'OR'; 'NAND') other than a monadic operator. (Logical operators such as AND and OR do not specify dyadic Boolean operations because they may have any number of inputs; they are 'dyadic operators' in computer usage because the computer performs these operations on only two operands at a time.) See *dyadic Boolean operation; relational operator; arithmetic operator; monadic*.

dyadic processor Two integrated processors (control units) that perform interleaved instruction execution.

dynamic address translation In a virtual storage system; the conversion of virtual addresses to real addresses as instructions are executed.

dynamic allocation In a multiprogramming system; to allocate system resources (peripherals; storage locations) to meet the changing needs of programs during execution. See *static allocation*.

dynamic buffering The flexible allocation of storage space for use as buffers to meet the varying input/output requirements during processing (in a transaction processing or mixed-mode system).

dynamic dump See *dump*.

dynamic mapping system (DMS) In a virtual storage system; to move pages/segments between primary and secondary storage to meet the changing needs of executing processes. See *virtual storage transfers*.

dynamic memory A memory in which each storage cell consists of an MOS transistor and an integral capacitor. A charged capacitor represents a 1-bit and a discharged capacitor a 0-bit. Because the capacitor charge tends to leak away, it must be 'refreshed' at short intervals (typically, every 2 milliseconds). The figure shows the basic organisation of the memory. A 1-bit is written to a cell by placing a high (+5 V.) on a column line at the same time that a high (+10 V.) is present on a row line. Charge then flows from the source to the drain of the selected transistor and charges the capacitor. In a refresh cycle, the row line is again high causing the capacitor to discharge through the source and the column line and when the pulse is detected in the refresh circuit, high is again placed on the column line to recharge the capacitor. A typical dynamic RAM holds 16K bits

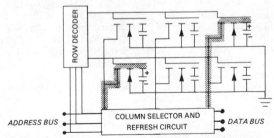

in 128 rows and 128 columns. (Single-chip devices have been produced with capacities up to 256K bits.) The memory is compact and inexpensive though it is relatively slow (100-400 ns.) and has the disadvantage of requiring external refresh circuitry.

Refresh, typically, takes about 50 microseconds and is performed every 2 milliseconds; it is commonly done by 'stealing' clock cycles from instruction execution. Like other semiconductor memory, dynamic memory is 'volatile' (data is lost if electric power is removed). See *static memory*.

dynamic memory management Variable partitioning. (The term is used with respect to some minicomputer systems in which adjusting partitions is the main or only way of managing storage for multiprogramming.)

dynamic parameter A program-generated parameter.

dynamic RAM Dynamic memory; a semiconductor random-access memory that requires short-interval refreshing to retain its contents. See *dynamic memory; static RAM*.

dynamic relocation The relocation of programs in main storage during execution in order to meet the varying space requirements of different programs. See *compaction; fragmentation*.

dynamic resource allocation Dynamic allocation.

dynamic set (1) In a data base; a set without any declared member type; a set that can be used for different purposes. **(2)** The pages/segments of a process image that are required for a particular run. See *process image; virtual storage system—processing units*.

dynamic stop A breakpoint halt.

dynamic storage (1) Dynamic memory. **(2)** Cyclic storage.

dynamic storage allocation The allocation of main storage to programs according to their changing needs during processing.

dynamic subroutine A subroutine in which certain parameters (scale and form of numeric results; number of times to be performed) are supplied each time it is called.

dynamiciser A term that has been applied to the 'read' circuits of coordinate-addressable storage. See *staticiser*.

E

E *Electromotive force*.

E-beam *Electron-BEAM*. A term applied to beam-accessed semiconductor memory. See *BEAMOS*.

EAM *Electronic Accounting Machine*.

EAROM *Electrically Alterable Read-Only Memory*.

earth See *ground*.

earth station A transmitting and receiving station that handles communications via a satellite. See *satellite communications*.

easy axis See *orthoferrite*.

EAX *Electronic Automatic eXchange*.

EBAM *Electron Beam Accessed Memory*.

EBCDIC ('ebb-sid-ick') *Extended Binary Coded Decimal Interchange Code*. An 8-bit internal storage code used by IBM (and most other) mainframe computers. See *code*.

EBR *Electron Beam Recording*.

EC *Engineering Change*.

ECC (1) *Error Checking and Correction*. **(2)** *Error Correcting Code*.

ECD *Energy Conversion Devices*. (Troy, N.Y.)

echo (1) On a data transfer or transmission line; elements of a transmitted signal that are reflected back from an impedance change in the conductors; for example, where they pass through a switch or from the end of an unterminated cable. **(2)** The common method of operating an unintelligent CRT terminal on a full-duplex link; each character that is keyed in is returned from the destination (usually a local computer or a terminal control unit) before it is displayed on the screen.

echo check Echoplex.

echo suppressor A device installed in many long-distance telephone lines to disable the receiving channel when the transmitting channel is in use (when there is a certain energy level in the transmitting channel). The purpose is to prevent a speaker from hearing distracting echoes. Typically, this blocking is disabled when energy in a channel drops to a preset level for 100 milliseconds (indicating that a person has stopped talking). Echo suppressors are not used on leased lines and they are commonly disabled when PSTN lines are used for data in order to reduce turnaround time. Disabling is accomplished by sending a distinctive 'answer tone' at the beginning of a transmission and by maintaining a low-frequency 'dither tone' on the line when no data is being transmitted.

echoplex Also *echo check*. A method of error detection in which data that is sent to a receiving location is retransmitted back to the sending location where it is compared with the original (held in buffer) to reveal any errors introduced in the transmission line/circuit.

ECL *Emitter-Coupled Logic*.

ECMA *European Computer Manufacturers' Association*. (Geneva)

ECOM *Electronic Computer-Originated Mail*.

ECOMA *European COmputer Measurement Association.*
ECS *Extended Core Storage.*
ECSA *European Computer Services Association.*
EDAC *Error Detection And Correction.*
edge connector On a replaceable printed circuit board; an etched (and usually gold plated) connector on one edge of the board. A row of such connectors are used to join the circuits on the board with those in the device in which it is installed. See *printed circuit board.*

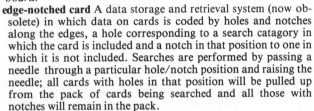

edge-notched card A data storage and retrieval system (now obsolete) in which data on cards is coded by holes and notches along the edges, a hole corresponding to a search catagory in which the card is included and a notch in that position to one in which it is not included. Searches are performed by passing a needle through a particular hole/notch position and raising the needle; all cards with holes in that position will be pulled up from the pack of cards being searched and all those with notches will remain in the pack.

edge-punched card A punched card that holds data in the punching of a paper tape code along its bottom edge. Cards typically hold about 70 characters and are supplied in fan-fold packs; they are often used without separation. They are a common input and storage medium in visible record computers.

edge-punched stationery A term sometimes applied to standard, continuous stationery (with sprocket holes punched along each edge).

edit (1) By system software; to prepare data for a subsequent operation by adding or deleting items and/or by formatting. Examples of operations performed include ordering, unpacking numeric data, zero suppression, formatting, and the addition or deletion of control characters. It is usually performed to prepare data for printing or display or for transmission on a data link. **(2)** By the operator of a VDU terminal; to examine displayed data and to make corrections prior to transmitting the data or writing it to a file. It is a common operation of word processing and on-line program development. **(3)** To make changes to a typescript to prepare it for typesetting.

edit facility A facility of an intelligent VDU that permits the operator to alter the refresh memory and, thus, to change the displayed data and the data that is to be transmitted or printed.

Typical facilities are character and line insertion and deletion.

editor (1) A system routine used to analyse, organise, or format code or data; for example, in maintaining library source files or preparing results for output via a printer or VDU. **(2)** A language processor used to organise and combine instruction sequences. See *linkage editor.* **(3)** A text editor.

EDP *Electronic Data Processing.*
EDS *Exchangeable Disc Storage.*
EEROM *Electrically Erasable Read-only Memory.* EAROM.
effective address A hardware address (produced by address modification). See *address; presumptive address.*
effective data transfer rate The average number of data units (characters; blocks) transferred on a communications channel per unit time and accepted as valid by receiving hardware. See *data transfer rate.*
effective instruction Also *absolute instruction.* An instruction with operands in effective address form; an instruction for which address modification has been completed. See *effective address; presumptive instruction; immediate instruction.*
effective speed With respect to processing or some other computer operation; that speed that can be maintained over some period of time.
EFTS *Electronic Funds Transfer System.* A data network system for making direct debits and credits between banks without the need for movement of paper. See *SWIFT.*
EIA *Electronic Industries Association.* (U.S.)
eight-level code A code, such as EBCDIC, in which each character is represented by an 8-bit group.
eighty-column card A (standard) punched card with 80 vertical columns. See *punched card; Hollerith code.*
EIN *European Informatics Network.*
either-or operation An inclusive OR operation.
either-way communications Communications in either direction but not in both directions simultaneously. See *half-duplex.*
elapsed time The time between the commencement of an operation and its completion. See *processing time.*
electric A term applied to a device that operates by electricity.
electrically alterable read-only memory (EAROM) Also *erasable read-only memory (EROM).* A read-only memory that can be erased and reprogrammed in the field. Programming is done by applying voltage to selected pins to write 1-bits where required. Erasure may be either by exposure to ultraviolet light (FAMOS) or by reversing the polarity used in writing (MNOS). Unless

otherwise indicated, MNOS is understood rather than FAMOS. The basic programming operation consists of establishing a semi-permanent gate charge that influences the source-drain conduction path to change the threshold voltage of conduction and, thus, to differentiate between holding a 1-bit and a 0-bit. See *electrically programmable read-only memory; MNOS; FAMOS; programmable read-only memory.*

electrically programmable read-only memory (EPROM) A read-only memory that can be programmed in the field by applying voltage to selected pins to write 1-bits where required. The term usually denotes a FAMOS (ultraviolet erasable) device, though it has also been used to include 'fuse PROM' and amorphous devices. See *programmable read-only memory.*

electricity A flow of electrons. The flow may be a discharge of electrons in a burst which is **static electricity** or a controlled flow through wires which are **conductors** in an outward and return path which is a **circuit**. Useful work is performed by connecting a **load** such as a motor or electric light in the circuit so that the electrons can flow through it. For illustration purposes, consider an electrical system in which the load is an electric motor, say, one that provides power for a flour mill. Such a system is like a water system in many ways; an electron equates with a quantity of water (say, a gallon), a conductor to a pipe, and the motor to a turbine or waterwheel. If the motor operates from a battery (an unlikely possibility for one that drives a mill), the battery equates to a reservoir or millpond. In a natural water system, the sun performs a 'pump' function (evaporation; rain) to replenish the reservoir and in an electrical system operated from a battery, this function is performed by a **generator** which forces electrons 'up hill' to **charge** the battery. In a water system in which conditions provide a stream that runs continuously at the same volume, there is no need for a reservoir and, similarly, in an electrical system in which the generator runs continuously there is no need for a battery. In a water system, the term 'head' is used to indicate how far the water falls from the reservoir to the turbine or waterwheel and the equivalent in an electrical system is **voltage** (V.) which may also be termed **electromotive force** (E). Both voltage and head are, in effect, measures of pressure. The greater the head and the larger the flow of water, the more work a waterwheel or turbine is capable of performing and, similarly, the greater the voltage and the larger the flow of electrons, the more work a motor is capable of performing. The term **current** is applied to electron flow and its unit of measurement is the **ampere** (amp.; I); it is equivalent to a measure of flow such as 'gallons per minute'. As the probable power of a waterwheel or turbine is indicated by the head and flow, so that of a motor is indicated by its volts and amps. In an electrical system, the unit of power is the **watt** (P; W.); it is equal to 1 volt $\times$ 1 amp. If, for example, the motor is using 50 amps. at 220 V., it is using 11,000 W. (11 **kilowatts**) and this is an indication of its power, as 746 watts is equal to 1 'horse-power'. (Like a waterwheel or turbine, the actual power depends upon a number of design factors.) If a waterwheel or turbine of a particular power is supplied with water through a pipe, then a large pipe will be required to carry a large flow if the head is low and, if the head is high, a smaller flow will be required and, hence, a smaller pipe can be used. Similarly, an electric motor of a certain power must be supplied by large conductors if the voltage is low and smaller conductors will do if the voltage is high. In a water system, the term 'restriction' is applied to that which limits flow and the equivalent in an electrical system is **resistance** (R). Large pipes have small 'restriction' and large conductors have small (low) resistance. The unit of resistance is the **ohm** (Ω). A water system with a high head can, then, provide a high flow through small pipes (ones with high restriction) and an electrical system with a high voltage can supply a high current through a high resistance. In electricity, this relationship is known as **Ohm's law**; it is the fundamental equation for electrical calculations:

$$E = IR$$

electrode (1) A term sometimes applied to a stylus in a thermal matrix printer. (2) A conductor that passes current between two different conducting mediums.

electroluminesence A term applied to a 'cool' conversion of electricity to light as, for example, by the phosphors in the screen of a cathode ray tube or by a light-emitting diode.

electromagnet A magnet with flux created by electric current passing through a coil; direct current is usually used and the coil is wound around an iron 'core'. Electromagnets are used to operate print hammers in impact printers. See *magnetisim.*

electromagnetic (1) Operated by an electromagnet or using electromagnets. (2) Concerning transmission (radio waves; light) by varying electrical and magnetic fields.

electromagnetic interference (EMI) High energy electrically induced magnetic fields as a cause of data corruption in cables passing through the fields.

electromechanical A term applied to a device that uses electricity to move or rotate elements; for example, a motor, a disc drive, or a relay.

electromotive force (E) Voltage. See *electricity*.

electron The smallest unit of electrical transfer; a negatively charged particle in the outer (valence) ring of an atom.

electron beam A focused stream of electrons originating from a heated cathode. See *cathode ray tube*.

electron beam accessed memory (EBAM) Memory in which data is read and written by an electron beam; the term includes electrostatic and BEAMOS.

electron beam recording (EBR) A method of recording data on microfilm in which an electron beam writes directly to the film. See *COM; recorder*.

electron tube Also *tube; valve; vacuum tube*. A switching or amplifying device that operates by controlling the flow of electrons in a vacuum. In its basic form, it consists of a filament 'B' which is an electrically heated resistance element, a cathode 'C' connected to the filament, a grid 'D', and a plate 'E'. The filament produces electrons which are 'gathered' by the cathode and directed towards the plate. If the grid is negative with respect to the cathode, the electrons are 'turned back' (repelled) and very few reach the plate. If the grid is high with respect to the cathode, electrons pass through to the plate and current flows through the circuit connected to the output. A tube as described performs as a switching device with a small grid current turning on and off a relatively large plate current. If the grid voltage is held within a band such that the highest level does not cause full plate current and the lowest value does not completely turn off the plate current, the tube performs as an amplifier; the higher the input signal, the higher the output signal. As compared to transistors, electron tubes are large consumers of power and are also expensive and have a short life expectancy. Cathode ray tubes are essentially the only electron tubes in use in computer-related equipment.

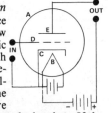

electronic A term applied to devices, circuits, and systems in which transistors and other semiconductor devices or valves/tubes are used to control electric currents.

electronic accounting machine (EAM) A device that uses electronic circuits to perform some accounting function; the term is now usually synonymous with 'visible record computer'.

electronic automatic exchange (EAX) A telephone exchange in which calls are routed by electronic circuits.

electronic calculating punch A device that performs arithmetic operations on numeric data read from a punched card and punches the result in another card.

electronic component An element of an electronic circuit other than an interconnection; for example, a resistor, a capacitor, a transistor, or an integrated circuit. See *element; electronic device*.

electronic computer originated mail (ECOM) A proposed service of a national postal system in which computer-originated mail for large users (insurance companies; government departments) is transmitted by a data communications system to regional centres where it is printed, enveloped, and addressed for posting to recipients in the area.

electronic data processing (EDP) A term sometimes applied to computers in general or to the computer industry. The term was once used to differentiate operations performed by electronic devices (computers) from those performed by mechanical devices such as card sorters and tabulators; in the actual processing sense, the term has been supplanted by 'data processing' and 'computing'.

electronic detent A small-movement servo system; a method of detecting a movement from a desired or normal position (say, of a read head from a track it is reading) and using an electronic circuit to provide a corrective movement. See *servo; feedback*.

electronic device (1) A device (radio; computer; calculator) that performs its functions by means of electronic circuits. (2) Also *active element*. A discrete (individually replaceable) semiconductor (transistor; integrated circuit) or a valve/tube.

electronic format control A printer facility for controlling vertical and horizontal tabulation by means of programmable memory; with respect to vertical tabulation, it accomplishes the same function as a paper tape loop with variations as required for particular jobs.

electronic funds transfer system See *EFTS*.

electronic mail A system that makes use of facsimile or other technique to transmit 'letters' over communications links; a term applied to a possible future system to replace some or all of an existing postal system.

electronic office See *paperless office*.

electronic point of sale (EPOS) See *POS*.

electronic switch A device in which transistors and/or other electronic elements perform circuit interconnections.

electrophotographic printer An electrostatic printer.

electrosensitive matrix printer A printer that uses electrically conducting styluses to selectively 'burn away' a conductive silver-grey coating on black paper and thus to produce dot matrix characters. Line widths are, typically, up to 32 characters and printing speeds are on the order of 50—80 characters per second. The following is a sample of the printing. See *matrix printer*.

```
HOME/HOBBY COMPUTOR
MICROPROCESSOR DEVELOPMENT SYSTEMS
```

electrostatic The term for electron deficits and surpluses not directly involved in a continuous current flow, as, for example, on the plates of a capacitor, on ungrounded magnetic tape when reading or writing, and in thunder clouds. An electron surplus in one place and deficit in another is a **charge** and the process of equalisation between the two places is **discharge**. The term **static electricity** may be applied to either the charge or the electron flow that constitutes discharge.

electrostatic field An attraction between two elements of unlike charge (one with an electron surplus and the other with a deficit) or a repulsion of two elements of like charge. See *electrostatic*.

electrostatic memory An early form of beam-addressed memory in which bits representing data were held as electrostatic charges in a special coating of the screen of a cathode ray tube. A plate in front of the screen could detect a small voltage difference depending upon whether the beam was directed at a charged or uncharged spot and thus could be used to read bits. Such a tube is termed a **Williams tube** after its inventor. See *BEAMOS*.

electrostatic plotter A plotter that operates on the same principle as an electrostatic printer except that the paper passes across a line of 'nibs' (electrodes) that are selectively energised to place electrostatic charges on special paper. The paper then passes through a toner where dark particles attach themselves to the paper where it is 'charged'. Plotters are available with widths up to 72 inches; common resolutions are 100, 160, and 200 dots per inch. The following are examples of a plot at 200 dots/in and characters at 160 dots/in. (Versatec plotter):

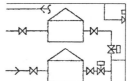

electrostatic printer Also *xerographic printer*. A computer output device that is similar in operation to a common dry-type office copier. A selenium coated drum is electrostatically charged in the dark and then exposed to data as displayed on a cathode ray tube. The ability of selenium to retain its charge is reduced by exposure to light and the charge thus leaks away in the 'background' area leaving charged areas representing the lines and characters of the data. The drum is then coated with an ink powder mixed with resin and this adheres to the drum where the charge has been retained and falls off the other areas. Paper is then rolled across the drum and receives the ink and resin particles; heating the paper melts the resin and fixes the data to the paper. The printer is a **page printer** and prints, typically, A4 sheets; a form overlay feature is incorporated to permit printing heads, column lines, etc. with the data. Models are available with speeds of between 2,000 and 13,000 lines per minute. See *printer; magnetic printer; form flash*.

electrostatic storage Electrostatic memory.

electrostatic storage tube A Williams tube.

electrothermal printer A thermal matrix printer.

element (1) A component of a larger system or unit; ('an element of an array'; 'an element of a computer system'). **(2)** An item that is part of an electronic circuit. An **active element** is one that performs a regulating or control function; for example, a transistor or a diode, and a **passive element** is a conductor, a resistor, or a capacitor. **(3)** A material in which all atoms are the same; not a compound or an alloy.

elementary field Of a record; a field that is not normally subdivided during processing; for example, a field that holds a customer's name, a part number, or the title of a book. See *field; group field; token*.

eligible Of a program; ready to be loaded and executed as soon as resources are available.

eligible list In some systems; a job queue.

else rule A specification of what is to be done if certain conditions are not fulfilled; of what is to be done in 'all other cases'. It may be expressed by a decision instruction such as:
IF TERM = 10 OR ENTRY > 5 GO TO PRINT-1 ELSE GO TO PRINT-2.

EM *End of Medium.*

embedded Included in something else; in source coding, the term refers to a declaration within another declaration or a statement within another statement. For example, in A = B + LOG (IF A = B THEN C ELSE D), the part in parentheses is said to be 'embedded'.

embedded servo A track-following servo system in which a servo track is recorded adjacent to each data track (on magnetic disc). See *track-following servo.*

embossment Of a document (as used in OCR), a raised area 'dimple' or wrinkle.

EMI *ElectroMagnetic Interference.*

emitter A P-N junction of a transistor or the external connection to the junction. See *transistor; collector; base.*

emitter-coupled logic (ECL) A type of extremely fast logic circuit that is also characterised by high power dissipation (about 40 mW. per gate). High speed is obtained by a design that prevents saturation. In the positive NOR gate shown, current flows through R1 and 'reference transistor' T3 unless either T1 or T2

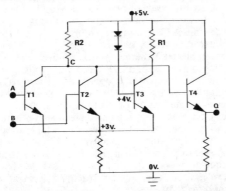

is ON. In this state, the gate of T4 is high, the transistor is ON and Q is high. When in this state, both of the inputs 'A' and 'B' are low. If either or both inputs go high, transistor T1 and/or T2 turns ON. This transfers conduction from T3 and drops point 'C' through R2 which lowers the gate of T4 causing it to turn OFF, thus dropping output Q. Heat and power considerations have prevented the use of ECL in high-density integrated circuits; the main application has been in high-speed mainframe computers in control unit circuits. Propagation delay can be as low as 1 ns. and access time as low as 15 ns.

empty set A null set.

emulation The process of using special software and/or hardware facilities to execute programs on a computer of a different type (word length; order code) than the one for which they were compiled. The **host computer** is the computer on which they are executed and the **target computer** is the one for which they were compiled. See *simulation; bridgeware.*

emulator (1) A program or hardware (logic array) that performs emulation. **(2)** Hardware or software that can be used in place of a missing facility; for example, a program that gives the responses of a data network for use in program development. **(3)** An adapter; a device that permits another device to perform a different function; for example, circuitry that 'emulates' a current-loop interface for a V.24 terminal. See *simulator.*

enable (1) To take some action that permits another action to take place; ('enable interrupts'). See *inhibit.* **(2)** To make a facility or functional unit operational; ('enable an error detection system'; 'enable a terminal control unit'). See *disable.*

encipher See *encryption.*

enclosure (1) Also, in some contexts, *frame.* Two delimiters between which a certain item or type of item can be placed; examples include a BEGIN and END statement enclosing a sequence of instructions and a start bit and a stop bit enclosing a character in start-stop transmission. See *delimiter.* **(2)** A cabinet; the external elements of a functional unit.

encode (1) To change the form of data in accordance with a set of rules (usually, as a step in changing the device or medium in which it is represented). For example, to read a graphic character on a document and press a key on a device that produces a bit pattern representation of the character for storage or transmission, or to produce a bit pattern in one code from a bit pattern in another code. See *code; decode.* **(2)** To encrypt; to change the form of date for security purposes.

encoded image A coded image.

encoded point An addressable point (raster graphics).

encoder (1) A device that performs an encoding operation. (2) A term sometimes applied to the 'write' elements of a storage device; ('a magnetic disc encoder').

encryption The process of converting data from a commonly interpretable form (English; EBCDIC) to a form in which a key or special knowledge is required for correct interpretation; a change of representation for security purposes. See *privacy code*.

end-around borrow In a register or numeric group of fixed size; the action of taking a borrow digit from the most significant digit position to the least significant digit position. See *borrow*.

end-around carry In a register or numeric group of fixed size; the action of moving a carry digit from the most significant digit position to the least significant digit position.

end-around shift A cyclic shift. See *shift*.

end-of-address (EOA) A control character used in some systems to indicate that the last character of the address has been transmitted and that the following characters are message characters.

end-of-block (EOB) A control character used in some systems to indicate that the last character of a block has been transmitted.

end-of-document (EOD) On a document intended for machine reading; a distinctive mark recognisable by a detector and circuitry to indicate that the last position where data can be entered has been passed.

end-of-job card A final card in a deck with punching to indicate to system software that all cards for the job have been read.

end-of-medium (EM) A control character used in some systems to mark the end of a medium (paper tape; magnetic tape) or of recorded data on the medium.

end-of-message (EOM) A control character used to indicate the end of a message; for example, in a transmission consisting of multiple messages.

end-of-tape (EOT) A mark on magnetic tape that is hardware detectable to indicate that the end of the permissible recording area has been reached.

end-of-text (ETX) A transmission control character used to indicate to receiving hardware that the previous character was the last character of message text.

end-of-transmission block (ETB) A block character.

end-of-transmission (EOT) A control character used to indicate that a transmission has been completed.

end office Also *local exchange*. In a telephone system; an exchange where local loops of a group of subscribers terminate.

end point In computer graphics; the position on a display surface to which the display writer is to be moved.

end-to-end protocol A single protocol that covers all interfaces between two users of a data network or two users on different, interconnected data networks.

end-to-end test A test of the internal circuits of two modems and a telephone link between them by which an operator at one modem causes a test pattern to be transmitted to the other modem where it is received, decoded, and passed to an error

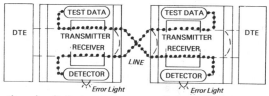

detection circuit that causes an error light to flash if an incorrect bit (say, a 0-bit in a sequence of 1-bits) is detected. (It may be used with four-wire systems or full-duplex two-wire systems.) Typically, the test is arranged by means of voice communications between operators at both sites. See *analogue loop test, digital loop test*.

end-use device A term sometimes applied to a device (typically, a VDU or printer) that puts the results of processing in final form for the user.

end user (1) Also *user*. A person or group that receives a data processing service from a particular computer system; for example, a business accounting department or a student doing research at a university. (2) The 'final user'; in this sense, a bureau could be the 'user' of an application package and the bureau's customer would be the 'end user'. (3) Of a hardware item sold to an original equipment manufacturer; the user of the equipment in which it is incorporated.

endpoint The destination of a (rerouted) message in a network; the final node.

engine A term sometimes applied to a hardware or software facility; ('a computing engine'; 'a queue management engine').

engineer In the computer sense; a person who designs or maintains computer hardware; when the term is used without qualification, 'maintains' is understood and the term is synonymous with 'field engineer'. See *software engineer*.

engineering test panel Also *maintenance panel*. On a functional unit; a group of circuit terminations identified in relation to a maintenance manual and used by an engineer to connect test equipment for diagnostic and trouble shooting purposes.

engineer's journal A file to which specified data relating to performance and errors is written; for example, details of system-recovered errors in transfers.

enhance Also *upgrade*. To improve the capability of a computer system by adding hardware or software or by replacing current units of hardware or software with improved versions.

enhancement (1)The process of improving a computer system by adding or replacing elements. (2)With respect to a display; to improve the appearance of an image by stretching or moving dots.

enhancement device An MOS transistor that is non-conducting except when a gate signal is present. See *MOS; depletion device*.

enlarge To increase size; for example, of a frame of microfilm that is to be visually examined. See *magnify; reduction*.

ENQ *ENQuiry*. A transmission control character used to request a response from the receiving station or to ask for identification.

enqueue To place items in a queue. See *queue; dequeue*.

enquiry Also, in some contexts, *transaction*. In a transaction processing system or multi-access system; a message from a terminal operator to the computer requesting some action to be taken. The term is applied with respect to 'instruction' messages ('Cancel Order 327') as well as to those requesting information, the entry of an order, etc. See *transaction processing; on-line; conversational mode*.

enquiry/response processing Transaction processing.

enquiry station A terminal; particularly a remote terminal in a transaction processing system.

enquiry system A transaction processing system.

enter (1)With respect to a sequence of instructions; to commence execution at some point other than the beginning; to commence execution at an 'entry point'. (2)Also, sometimes, *send; transmit*. At a terminal; to cause data held in the terminal buffer to be transmitted or moved to main storage.

Enterprise number In the U.S.; a telephone number to which a call can be placed without charge to the caller; a number of a (business) subscriber who has agreed to pay for incoming calls.

entity A general term for anything that is known to an operating system of a computer; for example, an employee, a customer, a data station, a file, a record, a volume, or a device. The term is also used in a more restrictive sense to mean anything (employee; customer; part; vehicle) for which a record is held in some file (or the equivalent in some other data structure).

entity identifier A number or other group of characters that uniquely identifies an entity; for example, a personnel number, a customer number, or a character group that identifies a particular peripheral device. See *entity*.

entity occurrence A specific entity; for example, a named employee. See *Bachman notation*.

entity record Also *attribute record*. A record as produced by normalisation and containing relatively long-term attributes. See *normalisation; relationship record*.

entity type A class of entity; for example, 'employee' or 'part'. See *entity occurrence; Bachman notation*.

entrance (1)A port. (2)An entry point.

entry (1)An element of a table or dictionary. (2)The commencement of execution of a sequence of instructions. See *entry conditions; entry point*. (3)The act of sending a message to a line. See *enter*.

entry conditions Also *initial conditions*. The values that must be supplied (or defaulted) before commencing execution of a sequence of instructions. In addition to the address of the first instruction (the entry point), they may include initial parameter values.

entry label Also *label; entry point label; entry name*. A source coding identifier of an entry point.

entry name An entry label.

entry point (1)An instruction address or label of a place in a sequence of instructions where execution can begin, for example, to selectively perform one of a program's functions. (2)An 'entry point' (def. 1) or a return address (a place where execution can be resumed).

envelope (1)The included frequencies of a signal; the range of frequencies that are represented in a transmitted or received signal. (2)Also *frame*. A pair of delimiters used to set off an item from other, similar, adjacent items. (3)A term sometimes applied to a special-purpose set of instructions or data; ('a testing envelope'; 'a simulation envelope').

environment (1)The set of physical conditions in which a device operates; the temperature, humidity, vibration, etc. to which it is exposed. (2)A mix of defining and restrictive elements; all of the relevant conditions considered as an entity; ('a computer environment'; 'a data capture environment'; 'a transaction processing environment'.) (3)With respect to a program; the mix of resources that is available for its execution in a particular computer system.

environment division That part of a COBOL program that identifies the resources (computer; peripherals; files) that will be used in its execution.

EOA *End-Of-Address.*
EOB *End-Of-Block.*
EOD *End-Of-Document.*
EOF *End-Of-File.*
EOM *End-Of-Message.*
EOT (1)*End-Of-Tape.* (2)*End-Of-Transmission.*
EPC *Edge-Punched Card.*

epitaxial layer A thin layer of doped silicon of one type deposited on a substrate or on a layer of another type (N-type on P-type or P-type on N-type). It is subject to masking and etching or metalisation in producing a semiconductor device such as a field effect transistor. See *semiconductor; diffusion; field effect transistor.*

EPOS *Electronic Point Of Sale.* See *point of sale.*
EPROM (1)*Erasable Programmed Read-Only Memory.* See *PROM.* (2)*Electrically Programmable Read-Only Memory.* Fuse PROM. See *PROM.*
EQ *EQual to.* See *relational operator.*
equal to See *relational operator.*

equalization (1)Conditioning; the process of improving the data carrying characteristics of a leased telephone line. (2)Also, sometimes, *balancing.* The process of adjusting circuit values to improve the performance of an electrical or electronic device. (3)An operation performed within a modem to compensate for phase and/or amplitude distortion introduced in a telephone line. The operation may be a relatively simple one of introducing fixed phase and/or amplitude compensation or a more complex operation in which received signals are compared with digital representations of 'ideal' signals with the differences (equalizer constants) used to provide a continuous 'running average' compensation.

equalizer In a modem; a circuit (pair of operational amplifiers) that adds a fixed phase and/or amplitude correction for distortion introduced in a telephone line. It may allow adjustment for the characteristics of a particular line or it may be a **statistical equalizer** that provides the correction that is expected to be required for the (dialed) lines of a particular telephone system.

equalizer constants In some modems; internal values that are computed at the end of each Baud and used to compensate for line-induced amplitude and phase distortion when receiving the next signal. They are differences between stored 'ideal' values and the values as received.

equivalence Exclusive NOR (logic operation).

equivalent binary digits With respect to a character set; the number of binary digits required to represent each character by a distinctive bit pattern. The number of equivalent binary digits is equal to the number required to express the final character of the set; for example, a character set of 30 characters requires five equivalent binary digits because 30 in binary is 11110 which is a 5-digit number.

equivalent four-wire circuit A frequency-divided two-wire circuit capable of providing the full-duplex operation of a (slow) four-wire circuit.

ER *ERror.*

erasable A term applied to a storage medium that permits data to be removed, leaving the medium in a condition to receive new data. Magnetic tape, for example, is 'erasable' and paper tape is not. The term is also applied to a read-only memory (integrated circuit) that can be reprogrammed by the user. See *PROM; MNOS; FAMOS.*

erasable programmed read-only memory (EPROM) See *PROM.*

erasable read-only memory (EROM) Electrically alterable read-only memory; memory that can be erased and reprogrammed in the field.

erase (1)To remove data from a magnetisable surface storage medium, usually by overwriting with zeros. See *zerofill; erase head.* (2)To return a read-only memory to the condition in which it can receive new bit patterns or internal interconnections. See *PROM.* (3)To remove stray magnetisation patterns from the sides of tracks. See *track trimming; straddle erase; tunnel erase; head.*

erase character A delete character.

erase head (1)In a magnetic tape unit; a head that erases previously recorded data from the tape before new data is written. (2)In magnetic disc recording; a head that performs track trimming. See *track trimming; straddle erase; tunnel erase.*

ergonomics The science or practice of considering the needs of people and reflecting those needs in the design of equipment and workspaces. It applies to such things as the height of chairs, the placement of keys on keyboards, the brightness of VDU screens, and the location of furniture and equipment in offices.

EROM *Erasable Read-Only Memory.*

ERP *Error Recovery Procedure.*

error (1) An action that produces an unintended and unwanted result or the result; ('a punching error'; 'a programming error'; 'an error in addition'). **(2)** Also *program error; software error.* An instance in which code or data fails to pass a validity test by a compiler/assembler, user program, or system hardware or software; an instance in which a computer or terminal input is rejected requiring reentry. **(3)** An instance where received data is not identical to the same data as transmitted. **(4)** An instance in which data read from a storage location is not identical to the same data as written to the location.

error burst In a data transmission; a number of bit transpositions that occur together or that are separated by no more than a certain number of correct bits. For example, a 'burst' may be considered to be terminated after three consecutive correct bits are received.

error/completion code A short (one or two byte) group that is returned to a user program by an operating system to indicate whether or not a command executed successfully and, if not, the reason for failure. See *status block.*

error condition A condition in which a computer operation cannot be continued because of an error detected by hardware or software. The detection of the condition causes a jump to an interrupt and, often, a jump to an error routine that initiates some corrective action or outputs an error message. See *error; recovery.*

error-control character A (final) character constructed to assist in the detection of errors in a block of transferred or transmitted data; for example, a block check character or a cyclic check character.

error correction code (ECC) A code that provides an inherent method of correcting errors detected in received data. The process is termed **forward error correction**. Such a code provides for the introduction of redundant bits as necessary to make all correct bit patterns conform to a particular rule according to some algorithm. The hardware with which the code is used provides for the analysis of bit patterns that deviate from the rule in order to determine which bits are in error and to change them. See *Hamming code.*

error detection and correction Forward error correction. See *error correction code; forward error correction.*

error detection code A code in which redundant bits are introduced as necessary to make all correct bit patterns conform to some rule. Hardware with which the code is used checks received bit patterns and signals an error when any are found that do not conform to the rule. See *error correction code; parity; M-out-of-N code; polynomial code; ARQ.*

error list A printout of source code errors as detected during assembly or compilation.

error message (1) A short message returned from a receiving station to the sender to indicate that an error has been detected in a unit of received data (block; message) and, usually, requesting retransmission of the unit. See *NAK; ARQ.* **(2)** A message from an operating system to a console operator indicating an error condition encountered during processing. **(3)** A message to a terminal or console operator indicating that an error has been detected in the operator's input.

error range (1) The difference between the highest and lowest error values detected in performing some operation. **(2)** A specification of the program-tested values that are to be regarded as in error; for example, a day of the month which is less than 1 or greater than 31 would be considered to be in the 'error range'.

error rate The number of detected errors per unit of data transferred or transmitted; in data communications, the unit is usually one million bits or one hundred thousand characters.

error ratio The ratio of error bits/characters to the total.

error recovery procedure (ERP) See *recovery procedure.*

error report An error list.

error retry The act of making a second or subsequent attempt to perform an operation that failed or in which an error was detected in the previous attempt.

error routine A routine to which a jump is made when an error condition is detected; it may, for example, output an error message, retransfer a block in which an error has been detected, or cause the suspension of a program.

ESC *ESCape.* A transmission control character used to indicate that one or more of the following bit patterns have no correct interpretations as characters in the code or link protocol of the system. See *escape; DLE*.

escape (1) In data communications; to indicate to receiving hardware that it is to change the interpretation of one or more bit patterns or to indicate that certain bit patterns are those of control characters rather than characters of the customer code. An escape is indicated by one or more special characters inserted in a message or block. It may apply to an entire block or message, to a single bit pattern, or to all those between two special characters. The affected bit pattern(s) may be identified in a transmission by means of an **escape character** (ESC), a **data link escape character** (DLE), a **shift character**, a **code extension character**, or a special group with a name and specific function depending upon the system. An escape may be made for one of the following reasons: 1. To disable the circuits in receiving hardware that identify control characters and thus to permit transmitting an alien code that may, inadvertently, contain bit patterns that are control characters in the system. 2. To change the meanings of control characters or to indicate to receiving hardware that a bit pattern is a special control character. See *DLE*. 3. To indicate to a terminal, computer, or other code-converting functional unit that certain bit patterns are to be interpreted with alternate meanings that are established within the system; for example, that they are to be interpreted as 'figures' rather than as 'letters'. See *shift character; code extension character*. **(2)** To terminate one type of processing in order to perform another; for example, in text editing, to 'escape' from the input mode and return to the command mode.

escape character The ESC character.

escape key (1) A key used to change a terminal (keyboard) function. **(2)** A code shift key.

estimator A value held by an operating system that indicates how much primary storage a process is likely to require for its active set during a particular phase of processing.

ETB *End of Transmission Block*.

etch To selectively remove metal; for example, in producing a 'printed' circuit board or forming the conducting channels from a metalised layer in manufacturing a microelectronic device. It commonly follows a photolithographic step in which a protective coating is created on those parts of a surface where metal is not to be removed. See *photolithography*.

Ethernet A local-area data network developed by Intel, Xerox, and Digital Equipment Co. It makes use of coaxial cable, operates at 10 megabits per second, and can support several hundred terminals.

ETX *End of TeXt*.

Eurocard A printed circuit board of standard European specification; it measures 100 mm. × 160 mm.

European Informatics Network A packet switching system used for interchanges between certain European research centres.

evaluate (1) To determine whether or not an item of hardware or software can perform a partiular required function or to determine which of two or more items can perform the function best. See *benchmark*. **(2)** To reduce an expression to its simplest form; for example, to change '$3^2 + 2$' to '11'.

event (1) An external condition of significance to an operating system or executing task; for example, the arrival of a transaction or the completion of a peripheral transfer. **(2)** An occurrence that is logged for statistical or fault control purposes; for example, a parity failure or a seek retry.

event driven Interrupt driven.

event-interrupt An event and a resultant interrupt. See *interrupt*.

exception An exception condition

exception condition A condition encountered during processing (overflow of significant digits; parity check failure on a transfer; no paper in the line printer) that causes an immediate transfer of control to an exception routine See *exception routine; interrupt*.

exception message An exception report.

exception report A report output on a printer or VDU indicating an abnormal condition encountered during processing; for example, a number in a sequence skipped, or a negative stock balance.

exception response A negative response.

exception routine A routine to which control is passed in order to deal with some abnormal condition that occurs during processing; for example, the inability to locate a referenced record or reaching the end of a file. Depending upon the condition, it may output an exception report.

excess-sixty four notation A common method used for representing a floating point exponent as a characteristic (typically of decimal value 127) from which 64 is subtracted. See *floating point*.

excess-three code (XS3) A transformation code used to facilitate adding decimal numbers by binary arithmetic; its purpose is to provide a carry digit in binary at the same place (after 9) as it occurs in decimal. Like binary coded decimal (BCD), it uses the first four binary digits, but 3 is added to the decimal digit before conversion. The following are examples of decimal numbers converted to BCD and XS3:

Decimal	BCD	XS3
0	0000	0011
1	0001	0100
5	0101	1000
7	0111	1010
12	1100	0100 0101
34	0011 0100	0110 0111

In decimal, a carry occurs after '9' and in a binary numeric it occurs after '1111' which, in decimal, is 15. Since computer addition is always performed on two numbers, if 3 is added to each decimal digit to be added, the total will be increased by 6 which is the amount that must be added to 9 to produce 1111, the point at which a carry occurs in binary. For example, the addition of 5 and 7 is performed as follows (remembering that 0011 is 'zero' in XS3):

```
                    5        0011 1000
                   +7        0011 1010
Without carry       2        0110 0010
Carry digit                         1
Total              12        0111 0010
```

The binary sum could be converted to 12 by subtracting 6 in the second digit position, however, the computer does it in two steps. If there is a carry digit, it subtracts 3 in the second digit position and adds 3 in the first to produce:

```
            0111   0010
           − 11   + 11
            0100   0101
```

It then subtracts 3 from both sides to produce:

```
            0100   0101
           − 11   − 11
            0001   0010
```

The result is, then, 12 in BCD.

exchange (1) To transpose; ('exchange storage locations'). **(2)** To replace one thing with another; ('exchange disc packs'). **(3)** Also *telephone exchange*. A location, facility, or item of equipment for routing telephone calls by selectively interconnecting circuits. **(4)** A message pair; a message from a terminal to a computer and a reply.

exchange sort Also *bubble sort; sifting sort*. A multiple-pass sequencing operation in which the first two items are tested and placed in the relative position they will occupy in the final sequence (exchanging them if necessary) with the second item then tested and placed in sequence with the third, and thus continuing until the last item of the group is reached at which point the operation is started again with the first two items. The process is repeated as necessary until a pass is made in which there are no exchanges and, thus, all items are in sequence.

exchangeable disc A magnetic disc that an operator can install on a drive and remove as required; it is, typically, part of an assembly with one or more other discs in a disc pack, though it may be a single disc in a disc cartridge. (Flexible discs, though 'exchangeable' are excluded in the usual contexts in which the term is used.) See *magnetic disc; disc pack; disc cartridge; data module, fixed disc.*

exchangeable disc storage (EDS) **(1)** One or more magnetic disc units with operator-replaceable disc packs. **(2)** A magnetic disc unit without any fixed discs. See *magnetic disc unit.*

exclusion Also *and-not; not-if then*. A logic operation with an output that is 'true' if the first of two inputs is 'true' and the second is 'false' and 'false' if the first is 'false' and the second 'true' or if both are 'true' or both are 'false'. See *logic.*

exclusion key On a telephone used for setting up dial-up data transfers, a button used to change between 'voice' and 'data'.

exclusive NOR (XNOR) A logic operation with an output that is 'true' if both of two inputs are 'true' or both are 'false' and 'false' if one is 'true' and the other false. See *logic.*

exclusive OR (XOR) Also *non-equivalence*. A logic operation with an output that is 'true' if one of the two inputs is 'true' and the other 'false' and 'false' if both are 'true' or both are 'false'. See *logic; identity.*

execute By a computer; to perform the operations specified by an instruction or sequence of instructions. See *execution.*

execute phase That part of a data processing operation in which instructions are executed, as contrasted, perhaps, with a 'compilation phase'.

execution (1) By a computer; to perform the operations specified by instructions. In this broadest sense, the term may be applied to a single instruction or to a program or other sequence of instructions and it includes all necessary data transfers but not the printing or display of the results; ('compilation followed directly by execution'; 'relocation during execution'). (2) By a central processor; to decode an instruction or the instructions of a sequence and to perform the arithmetic and/or logic operations specified. In this sense, the term excludes peripheral transfers which may be said to 'interrupt execution'. (3) By a central processor with respect to a single instruction; to fetch the operand(s), perform the specified arithmetic or logic operation, and to store the results. In this sense, instruction decoding is excluded and an 'execution cycle' follows a 'decoding cycle'. (4) By a central processor with respect to a single instruction; to perform all operations required including decoding, operand fetch, arithmetic or logic operation, and the storing of results. When loaded, instructions are placed in main storage in contiguous locations in the sequence in which they will be executed and the lowest numbered address (the address of the first instruction) is placed in the **program counter** (also **current address register**) in the control unit. In some cases (as when performing repeated calculations with different input values), operands can be located in main storage in the same way (in a table or array) but more often the operands are field contents of records and, since all fields are not usually required, they cannot be accessed in simple sequence as with instructions. The first instruction to be executed is then placed in an **instruction register** in the control unit and the program counter is incremented by a value (say, by 1 in a word-organised machine with instructions one word in length) so that it holds the address of the next instruction to be executed. The instruction in the instruction register is then decoded, which consists of comparing its bit patterns with those of the order code of the computer and the recognised formats of acceptable instructions in order to determine the meanings of the various elements and the operations that are to be performed. Essentially, this consists of identifying the **operator** and sending representative electrical pulses to the arithmetic logic unit and identifying the **operand(s)** and applying such **address modification** as necessary to produce a numerical value as electrical pulses which are sent to main storage in the **operand fetch** to cause the contents of a location to be read into a register in the arithmetic logic unit as pulses that set bits in the register. All the operations after decoding are said to occur at the **microcode level** and the bit patterns that determine the specific patterns of electrical pulses are **microinstructions** held in read-only memory contained within the control unit. The arithmetic logic unit performs its various operations using microinstructions in predefined sequences that may be termed **microprograms**. It consists of applying a sequence of pulses to appropriate 'control points' to cause the required movement of bits within registers and between registers. The execution of a single instruction may require more than a thousand such bit movements. When the arithmetic logic unit has finished performing its operations, one of the registers holds the result; it sends a pulse indicating completion to the control unit and it sends the appropriate pulses to cause the contents of the register to be written to another register or to a main storage location. The control unit circuitry then reads the program counter and sends the necessary pulses to cause the next instruction to be read into the instruction register. A fast computer may perform essentially this sequence of operations more than a million times per second. See *register; microinstruction; program; address modification; address; operator; operand.*

execution cycle A sequence of microcoded steps performed to execute an instruction; the time taken to execute a microprogram. (Most instructions require multiple cycles.)

execution path With respect to a program; one of the ways in which the various sequences can be executed.

execution phase Execute phase.

execution time (1) The time required to execute a program. (2) Run time; the time when execution begins.

executive A supervisor (in some systems); a group of programs used to control the execution of other programs. See *operating system; supervisor; system software.*

executive program (1) An executive. (2) An executive routine.

executive routine A supervisory routine; a unit of an executive, supervisor, or operating system.

exist To be present in main storage. The term may be applied to a program (usually in a multiprogramming system) or to a unit of code or data; for example, a page or segment in a virtual storage system. See *coexist; concurrency.*

existence time The time during which a program (or any of its segments) is present in main storage. See *concurrency; throughput.*

exit (1) A place where the execution of a sequence of instructions is (or can be) terminated as a normal step in processing. **(2)** To discontinue executing instructions of one sequence and transfer control to another sequence.

exit conditions With respect to a loop; the conditions (zero count; last card) that will cause a termination.

expand mode (1) With respect to a magnetisable surface storage device; to record data at the lower of two possible densities; for example, at 800 bits per inch instead of at 1600. **(2)** With respect to a printer; to widen characters or to introduce additional space between words and/or characters. See *compress mode*.

expanded addressing In a computer or other device in which the size of the standard storage and manipulation unit (word; byte) limits the amount of addressable storage; the use of additional bits to extend the addressing range. For example, an 8-bit microprocessor could normally address only 255 locations but this can be increased to 4095 locations by using 12-bit addressing circuitry and a 12-bit address bus.

expander A term applied to an add-on unit or fan-out device; ('a memory expander'; 'an input/output port expander').

expandor A device or circuit used in a telephone system to increase the difference in amplitude between weak and strong signals (and thus to restore their original relationship). See *compandor; compressor*.

expansion (1) With respect to a macro; to replace it with the source-code sequence of instructions that it represents. **(2)** Also *decoding*. By a control unit during processing; to break an instruction down into the microcode operations necessary for its execution.

expansion board A printed circuit board that provides for adding additional facilities; for example, one that increases the number of input/output ports or that interfaces with additional memory modules.

expert system A term sometimes applied to a data base for a particular scientific or technical specialty (renal diseases; petroleum geology) that is maintained and upgraded by 'experts' in the field. See *conceptual language; knowledge engineering*.

expiration data With respect to a file; a date after which it is no longer automatically protected from being overwritten.

explicit address An absolute address.

exponent (1) A number or symbol written at the upper right of a base number to indicate its power; for example, in x^3, the '3' is the 'exponent'. See *power*. **(2)** In floating point notation; the part that indicates the position of the radix point. See *floating point*.

exponentiation The process of evaluating a number with an exponent; for example, the process of producing '8' from 2^3.

express (1) To write or state; ('express a decimal number in binary'). **(2)** That which is fastest or has priority over others; ('an express channel'; 'an express stream').

expression (1) That which is written or stated. **(2)** A representation of a mathematical or logical condition; for example, $3x + 2y$, $c = b - d$, or A & B.

extended addressing Expanded addressing.

extended binary coded decimal interchange code See *EBCDIC*.

extended core storage (ECS) Bulk storage.

extended port With respect to a point-to-point communications system in which the remote-site modem has multiple ports; a port that interfaces with another modem (rather than with a DTE). The other modem provides for communications with one or more additional sites. See *onward link*.

extended port circuit An onward link; particularly one that connects to one port of a multiport remote site modem.

extended precision Multiple precision.

extender An expander.

extensible language A programming language that permits the user to define additional elements (macros; symbols) to meet particular needs.

extension In a telephone system; an internal circuit on a subscriber's premises.

extension character A code extension character.

extent (1) Also *range*. The inclusive locations in which something exists or operates; ('the extent of a variable'; 'the extent of an array'). **(2)** A limit or bound. **(3)** On a direct access volume; a number of contiguous storage locations allocated for a particular purpose.

external call A call to a sequence of instructions not compiled with the sequence in which it is used; a call implemented by a call routine. See *call; internal call*.

external decimal Also *unpacked decimal; zoned decimal; display format*. A term applied to decimal numeric data in character format in the storage code of the computer rather than in a computational format. Each digit is held as a bit pattern in one character or byte of storage. See *character format; computational format*.

external delays In classifying computer time utilisation; periods when the computer was unusable due to causes beyond the control of operators or maintenance engineers; for example, because of strikes or power failures.

external file name See *file name*.

external floating point Floating point as represented in source coding or data preparation. See *floating point; internal floating point*.

external fragmentation See *fragmentation*.

external interrupt An interrupt not caused by an event in the sequence of instructions that is interrupted; for example, one caused by the operator, by the arrival of a transaction in a mixed-mode processing system, or monitor detection of a fault condition.

external line A connecting telephone line outside the user's premises; a trunk line or a tie line.

external merge A merge made to a storage location that did not originally hold either of the sequences being merged.

external modem A free-standing modem; one not incorporated in the device it serves.

external name An identifier of an entry point in one sequence of instructions that is held in an exit instruction in another sequence.

external number A telephone number outside of a user's internal or private-line system. See *outside line*.

external number repetition A facility that permits a telephone subscriber to call any of a group of preselected external numbers by dialing only two digits.

external program parameter A run-time parameter.

external reference (1) An external call. **(2)** By an executing process in a virtual storage system; a reference to a page/segment that is not in primary storage.

external sort A sort in which the items to be sorted are written to a different storage location in their new sequence as they are identified. See *internal sort; exchange sort*.

external storage Also *backing storage*. Storage that is neither main storage or within the central processor. (Main storage is 'internal' even when physically separate from the central processor.) See *internal storage*.

external subprogram See *subprogram*.

external symbol In a compiled sequence of instructions; an address of an entry point in another sequence of instructions or the identifier of a routine to which control may be (or, will be) transferred during execution.

external symbol dictionary A list (for the operating system) of all the external symbols in a load module or other module of object code. See *load module*.

external transmit clock Transmit signal element timing provided by a repeater modem of an onward link or by a DTE. It is used to slave a modem transmitter to an external timing source, mainly from an onward link. (Where used, it is input on CCITT V.24 circuit 113.)

extract (1) With respect to a group of items in a particular storage location; to select those items that meet certain criteria and write them to another location. **(2)** With respect to a word or byte; to selectively read the contents of one or more bit positions. The operation is performed with a mask or filter.

eye pattern An oscilliscope trace that shows the X and Y coordinates of (received) data in a differential phase shift keying system. An eye pattern trace is commonly used to identify phase and amplitude distortions introduced in a line.

F

F (f.) *Femto*.

F-format *Fixed-length format*. In some systems; a term applied to a record that is of standard length for some purpose.

face A term used with respect to graphic characters to identify type or style; ('bold face'; 'an OCR face').

face change character A font change character.

facilities management (FM) The contract operation and management of a computer system; it may be performed on the owner's premises or the computer may be installed on the premises of the management company.

facsimile (FAX) The transmission of data as two-dimensional images (photographs; engineering drawings) over narrow band (non-video) communications links. It consists of scanning the original with a light beam and sensor that converts transmitted or reflected light into a voltage, sending the voltages and scan timing information as carrier wave modulations to a receiving station, and using their demodulated form in a scanning operation (photographic; thermal; xerographic) to produce a copy of the original.

facsimile signal level The maximum usable voltage produced in a facsimile scan; depending upon the system, it represents either black or white.

factor In multiplication; either of the numbers that are multiplied. In the expression 'A = 5 × C', both the '5' and the 'C' are 'factors'.

factorial (!) The total number of ways the elements of a set can be arranged; it is determined by multiplying the number of elements in the set by one less than this number and repeating (subtracting 1 each time) until there are no more multipliers. For example, factorial 5 (5!) is found by the multiplication: 5! = 5 × 4 × 3 × 2 × 1 (= 120).

fail To cease providing an effective service or function.

fail safe To fail in such a way that no loss or dangerous condition results. When the term is applied to a system, it implies the existence of backup facilities that can assume the full functions of certain primary facilities in event of their failure. See *fault; reconfiguration*.

fail soft To fail in such a way that some useful function continues to be performed. See *graceful degradation; fault*.

failure A complete loss of function. See *fault*.

fallback A change to a different (and, usually, more restricted) mode of operation as the result of a fault or failure encountered in the primary mode.

fallback data rate In data communications; a lower data rate that may be set automatically (by the DTE) when excessive errors are encountered at the higher rate.

false (1)One of two possible logic conditions; in computer operations it is represented by a 0-bit. (2)One of the voltages of a two-condition control circuit; for example, 0 volts in a circuit in which 'true' is represented by +5 volts. Typically, a circuit that is 'false' is neutral or in the 'inhibit' state. See *true; logical high*.

FAM *Fast Access Memory*.

FAMOS *Floating-gate Avalanche-injection Metal Oxide Silicon*. A type of programmable read-only memory in which the storage cells are similar to field effect transistors. A silicon gate is buried in glass between a source and drain. To program a 1-bit, a high voltage is applied to the drain while the source is held low, thus causing a breakdown and an avalanche of electrons to flow. Some of these electrons are trapped in the gate and form a static charge that reduces the threshold voltage thus permitting the element to conduct when a read signal of the correct voltage is applied. When exposed to ultraviolet (UV) light, the charge leaks away from the gates, thus permitting reprogramming. See *PROM; MNOS*.

fan fold A term applied to continuous stationery or cards, the individual sheets of which are folded successively in opposite directions to form a stack. As they are used, they are pulled up from the top of the stack. See *web; cut set; sheet feed*.

fan in To receive multiple inputs. In logic circuitry, the output of two or more circuits at one stage may be 'fanned in' to one circuit at the next. In data communications, the outputs of several terminals may be 'fanned in' to a single multiplexor. In data communications and storage transfer systems, the same device or circuitry normally handles movements in both directions and the term applied depends upon the direction. For example, when terminals are sending they are said to be 'fanned in' to a multiplexor and when receiving they are said to be 'fanned out' from it.

fan-in ratio (1)Of a functional unit or electronic circuit; the number of input circuits per output circuit. For example, a terminal control unit that interfaces between a single line and ten terminals would be said to have a 'fan-in ratio' of 10 to 1. (The term is used whether the terminals are considered as receiving or as sending.) (2)The ratio between the number of events and the number that affect a particular item; for example, the ratio of the number of transactions handled in a particular time and the number that access a particular file or the number of accesses to a file and the number that access a particular record.

fan out (1)To use a single source (channel; device; line) to provide multiple outputs. See *fan in*. (2)A measure of the 'driving power' of logic gates or electronic circuits; the number of gates or circuits (of standard or assumed impedance) that can be connected to the output.

far-end crosstalk Crosstalk that moves in the same direction as the signals in a channel. See *crosstalk*.

farad (f) The basic unit for measuring capacitance; it is the amount of capacitance that will limit a change of potential to 1 volt when 1 coulomb is received. The unit is too large for electronics purposes; capacitors are normally rated in 'microfarads' or 'picofarads'.

Faraday rotation The ability of certain magnetisable materials in thin films to deflect polarised light in a direction depending upon their magnetisation.

fast access memory (FAM) Also, sometimes, *secondary memory*. A memory with a speed between that of main memory and that of fixed-head disc (say, with an access time of between 5 μs. and 10 ms.).

fast Fourier transform (FFT) A processing technique for improving the detection and interpretation of signals in the presence of noise. It consists of determining the time-related characteristics of the signals to be detected, or for which improvement is required, and converting them to spectral lines in some frequency scale. The frequency representation of a single input wave is a 'discrete Fourier transform' (DFT). The calculation of DFT's is relatively complex, and when it is to be done in real time (say for radar or video image enhancement), it may require more than 200 million calculations per second. To reduce the necessary speed by combining calculations and eliminating redundant ones, an algorithm was developed which is termed a 'fast Fourier transform'. It is performed in an operation termed a 'butterfly' which consists of taking two stored input samples, performing multiplication and addition with them, and restoring them in memory. Though the operations can be performed on a standard computer, the regular performance of the operation in real time usually involves a special signal processor consisting of a multiplier-accumulator for the butterfly computations and a sine/cosine generator to produce the frequency representation.

fast select A facility of a packet switching system that provides for up to 128 bytes of user data to be sent with a Call Request.

father (1) A term sometimes applied to the file that was updated to produce the version being considered. See *generation*. **(2)** An owner. See *tree*.

fault An abnormal hardware or software condition that causes a reduction in performance or capability. By contrast, a **failure** is essentially a complete loss of capability. The term 'fault' is usually applied to a functional unit condition; it, typically, results from a 'failure' of a component. The term 'failure' can be applied to anything from a diode to a data network. When applied to software, the term 'fault' normally indicates defective logic or structure while an **error** is a programming condition that adversely affects compilation or execution. If the error is minor, it is usually termed a **bug** and the process of locating it and eliminating it is **debugging**. The identification of an error by the analysis of dumps is **dump cracking**. If an error is such that it prevents processing from continuing, a **crash** is said to occur. The term 'crash' may be applied to a system as well as to software; when applied to a system it can indicate either a hardware or a software failure. A minor fault in a functional unit may also be termed a 'bug'. The term 'debugging' is applied to hardware in the sense of locating and correcting 'bugs' in new equipment or a new system; the process applied to equipment in service is usually termed **trouble shooting** or, more formally, **corrective maintenance**. A system or functional unit in which a fault or failure prevents continued operation is said to be **down** and when it is corrected it is **up** or **back on line**.

FAX *FAXimile* (facsimile).

FC *Font Change*. A control character available in some systems to change the 'font' of a printing or display device, for example from Roman to italics.

FCC *Federal Communications Commission*. (Washington)

FCS *Frame Check Sequence*.

FD (1) *Full Duplex*. **(2)** *File Definition*.

FDD *Flexible Disc Drive*.

FDM *Frequency Division Multiplexing*.

FDS (1) *Fixed Disc Storage*. **(2)** *Flexible Disc Storage*.

FDX *Full DupleX*.

FE (1) *Format Effector*. **(2)** *Field Engineering*.

feasibility report See *feasibility study; systems analysis*.

feasibility study A preliminary investigation of the practical and economic factors involved in enhancing an existing computer system or implementing a new one. It usually results in a **feasibility report** to management giving a cost/benefit analysis of the possible courses of action. See *systems analysis; system design*.

FEC *Forward Error Correction*.

FEDS *Fixed and Exchangeable Disc Storage*.

feed (1) Also *line feed*. To move paper through a printer; unless otherwise indicated, it is assumed to be one line. See *throw; newline*. **(2)** With respect to paper tape or punched cards, to move through a punch or reader. **(3)** The mechanism that performs a 'feed' (def. 1; 2).

feed hole Also *sprocket hole*. A punched hole engaged by a sprocket pin to move continuous stationery through a printer (to advance it as each line is printed) or to move paper tape or edge-punched cards through a punch or reader.

feed pitch (1) The distance by which the paper of a printer is advanced between successive lines; the distance of a one-line 'feed'. (2)The distance by which a punched card or paper tape is advanced between successive punching positions.

feed track Also *sprocket track*. (1)In paper tape or edge-punched cards; a line of (small) holes that are punched at the same time as the data holes and are used to feed the card/tape during punching and reading. See *paper tape*. (2)In continuous stationery; either of the lines of pre-punched holes along edges that are engaged by the pins of a sprocket or tractor to advance the paper through a printer.

feedback (1)A representation of the output of a device or circuit as returned to the input side to control operation. In a typical **feedback system** the output is monitored for conformance to certain requirements (voltage; frequency; throughput; temperature) and when a variation is detected, an appropriate signal is sent back to modify the operation in such a way as to reduce or eliminate the variation. When the correction just counters the variation, the system is said to be 'stable'. A poorly designed system may be 'unstable', meaning that the output is subject to wide or erratic variation. The term **hunting** is applied to a limited oscillatory change resulting from over correction, for example, if the 'overvoltage' feedback of a power supply causes an undervoltage that, in turn, is corrected to cause another overvoltage condition. The reduction or elimination of hunting is **damping**; it usually consists of delaying the response to corrective signals. (2)A similar mechanism in other systems. See *heuristic.*

feedback loop The notionally circular arrangement of a feedback system in which part of the output returns to the input and is reflected in the output.

feedback system A system in which the output is sampled or monitored for system control purposes. See *feedback.*

feeder (1)A power distribution line or cable. (2)A telephone cable from a local exchange to a central exchange.

FEFO *First-Ended-First Out.*

femto- (f.) A combining form indicating 10^{-15}.

fence (1) In some multiprogramming systems in which the different concurrent programs have (or can have) different priorities; a priority threshold that is dynamically raised and lowered depending upon system load; only those programs with priorities higher than the 'fence' are allowed to process. (2)A partition.

FEP *Front End Processor.*

ferrite An oxide of iron; it is finely powdered and compressed with a binder to make **ferrite cores** for core memory and is the magnetisable part of the coating material of magnetic tapes and discs.

FET *Field Effect Transistor.*

fetch (1) To locate an operand or instruction in main storage and to load it into a control unit or arithmetic unit register. Unless otherwise indicated, an 'operand' is understood. See *execution.* (2)To locate a unit of code or data in backing storage and load it into main storage.

fetch cycle The part of execution in which an operand or instruction is read from main storage and written into a control unit or arithmetic unit register.

fetch routine A routine that handles the movement of a program or other sequence of instructions from backing storage to main storage.

FF *Form Feed.* A format effector used to cause a new form (say, that of an invoice) to be displayed on a VDU screen or to tabulate a printer to the beginning of the first line in the next form to be printed.

FFT *Fast Fourier Transform.*

FHDS *Fixed Head Disc Storage.*

Fibonacci number A number in the Fibonacci series.

Fibonacci search A search in which a sequence of numbers (usually record keys) is divided in accordance with the numbers of the Fibonacci series rather than into equal parts as in a 'binary search'. The first step is to add dummy numbers as necessary so that the highest number is one of those in the series. The sequence is then divided at the next lower number in the series and tests applied to determine if the number of the required item or group is above or below that point (as in a binary search). If the required number is below that at the division point, it is divided again at the next lower number in the series and the tests repeated. If the required number is higher than that at the division point, a new Fibonacci series is constructed from that point and it, in turn, is divided, the division point is tested, and one part is rejected. The process continues until the item or group is located or determined not to be present. See *search; Fibonacci series.*

Fibonacci series A series in which the first two numbers are 0 and 1 and subsequent numbers are equal to the sum of the immediately preceding two numbers. The first ten numbers of the series are thus 0, 1, 1, 2, 3, 5, 8, 13, 21, and 34.

fibre optics The technology of using thin glass filaments to transmit signals as pulses of light at frequencies of about 10^{14} Hz. A filament acts as a wave guide for the light (reflecting it back and forth from the inside walls) allowing it to be transmitted around bends and over long distances with minimal loss. Existing applications include use as a cable replacement for connecting terminals and peripherals and for internal light paths in optical mark and character readers. Problems of producing long, continuous filaments and of their interconnection have limited use over longer distances, except experimentally. It is considered as a possible replacement for coaxial cable in telephone systems.

fiche See *microfiche*.

field (1) A part of a form (source document) reserved for a particular item or type of data; for example, a place for a customer's name and address or a column for prices. **(2)** Also *card field*. On a punched card; two or more consecutive columns reserved for a particular purpose. **(3)** Of a record in computer storage; a subdivision that can be accessed as a normal step of processing. An **elementary field** is such a field that is not normally subdivided; for example, one holding a record key or a customer's name. A **group field** is a field holding several related elementary fields; for example, a customer's name, address, and account number. **(4)** A part of a source language instruction reserved for a particular purpose according to the syntax of the programming language; ('an operand field'; 'a modifier field'). **(5)** A part of a data transmission or of a storage location that holds a unit of data that is to be separately used or interpreted. See *field separator*. **(6)** A part of a printing or display surface to which data can be written; a print field or a display field. **(7)** A work area or other designated area of storage. **(8)** An area of magnetic or electrostatic influence. See *charge; magnet; field effect transistor*. **(9)** Where a product is sold and used (from the viewpoint of its manufacturer); ('trouble showing up in the field'; 'reports from the field'). See *field change*.

field effect transistor (FET) a transistor in which conduction is controlled, at least partially, by an electrostatic field. Though the term includes 'junction FET's', unless otherwise indicated it denotes a **MOSFET** (*Metal-Oxide-Silicon Field Effect Transistor*). MOSFET's are available as discrete devices and they are also the active elements in a wide range of integrated circuits. The basic structure, shown in Fig. 1, consists of a **substrate** of lightly doped silicon, a **source** and a **drain** of silicon of opposite type to the substrate (N-type if the substrate is P-type), a **channel** between source and drain, and a **gate** adjacent to the channel. The source is the functional

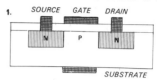

equivalent of a cathode and the drain the equivalent of an anode. The gate is a conductor area separated from the channel by a thin (1000 Angstrom) layer of silicon dioxide (glass). MOSFET's are also termed **unipolar transistors** because conduction is all through the same type of silicon. In operation, a thin layer of the substrate commonly 'inverts' in the channel to become, for practical purposes, the same as the source and drain. Such a transistor is **N-channel** if source, drain, and inverted channel are N-type silicon and **P-channel** if they are P-type silicon. An **enhancement mode** transistor is one that is normally OFF (no conduction between source and drain) and a **depletion mode** transistor is one that is normally ON. Most MOSFET's are 'N-channel enhancement mode' because conduction (and, thus, switching) is faster in N-type silicon than in P-type and because most circuit requirements are for transistors that are normally OFF. Figure 2a is the common symbol for an N-channel MOSFET and 2b is the symbol for a P-channel transistor. Figure 2c is the common symbol for a MOSFET of unspecified type; it is usually understood to be 'N-channel'. If there is a circle around the elements (as in 2a and

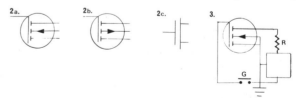

2b), it is usually understood to be a discrete device. Figure 3 shows an N-channel MOSFET in a circuit that is suitable for explanation purposes. When switch G is open, no potential is

applied to the gate and the substrate, effectively, forms back-to-back diodes with the source and drain, keeping the threshold high (say, 12 V) and preventing current flow through load R. Figure 4 is a 'silicon' illustration of the circuit. It shows depletion layers formed at the N-P junctions so there are no free 'carriers' to conduct between source and drain. In Fig. 5, switch G is closed making the gate 20 volts positive with respect to the substrate. This creates a 'field' that attracts electrons up

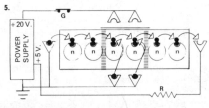

through the substrate, and into the thin channel adjacent to the gate. There are, then, a surplus of electrons in the channel (the P-type silicon has, effectively, been changed temporarily to N-type) and conduction takes place by electrons from the source successively 'bumping off' electrons which reach the drain and, thus, cause a current to flow through load R. (The inversion is not complete and the actual effect is to lower the channel conduction threshold to about 4 V.) In a depletion mode transistor, the substrate (or, in any case, the part which forms the channel) is lightly doped to be the same type of silicon as the source and drain. The threshold is, then, low and conduction takes place whenever the drain becomes sufficiently positive (say, +4 V.) with respect to the source. Figure 6 represents an N-channel depletion mode transistor. When switch G is closed, the substrate becomes 20 volts positive with respect to the gate, and this sets up a field that draws electrons out of the channel, thus creating depletion zones that cause the N-type silicon to temporarily appear to be P-type and to raise the source-drain conduction threshold. A P-channel transistor functions as 'mirror image' of N-channel; for example, a negative gate potential

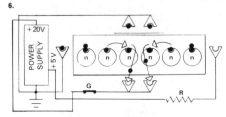

drives electrons from the N-type channel into the substrate, causing it to behave as P-type and to support conduction between the P-type source and drain. The transistors described are the common and inexpensive **thick oxide** type as used in dynamic RAM and in many ROM's and static RAM's. Most MOS devices are 'field effect transistors' though they may be known by other (or more specific) terms. See *MOS; junction FET; MNOS; FAMOS; programmable read-only memory; semiconductor; transistor.*

field engineer Also, usually, *customer engineer.* An engineer (typically, employed by a manufacturer) who performs corrective and preventative maintenance on equipment installed on users' premises.

field programmable logic array (FPLA) A logic array that can be (fuse) programmed by a user. See *programmable logic array.*

field-replaceable unit (FRU) An assembly or sub-assembly that is replaceable as a unit in event of a failure of one of its components. The most common ones in computer equipment are plug-in printed circuit boards.

field separator Also *field terminator.* A delimiter used to separate fields (or indicate a null field) in data communications or in packed data on magnetic tape or disc. See *FS; pack.*

FIFO *First-In-First-Out.* (1) An algorithm used in determining the order of handling or consideration; at any one time, the next item to be dealt with is that item among a group of items that has been waiting the longest (that was 'first in'). It is the inherent structure of a queue. (2) A queue; ('load a message into a transmitting FIFO').

FIGS *FiGureS shift.*

figurative constant A value (a literal) to which a standard data name has been assigned in a programming language; for example, in COBOL: ZERO, QUOTES, SPACE, or HIGH-VALUE.

figures shift (1) In a teletypewriter or similar device; to change key functions to output figures instead of letters. **(2)** (FIGS) A control character that causes a receiving device to change from 'letters' to 'figures'. See *code shift; letters shift*.

file (1) A named set of records and, often, access-related information. Though the term may be applied to a set consisting of source documents, punched cards, or other media, it is usually understood to be on magnetic disc or tape. By this definition, a file is a basic unit for storing and accessing user data; ('a master file'; 'the NSFX file'; 'a payroll file'). **(2)** Any individually accessible unit of storage (code, data, or empty locations). It is this definition that is implicit in such terms as 'file access', 'file transfer', and 'file protection'.

file access (1) The process of locating and reading files in backing storage. **(2)** The process of making transfers between main storage and backing storage. **(3)** The process of reading data from or writing data to a file.

file access mode (1) The type of access being performed (read; write; append). **(2)** The method of access used (serial; indexed).

file allocation (1) File placement. **(2)** The process of making files available to the programs or jobs that require them.

file assignment The process of designating a file in an assignment statement; the programming step of identifying a file that a program will access.

file attribute An item that identifies a file; for example, its name, size, or type of access supported.

file consignment In some systems; file allocation for the duration of a job.

file conversion (1) Also, usually, *data conversion*. The process of changing files from the code and format required for one type of computer to that required for another type of computer. **(2)** The process of changing the medium of a file; for example, from punched cards to magnetic tape.

file copy A backup file.

file creation The process of determining the attributes of a new file, opening it, writing data to it, and closing it.

file definition The process of identifying file attributes or, in some systems, identifying the input and output files a program will use during execution.

file description (1) In COBOL; an entry in the file section of the data division that identifies a file and specifies its size and structure. **(2)** An entry in an operating system catalogue that identifies a particular file together with its location and, usually, the access rights.

file directory (1) A list of all system and user files and their locations as maintained by an operating system. **(2)** A list of the files and their locations on a particular storage device or volume as kept in a reserved area (sometimes a **system control area**) on the device or volume.

file disposition A user specification of whether a file is to be temporary or catalogued and whether it is to overwrite an existing file or occupy another area of storage.

file gap A fixed length of unrecorded tape that separates two magnetic tape files on the same volume.

file generation number A generation number.

file index A volume table of contents.

file layout (1) The logical arrangement and structure of a file. **(2)** File placement.

file maintenance (1) The activity of keeping a file current by updating. See *update*. **(2)** File reorganisation.

file management The functions of an operating system relating to storing, allocating, and cataloguing files.

file map A tabular representation of the identities of files and their locations in a magnetic disc volume.

file name A character string that uniquely identifies a file. A **fully qualified file name** is a group identifying all the higher level owners of a file in a tree structure. An **external file name** is an identifier (often two characters) by which a file is known to an operating system and by which it is catalogued in a system catalogue. An **internal file name** is a (symbolic) name given to a file in source coding.

file organisation A method by which the records of a file can be accessed; the most common organisations are 'serial', 'sequential', 'indexed sequential', 'direct', and 'random'. A **standard file organisation** is one for which a computer manufacturer can provide the necessary software for access.

file placement Also *file allocation; file layout*. The process of organising the records of a file and writing them to a backing storage medium. Some operating systems perform all functions of file placement while others allow a degree of programmer control.

file protect An element (breakable tab; uncoverable hole;

removable plastic ring) that can be removed or set in such a way that it prevents writing to a storage volume.

file protected A term applied to a reel of magnetic tape from which the write-permit ring has been removed.

file protection The process of preventing corruption or loss of data; particularly by preventing the erasure or overwriting of data on magnetisable surface storage.

file reorganisation Also *file tidying*. The process of reloading a direct access file to eliminate or reduce overflow. It is, typically, done by a utility and consists of writing the records to a different volume while placing them in their correct order according to the file organisation.

file restore (1)De-updating. (2)A utility that performs the operation of de-updating.

file rotation In a system in which files are retained in versions corresponding to a fixed number of generations; the process of adding a new version and deleting the oldest.

file section A section of the data division of a COBOL program in which the files that will be used during execution are identified.

file separator A gap or other delimiter that marks the end of one file and the beginning of another on magnetic tape or in data communications. See *file gap; FS*.

file sharing A multiprogramming facility that permits two or more concurrent programs to access the same file.

file store Filestore.

file structure (1)The logical form of a file that results from applying a particular file organisation and layout to a group of records. (2)File organisation.

file tidying File reorganisation.

filename A file name.

filestore (1)In some virtual storage systems; that part of secondary storage that holds conventional files as contrasted to code and data held in pages and/or segments for automatic overlaying. (2)Backing storage.

fill To overwrite a storage location with 1-bits, 0-bits, or repeated bit patterns of a single character. See *one constant; zero constant; character fill; spacefill; zerofill*.

fill character (1)A character (often an asterisk or a dash) used to fill a line or space on a document; for example, to prevent altering the value of a cheque. (2)A pad character; a character (bit pattern) used to fill a storage location.

filler One or more (logically meaningless) characters added to a data item so that the total number of characters will equal some specified number.

film See *microfilm*.

filter (Data editing) A bit pattern or sequence of bit patterns (typically, of characters) used to control the combining of two bit strings. It operates by modulo-2 arithmetic and causes a character bit pattern to be moved from one string to the other only where 1-bits occur in the filter. In the following example, a single 1-bit is used to represent a 'character' of 1-bits in the filter:

Group A	0£00.000
Filter	01001001
Group B	00620154
New group, A + B	0£62.150

See *mask; modulo-2*.

filter (Electronics) A circuit containing resistive and capacitive elements that are balanced (tuned) to cause some frequencies to be attenuated more than others and thus to prevent certain input frequencies from appearing in the output. A **low-pass filter** is one that passes all frequencies below some specified frequency and a **high-pass filter** is one that passes frequencies

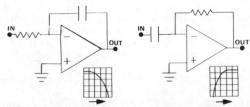

above some specified frequency. A **bandpass filter** combines a high-pass and a low-pass filter and, thus, can pass only those frequencies that are between the two. For example, a high-pass filter with a 'cutoff frequency' of 7 kHz. and a low-pass filter with a cutoff frequency of 8 kHz. will pass only those frequencies between 7 and 8 kHz. and thus constitutes a 1 kHz. bandpass filter. The figure on the left is a basic low-pass filter, the higher the frequency the more of the output passes through the capacitor as feedback and the less the gain. In the basic high-pass filter on the right, the higher the frequency the greater the amount of input signal that passes to the amplifier and the higher the output. See *band; frequency division* *multiplexing; operational amplifier.*

FINUFO *First-In-Not-Used-First-Out.* A discard algorithm; when space is required for a new page/segment, the one that has been in primary storage the longest time (or greatest number of instructions) without being used is the first (next) to be rolled out or overwritten. See *FIFO; discard algorithm.*

firmware A term applied to one or more sequences of instructions in read-only memory; for example to microcode contained in a control unit or to sequences of instructions that control peripheral transfers in a peripheral controller. The terms 'firmware' and 'microcode' or 'microcoded instructions' are often used interchangeably. See *hardware; software; microcode; read-only memory.*

firmware-driven Controlled by a program in read-only memory.

first fit See *allocation algorithm.*

first-generation computer A computer of the 1950's characterised by the use of vacuum tubes (valves) in arithmetic/logic and data transfer circuits.

first-in-first-out See *FIFO.*

first-in-not-used-first-out See *FINUFO.*

first-level address An absolute address or an effective address.

first-level memory First-level storage.

first-level storage Main storage. (The term may also be used to include cache or slave storage.)

first-remove A term applied to a routine or subroutine that is called from the main sequence and exits to the main sequence. One that is called by and exits to a called routine would be termed 'second-remove'. See *nesting.*

first variable A logic operation with an output that is 'true' if the first of two inputs is 'true' and 'false' if it is 'false'. See *logic.*

five-bit byte A quintet.

five-level code A code (Baudot; IA-2) in which each character is represented by a bit pattern consisting of five bits (plus, possibly, start-stop bits).

fixed and exchangeable disc storage (FEDS) A term applied to a magnetic disc unit in which some discs are fixed and others are operator-exchangeable. See *magnetic disc unit.*

fixed-cycle operation An operation that is performed in a fixed sequence of timed steps.

fixed disc A magnetic disc that is not operator-demountable from its drive. See *magnetic disc unit; exchangeable disc.*

fixed-disc storage (FDS) (1) Storage on fixed (non exchangeable) magnetic discs. (2) A magnetic disc unit in which all discs are 'fixed'. See *exchangeable disc storage; fixed and exchangeable disc storage.*

fixed-form Also *fixed-format.* (1) A term applied to a programming language in which each valid statement must conform to a pattern or to one of several patterns specified. (2) A term applied to an instruction in a fixed-form language in which each element (operator; modifier; operands) must be in a particular field. See *free-form.*

fixed-head disc storage (FHDS) A fixed-disc magnetic disc unit in which each recordable track has its own non-movable head.

fixed-length record A record that is of the same length as the other records with which it is stored and processed; a record with a length established by the system rather than by the data content.

fixed-length segment See *segment.*

fixed partitioning Partitioning in which the main storage space allocated to a task is not changed during its execution.

fixed-point A term indicating that numeric values are either integers or, if mixed numbers, the position of the radix point is preset (say, by a PICTURE clause) or inherent in the system (as in floating point). Unless otherwise indicated, the term indicates that numeric values are integers; the radix point is immediately to the right of the least significant digit.

fixed-point binary Synchronised binary integers as a computational format.

fixed-radix numeration See *numeration system.*

fixed storage (1) The storage of a fixed-storage device. (2) A term that has been used synonymously with 'read-only memory'.

fixed-storage device A device (fixed-disc; magnetic drum) in which the data medium is not changeable as a normal operating procedure. See *demountable device.*

fixed-word A term applied to a computer or other intelligent device in which the word is of a single, fixed length as established by the hardware design. See *variable-word.*

flag (1) An indicator that shows the existence of a certain condition when 'set' and the absence of the condition when 'clear'; for example, a bit position in which a 1-bit is placed in event of a size error or a character in a compiler print out that indicates 'unknown address'. See *semaphore; switch.* (2) In SDLC; a standard bit pattern (01111110) that begins and ends each frame; it is used for synchronisation and identifies a frame to receiving hardware. See *frame.* (3) A marker (note; red sticker) attached to a source document, card deck, volume, etc. to indicate some special condition. **(4)** A bit or bit pattern in a header of a storage location or unit of data that indicates some special condition (read-only; defective track). **(5)** To mark an item to indicate an unusual condition.

flag event An event that causes the setting of a flag (def. 1). See *event*.

flash (1) A high-intensity light of short duration as used in photography and 'form flash'. **(2)** To blink.

flat cable Ribbon cable.

flat file A relation; a two-dimensional array.

flat screen display A display (for computer output) that is relatively thin in relation to width and height. The term is applied to such devices as gas plasma panels, liquid crystal displays, and light-emitting diodes.

flatbed plotter A computer graphics output device in which a pen or stylus movable in two dimensions places designs on paper attached to a flat surface. See *drum plotter*.

flexible disc Also *floppy disc; diskette.* A flexible, plastic magnetic disc commonly used as inexpensive backing storage in computer systems and to hold text in word processors and typesetters. The disc most commonly used is 7.8 inches in diameter and is contained in an 8-inch by 8-inch plastic envelope that remains in place during reading and writing. The envelope has a radial slot to permit the read/write head to contact the disc, a centre hole to accomodate the drive hub, an index hole, and a write-inhibit slot that can be covered with tape when writing is required. In loading, the disc and envelope are inserted in a slot in the drive unit; closing the door causes a self-centering hub to engage the centre hole of the disc to drive the disc. A head-loading solenoid and a foam pad press the disc into contact with the read/write head during reading and writing. Indexing for data location is accomplished by photoelectrically detecting an index hole in the disc as it passes the index hole in the envelope. In standard drives, there are 77 tracks on the one surface of the disc that is recordable; usually 74 are available for data. Seek is by a stepping motor system that moves the read/write head one track with each actuation. The total capacity with the usual double-frequency recording (2FM) is about 246K bytes in the usual 'IBM 3740 compatible' format and 400K bytes unformatted (with no track space taken by headers). Access times are about 260 milliseconds average and transfer rates are about 30K bytes per second. Some systems use double-density recording (MFM) to provide an unformatted capacity of about 800K bytes. A flexible disc that is recordable on both sides is a **double-sided flexible disc** (also **flippy disc**); unformatted capacities are as high as 2M bits. A smaller version in a 5¼ inch square envelope is a **mini-flexible disc** (also **mini-floppy**); single-sided versions have a capacity up to about 250K bytes and double-sided to about 500K bytes.

flicker In a display on a VDU; a repetitive, visible change in brightness caused by a refresh cycle that is so long that the screen phosphors lose their charge between successive passes of the electron beam.

flip-flop Also *bistable circuit; trigger circuit.* A circuit with two stable output conditions that can be changed (inverted) by an input pulse or by an input pulse in combination with a static input. The basic type is the **R-S flip-flop** with logic representation

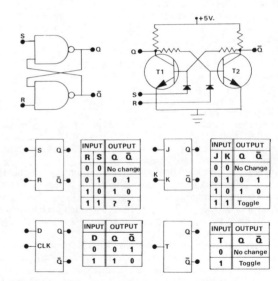

as shown in the upper left figure and a circuit as shown to the right. If input 'S' is pulsed high, transistor T1 turns on, its collector and output 'Q' go low and this low is applied to the gate of T2, turning it off and causing the collector and output '$\bar{Q}$' to go high. This condition of the outputs will be maintained until input 'R' is pulsed high causing T2 to turn on and reversing the output levels. If 'R' and 'S' are pulsed high simultaneously, the resultant outputs are indeterminate. (The end stable condition is determined by minor and residual circuit values.) The R-S flip-flop is the basic storage cell of bipolar semiconductor memory. A **J-K flip-flop** is the same as an R-S except additional circuit elements have been incorporated to eliminate the indeterminate condition when both inputs are pulsed high; when this occurs, the outputs invert. With a **D flip-flop**, whatever input is on D is output on Q and the inverse is output on $\bar{Q}$ whenever the clock signal goes high. With a **T flip-flop**, the outputs invert (toggle) each time T changes from low to high. Either an R-S or a J-K flip-flop can incoproprate an AND gate to permit clocked control; a transition can occur only when the clock signal goes high. All of the flip-flops described are available with PRESET (SET) and/or CLEAR (RESET). A low on PRESET sets Q to 1 and $\bar{Q}$ to 0 while low on CLEAR sets Q to 0 and $\bar{Q}$ to 1. (Some MOS flip-flops preset and clear with a high signal.)

float Of a circuit; to be at an indeterminate voltage with supply, if any, through high-impedance paths.

floating point A computational format used for performing arithmetic operations on numbers that have many digit positions. A number to be represented in the system is 'divided' into two parts, the first of which is the **fractional part** (also **mantissa**) consisting of the digits of the number (other than any leading or trailing zeros) and the second of which is the **exponent** that indicates the position of the radix point. The exponent is the power to which the **base** is to be raised. The 'base' is understood and not expressed numerically; it is usually either 10 (decimal) or 16 (hexadecimal). In decimal floating point, it is customary to express the fractional part as a number with a single integer; for example, 567.3 would be expressed as 5.673 02 in which the '02' is the exponent; the representation is equivalent to 5.673×10^2. (In many systems, the inputs are hexadecimal or octal and the fractional part has no integers and the base may be 16 instead of 10.) Bit 1 of the most significant byte is the 'sign bit'; '0' for positive and '1' for negative. The remaining bit positions of the byte hold the **characteristic** which is the representation of the exponent. Because floating point is used to hold very small values as well as very large ones, a method is required to distinguish between them and the method commonly used is **excess-64 notation**. Since the remainder of the byte has seven bit positions, it can hold a maximum value of 127 in decimal. This is divided by subtracting 64 to make the 'neutral' point of the characteristic 63. Large values are higher and small values are lower so 73 sets an exponent of +10 and 0 sets an exponent of —64. The following are the steps in representing 5673×10^{25} in decimal floating point in four bytes:

1. Rationalise the exponent: $\qquad 5673 \times 10^{25} = 5.673 \times 10^{28}$
2. Put the sign bit '0' in the first bit position of the high-order byte: $\qquad$ 00000000 00000000 00000000 00000000
3. Subtract the exponent from 64: $\qquad 64 - 28 = 36$
4. Add the exponent to 63 and place the total (99) in the remain-bit positions: $\qquad$ 01100011 00000000 00000000 00000000
5. Place the fractional part 5673 in the remaining three bytes: $\qquad$ 01100011 00000000 00010110 00101001

When a single computer word is used to hold floating point values (as above), it is termed **single precision floating point** or, sometimes, **short-form floating point**. If greater accuracy is required, one or more additional words are used and this is termed **multiple-precision floating point** or, sometimes, **long-form floating point**. The use of two words for **double-precision floating point** is common and computers with 16-bit words may use three or four words. Floating point in its bit-pattern representation in computer storage is termed **internal floating point** while a representation in some other form (say, in source coding) is **external floating point**. See *computational format*.

floppy disc A flexible disc.

flow (1) The movement of items between two points as in a stream or sequence. **(2)** A term applied to the path followed in performing a multi-part operation.

flow analysis (1) A compilation technique applied to determine the interdependent relationships of the elements of a program. **(2)** The consideration of instructions with respect to their sequence and timing of execution.

flowchart An aid to program design and a form of program documentation that consists of interconnected **flowcharting symbols**, each of which has a distinctive and accepted shape to indicate a type of functional unit, data medium, or operation. A written identification of each symbol (also 'box') is usually placed inside to show the function in the program. A **system**

flowchart makes use of many of the same symbols as program flowcharts and provides information on the structure and/or work flow in a system (say, a computer installation or a process control system). A **clerical flowchart** is used to show a method of handling paperwork, say, in an accounting department. Most computer manufacturers provide documents giving instructions for constructing programming flowcharts. The following are the relevant standards: ANSI X3.5; BS 4058; ISO 1028 and 2636. The following is the 'flowchart solution' to the example used in the *decision table* entry. See *decision table; program; programming language.*

flowchart symbol A mnemonic, graphic representation of an operation, device, interconnection, or relationship as used in constructing a flowchart.

flowcharter A utility available in some systems to construct flow diagrams from sequences of source code.

flowline A line in a flow diagram indicating a flow and its direction; for example, a line joining two flowcharting symbols in a flowchart.

fluid logic Fluidics.

fluidics The techniques or devices involved in performing sensing, control, and logic operations by the movement of fluids.

flux The invisible force that surrounds a magnet. Its presence is indicated by the deflection of a compass needle, by the attraction of iron, or by the generation of an electric current in a wire that is moved through it. It provides the operative force for core and magnetisable surface storage. See *magnet.*

flux transition In magnetisable surface recording; a place on a track where the orientation of particles reverses; a place where the direction of current in the write (or read/write) head was reversed during writing and where a data-significant signal is induced in the coil of the read (or read/write) head during reading. See *head; magnet; flux; data bit.*

fly By a read/write head in a rigid-disc magnetic disc system; to maintain an air-cushioned separation from the magnetisable surface that is correct for reading or writing. A representative figure for flying height is 50 microinches (about one-sixtieth the diameter of a human hair). The height is determined by the

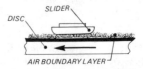

loading (the force exerted to push the head toward the disc), the shape of the air bearing surface (the part of the slider nearest the disc surface), the location and size of bleed holes (through which cushioning air escapes), the roughness of the disc surface, and the speed of disc rotation. See *head; land; load (Read/write head).*

fly-back In a scanning system (optical character recognition; cathode ray tube); the movement of the scanning element from the end of one scanned line to the beginning of the next. See *retrace time; scanner.*

flying head A read/write head that operates in proximity to (but not in contact with) a recording surface. See *head; fly.*

flying height See *fly.*

flying speed The minimum spindle rotating speed of a magnetic disc at which loading can take place; the speed at which the disc surface is moving fast enough to create an air cushion that will support the read/write head(s). Speeds vary from about 400

R.P.M. in lightly loaded Winchester-type systems to about 1800 R.P.M. in conventional rigid disc systems. See *fly; head loading zone; load.*

flying spot A point of light or the end of an electron beam that is movable at high speed back and forth across a field.

flying spot scan A scan, typically in a cathode ray tube or in a character recognition device, in which a flying spot places patterns on a field or detects patterns on the field.

flying spot scanner An optical character recognition device in which characters are identified by patterns of reflected or transmitted light from a flying spot.

FM (1)*Frequency Modulation.* (2)*Frequency Method.* (3)*Facilities Management.*

FNP *Front-end Network Processor.*

folding The process of dividing a number (or non-numeric bit pattern treated as a number) at its midpoint and adding the two parts. It is a method sometimes used as a step in producing storage addresses from record keys in a hashed random file. See *hashed random; hashing algorithm.*

folding ratio A term sometimes used with respect to a virtual storage system to indicate the size of the virtual storage in relation to the real storage.

font (1)Also *character set.* In a shaped-character printer; a set consisting of one of each of the type elements that can produce characters. A typewriter, thus, has a single font and a drum printer with 132 printing positions has 132 fonts. (2)The character-forming elements of a printer considered with respect to type size and style; ('an italic font'; 'a lower case font'; 'a 12-point Univers font').

font change The process of changing the size or style of characters that are printed or displayed.

font change character See *FC.*

forbidden combination A combination of bits or characters that cannot be used except in some special context (usually related to system operation); a combination that, if used incorrectly, may result in a malfunction or a misinterpretation of data. See *illegal; reserved word.*

forbidden combination code An error-detection code in which each valid character must conform to a particular pattern; any bit combination that does not conform to the pattern is interpreted as an error. Though the term can be applied to a parity system, it usually refers to an 'M-out-of-N code' or a similar code.

forceload The process of loading system software (say, from magnetic tape) under manual control rather than under program or firmware control. It is the method used with most microcomputers and many minicomputers. See *initial program load; teleload.*

foreground (1)A term applied to a job or program in a multiprogramming system that takes priority over other jobs or programs. (2)In some systems; that part of main storage allocated to foreground jobs. See *background; priority.*

foreground job A job that receives processing resources ahead of other jobs. See *background job.*

foreground processing In a multiprogramming system; the processing of higher priority jobs accomplished by reallocating resources from lower priority jobs as necessary. See *background.*

foreground program A program that, when active, is always given a high priority for processing.

foreground region Also *foreground.* A partition of main storage allocated to foreground jobs.

foreign Alien.

fork instruction An instruction that causes an operation (usually a data transfer) to be conducted in parallel with the execution of instructions. See *autonomous; channel activation command.*

form (1)A piece of paper printed to indicate the items to be placed on it and where they are to be placed; for example, a purchase order, an invoice, or a stock record card. (2)An image of such a form as projected and recorded with the data that it contains. See *form flash.* (3)On a printer; an arrangement in which fields are to be printed for a particular job as controlled by horizontal and vertical tabulation. See *paper tape loop; form feed; electronic format control.*

form feed (1)Also *form throw.* In a printer; a vertical movement of paper made to bring the first line of a form into printing position. See *FF.* (2)A mechanism or facility to accomplish 'form feed' (def. 1).

form feed character See *FF.*

form flash Also *form overlay.* The imposition of a form (say, a company's standard invoice) with computer output data onto paper (page printer) or film (computer output microfilm). The system, typically, incorporates a form on film, a stroboscopic light source, and a lens and mirror arrangement to project the form onto the data-recording medium. In the figure, the camera part of a recorder with lens A focuses through glass B to register data displayed on the screen of the cathode ray tube onto film C. The form to be superimposed with the data is on

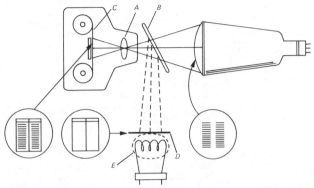

film D and when light E is flashed it is registered on the film as it is reflected from glass B. See *COM; page printer*.

form overlay Form flash.
form throw Form feed.
formal logic The study of the structure and form of valid argument without regard to the truth or falsity of the terms of the argument. See *logic*.
formal parameter Also *dummy argument*. A value entered in a program to establish the type, size, or structure of an item of data that will be inserted during compilation or at run time.
format (1)The physical organisation (spatial relationship of elements; placement on a field) of printed, displayed, or stored data. (2)To place data in a particular physical arrangement. (3)With representation by particular elements; ('binary format'; 'character format'). (4)With respect to a magnetic disc; to write access-related information to it. See *initialisation*.
format effector Also *layout character*. A control character that affects the placement of printed or displayed data; examples include 'space', 'tabulate', and 'newline'. See *code*.
format loop Also *paper tape loop*. A loop of paper tape (sometimes plastic tape) in which holes are punched to control the paper throw of a printer. A sequence of hole patterns is punched to meet the formatting requirements of a particular job and the loop is placed in a tape reader of a printer when the job is run. See *electronic format control; vertical format unit*.
formatter Also *disc formatter*. A device or section of a device (say, of a peripheral controller) used to initialise magnetic discs and, often, to perform transfer-related functions. See *initialisation; disc controller*.
formatting (1)The process of placing data in some format. (2) That part of disc initialisation in which track, head, and (possibly) sector identifiers are written. See *home address; certification; initialisation*.
formed character A shaped character.
FORTRAN *FORmula TRANslation*. A high-level programming language designed for scientific and mathematical applications.
fortuitous A term applied to random and unpredictable events; for example, 'fortuitous noise' on a telephone line.
forward channel A message channel; a communications channel used to carry user data in an asymmetric duplex system. See *channel; backward channel; asymmetric duplex*.
forward compatible Upward compatible.
forward error correction A recovery procedure in which receiving hardware is able to analyse bit patterns and correct small errors without retransmission of the block containing the error. See *error; Hamming code; error correction code*.
four-bit byte A quartet.
four-wire circuit Also *circuit*. A communications (telephone) circuit consisting of four wires (or the equivalent obtained, say, by frequency division multiplexing). Such a circuit can be used for simultaneous transmission of messages in both directions at full line speed. See *duplex; two-wire circuit; asymmetric duplex*.
FPLA *Field Programmable Logic Array*.
fractional part (1)In a radix numeration system; that part of a number to the right of the radix point; for example, the '136' in '21.136'. (2)A mantissa. See *floating point*.
fragmentation A term applied to the condition in which there is considerable wasted space in main storage with little if any of it being allocatable to meet processing needs. In an unpaged virtual storage system, **external fragmentation** results from unallocatably small spaces wasted between segments. In a paged system, **internal fragmentation** results from wasted space in unfilled pages. The condition in which space is wasted (for processing purposes) by allocating a high percentage of main storage to tables, catalogues, and the like is termed **table**

fragmentation. See *compaction; virtual storage allocation.*

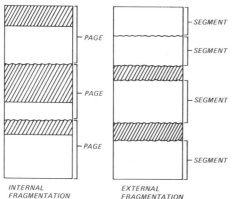

INTERNAL FRAGMENTATION   EXTERNAL FRAGMENTATION

frame (1)Also *row*. A group of bit positions extending across magnetic tape or paper tape; the bit positions that can contain one character. (2)Also *envelope*. A pair of delimiters used for identifying the data between them; for example, a start bit and a stop bit in asynchronous communications. (3) In microfilm; an area containing the image produced by a single exposure. (4) In SDLC, HDLC, and packet switching; the unit of data transfer beginning and ending with a flag. (5)A stack frame.

frame check character (FCC) A frame check sequence.

frame check sequence (FCS) A cyclic check character in a system (SDLC; HDLC; packet switching) in which the unit of data transfer is the 'frame'. See *cyclic check character.*

frame pointer A bottom-of-stack pointer; the address of the lowest register of a stack. See *stack; stack frame.*

frame rate Refresh rate.

framing The process of using a beginning and ending delimiter to identify data for handling or interpretation or to distinguish one data item from others.

framing bits Start-stop bits.

free-form language A programming language in which the elements of statements will be accepted by the compiler regardless of the order in which they appear in source code; the most common example is PL/1. See *language; fixed-format language.*

free list A table kept by an operating system to identify resources (main storage; backing storage; peripherals) that are available for allocation to executing programs.

free page reserve (1)In a virtual storage system; all the page slots available for allocation in primary storage. (2)Also *free list*. In a virtual storage system; a table of allocatable page slots as kept by an operating system. See *virtual storage transfers; allocatable space.*

free routing In a data communications system (say, a packet switching network); the use of any of a number of available circuits to send messages between stations.

free space Allocatable space.

free-standing (1)Of a functional unit; contained in its own cabinet; not enclosed with other elements of a system. (2)Also *stand alone*. Of a computer; capable of being used independently to perform general processing work. (3)Also *intelligent*. Of a terminal; containing its own video buffer and line interfacing elements. (4)Of software; capable of being used independently; not exclusive to a particular program.

frequency (1)Of wave transmissions (alternating current; sound); the number of times per second that a sequence of conditions (a cycle) is repeated. The measurement unit is the 'Hertz' (Hz.). See *wave; cycle; alternating current.* (2)A term used to indicate how often an event occurs; ('a high frequency of errors'; 'a frequency of about one per hour').

frequency band See *band.*

frequency division Also *frequency slicing*. The process of dividing a channel into frequency bands; the process of creating several or many narrow bands from one wider band. See *band; multiplexing.*

frequency-division multiplexing The operation (by means of filters) of dividing a wideband communications channel into narrow bands and using each of them to carry speech or data. In a telephone system, the wideband channel is usually 48 kHz. wide and is divided into twelve voice-grade channels. A voice-grade channel (typically, 3 kHz. wide) may be further divided into subvoice-grade channels (say, 250 Hz. wide) by frequency-division multiplexing. See *band; multiplexing; time-division multiplexing.*

frequency method (FM) See *frequency modulation (Data recording.*

frequency modulation (Communications) (FM) In a system using a carrier wave; the method of modulation in which the frequency of the carrier wave is changed in an analogue manner to transmit speech or data. See *modulation; frequency-shift keying.*

frequency modulation (Data recording) (FM) Also *frequency method; double-frequency recording.* A method of magnetisable surface recording in which the direction of current in the coil of the read/write head (and, hence, the direction of orientation of surface particles) is changed at intervals established by a clock sequence. The direction is also changed at the midpoint of an interval to write a 1-bit and if it is left unchanged at the midpoint a 0-bit is written. The method

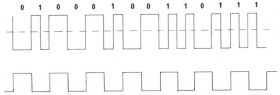

is self-clocking as the read circuitry interprets the evenly spaced changes as reference points to determine whether or not a change has also occurred between them. (Clock pulses are shown in the figure only for illustration purposes.) See *magnetisable surface recording; modified frequency modulation; modified modified frequency modulation.*

frequency-shift keying (FSK) A method of data transmission in which a carrier wave is modulated at only a limited number of frequencies, each of which represents a bit or an established pair or group of bits (say, a dibit). Typically, only two frequencies are used, one of which represents a 1-bit and the other a 0-bit. It is used for start-stop transmission at up to 150 bps. on narrowband channels and 1800 bps. on voice-grade channels. See *frequency modulation; start-stop transmission.*

frequency slicing Frequency division.

frequency zone In some magnetic disc systems; a group of adjacent tracks all of which are divided into the same number of blocks, the number of blocks being different than the number in other frequency zones. See *magnetic disc unit.*

friction feed A paper feed (as in an ordinary typewriter) that does not use sprockets or tractors to move the paper.

front-end A term applied to the user or communications line part of a computer or computer system; the external interface. By contrast, the term **back end** is applied to the interface between a computer and other processing facilities of an installation; for example, to peripheral transfer devices.

front-end network processor (FNP) A front-end processor that handles most or all of the functions of interfacing between a mainframe computer and a data network. See *front-end processor; back-end processor.*

front-end processor (FEP) An intelligent device (often a minicomputer) used to handle communications interfacing functions for another computer. Typical functions include polling, multiplexing, error detection and resolution, code conversion, buffering, editing and formatting of messages, and queue management. A number of different terms are used for the device in different systems. See *line adapter; communications controller; communications interface adapter; communications link controller; interface computer.*

front-strike See *impact printer.*

FRPI (f.r.p.i.; frpi.) *Flux Reversals Per Inch.*

FRPS (f.r.p.s.; frps.) *Flux Reversals Per Second.*

FRU *Field-Replaceable Unit.*

FS (1)*Field Separator.* A character that may be used as a delimiter for fields or other units of data in storage, transfer, or transmission. **(2)***File Separator.* A character that may be used as a delimiter for files or other units of data in storage, transfer, or transmission.

FSK *Frequency-Shift Keying.*

full adder See *adder.*

full-duplex See *duplex.*

full-wave rectifier See *rectifier.*

full word A complete computer word, as contrasted to a 'half-word' or 'double word'.

fully inverted file See *inverted file.*

fully perforated tape Paper tape in which chads are removed in the punching operation. See *chadless tape.*

fully qualified name A named member in a hierarchial data structure that contains (or consists of) the identification of the structure and its position in it; a member that is identified by the root and all intervening owners. See *tree structure.*

function (1) That which is done or performed; ('a computer function'; 'a read function'; 'a data preparation function'). **(2)** Also *expression.* A statement of a logical or mathematical relationship. See *logical function; switching function; mathematical function.* **(3)**A dependent variable or the value of a dependent variable. In the expression (also 'function' def. 2), 'a = 2b + c', the 'a' (the 'dependent variable') is a 'function' of the independent variables 'b' and 'c'. **(4)**Also *intrinsic procedure*. A sequence of instructions provided to accomplish a particular operation and included in the facilities of a programming language. It produces a single result for any input argument or set of arguments and is invoked by naming the procedure and supplying the argument(s). The most common are mathematical procedures such as those that provide trigonometric values, logarithms, or that perform exponentiation or derive roots. **(5)**A processing operation for which a computer has hardware or software facilities. **(6)**In some systems; an operator or operator field in an instruction. See *mode; offset*. **(7)**In data communications; a term applied to a device action; for example, to a carriage return or figures shift.

function character (1)A control character. **(2)**A control character that controls a mechanical operation of a receiving device in a communications system; for example, one that causes a carriage return or tabulation.

function code An operation code; a part of an instruction that specifies what is to be done.

function flowchart Also *logic flowchart*. A flowchart used to represent the major logical segments of a program and their interrelationships. See *flowchart; system flowchart*.

function key A key (on a console or terminal keyboard) that controls an operation affecting the format or transfer of data but not the content of the data; for example, a tabulator key, a shift key, a backspace key, or a carriage return key. In a computer graphics system, the term also includes keys that are used to control the display.

function operator An operator specifying an action by the control unit without involving the arithmetic logic unit except, possibly, in a transfer. See *operator*.

function processor In some mixed-mode, virtual storage computer systems; a subset of computer resources allocated to a particular processing stream; for example, 'a batch function processor' or a 'transaction function processor'.

function table A table that equates two or more related values; for example, angles and their trigonometric functions or numbers and their logarithms.

functional design That part of system design that specifies the functions of the components and their operating relationships.

functional test A test (for maintenance purposes) that duplicates or simulates an actual operation of a functional unit.

functional unit A term used to make a non-specific reference to a (free-standing) item of hardware in a computer system. A device that performs some 'function' in the operation of the system. (The term may be applied to the computer as well as to such items as peripheral controllers, modems, printers, and storage devices.)

fundamental A primary wave as produced by an oscillator; not a harmonic.

fuse (1)A protective, current-limiting device that contains an alloy conductor that melts when an excessive current flows through it and thus opens a circuit. **(2)**To place such a device in a (power supply) circuit. **(3)**To open a conductor path in a circuit by intentionally applying an excessive current. **(4)**To bond together by partially melting; ('a layer of fused silicon dioxide').

fuse PROM See *PROM*.

G

G Giga-.

gain The amount by which the output power or signal strength of an electronic circuit or device (repeater; amplifier) exceeds the input power or signal strength. See *decibel; attenuation*.

galactic Large and accessible from many places and by many applications; ('a galactic data base').

gang punch (1) To punch identical hole patterns in two or more punched cards. **(2)**A device that does this.

gap (1) Also *air gap*. An opening in the iron structure of a magnet where magnetic flux passes through air or some other medium. It is by means of the 'gap' in a read/write head that flux produced by the coil changes the orientation of particles in the recording surface during writing and registers such changes during reading. See *magnet; coil; electromagnet; head*. **(2)**An area of a magnetisable surface recording medium (disc; tape) that is left unrecorded for identification or access purposes; a space between successive units of data; for example, an 'interblock gap' or a 'file gap'.

gap length In a read/write head; the dimension of the gap as measured along a recorded track; it is a major factor in determining the practical recording density.

gap width In a read/write head; the dimension of the gap as measured across a recorded track; it is a major factor in determining the practical track density in magnetic disc recording.

garbage collection In a virtual storage system; the process of identifying unused pages/segments in primary storage and deleting them. See *virtual storage transfers; discard policy*.

gas plasma panel Also *gas panel; plasma panel*. A flat screen display consisting of a honeycomb matrix of cells filled with neon gas to form tiny neon lights. Transparent metal strips are deposited on the front and rear surfaces in a grid arrangement such that applying a voltage to one front strip and one back strip ionizes the gas in the cell at their intersection. Operation is usually on direct current with two voltages, a high 'strike voltage' that places selected cells in the glowing state and a lower 'maintain voltage' that will keep cells in this state but will not cause other cells to enter it. The device, thus, requires no refresh memory.

GAT *Graphics Art Terminal.*

gate (1) The control junction of a transistor or thyristor. **(2)** The electrical connection to the control junction of a transistor or thyristor. **(3)** A basic logic circuit; ('a NAND gate'). **(4)** To control by means of a 'gate'; ('gate characters into a buffer').

gateway (1) An interface between (packet switching) networks; a node that is an element of two networks. **(2)** A viewdata facility that permits direct user access to the computer of an information provider. See *viewdata*.

gauss A unit for measuring the intensity of a magnetic field.

gaussian noise White noise.

GCR *Group Code Recording.*

GE *Greater than or Equal to.* See *relational operator*.

general peripheral controller (GPC) A term sometimes applied to a peripheral controller that can handle transfers to and from devices of different characteristics; for example, printers and magnetic tape units.

general-purpose computer A computer that is designed to meet a variety of data processing requirements as arising in business, education, and government. Typically, it has an operating system capable of organising work and handling routine tasks, it is programmable in COBOL and other high-level languages, and it has the facilities for handling multiprogramming and, usually, transaction processing. The term is used to differentiate such a computer from a process-control computer, a scientific computer, a small business system, or a minicomputer or microcomputer. (Minicomputers of appropriate architecture are, increasingly, being considered as 'general-purpose'.) See *minicomputer; microcomputer; special-purpose computer; scientific computer; visible record computer; small business system.*

general-purpose language A programming language that can be used for a variety of purposes; particularly one (such as PL/1) that can be used in scientific as well as commercial applications. See *language*.

general-purpose register A control-unit register that is available to meet any of a variety of requirements; for example, to act as an index register, as an accumulator, or to hold return addresses. See *register*.

general-purpose terminal (GPT) A terminal that is intended to be used for different purposes; for example, for enquiries, for direct data entry, and for on-line program development.

general register (1) A general-purpose register. (2) An accumulator; a register with an associated full adder.

generalised program A program with selectively executable sequences that can be used to perform a variety of related tasks (say, sorts and merges) depending upon its input parameters.

generate (1) To implement an operating system or other major software. See *system generation*. **(2)** To produce a program with a 'generator'. **(3)** To produce a code string from a macro.

generating polynomial See *polynomial code*.

generating program A generator.

generation (1) The relation of a file in a hierarchy of files, each of which is an updated version (new generation) of the previous one. This may be indicated by a **generation number** in a continuous sequence from the creation file, or by such terms as 'grandfather', 'father', and 'son' with 'son' being the current generation. **(2)** A term sometimes used to indicate the technological state of development of computers. A 'first generation' computer (1950's) used valves/tubes for switching, arithmetic, and logic operations and any of a variety of storage methods including relays, electrostatic, delay line, magnetic drum and, towards the end of the generation, magnetic core. The 'second generation' computers (1960's) used discrete (separately wired) transistors and diodes for data manipulation and magnetic core main storage. The 'third generation' (the current one) uses semiconductors in integrated circuits for both data manipulation functions and main storage. (Some writers have used the term 'fourth generation' with respect to computers with virtual storage and/or dispersed intelligence.) **(3)** In microfilm and other graphic operations where copies are made; an indication of the relation of a copy to the original (and, thus, of sharpness or clarity); a copy from the original is termed 'first generation' and one from a copy is 'second generation'. **(4)**The process of creating a program or expanding a macro. See *generator*. **(5)**System generation.

generation number See *generation*.

generator (1)A program used to produce other programs of some particular type. It contains sections of coding (sometimes termed **skeletons**) and means for linking them and modifying them to meet the requirements of a particular application and computer system. Examples include a 'compiler generator', a 'sort program generator', and a 'report program generator'. **(2)** A program or other coding sequence that produces a result of specified type and format; ('a macro generator'; 'a microcode generator'). **(3)**A device that produces signals or electric power; ('a time base generator'; 'a direct current generator').

generic access An access to locate all data items of a particular type.

get To obtain a record from an input file.

ghost A faint, second image of a printed character caused by 'bounce' of the type elements or movement of the paper during printing.

giga- (G) A combining form indicating one billion (10^9).

gigahertz (GHz.) A frequency of one billion cycles per second.

GIGO *Garbage In, Garbage Out.* A term sometimes used to emphasise the fact that a computer can only produce good results from good (accurate; validated) inputs.

glass teletype An inexpensive VDU terminal designed to perform the functions of a Teletype or teletypewriter.

glide A synonym for 'fly'. See *fly*.

global (1) Of an instruction sequence (a subprogram) or a variable; defined in one section of a program and referenced in one or more other sections. **(2)**Available to several or many (but, probably, not all) application programs; ('a global segment'; 'a global variable'; 'a global file'). See *public; local; common*. **(3)**Applied with respect to the total rather than to a part; ('a global discard policy').

global discard policy In a virtual storage system; a discard policy applied to primary storage considered as a common pool for all active programs. See *discard policy; local discard policy*.

global extent An extent (sequence of magnetic disc tracks) that is available for use by several (or all) active programs.

global filestore A filestore available to all applications or to meet all (non virtual storage) backing storage requirements of a computer system. See *filestore*.

global memory In a multiprocessor system; memory that can be accessed by all processors.

global segment A segment that is shareable by two or more (but not by all) concurrent processes in a virtual storage system. See *segment; local; public*.

global sequence A subprogram; a sequence of instructions defined in one section of a program and used in others.

global variable A variable defined in one section of a program and used in one or more other sections.

glytch In magnetisable surface recording; a place where reading a track is impaired by a magnetisation pattern that 'crosses over' from an adjacent track. See *track trimming*.

go-ahead polling Hub go-ahead polling. See *polling*.

go-ahead tone An answer tone; a tone sent to an originating modem to indicate that data can be connected.

go channel See *channel*.

GOC *Graphic Options Controller.*

golfball Also *type element*. In some typewriters and printers; a type font in the form of a small (golfball-like) sphere with characters embossed on it. In operation, it is tilted and rotated to bring a keyboard-selected character to the printing position and then impacted against ribbon and paper to print the character.

golfball typewriter A typewriter with a type font in the form of a 'golfball'. Unless otherwise indicated, it is understood to be an IBM Selectric.

GPC *General Peripheral Controller.*

GPL *General-Purpose Loader.*

GPT *General-Purpose Terminal.*

graceful degradation The condition in which a system or device continues to be able to provide a useful service after one or more of its components have failed. Such a system or device usually contains **backup** elements; it is said to **fail soft**. See *fault; resilience*.

grade Of a circuit; a classification of speed or type of use; the ones usually recognised are 'broadband', 'voice', 'subvoice', and 'telegraph'.

grandfather A term sometimes applied to the second preceding update version (of a file). See *generation*.

graph A two-dimensional representation of numeric values consisting, typically, of one or more lines, bars, or curves superimposed on a grid. Examples include a number of bars with lengths indicating sales for each month of a year and a curve indicating the fuel consumption of a car at different speeds.

graph plotter A plotter usable for converting computer output to a graph. See *plotter*.

graphic (1)A meaningful, two-dimensional arrangement of elements (lines; dots) as printed, drawn, or displayed on a display device. Examples include a character, a symbol, a picture, and a diagram. (2)A term used to differentiate a visually recognisable character from a character in bit-pattern form (in data transmission or computer storage).

graphic arts terminal (GAT) A terminal with an output that is used for typesetting. The output is, typically, encoded alphanumeric characters and control characters on magnetic disc or paper tape. The terminal is used in conjunction with a photographic typesetter (which may be self-contained).

graphic character (1)Also *printable character*. A character with a form that is commonly used in printing and in displays as contrasted to a character identified by description or function (CR; TAB). (2)A character in the form in which it is printed or displayed rather than in its bit-pattern form.

graphic display program A program used to control the display or plotting of data.

graphic options controller (GOC) Add-on memory and control circuitry that provides an alphanumeric VDU with limited facilities of a graphics terminal.

graphics A term applied to the production, manipulation, or analysis of data as represented by two-dimensional images. See *computer graphics; micrographics*.

graphics plotter A plotter.

graphics terminal (GT) A terminal (VDU or plotter) that presents and/or receives data in two-dimensional form.

graphics VDU A visual display unit used for input and output in a computer graphics system; a VDU with the controls and circuitry to enable an operator to manipulate and change the display. See *light pen; display; computer graphics*.

grass See *background noise*.

graunch A term sometimes applied to a hardware failure. (It is often used as an informal synonym for 'head-disc interference'.)

gray code Reflected binary code.

greater than (GT) See *relational operator*.

greater than or equal to (GE) See *relational operator*.

grid Also *matrix*. Two sets of parallel elements (conductors; lines) that intersect at right angles. It is the basic structure of coordinate-addressable storage and of most graphs.

ground (1)Also *earth; protective ground*. In an A.C. distribution (mains) system; a connection of equipment or circuit elements to earth (often by a conductor attached to a water pipe). In a standard single-phase system, a 'neutral' and one of the current-carrying conductors connect to earth and the neutral is connected to the chassis or frame of any operated equipment. The purpose is to ensure that a fuse blows if the other current-carrying conductor contacts the chassis/frame, thus removing the risk of electric shock. (2)Also *signal ground; signal common*. A return path used by multiple circuits; for example, a fourth wire that is a conductor in 'common' for three circuits. A 'ground' by this definition is usually connected to a 'ground' (def. 1) but it consists of a separate wire or bus with provision for this connection to be broken.

group (1)A number of items present together or considered as a unit; ('a group of peripherals'; 'a storage group'; 'a frequency group'). (2)To place items in a 'group' (def. 1). (3)Also *channel group*. In a telephone system; a unit of broadband (coaxial cable trunk) transmission consisting of twelve frequency division multiplexed voice-grade channels occupying a 48 kHz. band. The 'basic' band occupies 60-108 kHz. Depending upon the system and distance of transmission, 48 kHz. bands may be further multiplexed in units of five to form a **supergroup** with the lowest (or only) supergroup occupying a band between 312 and 552 kHz. Supergroups may themselves be multiplexed to form a **hypergroup** (in the U.S. a **mastergroup**) consisting of from two to sixteen supergroups. The common hypergroup consists of ten supergroups and can carry up to 600 calls simultaneously.

group addressing In a data network; a method of addressing in which the data stations have receiving equipment that responds only to their own address (character group) and in which individual data stations are addressed by 'broadcasting' the address to all data stations.

group code recording (GCR) A method of magnetisable surface recording in which the data is divided into four-bit groups, each of which is represented as a five-bit group constructed to prevent the occurrence of more than two consecutive 0-bits. Quadbits and their GCR representations are as follows:

```
0000  11001         0110  10110         1100  11110
0001  11011         0111  10111         1101  01101
0010  10010         1000  11010         1110  01110
0011  10011         1001  01001         1111  01111
0100  11101         1010  01010
0101  10101         1011  01011
```

The purpose is to provide self-clocking and to give a relatively even density of flux reversals in order to reduce bit shift. It can also facilitate the use of on-the-fly error detection and correction. After the data is converted to GCR groups, the groups are encoded by NRZI. The method is 38% more efficient than phase encoding (PE) with respect to flux reversals per given

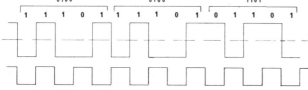

quantity of data. It is used mainly in half-inch magnetic tape systems to record at a density of 6250 characters per inch. Magnetic tape units that use GCR are considerably more complex and expensive than those that use PE or NRZI only.

group delay In a frequency division multiplexed group; the difference in transmission time between the slowest (high frequency) and fastest (low frequency) elements.

group field (1)In source coding; an identifier at one level that applies to data items at a lower level. (2)A field that contains two or more elementary fields. See *field*.

GS *Group Separator*. A character used to delimit two groups (or, possibly, other units) in a data transmission.

GT (1)*Greater Than*. (2)*Graphics Terminal*.

guard band (1)A band of unused frequencies (often, about 500 Hz. wide) used to separate adjacent speech or data bands in a frequency-division multiplexed system. It is a band of high attenuation created by filters to prevent an energy transfer between bands. See *band; frequency division multiplexing*. (2)On an initialised magnetic disc; a group of unused tracks that mark the inner or outer limits of the recordable surface. See *guard zone*.

guard disc An outer (top or bottom) disc of a disc pack; data can be written to its inner surface but its outer surface is left unused (because of the risk of damage during handling).

guard gap A guard zone.

guard zone In a track on magnetic disc; a length (say, of 80 bytes) that is left unrecorded (written with zeros) between two adjacent sectors. Its purpose is to ensure that data is never overwritten or unreadable because of inaccuracies in such things as the position of sector marks and the alignment of read/write heads. With respect to a particular sector, it is normally divided into a **preamble** (of, say, 60 bytes) at the beginning of the sector and a **postamble** (of, say, 20 bytes) at the end of the sector.

gulp A term that is sometimes applied to a group of several bytes. See *nibble*.

H

half adder See *adder*.
half-duplex (HDX) A term applied to a circuit, facility, or method of operating a communications system in which messages are sent in both directions but in only one direction at a time. See *duplex; simplex; asymmetric duplex*.

half-fit See *allocation algorithm*.
half path One wire of a two-wire circuit.
half-wave rectifier See *rectifier*.
half-word Half of a computer word; one end of a half-word is at a word boundary. (Eliminating the possibility of a 'half' taken out of the middle of the word.)
Hall effect A method of switching circuits that uses semiconductor elements to detect the presence or absence of a magnetic field. It is used in keyboards where the magnetic field is supplied by a permanent magnet that is placed in proximity with the semiconductor elements by depressing a key.
halt (1)To stop the execution of a sequence of instructions.(2)A point in a program or other sequence of instructions where execution is (temporarily) terminated.

halt instruction A breakpoint instruction or, possibly, a stop-run instruction. See *breakpoint instruction; exit instruction; stop-run instruction.*

hammer Also *anvil; print anvil.* In a back-strike impact printer (say, a barrel printer); a pivoted, solenoid-actuated element with a flat 'head' that strikes paper and ribbon against an embossed character to print the character image on the paper. See *impact printer.*

Hamming code A forward error correction code capable of detecting and correcting one-bit errors and of detecting, but not correcting, most multiple-bit errors. The following illustrates the method of applying it to the 7-bit character 1101010:

1. Reserve the first and the 2^n bit positions for the code, thus creating a 'skeleton' bit pattern: 000□000□0□□

2. Place the character bit pattern in the positions not reserved for the code: 110□101□0□□

3. Note the bit positions in which there are 1-bits and add the position numbers in binary using modulo-2. (There are 1-bits in positions 11, 10, 7, and 5 of the character being constructed.):

$$
\begin{aligned}
11 &= 1011 \\
10 &= 1010 \\
7 &= 0111 \\
5 &= \underline{0101} \\
\text{Modulo-2 sum:} &\ \ 0011
\end{aligned}
$$

4. Place this modulo-2 sum in the reserved positions to produce the complete character for transmission:

   1 1 0 0 1 0 1 0 0 1 1

5. At the receiving end, the bit positions with 1-bits are again added by modulo-2:

$$
\begin{aligned}
11 &= 1011 \\
10 &= 1010 \\
7 &= 0111 \\
5 &= 0101 \\
2 &= 0010 \\
1 &= \underline{0001} \\
\text{Modulo-2 sum:} &\ \ 0000
\end{aligned}
$$

Since there is no remainder from this addition, receiving hardware accepts the character as uncorrupted. Suppose the 1-bit in bit position 10 had been changed to a 0-bit during transmission, the following would have been the receive addition performed:

$$
\begin{aligned}
& 1011 \\
& 0111 \\
& 0101 \\
& 0010 \\
& \underline{0001} \\
\text{Modulo-2 sum:} &\ \ 1010
\end{aligned}
$$

This provides a 'direct reading' to tell recovery hardware to change the bit in the No. 10 position, in this case, from a 0-bit to a 1-bit. Again, if the 0-bit in position 6 had been changed to a 1-bit, the sum would have been 0110 and the bit in the No. 6 position would be changed from a 1-bit to a 0-bit.

Because the system is geometric ($1 + 2^n$ bits are reserved for the code), redundancy is very high for short groups, as that of the example. The code has, therefore, had little application in data communications though it has found some use in computer systems with large (say, 64-bit) internal transfers.

Hamming distance Also *signal distance.* The number of 1-bits in the modulo-2 sum of two binary numbers (the number of bit positions in which there is not identity). In the following, the Hamming distances are, respectively, 3, 5, and 2:

$$
\begin{array}{ccc}
1001110 & 10110 & 10011 \\
\underline{0011100} & \underline{01001} & \underline{00001} \\
1010010 & 11111 & 10010
\end{array}
$$

hand punch Also *spot punch.* A portable, hand-operated punch for punched cards; pressing a key punches a single hole in the row identified by the number on the key.

handler A term sometimes used synonymously with 'drive'; ('a disc handler'; 'a magnetic tape handler').

handshaking A term applied to the initial interchanges that are made between modems on a data communications link preparatory to transmitting data. See *modem interchanges.*

hard axis See *orthoferrite.*

hard copy A copy that can be preserved; particularly a copy on paper as produced by a printer. The term is used to differentiate such a copy from a 'soft copy' display on a VDU screen.

hard copy facility A term applied to a printer used in conjunction with one or more VDU terminals to make paper copies of displayed data.

hard core A term sometimes applied to locations in main storage (core or other) that are permanently occupied by units of system software. See *save area; locked down.*

hard disc Also *rigid disc.* A term used to differentiate a standard (aluminium) disc from a flexible disc.

hard error In magnetisable surface storage; an error that is detected consistently in data read from a particular storage location (indicating a defect in the recording surface). See *soft error; drop in; drop out.*

hard-sectored Of a magnetic disc system; with sectors (track divisions) established by some permanent method such as slots cut in the disc hub. See *soft-sectored; sectoring.*

hard stop An immediate termination of processing or (possibly) of some other operation.

hardware (1)Any tangible element (or group of elements) in a computer system. The term is applied to (or used to include) anything from a resistor to a computer with peripherals and all associated equipment; ('a hardware fault'; 'decreasing costs of hardware'). (2)Electronic circuitry. In this sense, the term contrasts task performance using such devices as data selectors, multiplexors, and logic arrays and performance by software (instruction sequences that can be changed by a programmer). The term is often used to indicate performance by firmware (instruction sequences in read-only memory); for example, 'hardware emulation' and 'hardware floating point'. See *software; firmware; bridgeware.*

hardware address Also, sometimes, *absolute address; real address; actual address; machine address.* A fixed numerical value (assigned by the computer manufacturer) that identifies a location in main storage. See *address.*

hardware check (1)A check performed by electronic circuitry; for example, a parity check. (2)A hardware failure that halts an operation.

hardware operation An operation performed by electronic circuitry; an operation not performed by software.

hardwired Also, often, *wired.* (1)Performed by electronic circuitry; ('hardwired exponentiation'; 'hardwired code conversion'). (2)Connected by a cable rather than by a communications link; ('hardwired terminals'). See *wired.*

harmonic A term applied to a wave with a frequency that is an integral multiple of the fundamental (the wave as generated); for example, if the fundamental is at 800 Hz., the 'first harmonic' is at 1600 Hz. and the second at 2400 Hz.

harmonic distortion Distortion of signals caused by the presence of harmonics of the carrier frequency.

hartley The decimal unit of information content equal to the decision content of a set of ten mutually exclusive events expressed as a logarithm to base 10. For example, the decision content of a character set of eight characters is 0.903 hartley.

hash (1)Computer output with no mathematical or logical significance. (2)To perform arithmetic operations with numbers that have no numerical significance. See *hash total.*

hash mark The symbol #. When placed in front of a number it indicates that it is binary coded octal.

hash total A control total formed by adding the contents of a field (customer name; account number) in each record of a group. The field contains a bit pattern that would not normally enter into arithmetic operations and, for the purpose, it is treated as a binary number. See *batch total; control total.*

hashed random file A random file.

hashing (1)Applying a hashing algorithm to record keys to generate addresses in direct access storage. (2)Forming hash totals.

hashing algorithm Also *randomising algorithm.* An algorithm used in constructing and maintaining hashed random files by which record keys are modified to produce their addresses in the address space of the file (on magnetic disc). A variety of algorithms are used, either singly or in combination; for example, folding, truncation, dividing by a constant and taking either the quotient or remainder, changing the radix, and squaring. Extraction (by mask) is often used to obtain an address of the required number of digits and various methods are used to select an output that is within the address space of the file. See *smoothing algorithm; hashed random.*

HASP *Houston Automatic Spooling Program.* A computer program that provides supplementary job management and data management functions such as control of job flow, ordering of tasks, and spooling.

HDI *Head-Disc Interference.*

HDLC *High-level Data Link Control.*

HDX *Half-DupleX.*

head An assembly consisting of one or more electromagnets (also **transducers**) used to read and/or write data in bit-pattern form on a magnetisable surface (magnetic disc; magnetic tape). Heads for use with magnetic tape may be either single-gap or dual-gap; a dual-gap head has separate coils and flux paths for reading and writing and thus provides a **read-after-write**

capability. Digital cassette magnetic tape heads read and write a single track, data cartridge heads read and write either two or four tracks, and heads for use with 'standard' half-inch tape operate with seven, eight, or nine tracks. Heads for magnetic disc systems are read/write heads for a single track. They commonly use separate read and write coils on a common ferrite structure. Most such heads incorporate an **erase head** which has separate coils and magnetic structure; the purpose is to remove stray magnetism at the sides of the track. Most heads use straddle erase, as shown. (Heads for flexible discs usually use tunnel erase.) In rigid disc systems, the head rides on an air cushion of

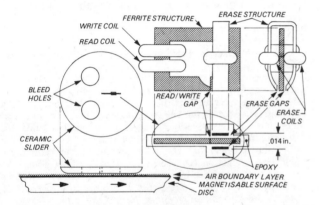

'captive' air that moves with the disc surface. The flying height of the head is determined by the shape of the **air bearing surface** which is the contoured lower surface of the slider. Height also depends upon the presence (and size) of bleed holes which allow some of the cushioning air to escape. The slider is of ceramic material and, usually, about 0.7 inch in diameter; it mounts through gimbals to the seek arm which is arranged to move it toward the disc (to 'load' the head) when the drive is up to speed, and to retract it on shutdown. (Heads for Winchester systems have a 'trimaran' structure and land on and take off from the disc surface.) The overall length of the ferrite and coil structure is about 0.3 inch; the gap is usually .001 - .002 inch.

The read/write and erase assembly is potted in epoxy and fastened into a slit in the slider with epoxy cement. Magnetic tape and flexible disc heads operate in contact with the recordable surface. See *magnetisable surface recording; magnetic disc unit; magnetic tape unit; servo system; track trimming.*

head carriage In a movable-head magnetic disc unit; the element that supports the head(s) and is moved by the servo for head positioning; in a multiple-disc system, it is often termed a **comb**. See *magnetic disc unit.*

head crash Head-disc interference.

head-disc interference (HDI) Also *head crash* and, sometimes *graunch*. A contact between a read/write head and a data-recordable area of the surface of a rigid magnetic disc; it often causes the loss of data and irreparable damage to the recording surface. See *magnetic disc; fly; loading zone; landing zone.*

head of form (HOF) The highest printable line on a page or the first line on which data is to be entered on a form. The term is also used with respect to continuous stationery to denote the first printing line; it is often the fourth line space below the fold.

head-per-track disc A disc in a fixed-head magnetic disc unit; a disc in which each track has a separate recording head.

head positioner A servo system; the elements of a magnetic disc unit that move the head(s) and maintain their position with respect to the tracks that are read and written.

head scatter The maximum possible difference in the position of a read/write head and the beginning of the recorded data of a sector at the instant reading begins. It is a cumulative total of errors in head mounting location, of errors in positioning sector slots, and of variations from designed spindle speed. See *sectoring; preamble.*

head-select A term applied to a circuit or operation that completes a data transfer circuit to a particular head of a multiple head magnetic disc unit.

header (1) Identifying or defining data placed at the beginning of a record, file, block, or other unit of data as stored or transmitted. (2) A location on a storage medium that is reserved for such data; ('a track header'; 'a block header'). In magnetic disc storage, there is, typically, a 'header' at the beginning of each sector; it contains the cylinder, head, and sector identifiers and is read when a seek is completed and compared with the location address to confirm that the correct track and sector have been located.

header card A punched card that contains data or instructions relating to the cards that follow it.

header label Also, usually, *file label*. Identifying and defining data at the beginning of a unit of data (typically, a file) on magnetic tape. It contains such things as name, owner, organisation of contents, generation number, and retention period. The data is checked by supervisory software as a step of accessing a file to ensure that the correct file has been located.

header record In some files; a first record that contains constants, information, or restrictions that apply to the other records.

header segment A part of a message that contains all or part of the header.

header table A header record (in tabular form).

heading Also *message header*. In data transmission, the first part of a message that contains such information as the identifier of the receiving station, priority, and routing instructions. It usually begins with the SOH character and ends at the STX character.

heading character The SOH character.

heat sink A semiconductor mounting, or a part of a semiconductor, that is designed to dissipate heat generated during operation. They are usually required only on high-power, discrete devices; for example, diodes, transistors, and thyristors used in power supplies.

helix printer A printer that forms dot matrix characters by means of linear, ridged print hammers that impact paper and ribbon against a helical ridge on a rotating cylinder. In one model that prints 132-character lines, each print hammer is wide enough to print six characters and a helix passes across the face of each print hammer once per revolution of the cylinder. During this revolution, the print hammer strikes the paper against the helix as many times as necessary to print all the dots on one line of all

UNIQUE ROTATING HELIX TECHNIQUE.

characters. The paper is then advanced to the next dot position in the characters; as many revolutions of the cylinder are required to print a complete line as there are dot positions on vertical lines in the characters (seven revolutions to print 5 × 7 characters). Printing speeds are, typically, from 300 to 600 lines per minute.

Hertz (Hz.) A standard unit of frequency equal to one cycle per second. See *frequency; alternating current*.

hesitation Cycle stealing.

heterogeneous Containing unlike elements. In computer usage, the term may be applied to a system or network using computers (or, possibly, other functional units) of different type or manufacture.

heuristic A term applied to a problem solving technique in which experience, guesses, and trial-and-error methods are used.

hexadecimal A number system with a radix of 16. It is frequently used to represent binary numbers in instructions and explanations, in computer input, and in listing binary values. The system employs digits and letters as follows:

Binary	Decimal	Hexadecimal
0000	0	0
0001	1	1
0010	2	2
0011	3	3
0100	4	4
0101	5	5
0110	6	6
0111	7	7
1000	8	8
1001	9	9
1010	10	A
1011	11	B
1100	12	C
1101	13	D
1110	14	E
1111	15	F

The positional value of digits increases by a multiple of 16 per digit position so the first four have decimal values of:

4096　　256　　16　　1

The hexadecimal for 256 is then '100' and for 4096 is '1000'. The following are some other equivalents:

16	10	32	20
17	11	150	96
30	1E	235	EF

See *binary; decimal; octal*.

hidden line In the display of a three-dimensional object (computer graphics) a line that could not be seen when viewing the 'real' object and which, therefore, should not appear in the display image. In the cube, the dotted lines are the 'hidden lines'.

hierarchy (1) An organisation of items on different levels in which the upper items have a precedential or control relation to the lower items. Such a relationship is, for example, expressed by a company organisation chart. **(2)** Also *tree structure*. A data structure consisting of 'owners' and 'members' in which each member can have only one owner and each owner can have any number of members. See *tree; net; access path*.

high Also, often, *logical high*. In control and logic circuits; the higher of two possible voltages; for example, + 5 V. in a system in which the other possible voltage is 0 V. Unless otherwise indicated, the term denotes a control voltage rather than clock or data signals.

high-level data link control (HDLC) An ISO definition of a standard data communications interface for the transfer of data to and from packet switched networks. With respect to data format, it is the same as SDLC in almost all respects. See *synchronous data link control*.

high-level language A programming language that does not reflect the structure or facilities of any particular computer and can, thus, be used to write programs for computers of different type and different manufacture. Examples include COBOL, FORTRAN, ALGOL, and PL/1. See *language; low-level language*.

high-level recovery A recovery other than one performed automatically; a recovery made by facilities external to the unit in which the failure occurred; for example, reloading an operating system, reading from a duplicate file, or switching to another peripheral.

high-level scheduler A master scheduler.

high-order position The leftmost position in a number or a character string or the highest and leftmost position in a matrix. See *most significant digit*.

high-pass filter See *filter*.

high-priority A term applied to a program or job that has processing precedence over others. See *priority*.

high-speed A term applied to a data communications device or facility capable of handling more than 4800 bits per second.

high-speed carry In mechanised or computer addition; a method of eliminating steps when a carry into one digit position results in an immediate carry to the next higher digit position (for example, when adding 1 to 99). See *standing on nines*.

high-threshold logic (HTL) A term applied to low-voltage logic circuits with higher-voltage inputs and/or outputs; the voltage difference is commonly obtained by the use of zener diodes. See *zener diode*.

highlight To change the appearance of the display of part of an image on a VDU screen, for example, by blinking or using 'inverse video'. It is a method of drawing the attention of the operator to a particular place.

highway Also *trunk; bus*. A major data transfer path within a computer or other functional unit. It, typically, consists of a number of wires or a multi-conductor cable.

highway width The number of bits that can be transferred simultaneously on a 'highway'.

histogram (1) A plot of the frequency of occurrence of quantised values; for example, one showing the number of days per year in which the sun shone for less than 1 hour, between 1 and 2 hours, between 2 and 3 hours, and between 3 and 4 hours. **(2)** A computer graphics plot containing shaded areas.

history file An archive file.

hit (1) To access, stop at, or consider a particular item in a group of items. See *hit rate*. **(2)** A transient disturbance (momentary open circuit; burst of impulse noise) on a communications circuit.

hit-on-the-fly See *on-the-fly*.

hit-on-the-line A 'hit' (def. 2).

hit rate Also, sometimes, *hit ratio*. **(1)** The number of successes in relation to the number of tries. In this sense, the term is applied to such things as finding referenced operands in a cache or slave store. **(2)** The number affected in relation to the number present or considered. An update run in which changes are made to most of the records of a file has a 'high hit rate'. **(3)** The number of times a particular item is accessed in relation to the number of accesses to the group in which it is contained. For example, in a transaction processing system, a routine that is seldom executed would be said to have a 'low hit rate'.

HLL *High-Level Language*.

HLS *High-Level Scheduler*.

HMOS *High-speed Metal Oxide Silicon*. (Intel)

HMOS-E *High-speed Metal Oxide Silicon-Erasable*. A programmable read-only memory that has been produced with up to 64K bits per chip.

HOF *Head Of Form.*

hold queue A queue of jobs that are ready to run and are waiting for release by the operator.

holding current In a volatile semiconductor memory system; a low current (say, resulting from about 1.5 V.) required to keep transistors in a conducting (and data retaining) mode when data is not being read or written. See *semiconductor memory; volatile.*

hole (1) A small, punched opening in a punched card or paper tape; a 'data hole' or a 'feed hole'. **(2)** An electron carrier in P-type silicon. See *semiconductor.*

hole pattern A data-related arrangment of holes as punched in a punched card or paper tape. Unless otherwise indicated, it is understood to represent a single character in some code. See *bit pattern; card image.*

Hollerith card An 80-column punched card.

Hollerith code A code widely used to represent data as hole patterns in punched cards with 80 columns and 12 rows. See *code.*

holographic memory A memory system in which bits are held as interference patterns of light in two-dimensional arrays. A laser A projects a beam of coherent light B to a lens system that divides it into a reference beam C and an object beam D. The object beam passes through a 'page composer' E where in-

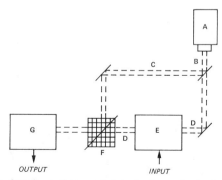

coming data is used to modulate the beam in the hologram F. Data is read by a photodetecter G. Packing densities exceeding 70 megabits per square inch have been achieved. The system is experimental; the most promising application has been in making microfiche read-only memories.

home address (1) In a magnetic disc file; an address of a home location; a record key that places a record in a home location rather than in an overflow location. **(2)** A track label; an area at the beginning of a magnetic-disc track that identifies the track (by track number and read/write head number).

home brew A term applied to software produced as a hobby or on a free-lance basis.

home location A magnetic disc file location identifiable by key; a location that is not in an overflow area. See *overflow.*

home loop A data transfer circuit of a local terminal that does not connect to communications lines; for example, a connection between the terminal and an adjacent printer.

home record (1) In a chained file; the first record in a chain; the record that must be accessed in order to access any other records in the chain. **(2)** A record in a home location.

hook A sequence of instructions (a branch) that cannot be executed during normal processing.

hop A direct connection between two nodes of a data network (as considered for message/packet routing purposes).

hopper In a card punch or reader; the element in which the input cards are placed.

horizontal distributed system A data network in which all data stations (including the master station, if there is one) have computers of equivalent size and capability.

horizontal feed A term applied to a card punch or reader that receives and handles punched cards long-edge first. See *vertical feed.*

horizontal microinstruction See *microinstruction.*

horizontal parity See *parity.*

horizontal tabulate Also *tabulate.* To move a printing position or VDU cursor a preset distance to the right along the same line. See *vertical tabulate; HT.*

horizontal tabulation character See *HT.*

host computer (1) computer that prepares programs to be run on a different type of computer. **(2)** A computer that can execute programs that were written for a different type computer. See *emulation; target computer.* **(3)** Also, often, *mainframe.* The controlling or main computer in a data network in which there are other computers, or the main computer in a multiprocessor installation.

host language A programming language from which a subset or variant is derived (as COBOL is the 'host language' of DML).

host machine A host computer.

host processor The central or controlling processor in a multiprocessor system.

host system (1) A system that supports or controls; for example, a particular computer installation may be the 'host system' for a data network. **(2)** A system that contains an item or in which a function is performed; for example, a particular mainframe may be considered the 'host system' of an auxiliary computer.

housekeeping (1) A term applied to a routine that performs some processing-related function, particularly with respect to storage management; for example, opening and closing files, performing read and write operations, and checking access rights. **(2)** A term that is applied to instruction sequences not directly involved in performing the task of the program in which they are used; for example, to those used in setting initial conditions and formatting the output.

housekeeping operation An operation that facilitates the processing or handling of data but does not affect data content. See *housekeeping*.

housekeeping routine A unit of system software that performs a processing-related function. See *housekeeping*.

HP *Hewlett Packard*. (Cupertino, Calif.)

HPIB *Hewlett Packard Interface Bus*. A 16-line, parallel, instrumentation bus now standardised as IEE-488-75.

HR *High Reduction*. See *reduction*.

HT *Horizontal Tabulate*. A format effector that causes a printing position or a VDU cursor to move to a preset position to the right along the same line. See *VT*.

HTL *High Threshold Logic*.

hub go-ahead polling Hub polling.

hub polling See *polling*.

human-oriented language A term sometimes applied to a programming language (say, to BASIC) that has features similar to those of a natural language.

hunt group The group of telephone circuits that are tried in sequence (by automatic equipment) when routing a dialed call between locations in different dialing areas. The most direct available circuit is tried first.

hunting In an electronic circuit or device; a slow, repeated, oscillation or change of values between two limits; a form of instability usually caused by overcorrection in a system designed to use feedback or an unintended feedback in a system not so designed. See *oscillation; feedback*.

hybrid (1) A term sometimes applied to a 'composite' device; to a device incorporating multiple elements of different type. **(2)** A hybrid coil. **(3)** A circuit that operates like a hybrid coil (by common mode rejection).

hybrid coil A transformer device used in a telephone system to connect two wires of a local loop to a four-wire circuit used within and between the exchanges of the telephone system.

hybrid computer A computer that combines digital and analogue elements.

hybrid integrated circuit (1) An integrated circuit in which the substrate is passive; for example, silicon on sapphire. See *monolithic*. **(2)** An integrated circuit device containing two or more chips that are interconnected and encapsulated as a unit.

hybrid microwave Microwave that carries both data and speech on the same channel. See *data under voice*.

hybrid RAM An integrated circuit RAM composed of multiple, interconnected elements; for example, a 64-bit device formed of four 16-bit chips with common mounting.

hypergroup See *group*.

hysteresis A lag between a change in a condition and a change of the force or influence that produces the condition; a difference between cause and effect. See *magnet*.

Hymu erase Straddle erase.

HZ (Hz.) *HertZ*.

I

I The standard symbol for 'current'. See *ampere*.

I-field *Information* field. Also *data field*. That part of a message that has relevance to the addressee rather than to the communications link; a message excluding flags, addressing, and control characters.

IA (1) *Interchange Address*. **(2)** *International Alphabet*.

IA orientation Cine mode.

IA-1 *International Alphabet number 1*. Baudot code. See *code*.

IA-2 *International Alphabet number 2*. The standard 5-bit telegraphy code. See *code; Baudot code*.

IA-5 *International Alphabet number 5*. Also *ISO-7*. A standard 7-bit communications code. See *code*.

IAM *Intermediate Access Memory*.

IB orientation Comic mode.
IBG *InterBlock Gap.*
IBI *Intergovernment Bureau for Informatics.* (Rome)
IBM *International Business Machines.* (White Plains, N.Y.)
IC *Integrated Circuit.*
ICA *International Communication Association.*
ICL *International Computers Limited.* (London)
ID (1)*IDentification character.* **(2)***Insulation Displacement.*
identification character (ID) In a data communications system that operates by polling or contention; a character (possibly one of two or more) that identifies a remote data station to the central station.
identification division The part of a COBOL program that contains the name of the program and, possibly, other information about it.
identifier (1)A value by which an operating system distinguishes an entity (file; volume; device; user) from other entities in a computer system. **(2)**Also *indicator.* A named field that holds integers to identify the branches that can be followed from a branchpoint; for example, a field TAB-IN that holds integers 1 through 5, each of which specifies a branch to a different address. **(3)**The value held in an 'identifier' (def. 2). **(4)**Identification characters; the address of the sender of a message.
identity (1) The condition in which two or more entities have the same set of attributes. **(2)**Exclusive NOR; the condition in which two bit patterns have identical bits in all bit positions. The two bit patterns to be checked are loaded into registers and the bits in each bit position are added by modulo-2 (exclusive

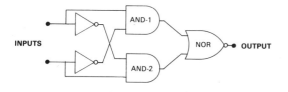

OR) and the result negated into a third register. This register is then shifted out and the presence of any 1-bits indicates non-identity. The figure shows the logic to test the two bits in each bit position. If both inputs are high (1-bits), the output of AND-1 will be high, AND-2 will be low, and the NOR output will be low (a 0-bit). If both inputs are low, the AND-1 output will be low and the AND-2 high and the NOR output will, again, be low. If the inputs are different, both AND outputs will be low and the NOR output will be high (a 1-bit).
identity operation A logic operation to determine whether or not two bits or bit patterns are identical; if there are only two inputs it is also an **equivalence operation**. See *identity.*
identity unit A device that performs identity operations.
idle Of a functional unit; ready to operate and waiting for inputs.
idle character On a data link; a character that may be transmitted repeatedly when no messages are being sent; it may be used for synchronisation and/or to provide verification that the link is functional. See *synchronous idle.*
idle time The time that a functional unit is operable but not being used.
IDMS *Integrated Data base Management System.*
IDP (1)*Integrated Data Processing.* **(2)***Institute of Data Processing.* (London)
IEEE *Institute of Electrical and Electronics Engineers.*
IEEE interface A widely accepted standard for instrumentation (data loggers; sensors; telemetry) interfaces. It defines the type of connector, the numbering and function of circuits, driver and receiver parameters, and a data transfer protocol. The interface has sixteen lines of which eight are used for handshaking and control and eight carry data asynchronously in bit parallel. Logical high ('false') is $+2$ V. and logical low ('true') is less than 0 V. Line lengths may be up to 20 meters and a single interface is limited to fifteen devices. (The interface was originally defined by Hewlett Packard.)
if-and-only-if Equivalence (logic operation).
if-then Implication.
IFIP *International Federation for Information Processing.* (Amsterdam)
IGFET *Insulated Gate Field Effect Transistor.*
ignore character A cancel character.
IL *Intermediate Language.*
I²L *Integrated Injection Logic.*
illegal Not interpretable or recognised in the system in which it occurs. See *forbidden combination; reserved.*
illegal character A character-length bit pattern that is not a member of the character set(s) used in the system in which it occurs.

illegal instruction An instruction that is not in a form recognised by the compiler or that contains an operator not included in the instruction set of the computer.

ILR *Instruction Location Register.*

image (1) A visually interpretable representation as displayed, plotted, or printed. **(2)** Also *binary image*. A representation in storage by a means other than the storage code of the computer or device in which it is held. Examples include the bit patterns of an alien code, and bit-pattern matrices of such things as the punching pattern of a punched card or of a character to be displayed.

image dissector A scanner; the element of an optical character recognition device that detects light transmission or reflection along lines (scan lines) that 'dissect' the image space.

image graphics Computer graphics in which a display is generated by means other than interpreting stored vector coordinates; for example by raster scan or form flash.

image mode Of data from a punched card; held in storage in bits representing the punching pattern rather than in characters. See *card image*.

image processing The use of computers to analyse, enhance, or interpret images.

image space (1) The bit-pattern storage space occupied by a coded image. **(2)** An area of paper or film where a graphic image may be present.

image tube (1) A tube for a television camera; a tube that can register and transmit 'images'. **(2)** An indicator tube; a vacuum tube that can display character images one at a time. **(3)** A tube that is capable of presenting an 'image' (as contrasted to performing amplification or some other function); for example, a cathode ray tube or an indicator tube.

imaginary number See *number*.

imaging The process of placing an image on a (photographic) medium; for example, in microfilm recording. See *recorder*.

immediate access storage (1) Random access storage. **(2)** Direct access storage. **(3)** A term sometimes used to include both random-access and direct-access storage.

immediate address A literal.

immediate instruction An instruction with operand(s) in literal form. See *effective instruction*.

immediate mode A method of executing a program in which statements are translated and executed one at a time; the method provided by an interpreter. See *interpreter*.

impact matrix printer A printer that produces dot-matrix characters by striking small rods (stylii; needles) against ribbon and paper. See *matrix printer*.

impact paper Carbonless copy paper.

impact printer A printer that uses mechanical pressure to apply character images from a type font to paper through an inked ribbon. In a **front-strike printer**, the type character strikes the ribbon and forces it against the paper (the most common form is an ordinary typewriter). A **back-strike printer** is one in which a flat-headed hammer strikes the paper and forces it against

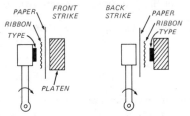

ribbon and a type character; common forms are barrel printers and chain printers. Impact printers can produce multiple copies using interleaved carbon paper or carbonless copy paper in multipart stationery. Inertia in the moving parts limits top speeds to about 30 impacts per hammer per second in a character printer. (Though the term includes matrix printers, a printer that prints a character per impact is understood unless otherwise indicated.) See *matrix printer; non-impact printer; printer; helix printer*.

impedance (Z) A value, expressed on ohms, that represents the total opposition to the flow of alternating current in a circuit. It depends upon the values of resistance, inductance, and capacitance with high values of resistance and inductance causing high impedance and, usually, any capacitance reducing the effect of inductance.

impedance matching The process of adding resistance (sometimes inductance or capacitance) to a circuit to make its impedance equal to that of another circuit to which it is connected. The usual reason is to prevent echoes or distortion in signals that pass from one of the circuits to the other. See *echo*.

imperative instruction An instruction that translates into object code (as contrasted, perhaps, to annotation or other non-executable source code).

imperative statement An imperative instruction (in a high-level language).

implement (1) With respect to a system; to design it, procure the necessary elements, install it, and place it in operation; ('implement a batch system'; 'implement a data network'). **(2)** With software; to place it in operation and test it; ('implement a new operating system'; 'implement a data base').

implementation (1) The process of implementing. **(2)** That which has been implemented.

implication Also *if-then; inclusion*. A logic operation with an output that is 'true' if the first of two inputs is 'false' and the second is 'true' and 'false' if the first is 'true' and the second 'false' or if both are 'true' or both are 'false'. See *logic*.

implicit address In assembly-language source code; a symbolic address or other group that translates into an operand address in object code.

impulse dialing The dialing method of a standard rotary-dial telephone (as contrasted to pushbutton dialing or, possibly, to automatic dialing). See *dial pulse*.

impulse noise Also, sometimes, a *hit* or *black noise*. A transient disturbance on a communications circuit caused by such things as making and breaking relay contacts, intermittent short-circuit or grounding, or energy transfer from a non-communications circuit. See *noise*.

impure code Code that contains parameters that are subject to change during execution. See *pure code*.

impurity Also *dopant*. An element added to silicon or germanium to form a semiconductor. See *doping*.

in connector An inconnector. See *connector*.

in-flight During transfer; without interrupting the flow of data; ('in-flight error detection and correction').

in-house Done on the (user's) premises and by own staff; ('in-house training'; 'in-house program development').

inactive (1) Also *idle; available*. Ready for use but not being used; ('an inactive printer'; 'an inactive data transfer channel'). **(2)** Of a program; not being executed. **(3)** Out of service; not available for use; ('an inactive line'; 'an inactive data station'). **(4)** Characterised by infrequent use during a particular period; ('an inactive file').

inclusion Implication (logic operation).

inclusive OR (IOR) OR (logic operation).

inclusive segments In an overlaid program; segments that can be in main storage at the same time.

incoming In process of being received; ('an incoming message'; 'an incoming character').

incoming circuit A circuit on which messages are received.

inconnector See *connector*.

increment (1) To add to; ('increment a number'). **(2)** To add a constant (often 1) in a sequence of such additions; ('increment a count with each iteration of a loop'). See *decrement*. **(3)** The constant added by 'increment' (def. 2). See *decrement*. **(4)** To move a punched card through a punch or reader by an 'increment' of one column; to move it to the position where the next character can be read or punched.

increment size (1) The number of units constituting an increment (def. 3). **(2)** In a raster system; the distance between addressable points.

incremental compiler A compiler that translates each source code statement into object code as the statement is entered. See *interpreter; compiler; load-and-go*.

incremental computer A computer in which the processing units are differences in values rather than absolute values.

incremental recording A term applied to the recording of one character at a time (as keyed in from a keyboard) to magnetic disc or magnetic tape. The facility permits a (flexible) disc or (cartridge) tape to be used as a functional replacement for paper tape in applications such as word processing and typesetting.

independent control point A control point that causes the movement of two or more bits within a register or between registers when a single pulse is applied to it; a control point that connects to multiple AND gates. See *control point; register*.

independent variable See *variable (Mathematics)*.

index (1) Also *table; index table*. A list of items and their locations maintained for access purposes; for example, of the records in a file, of the files in a volume, or of the tracks on one surface of a magnetic disc. See *catalogue*. **(2)** Also *table; index table; mapping table*. A group of storage locations used to hold values for address modification. See *address modification*. **(3)** The contents of one storage location in an 'index' (def. 2). See *pointer; index register*. **(4)** Also *subscript*. A value used to identify a location in an array. See *subscript*. **(5)** The value in an index field of an instruction; the address of an index register. **(6)** In some microfilm systems; a visual aid to locating particular frames. **(7)** In a magnetic disc system; a hardware-identifiable item (hole; slot cut in hub) used to mark the beginning of tracks. **(8)**To form an 'index'; to list items and their locations.

index field Also, in some systems, *modifier field*. A location in an instruction where an index or modifier can be placed.

index file (1)A file consisting of an index. **(2)**An indexed file.

index gap An index slot.

index hole (1) In a flexible disc; a photoelectrically detected hole that marks the beginning of tracks for access purposes. **(2)**A hole in the plastic envelope of a flexible disc through which the 'index hole' (def. 1) is detected.

index register A control-unit register used to hold a value that is required in a particular phase of execution. It may be used to hold a count, modifier, index, pointer, switch value, or flag, or to control the execution of a loop. When used to control the execution of a loop, it holds the hardware address of the first operand input and is incremented (possibly decremented) to provide a different operand for each iteration; the value by which it is incremented or decremented may be held in another index register. See *general register; loop; address modification*.

index sensing In a magnetic disc system; the process of detecting an index (def. 7) for purposes of locating data on tracks and timing read and write operations. It may be done by detecting flux transitions in a special head as an index slot passes or by photoelectrically detecting a hole or slot. See *indexing*.

index slot In a disc pack; a slot cut in the hub. It is detected by an index transducer. See *index sensing*.

index transducer A sensing element used to detect index slots or holes (and, possibly, also sector slots).

index word (1)A computer word that is an element of an 'index'. **(2)**A word by which text material can be located in a (back-of-the-book) 'index'.

indexed file (1) Any file for which there is an index of contents. **(2)**An indexed non-sequential file.

indexed non-sequential file Also *indexed random file*. A file in which records can be placed in any available location with access being made by keys that are held sequentially in an index with one index entry per record.

indexed random file An indexed non-sequential file.

indexed sequential file A magnetic disc file in which records are placed sequentially by key and which contains an index on one or more levels to help in locating particular groups of records when the file is processed non-sequentially. Typically, an index at the beginning of the file provides the highest key number in each file area, which, on a large file, would be a cylinder. A second-level index at the beginning of each cylinder provides the highest key number on each track and a third-level index at the beginning of each of the tracks provides the highest key number in each block. A smaller file would have fewer levels of indexing.

indexing (1) The placement of items in indexes. **(2)**Address modification; particularly when the values used in the modification are held in index registers. **(3)**The operation of providing a timing reference for access purposes on a magnetic disc unit. It is accomplished by an **index transducer** that detects an **index slot** in a rotating element of a drive or disc pack or, in a flexible-disc system, an **index hole** in the disc. The index transducer produces an **index pulse** each time the slot or hole passes. This is used by the host system (computer; peripheral controller) to mark the beginning of all tracks on the discs of the device. The index pulse is normally (rigid disc system) indistinguishable electrically from a sector pulse but is identified by its positional relation to them. The index pulse indicates that the following pulse is that for a sector and, thus, initiates the sector count on which access depends. The pulse is also used as the reference for rotational position sensing in systems with this facility. See *sectoring; index sensing; index hole; index slot*.

indicator (1)A field that can be 'set' (a 1-bit written) when a particular condition occurs during processing; a field that is used to hold a flag. **(2)**Also *indicator light*. A light (as on a control or display panel) that informs an operator that some condition exists; for example, that a particular switch is turned off or that a communications line is in use. **(3)**An identifier (def. 2; 3). **(4)**A switch indicator (a flag).

indirect address Also *multilevel address; presumptive address*. In an instruction in object code; a value that is input to one or more steps of address modification. See *direct address; address; indirection; address modification*.

indirect command file A file that supports an operator input from a terminal by displaying (asking) a sequence of questions; for example, in system generation.

indirect instruction A presumptive instruction; an instruction that contains a presumptive (indirect) address.

indirection Indirect addressing; particularly as considered with respect to the mechanism that performs it. The term **levels of**

indirection is used to denote the number of steps (table look-ups) that are required to produce a hardware address from an indirect address.

inductance (L) That which restricts current flow in a circuit as caused by reversing a magnetic field in such **inductive devices** as transformers, solenoids, and electromagnets. The unit of measurement is the 'henry'. See *resistance; capacitance.*

inductive switch A keyboard switch in which a permanent magnet moved by a key passes through the centre of an inductor core on which is wound a one-turn primary and a one-turn secondary, with pulses applied to the primary. When a key is in its unoperated position, the magnet is centred in the core and its flux saturates the core preventing pulses from transferring to the secondary. When the key is depressed, the magnet moves out of the core causing pulses to transfer from primary to secondary and to appear on the sense line.

inductor A device that introduces inductance in a circuit (for purposes of circuit balancing).

infix notation The usual method of expressing mathematical relationships in which the operators are placed between the entities with which the operations are to be performed (rather than separately as in Polish notation). See *Polish notation.*

infix operator An operator that is placed between operands.

Infonet An international bureau network operated by Computer Sciences Corp. to provide subscribers with interactive access to a number of large data bases.

informatics The science or technology of providing information exchange by means of computer-based systems. (The term is more widely used in continental Europe than elsewhere.)

information (1)An element of knowledge; that which a person may obtain from experience, observation, or, possibly, from the examination of data. (2)A term sometimes used synonymously with 'data'. See *information and data.*

information and data The terms 'information' and 'data' are sometimes used synonymously with 'information' supplanting 'data' in contexts where the emphasis is on the broad, grand, or useful aspects; ('information processing'; 'information network'; 'information interchange'). In a more restrictive sense, 'information' is that which results when some human mental activity (observation; analysis) is successfully applied to data to reveal its meaning or significance. In this sense, data is the vehicle and information is that which can result from its interpretation.

information bits Bits that are part of character bit patterns as contrasted to parity bits or other bits added to a character or block for purposes of error detection.

information channel (1)A message channel. (2)An assembly of data communications equipment and circuits used to transfer data between geographically separated locations; a message channel and a supervisory channel (if used).

information character In a message; a bit pattern that represents a letter, digit, or symbol rather than one that performs a control, error detection, or delimiting function.

information content A measure of information conveyed by the occurrence of an event of definite probability; it is equal to the logarithm of the reciprocal of the probability. For example, the information content of an 8-character character set when each character has an equal probability of occurring (in a message) is the logarithm of 8 or 0.903 hartley or 3 shannon.

information feedback (1)An indication of the effect of an action as used to modify a subsequent action. (2)Loop check.

information field See *I field.*

information interchange The process of sending and receiving data without altering content or meaning during transmission.

information message A message that has significance to the sender and receiver as contrasted to a supervisory or control message.

information processing (1)A term sometimes used in place of 'data processing', particularly as applied to a large interactive system with a data base. (2)A term sometimes applied to those functions of a computer system relating to the storage and internal manipulation of data as contrasted to interfacing or network management. See *network processing.*

information processor A term sometimes applied to the main processor of a computer installation to contrast it to auxiliary processors.

information retrieval (1)A term applied to a system or process in which large amounts of data are catalogued and arranged for selective access to meet different requirements; for example, to that of a university library. (2)The operation or facilities of a word processor in which stored data can be selectively located for purposes of change or review.

information separator (IS) A delimiter; particularly one used to separate units of like data; for example, a 'file separator' or a 'group separator'.

information system (1)A set of programs and a data base constructed to provide an organisation with a particular type of information. **(2)**An interactive network system that provides users with access to information (from multiple data bases).

information technology The field of creating systems and devices for use in storing and disseminating information.

information theory The branch of learning concerned with the study of measures of information and their properties.

inherited Carried over from a previous operation or stage of processing; ('an inhereted error').

inhibit To prevent an action from taking place; for example, by setting a control bit or changing a circuit value.

inhibit wire See *core memory*.

initial program load Also *cold restart*. The process of loading the system software of a computer. See *bootstrap*.

initial program loader (IPL) A utility that loads the initial modules of an operating system or, possibly, some other large program. See *bootstrap*.

initialise (Processing step) To establish prescribed starting conditions prior to executing a program or starting a run. Typically, it includes resetting counts, supplying run-time parameters, erasing locations to be used as work areas, and resetting flags. Unless otherwise indicated, the initialisation of alphanumeric and alphabetic fields consists of overwriting with space characters and that of numeric fields consists of overwriting with zeros.

initialise (Magnetic disc) To prepare a (new) disc or disc pack to receive data. The operation consists of checking each track for defects and writing identifying and control data required for access purposes. It is divided into **certification** which is the process of checking individual tracks, and **formatting** which is the process of writing track flags and identifying data. The operation is performed by an **initialisation program** that, typically, checks tracks and rechecks those with indicated defects, writes home addresses, assigns alternate tracks to replace defective primary tracks, and prints the results indicating which tracks are defective and which have been assigned as their alternates. See *certification; formatting*.

initiate **(1)**To take an action that causes an operation to be performed; ('initiate a search'; 'initiate a data transfer'). **(2)**To begin; to take the first action; ('initiate a message exchange').

ink-jet printer A printer that forms dot matrix characters by applying ejected droplets of ink to paper. In one method, a continuous stream of electrostatically charged droplets are ejected toward the paper with their paths controlled by deflector plates in a method that is similar to that used to control an electron beam in a cathode ray tube. Where no dot is to appear on a particular vertical line (say, above and below the 'bar' of an 'H'), the droplet that would have been placed there is deflected into a tube. Droplets caught in this way are reconstituted and return to the ink reservoir. The other method in use is the drop-on-demand method in which an ink cartridge supplies ink to a printing head that contains small reservoirs. There are as many reservoirs in the head as there are dots on

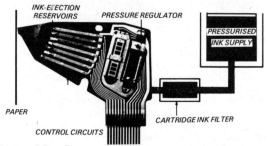

vertical lines and each has an outlet 'nozzle' directed toward the paper. Each reservoir has a piezoelectric crystal built into one wall and when the crystal is energised it reduces the volume of the reservoir, causing a droplet to be ejected from the nozzle. In operation, the head moves along the print line and characters are constructed by selectively energising piezoelectric crystals using circuitry similar to that which operates the needles in an impact matrix printer. As ejected, the droplets are about 6 mils in diameter and they fly about 35 mils to the paper surface where they flatten to form dots about 15 mils in diameter. Dot size (and, hence, character density) can be controlled by the pulsing current. Both methods produce printing of a quality equal to or better than that produced by the best impact matrix printers; the printing rates are on the order of 250 characters per second. The figure shows the elements of a (Silonics) drop-on-demand print head and beneath it is a sample of the printing produced.

input (1) That which is received or intended to be received; ('a programming input'; 'a circuit input'; 'a computer input'). **(2)**

A movement of data to main storage from an input or storage device; the software that handles the movement is an **input routine**. (3)A movement of data from an input device to magnetic tape or magnetic disc. (4)A movement of data from an external environment to a computer environment. (5)A term applied to the data received (or normally received) by a functional unit or computer. See *output; migration; staging; data acquisition, collection, and capture*. (6)A signal (voltage) that is received by a logic circuit and which (possibly, with other signals) determines the output.

input area A part of a program's workspace that is used to hold inputs.

input block An input area.

input buffer (1)Memory used to hold inputs (from communications links) awaiting processing. (2)An input area.

input data Data that is received or data of the type that is intended to be received.

input device A device used to convert data from some other form (keystrokes; punched holes; shaft rotation) into bit patterns that can be written (possibly after a code translation) to the magnetic storage of a computer system. Common devices include direct data entry stations, analogue to digital converters, punched card and paper tape readers, and optical mark readers. See *input; input medium; output device*.

input document A source document.

input field In a graphics display; an unprotected area in which the operator can enter or modify data.

input job A job in the job queue.

input medium A medium in which data can be represented in a machine-readable form or a medium containing such data. Though the term can include magnetic disc and tape, it is more commonly applied to punched cards, paper tape, and forms that are to be read by OMR, OCR, or MICR.

input mode (1)Of a terminal; the condition in which an operator can enter data. (2)Of a functional unit; the data-receiving condition (as contrasted to the data-sending or data-output condition).

input/output (I/O; IO) A term applied to a device, circuit, program, or operation involved in transferring data between the central processor (main storage and/or control unit or arithmetic unit registers) and an external device or circuit, for example, a peripheral device or a modem. (Unless otherwise indicated, the term applies to peripheral transfers.) In a microprocessor system, the term usually denotes a transfer through a UART. See *input; output; radial transfer; peripheral controller; UART*.

Print results.

input/output area A part of a program's workspace that is used to hold inputs and outputs.

input/output buffer Memory in computer main storage or in an interface device that is used to hold output data awaiting transfer and input data awaiting processing.

input/output channel A data channel.

input/output controller (IOC) A peripheral controller.

input/output coupler In a terminal control unit or other (small) intelligent device; the section or elements that handle interfacing functions.

input/output device (1)A device used to handle transfers to and from main storage; for example, a peripheral controller. (2)A device used to handle transfers to and from a computer terminal. (3)A semiconductor device that performs inputs and outputs (for a microprocessor). See *UART*.

input/output interrupt See *I/O interrupt*.

input/output multiplexor A device (or part of a device such as an access controller or interface computer) that performs multiplexing of peripheral transfers, thus allowing interleaved transfers to and from several devices simultaneously. The method used is 'time division multiplexing'. See *time division multiplexing; multiplexor*.

input/output processor (IOP) An auxiliary computer that handles interfacing functions for a larger mainframe computer. The term can be applied to a data channel or peripheral controller, to a front-end processor, or to a unit that handles both peripheral interfacing and communications line interfacing.

input/output queue A queue that holds incoming messages waiting for processing and outgoing messages waiting for lines.

input/output section In the environment division of a COBOL program; the section that names the files and external media that will be used by the program during execution.

input/output unit An input/output device or the part of a device that performs input/output functions.

input queue Also *task input queue; input work queue*. A group of job definitions, typically on magnetic disc, arranged in the order in which the jobs will be executed during a run.

input routine See *input*.

input stream (1) An input queue for jobs of a particular type or priority; for example, for high-priority jobs or for batch jobs. (2) A sequence of job control statements that control the way a job is to be run.

inquiry See *enquiry*.

insert To place an item in correct sequence among other items, moving other items as necessary. In text editing, it denotes adding new copy in the body of existing copy. In a sequential file, it denotes adding a new record in the location determined by key and moving all following records.

insertion (1) The process of inserting. (2) That which is inserted.

insertion sort A sort performed by placing each item to be sorted into the group of items already sorted in the location established by some criteria. See *sort*.

installed (1) Of a magnetic disc or tape volume; mounted on its drive. (2) Of a program; in main storage or on a mounted volume and accessible to the operating system.

installation (1) A computer and its associated peripherals and other devices as set up at a particular user's location. (2) A site. (3) With respect to an applications package or other software; the process of making it operational on a particular computer. (4) The process of placing hardware in location.

instruction (1) An element of a program that specifies an operation to be performed on or with data. A **programming instruction** (also **source language instruction**) is an instruction as written by a programmer in a programming language. When written in a high-level language, the term **statement** is used in preference to 'instruction'; thus, a 'MACRO-11 instruction' and a 'COBOL statement'. In either case, it is a (short) string of words and/or symbols that conforms to the rules and syntax of a particular programming language. Typically, it is composed of an **operator** that specifies what is to be done and one or more **operands** that identify the data that is to be used. When an instruction produced by a programmer is converted (punched card; keyboard to disc or tape) to a sequence of bit patterns in the computer storage code on some magnetic medium, it is termed a **source instruction** or, possibly 'source statement' when the written form was in a high-level language. When the program containing the instruction is assembled (low-level language) or compiled (high-level language), the result is one or more **machine instructions** (also **object instructions**). These are also bit patterns but in a condensed and precise form that can be interpreted by the control unit during execution. In a high-level language, a single source instruction may be expanded into a large number of machine instructions while, in a low-level language, there is, typically, a one-for-one correspondence. The term 'instruction' is used freely for all three forms (programming language; source code; machine code) and the one intended can be determined only by context. See *execution; address; modifier; operator; operand; program; branch instruction*. (2) A unique bit pattern that, when read by the control unit, causes the electronic-level performance of one of the designed operations of the computer. Such an instruction is one of the elements of the **instruction set** (also **order code**) of the computer. Each operator in a 'machine instruction' is a bit pattern that is identical to one 'instruction' by this definition. See *execution; microcode; instruction set*.

instruction address (1) An address in an instruction; usually the address of an operand. (2) The address of an instruction as used in an instruction fetch.

instruction address register A current address register.

instruction code See *instruction set*.

instruction control unit (1) An instruction processor. (2) A control unit.

instruction counter A current address register.

instruction cycle See *execution*.

instruction decoder The elements of a control unit involved in decoding instructions. See *execution; microinstruction; decode*.

instruction fetch A control unit operation of using an address from the current address register to read the next instruction to be obeyed from its storage location and loading it in the instruction register. See *current address register; execution; fetch*.

instruction field A part of an instruction that is used, according to the syntax of the programming language, for a particular purpose; ('an operand field'; 'a modifier field').

instruction format An arrangement of instruction elements (operators; modifiers; operands) that is permissible according to the rules of a programming language.

instruction location register A current address register.

instruction modification The changing of an operand within an instruction in order to cause the operation of the instruction to be performed on or with a different item of data the next time it is executed. The method is only possible with a low-level language. It is not often used because of the need to initialise the address each time the program containing the instruction is run. See *address modification*.

instruction modifier A value that is used to increment an address in instruction modification or, possibly, to change the operation it performs.

instruction processor Also, in some systems, *order code processor; instruction control unit.* In a multiprocessor computer; the processor used to decode and execute instructions (of user and system programs). It is usually also the 'control processor'.

instruction register Also *control register.* A control-unit register that holds the instruction currently being decoded and obeyed. See *current address register; execution; register*.

instruction repertoire The instruction operators available for use in a particular programming language; a group of symbols that represent all the operations that can be performed within the facilities of the language.

instruction scheduler A term sometimes applied to a control unit or to the elements of a control unit that decode instructions, fetch instructions and operands, and store results.

instruction set Also *order code; instruction code.* A set of bit patterns (instructions) in control-unit memory that control the operations of a computer and, collectively, define all the operations that the computer can perform. See *execution; register; microcode; microinstruction*.

instruction stream A flow of instructions (operators in bit-pattern form) from a control unit to an arithmetic unit during processing. (The term is applied mainly to such a flow in a multiprocessor computer.) See *stream; data stream*.

instruction time The time taken to fetch an instruction and load it into the instruction register for decoding.

instruction word A word used to hold an instruction.

instrumentation (1)The operation of using or installing 'instruments'; say, in process control. (2)A collective term for the instruments (meters; sensors) used in a system. (3)In some systems; a term applied to the subset of computer resources involved in performing monitoring and journalising operations.

insulated gate field effect transistor (IGFET) An MOS transistor in which the gate has no connection to an external circuit. See *FAMOS*.

insulation A dielectric material used to isolate an electrical conductor from contact with other conductors or non-circuit elements in its environment; for example, a plastic coating extruded on a wire as a step of manufacture.

insulation displacement (ID) A term applied to a method of making electrical contact with the conductor(s) of an insulated wire or cable that does not involve removing insulation. Most methods use pins that are driven into the ends or through the insulation of ribbon cable.

insulator (1)A non-conducting element used to support and/or separate electrical conductors. (2)A dielectric.

integer (1)A 'whole' number; a number without a fractional part; for example, —2, 1, 9, 15, or 27,654. See *number; mixed number*. (2)A numeric data item in which the radix point is assumed to be at the right of the least significant digit; a data item with no representation of a fractional part.

integer constant A string of decimal digits containing no decimal point.

integral (1)Consisting of or concerned with integers; ('integral numbers'; 'integral calculus'). (2)Contained within; not separate; ('an integral clock'; 'an integral modem').

integral boundary A main storage location to which a fixed-length field (half-word; double word) must be positioned. Its address is an integral byte multiple of the length of the field.

integral disc A fixed disc.

integral number An integer.

integrated (1)Of separate items (or items that are usually considered to be separate); included as a unit or intended to function as a unit. (2)Also *integral*. Built in; contained in the same enclosure.

integrated adapter An adapter that provides a direct data transfer path without using input/output channels; for example, between main storage and a cache memory.

integrated circuit (IC) (1)An electronic circuit in which the elements (transistors; diodes; connectors) are produced on a single small substrate (chip) by a process involving masking, etching, and diffusion. See *semiconductor; chip; microelectronics; SSI; LSI; VLSI; MSI.* (2)One or more 'integrated circuits' (def. 1) in an enclosure with connectors for mounting (usually onto a printed circuit board). See *DIL*.

integrated data base See *data base*.

Integrated Database Management System (IDMS) A CODASYL specified proprietary system (Cullinane Corp., Boston) that provides the facilities for structuring and using a large data base.

integrated data processing (IDP) A term that is sometimes applied to data processing in which all operations from data acquisition to dissemination of results are performed at a single location under common management and control.

integrated data store (IDS) In some systems; a data access management method (file organisation and utilities) that uses chained records.

integrated disc A fixed disc.

integrated filestore Also *secondary storage*. In some virtual storage systems; that part of backing storage held in pages and/or segments in a fast-access magnetic disc unit (a primary or secondary paging device).

integrated injection logic (I^2L) A type of logic circuit characterised by high packing density, medium propagation delay (20 ns.) and extremely low power dissipation (0.05 milliwatt/gate). The basic circuit is a bipolar R-S flip-flop in which a single multi-collector PNP transistor provides power (+5 V.) for each flip-flop via two of the collectors. Each flip-flop consists of two dual-collector NPN transistors, all such transistors having common emitters (the substrate). In the circuit shown, when in-

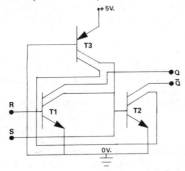

put R is high, transistor T1 conducts and Q is low. The other collector of T1 applies low to the gate of T2 preventing it from conducting and allowing $\bar{Q}$ to float high (with positive from an external circuit). If input S goes high, T2 conducts causing $\bar{Q}$ to go low. The other collector of T2 applies low to the gate of T1 and (unless R is held high externally) causes it to turn off, allowing Q to float high.

integrated modem A modem that is incorporated in the device that uses it; for example, in a terminal control unit.

integrated network processor In some systems; a front-end processor that is used to control both peripheral transfers and communications lines.

integration (1)The process of finding the area (or other attributes) of irregularly shaped objects by mathematical operations that are the equivalent of dividing the irregular area or volume into a finite number of units of regular shape that can be added or multiplied to find the required total. (2)The process of incorporating separate items to form a single unit or structure; for example, the incorporation of a large number of transistors into an 'integrated' circuit. (3)The process of combining multiple analogue inputs to produce a single output.

integrator A device with an output that is an analogue representation of two inputs; for example, a watt-hour meter in which the output is a function of electric current and time.

integrity (1)A term applied to data when considering its accuracy, validity, or freedom from corruption. (2)A term applied to a computer system, spaces, or operating procedures when considering the protection of data from corruption or unauthorised access.

intelligence Of a device; the ability to perform operations and/or to modify the way they are performed in accordance with self-contained instructions in memory.

intelligent Also *smart*. A term applied to devices with control provided by instructions in an integral memory; ('intelligent terminals'; 'intelligent machine tools'). See *unintelligent*.

intensity Brightness; the amount of light emitted by the elements of a display (LED's; screen phosphors).

interaction A message pair.

interaction time In some systems; the time required by a computer to accept one line of input from a (multi-access) terminal. See *response time*.

interactive Also, usually, *conversational*. A term applied to a computer system in which a terminal operator and a computer can jointly perform some operation by means of initiating actions and responses. The term is used to include both transaction processing and multi-access. See *on-line; conversational mode; message pair*.

interactive graphics The facilities or operation of a computer graphics system in which an operator of a graphics VDU can change the display. See *passive graphics*.

interactive mode Conversational mode.

interactive system A system that supports multi-access and/or transaction processing.

interblock gap (IBG) Also *interrecord gap; record gap*. In magnetisable surface storage in which the block is the unit of data recording and transfer; a space between blocks that is not recorded with data. (In magnetic disc, it may contain a block identifier or count.) With magnetic disc it is usually between 0.125 and 0.75 inches in length and with magnetic tape, between 0.4 and 0.75 inches in length. In magnetic tape recording, it serves both as a delimiter and as a zone where the tape is accelerated and decelerated.

intercept (1) With respect to a dialed telephone call; to route it to a special operator or to equipment that produces a recorded message, for example, when the number dialed is out of service. **(2)** With respect to a message in a packet or message switching system; to receive it in an exchange and hold it (say, for a station that is temporarily out of service). **(3)** The part of a line that appears between two other lines or specified points in a graphics display.

intercepted terminal An interactive terminal that cannot accept messages.

interchange (1) To transpose. **(2)** Also *conversation; dialogue*. A sequence of related messages between a computer and a terminal in a transaction processing system. See *message pair*. **(3)** An exchange; the location or facilities involved in routing messages or calls.

interchange address (IA) A combination of characters that uniquely identifies an interchange (def. 3) in a data network. See *address (Communications); terminal address*.

intercom *INTERCOMmunications system*.

intercommunications system (intercom) A communications system for internal (in-plant; inter-office) communications that does not use a switchboard.

interface (1) A boundary between systems or functional units with different characteristics; a place where signals or data in a form suitable for transmission on one system pass for conversion to a form suitable for another. The term may be applied to a cable or a connector, to a device that performs a conversion operation, or to a conceptual boundary. **(2)** To interact or to share facilities. In this sense, a program can 'interface' with an operating system. **(3)** To interconnect devices or systems with different characteristics; to create an 'interface' (def. 1).

interface computer (1) A computer (typically, a minicomputer) that performs conversion functions at an interface. The term includes front-end processors that provide interface functions between a mainframe and communications links and such devices as data channels that perform peripheral transfer functions. **(2)** A computer that performs conversion functions between computers with incompatible characteristics.

interface control unit Also *interface controller*. An intelligent device that performs interface functions; for example, a peripheral controller or a communications controller.

interface device A device that performs one or more interface functions.

interface function A function performed at an interface in order to permit signals or data to be passed between systems with different characteristics. Typical functions include code conversion, conversion between bit-serial and bit-parallel, synchronisation, and the matching of electrical characteristics of lines and cables. Additional functions may include buffering and queue management, error detection and resolution, multiplexing, and, in the case of a communications interface, polling and implementing a link protocol.

interface unit An interface device.

interference On a communications link; noise or unintended signals (echo; cross-talk) that impairs the receipt or correct interpretation of speech or data. See *noise*.

interlace sync In a VDU display; a method that can be used for enhancing dot matrix characters by introducing a delay in beginning alternate vertical scans in order to displace the scan to double the number of dots on vertical lines. By contrast,

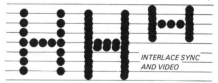

interlace sync and video retains the number of dots of normal synch but places them on half scan line spacing; the purpose is to provide vertical compression and, thus, to permit doubling the number of lines displayed.

interleave (1) To combine two or more groups in such a way that the elements of the different groups are interspersed but with the groups retaining their individual identities. **(2)** To allocate a resource in turn to each of two or more claimants; for example, to allocate processing time to different programs in a multiprogramming system or to allocate line use to different terminals in a multiplexed communications system. See *time division multiplexing; multiprogramming.*

interlock (1)Electrical or mechanical elements that prevent an action from taking place unless a particular condition exists; for example, a microswitch and rod used to prevent the drive motor of a magnetic disc unit from starting unless the cover is closed. (2)To arrange two operations so that events in one enable or inhibit events in the other.

intermediate access memory (IAM) Also *fast access memory* and, sometimes, *secondary memory*. Memory with an access time between that of main storage (core or semiconductor) and that of fast backing storage (drum or fixed-head disc). The term is applied to devices with access times between about 5μs and 15 ms. Technologies include CCD and bubble.

intermediate language A language other than machine code that is produced by a compiler as a step in compiling a high-level language program. Where used, it provides an optimised version of the program with respect to the facilities of the language. Further steps of compilation convert this version to machine code for the particular computer. See *language; compiler.*

intermediate result In performing a (complex) mathematical operation; a result produced in one stage of processing that is used as input to another stage. Such results are, typically, produced by called mathematical routines.

intermediate text language (ITL) A language intermediate between a natural language and a programming language; a language to retain the communicating ability of a natural language while eliminating the imprecision and inconsistencies that have prevented the use of natural languages in writing machine instructions.

internal block A block that is contained in another block.

internal call A call (often made by a PERFORM or DO statement) to a sequence of instructions compiled at the same time as the sequence in which it is called. See *call; external call.*

internal decimal Packed decimal.

internal file name See *file name.*

internal floating point Floating point in a bit-pattern representation as held in main storage or control unit registers. See *floating point; external floating point.*

internal fragmentation See *fragmentation.*

internal memory unit (1)The memory of an intelligent device other than a computer. (2)Main storage.

internal processing unit A central processor (control unit and arithmetic unit).

internal reference An internal call.

internal sort (1)A sort performed in main storage. (2)Of items identified by keys; a preliminary sort in which the keys only are sorted in a work area; it is followed by an (external) merge in which the actual items are written to a file in their new order.

internal storage That part of the storage of a computer system that can be accessed by the control unit without going through input/output channels. The term includes main storage (wherever located) plus any storage within the control unit or arithmetic logic unit such as slave, cache, or scratchpad. See *storage; external storage.*

internal storage code Storage code; the set of bit patterns in which data in character form is held in a computer.

internal subprogram See *subprogram.*

internal subroutine See *subroutine.*

International Organization for Standardization (ISO) An organisation of member countries that promotes the development and use of product and terminology standards to facilitate international trade.

internetworking The practice or techniques of passing data between data networks with different protocols.

interpret (1)To evaluate or to translate; ('interpret an error listing'; 'interpret a hole pattern'). (2)With respect to a source program; to translate and execute statements one at a time in sequence. See *interpreter.*

interpreter (1)A language processor that translates and executes source code one instruction at a time, usually without retaining the object code; the process may be termed **immediate mode**. Interpreters are used in performing one-off jobs (for example, using the computer as a calculator) and in debugging. See *incremental compiler; immediate mode.* (2)A device that 'interprets' the hole patterns punched on a punched card and prints the corresponding characters on the card. A **transfer interpreter** prints the characters on a different card.

interpretive code Code that is intended to be executed by an interpreter (def. 1).

interpretive program An interpreter (def. 1).

interrecord gap (IRG) An interblock gap; particularly such a gap in a file in which each record occupies a block.

interrogate To provide the parameters for a search; to identify a required item of data; ('interrogate a file'; 'interrogate a data base').

interrogation (1)The process of identifying and locating a required item of data in a data structure. See *interrogate*. (2) The process of requesting a terminal or data station to identify itself or to indicate status.

interrupt With respect to a sequence of instructions being executed; to stop the execution and transfer control to another sequence of instructions while retaining the values (register contents) necessary to resume the execution. Though the cause may be within the sequence of instructions being executed (looping; bound violation) the condition is detected and the transfer of control is performed by an **interrupt routine** which is a unit of system software. Depending upon the system, interrupts can occur when peripheral devices change status, when preset values are exceeded, when a hardware or software failure occurs, when a higher priority task is received, or when a program can no longer continue to execute. A **simple interrupt** is an interrupt in a system with provision for only one interrupt condition. A **vectored interrupt** is one in which the cause is identified. A **priority interrupt** is a vectored interrupt that indicates when it should be dealt with in relation to other interrupts that may be receiving or awaiting attention. An **external interrupt** is an interrupt that does not result directly from processing; for example, one that is caused by an operator or by a timer. (The term may include interrupts caused by changes in status of peripherals.) An **internal interrupt** is either one that is caused within the interrupted sequence or any interrupt resulting from processing (and not outside intervention). See *context switching*.

interrupt driven A term applied to an operating system that handles multiprogramming by allowing processing to continue for one program until an interrupt occurs (usually for a peripheral transfer) and then changing processing to another program. See *multiprogramming; multistreaming*.

interrupt event An event that causes an interrupt; a detected variation from a normal or preset condition that requires intervention by the operating system and, possibly, the operator.

interruption network A network of circuits in a computer system that continuously monitors its operation and produces interrupts when specified conditions differ from normal or preset.

intersection (1)A place where two lines cross; a place identifiable by coordinates. (2)An AND logical operation.

interstage punching The punching of card columns between those normally punched; when it is used, a standard 80-column punched card contains 159 columns.

intertask communications The exchange of data and/or control information between (user) tasks on different computers.

interval A separating time between successive events or a separating distance between adjacent entities.

intervention (1)To interrupt or change an operation while in process. (2)Cycle stealing.

intrinsic call A call to an intrinsic procedure.

intrinsic procedure Also *function*. A multistep operation initiated by a macro that is part of the facilities of a programming language.

intrusion tone An audible signal that may be superimposed when a third party connects to (wire taps) a telephone call.

invalid Cannot be used, considered, or performed because it fails to meet established standards or criteria; ('an invalid address'; 'an invalid name'; 'an invalid instruction'). See *illegal*.

inverse video On the screen of a cathode ray tube; a display in which the background is light and the display elements dark.

inverted file A file organised specifically to facilitate locating records by means of their auxiliary keys. Such a file is, typically, indexed sequentially in order of the auxiliary keys to be considered with each index entry holding one of the auxiliary keys and all of the primary keys of records that hold that auxiliary key. For example, in a library information system one of the auxiliary keys could be for 'polar bears' and this entry in the index would contain the primary keys by which all periodicals could be identified that had articles on polar bears. The alternative method of indexing such a file is the non-inverted form in which the index is sequential by primary keys with each entry containing a primary key followed by all relevant auxiliary keys. For example, the primary key for an issue of Geographical Magazine might be followed by ten or more auxiliary keys, one of which would be for 'polar bears'. If the inverted file structure is used, a student interested in polar bears would need to input only one key and the system could quickly print out the names and dates of all periodicals containing information on the subject. By contrast, the same request of a non-inverted file requires the reading of every auxiliary key in the index in order to locate the periodicals. A **partially inverted file** is one in which the index has the organisation of a non-inverted file with a second index by those auxiliary keys that are known to require frequent reference. Such a file could, for example, provide a rapid reference to articles on polar bears but a much slower location of those relating to, say, areca palms. A **fully inverted file** is one that is indexed only by auxiliary keys, each of which is followed by the relevant primary keys. A file so organised would be very slow when interrogated, for example, for the contents of a particular issue of Geographical Magazine but would be very fast for references by subject matter.

inverted tree A block diagram of a tree structure with the 'root' shown at the top. It is the usual way in which a tree is diagramed and considered when representing organisations and data structures. See *tree*.

inverter (1) A device that is used to convert direct current to alternating current; it may be a motor-generator or a **static inverter** which performs the function with power transistors/thyristors. **(2)** A circuit that has an output of logic level opposite to its input. On the left is the symbol and usual circuit of a high-input inverter; when the input goes high (say, +5 V.), the transistor turns ON and the output drops from high to low (to nearly 0 V.). The other symbol and circuit is of a low-input inverter; when the input goes low, the transistor turns OFF and the output goes from low to high.

invisible A term applied to an operation (say, parity checking) or to a hardware element (say, microcode storage) that is not evident to a user program and need not be considered by a programmer. See *transparent*.

invitation In a data network; the process by which a data station is requested to send any messages it may have. The term may be used to include both polling and enabling, in which the 'invitation' is made by connecting a line. See *polling; selection*.

invitation list A polling list.

invitation to send (ITS) A transmission control character used in an (ASR) teletypewriter system to cause the tape transmitter of a remote device to send its data to the line.

invoice A document sent by a supplier to a customer giving details of particular supplies or services provided and the amount owed for them.

invoke (1) To cause to be executed. The term is usually applied to a utility or other unit of system software rather than to an application program. See *call*. **(2)** To cause to be brought into main storage; ('invoke a segment'; 'invoke a compiler').

I/O *Input/Output*.

I/O controller A peripheral controller.

I/O device See *input/output device*.

I/O interrupt An interrupt that occurs at a point where a program requires a peripheral transfer; where it needs to input additional code or data or to output results or perform a dump.

IO *Input/Output*.

IOC *Input/Output Controller*.

IOM *Input/Output Multiplexor*.

IOP *Input/Output Processor*.

IOQ *Input/Output Queue*.

IOR *Inclusive OR*.

IPC *Independent Control Point*.

IPL *Initial Program Loader*.

IPS (1) *Instructions Per Second*. **(2)** *Inches Per Second*.

IPSS *International Packet Switched Service*. A packet switching system between the U.S. and Europe.

IR *Information Retrieval*.

IRG *InterRecord Gap*.

irrational number A number that cannot be formed by dividing one integer by another. See *number*.

IS *Information Separator*.

ISAM *Indexed Sequential Access Method*.

ISO *International Organization for Standardization*. (Geneva)

ISO-7 Also *ASCII; USASCII; IA-5; ANSI X3.4*. A common 7-bit (usually 8-bit with parity) code for data communications. It is also used as the storage code for many communications-related devices such as terminals and terminal control units. It contains 128 characters including control characters, upper and lower case letters, decimal digits, symbols, punctuation marks, and national characters. ISO-7 is identical to ASCII with the exception that ten bit patterns can be optionally allocated to national characters. See *CODE TABLE; national characters.*

isochronous Asynchronous; with fixed timing for bits and characters. See *anisochronous.*

isolate (1)To identify the part of a computer system in which a fault is located and to change configuration or adopt procedures to permit processing to continue. See *resilience; reconfiguration; fault.* (2)To separate two electrical circuits. See *circuit isolation.*

isolation test routine (ITR) A diagnostic test program.

ITA *International Telegraph Alphabet.*

iteration (1)The use of a loop in processing; the repetition of a sequence of instructions in order to perform an operation successively with different operands. See *loop.* (2)The repetition of a step or a sequence of steps as a method of solving a problem and/or refining a solution. For example, a method of obtaining a square root by making an initial estimate and refining it in successive, repetitive steps. See *recursive routine.* (3)One performance of the step or pass-through of the sequence of an 'iteration' (def. 1; 2).

iterative Performed by iteration.

iterative routine (1)A loop. (2)A routine that contains a loop. See *loop.*

ITL *Intermediate Text Language.*

ITR *Isolation Test Routine.*

ITS *Invitation To Send.*

ITT *International Telephone & Telegraph Co.* (Fort Wayne, Ind.)

ITU *International Telecommunications Union.* (Geneva)

J

jack A recessed electrical connector in which a round plug can be inserted; it is commonly used on test equipment.

jagging The condition in raster scan graphics in which curved and diagonal lines are represented on the screen in 'stair steps' with the distance between adjacent steps equal to the spacing of the scan lines.

JCL *Job Control Language.*

jitter A rapid, incidental phase modulation in data transmission. Its cause is poorly regulated or overloaded power regulators in the telephone system. It is usually at a harmonic of the ringing tone or the mains frequency.

job Also, in some systems, *task.* One or more application programs and their data submitted together for processing. It is the common unit of work for scheduling and resource allocation in batch processing. See *task; batch; run.*

job batch Two or more job definitions arranged in the order in which the jobs they control will be processed.

job control (1)Control over the way processing is performed and the allocation of processing resources as provided by a programmer or operator by means of instructions to the operating system in a job control language. (2)Control over processing methods and resources as exercised by an operating system. (3)Those steps performed by system software in preparing a job to run; for example, initialisation, assigning devices, logging job control statements, and fetching the first instruction to be executed.

job control card A punched card that contains job control statements for a particular job.

job control language (JCL) Also, in some systems, *command language.* A computer-specific language used to instruct the operating system with respect to the way processing is to be performed. It consists of all the job control statements that can be used to control processing performed by a particular operating system and computer. See *job control; job control statement.*

job control statement A statement, within the facilities of a job control language, that identifies a job or describes its requirements to the operating system. Statements are, typically, available to identify terminal users for security purposes, to identify jobs for accounting purposes, to identify resources (devices; files; compilers; storage) that will be required, to specify file organisations, to specify exception conditions and actions, and to specify the form of results.

job definition Also *job description.* A sequence of job control statements that define the processing environment of a particular job.

job description A job definition.

job input device A peripheral used to input job definitions and any accompanying data.

job input file A file containing a series of job definitions and accompanying data.

job input stream An input stream.

job management Job control (def. 1).

job name A jobname.

job-oriented terminal A dedicated terminal; a terminal used for only a particular type of job; for example, order entry or direct data entry.

job output device A peripheral used to output the results produced by one or more jobs.

job output file A file containing the output produced by one or more jobs.

job output stream An output stream.

job priority An assigned value that determines the scheduling and resource allocation for a job in relation to other jobs.

job processing (1)Processing in which the 'job' is the unit of scheduling and accounting. (2)The reading of job definitions and data from an input stream and initiating the specified actions.

job queue Those jobs that have been cleared for processing and are awaiting the allocation of processing resources.

job scheduler A scheduler.

job stacking The formation of a job queue by placing job definitions and data in a job input device in the order in which they will be processed. See *job batch*.

job statement The job control statement that begins a job definition; it, typically, contains the name of the job, the account number, and the assigned priority.

job step A job or a portion of a job that constitutes a single load module.

job step initiation The process of selecting a job step for execution and assigning required input and output devices.

job step restart A step restart.

job stream An input stream.

jobname The name of a job as input via a job statement.

joggle To align the edges of the punched cards in a deck (as by tapping on a flat surface) prior to loading in a card punch or reader.

Josephson junction A storage or logic element in some types of cryogenic memory.

JOSS *Johnniac Open-Shop System*. A programming language designed to provide fast calculations for solving complex mathematical problems.

journal Also *journal file*. A (magnetic tape) file to which selected data is written for such purposes as accounting, performance evaluation, or for maintaining a record of processing events. Depending upon the purpose, it could be used for logging communications between an operator and the operating system, recording resource utilisation chargeable to different accounts, and logging details of errors as they occur. A journal may also be used to record transactions affecting a particular file for possible use in de-updating.

journaling Journalising.

journalising The operation of writing to a journal.

JOVIAL *Jule's Own Version of International Algorithmic Language*. A multipurpose language used in command and control applications.

joy stick On some graphics VDU's; an operator control used to move display elements simultaneously in two directions.

jump Also *branch*. To discontinue executing one sequence of instructions and commence executing another. When 'branch' and 'jump' are differentiated, 'branch' usually refers to a transfer of control from a main sequence of instructions to another sequence (often a subprogram) that performs a processing function for the program whereas a 'jump' can be any transfer of control; for example, to or from an interrupt routine. See *branch*.

jump instruction An instruction that specifies a jump; an instruction that produces the address of an entry point in another sequence of instructions.

jumper Also, sometimes, *strap*. A wire or cable used to make a (short distance) connection as between two electrical terminals. See *strap*.

junction In a semiconductor; an interface between N-type and P-type silicon. See *semiconductor*.

junction FET A transistor that operates partly by 'field effect' and partly as a bipolar transistor. Figure 1 shows the symbol and a common circuit connection and Fig. 2 shows the

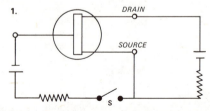

construction. The N-type layer is formed by deposition on a P-type substrate and the P-type gate is formed by diffusion in the N-type material that constitutes the source, drain, and connecting channel. The operation is complex at the electron level but certain combinations of gate-source and drain-source voltage

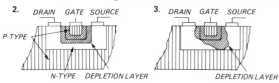

set up a field and cause an electron transfer that extends the depletion zone into the channel to cut off conduction, as indicated in Fig. 3. See *field effect transistor*.

justify (1) To position data that does not fill a field or register so that it is 'blocked' to the left or right boundary. If the data is blocked to the right it is said to be 'right justified' and if to the left 'left justified'; unless otherwise indicated, it is understood

RIGHT JUSTIFY	0	0	0	0	1	0	1	1	0	1
LEFT JUSTIFY	1	0	1	1	0	1	0	0	0	0

to be right justified. (2) In print preparation and word processing; to format copy so that lines are of equal length with left-hand ends aligned on one vertical line and right-hand ends aligned on another vertical line (as in this dictionary).

K

k (1)(k.) *Kilo-*. An abbreviation indicating 1000 in decimal notation. (2)(K) *Kilo-*. An abbreviation that, when capitalised and used relative to computers, indicates 1024. For example, a computer with 16K words of memory has 16,384 words.

Karnaugh map A form of truth table used to describe the logic of relatively complex circuits; (logic arrays; data selectors; multiplexors). The example is a map for the circuit of the *data selector* entry. It shows, for example, that if the Select A signal is high (1) and B is low (0), the

D_1 data input passes through as the output. Each intersection of the map is a 'mintern' and these are often identified by their binary numbers, for example, '11' identifies the D_4 mintern. See *data selector; mintern*.

KB *KiloByte*.

kernel (1) That part of an operating system that must always be in main stoge when any part of it is loaded. It consists of rigorously tested routines that perform basic loading and superisory functions including the 'bootstrap' operation of loading the rest of the operating system. (2) That part of a segmented program that must always be in main storage when any other segment is loaded.

kernalised Of an operating system; constructed with a 'kernel'.

key (File organisation) A value that identifies a record and is used to locate it in storage. Keys are, typically, numeric (customer number; part number), but they may be alphabetic (employee name) or alphanumeric. Within the same file, each record's key is held in the same field (the **key field**) that is usually the first field in the record or one of the first fields. (In some systems, the keys are held in a separate table that references them to 'record numbers' which are values held in the records.) In sequential and indexed sequential files, records are written to the file in ascending or descending order of their keys. In a random file, records are placed in order according to numbers produced by applying an algorithm to their keys. An access in which a record or group of records is located by key is a **keyed access** (as contrasted to a serial access, a sequential access, or a content access). (A sequential access is a form of 'keyed access' but is not normally included by the common usage of the term.) Unless otherwise indicated, the term 'key' is synonymous with **primary key**; it uniquely identifies a record in a file. In some files, two or more records may have the same primary keys (say, of a customer with several branch offices) in which case one or more **secondary keys** (say, giving location) are required to make a unique identification. In many files, it is necessary to locate records by attribute (for example, to determine which parts are supplied by a particular manufacturer). A key that identifies an attribute (say, the manufacturer of each part) is an **auxiliary key**. (More than one auxiliary key may be required to make a unique identification.) See *inverted file; associative storage; search; content access*.

key (Privacy code) The reference or algorithm necessary to represent data in a privacy code or to reconstruct the original from such a representation.

key (Storage protection) In some multiprogramming systems; a value used to define or limit the access rights of programs. See *storage protection*.

key (Telegraphy) (1) A device with a finger-operated lever with contacts that make and break a circuit to send characters by means of dots and dashes or spaced clicks. **(2)**To send characters or a message by means of such a device.

key (Typewriter or terminal) **(1)**An element of a keyboard; a button or switch actuator that, when pressed, causes the printing, display, or transmission of a character or performance of a control function. **(2)**To send or enter data by means of a keyboard; ('key data from a source document'; 'key a message').

key entry The use of a keyboard to enter data. See *direct data entry*.

key field A field of a record that can contain a primary, secondary, or auxiliary key. See *key (File organisation)*.

key in With respect to a message or item of data; to enter it by means of a keyboard.

key pulse A pulse (electrical signal) produced by pressing a key.

key rollover In a terminal or other keyboard device; a facility for buffering characters produced by key operation to prevent loss of data that could be caused by short, rapid bursts of key operation that exceed the printing or other handling capability of the device for a short period. See *n-key rollover*.

key sort An internal sort.

key station A terminal with a keyboard (it may be a full keyboard or may consist of only a few special-purpose keys).

key-to-disc A direct data entry system in which data entered at a key station is assembled on magnetic disc.

key-to-tape A direct data entry system in which data entered at a keystation is placed on magnetic tape.

keyboard That part of a terminal or operating station that consists of keys, each of which, when pressed, causes a formatting operation (carriage return; tabulate), a control operation (acknowledge; enter) or the printing, display, or transmission of a character. (In most computer equipment the keyboard is an expanded version of that of an ordinary typewriter.)

keyboard entry The use of a keyboard to enter data; for example, from a terminal or by a card punch.

keyboard lock See *lock*.

keyboard monitor A program that controls message transfers between a console typewriter/printer and the operating system of a computer.

keyboard punch A keypunch.

keyboard send and receive See *KSR*.

keyboard typing reperforator See *KTR*.

keyed (1) Containing or using (record) keys; ('a keyed record'; 'a keyed access'). **(2)**Entered by means of a keyboard.

keyed access Access in which a record or a group of records is located by key or by a combination of keys.

keyed serial file An ordered serial file.

keying (1) The operation of using a keyboard. **(2)**The operation of using a telegraph key.

keying wave The unmodulated signal transmitted in a telegraph system when a key is operated.

keypad terminal A terminal containing less than a full alphanumeric keyboard; for example, one containing ten numeric keys plus control keys.

keypunch A device with a keyboard used to punch data-related hole patterns in punched cards or paper tape. (Unless otherwise indicated, a 'card punch' is assumed.)

keyword (1)A predefined word in a programming language; a word with a specified meaning in the structure of the language. **(2)**A word by which a document, article, or book can be located in a library information system. **(3)**A descriptor.

kilo- (1)A combining form (abbreviated 'k') meaning 1000 as in 'kilogram' (kg.), 'kilocycle' (kc.) and 'kilometer' (km.). **(2)**A combining form (abbreviated 'K') meaning 1024 (2^{10}) as in 'kilobyte', 'kilobit' and 'kiloword'.

kilobit 1024 bits.

kilobyte 1024 bytes.

kilobyte second A unit of data transfer speed or computer storage utilisation. In the storage utilisation context, a program that uses 10 kilobytes of storage for 0.2 seconds during some phase of processing uses 2 'kilobyte seconds' of storage.

KIPS *K (1024) Instructions Per Second.*

knowledge engineering A term sometimes applied to the design and construction of information systems.

knowledge system An information system; particularly one with sophisticated data retrieval facilities.

KSR *Keyboard Send and Receive.* A designation of a common teletypewriter device with a keyboard used to send messages and a printer that prints both incoming and outgoing messages.

KTR *Keyboard Typing Reperforator.* A designation of a teletypewriter device with a keyboard, a paper tape punch, and a printer that prints the characters of incoming and outgoing messages on the paper tape adjacent to their punched bit patterns.

L

L The standard symbol for 'inductance'.

L-view In data base terminology; the view of a user or an application program; that which is apparent in a subschema.

label (1)Also *entry label; entry name*. A character string (a symbol) that identifies a sequence of instructions within a program that may be entered with its first instruction as the entry point. It is used to permit selective execution of particular sequences without executing the entire program or to permit one copy of a sequence to be used in different parts of a program. The sequence is usually termed a **subprogram**. (2)A symbolic address or data name; a character string that identifies a resource that a program will use during execution. (3) Housekeeping and identifying data written at the beginning of data on magnetic disc or tape; depending upon the system and context the term may be synonymous with 'header', 'header label', 'flag', 'track label', 'label block', or 'header record'. (4) A key, a 'record label'. (5)A piece of paper with identifying information as attached to a tape reel or cannister, disc pack, etc.

laced card A punched card with excess holes (and, hence, meaningless bit patterns) in some or all columns.

lag (1)By one event; to follow after another event. (2)The amount of time separating two related events.

lambda calculus A conceptual programming language used in evaluating language functions and in the study and notation of programming languages; it does not result in executable code.

laminar Existing in thin layers that have different flow patterns; for example, the air layers adjacent to a moving disc.

laminations Thin die-punched steel pieces fastened together to form the magnetic flux path of devices such as motors, transformers, and alternating current relays. See *coil*.

land By a read/write head in some (Winchester technology) magnetic disc units; to come into contact with the disc surface in a 'landing zone' as a normal step during deceleration of the disc. See *fly; take off; head-disc interference*.

landing zone In some (Winchester technology) magnetic disc systems; a band on a disc surface on which a read/write head takes off and lands and on which it rests when the disc is stopped. See *fly; loading zone*.

landline facilities A term applied to data communications facilities within the continental U.S.

language A set of sounds, symbols or characters, or a combination of these, that is used in accordance with certain rules or conventions to communicate between people or between people and machines. A **natural language** is one commonly used by people in communicating with each other; its rules and vocabulary evolve over a period of time. By contrast, an **artificial language** is one created for a particular purpose with usage governed by rules that are established with its creation. A **conceptual language** is either a natural language or an artificial language with facilities for expressing concepts and interrelationships in some particular field such as, possibly, semantics, physics, or medicine. A **programming language** is an artificial language designed for use by people in instructing machines. Its characteristic is a structure and syntax that prevents ambiguous constructions. With respect to a particular computer system, a programming language is often termed a **source language**; it is a language in which programs are written to control the operations of the computer system. The term **computer language** is sometimes used as a synonym for either a 'programming language' or a 'source language'. A source language may be either a **high-level language** or a **low-level language**. A high-level language is one (such as COBOL or FORTRAN) that is designed for ease of use in writing programs and is intended to be used to program computers of different manufacture and type. The term 'high-level' is used because a whole sequence of computer operations can be specified by writing a single, simple, 'instruction' in the language. By contrast, a low-level language is one that requires the programmer to tell the computer quite explicitly what is to be done at each step with, typically, a separate instruction required for each step that is to be performed. The term 'low-level language' is applied when considering such languages generally; the low-level language for a particular computer model or type is termed its **assembly language** or **assembler**. An assembly language is designed to make effective use of the storage and facilities of the computer though this is obtained at the cost of considerably more programming effort than is required when a high-level language is used. A low-level language may also be termed a **computer-oriented language**. High-level languages are often classified as 'problem-oriented' and 'procedure-oriented'. A **problem-oriented language** is one designed to solve a particular problem or class of problems; for example, calculating the stresses in steel beams or laying out printed circuit boards. They usually require little from a programmer other than a statement of what is to be done; most are intended to be used by people who are not professional programmers. The programming languages in most common use (such as COBOL and FORTRAN) are **procedure-oriented languages** that are designed to be used to perform a variety of tasks in some particular field; COBOL, for example, is designed for business use and FORTRAN is designed mainly for scientific use. A **general-purpose language** is a language with the facilities and flexibility to be used in a variety of applications; the most common example is PL/1. A **fixed-format language** is one in which each instruction must conform to some prescribed format if it is to be accepted as valid. A **free-form language** is one in which considerable latitude is allowed in the content and arrangement of instructions. Instructions in either a high-level or low-level source language are translated by one or more **language processors** into 'object code' which may be termed **machine language** or **object language** and has sometimes been termed **computer language**. A language processor may make use of an **intermediate language** in translating a high-level language into machine language; such a language is not visible to the programmer. An **intermediate text language** is an artificial language that is precise enough for constructing programs but which has many of the communicating facilities of a natural language. See *instruction; program; execution.*

language processor A program that performs some or all of the steps of producing an object code version of a program from a source code version. The term commonly includes compilers, assemblers, translators, interpreters, linkage editors, precompilers, and source converters.

language statement A statement in a source language or job control language that affects the way a program is compiled or processed.

language translator See *translator.*

large core storage (LCS) Bulk storage.

large scale integration (LSI) A term applied to semiconductor devices with between about 100 and 1000 gates formed on a single (silicon) chip. See *small scale integration; medium scale integration; VLSI.*

laser A device that produces 'tuned' light or light that is all of the same frequency (as contrasted to normal light that contains a wide spectrum of frequencies).

laser beam recording (LBR) A technique used in a microfilm recorder whereby characters of computer output are written directly to microfilm by a laser beam. In one system, the beam is produced by a helium-neon laser that is divided by prism into eight separate beams, seven of which are used to write 5×7 dot matrix characters by varying the on-off condition of the beams five times as they pass through each character position. The eighth beam is used to control a mechanical mirror system that scans the recording beams on lines across the frame. Each frame so recorded can contain up to 80 lines of 136 characters. See *COM; recorder.*

laser printer A printer that is similar in operation to an electrostatic page printer except that it uses a laser beam to write dot matrix characters onto the surface of the selenium coated drum instead of exposing it to data displayed on a cathode ray tube. Operating speeds are about 13,000 lines per minute. See *printer; electrostatic printer.*

last-in-first-out See *LIFO.*

latch A flip-flop; an electronic circuit that maintains a particular conducting condition of two possible conditions until changed to the other condition by the receipt of a pulse.

latency (1) A term applied to the delay between the initiation of an access and the receipt of the accessed data at its destination. **(2)** In a magnetic disc or magnetic drum access; the time taken for a unit of data to rotate from wherever it happens to be when the 'read' signal is received to the position of the read/write head where it can be read. The term **channel latency** is applied to the time a data transfer channel between a computer and a device is tied up while waiting for a transfer to begin (it includes any seek time as well as latency). See *seek time; rotational position sensing.* **drive latency** (1) The average latency of a magnetic disc unit. In milliseconds it is equal to 30,000 divided by the rotational speed in R.P.M. For example, a drive that operates at 2,400 R.P.M. has an average latency of 12.5 ms. (2) The time taken for a particular block to rotate to the position where it can be read or written. **(3)** In access of a recirculating memory device (delay line; bubble; CCD), the time required for an item of data to move from wherever it happens to be when called for to the position where it can be read.

lattice file See *net.*

layout character A format effector.

LBN *Logical Bucket Number.*
LBR *Laser Beam Recording.*
LC (l.c.) *Lower Case.*
LCB *Line Control Block.*
LCD *Liquid Crystal Display.*
LCN *Logical Channel Number.*
LCS *Large Core Storage.*
LDA *Logical Device Address.*
LDX *Long-Distance Xerography.*
LE *Less than or Equal to.* See *relational operator.*
lead (rhymes with 'feed') **(1)**By one event; to precede another event. See *lag.* **(2)**The amount of time by which one event precedes another. **(3)**A wire or jumper; for example, a 'test lead' used with a measuring instrument.
lead (rhymes with 'said') to introduce additional space (of less than a full line) between lines as printed or displayed.
leader The part of open-reel magnetic tape before the beginning-of-tape mark; the unrecorded part that is used to thread the tape when loading.
leading zeros Zeros that have no numerical or logical significance that may, because of processing method, appear before the most significant digit or character in a line or field of printout. See *zero suppression.*
leaf In a tree structure; an owner with no members. See *tree.*
leapfrog test A storage test in which a test routine copies itself from one storage location to the next to be tested.
learning By an intelligent device; the retention of pointers defining access paths in a data structure and the rejection of those combinations that define unsuccessful paths from those that will be followed in a subsequent trial.
learning sequence A training sequence.
leased line Also *dedicated line; private line.* A telephone circuit (usually with four-wire presentation) that is continuously connected between user equipment at two or more geographically separated locations. For data communications, such lines have an advantage over dial-up in that they are continuously available, call initiation delays are eliminated, and they are usually quieter because they bypass the switching relays of the telephone exchanges. Such lines are often 'conditioned' to improve their data-handling characteristics. See *dial-up; conditioning.*
least significant bit (LSB) In a bit group; the bit in the farthest right position; the bit that is transmitted first.

least significant digit (LSD) In a number; the digit in the farthest right position; the digit with the lowest weight.
LED *Light-Emitting Diode.*
ledger card A card that holds details of financial transactions; for example, a card in a 'sales ledger'.
left justified See *justify.*
left shift A movement of the contents of a register in increments (one bit, one character, or one digit position) to the left. With numeric data, it has the effect of multiplying by the radix. See *shift register.*
legal With respect to elements of source code (statements; commands; operators); capable of being executed or controlling execution in a particular computer system. See *illegal.*
length The number of smaller units (bits; bytes; characters; words) in a larger unit; ('word length'; 'block length'; 'message length').
lens Of a cathode ray tube; those elements that focus the random emissions from the heater into a coherent electron beam. A **lens magnet** is a magnet used for this purpose. See *cathode ray tube.*
less than (LT) See *relational operator.*
less than or equal to (LE) See *relational operator.*
letter An element of an alphabet. See *alphabet; character; symbol; graphic character.*
letters shift **(1)**(LTRS) A control character that causes a printer terminal (teletypewriter) to change from printing figures to printing letters. See *figures shift.* **(2)**A change from printing figures to printing letters.
level (1) That which distinguishes items or operations with respect to detail or degree of complexity; ('a high-level language'; 'implemented at machine level'). **(2)**A position in a hierarchial structure; ('first-level storage'; 'two-level addressing'; 'multi-level interrupts'). **(3)**Amplitude or signal strength; ('an audible level'; 'a level well above background noise'). **(4)**With respect to a code; the number of bits required to encode a character; for example, Baudot is a 'five-level code' and EBCDIC is 'eight-level'. **(5)**Also *channel.* A line parallel to the edge of paper tape along which data holes can be punched.
level number A reference number that indicates the position of an item in a hierarchial structure.
lexical scan A compilation step in which the elements of source-code statements are identified by type and repetitions are recognised. See *compiler.*

lexicographic A term applied to the recognition of character strings (usually symbolic addresses) by the order of their characters and the position of the characters in a collating sequence.

LF *Line Feed.* A format effector that causes a line feed. See *line feed; NL; VT.*

libname Library name.

librarian (1) A member of data processing staff who is responsible for organising and maintaining library files and controlling their access. **(2)** A program or set of programs used to organise and access the contents of a library.

library In a computer context; a magnetic disc or tape volume or set of volumes containing units of code and/or data that are available to be called by or incorporated in programs. Examples of contents include source programs held for record purposes or for use in constructing similar programs, mathematical routines, compilers and other language processors, and user routines that are frequently required.

library call A call to a library routine. See *call.*

library partition (1) A boundary within a library. **(2)** In some systems; an area of main storage used to hold shareable code or data.

library routine A routine in or from a library; a tested sequence of code available to be called by or included in programs.

LIFO *Last-In-First-Out.* An algorithm used to determine the order of use or consideration; the most recent item to arrive is the first item to be dealt with. It is the inherent structure of a stack. See *FIFO; stack.*

light-emitting diode (LED) A semiconductor device that produces light by electroluminesence when an electric current is passed through gallium phosphide (sometimes gallium arsenide). The most usual colour is red which is produced by gallium arsenide and zinc-oxide doped gallium phosphide; other dopants can produce colours ranging from blue to infrared. Typical operating current is 17-20 milliamps. LED's are used as discrete indicator lights, in segment and matrix displays, and as the light source for fibre optics communications. See *segment display; liquid crystal display.*

light mask A term applied to the use of interruptable light beams in counting and position sensing.

light pen A hand-held photosensitive stylus that detects light from the screen of a graphics VDU as the electron beam scans it and identifies particular places on the screen as points of interest for display change or manipulation. Ideally, a light pen would be able to detect a particular addressable point, but since its field of view is considerably larger than that, it operates in conjunction with an **aiming symbol** (typically, a cross) displayed on the screen. When the pen is placed over the aiming symbol, and the scan sweeps across it, circuitry determines whether or not the aiming symbol is in the centre of the field of the light pen and, if it is not, it causes the aiming symbol to move toward the centre of the field of the pen.

light pen attention A signal that causes the loading of the program that provides light pen functions that is produced when the light pen is placed against the screen.

light pen detect Light pen attention.

limit (1) A maximum or minimum value. **(2)** Also *bound.* The highest numbered or lowest numbered address of a particular area of storage, partition, array, or variable. See *storage protection.*

limited ASCII A subset of the ASCII code.

line (Communications) Also *circuit.* The transmission medium and equipment for carrying speech and/or data between separated locations. Though notionally four wires (a two-wire send channel and a two-wire receive channel), the term commonly includes all telephone facilities between the locations that are used for a particular transmission. In this usage, a 'line' may have either a two-wire or four-wire user termination and may consist of wires, coaxial cable, satellite link, or other sections. See *circuit; link; channel; path.*

line (Print or display) **(1)** A horizontal string of characters as displayed on the screen of a VDU or printed by a printer. **(2)** A horizontal 'band' that extends across sheet, page, form, or screen which is suitable for holding a 'line' (def. 1). **(3)** The distance between the base lines of successive 'lines'; the amount by which the paper must be moved in a printer in order to print the next line. **(4)** In many interactive terminal systems; the amount of data that is transmitted to the computer and processed at one time.

line access unit (LAU) Also *data access arrangement.* An interface switching device that enables an operator to set up half-duplex data transfers on a dialed PSTN line. (Some devices provide for setting up full-duplex transfers on two dialed lines.) Typical functions are to provide a connection for a telephone (used to set up data transfers), to switch between VOICE and DATA, and, usually, to provide automatic answering.

line adapter (1) A self-contained modem; for example, in a terminal control unit. (2) A transaction processing monitor; a unit of software that performs communications interfacing functions. (3) A line sharing adapter.

line code A code (bit-pattern representation of characters) that is used for data transmission (in a non-telegraph system). The most common is 'ASCII'. See *code; storage code*.

line condition In data communications; one of the possible data-significant conditions (frequency, phase, or amplitude of a carrier wave; carrier wave or line voltage on or off) that can be produced by transmitting equipment and detected and interpreted by receiving equipment.

line conditioning See *conditioning*.

line control (1) The supervisory function of selecting and monitoring circuits and routing traffic in a (large) data network as, for example, performed in a **line control centre**. (2) The procedures used to control interchanges and to monitor the performance of the lines and the associated equipment of a telephone or telegraph system.

line control block (LCB) A storage location in a (line interface) device that holds the characteristics (speed; modulation method) of a particular line.

line density The number of lines (per vertical inch) that can be printed by a printer or displayed by a VDU.

line driver (1) A transaction processing monitor; a unit of software that controls communications functions. (2) Hardware that performs such functions as bit-serial/bit-parallel conversion, adding outgoing control characters and interpreting incoming control characters, and buffering incoming data.

line feed(1) In a printer; an upward movement of the paper in one-line increments. (2) A repeat-action key that causes 'line feed' (def. 1). (3)(LF) A control character that causes the paper of a printer to advance by one line space.

line feed character See *LF*.

line group One or more communications lines that are intended to be activated and deactivated as a unit.

line hit A hit; a momentary disturbance on a communications line. See *noise*.

line impedance The resistance of a (local loop) telephone line as presented to user equipment; 600 ohms is standard.

line load (1) The percentage of time that a line is used. (2) The amount of current carried by a line.

line loss Attenuation (on a telephone line).

line noise Noise that is present on a (telephone) line; unless otherwise indicated, it is assumed to be 'white' noise.

line printer A printer that prints a single line of characters at a time by a method other than printing them in sequence from left to right or right to left. Typically, all the characters of the font are moved by each printing position during the cycle of printing each line and the selected character (if any) is printed by impacting paper and ribbon against the font character as it passes. The usual types are barrel printers, band, train, and chain printers, and helix printers. See *printer; character printer; impact printer; page printer*.

line protocol A link protocol.

line sharing adapter In some systems; an intelligent interface device that provides multiplexing and other line-related functions for multiple terminals that make use of a single leased telephone line.

line spacing See *pitch*.

line speed (1) The rated data handling capability of a leased telephone line in bits per second using a particular modulation method. (2) Also *data rate*. The number of bits per second actually transmitted on a line. (3) Baud rate; the number of times per second that line conditions are (or can be) changed.

line switching Circuit switching.

line termination equipment (LTE) Data circuit-terminating equipment (DCE); particularly for a non-telephone circuit.

line transition A change between line conditions. See *line condition*.

linear (1) Arranged or occurring along a line; having only one dimension. (2) Of an electronic circuit or device; having an output proportional to input; amplifying or attenuating all frequencies equally.

linear actuator An electric motor that provides linear movement rather than rotary movement; for example, in the seek mechanism of a movable-head magnetic disc unit.

linear addressing One-level addressing.

linear function A function that plots as a straight line; for example, $A = 2B$; $A = B \times C/3$.

linear optimisation Linear programming.

linear programming The production of programs that are designed to maximise or minimise relationships that can be expressed as linear functions. Such programs are used, for example, to determine the lowest cost method of producing electricity for different loads and fuel costs or a combination of ingredients that will produce the cheapest legal sausages considering the availability, costs, and characteristics of the different possible ingredients.

linearisation The process of adjusting/balancing circuits (say, in a voltmeter) so that the output values are a constant multiple of the input values.

lines of force A measure of the strength of a magnet or an indication of its flux path. See *magnet*.

link (Communications) The medium on which data is transmitted or transferred between locations. The term is usually synonymous with 'line' or 'circuit' though it denotes the data-carrying facility rather than the hardware. See *line; path; circuit; channel; link protocol*.

link (File organisation) To use pointers or a table to establish access paths between records of one file and records of another file. (As differentiated from **chaining** which is the establishment of access paths between the records of a single file.) A **linked file** is a file containing records that are 'linked' to one or more other files.

link (Processing control) **(1)**An instruction that passes control and parameters from one sequence of instructions to another during processing. **(2)**Also *return address.* An address in a calling routine to which control is returned when a called routine has finished executing. See *call*.

link (Task building) To join two separately compiled routines. See *linkage editor*.

link control protocol A link protocol.

link edit To create a load module by means of a linkage editor.

link pack A group of shareable modules of reentrant code retained in main storage during some phase of execution.

link protocol Also *line protocol.* A set of procedures and rules that control the interchange of data on a data link. Items covered by a protocol, typically, include the code to be used, the way data is to be represented (type of signals; modulation method), error recovery procedures, message formats, block length, control characters to be used, and, possibly, polling method.

linkage editor Also, depending upon the system, *consolidator; composer; collector.* A language processor that combines separately compiled routines to form a single load module. The functions, typically, include locating and inputting all the required modules, determining the total amount of storage space each will require and the total for the load module, merging the segments, and adjusting addresses as necessary so that they are all relative to the same value. The operation is commonly done disc-to-disc using temporary work files as necessary.

linkage instruction A link (Program execution, def. 1).

linkage loader A linkage editor that combines the functions of a loader. See *linkage editor; loader*.

linked file See *link (File organisation)*.

linked list (1)A list in which each item except the last holds a pointer to the next in sequence. It can be either a group of items in random order in one storage area or a group of items in different locations. **(2)**A chained list.

linked set See *set*.

linker A linkage editor.

liquid crystal display (LCD) A common 'segment' display as used in watches, calculators, and in other applications. With reference to the illustration, it consists of a 'sandwich' formed with a thin glass polarising screen A, a similar rear polarising screen B that is silvered on the back F to form a mirror, and liquid crystal C that fills the space between the screens. Thin, transparent conductors of tin oxide E are deposited on the in-

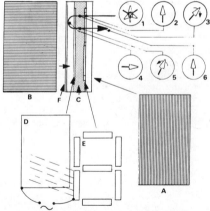

side of the front screen, typically, in the seven-segment pattern that is used to produce displayed numbers. The same conductor material D is deposited on the inside of the rear screen. Operation relies upon the inherent capability of the liquid crystal to rotate light by 90° as it passes through it. The arrows in '1' indicate the random orientation of light as it strikes the front glass polarising screen. The arrow in '2' indicates that the light that passes through the polarising screen has been oriented into a single axis. The arrow in '3' shows the rotating effect of the crystal as light passes through it and '4' shows that the light has been rotated by 90° as it leaves the crystal and passes through the rear polarising screen B which has an orientation 90° from that of front screen A. Light then reflects from the mirror surface and re-enters the liquid crystal where it is again rotated by 90°, indicated by the arrow in '5'. In '6' the light is shown as it passes back through the front polarising screen. As described, there is no display and the surface has the appearance of an ordinary mirror. When a weak electric field is applied to the crystal, light passes straight through it without rotation, and it is this characteristic that creates the display. Light that reaches the rear polarising screen is, then, of the same orientation as passed by the front screen and it cannot pass through the rear screen to the mirror surface. The light is then absorbed and the display element appears black. The device, typically, operates on alternating current in the range of 2—5 V. and from 25 to 30 Hz. (Direct current would cause darkening of the tin oxide conductors.) The display operates with a segment decoder and a drive circuit that shifts phase between the back conductor and selected segments in order to create a voltage difference. The device is inexpensive, reliable, and uses very little current (say 1 milliampere for a watch display). It operates reliably only between —10°C and +60°C. A one-way mirror and back lighting is used where viewing is required in low ambient light. Liquid crystal is also used in dot matrix displays and has been used experimentally to produce small television screens.

LISP *LISt Processing.* An interpretive language used in processing symbol lists; it is used in developing and modifying high-level languages.

list (1) Also *string; one-dimensional array.* An ordered set of data items. See *array.* **(2)**To print computer output; typically, by means of a line printer.

list handling List processing.

list processing The operation or facilities involved in locating and using data in chained lists and in structuring chained lists to meet particular processing needs.

listen mode By a data station in a polling system; the condition in which it is monitoring transmissions (waiting for its call) while other stations are being polled.

listing (1) Computer output in character format as produced by a printer. The term is usually applied to such output used for testing or debugging rather than the normal results of processing. The term may also be applied to a display (for debugging purposes) on a VDU. **(2)**The process of printing (possibly displaying) computer output.

listing paper Continuous stationery.

literal (1) In a source program; material that is to remain unchanged during compilation or other translation steps and, thus, will appear in output in the same form as input by the programmer. In source coding, it is commonly identified by quotation marks, for example: IF X = 0 PRINT "FAIL". **(2)** An operand that is itself a processing value rather than an address where such a value can be found; for example, the '12' in ADD 12 TO TOTAL-3.

live Functional and in use; ('...system expected to go live next month'; 'a live application').

live register A register with data manipulation circuitry (say, an accumulator) as contrasted to a storage location.

liveware A term sometimes (humorously) applied to members of data processing staff.

LLL *Low-Level Language.*

LO *LOw.*

load (Code or data) **(1)**With respect to a register (control unit or arithmetic unit); to place data in it (as read from main storage). **(2)**With respect to main storage locations; to read in code or data from backing storage. **(3)**With respect to a program or other sequence of instructions; to write it to main storage (as in a 'load module') preparatory to executing it.

load (Electrical) **(1)**To make a connection that causes the normal, working current to flow; ('load a transformer'; 'load a circuit'; 'load a transistor'). See *overload.* **(2)**That which is connected in a circuit; ('a lighting load'; 'switch off the load').

load (Facilities) That which is being carried or performed (at least notionally, as a percentage of capacity); ('a period of peak processing load'; 'a heavily loaded circuit causing message delays'; 'operating under light load').

load (Manual operation) To place a data medium in or on a peripheral; ('load a disc pack'; 'load a reel of magnetic tape'; 'load cards in a hopper').

load (Read/write head) In a movable head magnetic disc unit; to bring the read/write head and the disc recording surface to the correct proximity for reading or writing data. In a rigid-disc system, it is performed by a solenoid and spring arrangement that pulls the head toward the disc during acceleration (say to 1800 R.P.M.). As the head nears the disc surface, the slider of the head meets the boundary layer of air moving with the disc and it 'flies' on the layer during normal operation. When the disc decelerates in stopping, the operation is reversed and the head is 'unloaded' (retracted to its off-disc position). (In some rigid-disc systems, the head rises from the disc surface during 'loading'.) In a flexible disc unit, loading is accomplished by means of a solenoid that raises a foam pad against the non-recorded side of the disc to place the recording surface into contact with the read/write head. See *fly; head; magnetic disc unit; Winchester technology.*

load-and-go Also, sometimes, *compile-and-go; assemble-and-go.* Compilation (or, possibly, assembly) followed immediately by execution of the object code produced, with the compiler (assembler) remaining in main storage. See *interpreter; incremental compiler.*

load control (1)In a multiprogramming system; an operating function of controlling the number of programs being executed in order to optimise throughput with respect to job priorities and available resources. (2)In a virtual storage system; to delete programs when necessary to reduce the virtual storage interrupt rate (eliminate thrashing) in order to permit processing to continue on higher priority jobs.

load factor The percentage of system or device capacity that is being used at a particular time. See *load (Facilities).*

load map An operating system table containing the storage addresses of control sections and entry points of a loaded program.

load module A unit of object code suitable for loading into main storage for execution; it is usually the output of a linkage editor or collector. It, typically, consists of the executable code plus an **external symbol dictionary** and a **relocation dictionary**. The external symbol dictionary contains the addresses of all entry points with their labels and the relocation dictionary holds values required to map the addresses onto main storage. See *linkage editor; control section.*

load-on-call The facility (of a virtual storage system) in which pages/segments are brought into main storage as required by executing programs.

load point The beginning of the recordable area of a reel of magnetic tape.

load rules Engineering design specifications for circuit loading (current carrying) intended to assure that 'worst-case' operating conditions do not result in device failure or degraded performance because of excessive temperature.

loader (1)Also, sometimes, *fetch routine.* A system routine that places load modules in main storage preparatory to execution. (2)A linkage loader.

loading zone A band of unused tracks on a magnetic disc over which head loading takes place; it may be specially treated to resist the effects of head to disc contact during loading. See *load (Read/write heads); fly; landing zone.*

local (1)A term applied to that which is done or produced at a remote location rather than at the main computer facility of a system; ('local print-out' 'a local processing capability'). (2) Directly connected (to a computer); not using communications links; ('a local terminal'). See *remote.* (3)Defined and used in only one segment of a program; ('a local variable'). (4) Available only to a particular program; not shareable; ('a local segment'). See *shareable.* (5)Applied to a particular area or to less than the whole; ('a local discard policy'). See *global.*

local area network A data network implemented with direct cable links between terminals in a 'local' (manufacturing plant; office building) environment.

local batch processing (1)Batch processing performed at a remote location (rather than at the central computer facility). (2)Batch processing in which inputs are received and results distributed by means other than transmission over communications links. See *remote batch processing.*

local discard policy A discard policy applied to a partition of main storage (usually to the address space of a particular program). See *discard policy; global discard policy.*

local equalize An operation or modem facility by which a modem that loses signal quality can re-equalize by analysing the incoming data stream (without the need for a training sequence). Because of the relatively long time required (1 to 3 minutes), it is used mainly in point-to-point systems.

local loop In a telephone system; the line between a subscriber's telephone or modem and a local telephone exchange.

local name base register See *stack.*

local output Printed copy made at a remote location, often of the contents of VDU screens. See *hard copy.*

local processor An intelligent terminal or other device at a remote location that can perform some processing tasks as required at the location as well as (usually) handling interface functions with communications links.

local segment In a virtual storage system; a segment that holds unshareable code or data. The term may be applied to one that is specific to a particular application program or to one that holds system modules that are not available to application programs.

local service area In a telephone system; an area within which calls can be made for the minimum basic rate.

local station A local terminal.

local terminal A terminal that is part of a computer installation or one that is in proximity to the computer (say, in the same building or plant) and connected by means of a cable rather than a communications link. See *remote terminal*.

local variable See *variable*.

locality A term used with respect to virtual storage systems to indicate the amount of main storage a program requires during processing as a percentage (at least notional) of its total address space. A program is said to have 'good locality' if it can execute with a small average amount of main storage and if it avoids short-duration large requirements.

locality set An active set; those pages/segments that are being referenced by a program during a particular phase of execution. See *virtual storage system—processing units*.

locate To determine the location of an item of code or data; to perform a search or access.

location (1) An addressable position in computer storage; a place where code or data can be held for retrieval when required. Unless otherwise indicated, a position in main storage is assumed. **(2)** A site; a place where a computer is installed.

lock (1) A number associated with an item of data or a storage location to control its access. See *storage protection*. **(2)** With respect to a terminal keyboard; to engage a solenoid that prevents operation of the keys (as when an error has been detected).

lock and key See *storage protection*.

locked down In a virtual storage system; a term applied to a page or segment that must remain in primary storage during processing or during a particular phase of processing (to one that cannot be deleted). A location where such a page or segment is held is a **save area**.

locking A term applied to a control character that affects the interpretation of the bit patterns that follow it (and not just a single bit pattern); for example, 'Figures Shift' (FS).

lockout A term applied to the situation in which one program or job is allowed exclusive use of a resource (say, a file) until its processing is completed.

log (1) To record events (and often, the time of occurrence); for example, on a magnetic-tape journal. **(2)** A named record of this type, for example, a 'console log' or an 'engineering log'. **(3)** To transfer data from direct access storage to magnetic tape. **(4)** To record the contents of a VDU screen onto magnetic tape (or, possibly, by printing). **(5)** A common abbreviation for 'logarithm'.

log device A logger.

log in Also *log on*. To begin a session as a terminal or console operator by pressing a control key and entering a command (login; logon) followed by identification and, usually, a password.

log off See *log out*.

log on See *log in*.

log out Also *log off*. To end a session as a terminal or console operator by entering a command (logout; logoff).

log tables See *logarithm*.

logarithm Also *log*. A representation of a number that consists of the power (number of self-multiplications) to which another number is to be raised. The 'other number' is the **base** and is assumed to be 10 unless otherwise indicated. For example, the number 3 is $10^{0.477}$ and 0.477 is, thus, the 'logarithm' of 3. The purpose of logarithms is to facilitate the performance of arithmetic operations, either by machine or in place of a manual 'longhand' method. The following are the rules for their use:
- To multiply two numbers, add their logarithms.
- To divide two numbers, subtract their logarithms.
- To raise a number to a power, multiply the logarithm of the number by the power.
- To find the root of a number, divide the logarithm of number by the root.

Logarithms are given in **log tables** and a set of the tables is necessary for their use. A complete logarithm is composed of two parts, a **characteristic** which indicates where the decimal point is to be placed and a **mantissa** which is the value given in the log tables. For example, the mantissa of 554 is given as '7435'. The logarithm of 554 is 2.7435 which indicates that

$554 = 10^{2.7435}$. In this logarithm, the '2' is the characteristic; it indicates a value greater than 10^2 (100) and less than 10^3 (1,000). In like manner, the logarithm of 55.4 is 1.7435 and that of 5.54 is 0.7435. The following is an example in which 158 is multiplied by 55.4 using logarithms:

1. In log tables, find the mantissa of 158:	1987
2. Supply the characteristic; 158 is greater than 10^2 and less than 10^3 so this is '2':	2.1987
3. Similarly, find the logarithm of 55.4:	1.7435
4. Add them to obtain:	3.9422
5. In the log tables, find the number with a mantissa of 9422 (interpolation required):	8753
6. Place the decimal point for a characteristic of '3':	8,753.0

The following are the main steps to divide 158 by 55.4:

1. Find the logarithm of 158:	2.1987
2. Find the logarithm of 55.4:	1.7435
3. Subtract them to obtain this value for table lookup:	0.4552

The following is an example of exponentiation to find 158^3:

1. Find the logarithm of 158:	2.1987
2. Multiply by 3 to obtain this value for lookup:	6.5961

The following are the main steps to find the cube root of 158:

1. Find the logarithm of 158:	2.1987
2. Divide by 3 to obtain this value for lookup:	0.7329

In a computer, logarithmic numerical operations are performed using floating point. See *floating point*.

logger A device in a telemetry or instrumentation system that records data from multiple input channels. Typically, inputs are analogue (say, from flowmeters, thermocouples, or photocells) and the unit has the facilities to perform analogue to digital conversion, to sample the input channels in rotation, and to record the values (usually in RAM or on magnetic tape). It may also provide a display. The device often incorporates a microprocessor to perform linearisation, eliminate zero offsets, and to make comparisons and conversions. The output is usually a computer input via a spool file. A variety of devices are available to handle from 2 to about 1000 input channels and with scan (sampling) rates from, say, 50 channels per second to one per day. The term may also be applied to a magnetic tape or disc recorder that performs no function other than recording data from a single channel, say, for diagnostic purposes. See *journal*.

logging The process of recording events and, often, their time of occurrence.

logic (1) The science or art of reasoning correctly. (2) In one computer-related sense, the process of breaking down problems of reasoning and comparison to elementary operations that can be expressed as AND, OR, and NOT (or combinations) and can be performed by electronic circuits. This is an application of Boolean algebra and, as expressed in a program, is a form of **symbolic logic**. (3) In another computer-related sense, it applies to devices or hardware elements and is synonymous with 'logic gate' or a group of related logic gates; ('emitter-coupled logic'; 'diode-transistor logic'). The term is applied to semiconductor storage (consisting of exclusive-OR logic gates) as well as devices and circuits that perform manipulation and control.

logic array A (MOS) semiconductor device with AND and OR matrices used to perform some relatively complex operation such as code conversion. See *programmable logic array*.

logic circuit An electronic circuit that performs a logic operation. The following are the basic bipolar circuits to perform the NAND, AND, OR, and NOR functions. There are many varia-

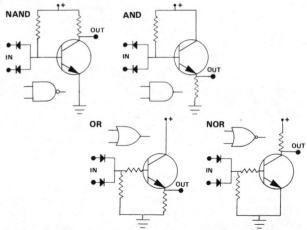

tions depending upon circuit requirements and the type of transistors used.

logic element (1) A logic gate. **(2)** A semiconductor device (transistor; diode) in a logic circuit.

logic flowchart A function flowchart.

logic function A function performed by a logic circuit; a logic operation.

logic instruction An instruction that specifies a logic operation; an instruction with a logic operator.

LOGIC OPERATION TABLE

INPUTS:

First (or only)	0 1 0 0 1 1 0 0 0 0 1 1 1 1
Second	0 1 0 1 0 1 0 1 0 1 0 1
Subsequent	0 0 1 1 0 0 1 1

OUTPUT FOR:

ONE CONSTANT	1 1 1 1 1 1 1 1 1 1 1 1
ZERO CONSTANT	0 0 0 0 0 0 0 0 0 0 0 0
VARIABLE	0 1
NOT	1 0
AND	0 0 0 1 0 0 0 0 0 0 0 1
Negated AND	1 0 0 0
NAND	1 1 1 0 1 1 1 1 1 1 1 0
Negated NAND	0 1 1 1
OR	0 1 1 1 0 1 1 1 1 1 1 1
Negated OR	1 1 1 0
NOR	1 0 0 0 1 0 0 0 0 0 0 0
Negated NOR	0 0 0 1
EXCLUSIVE OR	0 1 1 0
EXCLUSIVE NOR	1 0 0 1
EXCLUSION	0 0 1 0
IMPLICATION	0 1 0 0
FIRST VARIABLE	0 1 0 0 1 1 0 0 0 0 1 1 1 1
Neg. FIRST VARIABLE	1 0 1 1 0 0 1 1 1 1 0 0 0 0
SECOND VARIABLE	0 1 0 1 0 1 0 1 0 1 0 1
Neg. SECOND VARIABLE	1 0 1 0 1 0 1 0 1 0 1 0

logic level Either of the two available control voltages as used in most electronic, digital devices including computers, peripherals, and modems. The two voltages are, commonly, +5 V. (logical high) and 0 V. (logical low). The higher level usually enables or represents the 'mark' condition and the lower level disables or represents the 'space' condition.

logic operation (1) Also *logical operation*. An operation in which one or more inputs (each of which can have only one of two values) are evaluated or compared in accordance with some established rule to produce an output (which can have only one of two values) that indicates the result of the evaluation or comparison. See *LOGIC OPERATION TABLE*. **(2)** A computer operation performed in accordance with a logic instruction (as contrasted to an 'arithmetic operation').

logic operator Also *logical operator*. **(1)** Any of the operators AND; OR, or NOT used to form compound statements (often with relational operators), for example, IF COR-1 = 20 AND COR-2 NOT NUMERIC GO TO LP-FIRST. **(2)** Any operator other than an arithmetic operator; a 'logic operator' (def. 1), a relational operator, or an operator such as PRINT, MOVE, or GO TO.

logic-seeking A term applied to a bidirectional printer with the facility to move the printing position from the end of one line to the closest ending of the next line; if that ending is the right-hand one, it prints the line from right to left and if the left-hand one it prints it from left to right.

logic symbol A symbol that represents a logic operation or, possibly the symbol form of a relational operator. See *LOGIC OPERATION TABLE; relational operator*.

logic translator The elements of an interface device that make voltage changes, for example, from plus and minus 10 V. on an external circuit to +5 V. and 0 V. for internal (TTL) circuits.

logic variable A variable used to hold a flag; a one-bit variable that can be set to either 1 or 0.

logical (1) That which 'makes sense'; that which is straightforward and practical; ('a logical approach'; 'a program with a logical structure'). **(2)** Considered with respect to content rather than to structure or storage. For example, a 'logical record' is a record considered with respect to its information about, say, an employee, a customer, or a part. In this sense, the term is intended to contrast with 'physical'. **(3)** Considered with respect to access or identification. For example, a 'logical device' is a device (peripheral) considered with respect to its system identifier or, possibly, to its characteristics or access mode. **(4)** In order according to some collating sequence; for example, records that are read in 'logical order' are read in their (numerical) key sequence. **(5)** A term sometimes applied to an arithmetic operation with a result that has no numeric significance; ('a logical shift'; 'a logical total'). **(6)** A term used to identify a logic operation or gate; ('logical AND').

logical addition An OR operation.

logical address A presumptive address. See *syllable; presumptive address*.

logical bucket number (LBN) In some systems; an identifying number of each bucket that holds records of a particular file.

logical channel number (LCN) A number that identifies one end of a virtual circuit in a packet switching system.

logical channel program In some systems; a sequence of elementary commands and symbolic addresses that control a single data transfer operation (say, reading from magnetic tape).

logical character The necessary number of delimited bits to hold a bit-pattern character in a particular code (whether or not an actual character is present).

logical comparison An identity test. See *identity*.

logical device (1) A (peripheral) device considered with respect to its identifier in a system or to the facilities for its access. **(2)** A virtual device.

logical device name An identifier (symbolic address) by which a peripheral device is identified in source code written for a system with device independence. It is converted during compilation to a character string that identifies a particular type of device (say magnetic disc) and at run time this is used by the operating system, in conjunction with a configuration table, to select the actual device that will be used in the run. See *device independence; virtual peripheral*.

logical edit A term sometimes applied to a verification step in which checks are made on the values of numeric inputs in relation to preset values.

logical expression An expression specifying one or more logic operations.

logical file A file considered with respect to its data content or use. See *physical file*.

logical function A logic function.

logical link A path for transferring data between programs installed on different computers; a route through network software and user-transparent physical links.

logical operator A logic operator.

logical product An AND operation.

logical record A record considered with respect to its content or use rather than its structure or method of representation. See *physical record; logical; record*.

logical relation A relation as indicated by a relational operator.

logical segment A segment (virtual storage system) considered with respect to its content or use.

logical shift A shift that 'has no arithmetical significance; for example, a shift made to justify the contents of a register. See *shift; register; shift register*.

logical test Also *Boolean test*. The performance of a logic operation on inputs consisting of a preset value (a switch value) and a value contained in input data or produced during processing in order to determine if a particular condition exists. Logical tests use relational operators; for example, to determine if one number is greater than another. See *relational operator; switch; decision instruction*.

logical unit (1) A group of related entities considered as a unit. **(2)** A logical device.

logical unit number (LUN) In some systems; a number that is the equivalent of a 'logical device name'.

logical variable A logic variable.

logoff Log off.

logon Log on.

Long-Distance Xerography (LDX) The designation of a wideband facsimile service provided by the Xerox Corp.

long-form floating point Multiple precision floating point.

longitudinal parity Vertical parity. See *parity*.

longitudinal redundancy check (LRC) A vertical parity check or other check for errors applied to a message or block (rather than to a character). See *parity; redundancy check*.

look-ahead A term applied to a facility in which an operating system receives information on resource requirements at different stages of execution before a run begins and, thus, can perform staging and other management functions to ensure that the resources are available when required. See *look-behind*.

look-aside registers A set of control unit registers that holds the virtual addresses and hardware addresses of all pages and/or segments in primary storage. Each time a page/segment is referenced by an executing process, a parallel search of the registers is made to determine whether or not the page/segment must be rolled in from secondary storage. The registers are searched by content (virtual addresses) and the process may thus be termed **content addressing** or **associative addressing** and the registers are a form of **associative storage**. See *associative storage*.

look-behind A term applied to a procedure in which an operating system attempts to allocate resources to a program during execution on the basis of its requirements in previous stages of execution. See *look-ahead*.

look facility A facility that permits a programmer to selectively list single instructions or short segments of code during compilation.

look-up To read the contents of a location in a table or index as a step (or the only step) in finding the storage location of a unit of code or data. See *index; address modification*.

loop A sequence of instructions that is executed repeatedly, following a single initiation, in order to perform a single operation on or with different operands. The purpose of a loop is to eliminate the need to write, compile, and store multiple copies of an instruction sequence that is to be used repeatedly. The flowchart characteristic of a loop is that it returns control to a previous instruction in the same sequence, as shown to the right. A loop can be essentially an entire program (say, one that performs all payroll calculations) or a sequence with only a few instructions (say, to read a character from a punched card). A loop is initiated by an instruction that holds a label or address of the sequence and is terminated by the occurrence of some predefined event; for example, reading the last card or detecting a particular count value in a register. A loop is often implemented with three index registers; the first register holds the hardware address of the operand, the second register holds the amount by which the operand address is incremented with each iteration (if the operands occupy single words of main storage, this would be '1'), and the third holds a count that is incremented (or decremented) by 1 with each iteration. The loop contains instructions that increment (or decrement) the count and test for the final value or condition. A loop is

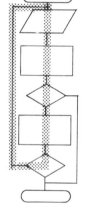

said to be **performed** and one execution of the sequence of instructions is termed a **performance**, an **iteration**, a **cycle**, or a **pass**. A loop may also be termed an **iterative routine** and the processing of data by means of a loop as an **iterative process**. If a value produced in one iteration is used as input to the next (as in exponentiation) it is **recursive**, and a loop in which this is done is a **recursive routine**. See *iteration; recursive routine; address modification*.

loop body That part of a loop that performs a processing function. See *loop control*.

loop check (1) Echoplex. **(2)** A check of a communications circuit and a remote site modem; an analogue loop or digital loop test.

loop control A term applied to those instructions of a loop that perform such functions as incrementing or decrementing a count and checking for the exit condition.

loop mode Of an interface device; operating as required for handling transmissions in a loop network. See *loop network*.

loop network A data network in which a primary (master) station and the secondary (tributary) data stations are connected by communications circuits that form a closed loop from the primary station to each of the secondary stations in turn and back to the primary station. In operation, the primary station sends an initiating message to the first data station; it adds any messages it may have and retransmits to the second data station, and this continues until all messages (and appropriate control signals) are received back at the master station, at which time a new initiating message is sent. The procedure may be termed **data streaming** and the transmismissions around the loop a **data stream**.

loop test Also *loopback test*. In a data communications system; a test of facilities made by sending a test pattern through all or part of a system and looping it back to the tester. See *analogue loop test; digital loop test*.

loop transmission frame The message and control structure of a loop transmission.

loopback test A loop test.

looping (1) The processing of a body of data by means of a loop; it is often initiated by a PERFORM statement. **(2)** The condition in which a sequence of instructions repeats until interrupted by an operator or monitor routine.

low Also *logical low*. In control and logic circuits; the lower of two possible voltages. See *high*.

low-level language (LLL) A language designed to facilitate the writing of efficient programs (ones that execute rapidly with minimum main storage space) without (usually) particular regard for their ease of use by programmers. Such languages, typically, produce one object code instruction for each source code instruction. They are designed for programming computers of particular makes and models. The term 'low-level language' is used when discussing such languages generally; the language for a particular computer type is termed its **assembly language** (also **assembler**). See *language; high-level language*.

low-order position The rightmost position in a number or in a character string or the lowest and rightmost position in a matrix. See *least significant digit*.

low-pass filter See *filter*.

low priority A term applied to a program or job that is processed when no higher priority program or job requires the resources needed. See *high-priority; priority; background*.

low-speed A term used in many data communications systems to indicate a transmission speed of less than 600 bits per second. See *high-speed; medium speed; Baud*.

lower case (lc.) The 'small' letters of an alphabet; letters that are not 'capital' letters. See *upper case*.

lower curtate See *curtate*.

LP *Linear Programming*.

LPI (lpi.) *Lines Per Inch*.

LR *Low Reduction*. See *reduction*.

LRC *Longitudinal Redundancy Check*.

LRU *Least Recently Used*. In a virtual storage system; a discard algorithm that provides that the first page/segment to be deleted from main storage when space is required is that one that has been in main storage the longest time without being used (referenced by an active process). The assumption is that the longer a page/segment has remained unused the greater the chances that the process that called it has finished with it. See *discard policy*.

LSB *Least Significant Bit*.

LSD *Least Significant Digit*.

LSI *Large Scale Integration*.

LT *Less Than*. See *relational operator*.

LTE *Line Termination Equipment*.

LTRS *LeTteRS shift*.

LTU *Line Termination Unit*.

LU *Logical Unit*.

Lukasiewicz notation Polish notation.

luminesce By screen phosphors and other substances; to give off 'cold' light. See *phosphors*.

LUN (lun) *Logical Unit Number*.

M

M (1)(m.) *Milli-*. **(2)**(M) *Mega-*.

M-out-of-N code Also *constant ratio code*. A data transmission code with a built-in error detection capability obtained by specifying that a certain number of the digits of an encoded character must be 1-bits. For example, in a 4-out-of-8 code there must be 1-bits in four digit positions of each 8-bit character. In this code, the characters 01101100 and 10010101 would be accepted as correct by receiving hardware and patterns 11001000 and 11101010 would cause initiation of an error procedure. The code provides only a limited error detection capability at a cost of high redundancy. See *parity; error; polynomial code*.

MA (mA.) *MilliAmperes*.

MAC (1)*Multi-Access Computing*. **(2)***Memory Access Controller*.

machine (1)A device that operates by power (often electricity) and performs some reasonably complex operation; ('an accounting machine'; 'photocopiers and other office machines'). **(2)**A computer. **(3)**Also *mainframe*. The central processor and directly associated units of a computer.

machine address A hardware address.

machine check A hardware check.

machine code Object code as compiled or assembled for a particular computer. The term may be used synonymously with 'object code' but, more often, 'object code' is used when discussing such codes generally or the result of compilation or assembly and 'machine code' refers to particular sets of bit patterns that control the operations of a certain computer. Thus, for example, compilers are used to convert source code to 'object code' while a short control sequence might be written in 'machine code'. See *object code; machine language*.

machine-independent (1) Of a programming language or, possibly, a procedure or technique; capable of being used on or with computers of different type or manufacture. **(2)**Also *plug compatible*. Of a peripheral or other device; capable of being used in computer installations with mainframes of different manufacture.

machine instruction An instruction in machine code.

machine instruction set A term sometimes used synonymously with 'instruction set' and 'order code'.

machine language The 'language' that a computer can understand and use; 'machine code' considered as a communications medium.

machine learning The ability of a device to improve its performance based upon previous trials. See *learning*.

machine operation An operation performed by a computer; particularly a hardware operation.

machine-oriented language An assembly language.

machine-readable In a form that can be translated by machine into bit patterns for computer storage. The term can be applied to such standard input media as magnetic tape, paper tape, and punched cards, though it is applied more frequently to documents that are to be read by OCR, OMR, or MICR.

machine-sensible Of data; in a form that is machine-readable.

machine time (1)Processing time. (2)Computing time as used or allocated; ('book an hour of machine time').

machine word A computer word. See *word*.

macro (1)In a programming language (usually an assembly language); an operator that, when used in an instruction, causes the generation of a sequence of instructions to accomplish a particular task. Tasks commonly performed by macros include initialisation, opening and closing files, reading records, and creating files. The term **macro instruction** may be used synonymously with 'macro'; more often it is a source-language instruction containing a macro. The process of producing a sequence of source-language instructions from a macro is **macro generation** (also **macro expansion**) and it is performed by a program (part of an assembler) termed a **macro generator** or, in some systems, a **macro processor**. The sequence of instructions that results from expanding a macro is taken from a **macro definition** which is the 'master copy' of the sequence. A **macro definition table** (in some systems, a **macro library**) is a table holding all of the macros and corresponding macro definitions that are available on a particular computer. It, typically, includes macros that are facilities of the job control language as well as those of the programming language. The term **macro prototype** may be applied to a macro, its definition, and an acceptable format for writing a macro instruction using it. A **user-defined macro** is one created to meet a particular user's needs rather than one defined by a language. The term **macro language** may be applied to a language used in creating the macro facilities of a programming language or to a language that makes extensive use of macros. (2)(MACRO) The assembly language of a Digital Equipment Co. computer.

macro call (1)A subroutine call to a macro; a reference used to execute a macro in a high-level language sequence. (2)A macro instruction.

macro processor A macro generator.

macroprogramming Programming (in an assembly language) that makes use of macros.

mag tape Magnetic tape.

magazine A term used with respect to some (mass) storage systems to denote a unit-accessible holder for a number of volumes such as magnetic cards.

magnet Ferrous material (iron; compressed iron oxide) with most of its molecules (basic particles) oriented in the same direction. One end of a magnet is its North **pole** and the other is its South pole; when the magnet is formed so that these are fairly close together (as in a read/write head), the space between them is the **air gap**. The invisible force that surrounds a magnet and passes through an air gap is a **magnetic field**; it is also termed **magnetic flux** or **flux**. The strength of a magnet is expressed in **lines of force** or in **maxwells**; the strength depends upon the amount of iron, the percentage of the molecules that become oriented, and the length of the air gap. The intensity of the magnetic field per unit of cross section of the air gap is expressed in **oersteds** or **gauss**. The process of orienting the molecules is **magnetisation** and in all practical applications it is done by passing an electric current through a coil of wire wound around the iron. The force causing the particles to align is termed **magnetomotive force** (mmf.) and its unit of measurement is the **gilbert**; it is proportional to **ampere turns** which is the product of the current and the number of turns of wire in the coil. The characteristics of a magnet depend on its alloy, its construction, and its method of treatment during manufacture. The degree to which particles become oriented in response to a particular magnetomotive force is termed **permeability** and **reluctance** is the resistance to particle orientation. The flux remaining when the electric current is turned off is the **remnance**. A **permanent magnet** is one with high remnance. A magnet that must change flux quickly (say, a read/write head) must have low remnance. The amount by which a change in flux lags a change in magnetomotive force is termed **hysteresis** and a plot of this through a full cycle (as produced by passing one cycle of alternating current through the magnetising coil) is termed a **hysteresis loop**. In the figure, voltage (which determines magnetomotive force) is indicated on the horizontal scale and magnetisation of one end (pole) is indicated on the vertical scale. Starting at A, with unmagnet-

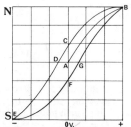 

ised iron, the pole becomes more strongly North as voltage increases and reaches a maximum at B. As voltage falls, the iron loses magnetism to a point C at which there is no voltage on the coil. At this point, the magnet could be removed from the coil and it would be a permanent magnet with one-third the strength it had at B; the distance A-C represents the 'remnance'. As the voltage goes negative, the flux continues to fall until some point D is reached at which there is no remaining magnetism. The magnetomotive force required to eliminate the 'residual' magnetism (from point C to point D) is the **coercive force**. As the voltage goes more negative, the pole becomes South and then more strongly South until maximum flux is reached at E. As the coil voltage drops, it again loses flux to point F where it has the same remnance as at C but of opposite polarity, then to point G where it is again of neutral flux, and, finally, as the voltage in the coil becomes increasingly positive, to point B. The area enclosed within a hysteresis loop represents the amount of work that must be done to change flux; the smaller it is the better the material for a read/write head or transformer. Computer-related elements that operate by magnetism include read/write heads, magnetic discs and tapes, core memory, control and actuating solenoids and relays, and hammer actuators of impact printers. See *head; magnetisable surface recording; core memory.*

magnetic Operating by means of changes in flux in magnet-like structures. See *magnet.*
magnetic bubble memory (MBM) Bubble memory.
magnetic card A plastic card with a magnetisable surface coating on which data can be stored. They are used as inexpensive storage media in word processors and visible record computers and also as the storage medium of some mass storage systems. In the latter application, a card holds about 200,000 characters and is stored with other cards in a 'magazine' that is addressable for access purposes and is moved automatically from its storage location to a read/write station. In reading and writing, cards are automatically wound around a drum which is then turned in the same manner as a magnetic drum.
magnetic cell A storage cell in a magnetic storage medium. The term would include a magnetic core, a magnetic bubble, and the length of track that can hold a bit on magnetic disc or tape.
magnetic core See *core memory.*
magnetic core memory Core memory.
magnetic delay line A delay line in which data is represented by propagated flux transitions.
magnetic disc A computer storage medium consisting of a rotatable disc with a magnetisable surface on which data is recorded by means of a read/write head. In 'mainframe' computer systems, the most common type is the 14-inch aluminium **rigid disc** (also **hard disc**) with a 50-70 microinch ferric oxide coating on both sides. They are used in a variety of single and multiple-disc configurations and may be fixed to their drives or replaceable. Many minicomputers use 8-inch or 5¼-inch rigid 'Winchester' discs and they (and microcomputers) often use **flexible discs** which are of Mylar and either 8 or 5¼ inches in diameter. Disc capacity depends upon size, recording method, and track density; the following are typical values in Mbytes per recording surface:

Rigid, 14-inch (Standard)	1.5 - 15
Rigid, 14-inch (Winchester)	9.0 - 80
Rigid, 8-inch (Winchester)	1.5 - 8.5
Rigid, 5¼-inch (Winchester)	1.5 - 3.2
Flexible, 8-inch	0.4 - 0.8
Flexible, 5¼-inch	0.2 - 0.5

See *magnetic disc unit; disc pack; disc cartridge; data module; flexible disc. magnetisable surface recording.*

magnetic disc storage The common direct access storage of most computer systems. It consists of one or more magnetic disc units and associated access hardware and software. The term may also be applied to disk packs or individual discs.

magnetic disc unit Also *disc unit; disc drive; drive; disc handler; disc transport; disc transport unit.* A direct access peripheral storage device that uses magnetic discs as the storage medium. Unless otherwise indicated, the term denotes a device that uses rigid discs rather than one that uses flexible discs. Data is

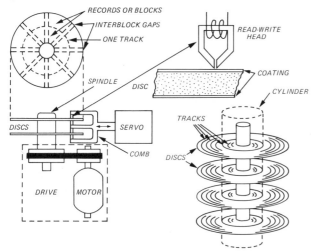

written to a disc and read from it by a **read/write head** that 'flies' a small distance above the surface; there may be more than one 'head' per surface. In writing, changes in direction of current in the coil of the head cause changes in the direction of orientation of the magnetisable surface particles along a narrow path which is a **track**. In reading, a small voltage is induced in the coil whenever the direction of orientation changes and these are analysed by electronic circuitry to determine their data significance. There are several different methods by which these **flux transitions** can be used to represent data. See *magnetisable surface recording*. A disc of 14 inch diameter (standard for rigid discs) may be recorded with from 200 to about 1500 concentric tracks, depending on the system. Depending on the recording method, the amount of data per track can range from about 4K bytes to over 200K bytes. Because a track holds more data than can be conveniently written to main storage at one time (and more than is required by an executing program at one time), the tracks are divided for access purposes into smaller units which are usually **blocks**. Though a few systems use variable-length blocks, most are fixed-length (say 512 bytes). Particular blocks are located for access by reading identifiers written in their 'block headers'. In most systems, the electronically accessible unit is the **sector** which, depending upon requirements, may contain one block or a number of blocks. Someplace on the rotating structure, there is an **index** which is physically detected by a transducer and used to establish the starting reference point for all tracks. Sectors may be located by the same means as the index (hard sectoring) or by variations in the synchronising pulses that are recorded at the beginning of sectors (soft sectoring). See *sectoring*. In some systems, sectors are not used and the only access at the track level is by reading block headers. In some systems, the unit of access is termed a **bucket** rather than a block. Some systems also divide the outer (longer) tracks into more blocks/buckets than the inner tracks. A group of tracks with the same number of divisions may be termed a **zone**. A magnetic disc unit in which discs can be removed and replaced by an operator is termed **exchangeable disc storage** (EDS) and, in some systems, those of high capacity are termed **mass storage**. Depending upon the device, between one and twenty discs are replaceable as a unit. The replaceable unit may be a disc pack, disc cartridge, or data module and its capacity may be from 2 megabytes to about 300 megabytes. Some devices have two spindles (the element that rotates the discs) and can read and write with two disc packs simultaneously; these may be termed **twin exchangeable disc storage** (TEDS). A magnetic disc unit that handles data modules may be termed a **data module drive**. See *disc pack; disc cartridge; data module*. Magnetic disc units in which one or more discs are permanently mounted to the spindle are termed **fixed-disc storage** (FDS). Both EDS and FDS units are **movable-head disc units**, unless otherwise indicated. In such a unit, the read/write heads are mounted on a **seek arm** which moves radially to position the heads at different tracks. The movement is provided by a **servo mechanism**; if it moves more than one seek arm, the assembly of seek arms may be termed a **comb**. There may be more than one head per seek arm in order to reduce the distance of movement (and hence, the time) to position a head at a particular track. The time required to move the head(s) to a particular track that is to be read or written is the **seek time**; it can vary from a few milliseconds to over 100 milliseconds depending on the distance moved and the system. Like numbered tracks on all disc surfaces of a disc pack constitute a **cylinder**. The tracks of a cylinder can be accessed by switching read/write circuits between heads and without moving the heads. Because it takes only a few microseconds to change the read or write function from one head to another, it is customary to place related data on the same cylinder rather than on adjacent tracks of a single disc surface. A fixed-disc unit with non-movable heads (permanently mounted heads) is termed **fixed-head disc storage** (FHDS) or **head-per-track disc**. Such units usually have a single disc and may have up to about 512 read/write heads for each of its surfaces. With fixed-head disc units, the access time consists only of **latency** which is the time required for a block to move from wherever it happens to be when the read or write signal is received to the position where it passes under the appropriate read/write head. Depending upon the rotating speed, this can average less than 12 milliseconds. The access time of a movable-head disc unit consists of both seek time and latency and is, thus, considerably longer when tracks must be changed. See *seek; latency*. Some systems have **rotational position sensing** which determines the rotational position of each of two or more required blocks or sectors and causes them to be read or written in the most rapid order. See *magnetisable surface recording; head; servo; track-following servo; rotational position sensing; magnetic disc*.

magnetic drum A direct access peripheral that holds data on a magnetisable surface of a rotating drum. The read/write heads are fixed tangential to the drum; in some units they are movable to read and write different tracks. (With magnetic drum a track is sometimes termed a 'band'.) Drums are usually eight to twelve inches in diameter, provide up to twelve megabytes of storage, and have access times between ten and twenty milliseconds. At one time, they were a common form of backing storage for general-purpose computers; units of small size continue to be used in military and other special applications, mainly in microprocessor systems. See *magnetic tape; magnetic disc*.

magnetic drum storage Storage on magnetic drum. (The term is sometimes applied to fixed-head disc storage.)
magnetic field The influence that surrounds a magnet.
magnetic head See *head*.
magnetic hysteresis See *magnet*.
magnetic ink Ink that has iron oxide powder mixed in it and is thus capable of forming a magnetisable surface coating when printed. See *magnetic ink character recognition*.
magnetic ink character recognition (MICR) The technique of machine reading characters printed in magnetic ink and generating their bit pattern representations for computer input. The standard character set consists of visually readable numbers plus symbols and special marks. Each character, as printed, has a distinctive pattern of inking on vertical lines, as

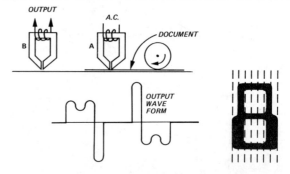

shown by the '8'. In reading, the document containing the characters is first passed across a transducer 'A' that induces flux reversals of fixed spacing in the deposited magnetic ink. The document then (in a device of simplest form) passes across a slit scanner 'B' which performs an operation similar to reading magnetic tape. Wherever there is a change in the flux, a pulse of measurable amplitude is induced in the coil of the head. Since each character has a distinctive ink pattern, each sequence of pulses one character wide can be analysed by electronic circuits to determine which character has been read. It is commonly used in sorting bank cheques; reading speeds are up to about 2000 cheques per minute. See *optical character recognition*.

magnetic ledger computer See *visible record computer*.

magnetic printer A printer with a drum that is coated with high-remnance nickel cobalt to which data is written in the form of magnetised dots that form dot matrix characters with electromagnet styli. Magnetic (ferrous oxylate) ink is then applied as a powder to the drum and it adheres wherever there is a dot. Paper is then fed through the machine in contact with the drum and the ink transfers from the drum to the paper; heating or chemical means are used to fix the ink to the paper. Speeds are about 2000 lines per minute. See *printer; electrostatic printer*.

magnetic storage A storage in which bits are represented in a magnetisable medium by direction of magnetisation (core; thin film; plated wire) or the space between areas of different magnetisation (magnetisable surface; bubble).

magnetic storage medium A medium in which magnetic flux can be changed in a data-significant way.

magnetic stripe A band of magnetisable surface coating (as on magnetic tape) on a ledger card, badge, product identification tag, or other item. See *magnetic card; visible record computer*.

magnetic tape A common data storage medium consisting of plastic (usually polyester) tape with a magnetisable surface coating. The tape in most common use is one thousandth of an inch thick, one-half of an inch wide, and has a ferric oxide coating approximately half a thousandth of an inch in thickness applied to one side. Magnetic tape is usually recorded in seven or nine channels by a multitransducer head that operates in contact with the magnetisable surface. Characters are written in bit-parallel across the tape, with one channel for each bit position and (usually) one channel for parity. The most common recording methods are NRZI and PE. Recording densities are 200, 556, or 800 bits per inch by NRZI on 7-track tape, and with 9-track tape, 800 bpi. by NRZI, 800 or 1600 bpi. by PE, and 6250 bpi. by GCR. Recording is bit parallel; the number of bits per inch is also the number of characters per inch. Tape is usually supplied in a length of 2400 Ft. on a 10.5 inch reel. See *data cartridge; digital cassette*.

magnetic tape cartridge See *data cartridge*.

magnetic tape cassette See *digital cassette*.

magnetic tape controller In some systems; a specialised, intelligent interface device between a magnetic tape unit and an input/output multiplexor. See *peripheral controller; device control unit*.

magnetic tape deck A magnetic tape unit.

magnetic tape drive (1) Also *tape drive; magnetic tape transport; magnetic tape deck*. The motors, capstans, reels, and controls involved in moving magnetic tape through a magnetic tape unit. **(2)** A magnetic tape unit.

magnetic tape encoder A key-to-tape data entry device. See *direct data entry*.

magnetic tape file A file on magnetic tape. See *serial access*.

magnetic tape label See *label*.

magnetic tape leader See *leader*.

magnetic tape reader A device that can read (but not write) magnetic tape.

magnetic tape storage Computer storage consisting of part of a reel, a reel, or multiple reels of magnetic tape. See *magnetic tape; magnetic tape unit*.

magnetic tape unit Also *magnetic tape drive; tape drive; magnetic tape transport; tape transport; magnetic tape handler; tape handler; magnetic tape deck; tape deck*. A common computer peripheral device that reads and writes data on

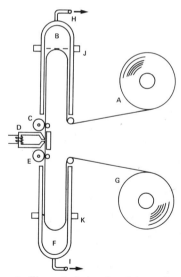

magnetic tape. A file reel A is placed into the unit by an operator when an item that it contains is required for processing. The tape passes through reservoir B, rewind capstan C, read/write head D, drive capstan E, reservoir F, and onto machine reel G. The drive capstan can move the tape at two speeds, a high speed for search and rewind and a slower speed for read/write. The reservoirs act to prevent breaking or damaging tape during acceleration and deceleration; they pull slack tape in by a vacuum pump that extracts air at points H and I. The movement of the tape reels is controlled by the photosensitive diodes J and K that detect a narrow beam of light passed through the reservoir. In the position in which the tape is shown in reservoir B, the tape has just uncovered the light beam; reel A will now feed tape until it is covered again. In reservoir F, the light beam is blocked by the tape and reel G will now take up tape until it is uncovered. During acceleration, tape is drawn from reservoir B and put in reservoir F and this imbalance continues while the reels accelerate to supply and take up the tape at the speed at which it is being passed by the capstan. Tape is read and written only when moving in one direction; it may be searched in both directions. It is normally read and written at a speed of about 10 feet per second and searched and rewound at a speed of about 40 feet per second. Some magnetic tape units use a spring-loaded swinging arm in place of vacuum chambers to take up tape slack; others eliminate the problem with microprocessor control that monitors the tape diameter on each reel and adjusts drive and takeup speeds to prevent the creation of slack. Another variation is a unit that uses two-inch wide 'video' tape; it has a capacity of about three terabits and searches at over 80 feet per second. A number of smaller units are available to handle cartridge tape and digital cassettes. See *magnetisable surface recording; data cartridge; digital cassette; streamer.*

magnetic tape volume A reel of half-inch magnetic tape, a data cartridge, or a digital cassette considered with respect to its use or data content.

magnetic thin film See *thin film memory.*

magnetic track See *track.*

magnetic wire storage Plated wire memory.

magnetisable surface A thin coating of magnetisable particles (ferric oxide) and a binder deposited on a substrate (aluminium disc; polyester disc or tape) as a data storage medium.

magnetisable surface recording The use of a magnetisable surface to receive, store, and output data in the form of bits and bit patterns. Data is written to a magnetisable surface by a **head** (often a **read/write head**) that has a coil in which the direction of an electric current can be changed as the surface passes the head (as moved, for example, by magnetic tape or a magnetic disc). Changes in direction of coil current change the direction of the magnetic flux in the 'air gap' of the head (the part next to the surface) and this changes the direction of magnetisation of the ferric oxide particles of the surface to represent bits and bit patterns in accordance with some code. In most systems (except phase encoding), the direction of magnetisation has no significance and all information is carried by the spacing between **flux transitions** where the magnetisation changes. A line (say, three thousandths of an inch wide) along which these flux transitions are placed is a **track** or, on magnetic tape, a **channel**. In reading, these flux transitions cause small, momentary currents to flow in the coil of the head as the track moves beneath it. These pulses are analysed by electronic circuits to determine their data significance. There

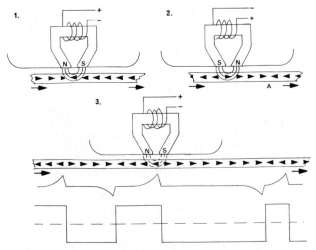

are a number of coding methods for representing data. The illustration is of a read/write head in a magnetic disc system. In Figure 1, the head is writing magnetic flux of one polarity while in Figure 2 it is writing flux of the opposite polarity. In both cases it is erasing previously written data from the track. In 2, a flux reversal is marked by 'A'. The reading operation is shown in Figure 3; as each flux transition passes beneath the head, it produces a small flux change which is detected by the coil and output to the read amplifier and logic circuitry. See *NRZ; NRZI; phase encoding; frequency modulation (Data recording); modified frequency modulation; modified modified frequency modulation; group code recording.*

magnetomotive force (mmf.) The force used to cause magnetisation in iron as created by passing a current through a coil. It is proportional to ampere turns; the unit of measurement is the **gilbert**. See *magnet; ampere turn.*

magnify (1) To increase the size of an image as displayed on a graphics VDU. **(2)** To enlarge; to increase size for display or copying. Typically, 'magnify' is applied to an image and 'enlarge' to an area; ('magnify a character'; 'enlarge a frame'). See *reduction.*

magnitude A term applied to a numeric value without considering sign; for example, +2000 and −2000 are of the same 'magnitude'. See *order of magnitude.*

mailbox Also *mailbox buffer.* A storage location for passing terminal-program or program-program data in some multiprogramming systems.

main control unit A control processor; an instruction control unit that performs scheduling and supervisory functions for other processors in a multiprocessor system.

main entry point In a program with multiple entry points; the one at which execution usually begins; it is, typically, the address of the first instruction in the first sequence. See *entry point; label.*

main file A master file.

main frame A mainframe.

main memory Main storage.

main processor unit A control processor; a processor that exercises control over other processors in a multiprocessor system.

main program (1) The principle program in a group of related programs. **(2)** A main sequence. **(3)** A control segment; a part of an overlaid program that is executed first and that remains in main storage throughout execution.

main sequence The sequence of instructions that represents the structure of a program and to which control is returned after branching.

main storage Also *main store; main memory; primary storage; first-level storage* and, in some contexts, *internal storage.* The coordinate-addressable (core; semiconductor) storage of a computer system that is external to the control unit and directly accessible to the control unit without using input/output channels. It is the principle fast-access storage of a computer and is used to hold the operating system and other system programs and those application programs and data that are being executed at a particular time. See *core memory; semiconductor memory; coincident-current selection; cache; slave store; bulk storage; storage; backing storage; random access.*

main task (1) The principle function of a computer; for example, process control, preparing a payroll, or order entry. **(2)** A program; the principle sequence of a load module. **(3)** In some multiprogramming systems; the main program held in a main storage partition.

mainframe (1) The main hardware unit of a computer system; a combination (usually within a single enclosure) that consists of the control unit, arithmetic unit, and main storage. In this sense, the term is synonymous with 'central processor' though with a hardware orientation. Also, where 'central processor' is quite explicit as to the units included, 'mainframe' may be used loosely enough to include directly associated units such as the console and peripheral controllers. **(1)** A computer considered with respect to its manufacturer; ('a magnetic disc unit that can be used with different mainframes'). **(3)** The principle computer in an installation where there are multiple computers. **(4)** A large, general-purpose computer (as distinct from a minicomputer or microcomputer). **(5)** In a data network; the computer at the central site; the main computer of the system.

mainframers A term sometimes applied to manufacturers of 'mainframe' computers or to people who consider such computers to be greatly superior to other types.

mainline A main sequence of instructions; ('subroutines called from a FORTRAN mainline').

maintainability A term sometimes used when discussing the amount of effort or lost time incurred in correcting hardware faults or preventing their occurrence. See *availability.*

maintained data Data that is kept current; data that is updated as changes occur, as contrasted, perhaps, to archive data.

maintenance (1) With respect to hardware; an activity undertaken to keep it in a condition in which it will perform its function (**preventative maintenance**) or to return it to operating condition following a failure (**corrective maintenance**). (2)With respect to programs; the activity of changing them to reflect changing processing needs and of documenting the changes. (3) With respect to files and other data structures; the operation of updating them as changes occur, changing their storage organisation, and adjusting pointers and indexes as required.

maintenance panel An engineering test panel.

maintenance program A diagnostic test program.

major control field See *control field*.

major key (1)The contents of a major control field. (2)A primary key.

major task A main task.

majority carrier In a semiconductor device; the carrier (holes or electrons) of the main conductor path. See *N-type; P-type*.

majority operation A threshold operation with Boolean (two-condition) inputs; the output is 'true' if more than half of the inputs are 'true' and it is 'false' if less than half are 'true' or if they are evenly divided. See *threshold*.

makeup time Computer time used in rerunning jobs that were interrupted or prevented from running because of system faults.

malfunction A fault; a condition in which a unit of hardware ceases to perform as designed or intended. See *fault*.

malfunction routine A diagnostic test program.

management information system (MIS) Computer programs and techniques designed to provide management with relevant, timely data in a form that facilitates use and analysis. It may consist of programs and data specifically designed to provide this service and/or facilities for selecting, extracting, and formatting data produced to meet other processing requirements. For example, a management information system may make use of payroll data to produce a summary containing the number of employees in each pay bracket by department, average hourly wage, hours of overtime worked, and a comparison with wages for the same period of the previous year.

Manchester code A method of encoding data for transmission (or, possibly, for magnetisable surface storage) in which a line transition occurs in the middle of each bit period with a high-low transition encoding a 1-bit and a low-high transition a 0-bit. A transition also occurs at the end of a bit period when encoding multiple 1-bits or 0-bits. See *phase encoding*.

Manchester terminal unit (MTU) A terminal that provides for bit-serial, time division multiplexed transmission in the Manchester code utilising a single twisted pair of wires (or the equivalent) as the data bus. All encoding, decoding, multiplexing, and control functions are, typically, implemented by a single CMOS integrated circuit.

manipulate With respect to data; to change its form or location; to perform arithmetic, logic, or transfer operations with it.

mantissa (1)That part of a logarithm that represents a number without considering its radix point; in the logarithm 1.74351, the '74351' is the 'mantissa'. See *logarithm; characteristic*. (2)A fractional part. See *floating point*.

manual (1)Performed by hand or with non-automatic equipment; ('manual data entry'; 'manual sorting'). (2)Of equipment; without a motor and intended for hand operation; ('a manual keypunch'; 'a manual typewriter'). (3)Requiring an operator in order to function; ('a manual exchange'; 'a manual executive'). See *automatic*.

manual control With respect to a computer operation; controlled by the operator from the console.

manual exchange A telephone exchange in which calls are routed by an operator. See *automatic exchange*.

manual executive An executive that is not part of or used with an operating system; system software that requires major scheduling and execution control by an operator.

manual file rotation File retention that is controlled by statements in job control language.

manual input An input made by a person, usually via a keyboard.

manual off-line operation A manual operation that is not a direct step in inputting data to computer storage. For example, sorting, checking, or transcribing source documents or decollating printed output.

manual on-line operation A manual operation in which an operator provides an input to a computer program, for example, via a console typewriter or a direct data entry terminal.

manual operation An operation performed by hand or partly by hand; for example, entering data at a keyboard or decollating multi-part printout.

manual originate The process of setting up a data transfer over a PSTN line by an operator at one data station dialing the telephone number of a line access unit at another data station and switching from voice to data when an answer tone is received.

manual overlaying Overlaying of program segments in the sequence specified by a programmer. See *overlay*.

map (1) To establish a one-to-one relationship between the entities of different sets. See *mapping*. **(2)** Also, often, *table; index*. A list of data units and their locations in computer storage; ('a map of main storage'; 'a file map').

mapping (1) Converting a program's addresses to hardware addresses and loading it in main storage; a program may be said to be 'mapped onto' main storage. **(2)** In a virtual storage system; the process of setting up the reference tables and values for accessing pages/segments in main storage. See *mapping table*. **(3)** The process of setting up a file index or directory and writing the necessary values for indexed access of the file.

mapping table Also, often, *index; table; directory; map*. A table of accessible entities and their locations; for example, a page table that holds the addresses of pages in main storage or an index of an indexed file as held at the beginning of its storage area on magnetic disc.

margin-notched card An edge-notched card.

margin-punched card An edge-punched card.

marginal Of equipment or an operation; unstable and error-prone; likely to fail or cause difficulty in use.

marginal check A maintenance technique in which an operating condition or environment (voltage; temperature) is varied in order to reveal intermittent or incipient faults.

marginal test A marginal check.

mark (1) A representation of data in an optically detectable, non-character form; for example, a pencil line in a preprinted box. See *optical mark recognition*. **(2)** Also *marker*. A delimiter; for example, an 'end-of-tape mark'. **(3)** In a telegraphy system; a pulse (often +80 V.) that represents a 1-bit. **(4)** A 1-bit considered with respect to transmission, representation, or some control function; ('mark idle'; 'a mark to space transition'; 'a DCD drop code consisting of 129 marks'). **(5)** In paper tape; a data hole.

mark hold On a data circuit of a modem or other communications or interface device; a continuous signal of the polarity and voltage used to represent 1-bits.

mark idle On a communications channel; the continuous transmission of 1-bits when no data is being sent; the usual purpose is to provide synchronising information.

mark reader An optical mark reader or a mark sense reader.

mark scanning Mark reading; the optical detection of marks on a document. See *optical mark reader*.

mark sense reader A reader that uses mark sensing.

mark sensing The electrical sensing of conductive marks as placed on a document or punched card by means of a special pencil. With punched cards, a mark indicates a position where a hole is to be punched.

mark sensing card A (punched) card preprinted with locations where conductive marks can be placed.

marking In a telephone system; the routing of calls by operating the appropriate relays.

marking wave In telegraphy; the line condition that is used to represent 'marks'.

Markovian A term applied to a probability model in which each event depends upon the previous event.

mask (1) A pattern of bits or characters that is used to control which bits or characters of input are to be included in output. A mask is, typically, a string with a 1-bit in each bit position where the input is to be moved to output and a 0-bit where it is not to be moved. It is an AND operation; the following is an example:

Input	0 1 0 0 0 1 1 1
Mask	1 1 1 0 0 0 0 1
Output	0 1 0 0 0 0 0 1

See *filter*. **(2)** In the manufacture of semiconductor devices; a photographically reduced representation of a circuit or element as used to establish an etching pattern. See *semiconductor; photolithography*.

mask programmable A term applied to an integrated circuit read-only memory that is produced as a chip with 1-bits 'written' in all bit positions. A special 'mask' is produced to customer specification for controlling an etching operation to remove sections of metalised channel and thus to write 0-bits were required. After etching, final stages of encapsulation and test are performed. Masks are computer-generated from (usually) paper tape or punched cards supplied by the customer. See *PROM*.

masked In some systems; a term used synonymously with 'disabled'.

masked ROM A read-only memory that is produced by an application-specific mask and etching process. See *mask programmable*.

mass storage (1) The storage of a mass storage system. **(2)** Any large storage that is directly accessible to the central processing unit of a computer. The term is often applied to magnetic disc storage with a capacity of more than about 200 megabytes.

mass storage controller A disc file controller; a specialised interface device between an input/output multiplexor (or other peripheral control device) and a large-capacity magnetic disc unit.

mass storage device (1) An element of a mass storage system. **(2)** A high-capacity magnetic disc unit.

mass storage system (MSS) Also, sometimes, *terabit storage*. A term that may be applied to any storage with more than about a terabit (10^{12} bits) capacity. Such systems, typically, provide rack storage for data cells with means for locating them, moving them to a read/write station, and replacing them after the required locations have been read or written. Systems have been designed with storage cells for a variety of media including photo-digital, laser holograms, magnetic tape cartridge and cassette, and magnetic cards. Access times are, typically, from about three seconds to about twenty seconds. They are used in many large virtual storage systems to hold data that is prestaged to magnetic disc under the control of a separate minicomputer.

mass storage unit (MSU) Also *mass storage device*. A term sometimes applied to a high-capacity magnetic disc unit.

master catalogue A catalogue that is accessed as a step in locating other catalogues; a table of catalogues.

master console In a computer system with multiple consoles; the console from which others can be controlled.

master file In a system in which there are multiple generations and/or copies of files; that file which is most up to date and authoritative.

master index An index whose elements are other indexes.

master key In some storage protection systems; a key (held by the operating system) that provides access to all locations in the system. See *storage protection*.

master mode The processing mode in which system routines are being executed. See *slave mode*.

master processor A control processor.

master scheduler In some systems; a control program that deals with commands input from a console or terminal.

master station Also *primary station; control station*. In a data network; the station that exercises network control. It is normally associated with the computer (or main computer) of the system. See *polling; tributary station*.

match (1) With respect to a particular item; to make a comparison with other items in order to locate those that have the same attributes. **(2)** With respect to two groups; to compare elements to identify those that are identical or that have certain specified attributes in common.

mathematical check An arithmetic check.

mathematical function A mathematical procedure.

mathematical logic Symbolic logic.

mathematical model A numerical representation of a system or operation.

mathematical procedure A program (usually a library routine) that is available to perform some mathematical calculation or class of calculations; for example, extracting roots, calculating logarithms, generating random numbers, or producing trigonometric relations.

mathematical programming (1) The construction of programs intended to solve non-linear mathematical problems; for example, finding maximum and minimum values. **(2)** The construction of source programs using an autocode or other numerical code.

mathematical subroutine A mathematical procedure.

matrix (1) An arrangement of items in rows and columns and, possibly, planes, each item of which can be identified by its coordinates. **(2)** A group of coordinate-addressable storage locations that has significance for some purpose. See *subscript; array*. **(3)** A grid; a two-dimensional arrangement of items or locations; for example, a 'dot matrix'.

matrix character A dot matrix character or, possibly, a character constructed of line segments in a matrix as in an LED.

matrix printer A printer that prints dot matrix characters (as contrasted to one that prints shaped characters). unless otherwise indicated, the term denotes an **impact matrix printer**. Such a printer, typically, has a print head with a vertical row of extendable styli (needles) with as many styli as there are dots on character vertical lines; for example, a printer that prints 7×9 characters would have a head with nine styli. The printer has a self-contained buffer that holds one or more lines of characters that are to be printed and a character generator that holds a two-dimensional bit pattern of each character in the character set. As the head moves along a line being printed, circuitry determines which dots are required in each printing position and causes solenoids (or hammers) to be energised to impact the selected styli against ribbon and paper to print the dots. In a printer that prints 7 × 9 characters, the circuitry makes this dot determination seven times as the head passes through each character position and such a printer can place dots in any combination of 63 locations in constructing each character. Most printers that print 7 × 9 characters (and some that print 7 × 7), can print on half spaces as shown with the 'Z'; a needle cannot impact adjacent half-space positions. Printing speeds are from about 45 characters per second to about 350 characters per second; the higher speeds are obtainable by bidirectional printers. Electrostatic and electrothermal matrix printers provide even higher speeds. Most 5 × 7 matrix printers print upper-case only (an ASCII 64-character set) while many 7 × 7 and most 7 × 9 printers handle both upper and lower case (ASCII 96 or 128 character sets). Matrix printers are commonly used for output of minicomputer and microcomputer systems, to provide a hard copy facility at locations using VDU terminals, and for printing tape in calculators and in systems such as those for stock market prices. The following are examples of printing (all impact

matrix); the first two are 5 × 7, the second two 7 × 7, and the last one is 7 × 9. See *electrothermal matrix printer; electrostatic printer; electrosensitive matrix printer; helix printer; dot matrix; print head.*

matrix storage Coordinate-addressable storage.

maxi-tape A term sometimes applied to standard, one-half inch magnetic tape (or to equipment that uses it) as contrasted to the narrower widths used in tape cartridges and digital cassettes.

maxicomputer A term sometimes applied to a minicomputer with more than about 500K words of main storage. See *minicomputer.*

maxwell The unit of measurement of the strength of a magnet. See *magnet.*

MB (Mb.) *MegaByte.*

MBM *Magnetic Bubble Memory.* See *bubble memory.*

Mbyte *Megabyte.*

MDR *Marked Document Reader.* An optical mark reader.

MDS (1)*Microprocessor Development System.* **(2)***Mohawk Data Sciences Corp.* (Herkimer, N.Y.)

mean Also *average.* A number that 'represents' a group of numbers; a number obtained by adding the numbers and dividing the total by the number in the group. For example, the 'mean' of 5, 5, 7, 8, 2, and 3 is obtained by adding them to obtain the total 30 and dividing the total by 6 because there are six numbers in the group. The result is, then, '5'. See *statistics; standard deviation.*

mean time between errors (MTBE) The average time (possibly number of instructions) that a computer operates without experiencing a system software error.

mean time between failures (MTBF) A term used to indicate the reliability of equipment; it is equal to the number of operating hours in the period under consideration, divided by the number of failures experienced.

mean time to repair (MTTR) A measure of the repairability of equipment and the effectiveness of support by its manufacturer or supplier; it is equal to the total time required to perform corrective maintenance during a period divided by the number of faults corrected.

media The plural of 'medium'; ('direct access media'; 'magnetic storage media').

media conversion The transcription of data from one storage medium to another; for example, from punched cards to magnetic tape. A change of media often requires a change of the way data is represented.

medium (1)A physical means used to represent data for storage or transfer. For example, a magnetisable surface coating or a magnetic disc unit or bubble memory can be termed a 'data storage medium'; 'data medium'; or 'storage medium' and a telephone line can be termed a 'data transfer medium'. **(2)**A term applied to that which is intermediate between maximum and minimum values.

medium scale integration (MSI) A term applied to semiconductor devices with from about 10 to about 100 gates per chip. See *semiconductor; large scale integration; small scale integration; chip.*

medium speed In data communications; a data transmission speed of from about 600 to 4800 bits per second. (In a particular system, the upper limit is commonly the highest practical speed using a PSTN line.)

mega- A combining form indicating one million (10^6).

megabit A million bits considered as a unit.

megabyte (MB; Mb.; Mbyte; M-byte) A million bytes considered as a unit.

megaword A million computer words considered as a unit.

member (1)An element; one of the units that make up a group or set; for example, a letter is a 'member' of an alphabet. (2)In a hierarchy; an element that is lower than, controlled by, or accessed via another element termed an 'owner'. For example, records are 'members' of files. See *tree*. (3)A term sometimes applied to a subprogram.

membership The condition of belonging to a group, set, or data structure.

memory Also, often, *storage; store*. A term applied to a medium or device capable of receiving, retaining, and outputting data in binary form. The term 'storage' is more often used when discussing particular units or types (main storage; peripheral storage) and 'memory' when considering the technology or method of access (semiconductor memory; read-only memory). See *storage; random-access memory; read-only memory*.

memory access controller In some systems; control unit hardware that converts instruction addresses to hardware addresses, checks for bound violations, and prevents attempts to execute data or to write to read-only areas of storage.

memory-based A term sometimes applied to a computer with little if any backing storage.

memory bus A circuit in coordinate-addressable storage on which bits move to and from their storage cells during access.

memory cell A storage cell; that which can hold a single bit.

memory cycle A storage cycle.

memory cycle time Storage cycle time.

memory protection Storage protection.

menu In an interactive system; a (displayed) list of items or services available with identifiers by which they may be selected (by pressing keys on a keyboard). A banking terminal may, for example, have a 'menu' by which a user can specify a cash advance, a display of exchange rates, or the balance in his checking account. Menus are often used on different levels with the first menu displayed used to select other menus.

menu operation A method of operating an interactive system in which a program causes options to be displayed at a terminal and performs processing according to the option selected by the terminal operator. See *menu*.

mercury storage A delay line memory in which mercury is used as the acoustic medium. See *delay line memory*.

merge With respect to two sets of items in key sequence; to combine them to form a single set in the same key sequence. For example, a set of records with keys 1, 3, 4, 6, and 11 would be 'merged' with another set having keys 2, 7, 9, 12, and 20 to form a set in the order 1, 2, 3, 4, 6, 7, 9, 11, 12, and 20. See *sort; collate; sequence by merge; internal sort*.

merge order A term that may be used to indicate the number of sets to be merged.

merge pass An operation of merging two sets as a step in performing a merge of three or more sets.

merge sort A sort of a (large) group of items in which the group is divided into smaller groups, each of the smaller groups is sorted, and the sorted groups are merged.

merged transistor logic (MTL) Integrated injection logic.

mesa An early type of transistor construction in which silicon between active areas was removed leaving 'mesas' which were hand-connected (with aid of a microscope). See *planar*.

message (1)In data communications; a unit of data and appropriate addressing and control characters transmitted as a unit (perhaps in separate blocks) between data stations. (2)A communiation from a computer to an operator.

message channel Also *forward channel*. The channel of an asymmetric duplex data circuit that is used to carry messages that have significance to the users of the system. See *asymmetric duplex*.

message control program A transaction processing monitor.

message exchange (1)An exchange (routing facility) in a message switching system. (2)A message and response. See *Message pair*.

message handler A sequence of user-specified macro instructions that examine and process control characters in message headers.

message header The first part of a message containing non-text material such as address, priority, and routing.

message pair Also *phase; interaction*. An initiating message and a response message in a transaction processing system. Typically, the initiating message is an enquiry from an operator at a remote station and the response message is a message returned by a computer giving information requested, indicating problems encountered, requesting further action by the operator, or confirming that the required action has been taken.

message queue A queue of messages awaiting processing or awaiting transmission.

message routing (1)The selection of the circuit on which a message is to be sent. (2)The specification of the interchanges through which a message will pass.

message sink A place or equipment that receives a message. See *message source*.

message source A place or equipment that sends a message. See *message sink*.

message switching A mode of operating a data service or data network in which a message exchange receives messages from senders and retransmits them to their destinations, possibly via other message exchanges. The operation may consist of consolidation and reformatting as well as performing routing functions. The term includes a telegraph system and store and forward systems and contrasts such systems with packet switching and the use of direct links in circuit switching. A system is available to Telex subscribers that makes use of a functional unit (a **message switch**) on the user's premises to receive, store, and route messages to other Telex subscribers. See *circuit switching; store and forward; packet switching*.

message text That part of a message that has content significance rather than routing or control significance. See *message header*.

metalanguage A language used to define or explain a language (either itself or another language).

metalisation In semiconductor manufacture; the process of creating conductive channels on a chip.

meter (1)A device used to visually present a measurement or a relationship; for example voltage, frequency, or amperes. The presentation is assumed to be analogue (with a needle) unless otherwise indicated. See *digital*. (2)To measure an analogue value; for example, flow or temperature.

metering pulses In some telephone systems; pulses that are sent at intervals during a dialed call and counted to determine the charge to be made. See *metering tone*.

metering tone In many telephone systems; a distinctive tone that is switched off when a call is connected and on when it is disconnected; in the off state, it enables a counter which determines the charge to be made for the call. In many systems, the tone is in the voice band (say, at 2800 Hz.) while in others it is 'out of band' (often at 12 or 16 kHz.). When 'in band', a notch filter prevents speech or data tones from being interpreted as the metering tone.

MF *MultiFrequency signalling.*

MF4 The British Telecom designation for a 'multifrequency signalling' service (push-button telephones).

MFM *Modified Frequency Modulation.*

MFR (1)*ManuFactuRer.* (2)*MultiFrequency Receiver.*

MFRS *Million Flux Reversals per Second.*

MFS *Multi-Frequency Signalling.*

MFT *Multiprogramming, Fixed Tasks.* Multiprogramming with a fixed number of tasks.

MH *Message Handler.*

MHD (1)*Multiple-Head Disc.* (2)*Movable-Head Disc.*

MHZ (MHz.) *MegaHertZ.* A frequency of one million cycles per second.

MICR *Magnetic Ink Character Recognition.*

micro A microprocessor.

micro- (1)(μ) A combining form meaning one-millionth as in 'microsecond'. (2)A combining form meaning 'very small' as in 'microcircuit'.

micro-based mini A minicomputer with a microprocessor as its central processor.

micro-Winchester A Winchester magnetic disc unit with 5¼ inch diameter discs. See *Winchester technology*.

microcircuit A circuit formed on a silicon chip; the electronics of an integrated circuit.

microcode (1)Bit patterns held in read-only memory (in a control unit) and read as pulses that are sent to logic gates associated with registers to cause a transfer of bits between registers or within a register. See *register; control point; microinstruction; microprogram*. (2)Microinstructions considered collectively. (3)To write control bit patterns to control unit memory. See *soft centered*.

microcode memory Also *control memory*. Memory used to hold microcode; read-only memory (possibly programmable) that holds control bit patterns.

microcode processor An arithmetic unit and/or a control unit; the elements of a computer or other intelligent device that use microcode to move bits. See *microcode; instruction scheduler*.

microcomputer A small computer with intelligence provided by a microprocessor. It is, typically, a portable or desk-top unit with keyboard and CRT display or a connection to use a television for the display. Backing storage is commonly cassette tape, flexible disc, or 5¼ in. Winchester disc. Programming is usually in BASIC and/or PASCAL plus assembler. Most are 8-bit devices; CP/M is a 'standard' operating system.

microcycle The time in which one microinstruction is executed.

microelectronic device A multi-element electronic device with elements that are so small that they cannot be visually identified or manually manipulated (except, possibly, with the aid of a microscope). With a few exceptions (bubble memory; silicon-on-sapphire) the term denotes a device formed on a silicon chip. When packaged, it is an 'integrated circuit'.

microelectronics The science, technology, or operation of designing and/or producing microelectronic devices.

microfarad (μf.) One millionth of a farad. See *farad*.

microfiche Also *fiche*. A piece of photographic film of standard size (148 mm. × 105 mm.) with a number of frames of microfilm arranged in a grid pattern and, usually, containing coordinate reference letters or numbers to facilitate the visual location of particular frames. The frames (as used in COM systems) are usually 42X reduction and such a fiche contains 208 frames arranged in 13 rows and 16 columns. See *COM; reduction; ultrafiche; recorder*.

microfilm (1) High-resolution film suitable for recording images with large reductions. Originals and masters for duplication are usually made on fine-grain **silver halide film** of the same type as used for black and white photography. Copies are usually made on **diazo film** which is exposed with ultraviolet light and developed by passing it through a chamber containing ammonia vapour; it produces blue negative copies from negative masters. Another film used for copies is **vesicular film** which is similar to diazo but with self-contained developer that is activated by exposure to ultraviolet light; it produces pink copies (either positive or negative) from negative masters. See *COM; duplicator*. **(2)** Film containing high-reduction images.

microform (1) That which contains microimages; for example, microfiche, roll film, or an aperture card. **(2)** A microimage of a form. See *form flash*.

microform reader Also *reader*. An enlarger or enlarger-projector for microforms.

microform reader-copier A reader-copier; a device that enlarges microforms for visual examination and can also produce paper copies of the enlarged images.

microform reader-printer A microform reader-copier.

microfunction A function implemented by microcode.

micrographics The branch of technology concerned with producing, preserving, and using microfilm recordings. Unless otherwise indicated, 'producing' is understood. See *COM; microfilm; microform; display*.

microimage An image (on microfilm) that must be enlarged or magnified for visual interpretation; the contents of a frame of microfilm. See *COM; frame*.

microinch One millionth of an inch (about one-fortieth of a micron).

microinstruction A sequence of **microcode** bit patterns held in read-only memory in a control unit or arithmetic unit and output to logic gates as a step in executing an instruction. It contains (consists of) the control point values where a movement of bits within a register or between registers is to take place plus the address of the next microinstruction to be executed in the microprogram being executed. A **packed microinstruction** (also **vertical microinstruction**) is a short sequence (a few bits plus next address) that is interpreted in a microinstruction decoder to produce one or more **unpacked microinstructions** (also **horizontal microinstruction**) with as many bit positions as there are control points to be set simultaneously (in one clock cycle). The use of a microinstruction decoder is said to constitute a **nanolevel** and an input to the decoder (a vertical microinstruction) may be termed a **nanoinstruction**. See *execution; register; control point; microprogram; microcode*.

micron One millionth of a meter; 39.37 microinches.

microprocessor (1)(MPU) A single integrated circuit ('chip') that performs instruction execution and monitor and control functions for an intelligent device such as a modem or a small computer. The usual elements are read-only memory (ROM) to hold the order code and microcode for instruction execution, an instruction register to hold the instruction currently being executed, a program counter register to hold the address of the next instruction, an arithmetic-logic unit to perform comparisons and arithmetic, and additional registers for holding addresses, input and output data, and information concerning processing status. Some MPU's also have integral clocks and small amounts of random-access memory (RAM) to hold transient data produced in processing; for example, intermediate results of arithmetic operations and addresses in external memory that must be 'remembered' for later use. The microprocessor has external interfaces consisting of an address bus by which it can select locations that are to be read or written in external memory chips, a bidirectional data bus on which transfers are made to and from memory chips and, possibly, devices such as flexible disc units, and single-pin connections for electric power, reset, and control of function, say, by switch position. Most microprocessors use CMOS or NMOS silicon gate technology and are 'TTL compatible' (inputs and outputs need be no higher than +5 V.). They are classified according to the number of bits their internal registers can hold and the number of bits that can be transferred in parallel on the data bus. The most common are 4-bit, 8-bit, and 16-bit devices. Four-bit MPU's are used in relatively simple applications such as in domestic appliances, toys, and car ignition control. Eight-bit devices are used in a wide variety of applications including test equipment, robotics, process control, data communications equipment, entertainment machines, and microcomputers. Sixteen-bit units are used in larger and more sophisticated applications of the same type as 8-bit units, and also to implement many minicomputers. A 'microprocessor' by this definition is an integrated circuit device as supplied by a manufacturer and it can only perform a useful function when mounted on a board and connected to other devices and circuit elements. **(2)**A 'microprocessor' (def. 1) plus supporting devices and circuitry as used to perform a particular function or range of functions. It is a 'microprocessor' by this definition that is implied in most (non-electronic) discussions of the subject. In addition to the MPU supplied by the manufacturer, such a microprocessor requires one or more ROM memory chips, usually at least one RAM chip, some form of input/output chip, and a clock generator (oscillator), unless a clock is included in the MPU. After development and prototyping, all chips (and, often, devices such as switches, resistors, capacitors, and relays) are mounted on one or more custom-designed printed circuit boards. The function(s) that can be implemented by a particular microprocessor depend upon the facilities provided by the MPU, the additional chips and components that are connected, and the way that it is programmed. Basically, a microprocessor can do the following things: 1. It can recognise external 'on-off' conditions such as provided by switch positions, counters, or detectors. 2. It can receive digitised information, for example, that indicates the temperature of a furnace, the position of a valve, or the key that has been depressed on a typewriter. 3. It can compare inputs with stored values in order to perform such operations as causing a valve to close if a temperature is too high, to open if it is too low, and to cause an alarm to sound if the temperature is above a certain level or if a valve fails to operate. 4. It can receive and hold in memory the instructions (bit groups) that are required to perform tests (comparisons) and to receive inputs and make outputs. 5. It can receive and

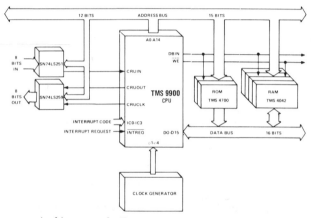

Architecture of a Texas Instrument microprocessor.

hold in memory those values used in tests/comparisons and also bit patterns that represent characters that are to be printed, displayed, or transmitted. 6. It can make data transfers internally and also to and from other devices; for example, a modem, a magnetic disc drive, or a computer. 7. It can detect and provide external indication of abnormal conditions encountered in processing; for example, a faulty address or an incorrect bit group. 8. It can manage and synchronise instruction execution and inputs and outputs. 9. It can provide useful outputs as on-off circuits (say, to operate relays or lights) or as digital groups (say, to cause a printer to print particular characters). The MPU manufacturer can, typically, provide all necessary additional chips for interfacing and control and the information required for programming (but not for program design). Programming consists of writing instructions (fixed length bit patterns) to memory in the order in which they will be required to perform the desired operation (add; move; compare) and the addresses where the affected bit patterns are located (say, the values that are to be added or compared). A sequence of instructions to perform a certain operation (say to read a temperature and cause a valve to open or close) is a 'program'; a microprocessor may have only a single user-written program or, if required, it may have a large number. If a microprocessor is required to perform a series of repetitive and reasonably simple operations (say in machine tool or process control), all instructions are commonly written to read-only memory. If only a few systems are required, this memory can be 'programmable ROM' (PROM) and devices are available to 'burn in' the bit patterns of the instructions. If more than about 100 are to be made, it is usually more economical to send the program(s) to the chip manufacturer (on punched cards or paper tape) for incorporation in special memory chips. The MPU usually requires a certain amount of external (on another chip) random access memory and such memory is also required for use in developing and testing programs. If the system is so complex that all programs cannot be held conveniently in ROM, then they must be held in external storage (say on flexible disc) and loaded into the required amount of RAM as they are needed during processing; the MPU has the facilities, in conjunction with a special interface chip, to make the transfers. The MPU manufacturers and others provide a wide range of programming aids from a simple hexadecimal keyboard and a chip to permit single instruction execution to a complete hardware and software package that provides high-level language programming facilities and sophisticated debugging aids. See *instruction; execution; program; bit slice; register.*

microprocessor development system (MDS) A set of programs and, possibly, hardware, designed to facilitate the development of microprocessor programs on a minicomputer. Typically, the package emulates the microprocessor instruction set and execution environment and allows programs to be developed and tested making use of the high-level language and debugging facilities of the minicomputer. When a program (or all programs) have been tested, the object code is written to the microprocessor memory.

microprogrammable Of a computer or other intelligent device; containing the facilities to permit users to write microcode routines and thus to extend or 'customize' the instruction set.

microroutine A microprogram.

microsecond (μs.) One millionth of a second; one thousand nanoseconds.

microwave An identifier of a communications system that uses a carrier wave with a frequency higher than 890 MHz. It is usually a line-of-sight system in which speech and data traffic are sent by radio waves between relay towers, each of which amplifies and retransmits received signals.

middleground In some systems; a classification of jobs in a multiprogramming environment that are neither 'foreground' (high priority) nor 'background' (low priority).

middleware (1) Bridgeware (in ROM). **(2)** Firmware; particularly an element of a software 'package'.

midicomputer A term that is sometimes applied to a minicomputer with from about 250K to 500K words of main storage. See *minicomputer; maxicomputer.*

midnight line A service of the U.K. Post Office that permits subscribers to make unlimited telephone calls to inland points between the hours of midnight and 6:00 A.M.

migration any movement of data made because of changed access requirements; for example, a file relating to a particular aircraft flight 'migrates' from magnetic disc to magnetic tape the day after the flight is completed. See *staging; spooling.*

mil One thousandth of an inch (25.4 microns).

MIL *MILitary.* (Chiefly U.S. usage)

mill A term sometimes used synonymously with 'arithmetic unit'. See *number cruncher.*

milli- A combining form meaning one thousandth.

millisecond (ms.; msec.) One thousandth of a second; one thousand microseconds.

MIMD *Multiple Instruction stream Multiple Data stream.* A designation of a parallel processor that is essentially two or

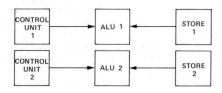

more individual computers with facilities for interaction and work sharing. See *SIMD; SISD; MISD*.

mini A minicomputer.

mini- A combining form meaning 'very small' (but not as small as 'micro-').

mini-cartridge A small data cartridge that can hold about 700 kilobytes of data. See *data cartridge*.

mini-flexible disc Also *mini-disc; mini-floppy disc*. A flexible magnetic disc 5¼ inches in diameter with, typically, 35 or 40 tracks per side and unformatted capacities from about 100K bytes (single-sided single-density) to 500K bytes (double-sided double-density). See *flexible disc*.

minicomputer Also *mini*. A small computer that is intended to be used in an ordinary office environment without subfloor or airconditioning. Typical main storage capacities are from 16 kilobytes to 2 megabytes and word length may be 8, 16, 32 or 48 bits (16 bits is the most common). Configurations include desk-top units similar to VDU's, free-standing desk units, and units with cabinet or rack-mounted central processors and multiple operating terminals. Peripherals range from data cartridge and flexible disc units to conventional 'mainframe' magnetic disc and magnetic tape units. They are used as general-purpose computers and in special applications such as process control and for performing interface functions for a larger (mainframe) computer. A minicomputer with from about 250K to 500K words of main storage is sometimes termed a **midicomputer** and one with more than about 500K words a **maxicomputer**. Configurations are available with up to about 5 megabytes of main storage. A minicomputer is usually programmable in assembler plus COBOL, FORTRAN and other high-level languages; it usually has facilities for floating point, multilevel interrupts, and advanced storage management. There are no distinguishing performance or capability differences between larger minicomputers and the small to medium-size 'mainframe' computers. (Digital Equipment Corp. defines a minicomputer as a computer that sells for between $20,000 and $200,000.) See *mainframe; microcomputer; microprocessor; general-purpose computer*.

minidisc (1) A mini-flexible disc. (2) In some systems; a 'virtual disc'.

minimum delay programming Programing to provide access frequency loading.

minimum distance code A code in which the signal distance is always greater than some specified value.

minimum truncation The shortest form of a command that will be accepted by a program as valid (that will make a unique identification); for example, 'LOGI' for 'LOGIN' or 'EDI' for 'EDIT'.

minitape cartridge A mini-cartridge. See *data cartridge*.

minor control field See *control field*.

minor key A secondary key. See *major key*.

mintern In a multi-input logic circuit; a unique condition or result that is produced by a particular combination of variables. It is often represented by a 'cell' of a Karnaugh map. In the example of the *Karnaugh map* entry, each of the cells D_1, D_2, D_3, and D_4 is a 'mintern'.

minuend In subtraction; the number from which another number (the **subtrahend**) is subtracted. For example, in the expression $X = 5 - 3$, the 5 is the 'minuend' and the 3 the 'subtrahend'.

MIPS (mips.) *Million Instructions Per Second*.

MIS *Management Information System*.

MISD *Multiple Instruction stream Single Data stream*. A parallel processor in which multiple control units operate on a

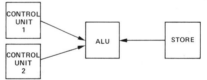

single data stream. See *SISD; SIMD; MIMD*.

missing clock In magnetic disc recording using double frequency recording; a method of marking the beginning of sectors by eliminating one clock pulse (flux reversal) in each of two adjacent bytes of each sector header. The distinctive pattern is recorded during disc initialisation and is detected and counted by circuitry to locate a particular sector. The method is termed **soft sectoring** as contrasted to 'hard sectoring' in which sectors are identified by 'sector slots'. See *sectoring; index*.

missing page interrupt A page fault.

mixed-base numeration system A numeration system in which a 'number' consists of the sum of two or more terms, not all of which have the same base; for example, time expressed as hours and minutes or value expressed in pounds, shillings, and pence. See *mixed-radix numeration system*.

mixed-mode operation An operation performed on or with items of different types; for example, addition in which some of the numbers are in fixed-point binary and others in packed decimal.

mixed-mode processing Processing in which a computer concurrently executes interleaved programs of different types; for example, a mix consisting of local batch work and transaction processing.

mixed number A number that is not an integer; for example, 1.3, 9⅓, or 2367.001. See *integer; number.*

mixed processing Mixed-mode processing.

mixed-radix notation A mixed-radix numeration system.

mixed-radix numeration system A mixed-base numeration system in which bases are in descending order of magnitude and each base is an integral multiple of the next lowest. An example would be a method of representing time in hours, tens of minuites, and minutes. The base of the first is, then, 60, the second, 10, and the third (the lowest order), 1. There are few examples with practical application and using modern units of measurement. See *mixed-base numeration system; numeration system; radix.*

ML *Machine Language.*

MMDS *Martin Marietta Data Systems.* (Towson, Md.)

MMF (mmf.) *MagnetoMotive Force.*

MMFM (M²FM) *Modified Modified Frequency Modulation.*

mnemonic A term applied to something that is used to aid the memory; for example, a circle drawn around a date on a calendar or the letters 'mpy' to indicate 'multiply'. In computer-related usage, the term is applied to elements of programming languages (BNZ— *Branch if Not Zero*) and to symbolic addresses. (Because a symbolic address is a 'symbol' or contains a symbol, it is also a 'mnemonic' whether selected as an aid to memory or for other reasons.) See *acronym; symbol; symbolic address.*

mnemonic name A programmer-supplied word associated with a specific function name (in the environment division of a COBOL program).

mnemonic symbol A character or group intended to serve as a mnemonic; for example, a '✓' placed by an item that has been counted or a '?' by an item that needs checking.

MNOS *Metal-Nitride-Oxide-Silicon.* A type of electrically alterable read-only memory (EAROM) that can be programmed by means of electrostatic charges in silicon nitride (Si_3N_4)

gate regions. The device is similar to one containing low-threshold 'nitride' MOS transistors, except that the silicon dioxide between the nitride and the substrate is extremely thin (20 Angstroms) in the location of source-drain conduction channels. The construction is indicated in Fig. 1. By convention, erasing consists of placing storage cells in their low-threshold state which writes 1-bits in all locations. This is ac-

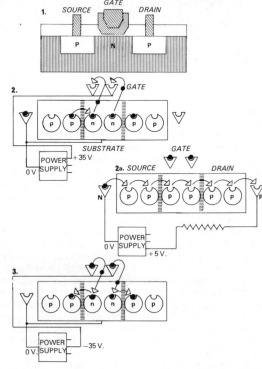

complished by placing the gate strongly positive (+35 V.) with respect to the substrate. This causes electrons to 'tunnel' out of the source-drain channel and to become 'trapped' by positive charge in the nitride gate region. Silicon nitride is a good insulator and the charge remains after the erase voltage is removed. This, effectively, creates 'holes' which reduce the source-drain threshold voltage to about 2 V. To program (selectively write 0-bits), the gate voltage at these locations is placed low (—35 V.) with respect to the substrate. This causes electrons to be expelled from the silicon nitride and to 'tunnel' back through the dioxide and into the source-drain channel where they neutralise P-carriers (fill holes) and return the channel to its high-threshold (12 V.) state. Fig. 2 illustrates the effect of erasing and Fig. 3 of writing a 0-bit. To erase and write takes about 40 milliseconds per word; read access time is about 1 microsecond. MNOS has an advantage over FAMOS in that individual word positions can be erased and rewritten and that reprogramming does not require the removal of devices from their printed circuit boards. See *MOS; field effect transistor; FAMOS.*

mode (1) A term applied to an operating condition that is one of two or more such conditions; ('receive mode'; 'write mode'; 'batch mode'; 'sequential access mode'). **(2)** In some systems; the part of an instruction that indicates how the operand is to be obtained (literal; direct; indirect). See *function; offset.*

model (1) Also, often, *mathematical model.* A representation of a structure, system, or process by its essential elements and in terms that facilitate analysis and manipulation. **(2)** A term applied to an item of equipment that is different in construction or operation than another item of equipment that performs the same basic function.

modem (*MODulator-DEModulator*) A functional unit of a data communications system that modulates and demodulates a carrier wave in order to represent data on a telephone circuit. When transmitting, it receives data as direct-current pulses from a computer or terminal (DTE), generates a carrier wave, and modulates the carrier wave to represent the data. When receiving, it converts modulations to direct-current pulses and passes them to the associated DTE. The most common modulation methods are frequency shift keying (FSK) for transmission speeds below 2400 bits per second and differential phase shift keying (DPSK) for speeds of 2400, 4800, 7200, and 9600 bits per second. In addition to modulation and demodulation functions, a modem, typically, has facilities for establishing and maintaining synchronisation with another modem, for testing the circuit, and for changing the speed of transmission. Some modems also have limited facilities for multiplexing and/or for changing between 4-wire leased circuits and 2-wire switched (dialed) circuits. A number of modern modems are microprocessor controlled. See *carrier; modulation; modem interchanges.*

modem eliminator A functional unit that establishes a standard interface for connecting terminals intended for use on communications (telephone) links to local cable systems.

modem interchanges Communications between a modem and its associated data terminal equipment. The most commonly used system is that of the CCITT V.24 and V.28 recommendations. These are, basically, as follows for a switched carrier (polled) system: When the modem has power, and is not in a test mode, it maintains a constant high (say +5 V.) **data set ready (DSR)** signal to the DTE. When the DTE has a message to send, it raises the **ready to send (RTS)** signal to the modem. When the modem receives this signal, it starts generating and transmitting the carrier wave and then a 'training sequence' that is used by the modem at the other end to establish synchronisation. When the training sequence is completed (in 18-253 milliseconds), the modem sends the DTE a **clear to send (CTS)** signal. When this signal is received, the DTE commences sending data. When a message is to be received, the modem detects the incoming carrier wave and notifies its DTE by raising a **data carrier detect (DCD)** signal. In a point-to-point (constant carrier) system, both DTE's maintain RTS at constant high and transmit immediately whenever they have data to send.

modem simulator A modem eliminator.

modem turnaround time The time required for the modems in a half-duplex system to change from the condition in which modem A is sending and modem B is receiving to the condition in which modem A receives and modem B transmits. The time is usually between 100 and 300 milliseconds, depending upon the training sequence used and whether or not echo suppressors are enabled.

modified frequency modulation (MFM) A method of magnetisable surface recording (on magnetic disc) that is similar to frequency modulation except that fewer flux reversals are required to encode a given amount of data. In MFM, a change of direction of current in the coil of the read/write head (and, hence of the flux along the track) is made between clock pulses to write a 1-bit, in the same manner as in FM. Unlike FM, where the flux is changed coincident with clock pulses, the flux is changed at a clock pulse only if the bit to be written is a 0-bit and the previous bit was also a

0-bit. Though it provides less synchronising information than FM, it has proved to be adequate. In the figure, it will be noted that the group can be written with only 10 flux reversals as compared to 20 for the FM method. (Clock pulses are shown

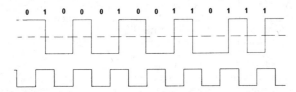

only for illustration purposes.) Because recording density is limited by the number of flux reversals that can be made per inch of track, it is possible to record twice as much data per disc surface by MFM as can be recorded by FM. See *magnetisable surface recording; frequency modulation (Data recording); double density recording; double frequency recording.*

modified modified frequency modulation (MMFM; M²FM) A method of magnetisable surface recording similar to MFM except that a flux reversal for clocking purposes is only made

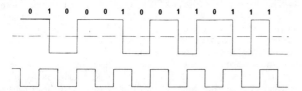

when a 0-bit is to be recorded and no flux change was required to encode the previous bit. It thus eliminates the flux change used in MFM to record the second of two 0-bits when a flux change was made to record the first. The method reduces by half the number of flux transitions required to encode a string of 0-bits. See *magnetisable surface recording; modified frequency modulation.*

modifier (1)A value (generally the contents of a modifier register) that is added to an operand address each time a loop is performed; it has the effect of providing a different operand for successive iterations. See *loop; address modification.* **(2)** A value (say, a base address) that is applied to a presumptive address as a step (or the only step) in obtaining an effective address. **(3)**Also, sometimes, *index*. In an instruction; a value in a modifier or index field that indicates if a modifier or index register is to be used and, if there is more than one such register, the particular one to be used.

modifier field Also, sometimes, *index field*. In an instruction in a fixed-format language; a field where a 'modifier' can be placed.

modifier register A register (usually a general-purpose register) that is used to hold a modifier. If the modifier is a base address, it may also be termed a 'base address register' See *index register.*

modify (1) To change an item of hardware or software, say, to improve performance or reliability. **(2)**To apply a value to a presumptive address as a step (or the only step) in producing an effective address. See *modifier.* **(3)**Also *increment.* To add a value to an effective address in order to form a different effective address. See *loop; address modification.* **(4)**To change the action of an instruction as, for example, by substituting one label for another in an unconditional jump instruction (as by use of the COBOL 'ALTER' statement).

modular Consisting of modules.

modular programming Programming in which the problem is broken down into logical subdivisions, each of which is coded and tested as a unit. See *structured programming.*

modularity The degree to which an item is composed of modules. See *monolithic.*

modulation (1) The process or technique of changing a carrier wave in a data-significant way. Some of the methods used are **amplitude modulation** in which the height of the wave is changed, **frequency modulation** in which the frequency is changed, **frequency-shift keying** in which the frequency is changed between two values, **phase shift modulation** in which phase is changed, **quadrature amplitude modulation** which is a form of phase shift modulation, and **pulse code modulation** which is a multiplexing technique. See *carrier wave; band; modulation rate; demodulation.* **(2)**A method of representing data in magnetisable surface storage; for example, 'modified frequency modulation'. **(3)**In magnetisable surface recording; differences in read amplitude that are not caused by differences in write amplitude; the condition usually results from variations in the thickness of the magnetisable surface coating material.

modulation rate The reciprocal of the duration of the shortest nominal time interval between successive data-significant conditions of a modulated carrier wave. If duration is in seconds, the modulation rate is in Baud. For example, if it takes .01 seconds to transmit a bit and change the line condition to transmit the next bit, then the modulation rate is 100 and the transmission is at 100 Baud. See *Baud; data signalling rate; modulation*.

modulator-demodulator A modem.

module A part of a whole that is capable of separate consideration, use, or creation. (1)A sequence of instructions that is written, compiled, and tested as a unit (before being linked with other parts of a program). (2)A functional unit that may be present, absent, or duplicated in a computer depending upon the needs of the user. (3)A 'volume' considered as hardware; for example, a reel of magnetic tape or a disc cartridge. (4)A term applied to an 'add-on' unit, particularly to a unit of main storage.

modulo-2 addition Binary addition without carry. It is an exclusive-OR operation and is the common method of forming check totals and comparing bit strings. The following is an example:

$$\begin{array}{r} 1100111 \\ \oplus 1010100 \\ \hline 0110011 \end{array}$$

See *identity*.

modulo-N A mathematical operation with a result that is the remainder from a division; for example, '5 modulo-3' is '2' and '187694 modulo-8' is '6'.

monadic Also *unary*. Consisting of a single item or performed on or with a single item. See *dyadic*.

monadic operation Also *unary operation*. An operation performed on or with a single input; the term includes 'one constant', 'zero constant', and 'inversion'.

monadic operator Also *unary operator*. In an instruction; an operator that specifies an operation on a single operand; for example, 'NEGATE' or 'MOVE'.

monitor (1)To check an operation as it is being performed; particularly such a check performed by automatic measuring or sampling. (2)A term sometimes applied to the routines of an operating system that perform physical operations; for example, peripheral transfers, inputs, and outputs. (3)An elementary supervisor (now obsolete) with function limited, typically, to initiating execution of the next program when another program execution is completed. (4)A device that monitors (def. 1). (5)A monitor program. (6)A non-interactive display device; particularly a television set in a closed-circuit system.

monitor display A display on a non-interactive VDU.

monitor mode The condition in which a device (terminal; communications controller) receives but does not initiate or respond. See *listen mode*.

monitor printer A printer that prints all messages carried by the circuit to which it is attached.

monitor program Also *monitor routine*. A unit of system software that performs some check on computer operations in progress in order to detect abnormal conditions (bound violations; seek failures; parity failures; looping) and to initiate the appropriate action which, typically, begins with a jump to an interrupt routine. The term is sometimes applied to a program that performs an 'observing' function related to normal processing; for example, to one that maintains the activity status of peripheral devices or tests input buffers to detect the arrival of data.

monitor routine A monitor program.

monitor system A computer with a monitor (an elementary supervisor). See *monitor*.

monocase A term applied to a type font consisting only of upper case letters or only of lower case letters (plus appropriate numbers, punctuation, and symbols). Unless otherwise indicated, 'upper case' is understood.

monolithic Not divisible; not modular; consisting of a single unit.

monolithic integrated circuit The most common type of integrated circuit in which the substrate has some of the active elements formed on it. See *hybrid integrated circuit; mesa*.

monolithic storage Computer (main) storage consisting of 'monolithic' integrated circuits. The term is often used with the intent of indicating 'bipolar' (TTL) rather than an MOS form. See *semiconductor memory*.

monotonicity In digital to analogue and analogue to digital converters; the ability to pass signals corresponding to a change in the least significant bit of the digital signal across the interface. An AD converter, for example, is monotonic if a change in voltage of the analogue signal that should be reflected in the least significant digit position actually causes a change in that position.

Monte Carlo A term applied to techniques for obtaining approximate solutions to mathematically expressed problems plus statistical indications of the reliability of the solutions. Basically, it consists of analysing the output produced from random inputs.

Morse code A telegraphy 'return to zero' code in which characters are represented by dots and dashes, a 'dot' being a short transmission of a voltage or carrier wave and a 'dash' a longer transmission. (It is not commonly used in computer-related data communications.)

MOS *Metal-Oxide-Silicon.* A class of semiconductor devices in which conduction is controlled by electrical fields produced in 'gates' that are physically separated (by silicon dioxide) from active semiconductor materials. Though the term includes CCD and BEAMOS, it usually denotes a field effect transistor or a device incorporating field effect transistors. An **NMOS** device is one in which conduction is through N-type silicon and a **PMOS** device is one in which conduction is through P-type silicon. A **CMOS** device provides conduction through both types of silicon. The circuit symbols and representative 'cross sections' of single elements are shown below.

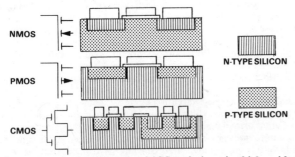

A common and inexpensive MOS technique is **thick oxide** in which about 1000 Angstroms (one-tenth micron) of silicon dioxide (glass) separates the metal gate from the channel that it controls. Such devices commonly require about a 20 V. difference between the supply (V_{DD}) and substrate (V_{SS}). The **threshold voltage** (V_T) at which the source-drain conduction channel forms is, typically, about 4 V. applied as gate voltage (V_{GG}) and it is not, therefore, inherently compatible with TTL (or other bipolar) circuits. Where lower threshold voltages are required, **silicon gate** devices are often used. The technique involves forming the gate of 'polycrystalline' silicon instead of metal and placing the gate very near (200-300 Å) to the source-drain channel, thus increasing the effect of the field created. Another type of device with a low threshold voltage is the **silicon nitride** MOS in which a layer of silicon nitride is formed between the metalised gate and the source-drain channel. This serves to extend the gate closer to the channel than is practical with metal and, thus, to increase the effect of the field. Most MOS devices are **enhancement devices** in which the application of a gate signal causes source-drain conduction. A **depletion device** is one that is normally in the conducting state and in which the application of a gate signal stops conduction.

mosaic printer A matrix printer with a programmable character generator (to permit printing non-Roman alphabets).

MOSFET *Metal-Oxide-Silicon Field Effect Transistor.*

most significant digit In a number in a positional representation system; the leftmost (and highest weight) digit. See *significant digits; least significant digit; numeration system.*

motherboard A (non-removable) printed circuit board to which other (removable) printed circuit boards connect.

motherplane Also, often, *backplane.* In a device in which the electronic elements are on removable printed circuit boards; a plane containing the connectors for the boards and associated interconnecting wiring to complete circuits between boards and to external interfaces.

mount With respect to a storage volume (disc pack; magnetic tape reel); to place it in the device where data can be written to it or read from it.

mount attribute The association between a volume and its drive; the condition(s) in which it is to be mounted and demounted.

movable-head disc See *magnetic disc unit.*

move To read data in one location and write it in another (leaving the data in the first location unchanged). Unless otherwise indicated, it is understood to be within main storage or between main storage and a register in the control unit or arithmetic unit. The term is also applied to changes of location in backing storage; ('move a file from magnetic tape to magnetic disc'). The term 'transfer' is commonly used when the movement is between main storage and backing storage. See *transfer; transmission; load; fetch.*

moving-head printer A printer in which a print head moves along a line as it prints characters on the line. Examples include Teletypes, daisy-wheel printers, golfball typewriters, and character matrix printers. See *print head; carriage.*

moving-medium storage device A magnetisable surface storage device; a device (magnetic disc unit; magnetic tape unit) in which the storage medium moves in relation to the location where it is read and written. See *cyclic storage*.
MPI *Magnetic Peripherals Inc.* (Minneapolis)
MPU *MicroProcessor Unit.*
MS (ms.) *MilliSecond.*
MSB *Most Significant Bit.*
MSEC (msec.) *MilliSECond.*
MSD *Most Significant Digit.*
MSEC (msec.) *MilliSECond.*
MSI *Medium Scale Integration.*
MSP *Management System Programmers Ltd.* (London)
MSS *Mass Storage System.*
MT *Magnetic Tape.*
MTBE *Mean Time Between Errors.*
MTBF *Mean Time Between Failures.*
MTC *Magnetic Tape Cassette.*
MTS *Million Transitions per Second.* A million flux reversals per second. See *MFRS*.
MTTR *Mean Time To Repair.*
MTU (1)*Magnetic Tape Unit.* (2)*Manchester Terminal Unit.*
multi- A combining form meaning 'more than one'.
multi-access computing (MAC) A processing mode in which a user enters and controls his job interactively from a terminal. The computer executes each statement as it is entered and advises him of the result so that he can decide what do do next. The mode is often used in program development and testing and is the common method of executing programs in computer aided design and graphics applications. It is also widely used in instruction. There is no absolute distinction between multi-access and transaction processing, though multi-access is assumed to use a local terminal and transaction processing a terminal connected by a communications link; in some systems, the term 'on-line' is used to cover both. See *on-line; transaction processing; conversational remote job entry; remote job entry*.
multi-address code In a Telex or other data communications system; a single 'address' that causes a message to be routed to each of a number of addressees.
multi-address instruction An instruction that specifies an operation on or with two or more operands.
multicomputer system (1)An installation consisting of two or more independent computers, each of which performs a particular function or combination of functions for the organisation. (2)A computer system consisting of a main computer and one or more auxiliary computers to perform specialised functions; for example, communications interfacing or storage management. (3)A term sometimes used synonymously with 'multiprocessor'.
multidimensional language A term sometimes applied to a communications medium that requires two (possibly three) dimensions; for example, 'flowcharting'.
multidimensional processing Mixed-mode processing.
multidrop line (1)A four-wire, leased telephone line that provides terminations at multiple, geographically-separated locations. Such a 'line' may incorporate multiple trunk channels and be connected through multiple telephone exchanges. It is, thus, not a single, physical line but a number of interconnected lines with routing that is usually unknown to the subscriber. By this definition, the term is synonymous with 'multipoint line'. in its most common usage. (2)A single local loop with 'drops' to more than one location. Such a line could be used for polled data communications, for telemetry, or to serve multiple telephone subscribers. When multiple telephone subscribers are served, it is a 'party line'.
multifrequency pushbutton set A pushbutton telephone that uses multifrequency signalling. See *multifrequency signalling*.
multifrequency signal A distinctive combination of audio tones that represents a digit for purposes of 'dialing' in a multifrequency signalling system.
multifrequency signalling In a telephone system; a method of 'dialing' numbers in which a pushbutton telephone generates two-frequency signals, each button causing the generation of a tone combination to represent a particular digit. Equipment at the exchange uses filters to identify the digits and route the call. Once a call is connected, the buttons can be used to transmit multifrequency signals to the receiver of the call. Where appropriate receiving equipment is present, such a telephone can be used as a low-speed data entry terminal. In some data communications systems (say, for handling calls from salesmen), the computer can generate 'spoken' replies, thus permitting the use of a pushbutton telephone as an audio reponse terminal. See *audio response terminal*.
multifrequency system A system that uses multifrequency signalling.
multifrequency terminal A terminal (presumably, other than a

push-button telephone) that makes use of multifrequency signals for transmitting and/or receiving data. See *multifrequency signalling*.

multijob operation Multiprogramming. If the two terms are differentiated, 'multijob' denotes interleaved execution in which jobs use separate subsets of the computer resources (sharing only the central processor) while 'multiprogramming' denotes a system in which resources are considered as a common pool and are allocated according to availability and the priorities of executing programs. See *multiprogramming*.

multileave To interleave data being transmitted in opposite directions on a single channel.

multilevel address An address with more than one part; typically, an address with a subscript.

multilevel addressing The addressing of items in data structures of two or more dimensions; for example, addressing an item in an array by the array name and one or more subscript, or, in a virtual storage system, by segment and page or by segment, page, and line. See *array; subscript; virtual storage addressing; one-level addressing*.

multilevel signalling A method of modulation in which a modem transmits with more than two line conditions, with each line condition encoding multiple bits. See *phase shift modulation*.

multilevel storage Storage with different access speeds and characteristics that must be considered by a programmer or operating system; backing storage that cannot be regarded as a single structure. See *one-level storage; storage hierarchy*.

multilist chain A chain of sequential items divided into segments with an index used to hold the lowest number in each segment. The method is used to reduce the time required to locate an item or consecutive group in a long chain; the index is searched first to find the segment that is to be read or where reading is to begin.

multimeter A meter (test equipment) that can measure several electrical values; typically, voltage and resistance in different scales as well as current in low values.

multipart stationary Continuous stationary with multiple sheets interleaved with carbon paper (or of carbonless copy paper) as used in an impact printer to produce multiple copies. See *continuous stationary; one-time carbon; carbonless copy*.

multiphase transaction In a transaction processing system; a transaction (say entering an order or checking availability of a part) that requires more than one phase (message to a computer and reply). See *phase*.

multiplatter disc See *disc pack*.

multiple addressing The addressing of messages to more than one destination.

multiple assignment Giving the same value to two or more variables. See *assignment statement*.

multiple-head disc See *magnetic disc unit*.

multiple key A single key used to access two or more (logically linked) records.

multiple length A term applied to a unit of code or data that is contained in more than one word of storage.

multiple precision The use of two or more computer words to hold a number (and, thus, to increase the precision to which a value can be expressed). See *floating point*.

multiple punching In a punched card; to punch more than two holes in a single column. See *laced card*.

multiple recording The process of writing data simultaneously to a master file and a backup file.

multiple routing The sending of a message to two or more addressees.

multiple task operation Multijob operation.

multiplexing (1) A method of using a single communications channel (pair of wires; coaxial cable) to carry multiple speech and/or data transmissions simultaneously. The two methods in common use are **frequency division multiplexing** and **time division multiplexing**. In frequency division multiplexing, a channel that can carry a wide band of frequencies is divided (by transmitter and receiver filters) into multiple channels of narrower bandwidth, each of which can be allocated to a different user or for a different purpose. The method is used mainly with coaxial trunk lines of a telephone system. See *frequency division multiplexing; group; band; translation; carrier system*. In time division multiplexing, the use of the channel is 'switched' between users or between functions, each receiving a (small) time slice in rotation. Depending on the system, the time slice is of the length required to send a bit, a character, a byte, or a computer word. See *time division multiplexing; pulse code modulation; interleave; scan*. **(2)** In a computer system; a method of making peripheral transfers in which a unit of data (usually a block) is sent to or received from different peripherals in turn or in rotation to provide multiple tasks with (apparently) simultaneous transfers.

multiplexor (1) A device that performs multiplexing. In a data communications system, it is, typically, an element of an interface device (terminal control unit; front-end processor) and provides time division multiplexing. (In a telephone system, a multiplexor performs frequency division multiplexing and is termed a **translator**.) See *concentrator; line sharing adapter; terminal control unit; multiplexing*. **(2)**(MUX) A data selector; a device (integrated circuit) in which multiple input circuits are selectively connected to a single output circuit.

multiplicand In multiplication; the number that is multiplied by another number which is the **multiplier**. See *multiplication*.

multiplication The arithmetic operation usually specified by the symbol '×' that is performed to determine the total from adding one number to itself as many times as specified by another number. In the expression 'A = 2 × 120', the '2' is the **multiplier** and the '120' is the **multiplicand**. Since multiplication is performed 'mutually' by two numbers, there is no way to determine which item in an expression is to be considered the multiplier and which the multiplicand; the larger number is generally considered to be the multiplicand. Both the multiplier and the multiplicand are **factors** and the result is the **product**. In computers, calculators, and other digital devices, multiplication is performed using three registers, one for the multiplicand, one for the multiplier, and one for the cumulative total. The multiplicand is added to the cumulative total as many times as 'specified' by the units digit of the multiplier, which is decremented by '1' with each addition. When this digit is '0', the multiplicand is shifted left one digit position and added to the total while decrementing the '10's' digit of the multiplier. Adding, decrementing, and shifting continue until the multiplier register is '0' in all bit positions.

multipoint connection A communications link that joins three or more data stations. It is considered to be a linear arrangement in which a link goes from one station to another rather than a 'star'. See *star network*.

multipoint line **(1)**Also *multidrop line*. A four-wire leased telephone line with presentation at multiple geographically separated locations. It is the usual line of a data network that operates by polling. **(2)**Separate leased telephone lines terminated at a central site with each line providing a link to a remote site. Such a system may be termed a 'star network'. The difference between a multipoint line by this definition and definition 1 is that the subscriber must provide interface equipment (multiplexor; concentrator) and a modem for each line.

multipoint network A data communications network using a multipoint line. Though such networks can be operated by contention, it is assumed to be a polling system unless otherwise indicated.

multiport Containing multiple interface ports; for example, the term is applied to a modem with facilities for connecting multiple DTE's.

multiport storage Coordinate addressable storage with the circuits and interfaces to permit two data transfers to be made concurrently.

multiprocessing **(1)**The processing of a multiprocessor. **(2)** Multiprogramming.

multiprocessor Also, often, *parallel processor; array processor; parallel computer; array computer.* A computer system with two or more processors under some degree of control by a single operating system. It may be MISD in which all processors access data from a single 'main storage' or MIMD in which each has its own storage module. It is assumed that there is a single pool of data for the system and that interface units, data transfer channels, and peripheral devices are allocated as necessary to meet the needs of all processors. The term may sometimes be applied to a system consisting of a main computer and one or more specialised, auxiliary computers. See *multicomputer system; array processor; distributed array processor.*

multiprogramming A method of computer operation in which two or more application programs are being executed simultaneously by the interleaved allocation of a single set of computer resources. The time during which the instructions of a particular program are being executed is a **time slice**. If the active programs service multiple terminal users, it is a **time sharing system**. (The system may also perform batch processing.) An operating system may manage multiprogramming by allocating a fixed time slice (say, 20 milliseconds) to each program in turn, it may allow a program to execute a fixed number of instructions before control is switched to another

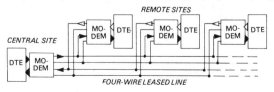

program, or it may transfer control only when an interrupt occurs. Most systems are of the latter type and may be termed **interrupt driven** (also **event driven**); the instructions of a particular program continue to be executed until an instruction generates an interrupt which is, often, because a peripheral transfer is required. Interrupts may also be caused by events external to the program; for example, the arrival of a transaction in a system that is executing a batch program. Some systems are both time interleaved and interrupt driven; instructions of a program continue to execute until either an interrupt occurs or the end of the time slice is reached. See *multistreaming; multitasking; multithreading; interrupt; peripheral transfer.*

multistreaming (1) Multiprogramming in which multiple job queues (streams) are used to input work according to priority. **(2)** Mixed-mode operation; processing performed with, for example, a 'batch stream' and a 'transaction processing stream'. **(3)** The system of a parallel processor in which an arithmetic logic unit receives multiple data and/or instruction streams. See *stream.*

multitasking (1) The operation of simultaneously executing a main task and subtasks that are either interleaved (by a single processor) or executed concurrently (by a multiprocessor). **(2)** Multiprogramming in which the interleaved units are segments of the same program. **(3)** Multiprogramming (in which resources are shared) as contrasted to a multijob operation. See *multiprogramming; multijob operation.*

multiterminal Including or supporting more than one terminal (usually understood to be at the same location rather than joined by communications links).

multithreading (1) A method of multiprogramming used to handle transaction processing in which the routines required to process a transaction are organised in a 'pipeline'. An incoming transaction might, for example, be dealt with first by an analysis routine then a validation routine and then through a number of access, processing, and editing routines until the reply is formulated and transmitted to the originating terminal. The various routines that are used successively may be termed 'beads'. See *multiprogramming.* **(2)** A term sometimes applied to accesses of data in a data structure that provides multiple access paths.

multivibrator A circuit with two output states and the capability to change from one to the other. An **astable multivibrator** basic circuit is shown in Fig. 1. When voltage is connected, the capacitor is discharged and point 'a' is low; the transistor is then OFF and the output is high. The capacitor then charges through R1 and, after a certain time, it reaches a level high

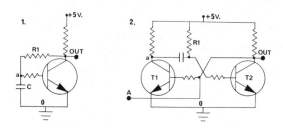

enough to turn the transistor ON. This changes the output to low and causes the capacitor to discharge through R1 to a point at which the transistor turns OFF causing the output to, again, go high. Such a circuit is an **oscillator** and, depending on the values of R1 and C, may have a frequency between about 5 Hz. and 1 MHz. A **monostable multivibrator** is shown in Fig. 2. In its normal state, transistor T2 is ON and the output is low. If a positive pulse is applied to input 'A', T1 turns ON, dropping the voltage at point 'a' and, through the capacitor, the voltage on the base of T2. This causes T2 to turn OFF, thus changing the output to high. When point 'a' goes low, the capacitor begins charging through R1 and, after a short time, it is sufficiently charged to raise the voltage on the gate of T2 to the point where it turns ON again, dropping the output to low, which is the single stable state of the circuit. A **bistable multivibrator** is one with two stable states with an input pulse causing a transition between them. See *flip-flop.*

Murray Code The Western Union telegraph code; it differs slightly from IA-2.

MUX *MUltipleXor.*

MVT *Multiprogramming with a Variable number of Tasks.* An IBM OS/360 control program that supervises the execution and resource allocation for a variable number of concurrent programs in main storage.

Mylar A DuPont trade name for a polyester film widely used as the medium on which a magnetisable surface coating is applied in the manufacture of magnetic tape and flexible discs.

N

N (n) **(1)** A symbol used in mathematical expressions to denote an unspecified parameter that must be supplied as an input. For example:

$$X = 2^n \qquad A = \frac{X_1 + X_2 + \ldots X_n}{n}$$

The first expression states that X is equal to some power of 2 and the second is the formula for finding the average of 'n' terms. **(2)** *Nano-*.

N-channel A term applied to a unipolar semiconductor (field effect transistor or related) in which the main source-drain conduction path is through N-type silicon.

N-channel MOS (NMOS) A term applied to an MOS device (usually a transistor) in which all conduction is through N-type silicon. See *P-channel MOS; field effect transistor; MOS*.

n-key rollover A facility of a keyboard-operated device that enables it to print/display the character for the most recently depressed key, whether or not previously depressed keys have been released.

n-plus-one address instruction An instruction that contains 'n' operand addresses (presumptive addresses) plus the address of the next instruction in the sequence.

n-tuple relation A relation (table) with any number of tuples (entities); if, for example, there are 16 tuples, it is a '16-tuple relation'.

N-type An identifier of a semiconductor material (usually silicon) in which the majority carriers are electrons. (In which the primary means of electrical conduction is by the movement of loosely bonded electrons.) See *semiconductor; P-type*.

NAG *Numerical Algorithm Group.* (Oxford)

NAK *Negative AcKnowledge.* A transmission control character sent by a receiving station to a sending station to indicate that an error has been detected in a received message or block and requesting its retransmission. See *ACK*.

naked A term sometimes applied to an electronic device that is supplied as only the basic elements (say as a printed circuit board) and without the usual cabinet, fittings, etc. ('a naked modem'; 'a naked minicomputer').

name A character string (assumed to be in source coding) that identifies a program, file, variable, array, storage location, device, user, or other entity. According to the rules of most systems, it is an alphanumeric string in which the first character is a letter. See *data name; symbolic address; identifier; label*.

name space The address space of a named application program. See *address space*.

named A term applied to an entity (storage location; volume; file; peripheral) that has been assigned an identifier by which it is known to the operating system.

NAND Also *non-conjunction*. A logic operation with an output that is 'true' if any of its inputs are 'false' and 'false' if all of them are 'true'. See *logic operation*.

nano- **(1)** (n) A combining form indicating one billionth (10^{-9}). **(2)** A combining form meaning 'basic-level' or 'very small'.

nanolevel See *microinstruction*.

nanometer (nm.) One billionth of a meter; ten Angstroms.

nanosecond (ns.) One billionth of a second; one thousandth of a microsecond.

narrowband A band of limited width; a subdivision of another band. See *band; wideband*.

narrowcasting A term sometimes used in place of 'broadcasting' when the receiving group is small and selected; for example, in a viewdata system.

national characters In an international alphabet (ISO-7); bit patterns that can be assigned with national meaning; for example, to encode a tilde or £. See *CODE TABLE*.

native mode A term applied to an operating system (possibly to other items) that is designed to take maximum advantage of the hardware facilities of a particular computer make and model; for example, VME/B is the 'native mode' operating system of the ICL 2980 and GCOS is the 'native mode' operating system of Honeywell Series 60. The term is used to contrast execution using such an operating system with emulation or, possibly, with using an operating system that is the 'native mode' system of a different computer.

natural language A language of everyday use such as Urdu, Swahili, or English. See *language; artificial language*.

natural number A non-negative integer.

NC *Numerical Control.*

NCC *National Computer Centre.* (Manchester)

NCR *National Cash Register Co.* (Dayton, Ohio)

NDR *Non-Destructive Read.*

NE *Not Equal to.* See *relational operator.*
NEC **(1)***Nippon Electric Co.* (Tokyo) **(2)***National Electronics Council.* (London)
needle **(1)**Also *stylus; wire.* An element of a print head that places dots to form dot matrix characters in an impact matrix printer. See *matrix printer.* **(2)**A thin, pointed rod used in sorting edge-notched cards. See *edge-notched card.*
needle printer An impact matrix printer. See *matrix printer.*
NEG (neg.) *NEGative.*
negate To perform negation.
negation **(1)**The change of a numeric value from negative to positive or from positive to negative. **(2)**With respect to a binary digit, number, or string; to change all 1-bits to 0-bits and all 0-bits to 1-bits. See *complement representation.* **(3)**Also *NOT.* A logic operation with an output that is 'true' if the single input is 'false' and 'false' if it is 'true'. **(4)**Inversion.
negation first variable A logic operation that is 'true' if the first of two inputs is 'false' and 'false' if it is true'. See *logic operation.*
negation second variable A logic operation with an output that is 'true' if the second of two inputs is 'false' and 'false' if it is 'true'. See *logic operation.*
negative **(1)**(—; neg.) Of a number; less than zero; for example, —5, —120, and —.003 are 'negative numbers'. See *positive.* **(2)** (NEG.; —) Of a battery, rectifier, or other direct-current device or circuit; the position from which electrons flow toward 'positive'; the electron source. See *positive; cathode.* **(3)**A term used in various contexts to indicate 'no cause found', 'something wrong', 'nothing to report', or 'no'; ('a negative poll response'; 'a negative reply'; 'a negative result of a test'). See *positive.*
negative acknowledgement On a data communications link; a short message sent by the receiving station to indicate that an error has been detected in the current block or message and requesting the sending station to retransmit it. See *acknowledge; NAK; ACK.*
negative acknowledgement character The NAK character.
negative poll response In a polling system; a short message from a polled station to the master station indicating that the polling message has been received and that there are no other messages to be sent.
neither-nor operation A NOR operation. See *logic operation.*
NEL *National Engineering Laboratory.* (Glasgow)

nest To incorporate a structure into another structure of the same type in such a way that the incorporated structure retains its individual identity. See *nesting.*
nested loop A loop that is initiated by an instruction in another loop. See *loop; nesting.*
nested routine A routine included in another routine. While the term may be applied to a routine that is executed in response to either an internal call or an external call, it generally refers to 'external call' and, in particular, to a routine called by another called routine. See *nest; nesting.*
nesting **(1)**The process of including an item of separate identity within another item of the same type; for example, a message could be nested within another message or a file nested within another file. **(2)**The programming operation of specifying a separately compiled sequence of instructions that will be executed within the main sequence of instructions. Though the term may be used synonymously with 'calling', it is usually applied to the situation in which called routines themselves include called routines. See *call.* **(3)**Embedding; the writing of instructions that include other instructions. See *embedded.* **(4)** The placement of items in a push-down stack. See *push; stack.*
net Also *network; plex; lattice file.* A data structure that supports multiple access paths and in which the entities (**nodes; occurrences**) need not be in hierarchical relationship. An **owner** is an entity that, on a particular access path, must be accessed prior to any other entity on that path; any other entity is a **member**. An entity that is a member may also be an owner of any number of entities and it may also have any number of owners on different access paths. The access paths and member-owner relationships are established by **pointers** which are addresses of entities held by other entities; an entity that holds a pointer to another entity is that entity's owner (on one access path). A pointer-established link between an owner and a member is termed a **relationship** (also **connector**). An **access path** (also a **chain**) is a sequence of relationships that provide the entities required for some processing operation; for example, printing the numbers of the parts that are supplied by a particular manufacturer or those that are components of a particular assembly. If a net is hierarchial, it may also be termed a **set** or a **tree** and a net that is not hierarchial may contain hierarchial sets. A set is a group of entities (with common attributes) that can be accessed via a single owner. A **linked set** is a set with members on different access paths.

network (1) A data network; an organisation of lines, equipment, and control procedures that provides a data communications service (and, often, a computing service) for geographically separated locations. See *data network; distributed processing; communications; on-line*. **(2)** An organisation of distributed but related entities under common control; ('a telephone network'; 'a distribution network'). **(3)** A net; a data structure that supports a variety of access paths. See *net; tree*. **(4)** A term applied to a complex electronic or electrical circuit; ('a phase-shift network'; 'a pulse-shaping network'). **(5)** A term applied to multiple (identical) circuit elements in a single package; ('a resistor network'; 'a transistor network').

network address A character group that identifies a data station in a data network.

network analysis (1) Project planning aided by a schematic representation of events and activities. See *PERT*. **(2)** The use of mathematical models to study electrical circuits.

network control The activity of supervising circuit use and message interchanges for a data network. See *link protocol*.

network control program A program (as executed by a communications controller) that performs some function of network control; for example, polling or error detection.

network generation (NETGEN) The operation of implementing the network-related facilities of an operating system that are required by a computer at a network node.

network interface module (NIM) In some systems; a subset of the facilities of a communications link controller that is used to perform functions for a particular group of lines.

network processing (1) Distributed processing. **(2)** In a distributed processing system; that part of processing (by the main computer) applied to network control and, possibly, to functions relating to handling transactions within the computer system. See *information processing*.

network processor A front-end processor; a computer that handles communications-related functions for another computer.

neutral signalling Unipolar signalling.

neutral transmission Data transmission by unipolar signals.

new line Newline.

new range A term sometimes applied to a manufacturer's product that is under advanced development or that has just been released for sale. In the same contexts, the term 'current range' may be applied to the product that is currently being manufactured and sold and 'old range' to that which has been superseded.

newline A term applied to the movement of a printing position or VDU cursor from wherever it happens to be in one line to the beginning (at the left margin) of the next line. In some systems, it is the equivalent of 'carriage return' while in others it denotes a line feed. See *NL; carriage return; line feed*.

newline character See *NL*.

new sync An interface signal from a DTE that causes a modem to request a training sequence from the other modem of a link. Its use requires the DTE to have facilities for monitoring signal quality as indicated by the error rate.

next instruction register (NIR) A current address register.

nibble A term sometimes applied to a quartet (half of a 'byte').

nines complement The diminished radix complement of decimal numbers. See *diminished radix complement*.

NIR *Next Instruction Register*.

NL *NewLine*. In some systems; a control character that causes a VDU cursor or a printing position to move to the beginning (left-hand margin) of the next line. In such a system, carriage return (CR) causes a movement to the beginning of the current line. See *carriage return*.

NM (nm.) *NanoMeter*.

NMOS *N-channel MOS*.

no-operation instruction Also *do-nothing instruction; null instruction*. An instruction that, when executed, does nothing except cause the next instruction to be executed.

nodal Located at a node or occurring at a node.

nodal addressing The addressing of messages by the node identifier of the receiving station and the node identifiers of any intermediate stations through which messages are routed.

nodal switch A rerouting facility at a node in a data network. The term may be applied to such facilities at an exchange in a message switching or packet switching system or to an intelligent device, say a terminal control unit, that handles multiplexing and message routing for terminals or branch lines.

node (1) A termination or interchange point in a data network; a place that has significance for data routing. (The term is more often applied to a place in a circuit or message switching system than to a multipoint system.) **(2)** In a data structure; an entity on two or more access paths. See *net*.

node identifier An interchange address.

node processor A processor that performs message routing and/or multiplexing at a node; it may also perform local processing.

node switch A nodal switch.

noise On a communications link; any detectable electrical events that were not intentionally placed on the link by a sending station. Though noise may cause errors in data sent on circuits in which there is no conversion to audible form, it would appear as sound if an appropriate earphone or speaker was connected. There is always some **background noise** on any circuit; it may appear as hissing or humming sounds during periods when no signals (data or speech) are present. If it is composed of random frequencies (hissing but little if any 'hum'), it is termed **white noise**. A noise that has a distinct clicking or crackling sound is termed **impulse noise** (sometimes **black noise**). See *hit; crosstalk*.

noise word An optional word.

non-conjunction NAND (logic operation).

non-contiguous Not adjacent; separated; ('non-contiguous areas of storage').

non-destructive cursor A cursor that can be moved through a display without changing or destroying elements of the display. See *destructive cursor*.

non-destructive read In coordinate-addressable storage; a read operation that leaves data in a state in which it can be immediately read again. It is the type of read of semiconductor memory (as contrasted to that of core memory, which is 'destructive'). See *destructive read*.

non-disjunction NOR (logic operation).

non-equivalence Exclusive OR (logic operation).

non-erasable memory A memory that, once written to, cannot be erased. The term is applied to a read-only memory such as fuse PROM or photo-digital. See *PROM*.

non-exchangeable disc A fixed disc.

non-identity A logic operation with an output that is 'true' if the inputs are mixed and 'false' if all are 'true' or all are 'false'. See *identity; logic operation*.

non-impact printer A printer that operates by some method other than impacting a character (or element) and ribbon against paper. See *printer; impact printer*.

non-linear (1) Of an electronic circuit; with an output that is not directly proportional to input(s). **(2)** Of a mathematical operation; with an output that does not plot as a straight line.

non-linear programming The production of programs that are designed to determine maximums or minimums of functions that are represented (at least partly) by non-linear expressions. See *linear programming*.

non-locking A term applied to a code extension character to indicate that it applies only to the immediately following bit pattern. See *code extension character; escape character; shift character; locking*.

nonnegative number A natural number.

non-numeric Not a number or not containing numbers.

non-numeric literal A character or character string in a source program that is to remain unaltered in compilation and storage and, thus, will appear in printed results in the same form as written. See *literal*.

non-polarised-return-to-zero-encoding Dipole encoding; unipolar signalling.

non-printable character An unprintable character (usually a control character).

non-recoverable error (1) An error that results in loss of data; for example, one that results in overwriting data on a magnetic disc or erasing a buffer. **(2)** A hard error; an error (in reading from backing storage) that cannot be resolved by automatic recovery facilities. See *high-level recovery*.

non-reflective ink Ink that prints with a dull finish (and may enhance the readability of characters by optical character recognition).

nonresident Not in main storage; ('a nonresident segment of a program').

non-return-to-reference Non-return-to-zero.

non-return-to-zero See *NRZ*.

non-return-to-zero, change on ones Non-return-to-zero inverted. See *NRZI*.

non-return-to-zero inverted See *NRZI*.

non-reusable Not reentrant; subject to values being changed during processing. See *reentrant code*.

non-specific volume request In job control language; a request for a volume that allows the operating system to make the selection.

non-volatile memory Memory that can retain its stored data in absence of electric power. It includes core and bubble memory and semiconductor read-only memory. The term may also be applied to a unit of inherently volatile semiconductor memory that is provided with a battery and an automatic power transfer circuit. See *volatile memory*.

NOR Also *non-disjunction*. A logic operation with an output that is 'true' if all of the inputs are 'false' and with an output that is 'false' if any input is 'true'. See *logic operation*.

normal distribution The usual distribution of randomly occurring events or values such as heights of children at a particular age, the lengths of messages, or the number of sunspots per year. A distribution is 'normal' if 67% are within one standard deviation from a central value, if 95% are within two standard deviations from that value, and if 99.7% are within three standard deviations. The figure is a curve of 'normal

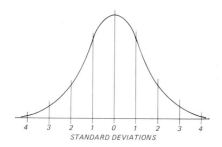

distribution' with the values representable on the vertical axis and the number of occurrences of each value (usually quantised) on the horizontal axis. See *standard deviation*.

normalisation (1) A formalised process for analysing unstructured data in order to produce the fewest possible records to hold all processing-significant relationships. The operation is performed in three steps, the last of which produces the **third normal form** (3NF) consisting of one or more **relationship records** and one or more **entity records**. If, for example, the method was applied to a lot of purchase orders from different customers for different products, the relationship records would hold such 'this time only' information as the 'relationship' between customer numbers and their order numbers, between order numbers and product numbers of items ordered, and between product numbers and order quantities. The entity records hold relatively permanent and 'identifying' information; for example, the 'relationship' between customer names and customer numbers, between customer numbers and sales areas, and between product numbers and product prices. The characteristic of the third normal form is that every item in the input data that is to be considered in processing is represented by a value or key and that no record holds multiple occurrences of any value or key. **(2)** The process of adjusting the representation of the exponent and fractional part of a floating point number so that the fractional part has a radix point position that is standard for the system. If, for example, the fractional part is specified as having a single integer, then normalisation is the process of converting, say, 2375 to 2.375×10^3. See *floating point*.

normalised form Also *standard form*. Of numeric data; in the form required for an arithmetic operation with the facilities of the particular computer.

NOT Also *negation; inversion*. A unary logic operation with an output that is 'true' if the single input is 'false' and 'false' if it is true. See *logic operation; inverter*.

not-AND NAND (logic operation).
not-both NAND (logic operation).
not equal to (NE) See *relational operator*.
not-if-then Exclusion (logic operation).
not-OR NOR (logic operation).

notch filter A filter that is designed to give a high attenuation of a narrow band of frequencies. The purpose is to permit these frequencies to be used for a control or metering function (by telephone system equipment) or to separate two channels (in an asymmetric duplex or two-wire, full duplex system). The notch frequencies are deleted from the carrier wave by transmit and receive notch filters in the modems. Some modems can provide multiple notches. See *band; filter*.

note Comment.

noughts complement Radix complement.

NPN A designation of a bipolar transistor in which the emitter and collector are of N-type silicon and the base of P-type silicon. See *PNP; semiconductor; transistor*.

NRZ *Non-Return-to-Zero*. A method of data transmission in

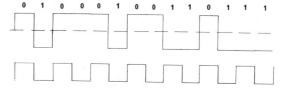

which a circuit carries data whenever it is enabled and in which a voltage of one polarity represents a 1-bit and of the other polarity a 0-bit. Conventionally, negative signals represent 1-bits and positive, 0-bits. It is the usual method of data transfer between a computer or interface controller and modems or peripherals. The method has also been used for magnetisable surface recording. See *NRZI; polar signalling.*

NRZI *Non-Return-to-Zero Inverted.* A method of magnetisable surface recording in which the current in the coil of the read/write head is reversed to write each 1-bit and is left unchanged (at the polarity used to write the last 1-bit) to write a 0-

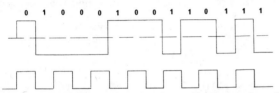

bit or sequence of 0-bits. There is, thus, a flux reversal on the track being recorded wherever a 1-bit is written and a place of unchanged flux of length equal to one clock cycle wherever a 0-bit is written. It is a common method of recording magnetic tape. See *NRZ; magnetisable surface recording.*

NRZI encoding The representation of bit patterns in data transfer by signals constructed in the same way as those used in NRZI recording.

NS (ns.) *NanoSecond.*

nucleus (1)That which is central; that on which other items depend for control. (2)A control segment. (3)In a virtual storage system; those parts of the operating system that must remain in primary storage during execution. See *save area; locked down.*

NUL *NULl.* A character (considered to be a control character or format effector) that can be inserted in a sequence of characters without changing the meaning or interpretation. In some systems, it may be the equivalent of a space character used for a function other than delimiting; for example, to provide additional inter-group space required for justification.

null A term indicating an absence of signal, element, or value; a gap that may have some media-related purpose but which can be ignored in the interpretation of data.

null character (1)See *NUL.* (2)A bit pattern consisting of 0-bits in all bit positions.

null device A peripheral address available for use in testing or program development.

null instruction A do-nothing instruction.

null line A line space (printer; VDU) considered as a line; a line with no characters.

null representation A mark or pattern that indicates that the items on both sides of it are to be treated as forming a continuous unit; for example, a feed hole or error punching on paper tape.

null set A set that has been named or allocated space but which has no elements.

null string A sequence of positions in which a 'string' could be placed or from which a 'string' has been removed.

null suppression The elimination of null representations from data as transcribed or transmitted.

null value That which represents a 'null'; it is, conventionally, zero for numeric items, spaces for alphabetic and alphanumeric items, and unpunched locations for data on punched cards and tape.

number (1)In common usage; a digit or digit string that represents a value, quantity, or relationship. (2)A quantity as an abstraction; though not definitively named, one of them can be recognised as that sense represented by 'four' in English, 'empat' in Malay, and by the **numerals** (discrete representations of numbers) '4' in decimal, '100' in binary, '////' in tally, and 'IV' in Roman. An **integer** is a number without a fractional part and may be '0', positive (2; 65), or negative (—2; —37). A **natural number** is a positive integer. A **mixed number** is a number with a fractional part (4⅔; —62.4; 1.007). A **prime number** is an integer that, when divided by any integer other than itself or '1' produces a non-integer; examples include 2, 3, 11, and 23. A **composite number** is any number other than a prime number, for example, 8, 25, or 62. A **transcendental number** is a value that cannot be expressed with complete accuracy; for example, 'π' (usually expressed as 3.14 or 3.14159) which can always be expressed with greater accuracy with the use of an additional digit position. A **rational number** is one that can be formed by dividing some integer by another; most numbers are 'rational', for example, 2 can be formed in many ways including dividing 6 by 3 and 5.015873 can be formed by dividing 316 by 63. An **irrational number** is one that cannot be formed by dividing integers; transcendental numbers are 'irrational'. A **real number** is a number that can be represented in a fixed-radix numeration system (such as decimal or binary); all of the foregoing numbers are 'real'. An **imaginary number** is a number other than a real number; they are usually considered to be numbers that, when squared, produce negative numbers. Such numbers have never been 'seen' because the square of a negative number is positive; they are manipulated by using 'i' to represent the square root of —1. A **complex number** is a number that combines real and imaginary parts in the form $a + bi$ where a and b are real numbers; they are used in some advanced calculations. See *numeration system; binary; decimal; digit*.

number cruncher An informal term for an arithmetic logic unit with extensive hardware facilities for performing arithmetic operations (usually in a scientific computer). See *mill*.

numeral (1) In common usage; a decimal digit. **(2)** A discrete (single-element) representation of a number; for example, a decimal or binary digit, 'K' indicating 1024, or, possibly, a position of flags in 'semaphore' code. **(3)** A discrete (single-element or 'recognised' group) representation of a number; for example, such representations of the 'number' dozen as 'twelve', '12', 'XII' or the binary group '1100'. See *number; digit*.

numeration system A set of symbols and rules for representing numbers. Most numeration systems are **positional representation systems** in which digits have **weights** which are multiplier values that depend upon their **digit position** in relation to the other digits of a number. Both the decimal system and binary system are 'positional representation systems'. The difference between the weights of digits in adjacent digit positions is the **radix** of the system. For example, the decimal system has a 'radix' of 10 and a digit is effectively multiplied by 10 when moved one digit position to the left and divided by 10 when moved one position to the right. (The 6 in 600 has ten times the value of the 6 in 60 and one-tenth the value of the 6 in 6000.) A **radix numeration system** is one in which the weight difference between adjacent digit positions is always an integer (though not necessarily the same integer between all positions). A **fixed radix numeration system** is one, such as decimal or binary, in which the weight difference between two adjacent digit positions is always the same integer, for example, '10' in decimal and '2' in binary. A **mixed-radix numeration system** consists of two or more related radix numeration systems with different radices. Each radix (except the lowest-order) is an integral multiple of the next lower and the multipliers are in ascending order; for example, the radices could be 16, 8, and 2. In a radix numeration system, a **radix point** divides a mixed number into integral and fractional parts; in the decimal system, it is a **decimal point**. See *number; base; radix*.

numeric (1) Consisting of digits or numbers; not alphabetic or alphanumeric; ('a numeric input'; 'a numeric value'; 'a numeric string'). A numeric item (in the strictest sense) must be formed from a set consisting of digits, a 'plus' sign, a 'minus sign' and a character suitable for marking the radix point. **(2)** A group of four binary digits (as used to represent a decimal digit). See *binary coded decimal*. **(3)** The least significant four digit positions of an EBCDIC character. **(4)** A numeral.

numeric character A term applied to a digit in a computer storage code (as contrasted to a digit in a computational format).

numeric character set A character set consisting of digits and, possibly, signs, symbols, spaces, and control characters (but with no letters included).

numeric code A code in which data is represented by elements of a coded character set.

numeric constant An integer, real, or complex constant.

numeric literal A value in an instruction that is itself an operand for an arithmetic operation. See *literal*.

numeric pad A group of keys (pushbutton telephone; terminal keyboard), each of which represents a decimal digit.

numeric punch A digit punch.

numeric set A numeric character set.

numeric shift A figures shift.

numeric word (1) A computer word that holds a numeric value. **(2)** A number that, by usage, has become accepted in a non-numeric meaning; for example, an '88' (piano) or a '360' (IBM computer).

numerical analysis Mathematical modelling; the use of mathematics to study real-world conditions and systems.

numerical control (NC) The control of a manufacturing operation (welding; cutting; machining; lifting) in an essentially automatic mode by means of coded instructions in numeric form. Typically, a complex operation is analysed with the aid of a computer and broken down into a sequence of discrete steps that can be represented on paper tape (or some other medium) for input to a control unit on the machine. The control unit reads and interprets the inputs and uses them to control physical movements such as positioning of jigs, movements of cutting tools, and speeds of drive motors.

numerical order Of items consisting of numbers or using numbers as keys; arranged in an ascending or descending order that corresponds to the relative values of their numbers. See *alphabetical order; collating sequence.*

NV *Non-Volatile.*

O

O/A *On Application.* In a price sheet; a term indicating that the price will be supplied if requested.

OAP *Orthogonal Array Processor.*

obey With respect to an instruction; to perform the operations it specifies. In some contexts the term is used synonymously with 'execute' though 'obey' is from the viewpoint of the instruction and 'execute' from that of the computer or control unit. The terms may also be used in the sense that 'execute' includes instruction decoding and 'obey' does not. See *instruction; execution; control; decode.*

object (1) An entity. **(2)** That which results.

object code Also *machine code.* The final result of a language translation; a set of bit patterns interpretable by the electronic circuitry of a computer. The term 'object code' is more often used when discussing programming and compilation and 'machine code' when discussing the execution or computer facilities. See *machine code; compiler.*

object computer The make and model computer on which a particular program is intended to be executed.

object language (1) A language that is defined by a particular metalanguage. **(2)** A target language; a language that results from a translation. See *source language.*

object-level program A program in its object code version.

object library A library used to store modules of object code that can be called by (or included in) programs. See *source library.*

object machine An object computer.

object module A program unit as output from an assembler or compiler; it is the usual input to a linkage editor or loader.

object program A program that is to result from compilation and linkage; a program as a load module or group of load modules. See *source program.*

object time Execution time.

occurrence (1) An event; a thing that happens or appears; ('an occurrence of impulse noise'). **(2)** In data base terminology, a single instance; ('a set occurrence'; 'a record occurrence').

occurrence diagram In Bachman notation; a diagram in which the elements are 'occurrences'.

OCL (1) *Operator Control Language.* **(2)** *Operation Control Language.*

OCP *Order Code Processor.*

OCR *Optical Character Recognition.*

OCR font A set of characters designed to be read by OCR.

octal (1) Also *pure octal.* A numeration system with a radix of 8; it is often indicated by an '8' subscript as in 123_8. The digits of the system are the same as the decimal digits 0—7. The following are the weights of the first five digit positions:

$$4096 \quad 512 \quad 64 \quad 8 \quad 1$$

The following are some examples:

Decimal	Binary	Octal
0	000	0
3	011	3
7	111	7
8	1000	10
10	1010	12
15	1111	17
15	1111	17
24	11000	30
176	10110000	260

(2) Also *binary coded octal.* A common form of computer input and output of binary values in which each three binary digits are represented by a single octal digit. It is commonly indicated by the 'hash' mark as in #123. As an example, the 16-bit binary word 0110010101110111 is represented in octal as 062567. The octal string is formed from right to left (the three lease-significant binary digits are converted first); additional zeros are added in most-significant positions if the number of binary digits is not evenly divisible by three.

octet Eight contiguous bits considered as a unit. In data communications contexts, the term may be used in preference to 'byte'.

odd-even check A parity check.

odd parity Parity in which there is an odd number of 1-bits. See *parity; even parity*.

OEM *Original Equipment Manufacturer*. A term (applied by a manufacturer or supplier) for a customer who is a manufacturer who uses (or may use) their purchased items in the manufactured product. Such a customer is expected to purchase in quantity and usually receives the largest discount allowed.

OEM discount A long (typically, 40-50%) discount extended to OEM customers.

oersted A unit for measuring the intensity of a magnetic field. See *magnet*.

off-bit A term sometimes applied to a 0-bit as an indicator or flag. See *flag; on-bit*.

off-hook The status of a telephone or automatic dialing or answering equipment in which incoming calls are inhibited. It is the state in which dialing is performed and in which messages are sent and received. See *on-hook*.

off-line (1) A term applied to devices or operations that are not under the control of the central processor of a computer, or that are not under continuous control of the central processor. Paper tape and punched cards are, for example, considered 'off-line storage' though the readers and punches may be under control of the central processor while reading/punching is being performed. See *on-line (Relation to central processor)*. **(2)** To remove from control of the central processor; ('off-line a file to punched cards'; 'off-line a printer for repairs').

off-line operation A manual off-line operation.

off-line storage (1) A medium that must be loaded by an operator each time it is read; the usual forms are punched cards and paper tape. **(2)** Any storage that is not under the control of the operating system. By this definition, the term includes the off-line storage of definition 1 plus unmounted magnetic disc and tape volumes. See *on-line storage*.

off-line volume A volume that is not mounted on a drive.

off-the-shelf (1) A term applied to a product that is an item of standard production and sale (as contrasted to one that must be specially designed, manufactured, or adapted). See *bespoke; one off*. **(2)** A term applied to a product that is in stock (by a supplier or manufacturer).

office In some countries; a telephone exchange.

offset (1) A displacement; a difference between a location and a reference location; for example, a relative address is an 'offset' from a base address. **(2)** To compensate or balance; ('plus errors that offset minus errors'). **(3)** Lithography; the printing process in which an intermediate roller carries ink from the plate to the paper. **(4)** A command that can only execute following the execution of another command. It is used to expand the first command; for example, to set up a buffer to hold data that will be produced when the first command executes.

offspring A term sometimes used synonymously with 'member' or 'group of members'. See *tree*.

ohm (Ω) The standard unit of measurement for electrical resistance; it is equal to voltage divided by current. See *electricity; volt; ampere*.

Ohm's law See *electricity*.

OMR *Optical Mark Recognition*.

on-bit A term sometimes applied to a 1-bit as an indicator or flag. See *flag; off-bit*.

on-board On the same printed circuit board as other components; ('an on-board power supply').

on-chip On the same integrated-circuit chip as other elements; ('an on-chip clock').

on-demand When required/requested (by an executing program); ('on-demand staging').

on-hook The status of a telephone (or automatic equipment) in which it can receive an incoming call. See *off-hook*.

on-line (Operational status) Of a system or item of equipment; connected and ready to perform its function.

on-line (Processing) A term applied to a system or to the facilities that provide an interactive data processing service at a location that is geographically separated from the computer that performs the processing; ('an on-line terminal' 'on-line order entry'; 'an on-line seat reservation system'). The term **communications** is often used in preference to 'on-line' when emphasis is on facilities; ('part of the communications setup'). An on-line system is also a **distributed processing system** that is used interactively. In some systems, the term 'on-line' is used to include local interactive computing facilities as well as remote. If there are multiple remote terminals, an on-line system is also a **data network**; it may be 'transaction processing', 'enquiry', or 'real-time'. 'Transaction' may be used synonymously with 'message' ('an incoming transaction') though it has connotations of 'making agreements' and, thus, the term

transaction processing system is, typically, applied to a system in which there is a 'negotiation' between a terminal operator and a computer which involves the computer taking some action. Examples include order entry systems, airline seat reservation systems, and stockbrokers' systems. The term 'transaction processing' may also be used in place of 'on-line' as the general term for remote, interactive systems. The term **enquiry system** is applied to a system in which the computer provides information at the request of a terminal operator without taking any action other than providing the information. Examples include credit checking systems and police information systems. A **real-time system** is one designed so that the computer can receive and process an enquiry and return an answer in a very short time (say, within three seconds). The purpose is to permit a smooth, 'conversational' flow between the terminal operator and the computer and, often, to provide an answer for someone who is waiting at the terminal location. A real-time system is, then, an enquiry or transaction processing system with a very short response time. The term 'on-line' assumes a continuously maintained communications link between the terminal(s) and the computer. Unless otherwise indicated, it applies to a system in which the terminals are remote (rather than local) and in which the communications link is a leased telephone line. The term **information system** may be applied to an on-line system (such as 'viewdata') that serves a number of users on a subscription basis. See *multi-access; data network; communications; information system; conversational; interactive.*

on-line (Relation to central processor) A term applied to a peripheral device or volume that can be accessed by the central processor without the need for any action (loading; connecting) by an operator. It is commonly applied to printers, magnetic disc and tape units, and to mounted tape and disc volumes. The term may also be applied to a slow-speed device (card punch or reader) when it is connected and in condition to make or receive a data transfer under control of the central processor. See *off-line.*

on-line program development On-line programming; program development using an interactive terminal.

on-line programming Program development using an interactive terminal and a language processor that checks statements as they are entered and outputs appropriate error messages and other aids. It is usually a multi-access operation using a terminal local to the computer. See *programming.*

on-line storage Storage that is accessible to the central processor via input/output channels and which can be read or written without operator intervention. The term is applied to drum and fixed disc storage and to mounted magnetic disc and tape volumes. See *off-line storage.*

on-the-fly (1) A term applied to a printing method that uses a moving font; for example, the method of a barrel, band, or train printer. **(2)** With respect to error detection and correction; performed automatically and without apparent delay in processing or data transfer.

one-address instruction An instruction with a single operand; an instruction that specifies a unary operation.

one-bit (1-bit) A binary digit; a basic unit of binary storage and transfer. See *mark; zero-bit.*

one-constant The operation of outputting continuous 1-bits; a logic operation with an output that is 'true' whether the single input is 'true' or 'false'. See *logic operation; zero-constant.*

one-dimensional Linear; for example, a row or string.

one-dimensional array See *array.*

one-dimensional language A language (English; COBOL; FORTRAN) that is customarily written as character strings. See *multidimensional language.*

one-for-one translation A translation in which an object code instruction is produced for every source code instruction; it is a characteristic of assemblers and assembly languages. See *high-level language; low-level language.*

one-level address A direct address.

one-level addressing (1) The addressing of locations in one-dimensional data structures. See *multilevel addressing.* **(2)** Direct addressing; addressing that requires no index reference or table look-up. See *direct addressing; indirect addressing.*

one-level storage (1) From the viewpoint of a programmer or user program; all of the storage that can be accessed without specifying physical locations or devices; all the storage for which allocation can be left to the operating system. **(2)** From the viewpoint of an operating system; all of the backing storage that can be accessed by a single type of channel activation command; all of the backing storage that can be read or written without specifying details (or changing details) of interfacing. The term usually implies intelligent interface devices (interface computer; access controllers) to resolve any device-related differences in data formats and transfer speeds. See *bus-*

organised; staging; interface function. (3)A term sometimes used with respect to a data-base system to denote all storage except primary (main) storage.

one-off (1)Done one time only; not likely to be repeated. (2)A term applied to a manufactured item that is produced (possibly modified) to meet a customer's specification.

one-plus-one address instruction See *n-plus-one address instruction*.

one-shot (1)A single pulse, as for event timing; ('a sector-mark one-shot'). (2)A term that may be applied to an operation that is performed once only.

one-time carbon (OTC) A term applied to continuous stationery with interleaved carbon paper (that is used only one time).

one-way communications The communications of a simplex system; communications in one preassigned direction only. See *two-way; simplex*.

one-way trunk A trunk line that carries traffic in one direction only (between telephone exchanges).

ones complement The diminished radix complement of binary numbers. See *complement; diminished radix complement*.

oneshot A one-shot.

online On-line.

onward link Also, sometimes, *extended port circuit.* In a data network; a secondary data link that connects with the main network through a remote site modem. The connection is through a 'repeater' modem that connects to an interface port of the remote site modem in the same manner as a local DTE. A special interface cable is used to 'invert' certain signals between the two modems; for example, DCD from the repeater modem becomes RTS to the remote site modem and receive data becomes transmit data. See *RTS-DCD simulation*.

op-amp *OPerational AMPlifier.*

opcode *OPeration CODE.*

open (1)With respect to a file; to locate it in backing storage and to read the header label to determine that the correct file and version has been found and that the access permitted is that which is authorised to the user program. The operation is performed by system software in response to an instruction in the program that requires the file. (2)With respect to an electrical circuit; to operate a switch or other device to stop the flow of current.

open box A term sometimes applied to software to indicate that its structure and methods are understandable to users. The term is applied to critical and decision-making programs (for example, in medical diagnosis) whose results could only be trusted if the method of arriving at them is known. See *black box*.

open circuit The condition in which current is not flowing in a circuit because of a break in the conducting path. The term is applied mainly to an abnormal condition resulting from, say, a blown fuse, broken wire, or unsoldered connection.

open-contact tone In a telephone system; an audible tone that indicates that a relay contact has failed to close.

open ended A term applied to a process or system to which other elements can be added; not limited to a specific set or fixed number.

open-reel A term sometimes applied to standard half-inch tape in 'open' demountable reels (as contrasted to tape in cartridges or cassettes).

open shop A term applied to a computer system (as at many universities) in which users can program and run their own jobs, often via interactive terminals. This contrasts to a **closed shop** in which execution (and, usually programming) is performed only by data processing staff.

open subprogram See *subprogram*.

open subroutine See *subroutine*.

open system A term applied to a (large) data network in which flexible interfacing facilities are provided to permit the connection of a variety of user devices.

open-wire A term applied to a communications link consisting of bare wires strung between insulators on poles.

operable Also *in operating condition.* Of a functional unit or system; capable of being operated when required; not prevented from being used because of failure or need for maintenance.

operable time Also *up time.* The time during which a system or functional unit is capable of being operated. See *failure; down time*.

operand (1)The basic unit of data that enters processing; a value that is used or manipulated during the execution of an instruction. It is a bit pattern identified for access by an **operand address** which is a hardware address in main storage. See *R-value; fetch*. (2)A bit pattern in a field of a record (say in a magnetic tape file) that becomes an 'operand' (def. 1) when the record is read into main storage. (The term is 'access' and 'programming' oriented, and this would not be a common meaning.) **(3)**In a source language instruction; a value that is either a 'literal' or that identifies or names the location of an 'operand' (def. 2). It is a value that provides the compiler and operating system with the means for locating the value when it is required during execution; if it is in symbolic form, it is a **symbolic address**. See *literal; L-value; address modification; direct addressing; indirect addressing.* **(4)**A bit pattern in a compiled (object code) version of a program that is a translation of an 'operand' (def. 3); it is a value that is used directly or via address modification to locate (fetch) an 'operand' (def. 1) during execution. See *operator (Data); instruction; execution.*

operand field A place in a source language instruction where an operand can be placed or where it has been placed.

operand part An operand field.

operating (1) The work function of a computer operator. **(2)**Of a functional unit or a system; in use, performing its function.

operating condition (1) Operating status. **(2)**Capable of being used. See *operable.*

operating station A terminal, console, or location that is used by a computer operator to exercise control over processing.

operating status Of a functional unit; its condition with respect to the function it is intended to perform; for example, 'in use', 'standby', 'available', or 'out of service'.

operating system A set of tested, interrelated programs provided by a computer manufacturer to exercise management and control functions over processing. As compared to an 'executive' or 'supervisor' system, it is intended to increase throughput, improve resource utilisation, and to reduce the amount of supervision and intervention required from the operator. There are many differences between systems but, generally, an operating system provides the following:

Storage management— It transfers data and instructions between peripheral devices and between peripheral devices and main storage, it keeps track of where items are in main storage and in backing storage, and it allocates main storage space to meet processing requirements.

Processing management— It monitors the hardware activities of execution and deals with error conditions and interrupts, it maintains a record of peripheral utilisation and availability, it initiates and monitors transfers for executing programs, and it implements processing priorities.

Protection— It performs checks to prevent the unauthorised access of code and data or the overwriting of required data, it maintains backup copies of specified items to reduce the effects of hardware or software failures, it performs validation of inputs, and it takes appropriate action to resolve errors.

Human interface— It receives and acts upon operator instructions and outputs messages acknowledging them and also messages indicating the status of work and any problems encountered.

Accounting— It keeps track of the time and resources used by the various jobs and users of the system and produces totals for charging, performance analysis, and maintenance scheduling.

Logging— It maintains records of communications with the operator and of errors or other conditions encountered during processing.

Strictly speaking, an operation can be said to be 'performed by the operating system' only if it is done by a utility or other unit of supervisory software. In practice, it is common to 'credit' the operating system with functions that may actually be performed by hardware (read-only memory). In modern computer systems, the hardware and software are often so interrelated that only the design engineers would be able to state with certainty which functions were performed by hardware and which by software. See *supervisor; monitor; manual executive.*

operating system nucleus Those elements of an operating system that must be in main storage whenever processing is being performed. See *nucleus; kernel.*

operating time The time when a system or functional unit is actually being used. See *operable time; idle.*

operation (1) That which is done; ('a computer operation'; 'a collating operation'; 'a printing operation'). **(2)**During execution; that which is performed on or with data; ('an arithmetic operation'; 'a logic operation').

operation code (1) Also *function code.* That part of an object code instruction that consists of the operator; that part that determines what is to be done during execution. See *operator; instruction.* **(2)**An instruction set.

operation control language (OCL) An operator control language.

operation table A truth table.

operational amplifier (op-amp) A stable, high-gain, direct current coupled amplifier that is usually used with a large amount of negative feedback. Function largely depends upon the feedback elements used. Common variations include an inverting amplifier, non-inverting amplifier, current to voltage con-

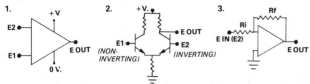

verter, voltage follower, summing amplifier, zero crossing detector, low-pass filter, high-pass filter, and bandpass filter. Figure 1 shows the operational amplifier symbol and its connections and Figure 2 shows the basic circuit. Figure 3 shows a basic inverting amplifier.

operations analysis Operations research.

operations research (OR) The study of resource utilisation systems and techniques (factory production; aircraft operation; electricity generation) by means of mathematical models. The purpose is to provide the basis for making decisions on resource allocation in complex systems. See *linear programming*.

operator (Data) That part of an instruction that specifies the operation to be performed on or with the operand(s). It is a bit pattern that is identical to some bit pattern in the instruction set of the computer and it, thus, specifies one of those operations that the computer is designed to perform. An **arithmetic operator** is one with numeric inputs and outputs, the usual ones are 'add'. 'subtract', 'multiply', 'divide', 'exponentiate', and 'compute'. A **logical operator** is one that provides for a test of inputs in accordance with the rules of symbolic logic. See *logic operation*. A **relational operator** is one that determines the similarities or differences between two inputs. A **function operator** is one that specifies an execution-related step; for example, 'get', 'move', 'read', 'write' and 'go to'. The term 'operator' can be applied to an element of an instruction in either source code or object code; when applied to an object code version, it is synonymous with 'operation code'. See *operand; instruction; execution; instruction set*.

operator (Mathematics) A symbol indicating a mathematical operation to be performed; for example, the '+' in the expression $A = B + C$.

operator (Person) Also *computer operator*. A person who performs processing related tasks at a computer installation; in particular in a computer room, and who is present during processing to control computer operations, to receive messages from the supervisor or the operating system, and to take such action as they indicate. The term is usually understood to mean **console operator** which is the person directly in charge of the controls and message sending and receiving facilities of the console. A **peripheral operator** is one who attends to peripheral devices and performs such tasks as replenishing supplies and loading and unloading punched cards and magnetic disc and tape volumes. A **terminal operator** is a person who initiates processing and receives results by means of a terminal.

operator command A command to an operating system (control program) as entered by an operator (via a console typewriter).

operator console A console.

operator control command A statement in an operator control language.

operator control language (OCL) A set of commands and rules for their use that enable a computer operator to instruct an operating system to perform, change, or terminate a processing operation. In some systems, the term 'job control language' is applied to all commands and rules for controlling execution, whether input by punched cards/paper tape or via the console. In other systems, they are considered as separate languages and together they comprise the **system control language**. See *job control language*.

operator control panel A group of switches and indicator lights that is associated with the console (or considered part of it) and by which the operator can monitor and control certain functions of the system. See *console*.

operator field A place in a source language instruction where an operator can be placed or where it has been placed.

operator ID A character group by which an operator is known to an operating system; a group input by a terminal operator or console operator during log-on and which is checked by the operating system to establish the person's authorisation to use or control the facilities of the system. See *operator's access code*.

operator message A message from an operating system to an operator as printed by a console typewriter or displayed on a console VDU.

operator part An operator field.

operator's access code A value held in a system table that is related to each operator ID and defines the access rights permitted to the person with the particular ID.

OPM (opm.) *Operations Per Minute.*

OPS (1)*OPeratorS.* **(2)**(ops.) *Operations Per Second.*

optical In the computer-related sense; a term that denotes sensing and input by means of photoelectric devices.

optical character reader A device that identifies characters by their patterns of reflected or transmitted light. See *optical character recognition*.

optical character reading Optical character recognition.

optical character recognition (OCR) Computer input equipment and techniques for identifying printed (sometimes handwritten) characters by photoelectric sensing and analysis of their patterns of reflected or transmitted light. One of the simplest methods uses a matrix of photodiodes onto which characters from a document are projected by a lens system. Those photodiodes that receive a high level of light (reflected from white paper) turn on while those that receive less light (reflected

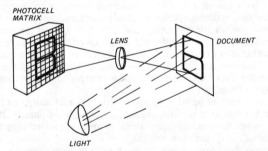

from the black ink of the character) remain off. The matrix is then scanned and read into a storage-cell matrix where the bit pattern is compared with character bit patterns in read-only memory to determine which one it most closely resembles. See *magnetic ink character recognition; optical mark recognition*.

optical coupler Also *optocoupler; optical isolator*. A sealed device containing an infrared-emitting photodiode and a phototransistor. When current flows in the input circuit to the photodiode, light passes to the phototransistor, turning it on and causing current to flow in the output circuit. The purpose is to isolate the two circuits and prevent noise and peak pulses from passing to the output circuit. They are used in current loop

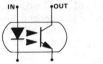

systems and in systems with inputs from switches and sensors located in electrically noisy environments.

optical fibre A thin, glass filament as used in fibre optics. See *fibre optics*.

optical mark reader A device that identifies marks on a document by means of changes in reflected or transmitted light as the document passes through the device. See *optical mark recognition*.

optical mark reading Optical mark recognition.

optical mark recognition (OMR) Computer input equipment and techniques for identifying and interpreting marks (short lines; filled-in squares) on documents by means of changes in reflected or transmitted light. The system uses a light source and photocells positioned across the document path to detect the presence and absence of marks as the document passes through the reader. The reader is set up according to the document format so that the significance of marks can be determined by registering their coordinate positions on the document. The output is a bit-serial stream with encoded timing which is input to a computer program. OMR is used in grading examination papers and entering data from marked forms; for example, purchase orders and lottery cards.

optical reader A reader that uses photoelectric detection; an optical mark reader, an optical character reader, or a bar code reader.

optical scanner (1) An element of an optical character reader or similar device that senses the light reflectivity or transmission of a pattern (say, of a printed character) on a sequence of spaced 'scan lines'. See *scanner*. **(2)**A wand; a hand-held optical device for reading bar codes. See *bar code; point of sale*.

optical type font A set of alphanumric characters that are particularly designed for 'unambiguous' machine reading.

optimisation (1) The (mathematical) process of determining the best course of action or combination of inputs with respect to some desired condition. See *linear programming*. **(2)**Also, in some contexts, *tuning*. The improvement of a system or process to the point where it is neither time nor cost effective to seek further improvement. The term is often applied to the rewriting and testing of (frequently used) programs to improve their running speed.

optional parameter A value that can be supplied by a programmer or operator but need not be supplied; if nothing is supplied, the compiler, operating system, or program provides a 'default parameter'. See *default; parameter.*

optional-pause instruction An optional-stop instruction.

optional-stop instruction An instruction that will cause a halt in the execution of a program at a particular point if required by the operator.

optional word Also *noise word*. A word that is acceptable in source coding according to the rules of a programming language but may be omitted at the discretion of the programmer. Such words are often used in order to make coding more readable. For example, in the COBOL statement WRITE TEXT-2 AFTER ADVANCING 3 LINES, the 'ADVANCING' and 'LINES' are 'optional words'; the statement could have been written: WRITE TEXT-2 AFTER 3.

opto-coupler An optical coupler. See *optical coupling.*

optodeflector Also *deflector plate*. In a cathode ray tube; a (aluminium) plate that can be capacitively charged in a controlled way to attract and repel the electron beam and thus to control its movement in scanning the screen. See *cathode ray tube.*

optoelectronics The science, practice, or equipment involved in using light (usually understood to be in fibre optics) in conjunction with electronic circuitry to accomplish a switching or data transfer function.

OR Also *inclusive-OR; disjunction*. A logic operation with an output that is 'true' if any input is 'true' and 'false' if all are 'false'. See *exclusive-OR; logic operation.*

order (1)A term used to indicate the physical relationship of the items of a group; ('alphabetical order'; 'in order of receipt'; 'numerical order'). (2)Also, often, *arrange; sequence; sort*. To place the items of a group in physical relationship according to some rule. The term 'order' is the broadest of the available terms and can be used to include multi-dimensional positioning. The term 'arrange' is a near synonym but may have a 'two-dimensional' bias. A 'sort' is the usual computer method of 'ordering' items. Items that are 'sequenced' are given relative positions according to number or key and, while this is the usual case with items that are 'ordered' or 'sorted', it is not a definitive requirement. See *sort; collate*. (3)A command. (4)A purchase order. (5)A term used to indicate that a value is an approximation; ('packing densities on the order of 60%').

order by merge See *sequence by merge.*

order code An instruction set.

order code processor (OCP) An instruction processor; a processor in a modular computer system that decodes instructions of user programs and performs the required arithmetic/logic operations. It is the 'central processor' of a system that may have separate 'processors' to perform storage management and interfacing functions and/or multiple processors for executing the instructions of user programs.

order entry The process of entering purchase orders into a computer system; particularly a process in which a terminal operator reads the orders and enters their details by keyboard.

order of magnitude A term used with the general sense of 'multiply by 10'; to increase processing speed by 'two orders of magnitude' would, then, be to increase it by 100 times.

ordered serial file Also *keyed serial file*. A sequential file on a serial medium (magnetic tape). See *serial file; sequential file.*

ordering bias Of a set of items that are to be sorted; the degree to which they are already in the order to be produced by the sort. A group with a 'high ordering bias' will, for example, require very little time or effort to sort.

orderly In accordance with usual or standard procedures; not emergency or 'crash'; ('an orderly shutdown').

origin (1)Also, sometimes, *base address*. The lowest numbered address in an area of coordinate-addressable storage. See *base address*. (2)A root. See *tree.*

original document A source document.

original equipment manufacturer See *OEM.*

originate To initiate or to be the source of; ('originate a call'; 'originate a data transfer').

originate mode The mode of a line access unit or automatic dialer in which it is dialing a data station in order to set up a transfer on a PSTN line. The term is also used to identify this modem when discussing handshaking or the actual transfer; ('the modem in originate mode transmits on low channel'). It can be either **manual originate** in which dialing and changing from voice to data is done by an operator or **automatic origin-**

ate in which these functions are performed by an automatic dialer with initiation from the DTE. See *answer mode*.

origination (1)The process of converting input data into computer-readable form. (2)The process of setting up a data transfer on a PSTN line. See *originate mode*. (3)The process of formatting and sending a message.

orthoferrite A term applied to a magnetisable material that can be more easily magnetised along one axis than along another. The axis requiring least magnetising force is the **easy axis** and the other is the **hard axis**. See *magnet; bubble memory*.

orthogonal (1)Having the characteristics of a matrix; with elements that are accessible at the intersection points of two or three coordinates that (notionally) intersect at right angles. (2)A term sometimes applied to coordinate-addressable storage (which is normally accessed in bit-parallel) that has another set of access paths that allow individual bits to be read or written (as a test or diagnostic procedure).

orthogonal array processor An array processor. See *array computer*.

OS *Operating System*.

OS/360 The IBM System/360 operating system.

OS/MFT The IBM System/360 operating system that supports multiprogramming with a fixed number of tasks.

OS/MVT The IBM System/360 operating system that supports multiprogramming with a variable number of tasks.

OS/VS *Operating System/Virtual Storage*.

OS/VS1 A virtual storage operating system that is an extension of OS/MFT.

OS/VS2 A virtual storage operating system that is an extension of OS/MVT.

oscillate To make a repetitive change of state or value; to move between limiting values or positions.

oscillating sort A merge sort in which sorting and merging operations alternate. See *merge sort*.

oscillation (1)A change that produces alternating current. See *oscillator*. (2)A single instance of changing polarity and returning to the original condition. See *cycle*. (3)Hunting; a slow, repetitive change of circuit values.

oscillator A device that generates high-frequency pulses (usually a square wave) for purposes of synchronisation and event timing. Most are **crystal oscillators** that take advantage of the inherent resonance of a (quartz) crystal to obtain frequency stability. See *timer; time base; clock*.

oscilloscope A cathode ray tube with time base generation and control circuits that enable it to time the display of events (waves; pulses) to their frequency of occurrence and, thus, to 'stop' them in order to permit an operator to make timing measurements or to observe the wave form. An oscilloscope is a common item of test equipment for use with electronic circuits and devices.

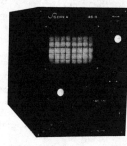

OTC *One-Time Carbon*.

out-of-frame A term applied to a signal or character (data communications) that is outside of its time frame or other delimiters.

outconnector See *connector*.

outgoing circuit A circuit on which messages are sent.

output (1)To produce as a result of processing; ('output a message on a screen'; 'output data on a printer'). (2)That which is produced during processing; ('a printed output'; 'an output from a logic operation'). (3)A transfer to a peripheral device. See *input; input/output*. (4)An identifier of something used in an 'output' (def. 3); ('an output routine'; 'an output channel'). (5)That which is produced by a circuit or device; ('a 12 V. output'; 'a square-wave output').

output area An area of main storage that is used by one or more programs to assemble results.

output buffer In a computer or communications interface device; storage used to hold data that is awaiting transfer.

output channel A path on which data is sent to another location.

output device A device used to convert data from its bit pattern representation in computer storage to a form in which it can be used outside the computer system. Examples include printers, card and tape punches, VDU's, and COM recorders. See *input device*.

output medium A medium on which output data is represented; for example, continuous stationary, punched cards, or microfilm. (The term 'output media' would include VDU screens but the term 'output medium' would probably not be applied to other than a 'permanent record' material.)

output routine A utility that organises or performs an output (peripheral transfer).

output unit An output device.

output writer A utility that performs output peripheral transfers (usually understood to be from main storage directly to a printer or other slow-speed device). See *spooling; dump routine*.

outside line A telephone connection on which calls are made to locations outside the user's premises.

overflow (1)That part of a unit of data that will not fit into a storage location intended to receive it. The term may be applied to the 'excess' data whether it is lost (by truncation) or stored elsewhere. (2)The process of storing all or part of a unit of data in another location when there is not room for it in the location in which it would normally be placed. For example, the process of writing a record to an 'overflow area' when the block to which it would be allocated by key is already occupied. (3)To attempt to add an item to a full stack. See *underflow; stack*.

overflow area On magnetic disc storage; a location to which records can be written that cannot be contained in the blocks in which they would normally be placed. See *overflow record*.

overflow pointer An address of a record in an overflow area as held in the location from which it overflowed.

overflow record In a random file; a record placed in an overflow area because the value generated by the randomising algorithm is that of a full block or a home record. See *random file; overflow*.

overhead (1)With respect to processing; time or operations that are devoted to system functions rather than to user jobs. See *housekeeping*. (2)With respect to a business; fixed (monthly) costs that are independent of sales.

overhead operation A housekeeping operation.

overlap (1)Also, often, *parallel*. By an operation; to be performed during the same time that another operation is being performed; one such operation is said to 'overlap' the other. They may also be said to be performed 'concurrently' or 'in parallel'. (2)With respect to two operations that begin and/or end at different times; the amount of time during which they are both being performed; ('a twenty millisecond overlap'). See *lag; lead*.

overlapping seek A facility of a peripheral controller for magnetic disc units that permits it to perform a seek on one unit while reading or writing on another.

overlay (1)Also *overlay segment*. A part of an 'overlay program' that is intended to be loaded when it is required during the execution of the program and overwritten when no longer required. (2)The operation of loading an 'overlay segment' when it is required during execution. (3)An image (say, of an invoice form) superimposed on data. See *form flash*.

overlay module A load module that has been divided into overlay segments plus the information required by the overlay supervisor to cause the segments to be loaded as required.

overlay path The sequence in which overlay segments are to be overlaid during execution.

overlay program A program that has been divided into overlay segments and a control segment.

overlay segment A sequence of instructions in an overlay program that is intended to be loaded and executed when required and overwritten when the space it occupies is required for another overlay segment.

overlay supervisor A system routine that controls the sequencing and transfer of overlay segments during the execution of an overlay program.

overlay tree A graphic representation of the sequence in which overlay segments are overlaid on different execution paths of a program.

overlaying (1)The operation of bringing a unit of code or data (overlay segment; page; segment) into main storage when required during execution. The process performed by an operating system in a virtual storage system of locating a required page or segment in backing storage and reading it into main storage may be termed **automatic overlaying**. See *discard; virtual storage system*. (2)By a programmer; to divide a program into 'overlay segments' and to write the necessary instructions to locate them when they are required during execution; the operation may be termed **manual overlaying**.

overload (1)To exceed the designed work capacity of a system or functional unit. (2)To exceed the safe current carrying capacity of an electric circuit. (3)The amount by which designed or safe capacity is exceeded; ('a 20% overload').

overpunch (1)To place a punched card or paper tape back to a particular punched hole pattern and to punch one or more additional holes (usually to delete a character or correct a mistake in the first punching). (2)To form a special character (a method of code extension) by adding one or more holes to the punching pattern of some existing character. (3)An accidental repunching of a paper tape or punched card that has already being punched. (It may also be done to cause rejection or to produce a read stop.) See *laced card*.

overrun (1)The operation of producing more of something than was ordered or intended. (2)A term sometimes applied to the condition in which data is lost because a receiving device cannot accept data at the speed it is sent to it.

overwrite With respect to data in a storage location; to write new data to the location, thus destroying the existing data.

ovonic memory A form of amorphous memory in which bits are held as differences in electrical resistance of small (5 micron) areas of germanium or tellerium alloy amorphous material. The device is formed by sputter coating the amorphous material onto an insulating layer through which holes have been etched to a conductive substrate. The amorphous material is then etched away except for that deposited in the holes (termed 'vias'), each of which becomes a 'pore' capable of holding one bit. A further masking and metalising step produces a matrix of conductors by which each pore can be 'addressed'. In an unwritten device, the amorphous material is in the fully amorphous condition and each pore has a resistance of about 100,000 ohms. To write a 1-bit (to 'set' a pore) a small current (6 mA.) is passed through a pore and by 'threshold switching' (a process that is not well understood) the material changes to a semi-crystalline form with a resistance of 500 — 1000 ohms. To reset the pore (set a 0-bit), a pulse of higher current (25 mA.) is sent through it which heats the material and returns it to the fully amorphous (high-resistance) state.

owner (1)In a hierarchial structure; an entity that has some degree of control or privilege with respect to entities (**members**) on a lower level. (2)In a data structure (not necessarily hierarchial); an entity that must be accessed first in order to access other entities (members) or to access other entities on a particular access path. As an example in a hierarchial structure, a file is the 'owner' of its records and the records are 'owners' of their fields. See *net; tree*. (3)Also, sometimes, *controller; user*. With respect to certain programs or data; the individual or organisation with full access rights.

P

P (1)*Program*. (2)*Permutation*. (3)*Positive*. (4)*Power* (electrical). (5)(p) *Pico-*.

P-channel MOS (PMOS) A term applied to an MOS device (usually a transistor) in which all conduction is through P-type silicon. See *N-channel MOS; field effect transistor; MOS*.

P-counter *Program* counter.

P-record *Primary* record.

P-type *Positive* type. An identifier of a form of semiconductor material in which the primary conduction is by means of 'holes'. See *semiconductor; N-type*.

PABX *Private Automatic Branch eXchange*. A private telephone exchange (say, for a company's offices) that automatically connects internal 'branch' lines to the external circuits of a telephone system.

pacing In data transmission or transfer; a system in which the receiving device controls the speed of transfer to prevent overrun. For example, the method of a paper tape punch in which a signal that punching has been completed is sent to initiate the transfer of the next character.

pack (1)To reduce the transmission time or required storage space for data in character format by eliminating such elements as null representations, non-significant zeros, and spaces. See *data compression*. (2)With respect to numeric data; to place it in 'packed decimal' format. See *packed decimal*. (3)A disc pack. (4)A card pack.

package (1)A term applied to a group of related items (say, a computer and its software and peripherals) sold at a single, all-inclusive price. (2)An application package; ('a bill-of-materials package'; 'a stock control package'). (3)The enclosure and terminal arrangement of a semiconductor device; ('a TO-72 package'). (4)A set of instructional materials; ('a COBOL package'). (5)In equipment design; the function of deciding the location of components and the form of the cabinet or other enclosure. (6)An item of equipment considered with respect to its physical size and form; ('an attractive package'; 'a small package'). (7)To specify the contents and/or gather together the elements of a 'package' (def. 1; 2; 4).

package count On a printed circuit board; the number if integrated circuits and, possibly, other separately connected components.

package generator A program used in producing some type of application package.

packaged (1)Included within a 'package'. See *package*. (2)A term applied to a computer (or, possibly, some other system) that is contained within a single enclosure, desk, etc.

packed decimal Also *internal decimal*. A computational format in which decimal data is represented by two BCD digits per byte. In **signed packed decimal**, the least significant byte holds one digit and the sign code. The sign code is 1100 for 'positive' and 1101 for 'negative'. Decimal 782 would, then, be represented in two bytes as 01111000 00101100 and —9 would be represented in one byte as 10011101. See *external decimal*.

packed microinstruction See *microinstruction*.

packet A unit of data and necessary routing and control characters intended to be transmitted as a unit; particularly in a 'packet switching system'. See *packet switching*.

Packet Assembly/Disassembly Facilities (PAD) The facilities of a packet switching system that provide for the connection of asynchronous (start-stop) DTE's. See *packet switching system*.

packet mode The operation of a data network by means of packet switching.

packet sequencing In a packet switching system; the operations performed to assure that (related) packets are sent to the receiving station in the same order as they were received from the sending station.

packet switching A means of operating a data network or data communications system for a number of users in which addressed 'packets' are routed by system facilities. Typically, a user sends a message (packet) by means of a leased or dialed telephone line to the nearest 'packet switching exchange' where it is buffered, checked, and retransmitted over a high-speed circuit to the packet switching exchange that serves the addressee (possibly passing through other exchanges on the way). At the destination exchange, it is sent over local telephone lines to the addressee. The main advantages are that it can provide a high-speed data service to users without enough traffic to justify leased lines and it makes efficient use of the high-speed circuits. Systems may also include reformatting facilities to permit different types of equipment to be connected. See *message switching; circuit switching; packet switching system*.

packet switching exchange (PSE) The computer facilities that provide the interface between users and the node-to-node circuits of a packet switching system. Functions include routing, packet sequencing, and implementing the network protocol.

packet switching network (PSN) A packet switching system.

packet switching system (PSS) A data network by which users communicate with each other by means of 'packets' of standard format. Such a system consists of a number of 'packet switching exchanges' that are interconnected, usually, by broadband telephone circuits that permit high-speed (48K or 52K bits per second) transmission. Users that have equipment for bit-synchronous transmission usually connect to their nearest packet switching exchange by means of a leased telephone line. Users with asynchronous (start-stop) equipment can connect by leased line or by dial-up. The common type of system is that defined by CCITT Recommendation X.25. Such a system uses three levels of protocol. Level 1 is the circuit level and describes the connection of a DTE (computer or terminal) to the DCE (circuit equipment including the local modem and equipment at the exchange). Only the connection to the modem is defined and the system currently used is as defined in V.24. Level 2 is the frame level. It specifies that each packet will begin and end with a 'flag' (the pattern 01111110), a control byte as the second byte, and a frame check sequence (FCS) that occupies the two bytes preceding the final flag. (An FCS is a group more commonly known as a 'cyclic check character'.) The control byte identifies the type of packet as either 'information' or 'supervisory'. An information packet contains an 'I-field (user data) and two 3-digit binary numbers, one of which is the 'send sequence number' and the other the 'receive sequence number'. The send sequence number N(S) is, in effect, the serial number of the frame and the receive sequence number N(R) is the expected N(S) of the next packet to be received. The numbers are in modulo-8 sequence (0 follows 7) and they are used for sequencing and to detect errors in sequencing. An N(R) serves to acknowledge receipt of all packets of lower N(S). A supervisory packet contains an N(R) if it relates to packet handling ('ready for next packet') and is unnumbered if it relates to the link ('disconnect'). Level 2 protocol is implemented by the DTE or by a special interface device between the DTE and modem. Level 3 is the 'packet level' protocol and is implemented by special DTE software. It covers the procedures for initiating calls and for sending and receiving packets. Basically, the system operates in full-duplex with two 'logical channels', each of which carries packets in one direction. When joining a network, a user is assigned a range of logical channel numbers (LCN's). To set up a virtual circuit (two logical channels—send and receive), a user sends a 'call request packet' containing one of these LCN's and the address of the location (node; DTE) to which a message is to be sent. The exchange interprets this and sends appropriate details to the exchange with which the intended recipient is connected.

This exchange selects one of the recipients available LCN's and uses it in an 'incoming call packet'. If the intended recipient can accept the call, it returns a 'call accepted packet' and the exchanges set up the two-way virtual circuit. Data packets can then be exchanged. A data packet contains the single LCN that identifies the virtual circuit to the sender. The method described sets up a 'switched virtual circuit' (SVC) which is set up and terminated as required. Most systems also provide for 'permanent virtual circuits' which are the equivalent of a leased line between users. Level 3 also provides for sequencing numbers P(S) and P(N) which operate in the same way as the frame-level N(S) and N(R) though the rotating sequence can, optionally, be 128 instead of 8. The P(S)-P(N) sequencing is end-to-end and permits the DTE's to check for improperly sequenced packets. (It also allows for multiple DTE's operating through a single interface device that handles N(S) and N(R) sequencing.) The N(S)-N(R) sequencing is only between a DTE and the packet switching exchange with which it connects. The advantage of packet switching over leased line or dial-up systems is that users with different types of equipment (and operating at different speeds) can be connected and costs should be less as packets for many users can be transmitted by time interleaving on the same telephone circuit. The system provides 'packet assembly/dissassembly' (PAD) facilities to permit the use of asynchronous equipment operating at speeds up to 300 bits per second. Synchronous operation is commonly at 9600 bits per second though provision is made for user equipment to operate at full network speed (say, 48K bps.).

packing density (1) Also *storage density* and, on magnetisable surface media, *recording density*. The number of bits that can be held in a unit length, area, or volume of a storage medium. See *recording density*. (2)The percentage of the address space of a magnetic disc or magnetic tape file that is occupied when the file is created or reformatted. The value is usually input to a file loading utility. (3)The number of integrated circuits (or other devices) mounted per unit area of a printed circuit board.

packing factor Packing density (of a file).

pad (1) To add logically meaningless characters to a data item to bring it up to some prescribed or minimum length. See *fill; character fill; null value*. (2)A sequence of 0-bits recorded at the end of a sector on a magnetic disc track during disc initialisation. Its purpose is to provide a blank space at the end of the sector to assure that the last data in the sector is not overwritten when data is written to the next sector; ('a two-byte pad'). (3)To add logically meaningless characters to a data item or write them to a storage location. (4)A group of adjacent, functionally related keys that do not comprise a 'standard' alphanumeric keyboard. The term may be applied to a group of buttons on a simple terminal, to the 'numeric pad' of a pushbutton telephone, or to a separately identified set of keys (often numeric) on the keyboard of a terminal or console. (5)A term often applied to edge connectors; the circuit terminations of a printed circuit board. (6)A slider; the part of a magnetic disc read/write head that is in closest proximity to the disc surface when reading or writing. See *head; fly*. (7)An attenuator; a device for introducing impedance in a telephone line. See *conditioning*.

PAD *Packet Assembly/Disassembly (facilities)*.

pad character (1) Also *null character*. A logically meaningless character (sometimes represented by #) that is used to extend data or fill unused positions in a storage location. See *pad; fill character; character fill*. (2)An operationally neutral character added in a control sequence for purposes of filling time, often to permit a mechanical operation (carriage return; form feed) to be performed.

padding (1) The process of adding pad characters to data items, storage locations, or control sequences. See *pad character*. (2)A collective term for all the pad characters used in a location or added to a data item or control sequence.

padding character A pad character.

page (1)A standard unit of storage and transfer in most virtual storage systems; a fixed number of words or bytes that is identifiable as a unit by the operating system. See *segment; virtual storage allocation; paging*. (2)Of fan-fold continuous stationery; the amount of stationery between two successive folds. (3)One side of a piece of paper; the printing unit of a 'page printer'. (4)The data displayed at one time on the screen of a VDU. See *page turning; scrolling*. (5)To move a 'page' (def. 1) between main storage and backing storage. See *paging*.

page-at-a-time printer A page printer.

page fault See *virtual storage interrupt*.

page fixing The process of designating those pages that must remain in main storage during processing. See *save area*.

page frame Also *page slot*. A primary storage location that can hold a page. See *virtual storage allocation; virtual storage transfers*.

page in Also *roll in*. To transfer a page from secondary storage to primary storage. See *virtual storage transfers*.

page out Also *roll out*. To transfer a page from primary storage to secondary storage. See *virtual storage transfers; discard*.

page pool A free page reserve.

page printer (1)A printer that prints an entire (A4) page at a time; a printer that does not print characters sequentially or line by line. See *electrostatic printer; laser printer*. (2)A term sometimes applied to a printer (thermal matrix) that prints on cut sheets or forms (typically, A4) rather than on continuous stationery.

page reader An optical mark reader or optical character reader for which a 'page' is the usual input.

page/segment table A 'page table' in a virtual storage system that uses both fixed-length pages and variable-length segments. See *page table*.

page slot A page frame.

page stealing A discard from the viewpoint of the process that loses a page from its resident set. See *discard*.

page swapping See *swap*.

page table In a virtual storage system; an operating system table that correlates virtual addresses with page numbers and indicates whether particular pages are in primary storage.

page turning (1)The operation of replacing the entire contents of a VDU screen at one time. See *scrolling*. (2)Paging; the exchange of pages between primary and secondary storage.

page wait A suspended status in which a process may be placed while waiting for a required page.

paged segment A short segment that is contained (with others) in a single page. See *segment*.

paged system A paging system.

paging (1)Using 'pages' to hold code and data in primary storage; ('a paging system'; 'paging storage'). (2)The operation of moving pages between primary and secondary storage. See *swap; roll in; roll out*.

paging algorithm See *discard policy*.

paging device (1)A magnetic disc unit used to hold pages and/or segments required for a particular run in a virtual storage system. (2)In some systems; a utility that manages paging operations.

paging policy See *discard policy*.

paging rate VSI rate; the number of page transfers per unit time See *virtual storage interrupt*.

paging storage Secondary storage used to hold pages; storage on a paging device.

paging system Also *paged system*. A virtual storage system in which the fixed-length 'page' is a primary (or the only) unit of storage allocation and transfer. See *virtual storage allocation; virtual storage terms; page; segmentation system*.

painting In computer graphics; the operation of shading some area of a display image; for example, with dots or cross-hatching. See *histogram*.

PAM *Pulse Amplitude Modulation*.

panel (1)A part of the cabinet (enclosure) of a functional unit; ('remove the back panel'). (2)A group of control or test elements (lights; switches; terminals) on a functional unit; ('a display panel'; 'an engineering test panel'). (3)An area of a VDU screen used to hold a predefined display; ('an operator instruction panel').

paper In a computer system; 'continuous stationery'. (The usual meaning unless otherwise indicated.)

paper feed (1)Also *feed* and, sometimes, *throw*. A vertical movement of paper in a printer. (2)The electrical and mechanical components that move paper through a printer. See *tractor*.

paper skip Paper throw.

paper tape Also, sometimes, *punch tape*. A data input and storage medium consisting of paper tape of standard specification in which data is represented by hole patterns punched across the tape. Standard widths are 11/16 in. (5 channel), 7/8 in. (6 channel), and 1 in. (8 channel). It is commonly used in

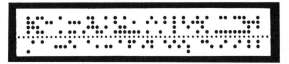

teletypewriter communications systems, for numerical control, and in typesetting systems. (It has largely been superseded by magnetic media in computer input applications.) See *level; frame; data hole; feed hole*.

paper tape code Also *tape code; punch tape code*. A relationship between the characters of a character set and the hole patterns by which they can be represented on paper tape. Common codes are ASCII, BCD, and IA-2 (Telex).

paper tape loop A format loop; a loop of paper tape with punching to control paper throw in a printer. See *vertical format unit*.

paper tape punch Also *perforater; tape punch*. A device that punches hole patterns in paper tape to represent characters for storage and/or transfer. The term is applied to different devices including a key punch that punches the patterns as the operator presses keys, a computer output device that punches data on tape for storage purposes, and to an element of a teletypewriter that performs the function of a key punch and may also record received data on tape. Punching speeds are, typically, about 50 characters per second maximum. See *ASR; KSR; paper tape; paper tape reader*.

paper tape reader A device that converts punching patterns on paper tape to electrical signals. It is usually accomplished by means of a light on one side of the tape and a photodiode aligned with each channel on the other side of the tape. An alternative method is to use 'brushes' that make an electrical contact through the holes. Paper tape readers are used in numerical control, in printer format control, in typesetters, and in teletypewriters. They were once widely used for computer inputs.

paper tape verifier A data preparation device on which an operator duplicates the punching of paper tape to locate any errors before inputing data to a computer.

paper tape winder A hand-cranked or motor-driven reel that receives and winds paper tape output from a punch or reader.

paper throw Also *throw* and, sometimes, *paper feed; slew; vertical tabulate*. A movement of paper through a printer. It is usually expressed in lines and is assumed to be by an amount greater than a single line; ('a ten-line throw'). See *line feed; newline*.

paperless office The 'office of the future' in which all records are held in computer-readable form, operations are performed largely by computer, and inputs and outputs are made by electronic means.

parallel (1)Also *concurrent; overlapping*. Of independent operations; performed simultaneously or within the same time period; ('data transfers in parallel with processing') See *overlap*. (2)Simultaneous; ('parallel execution'; 'a bit-parallel data transmission'). (3)Capable of performing two or more operations simultaneously; ('a parallel adder'; 'a parallel processor'). (4)Duplicated (for backup purposes); ('parallel recording'; 'a parallel line'). (5)An identifier of an electric power circuit in which all loads are connected to full terminal voltage. See *series*.

parallel adder An adder that adds digits in all digit positions simultaneously. See *adder*.

parallel addition The addition of a parallel adder.

parallel allocation The allocation of a single resource to two or more concurrent programs. See *shareable*.

parallel computer A computer with multiple control units and/or arithmetic logic units and, thus, with a capability to perform multiple operations simultaneously. See *array computer; multiprocessor; dataflow processor; SIMD; MISD; MIMD*.

parallel operation An operation that is performed at the same time as some other operation.

parallel processing Processing in which some unit of processing (program; instruction) is divided into smaller units, all of which are executed at the same time using multiple sets of facilities. See *parallel computer; dataflow processor*.

parallel running The duplicated performance of (computer) work by a new system and by the system it is intended to replace. The purpose is to compare results to assure that the new system is functioning properly before the old one is replaced. The operation may be performed with two computers, with a computer and a manual system, or with different versions of programs to perform the same application.

parallel search storage Storage (control unit registers; magnetic disc) in which a search is performed simultaneously on two or more storage locations. Such storage has, typically, been searched by content rather than address. See *look-aside registers; content-addressable filestore; associative storage*.

parallel storage Also, usually, *coordinate-addressable storage*. Storage in which the entire contents of a multi-bit location can be read or written at one time. Examples include main storage and control and arithmetic unit registers.

parallel transfer (1)A bit-parallel transfer; the simultaneous transfer of all the bits of one or more words, say, from main storage to the control unit. (2)An asynchronous transfer; a peripheral transfer that does not interrupt execution of instructions. (3)A transfer that takes place at the same time as another transfer.

parallel transmission (1)The simultaneous transmission of all of the bits of an encoded character. See *bit parallel*. (2)The transmission method of multifrequency signalling in which a single signal contains all of the frequency components necessary to identify the digit (possibly, other character) to receiving hardware. **(3)** The simultaneous transmission of data over parallel lines or circuits.

paralleled Also, often, *duplicated; duplexed.* Backed up by another unit or facility with the same capability. A file would be said to be 'paralleled' if a backup copy is created and a peripheral controller would be 'paralleled' if a system contains a similar or identical unit that can be used in event of its failure. See *backup; standby; failure.*

parameter (Data processing) A value used in processing that controls how processing is performed or the results produced and which can be changed to affect processing or results. A parameter can be input by a programmer or operator, supplied by a compiler or operating system, or generated as an intermediate result during processing. It can be a numeric value for an arithmetic operation, an address, or the object-code version of a declaration. A **parameter word** is a 'declaration' in source coding by which a programmer makes his requirements known to a compiler or operating system. An **actual parameter** (also 'link') is an address in a main sequence of instructions to which control will be returned by a called routine when it has finished executing. A **default parameter** (also **default; default value**) is a value supplied by a compiler or operating system in absence of a specific input by a programmer or operator. A **formal parameter** (also 'dummy argument') is a source coding input that establishes the size and structure of a variable or indicates a value that will be supplied at run time or during execution. See *default; variable; program-generated parameter.*

parameter (Mathematics) An input to a calculation other than an argument; for example, the limits of an integration, the first or last value of a series, or a value that establishes the origin of a vector.

parameter (System and design) **(1)** That which is to be provided in a new system or design; for example, the printing speed to be provided by a new printer or the number of terminals to be catered for in a data network. **(2)** That which limits capability or performance of a system; for example, the amount of main storage of a computer.

parameter word A word that provides or identifies a value required in processing. See *parameter.*

parametric Concerning parameters.

parent (1) The previous generation (of a file). See *generation.* **(2)** An owner.

parentheses-free notation A method of forming mathematical expressions without the use of parentheses. See *prefix notation; postfix notation; Polish notation.*

parity A system of detecting errors in data transmissions and transfers that consists of selectively adding a 1-bit to bit patterns in order to cause the bit patterns to have either an odd number of 1-bits (**odd parity**) or an even number of 1-bits (**even parity**). Receiving hardware checks the number of 1-bits in each pattern and indicates an error condition if a pattern with an even number of 1-bits is found in an odd parity system or an odd number in an even parity system. The bit that is selectively added is a **check bit** which, in a parity system, is termed a **parity bit.** Typically, the unit to which the parity bit is selectively added is the bit pattern of a character in some code. If, for example, the code is a 7-level code, an additional bit position will be reserved for a parity bit and it thus becomes an 8-level code as transferred or transmitted. Parity may also be applied to a block or message and, in this case, the number of 1-bits is totalled for each bit position of all the characters of the message or block and a 1-bit is added, if necessary, at the end. The application of parity to a block or message is **block parity** (also **vertical parity; longitudinal parity**). (Where the term 'vertical parity' is used, parity as applied to individual characters is termed **horizontal parity**). (Many systems use both character and block parity; character parity is usually 'odd' and block parity 'even'. The following is an example of character and block parity applied to a 'message' consisting of just the word PARITY (in ASCII):

Character parity   *8 7 6 5 4 3 2 1   Bit Position*
P   **1 1 0 1 0 0 0 0**
A   **1 1 0 0 0 0 0 1**
R   **0 1 0 1 0 0 1 0**   *Message*
I   **0 1 0 0 1 0 0 1**   *characters*
T   **0 1 0 1 0 1 0 0**
Y   **1 1 0 1 1 0 0 1**
      1 0 0 0 0 1 1 1   *Block Check Character*

The final character of the 'message' consisting of the vertical parity bits (10000111, above) is the **block check character** (BCC). A parity system as described can detect all one-bit errors and most mutliple-bit errors. It cannot detect errors in a rectangular pattern, as can be demonstrated by reversing the circled bits in the following:

```
0 1 1 0 0 1 1 1
0 ① 1 0 0 ⓪ 1 0
1 1 1 0 1 1 1 1
0 ⓪ 1 0 1 ① 0 0
1 1 1 0 0 1 1 0
```

See *polynomial code; error; Hamming code; check digit; check sum.*

parity bit A 1-bit selectively added to a column or row of bits to make the total of 1-bits in the column or row either an odd number or an even number (depending upon the system). See *parity; check bit.*

parity check A redundancy check in a parity system; a test performed by receiving hardware to determine if received bit patterns have either an odd or even number of 1-bits (depending upon the parity system in use) and to initiate error recovery procedures when bit patterns do not conform. See *parity; redundancy check.*

parity error The condition in which a bit pattern with an even number of 1-bits is detected in a system that uses odd parity or one with an odd number of 1-bits is detected in a system that uses even parity. See *parity.*

parity sum In a parity system; the number of 1-bits in a bit pattern which determines whether the pattern has been corrupted. The bits are added by modulo-2; a total of '1' indicates an error in an even parity system and a total of '0' indicates an error in an odd parity system. See *parity.*

parity system A data transfer or transmission system in which parity checks are made on received data to determine whether or not corruption has occurred. See *parity.*

parsing A compiler operation of identifying the elements of instructions in terms of the programming language.

partial screen transmit A facility of a VDU terminal that permits the operator to transmit only a selected part of the contents of the screen (but more than one line).

partially inverted file See *inverted file.*

partially qualified name A name of a member in a hierarchial data structure that includes (or consists of) some of its owners but not all of them. See *fully qualified name.*

partition (1) A boundary within main storage maintained by an operating system to separate areas that are allocated for different purposes or to which different priorities or access rights apply. **(2)** An area of main storage between 'partitions' (def. 1). **(3)** To divide into parts; for example, to 'partition' a program into sections for overlaying or to 'partition' an area of storage.

party line A multidrop line that serves different telephone subscribers.

party line bus A term sometimes applied to the major internal transfer bus of an intelligent device.

PASCAL A highly structured programming language related to ALGOL.

pass (1) One processing cycle of a multi-cycle operation; ('a sort pass'; 'a compile pass'). **(2)** An iteration. See *loop.* **(3)** By a filter; to allow certain frequencies to go through without attenuating them.

passband A range of frequencies that goes through a bandpass filter without introduced attenuation.

passivated Of a semiconductor device; constructed with a sealing layer of glass.

passive element An element of an electronic device or circuit that is not capable of performing a switching, amplification, or current directional control function; in a semiconductor circuit or device, an element other than a transistor or diode. The most common are resistors and capacitors. See *element.*

passive graphics (1) Computer graphics in which display elements cannot be manipulated by an operator; the term is usually applied to computer output on microfilm, plotters, and monitor displays. See *interactive graphics.* **(2)** The operation of interactive graphics terminals in passive mode.

passive mode (1) A method of operating an interactive graphics system that permits a terminal operator to observe a display but not to change or manipulate it. **(2)** Also, sometimes, *listening mode.* Of a data station or communications equipment; not, at that time, capable of sending or receiving a message. The term may, for example, be applied to the condition of a data station when it is not receiving a polling message or responding to one.

passive station A data station that, at that time, is neither sending or receiving a message. See *passive mode*

password A group of characters (in a system table) associated with a unit of code or data, or a subset of system facilities, to which access restrictions apply. An application program or terminal operator must provide the operating system with an identical copy of the 'password' in order to be allowed access to an item to which access restrictions apply.

PAT *Peripheral Allocation Table.*

patch (1) A section of code inserted in a previously written sequence to make an alteration or correct an error. **(2)** To insert a section of code in a previously written sequence. **(3)** To modify a sequence of instructions by changing the object code rather than the source code. **(4)** To make a temporary electrical connection.

patch cord A length of wire with end connectors as used to make connections in a plugboard.

patch panel A plugboard.

path (1) That which carries data or signals between two locations. In a communications context, the term may be used in place of 'line', 'circuit', 'channel', or 'link' and in a data transfer context, in place of 'bus', 'circuit', 'highway', or 'cable'. **(2)** With respect to a program containing branches; one of the combinations of instructions of the main sequence and one or more branch sequences that can be followed during execution. See *branch; jump; path length*. **(3)** An access path; a sequence used to locate data with particular attributes in a data structure. See *net*. **(4)** In a data network or data communications system; a route between a sending and receiving location as defined by the nodes through which a message or packet must pass.

path length (1) A count or estimate of the number of machine instructions in a particular 'path' through a program. **(2)** The distance between sending and receiving points in a data transfer or communications system.

pattern (1) A physical arrangement of elements; ('a bit pattern'; 'a dot-matrix pattern'; 'a storage pattern'). **(2)** Repeating; with some degree of correspondence in successive trials or observations; ('a pattern of message traffic'; 'a pattern of hardware failures').

pattern matching The performance of logic operations to determine if two bit patterns are identical. See *identity*.

pattern recognition The machine identification of two-dimensional representations as, for example, in 'optical character recognition'.

pattern-sensitive fault A fault that becomes evident only when certain patterns of data are being accessed. See *program-sensitive fault*.

pause instruction A halt instruction.

pause-retry After an error; a retry after a short delay (during which the condition causing the error may disappear).

PAX *Private Automatic eXchange.*

PBX *Private Branch eXchange.*

PC (1) *Printed Circuit.* **(2)** *Program Counter.*

PCB *Printed Circuit Board.*

PCK *Processor Controlled Keying.*

PCM (1) *Pulse Code Modulation.* **(2)** *Plug Compatible Manufacturer.* **(3)** *Punched Card Machine.*

PCS (p.c.s.) *Plastic Coated Silicon.*

PCU *Peripheral Control Unit.*

PDC *Peripheral Device Controller.*

PDN *Public Data Network.*

PDP-11 A Digital Equipment Corp. minicomputer.

PDT *Physical Device Table.*

PDX *Private Digital eXchange.*

PE (1) *Phase Encoding.* **(2)** *Processing Element.* **(3)** *Parity Error.*

peak shift Bit shift; a movement of bits as read from the time frames in which they were recorded.

pel *Picture Element.* An addressable point; a basic element of a display image.

perforated With punched holes.

perforated tape Paper tape with punched data holes.

perforator A paper tape punch. (The term is used mainly with respect to communications-related equipment.) See *paper tape punch; reperforator.*

performance Speed and reliability. The term is used when discussing the capability of devices and systems, often in contexts in which the emphasis is on 'speed' with 'reliability' assumed; ('a high-performance printer').

peripheral Also *peripheral device; device*. In a computer system; a functional unit that makes and/or receives data transfers with initiation (and, possibly, other control) by the central processor. The term includes **storage devices** (magnetic tape units; magnetic disc units), **input devices** (punched card and paper tape readers), and **output devices** (printers; plotters; card and paper tape punches; microfilm recorders). The term is not normally applied to terminal devices (DDE systems; MAC terminals) or 'cartridge' mass storage. In its most common usage, the term denotes a magnetic disc unit, a magnetic tape unit, or a printer. See *backing storage; input device; output device.*

peripheral allocation table (PAT) A system table that holds the availability status of the peripheral devices of a computer system.

peripheral bound (1)Of a program; prevented from continuing to execute because a peripheral transfer is required. (2)Of a program; prevented from executing at normal or satisfactory speed because of limited availability of a peripheral.

peripheral control unit (PCU) A peripheral controller.

peripheral controller Also *peripheral control unit; input/output controller; device control unit*. A functional unit (or section of a functional unit) that handles transfers between main storage and peripheral devices. Typical functions include buffering, making circuit connections, bit-serial/bit-parallel conversion, error detection and resolution, performing seeks and searches for required items, reading headers to verify that required items have been located, and maintaining a record of the status of the various devices under its control. The actual functions performed depend upon the system; a system may have multiple peripheral controllers and they may be specialised according to the devices they control. They may also be in hierarchial order with a 'general' controller handling transfers to and from several 'device-specific' controllers. The device is assumed to be intelligent (usually with programs in read-only memory) and capable of making autonomous transfers whenever initiation and addresses are received from the central processor. A device that performs a range of transfer-related functions or that controls other controllers is often termed a **data channel** or **interface computer**. A section of a small or specialised computer that handles peripheral transfers is often termed an **input/output coupler**. See *interface computer; device control unit; front-end processor; input/output processor; data channel; channel program*.

peripheral device See *peripheral*.

peripheral device controller In some microprocessor systems; a programmable input/output chip.

peripheral equipment (1)Peripherals. (2)Any unit of a computer system other than the central processor.

peripheral interface (1)The programs and devices used to make peripheral transfers. (2)The conductor and connector pin arrangement used in making a cable connection to a peripheral. See *plug compatible*.

peripheral interface adapter (PIA) In common bus-organised microprocessor systems (and, perhaps, larger systems); a device (sometimes a single integrated circuit) that provides interface functions between the bus and peripherals. Typical functions include bit-serial/bit-parallel conversion, buffering, addressing, monitoring status, and generating interrupts. See *communications link adapter*.

peripheral interface channel A circuit on which peripheral transfers are made.

peripheral limited (1)Peripheral bound (def. 2). (2)Of processing in a particular computer system; limited in speed because of insufficient peripherals· or lack of peripherals of the required type. See *processor limited*.

peripheral manager A term sometimes applied to a set of utilities used to perform peripheral transfers.

peripheral operator In a large computer system; an operator who handles mounting and demounting of tape and disc volumes, replenishing supplies, and other functions relating to the peripherals.

peripheral prompt A message from an operating system to a console operator concerning the status of a peripheral or the need to load a volume.

peripheral storage Also, usually, *backing storage*. That part of the storage of a computer system accessible to the central processor via input/output channels; storage provided by peripheral devices. (The term 'backing storage' includes 'cartridge' mass storage while 'peripheral storage' does not.) See *storage; storage device; backing storage; secondary storage; filestore*.

peripheral transfer Also, usually, *data transfer*. A movement of a unit of code and/or data between main storage and a peripheral device or between peripheral devices. Unless otherwise indicated, the term denotes a movement between main storage and a printer or storage peripheral to meet the needs of an executing program. A **synchronous transfer** is a transfer in which instruction execution is suspended during the transfer; an **asynchronous transfer** is one that is performed concurrently (in parallel) with instruction execution. An asynchronous transfer may be an **autonomous transfer** performed by another intelligent device with initiation from the central processor. It may also be performed by 'cycle stealing' in which a data transfer utility has its instructions executed during short bursts of clock cycles 'stolen' from instruction execution. See *spooling; staging; fetch; peripheral; peripheral controller*.

peripheral unit A peripheral.

permanent error A hard error.

permanent file A term sometimes applied to a file other than a scratch file.

permanent storage (1)Non-erasable memory. (2)Non-volatile memory.

permeability The ease with which iron becomes magnetised. See *magnet*.

permutation (P) Of a set of items; a subset (smaller group) that has separate identification both because of the items included and their order. For example; 5-7-3 is one 'permutation' of the ten decimal digits and it is considered be diffrent than, say, 3-5-7 or 7-5-3. The formula for finding the numberof permutations of a given size in a particular set is:

$$nPr = n!/(n-r)!$$

The 'n' is the number of items in the set, 'r' is the number in the permutations, and '!' denotes 'factorial'. The expression for finding the number of 3-digit permuations in a 10-digit set is then:

$$10P3 = 10!/(10-3)!$$

It is solved by dividing factorial 10 by factorial 7:

$$10! = 10 \times 9 \times 8 \times 7 \times 6 \times 5 \times 4 \times 3 \times 2 \times 1 = 3,628,800$$
$$7! = 7 \times 6 \times 5 \times 4 \times 3 \times 2 \times 1 = 5,040$$

There are, then, 720 3-item permutations in a 10-item set. See *combination*.

personal code A number that is assigned (say, by a credit card company or bank) to uniquely identify one person.

personal computer An inexpensive microprocessor-based computer intended for the hobby or small-business market. It, typically, has a keyboard and screen (or TV adapter), up to 64K of random-access memory, and backing storage consisting of digital cassette (sometimes audio cassette) or flexible disc. Though they may be classifiable as 'microcomputers' the term is not often used by their manufacturers. See *microprocessor*.

personal terminal (1)A terminal intended for use by one (managerial) person. (2)A small and inexpensive terminal (usually a VDU).

personalise With respect to a unit of hardware or software; to adapt it to meet the needs of a particular user.

personality card (1)An element of automatic test equipment; a printed circuit board that holds the logic to test a particular device, component, or circuit during manufacture. (2) A printed circuit board that, when installed, gives a device a particular capability; for example, a board that changes a single port modem to multiport.

PERT *Project Evaluation and Review Technique.* A system of network analysis for scheduling and controlling large projects (often, engineering construction). It consists of identifying the events that must take place between initiation and completion, making a 'network diagram' showing their sequence of occurrence and interdependencies, and making an estimate of the time required for each. Central to the method is identifying the 'critical path' which is the sequence of events with the longest total time. This time is, thus, the shortest time in which the project can be completed and a delay in occurrence of any event on the path must result in delayed completion. Application packages are available to perform the analysis and to provide forecasts based upon different possibilities.

PET *Personal Electronic Transaction computer.* A personal computer produced by Commodore Business Machines.

petal printer A term often applied to a printer that uses a daisy wheel; speeds are up to about 45 characters per second. See *daisy wheel; word processing*.

PF (1)*Power Factor.* **(2)**(pf.) *PicoFarad*.

PH *PHase*.

phase (1)A particular time or sequence of events; ('a phase of execution'; 'the compilation phase'). **(2)**The time relationship between two waves of the same frequency. The two waves are assumed to be sine waves and since these are typically generated by coils rotating in magnetic fields, it is customary to express the relationship in degrees. If two waves go from positive to

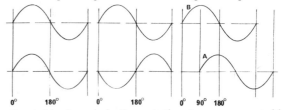

negative and back again in the same time (say, as generated by two synchronised alternators) they are said to be 'in phase' meaning that there is no angular difference between their generating coils. If the waves do not go through their cycles concurrently, they are said to be 'out of phase' and the amount they are 'out' is given in degrees. Since a cycle takes place in each 360° of coil rotation, the maximum amount that two waves can be out of phase is 180°; this relationship is shown in the centre figure. When waves are out of phase by less than 180°, one is said to 'lead' or 'lag' the other. In the right-hand figure, Wave B is shown leading Wave A by 90°; the relationship could also be expressed as 'Wave A lagging Wave B by 90°. In some communications systems, it is necessary to consider waves as lagging or leading by as much as 315°. See *alternating current; sine wave; phase shift modulation*. (3)A message pair; a message from a terminal operator to a computer and a reply from the computer.

phase angle The amount in degrees by which one wave lags or leads another. See *phase*.

phase distortion See *delay*.

phase encoding (PE) A common method of magnetic tape recording in which a flux reversal in one direction encodes a 0-bit and in the other direction a 1-bit. The reversal is made at the centre of the clock pulse and if a sequence of 1-bits or 0-bits is

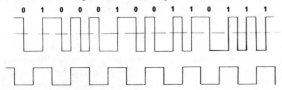

to be written, a flux reversal also occurs coincident with the transition of the clock signal. Receiving equipment ignores any transitions that coincide with clock transitions. Commonly, a positive to negative transition encodes a 0-bit and a negative to positive transition encodes a 1-bit. Phase encoding is used to record half-inch magnetic tape at 1600 (sometimes 800) characters per inch.

phase equalizer Also *delay equalizer*. A circuit in a modem transmitter or receiver that reduces or eliminates the effect of signal frequency distortion introduced in a line. See *equalizer; statistical equalizer*.

phase-locked A term applied to a device or operation that obtains its timing from input signals and which incorporates a feedback circuit to maintain synchronisation.

phase-locked oscillator An oscillator that receives its timing from input signals and which has circuitry to modify the phase of its output to maintain synchronisation with the input.

phase modulation encoding Phase encoding.

phase shift modulation Also *differential phase shift keying; phase encoding; phase modulation* and, in some forms, *quadrature amplitude modulation*. A method of modulation in which data is transmitted as different amounts of change of phase of a carrier wave. In a typical system, the output of an oscillator goes to two 'phase modulators'; it goes to the first one directly and to the second one through a delay line that introduces a 90° delay. The phase modulators output two waves, the wave as input or an analogue wave 180° out of phase. There are, then, four waves of different phases available to constitute the carrier

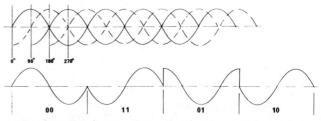

wave, these are the wave as output by the oscillator, a wave delayed by 90° as the 'straight-through' wave from the second phase modulator, a wave delayed by 180° as the analogue wave of the first modulator, and a wave delayed by 270° as the analogue wave of the second phase modulator. These waves are shown on a time scale in the upper part of the figure; the waves output from the first phase modulator are shown as solid lines and those of the second phase modulator as dotted lines. The system transmits data as 'dibits' which are two-bit combinations; the following four are possible: 00, 01, 11, and 10. While it would be possible to encode dibits by associating each with a wave of particular phase, synchronisation is simplified by using change of phase rather than actual phase. Typically, a dibit is transmitted about every 1.5 cycles (depending upon the frequency of the carrier wave and speed of transmission). The receiving equipment has registers that enable it to compare the phase of an incoming signal with that of the previous signal and to determine the phase difference and, thus, the dibit being received. In one encoding convention, a 01 dibit is transmitted by shifting phase by 90°, a 11 by shifting phase 180°, a 10 by shifting phase 270°, and a 00 by continuing to transmit an unchanged wave (making no shift). The lower part of the figure shows the phase shifts necessary to transmit the character 00110110 by this method. Phase shifts are shown as occurring every cycle instead of every cycle and a half. Because receiving hardware requires fairly continuous phase shifts to maintain synchronisation, there is some risk of losing synchronisation when long strings of 00 dibits are transmitted. For this reason, another encoding convention specifies a shift of 45° to transmit the 00 dibit. The modulation and demodulation described is usually performed by a modem. In some modems, the operations are performed with waves in digital representation with only the inputs and outputs in analogue form. The method described using dibits is typical for transmission at 4800 bps. For transmission at 7200 bps., the carrier wave is shifted in phase in 45° increments and the unit transmitted at one time (in one Baud) is three bits or a 'tribit'. For transmission at 9600 bps., two different amplitudes are used in conjunction with shifts in 45° increments to give sixteen data-significant combinations. In such a system, four bits (a 'quadbit') are transmitted each Baud.

phosphors The interior coating material of the screen of a cathode ray tube that emits visible light when an electron beam strikes it. They continue to emit light for a short time (a few milliseconds) after the beam passes and thus serve to maintain a visually continuous display. The commonly used phosphors are P4 (White; medium-short persistance), P31 (Green; medium-short), P39 (Yellow-green; long), and P42 (Yellow-green; medium). See *cathode ray tube*.

photo-digital memory A memory consisting of photographic film on which data is written by laser beam or focused light beam in the form of exposed dots (1-bits) and unexposed areas of dot size (0-bits). When the film is developed, it becomes a permanent read-only memory. It is read by scanning with a light beam and using a photosensitive diode to determine the bit positions in which the light passes through the film.

photochronic tube Also *dark trace tube*. A cathode ray tube with screen phosphors that darken (rather than luminesce) where they are contacted by the electron beam.

photodiode A light-sensitive semiconductor; a device with conductivity that depends upon the amount of light it receives.

photolithography The process of controlling an etching operation by means of selectively exposing a coated surface to light, the coating having the ability to protect the surface from the etching fluid in the areas where it has been exposed to light. The pattern to be etched on the surface is held in a 'mask' that is clear where the coating is to be exposed to light and opaque in

GLASS-EPOXY 'BOARD' WITH BONDED SHEET COPPER

WITH SPRAYED OR CENTRIFUGALLY APPLIED COATING OF PHOTO-RESIST

WITH MASK IN PLACE AFTER PHOTO-RESIST HAS DRIED

AFTER EXPOSURE TO LIGHT AND REMOVAL OF THE MASK

AFTER WASHING AWAY THE UNHARDENED (UNEXPOSED) PHOTO-RESIST

AFTER ACID OR POTASSIUM-CHLORIDE ETCHING FLUID HAS REMOVED COPPER EXCEPT WHERE PROTECTED BY PHOTO-RESIST

THE COMPLETED PCB AFTER REMOVAL OF THE PHOTO-RESIST

remaining areas. It is a basic operation of producing microelectronic devices and printed circuit boards. Following coating, masking, and exposure to light, the coating is dissolved away from the unexposed areas and the surface is then exposed to the etching fluid, usually by immersion. For printed circuit board production, the copper surface coating is selectively removed by the etching in order to leave a pattern of conductors. In producing microelectronic devices, the surface is usually glass that is selectively removed to permit ion implanting or metalisation of the silicon material on which the glass was formed. The construction of a microelectronic device involves multiple photolithographic steps. Current technology is capable of defining areas between 3 and 5 microns wide. See *mask; semiconductor*.

photoresist A light-sensitive coating used in photolithography in conjunction with a mask to define the etching pattern.

photosensitive (1) Of a device (usually a semiconductor); with electrical characteristics that depend upon the amount of light that it receives. See *photodiode; phototransistor; photovol-*

taic. (2)Of a coating substance (silver halide; photoresist); changing characteristics (opacity; solvent resistance) where exposed to light.

phototransistor A transistor with collector-emitter conduction controlled by the amount of light striking a gate area.

photovoltaic A term applied to a light sensitive device that produces a voltage dependant upon the amount of light received (rather than changing resistance, as a photodiode).

physical (1)Considered with respect to storage rather than use or content; ('a physical record'; 'a physical block'). (2)Real or hardware; not virtual; ('physical storage'; 'a physical address'). (3)A term sometimes used to distinguish a 'real' unit from its address, attributes, access method or the like; ('a physical device'; 'a physical track'). (The usage is often tautological.) See *logical.*

physical address (1)In a virtual storage system; an address other than a virtual address; a hardware address in either primary or secondary storage. (2)An address in secondary storage. (In this sense it contrasts with 'hardware address' which is an address in primary storage.) See *address.*

physical data Data considered as bit patterns or the content of storage locations.

physical device A device; a peripheral or, possibly, a terminal.

physical device address In a data network; an address of a particular device (terminal; computer) rather than the address of a data station. See *terminal address.*

physical file A file considered with respect to its organisation or storage (as contrasted to use or content).

physical order The order in which items are arranged or held in storage.

physical record (1)A record considered with respect to its storage location, its position in a data structure, or its method of access. See *record; logical record.* (2)A unit of storage that holds a record or is suitable to hold a record; for example, a fixed-length division of a block.

physical storage (1)Also, often, *real storage; actual storage.* In a virtual storage system; primary and secondary storage. (2)In a virtual storage system; secondary storage only. In this sense, it contrasts with primary storage which is usually termed 'real storage'. See *virtual storage system; virtual storage terms.*

PIA *Peripheral Interface Adapter.*

picking list A (computer-produced) list of the items required to fill a purchase order or group of purchase orders. It is used by warehouse staff to 'pick' the items from storage for shipment.

pico- (p) A combining form meaning 10^{-12}.

picofarad (pf.) A unit of capacitance equal to a trillionth of a farad.

picojoule (pj.) A measure of logic gate efficiency obtained by multiplying propagation delay in nanoseconds by power dissipation in milliwatts. See *speed-power product.*

picosecond A trillionth of a second; one thousandth of a nanosecod.

picture In a programming language; dummy characters used to indicate the properties of a character string. For example, in COBOL, PIC XXX would indicate three alphanumeric characters and PIC 9999, four decimal digits.

picture clause A (COBOL) statement containing a 'picture'.

piezoelectric The property of changing electrical characteristics when physical pressure is applied and/or of changing physical dimensions when an electric current is applied. Unless otherwise indicated, the term denotes 'piezovoltaic' rather than 'piezoresistive'.

piezoresistive With an electrical resistance that depends upon the physical pressure applied. This property of carbon is used in making some types of voltage regulators. See *piezoelectric; piezovoltaic.*

piezovoltaic Also, often, *piezoelectric.* The property of a crystal that produces an electrical pulse when pressure is applied along one axis and which elongates along that axis when an electrical pulse is applied from an external source. See *piezoresistive.*

pilot running In proving and testing a new system; running with inputs that are representative of the work that will actually be performed. A new payroll system might, for example, be 'pilot run' with the records of one department before being implemented throughout a company. See *parallel running.*

pin (1)In a multi-circuit electrical connector, a mating element that joins two conductors (and completes one circuit); ('with data output on Pin 16'). (2)A conductor of an integrated circuit

(or other device) by which it is connected to a printed circuit board or socket. (3)A 'tooth' on a sprocket or tractor as used to move paper through a line printer.

pin feed See *sprocket feed*.

pin-feed platen A platen roll that incorporates a 'pin-feed' sprocket at each end.

pinboard A (small) plugboard.

pinout (1) The relation between the internal circuits of an integrated circuit and its connecting pins; ('a similar device with a different pinout'). **(2)** A diagram or table showing the circuit functions of the various pins of an integrated circuit.

pinout diagram A diagram showing the internal elements of an integrated circuit and their connections to pins. The diagram

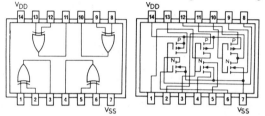

on the left is of a quad exclusive-OR gate and on the right is a dual CMOS inverter.

pinwheel A daisy wheel.

PIO (1) *Programmable Input/Output chip.* **(2)** *Parallel Input/Output.*

pipeline (1) In an instruction control unit; a sequence of registers with associated microcode and circuitry, each of which is capable of performing some phase of instruction execution and passing the instruction and partial results to the next register in the sequence. The first register might, typically, perform instruction decoding, the second operand fetches, the third would control arithmetic and logic operations (probably performed in registers in addition to those in the pipeline) and a fourth would store the results. In such a system, a register that has completed its operation with respect to one instruction immediately receives inputs for the next instruction so there would, usually, be four instructions in different stages of execution simultaneously. Pipelines with two to eight stages can be implemented on SISD computers; larger and more complex versions are possible on computers that use multiple instruction and/or data streams. **(2)** A sequence of processing units (not necessarily in the same computer), each of which performs some part of a processing task and outputs results that are used as inputs to the next processing unit. The process may be termed **stream computing** and a computer designed to perform it a **stream computer**. See *processing element; stream*.

pitch In a physical sequence (punched characters on paper tape; printed characters), the number per unit length; ('a pitch of 10 characters per inch').

pixel (1) A bit cell in a display memory. **(2)** A term sometimes applied to an addressable point in a graphics display.

pixel store Memory that holds the bit-pattern representation of a display in a graphics VDU.

PL/1 A programming language with a wide range of facilities intended to meet the needs of both business and scientific users.

PL/M A high-level language for programming microprocessors as developed by Intel; it is a PL/1 dialect.

PLA *Programmable Logic Array.*

PLAN *Programming LAnguage Nineteen hundred.* The assembly language of the ICL 1900 Series.

planar Of a semiconductor; with all active elements formed (by ion implant) in the substrate and/or in epitaxial layers (without removal of silicon as in 'mesa' devices).

plasma panel A gas plasma panel.

plastic coated silica (PCS) Monofilament glass with a plastic coating as used as the transmission medium in a fibre optics communications system. See *fibre optics*.

plated wire memory A memory system in which bits are held as the magnetisation direction of a magnetisable coating plated onto intersecting wires. Though the magnetisation patterns are somewhat more complex, it is essentially the same system as core memory. (At one time it appeared to offer some manufacturing advantages over high-speed core.)

platen A surface against which paper and ribbon are impacted by a character or character element in an impact printer.

platen anvil A print hammer. See *impact printer*.

platen roll In a typewriter and many impact character printers; a roll with a resilient surface that supports and feeds the paper during printing.

platter (1) A single magnetic disc. **(2)** A replaceable printed circuit board.

plex A net; a data structure that supports a variety of access paths. See *net*.

PLO *Phase-Locked Oscillator.*

plot To place graphic images on paper; in computer graphics, the function of a plotter.

plotter Also *graph plotter*. A computer-output device that places two-dimensional patterns (graphs; engineering drawings; maps) on paper. Unless otherwise indicated, the pattern is formed by a moving pen; other methods include xerographic and thermal printing of dots. See *computer graphics; graphics terminal; flatbed plotter; drum plotter*.

plotter step size The minimum distance between plottable points.

plotting head The display writer of a plotter.

plug Also, usually, *connector*. A separable, two-part device by which the conductors of two cables are joined or by which the conductors of a cable are joined to those of a functional unit.

plug-compatible A term applied to equipment of one manufacturer that can be operated with equipment of another manufacturer when joined by a cable and 'plug'.

plug compatible manufacturer (PCM) A manufacturer who produces plug-compatible equipment. Unless otherwise indicated, the term is understood to mean 'plug-compatible' with IBM equipment.

plugboard Also *patch panel*. An array of board-mounted plugs (electrical connectors) that are connected (behind the board) to different circuits (say, to different internal telephone circuits). In some units (PBX), plugs on flexible cords are used to complete connections to the various circuits. In other systems, **patch cords** with electrical connectors on both ends are used to complete circuits between plugs on the board.

PMOS *P-channel MOS*.

PNP A designation of a bipolar transistor in which the emitter and collector are of P-type silicon and the base is of N-type silicon. See *NPN; semiconductor; transistor*.

PO *Post Office*.

pocket In a card or document sorting device (say, one that sorts bank cheques); a receptacle to receive all items with a common sort attribute (for example, all the cheques for a particular bank or customer).

POF *Point Of Failure*.

point (1) A place or time in a sequence of events; ('a point during execution'; 'a breakpoint'). **(2)** A place; ('point of sale'; 'point-to-point communications'). **(3)** A position in a sequence; ('a division point'; 'a decimal point'). **(4)** To hold or produce the address of another storage location. See *pointer*.

point of failure (POF) A place in a program where execution is stopped because of an error. See *interrupt; restart*.

point of sale (POS) A place where a customer pays for (or charges) goods or services; for example, a cash register station in a store. The term is applied to terminals and other equipment used to read labels on goods and/or to receive operator inputs relating to transactions.

point-to-point An identifier of a data communications system in which two data stations are connected by a full-duplex circuit with constant carrier on both channels. See *constant carrier; multipoint; switched carrier*.

point-to-point connection A connection between two locations (usually understood to be by a four-wire leased line).

pointer An address of one storage location or register as held in another storage location or register. It is a value used to locate the next item to be accessed. See *access path; net*.

pointer array A table consisting of pointers.

pointer chain A sequence of pointers that establishes an access path. See *pointer; chain; access path*.

Poisson distribution A distribution in which the variance equals the average. In designing computer and communications systems, it is used to estimate maximum and minimum load conditions when the average load has been determined or estimated. For practical applications, the distribution is obtained from a plot which is reproduced below. This shows, for

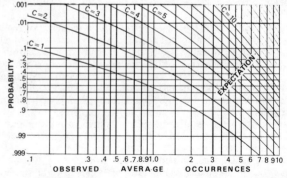

example, that if an average of 30 transactions are received per hour, that the probability of at least 13 being received in a particular hour is 90%.

POL *Procedure-Oriented Language*.

polar Concerning poles (either magnetic or electrical).

polar relay A relay incorporating a permanent magnet that senses the polarity of coil current and makes (or breaks) different contacts depending upon the polarity.

polar signalling Also, in some cases, *NRZ*. Signalling (as used in telegraph on non-telephone lines) in which a direct current signal of one polarity represents a 1-bit (mark) and a signal of the opposite polarity represents a 0-bit (space). When there is no zero-voltage line condition between pulses, the method is often termed 'NRZ'; when the line is at zero voltage in absence of signal, it may be termed 'polarised return-to-zero. See *NRZ; unipolar signalling*.

polar transmission Transmission of data by polar signalling.

polarised return-to-zero A three-condition signalling method in which positive and negative signals have data significance and in which the line condition returns to zero voltage between signals. See *NRZ; single-current signalling*.

polarity (1)Of direct current or a pulse; the condition of being either positive or negative. (2)The direction of magnetisation of particles; the condition of being either North or South. See *magnet*.

pole (1)One end of a magnet; either a North pole or a South pole. See *magnet*. (2)The pair of contacts of a relay that carries one circuit; ('a double-pole relay').

Polish notation Also *prefix notation; Lukasiewicz notation*. A method of facilitating the computer performance of mathematical operations in which the operators are placed in the order in which they will be dealt with rather than in the order they occur in conventional ('infix') notation. In Polish notation, the 'collected' operators are placed before the operands and in **reverse Polish notation** ('postfix notation') they are placed after the operands. Commonly, operands are held in one stack and operators in another during evaluation. An example is the expression $E = -2 \times (B + C)/D$ which a compiler would change to reverse Polish notation as $BCD2 +/\times -$. (There are variations in compilers.)

poll (1)By a master station in a data network; to send a short message to each data station to invite the station to send any messages it may have. See *polling*. (2)By a monitor program or other supervisory routine; to determine the status of each of a group of flags or indicators; for example, to determine which peripheral devices are in use at a particular time. (3)A polling message.

pollable A term sometimes applied to a terminal that has the circuitry and firmware to respond to polling messages.

polling (1)A method of operating a data network in which the central site DTE and modem (the master station) send short 'polling messages' to each remote site data station in rotation. The remote site modems and DTE's have the necessary circuitry and firmware to recognise their addresses and to respond to polling messages destined for them. When a polling message is received by a remote site DTE, it either returns a short acknowledging message (a 'negative poll response') or sends any data that may have become ready for transmission since the previous polling message was received. When a central site DTE has a message for a remote site, it sends it in place of the polling message for the site. Such systems are, typically, 'switched carrier' and use a four-wire telephone circuit (a leased line) that connects the central site modem to each of the remote site modems. (It often consists of a number of individually leased lines interconnected at telephone exchanges.) In such a system, the carrier is transmitted continuously from the central site modem via one channel (two wires or the multiplexed equivalent) to all remote sites. (RTS is constant high at the central site and DCD is constant high at the remote sites.) The channel to the remote sites is usually termed the 'down line'. The other channel (the 'up line') is used by the remote sites when transmitting to the central site. When a remote site DTE receives its polling message, it raises RTS causing its modem to send a 'training sequence' to the central site and this is followed immediately by a data message (if there is one) or a negative poll response. When discussing facilities rather than operation, a 'polling system' is usually termed a 'multipoint system' or a 'multidrop system' with 'multipoint' preferred when considering a data network and 'multidrop' when considering telephone lines and equipment. Most systems use **roll call polling** in which the remote sites are polled in 'round robin' rotation. In **hub polling** (also **hub go-ahead polling**), the central site DTE sends a polling message only to the first remote site at the beginning of each polling cycle. This site sends any message(s) it may have to the central site but if it has no message, it sends a polling message to the next remote site rather than sending a negative poll response to the central site. When this second remote site receives its polling message, it acts upon it in the same way and this continues from site-to-site until all remote sites have been polled; the final remote site sends a response to the central

polling characters The characters of a polling message that identify it as a polling message to the data stations that receive it.

polling cycle The sending of a polling message to each remote site of a network; a 'round' that begins with sending a polling message to one site and ends when the time arrives to poll that site again.

polling interval The time between transmitting successive polling messages to a particular data station.

polling list In a data network that uses polling; a list of the addresses of the data stations in the sequence in which they are to be polled.

polling message A short message (polling characters plus address and error detection characters) sent to a data station by a master station inviting it to send any messages it may have accumulated since it received the previous polling message.

polling ratio For a node; the number of polling cycles that intervene between successive polls; for example, a node with a polling ratio of 5 would only be polled once every five polling cycles. (The use of polling ratios permits inactive nodes to be polled less frequently than active nodes.)

polynomial code An error detection code in which a mathematical operation is performed on data at a sending location and duplicated at the receiving location where it is compared with a known 'correct' value in order to reveal any errors introduced in transmission. Typically, an arbitrarily selected constant (the **generating polynomial**) is divided into the (logically meaningless) total obtained by adding the bit patterns of the characters of a block or message as if they were binary numbers. The remainder is then transmitted as the **cyclic check character** at the end of the message or block. At the receiving location, the message or block is totalled (including the cyclic check character) and divided by the generating polynomial; if there is no remainder, the message or block is accepted as uncorrupted. For example, if the generating polynomial is 11011 and the 'data total' is 11010110110, the following operation is performed at the sending station:

```
                    10001010001   Dividend (Unused)
          11011 √ 110101101100000 Data total plus
                  11011                   five 0-bits
                  ─────
                   11101
                   11011
                   ─────
                    11010
                    11011
                    ─────
                     10000
                     11011
                     ─────
                      01011   Remainder (Cyclic
                                   Check Character)
```

At the receiving station, the cyclic check character is added to the data total:

```
       1101011011    Data total
            01011    Cyclic Check Character
       ──────────
       110101101101011  Block total
```

And the same division is performed:

```
                    10001010001   Dividend (Unused)
          11011 √ 110101101101011 Block total
                  11011
                  ─────
                   11101
                   11011
                   ─────
                    11010
                    11011
                    ─────
                     11011
                     11011
                     ─────
                     00000   Remainder
```

This 'zero' remainder indicates an uncorrupted message or block. If the data total obtained at the receiving station had been different from that obtained at the sending station, there would have been a remainder from the division and this would initiate error recovery procedures. Tests have shown that a polynomial code is several times more effective than a parity system in detecting errors and it has the advantage of much less redundancy as the only non-data bits required are those of the single cyclic check character. See *error; parity; Hamming code.*

POM *Print-Out Microfilm.*

pop To remove an item from the top of a push-down stack. See *push*; *stack*.

pore A storage cell in some amorphous memory devices. See *ovonic memory*.

port (1)An interface by which data enters and/or leaves a functional unit. It is, typically, a multiple pin electrical connector or a termination of a coaxial cable. (2)A functional unit (terminal) by which data can enter or leave a data network at a node.

port width The amount of data that can be transmitted simultaneously (in bit parallel) through a port of a functional unit.

portability The extent to which items can be used on or with different systems. The term may be applied to programming languages and different types of computers or to programs and different operating systems.

POS (1)*POSitive*. (2)*Point Of Sale*.

position seeking Logic seeking; the facility of a bidirectional printer that permits it to minimise the amount of head movement when changing from one line to the next.

positional notation Positional representation.

positional representation Of a numeric value; its expression by means of digits that have values that depend upon their locations with respect to other digits. See *numeration system*.

positional representation system A numeration system in which digits have positional values. See *numeration system*.

positional value Weight; the part of the value of a digit that depends upon its location with respect to the other digits of a number. See *number*.

positioning time (1)Seek time. (2)Seek time plus latency (def. 2).

positive (1)(+; pos.) Of a number; greater than zero; not a negative number. See *negative*. (2)(+; POS.) Of a battery, rectifier, direct-current device or circuit; a terminal or position towards which electrons flow from 'negative'. See *negative*; *anode*. (3)A term used in various contexts to indicate 'cause found', 'condition normal', 'something to report', or 'yes'. See *negative*.

positive acknowledge character The ACK character. See *ACK*.

positive acknowledgement In a binary synchronous communications system; a short message sent from a receiving station to a sending station to indicate that no error has been detected in a message or block. See *ACK*.

positive integer A natural number. See *number*.

positive poll response In a polling system; the action of a polled data station when it sends one or more messages to a master station following receipt of a polling message. See *polling*; *negative poll response*.

positive response A positive acknowledgement or a positive poll response.

post (1)In bookkeeping; to enter details of a transaction in a ledger. (2)A peg or pin used as an electrical connector (say, for connection by 'straps' on a printed circuit board). (3) A postal system. (3)To send by a postal system.

Post, Telephone, and Telegraph Authority (PTT) A term commonly applied to the government departments that provide the indicated services in many countries other than the U.S.; for example, the Bundespost in Germany or British Telecom.

postamble A sequence that comes after another. (1)In magnetic disc recording; an unused portion of a track at the end of a sector. See *guard zone*. (2)In magnetic tape recording; a group of synchronising characters recorded at the end of a block (for synchronising in reverse reading).

postfix notation Reverse Polish notation. See *Polish notation*.

postmortem (1)An analysis of an operation performed after its completion; an investigation made to determine 'what happened'. (2)A postmortem dump.

postmortem dump (1)A dump of a task's register and main storage locations (and an indication of the status of event flags and outstanding I/O requests) as made by a system utility when a task terminates abnormally. (2)A 'dump' (def. 1) as listed for debugging and analysis purposes.

postprocessor (1)A term sometimes applied to a program that performs some final stage of processing, for example, editing or outputting. (2)In emulation; a program that produces the form required by the host computer.

potential Voltage.

potentiometer Also *pot*. A variable resistor with resistance controlled by turning a shaft to position a sliding contact on a

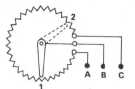

circular resistance element. In the figure, if the total resistance is 1000 ohms, then the resistance measured from A to B would be about 250 ohms with the contact in position 1 and about 900 ohms with it in position 2. See *resistor*.

power (1)The value of an exponent; the number of times a number is to be multiplied by itself in exponentiation. For example; 6^3 can be expressed as 6 to the 'power' of 3. See *exponent*. (2)Electricity use measured in watts. (3)A general term for electricity; ('connect power'; 'a power supply'). (4)With respect to a computer; an indication of processing speed. (5)A term used to indicate capability. See *powerful*.

power delay product Speed-power product.

power down (1)To make an orderly shutdown (as contrasted, possibly, to one under power fail conditions). (2)With respect to volatile semiconductor memory; the condition in which resistance is introduced to reduce power consumption to a minimum required to prevent loss of data during periods of inactivity. See *standby*.

power factor (PF) The ratio of the amount of electrical power productively used by a device to the amount supplied at its input terminals. It depends upon the phase relationship of the voltage and current. In resistive circuits (heaters; filament lights), they are in phase and the power factor is 1 (the maximum) while in inductive circuits (motors; transformers), the current lags the voltage and the power factor is lower (say, about 0.8). This effectively says that, in an inductive circuit, some of electric power is used unproductively to change the direction of magnetic flux.

power fail restart A facility of a computer or other device that can detect a power failure in progress and use available time (say, 50 milliseconds) to dump register contents to non-volatile (battery sustained) storage from which they can be retrieved for restart purposes.

power level The ratio of power (often signal strength) as measured at some point to an arbitrary level which is usually a watt or milliwatt. It is expressed in decibels with the reference indicated, for example; dBm indicates a measurement based upon a milliwatt and dBw indicates one based upon a watt. See *decibel*.

power supply A device that provides the direct current voltages required by the internal circuits of one or more functional units. Typically, it contains a transformer with a primary that connects to the mains supply and a secondary that is tapped for the different voltages required. The secondary voltages are then rectified and, usually, voltage regulated and filtered.

power transistor A transistor with a rated collector current in excess of about one ampere. Such a transistor contains a built-in heat sink and may be mounted with an additional heat sink. They are extensively used in power supplies and voltage regulators. See *transistor*.

power typing The preparation of letters or other documents by an electric typewriter with facilities for reading characters and format instructions from punched tape or some other recorded input medium.

power-up To apply electric power to a functional unit or the various units of a computer system and, possibly, to make pre-operating checks.

powerful A term used in various ways to indicate capability or versatility. For example, a computer with a 'powerful instruction set' can perform many different operations and a 'powerful macro' is one that expands to produce a sequence of many individual instructions.

POWU *Post Office Work Unit*. A unit for measuring computer performance devised by the U.K. Post Office.

PPS *Page Printing System*. See *page printer*.

PPSN *Public Packet Switching Network*.

PPSS *Public Packet Switched Service*.

pragmatics The relationship of characters or groups of characters to their interpretation and use.

preamble A sequence at the beginning. (1)A sequence of synchronising characters at the beginning of a block in a synchronous data transmission or at the beginning of a block on magnetic tape (when phase encoding is used). (2)In magnetic disc recording; an unused portion of a track at the beginning of a sector. See *guard zone*.

preamplifier A first stage of amplification, typically, to bring input signals into the range required by an automatic gain control circuit (say, in a modem).

preassembly An assembler operation of conditional assembly and macro generation.

precedence (1)The order in which items are processed or considered. (2)Also, often, *priority*. The order an item is to be dealt with; the position in which an item is placed in a queue.

precedence prosign A group of characters that indicates how a message is to be handled.

precedence rule The order in which a compiler places the operators of an arithmetic expression and, hence, the order in which operations are performed during execution. The usual order is: 1. Monadic plus and minus. 2. Exponentiation. 3. Multiplication and division. 4. Addition and subtraction. When an expression contains two or more operators at the same level (say, two additions or an addition and a subtraction), they are dealt with in the order they appear in the expression from left to right. Brackets may be used to change the order; a bracketed item is dealt with first.

precision The accuracy of a number as limited by the maximum number of digits that can be used to express the fractional part. The term **single precision** indicates that a numeric value is held in a single computer word and **multiple precision** that it is held in two or more words. Most computers provide for single precision and double precision; scientific computers and those with a short word length may provide for triple and quadruple precision. See *floating point*.

predefined Defined or fully identified elsewhere.

predefined process A routine or subroutine that is identified by name or label and which is located and documented elsewhere. The term usually denotes a separately compiled routine that is to be included in-line.

preemptible Also, usually, *swappable*. A term applied to a program (usually system software) that is normally resident in main storage but which can be deleted in certain circumstances. See *save area; locked down*.

preemptive A term applied to a program or job that interrupts regular (or lower priority) processing.

pre-erase In magnetisable surface recording; to use a second head to erase a track before data is written to it.

prefetch To move the contents of main storage locations to control-unit storage (slave; scratchpad) before they are required in execution.

prefix (1) A part that precedes; for example, the operators of an expression in Polish notation. **(2)** Digits dialed before those of a subscriber's number (usually to identify a dialing area).

prefix notation Polish notation.

preformatting An operation performed to place input data in the format required by (or most efficiently used by) the computer that will process it.

prepaging The roll-in, at one time, of all the pages that constitute the working set of a process at a particular stage of execution. It may be used when processing is initiated or to permit a reactivated process to continue execution from the point at which it was suspended. See *demand paging*.

preparation A term applied to an operation that must be performed before the main or succeeding operation. It is usually performed by a utility; for example, opening a file, zeroising a count, or resetting flags.

preprocessor (1) A program that performs some preliminary or organisational step of processing; for example, reformatting or validation. **(2)** A processor (a separate intelligent device) that performs some preliminary functions; for example, analogue to digital conversion and buffering.

preset (1) To establish an initial condition; for example, the number of iterations of a loop, or the bound value of a parameter. **(2)** A parameter that is provided prior to execution. **(3)** An input to a flip-flop that sets $\overline{Q}$ to 0 and Q to 1 independent of clock or other inputs. See *flip-flop; reset*.

preset parameter A parameter that is bound in the source code or during compilation.

prestaging Anticipatory staging. See *staging*.

Prestel The viewdata service of British Telecom.

prestore To write the code and/or data of a program to the (backing storage) locations from which it will be read during execution.

presumptive address An address as contained in an instruction; a symbolic, relative, or virtual address; an address that is to be modified during execution to produce an 'effective address'. See *effective address; address modification*.

presumptive instruction An instruction with operand(s) in presumptive-address form. See *presumptive address; effective instruction*.

preventative maintenance Maintenance performed for such purposes as cleaning, adjustment, and the detection of incipient faults. See *corrective maintenance*.

primary coil See *transformer*.

primary function (1) The main task of a system or functional unit that is capable of performing other (secondary) functions. **(2)** The function of a data station (a control station or master station) that exerts overall control over a data link according to the link protocol.

primary key The main (or only) value by which a record is identified for access purposes. See *key; secondary key; auxiliary key*.

primary key field A field in a record that holds its primary key.

primary paging device In a virtual storage system; a direct access device (usually, a large magnetic disc unit) that holds the pages/segments that are required for a particular run or for a particular type of processing. It is the device to and from which pages/segments are regularly moved during processing. See *virtual storage transfers*.

primary processor A control processor.

primary record (P-record) In an indexed file; a record for which there is an index entry; it, thus, constitutes an entry point for accessing complementary records. See *complementary record*.

primary station A master station or control station; a data station that performs the primary function.

primary storage Also, often, *main storage; real storage*. The main internal storage of a virtual storage system. See *secondary storage; storage; virtual storage system; virtual storage terms*.

primary track In magnetic disc systems; a track that, by number, would normally be allocated (during initialisation) for data recording. If it is found to be defective, it is so flagged and an 'alternate track' is substituted. See *initialise (Magnetic disc); alternate track*.

prime number A number that cannot be produced by multiplying integers (other than itself and 1). The largest number known to be 'prime' contains 6,533 digits. See *number*.

primitive file (1)A physical file. (2)A physical file as duplicated in different volumes; an original and all copies.

primitive instruction A microinstruction.

primitive operation (1)A basic step of data processing that consists of moving one or more bits between registers or within a register. It is the operation performed in executing a single microinstruction. See *register; microinstruction*. (2)Any central processor operation smaller than the execution of a complete instruction; for example, fetching an operand or performing an addition. (A single 'primitive operation' by this definition includes several or many primitive operations by definition 1.) See *execution; instruction*.

print (1)To convert data from representation by key strokes or electrical pulses to representation by characters on paper. In this sense, the term applies to an operation by a typewriter, terminal, or computer peripheral. See *printer*. (2)To make multiple copies of a single master image. In this sense, the term applies to an operation by a printing press, copier, or duplicator.

print anvil A hammer; the moving printing element of a backstrike printer.

print bar A type bar.

print barrel Also *barrel; drum; print drum*. The rotating element of a barrel printer that contains embossed characters on its surface; the element that ribbon and paper are struck against in printing. See *barrel printer*.

print control character A format effector (that controls a printing operation rather than a display).

print drum (1)A print barrel. (2)The rotating element of a xerographic or laser printer that receives the printing image.

print field (1)The part of a page that is printed. (2)The total area (rectangular measurement) that can be printed by a particular printer or that is to be printed using a particular format. (3)A part of a form (preprinted or programmed) that is used to hold a particular item or type of data.

print hammer See *hammer; impact printer*.

print head The element of a matrix printer that forms characters on paper. Though the term may be applied to such an element of a thermal matrix printer, it usually denotes a part of an impact matrix printer. The head moves along the line as

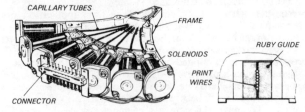

characters are being constructed. Typically, such a head has as many **print wires** (also **needles**) as there are dots on vertical lines of the characters. The wires are attached to solenoids that are selectively energised to extend the wires and, thus, to impact ribbon against paper.

print inhibit A feature of a word processor or terminal that permits data to be transmitted, displayed, or recorded without printing.

print magnet An electromagnet or solenoid that actuates the printing element in an impact printer.

print pel A print point.

print point A place on paper where a plotter can place a point (a 'dot' display element).

print wheel A daisy wheel.

print wire Also *needle*. A wire that is driven by a solenoid or electromagnet to impact ribbon against paper to print dots that form characters in an impact matrix printer. It is an element of a print head; there are, typically, as many magnets and print wires as there are vertical dot positions in the characters. See *print head*.

printable character A character for which there is an agreed representation by means of lines and/or dots; for example, a letter, number, or punctuation mark. See *character; unprintable character*.

printed circuit board Also *PC board; PCB; board; card.* **(1)** A thin 'board' (typically, of phenolic or glass-epoxy) to which sheet copper two to five thousandths of an inch thick has been bonded to one or both sides. **(2)** Such a board on which copper has been selectively removed by a photolithographic and etching process to leave a pattern of electrical conductors and

connection points. **(3)** Such a board on which electronic elements (integrated circuits; resistors; capacitors; diodes) have been mounted and soldered in place (through holes drilled or punched in the connection points) to form an electronic circuit or group of circuits. Such a board is, typically, replaceable and mounted in a 'card cage' with connections to external circuits being made by **edge connectors** that are etched along one side of the board. In modern computers and other electronic functional units, all electronics circuits are, typically, contained in printed circuit boards. See *photolithography*.

printer A device that inputs data in the form of keystrokes and/or electrical pulses and outputs it as characters on paper. The term does not normally include an ordinary typewriter but does include similar devices (Teletype; console typewriter) that are used by an operator to enter data as well as to receive it. An **impact printer** is one that prints by striking character-forming elements against ribbon to transfer ink or pigment from the ribbon to paper. The printer may be either a **matrix printer** or a **shaped-character printer**; unless otherwise indicated, 'shaped character' is understood. A shaped-character printer may be either **front strike** in which embossed type is impacted against ribbon to print or **back strike** in which a hammer impacts paper and ribbon against embossed characters. Common front-strike printers include Teletype and daisy wheel. Most high-speed impact printers are back-strike; these include **barrel printers** in which the embossed characters are on a rotating drum, **train printers** and **chain printers** in which the embossed characters are on 'slugs' that are driven along the line as it is printed, and **band printers** which are similar to train and chain printers except that the type characters are embossed on a continuous steel band. Back-strike impact printers are, typically, **line printers** meaning that they construct an entire line of characters by selectively impacting paper and ribbon against the embossed type characters as they pass the various printing positions along the line. By contrast, a **character printer** (typewriter; Teletype) prints characters in sequence along the line, usually starting each line at the left margin. (A 'bidirectional' printer prints lines from right to left as well as from left to right.) A **matrix printer** may be either a front-strike impact printer that impacts the ends of wires against ribbon and paper to form dot-matrix characters, or a **non-impact printer** that prints by heated styli, xerography, ink jet, or other means. Small matrix printers are universally character printers. A **page printer** is a printer that can form and print an entire page in one continuous operation; it is, typically, a matrix printer that prints by xerography or other non-impact method. Printers are commonly used as terminals (or incorporated in terminals) for both remote and local communications with a computer, and as computer peripherals. Those that are in terminal applications are usually character printers and printers as peripherals are usually line printers, except in very small systems. Those in terminal applications often incorporate keyboards and are used to send messages as well as to receive them. The electrical pulses that constitute the non-keyboard inputs to a printer are bit-pattern representations of characters in some code. Because printing is a relatively slow operation, printers associated with computers (either as peripherals or terminals) require 'buffers' to receive the bit patterns and hold them as they are interpreted and the corresponding characters printed. See *belt printer; barrel printer; band printer; chain printer; electrosensitive matrix printer; electrostatic printer; electrothermal printer; helix printer; impact printer; ink jet printer; laser printer; magnetic printer; matrix printer; page printer; petal printer; rotating belt printer.*

printing element That part of a printer that forms printed characters; for example, a typebar, a golfball, a print hammer, an electrode, or a stylus.

printing position A place along a horizontal line where a character can be printed; one of the positions that can be printed in a line of text. The line length of a printer is the number of printing positions in its longest possible line.

printout Data in character form as produced by a printer; unless otherwise indicated, it is on continuous stationery and produced by a line printer. See *hard copy.*

printout microfilm (POM) Microfilm in which each frame is recorded with the data that would otherwise occupy one page of continuous stationary as printed by a line printer.

prioritized Arranged according to priority.

priority (1) An assigned rank or value that indicates when a particular item (task; message; interrupt) is to be dealt with in relation to other items awaiting attention or the allocation of a resource. An item that takes precedence over most or all other items is termed **high priority** and one that takes precedence after most or all of the other items is termed **low priority**. See *foreground; background*. **(2)** High priority; ('interrupted by a priority job').

priority indicator A character or group sometimes used in the heading of a message to indicate priority and, hence, the order in which it is to be transmitted.

priority interrupt An interrupt that takes precedence over other interrupts and indicates its priority number so that the system can give it attention in relation to other interrupts.

priority scheduler A job scheduler that initiates execution according to job priorities.

privacy code An algorithm for transforming data from a standard alphabetic or numeric form to another form from which the original can only be recovered by reapplying the algorithm. See *encryption.*

privacy transformation The operation of placing data in a privacy code.

private automatic branch exchange (PABX) A private automatic exchange that provides for routing calls between internal telephones and the public telephone network as well as for routing internal calls.

private automatic exchange (PAX) A private (company) telephone exchange that automatically routes dialed calls between internal lines but does not connect internal lines with outside lines.

private branch exchange (PBX) A telephone exchange (on a subscriber's premises) with facilities to permit an operator to route internal calls and to connect internal and external lines.

privilege An indication of the access rights of a user or user program to the data of a computer system. If given a numeric value, it may be termed an 'access control level'.

privileged Of a program or routine; having access rights or a claim to resources not granted to other programs or routines. (The term usually applies to system software.)

privileged instruction An instruction that implements some system function and can occur only in a supervisory routine.

problem Also, often, *application*. A 'real-world' situation for which data is processed by a computer or for which such processing is being considered. The term may be applied to anything from an accounting system to counting bottles on a production line. See *application.*

problem description That part of a feasibility study that defines the problem that is to be solved or function to be implemented.

problem-oriented language A programming language designed for writing programs to perform some particular type of calculation or analysis. See *language.*

problem program An application program.

problem programmer An application programmer.

procedural language A procedure-oriented language.

procedural stack See *stack.*

procedure (1) The steps by which something is accomplished; ('a programming procedure'; 'a maintenance procedure'). **(2)** A short sequence of system instructions that is available to be called by (or incorporated in) a user sequence to perform some standard operation; for example, returning a root or copying a file. With respect to sequences nonteined n e library, the terms 'procedure' and 'subroutine' are often used interchangeably. **(3)** A short subprogram; a user-written sequence that is called by label where required; for example, to perform a validation or check a flag. (4)In some systems; a term applied to any executable sequence of instructions. See *function*.

procedure call An external call.

procedure call mechanism A call routine.

procedure division A division of a COBOL program that contains the statements required to input, process, and output data.

procedure library In some systems; a direct-access library of job definitions.

procedure name In COBOL, a label within a particular module; either a paragraph name or a section name.

procedure-oriented language A programming language designed to help a programmer to express a procedure (for performing an operation or solving a problem) in a concise sequence of instructions. Such languages include facilities that are useful for a variety of applications and are, commonly, oriented to either business or scientific use. Examples include COBOL, FORTRAN, ALGOL, PASCAL, and PL/1. See *language; problem-oriented language*.

process (Operation) (1)To execute an application program or a related group of application programs; ('process a payroll'; 'process an enquiry'). (2)To execute instructions; ('process until an interrupt'; 'continue processing from a breakpoint').

process (Processing unit) (1)Also, in some systems, *activity*. In a virtual storage system; an application program in process of execution; a program with at least some pages/segments in primary storage. See *virtual storage system—processing units*. (2)Any executable sequence of instructions.

process (Industrial) A set of facilities and methods used to produce a product.

process control The use of monitoring and measuring equipment and, possibly, a computer to regulate a manufacturing or processing (food; chemical) operation.

process descriptor In some systems; an entry in a system table holding details of a process (status; address space; exception conditions).

process image (1)The code and data available to a process in a virtual storage system; all of the non-hardware resources of a virtual machine. See *process; virtual storage terms; virtual machine*. (2)A storage image.

process number A number assigned to a process by an operating system.

process state The activity condition of a process: 1. Active—With instructions being executed. 2. Ready—Capable of being executed when resources are allocated. 3. Suspended—Prevented from being executed.

processible Capable of being processed (by a computer).

processing The operation of executing user programs with appropriate data. See *execution; data processing*.

processing mode Of a file; the type of processing in which it is to be used (input; output; update).

processing operation A computer operation in which an instruction in a user program is executed. It is a step in which an arithmetic or logic operation is performed and/or in which a storage transfer is made.

processing resource That which must be made available to a program in order for its instructions to be executed. The usual ones are main storage space, central processor time, and peripherals for data transfers.

processing speed The number of instructions executed per second by a central processor. See *data rate; MIPS; KIPS*.

processing system A computer system.

processing time (1)Also *computer time; machine time*. The time when a program or job is active; the elapsed time between loading the producton of final results. (2)Also *processor time; mill time*. The total time spent by the central processor in executing the instructions of a program or job.

processing unit (1)Also, often, *load unit*. An instruction sequence to which computer resources are allocated. (2)A central processor.

processor (1)An intelligent element of a computer or functional unit; storage, stored values, and circuits that can interpret and executing instructions. (2)A central processor; the primary (or only) intelligence of a computer.

processor bound (1)Of a program; prevented from executing at a particular time because of lack of availability of the central processor. (2)Of a computer system; unable to provide a satisfactory throughput because of limitations of the central processor.

processor-controlled keying The operation of a direct data entry system in which a central processor (or a self-contained microprocessor) provides prompts and performs validation and formatting functions to assist a keyboard operator.

processor storage Also , usually, *internal storage*. Storage within the central processor; it, typically, includes main storage and any cache, slave, or scratchpad storage of the control or arithmetic logic units. See *storage; internal storage.*

processor subsystem Any of the integrated, separately identifiable elements of a central processor; for example, a control unit or arithmetic logic unit.

processor time Also *processing time.* The time spent by a central processor in executing the instructions of a program or job. The term 'processing time' is used when considering a program or system utilisation and 'processor time' for accounting and charging purposes.

product (1) The result of a multiplication; in '3 × 5 = 15' the '15' is the 'product'. **(2)** That which is produced or manufactured.

product code (1) An identifier of a product as used, for example, on an invoice, stock control record, or discount schedule. **(2)** An identifier (say, a bar code or on a magnetic stripe) by which a product is identified at a point-of-sale terminal. See *Universal Product Code; bar code; point-of-sale.*

production (1) By a computer; the processing of user data to produce usable results (as contrasted to testing, program development, etc.). **(2)** The manufacturing or processing operation; the creation of goods for sale.

production control Process control; particularly as applied to an assembly-line manufacturing operation.

production run A run in which a program operates with real data to produce usable results (as contrasted, possibly, to a test or debugging run).

profile A term sometimes used when discussing the characteristics that distinguish different entities or systems.

program (1) One or more sequences of related instructions that, when executed by a computer, perform some function or operation. Examples of the function or operation include mathematical computation, searching and sorting lists of items, comparing items according to certain criteria, encoding and decoding, moving encoded forms of words and numbers in computer storage, and outputting results that are to be printed or displayed. In this broadest sense, the term includes **application programs** (also **user programs**) that perform work for users (for example, preparing a payroll), **system programs** that are part of a computer's facilities and **sequence control programs** used in a device (printer; washing machine; machine tool) control. Application and system programs are written by programmers and converted to computer form with the aid of special programs termed 'compilers' or 'generators'. Programs of the foregoing types are, collectively, **software**. They are, typically, recorded on magnetic disc or tape and are movable within a computer system as required. Sequence control programs are usually in read-only memory and are often encoded in integrated circuits during their manufacture; such programs are known as **firmware**. Unless otherwise indicated, the term 'program' denotes a software program rather than a firmware program and, within software programs, it denotes an application program rather than a system program. An application program as written by a programmer in a programming language (COBOL; BASIC) is a **source program**; this term may be applied to a handwritten version (on a coding sheet), to an intermediate form (punched cards) or to the bit-pattern representation of the characters as entered in computer storage (magnetic tape). This bit-pattern form is the input to a compiler which makes a translation into the particular form and code required by the computer. This consists of a number of executable instructions and is termed an **object program**; it is this version that tells the computer exactly what is to be done during execution. A system program is an object program that is supplied with the computer (or purchased separately) to perform some repetitive or frequently required operation. Collectively, system programs are known as **system software**. A **supervisory program** is a system program that performs some essential function relating to executing application programs or to managing the computer system; examples of functions include transferring programs and data within the system, locating required files and records, communicating with the operator, and checking for errors and abnormal conditions. Collectively, supervisory programs are termed **supervisory software** and the supervisory software for a particular computer is its **operating system**. A **microprogram** can be considered as an extension of system software; it is a sequence of highly detailed 'microinstructions' that control the electronic operations of executing a program instruction. A number of different supervisory programs are separately named, for example, a **utility program** performs some (small) operation that is frequently required during processing, a **monitor program** checks for errors and abnormal conditions, and a **control program** handles some scheduling or storage management function. A **library program** is a program of any type held on a library volume (usually magnetic tape) for incorporation in other programs. There is no clear distinction between a program and a 'routine', though the term 'routine' would not be applied to a complete, user-written sequence. The term 'supervisory program' is, then, synonymous with 'supervisory routine'. See *instruction; execution; software; language; call; coding; subprogram; routine.* (2)By a programmer; to write a program or group of programs; ('program an inventory control system'). (3)To provide all the programs required to perform some operation or group of operations; ('program a computer'). (4)With respect to an (integrated circuit) read-only memory; to write (permanent) bit patterns to it. See *PROM.*

program address counter (PAC) A current address register, particularly in a microprocessor system.

program attention A key or combination (often CTRL C) that a terminal operator can press to invoke the command line interpreter (to log on or log off).

program block A major division of a program written in a block-structured language. See *block.*

program chain A number of programs that are arranged to be executed in sequence without operator intervention. The linking may be done by a supervisor or by job control cards input with the program cards.

program check An interrupt caused by a (user) program error. See *machine check.*

program controller A controller (device or process control) that operates under supervision of a stored program.

program counter (PC) A current address register.

program design The process of determining and specifying the function and structure of a program.

program development (1)The process of producing computer programs for some application. By this definition, the term includes all steps from initial design to live running. (2)The programmer activity involved in writing, compiling, debugging, and testing programs.

program development time Computer time used in compiling, testing, and debugging programs.

program-driven Of a functional unit; intelligent; operating under the control of a stored program.

program error A defect in a (user written) instruction sequence that prevents correct compilation, linking, or execution. See *error; software error.*

program exception error A program error that causes an interrupt during execution; for example, truncation of significant digits or a bound violation.

program fetch The operation of locating an instruction sequence in backing storage that is to constitute a load module or be included in a load module. See *load module.*

program flowchart A flowchart used to design or document a program (as contrasted, possibly, to a system or clerical flowchart). See *flowchart.*

program function key (1)A key that invokes a utility; for example, to perform scrolling or page turning or to display the contents of a print queue. (2)A soft key; a key that can be user programmed; for example, to set terminal operating conditions or to insert a repetitive line of data.

program-generated parameter Also *dynamic parameter.* A parameter that is bound during execution; for example, a mathematical result that is produced by one sequence of instructions and passed to another sequence.

program generator A program used in the construction of other programs (as contrasted, possibly, to a macro generator).

program instruction An instruction in a user program (as contrasted, perhaps, to one in a job control sequence).

program interrupt Also *program check.* An interrupt caused by a program error. See *interrupt; error.*

program language (1)The programming language in which a program is written. (2)A programming language.

program library A source library; a library that contains the source-language versions of the application programs of a computer system. See *library.*

program maintenance The programmer activity of correcting program errors and revising programs to meet changing needs.

program management A term sometimes applied to operating system functions relating to fetching and deleting programs and allocating main storage space to them. It may also include recording resource utilisation for accounting purposes.

program name A character group that uniquely identifies a particular program within a computer system.

program origin The lowest numbered location in the main storage space allocated to a particular program.

program parameter An external program parameter; a parameter bound at run time.

program request (1)A message from a terminal operator identifying the application program required for operator-program interchanges. (2)Program attention.

program segment (1) A logical division of a program. (2) An overlay segment. (3) In a virtual storage system; a segment containing code rather than data.

program-sensitive fault A fault that occurs only when certain types or sequences of instructions are being executed. See *pattern-sensitive fault*.

program specification The product of program design; a description (function; structure; validation procedures) of a required program as produced, usually, by a systems analyst.

program status word (PSW) In a multiprogramming system; a word used by the operating system to hold the execution status (executing; ready) of a program and, for a waiting program, an identifier of the resource required and the address of the next instruction to be executed.

program suite A term sometimes applied to a group of related programs; for example, those of a particular application package.

program support The assistance a computer manufacturer (or software supplier) provides to users with respect to correcting, modifying, and updating proprietary software.

program support representative (PSR) An employee of a computer manufacturer who provides program support functions to users in the field.

program swapping Roll-in/roll-out; the movement of programs to and from main storage to meet processing requirements of different priorities.

program switching Interleaving; the process of changing execution between different concurrent programs in a multiprogramming system.

program tape Magnetic (or, possibly, paper) tape used to hold the object code of one or more programs.

program testing The process of running a new or changed program (usually, with test data) to ensure that it performs correctly and is free of errors.

program unit A main program or a subprogram.

program validation Program testing.

programmable (1) Also, sometimes, *intelligent*. With a function that can be established or changed by means of a program; ('a programmable terminal'; 'a programmable machine tool'). (2) Of a memory unit or type of memory; using storage cells of a type that permit bit patterns to be set and/or changed to meet different user requirements; ('programmable read-only memory').

programmable input/output chip (PIO) In a microprocessor system; a chip that provides tri-state bit-parallel interfacing between the data bus of the microprocessor and multiple input/output ports.

programmable logic array (PLA) A read-only memory that has been programmed to perform logic operations. The elementary device shown is programmed to perform the AND, OR, and NAND operations on Inputs A and B. See *read-only memory*.

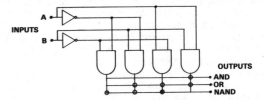

programmable read-only memory (PROM) Read-only memory in which bit patterns can be written by users. The term includes **FAMOS** in which bits can be erased by ultraviolet light to permit reprogramming, and **fuse PROM** in which bits are written permanently. The basic elements are an AND address (select) matrix and programmable OR matrix. In fuse PROM, each intersection of the OR matrix has a diode or link connection which, effectively, writes 1-bits in all positions. The matrix lines are brought out on pins that can be selectively connected to high voltage (in a 'PROM burner') to write 0-bits where required. PROM's are used in prototyping and in short-run production. For a given amount of data, they are larger and more expensive than ROM's which are mask programmed during manufacture. See *read-only memory; electrically alterable read-only memory; FAMOS; MNOS*.

programmed (1) Of a computer or functional unit; with programs to accomplish a particular function or range of functions; ('programmed for inventory control'; 'programmed for milling key slots'). (2) Of read-only memory and logic devices; with bit patterns or logic functions established.

programmer A person with necessary skills who is employed to write, test, modify, document (and, possibly, design) programs (in a particular programming language); ('a FORTRAN programmer'). The term includes a person who writes and tests system software but, unless otherwise indicated, it is understood to mean a person who works with application programs and is synonymous with **application programmer** (also **problem programmer**). See *system programmer*.

programming The activity of writing (and, possibly, designing) computer programs.

programming instruction A program instruction.

programming language An artifical language suitable for writing computer programs. See *language*.

PROM *Programmable Read-Only Memory.*

PROM burner A device used to program PROM's by selectively burning out (fusing) diodes or transistor elements to write 0-bits. See *programmable read-only memory*.

prompt (1) A message (of any type) from an operating system to a computer operator as printed on a console typewriter or displayed on a console VDU. **(2)** A message from an application program to a terminal operator that provides assistance in making an entry; for example, a message that causes the display of the characters CUSTOMER NAME adjacent to the location where the name is to be entered. See *menu operation*.

propagated error An error in one operation that causes errors in one or more other operations (that use the output of the first operation as input). See *inherited error*.

propagation The process of carrying signals between separated locations by such means as electrical conduction, light, or radio.

propagation delay With respect to a semiconductor gate; the time that elapses between a change in the logic level of an input and a resultant change in the output. The delay depends upon channel length, interchannel capacitance, and whether the semiconductor path is N-type silicon or slower P-type. Usually a low delay is obtained at the price of a high operating current. The following are representative values:

ECL	1 - 5 ns.
TTL	3 - 10 ns.
I^2L	10 - 20 ns.
NMOS	20 - 30 ns.
CMOS	25 - 40 ns.
DTL	25 - 40 ns.
PMOS	40 - 60 ns.
EPROM	50 - 200 ns.

See *access time; speed-power product*.

propagation speed The speed at which signals or energy move between two points; the following are some typical values in miles per second:

Light	180,000
Radio	100,000
Direct wire	14,000
Coaxial cable	8,000

proper subset A subset (selected group of items) that does not contain all the items of the original set.

proprietary A term applied to an item that is produced and sold by a particular company, often under patent, copyright, or trademark protection.

protect mode The mode of operation of a display terminal in which it contains one or more protected fields.

protected (1) Of computer storage; with safeguards to prevent unauthorised access. See *storage protection*. **(2)** Of a storage area or direct access volume; with facilities to prevent data from being accidentally overwritten or erased. See *save area; file protect*. **(3)** Of an area of a display; prevented from having contained data erased or changed by an operator. See *protected field*.

protected field On a display device; an area of the display field in which messages from an application program can be displayed but which cannot be changed or overwritten by operator keying. Such an area is, typically, used to display instructions, prompts, and error messages.

protected location A storage location used to hold data to which access restrictions apply or a storage location that is protected from accidental overwriting or erasure. See *save area; file protect; storage protection*.

protection domain An area of protected code or data belonging to a particular program. See *storage protection*.

protection key A key used in lock and key storage protection. See *storage protection*.

protection ring (1) In some storage protection systems; a conceptual ring used to identify (and illustrate) access rights. The rings are concentric and those towards the centre have low numbers and identify broad access rights of supervisory software. The higher-numbered rings identify progressively lower access rights and the outer (highest-numbered) ring identifies the rights of a user program that is restricted to its own code and data. See *storage protection*. **(2)** A write-enable ring.

protocol (1) A set of rules for performing data interchanges between independent devices. See *link protocol*. (2)Characters added to data to implement a 'protocol' (def. 1); ('enclose a packet in protocol'; 'strip protocol from incoming data').

PSE *Packet Switching Exchange.*

pseudo address In a (message switching) communications system; an intermediate address by which an addressee may be known for routing purposes.

pseudo code Instructions in a form that must be translated before execution. (A term once applied to 'code' in a programming language.)

pseudo cursor On some display devices; a symbol that can be used to simulate a cursor (for test purposes).

pseudo device An identifier of a non-existent peripheral as used to simulate an actual peripheral for some purpose (testing; program development).

pseudo instruction (1)An instruction in a programming language (rather than in executable code). See *psuedo code*. (2)A term sometimes applied to any instruction that does not result in executable code.

pseudo off-line storage A term applied to storage that would normally be considered as off-line (magnetic card; photodigital) in a system with facilities for moving data from it to on-line (direct access) storage under program control. See *staging*.

pseudo off-lining Staging.

pseudo page fault A page fault occurring in one process that immediately transfers control to the next process ready to execute (thereby eliminating lost processing time while the required page is rolled in).

pseudo random numbers Numbers (produced by a randomising algorithm) that are sufficiently random for some purpose even though some pattern may exist. See *random numbers; randomising algorithm*.

pseudo sectoring In magnetic disc access; to subdivide sectors by timing pulses between sector marks; a facility to permit accessing locations smaller than sectors. See *sectoring*.

PSN (1)*Public Switched Network.* (2)*Packet Switching Network.*

PSR *Program Support Representative.*

PSS *Packet Switching System.*

PSTN *Public Switched Telephone Network.*

PSU *Power Supply Unit.*

PSW *Program Status Word.*

PTP *Paper Tape Punch.*

PTR *Paper Tape Reader.*

PTT *Post, Telephone, and Telegraph authority.*

public (1)Available to subscribers on a non-exclusive basis; ('a public telephone system'). (2)With respect to a page, segment, or other unit of code or data; available to any program/process that requires it; not subject to access restrictions. See *local; global; common*.

public data network (PDN) A data network provided by a common carrier or PTT.

public packet switched service (PPSS) (1)The service of a public packet switching network. (2)A public packet switching network.

public packet switching network (PPSN) A packet switching system operated by a common carrier or PTT and available to subscribing users; for example, the Spanish RETD system or the French TRANSPAC system. See *packet switching*.

public switched network (PSN) A communications system that connects circuits between subscribers. The term includes public telephone systems and other systems such as Telex.

public switched telephone network (PSTN) The facilities of a telephone system involved in providing dialed or operator-routed connections between subscribers.

pull-down resistor A resistor used to lower voltage at some point in a circuit.

pull-up resistor A resistor used to raise the voltage at some point in a circuit.

pulldown In microfilm recording; the amount of film advanced between exposures.

pulse A short-period presence of voltage (a positive or negative 'pulse'), or a voltage polarity change, as used for timing or control or to represent data. See *clock pulse; signal*.

pulse amplitude modulation (PAM) A method of modulation and multiplexing in which a wave (say, as produced by speech on a telephone line) is sampled at short intervals (say, every few microseconds) and a pulse transmitted with the amplitude of the wave when sampled. At the receiving end, circuitry amplifies and joins the pulses to reconstruct the original wave. During the time when a particular transmission (say, from a local telephone line) is not being sampled, other transmissions can be sampled in the same way, thus permitting a single circuit to carry multiple, multiplexed transmissions. See *pulse code modulation; time division multiplexing*.

pulse code modulation (PCM) A method of modulation (and

multiplexing) in which an analogue wave (representing speech or data) is transmitted by means of digital bit patterns, each of which represents (encodes) the amplitude of the wave at a particular sampling point in time. It is identical to pulse amplitude modulation except that a particular amplitude level is represented by a bit-pattern 'character' rather than by a single pulse in order to reduce the effects of any distortion that may arise during transmission. In one system, a 7-bit code is used in which each character represents one of 128 different amplitude levels. In a multiplexing system, an electronic scanner takes and

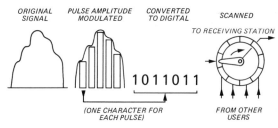

transmits one character in turn from each source (local telephone line; data terminal). At the receiving end, the characters representing each transmitted wave are separated from the others by a scanner that is synchronised with the scanner at the sending station. A signal of the amplitude represented by each character is then generated and used to form a 'quantised' wave that is, for practical purposes, identical to the original. The method is used by telephone systems to permit existing circuits to carry a greatly increased traffic; in a common implementation, a single four-wire circuit can carry 24 simultaneous transmissions. It has been determined that the scanning rate must be at least twice the maximum frequency to be handled; to transmit speech with a maximum frequency of 3000 Hz. then requires 6000 samples per second. See *pulse amplitude modulation; quantising; modulation; multiplexing.*

pulse crowding The condition in magnetisable surface recording in which the recording density is so high that the magnetic fields produced in recording alter previously recorded patterns. The common result is 'bit shift'; in extreme cases (or if no compensation is provided) it can result in corruption of data. See *bit shift.*

pulse repetition rate The number of (equally spaced) pulses per unit time (usually, per second).

pulse shaping A circuit operation of improving the form of pulses; for example, by steepening the leading edges and flattening the tops.

pulse string A pulse train.

pulse train A series of equally spaced pulses of similar characteristics.

PUMA *Programmable Universal MAnipulator.* A (Unimation) robot designed to be programmed to perform a variety of assembly operations in manufacturing.

punch (1) To put (data significant) hole patterns in paper tape or punched cards. **(2)** A keypunch or hand punch; a device for putting holes in paper tape or punched cards.

punch card See *punched card.*

punch column A card column; a vertical line of punching positions on a punched card.

punch row A card row; a horizontal line of punching positions on a punched card.

punch tape Paper tape.

punched card Also *card; punch card.* A rectangular card of standard material and dimensions (186 mm. × 82 mm.) in which hole patterns are punched to represent data. The rectangular holes are made by a **card punch** which may be either a **keypunch** that punches all the holes of a character when a single key on a keyboard is pressed or a **hand punch** (also **spot punch**) that punches one hole at a time. A character is represented, in accordance with some code, by one or more holes punched in a **card column** which is a line of punching positions parallel to the short edges of the card. There are 80 columns in the most commonly used card, which may be referred to as an **80-column card** or a **Hollerith card**. A card can hold as many characters as there are columns. A **card row** is a line of punching positions parallel to the long edges of the card. There are, typically, 12 card rows on a card numbered (from the top) 12-11-0-1-2-3-4-5-6-7-8-9. A hole punched in row 12, 11, or 0 may be termed a **zone punch** and one in a row from 1 to 9 a **digit punch**. The standard card has the upper left corner cut off diagonally to facilitate checking that all cards of a group are correctly aligned. A group of related cards is termed a **deck** or a **pack**. The term 'punched card' is commonly applied to cards whether holes have been punched in them or not; the term 'punch card' may be used synonymously with 'punched card' or it may be used to denote a card in which no holes have been punched. See *card punch; card reader; verifier; card image; Hollerith code; edge-punched card; edge-notched card.*

punched card reader A card reader.

punched tape Paper tape in which data holes and feed holes have been punched.

punched tape code A paper tape code.

punched tape reader A paper tape reader.

punching position A place where a hole or a hole pattern can be punched in a punched card or in paper tape.

punching rate (1)The number of cards that can be punched per unit time (usually, per minute). (2)The number of characters that can be punched in cards or paper tape per unit time (usually, per second).

punching station In a card punch; the location where holes are punched or the mechanical elements that perform punching.

purchase order Also *order*. A written request for goods or services as placed by a customer with a supplier.

pure binary A term sometimes applied to a numeric representation in the binary numeration system (as contrasted, possibly, to binary coded decimal or some other representation using 0-bits and 1-bits). See *binary*.

pure code Also *reentrant code*. A term applied to any sequence of instructions that remains unchanged during processing and between processing runs. Such code can be used repeatedly in one program or can be incorporated in or called by different programs. To be 'pure', code must neither incorporate run-specific parameters nor be modified during execution.

purge To remove a unit of data (typically, a file) from computer storage (because it has been superseded or, for other reasons, it is no longer required).

purge date The date after which a file can be deleted from storage by overwriting. See *retention period*.

push To add an item to the top of a stack. See *pop; stack*.

push button A device that operates by pressing with a finger; ('a push-button switch'; 'push-button dialing').

push-button dialing The initiation of a telephone call by pressing numbered buttons on a push-button telephone (rather than by means of a rotary dial of a 'standard' telephone). See *multifrequency signalling; impulse dialing.*

push-button telephone A telephone that provides for initiating calls by pressing numbered buttons rather than by means of a rotary dial. Each button, typically, produces a distinctive tone.

See *Touchtone; multifrequency signalling.*

pushdown list A group of items from which items can only be removed in inverse order from that in which they were placed in the group; a pushdown stack considered with respect to contents. See *LIFO; pushdown stack; pushup list.*

pushdown stack Also *stack; classic stack*. A data structure that provides for the addition and removal of items only at one end and in which all items in the structure move one item-space toward that end when an item is removed and away from that end when an item is added. See *stack; pushdown list; push; pop.*

pushdown storage Storage in one or more pushdown stacks.

pushup list A group of items to which items can be added only at one end and from which items can be removed only at the other end; a queue considered with respect to contents. See *FIFO; queue; pushdown list.*

pushup storage Storage in one or more queues.

Q

quad (1)A term applied to an electronic device or circuit that contains four (identical) circuit units; ('a quad inverter'; 'a quad amplifier'). (2)Four insulated wires (constituting a single telephone circuit) twisted together in a cable.

quadbit In data communications; four bits that are transmitted in a single Baud. See *phase shift modulation.*

quadruple-length register Four registers of standard length that, for some purpose, can be considered as a single register.

quadruple precision See *multiple precision.*

qualified name A multiple-part name that identifies an item (usually, a file) and indicates its place in a hierarchial structure; for example, 'SYS/FOR/CULIB'. If it identifies the root and all intervening owners, it is a 'fully qualified name'.

qualifier (1)That which identifies the location of an item of data in a hierarchial structure; any element of a qualified name except the last item (which is a 'simple name'). See *qualified name.* (2)In a (COBOL) data description; a data name that is used to provide a unique identification for a data name that would, otherwise, be non-unique. (3)A parameter entered by a job control statement; for example, the number of copies to be printed of an output.

quantising (1)The process of dividing a range of values into 'bands' or subdivisions, each of which can, for some purpose, be considered as a unit. For example; the process of dividing (classifying) insurance applicants into five-year age groups ('present age 25-30') for purposes of determining premiums. (2) In communications; the process of representing an analogue wave (say, of speech) by a sequence of discrete signals or characters, each of which represents the amplitude of the wave at some point in time at which it is sampled (measured). The sampled amplitude as transmitted by a single signal or character is a **quantising level**. At the receiving end, the signals (pulse amplitude modulation) or characters (pulse code modulation) are used to generate a wave that reproduces the original. Because there is no way of recapturing the characteristics of the original wave between samplings, a **quantising error** is introduced in the process; the more frequent the sampling the less the quantising error. See *pulse amplitude modulation; pulse code modulation.*

quantum The band or subdivision that is used in 'quantising'; for example, a five-year age bracket or the time between successive samples of a wave. See *quantising.*

quartet Four contiguous bits or bit positions; either a 4-bit byte or half of an 8-bit byte. In the latter (more usual) case, the most significant four bits are a **zone quartet** and the least significant a **numeric quartet**. See *numeric.*

query (1)An enquiry. (2)To request a programmed search; ('query a file'; 'query a data base'). (3)A message requesting a receiving station to indicate identity or status.

queue An inherently first-in-first-out (FIFO) data structure containing two or more items awaiting service or attention. In a computer context, it may be applied to programs waiting to execute, incoming messages waiting to be processed, or outgoing messages waiting for an available line. A new entry to a queue is termed an **arrival** and that which supplies service or attention is termed a **server**. The branch of mathematics and statistics that deals with queues is **queueing theory**; it attempts to predict the size of queues and the lengths of time items must wait for service or attention in different conditions. (2)To enter a queue. (3)To form items into a queue.

quiesce To enter or assume a quiescent state.

quiescent (1)Not active or not transmitting. (2)Of a computer or functional unit; operable but lacking work or inputs.

quietized Of an impact printer or other 'noisy' device; with a special enclosure or special design features intended to reduce noise (to permit operation in an office environment).

quintet Five contiguous bits treated as a unit; for example, the bits of a character in a five-level code.

quotient A result of division. See *division.*

qwerty A term sometimes applied to a keyboard in which the alphabetical keys are arranged in the same way as they are in a standard typewriter. (The term consists of the first six letters in the first alphabetical row of such a keyboard.) See *azerty.*

Qwerty Keyboard

R

R *Resistance.*

R-value A term sometimes applied to an object-code version of an item (instruction; address) to distinguish it from a source-language version which may be termed an 'L-value'.

R&D *Research And Development.*

rack up On a VDU screen; to move all lines up in one-line increments, causing the top line to drop off the screen if it is full. It is the usual procedure when each new line is entered at the bottom of the screen.

radial On or forming a radius.

radial transfer A transfer between two peripheral devices in which the device to which the transfer is made has a shorter access time (by the central processor) than the peripheral from which the transfer was made; for example, a transfer from magnetic tape to magnetic disc. See *spooling; staging; migration.*

radio frequency (RF) A frequency in the range used for radio transmission (about 15 kHz. to 900 mHz.).

radio frequency interference (RFI) A possible source of data corruption in (unshielded) data carrying cables in the vicinity of radio transmitters or other sources of high-energy RF emission.

radix Also *base.* A value that characterises a positional representation numeration system; a value by which all numbers in the system can be constructed by exponentiation and addition. For example, the number 125 in decimal is simply the short and conventional way of expressing 1×10^2 plus 2×10^1 plus 5×10^0. Similarly, 125 in hexadecimal is the 'short form' of 1×16^2 plus 2×16^1 plus 5×16^0. With respect to a numeration system; the terms 'radix' and 'base' are synonymous. See *base; number; numeration system.*

radix-50 A method of holding three alphanumeric characters in 16 bits. The character set is the alphabet, the decimal digits, a period, a space, and '$'. The '50' is in octal (decimal 40) and each character is assigned a numeric value in the range 1-50. The value of the low-order character is multiplied by '1', the middle character by 50, and the high-order by 2500 and the representation consists of the total of the three. The first character is recovered by dividing by 2500, the second by dividing the remainder by 50, and the third character is represented by the final remainder.

radix complement Also *noughts complement; true complement.* A complement that is obtained by subtracting the digits of the number to be complemented from a 'number' consisting of 1 less than the radix in each digit position and adding 1 to the value obtained. For example, the radix complement of 237 in decimal is 999 — 237 + 1 = 763. (The radix complement is the same as the diminished radix complement with a 1 added.) See *complement; diminished radix complement.*

radix-minus-one complement A diminished radix complement.

radix notation A representation in a radix numeration system.

radix point In a number containing an integral part and a fractional part; the (marked) location that separates the two parts; for example, the place of the full stop in 13.5. In the decimal system, a radix point is termed a **decimal point**.

rail An electric power distribution bus (or cable) that supplies functional units or electronic devices; ('a 28-volt rail'; 'using a common rail').

RAM *Random Access Memory.*

random access (1)An access of a random access memory; an access in which the time required to read and write data is a constant that does not depend upon the location being accessed within the memory. (2)An access of a random file. (3)A term sometimes used synonymously with 'direct access', or to include both direct access and 'random access' (def. 1).

random access device (1)An electronic device (integrated circuit) containing random access memory. (2)A term sometimes applied to a direct access device.

random access memory (1)(RAM) High-speed, read-write memory with an access time that is the same for all storage locations. The term includes core, thin film, plated wire, and semiconductor; unless otherwise indicated 'semiconductor' is understood. Semiconductor random access memory can be either **dynamic RAM** in which a storage cell consists of one transistor and a capacitor or **static RAM** in which the storage cell is a two-transistor flip-flop. Dynamic RAM is universally unipolar (MOS) while static RAM can be either unipolar or bipolar. Unipolar static RAM can be NMOS, PMOS, or CMOS. Bipolar static RAM can be TTL, ECL or I^{2}L. Core, thin film, and plated wire memory is 'non-volatile' while semiconductor RAM is 'volatile' (data is lost if electric power is removed). Random access memory is also **coordinate-addressable storage**. See *coordinate-addressable storage; dynamic RAM; static RAM; core memory; semiconductor memory.* (2)A term that has been used to include 'random access memory' (def. 1) plus other fast read-write memory such as magnetic disc and drum. See *direct access.*

random access storage Random access memory.

random file Also *direct file; hashed random file.* A file (on magnetic disc) in which records with keys are placed in storage locations with addresses that are produced by applying a randomising algorithm to their keys. Access is performed by applying the algorithm to the key of the record required and reading the data in the location with the address produced. Because a randomising algorithm is inherently capable of producing the same address when applied to different keys, only about fifty percent of the address space of the file is allocated to records when the file is created. Subsequent additions may bring the packing density up to the practical maximum which is about seventy percent. The main advantage of the random file is that it eliminates the need for an index with the attendant overheads that are involved in changing index entries when records are added or deleted. See *hashing.*

random logic Random access memory.

random number A number derived from a set in such a way that it has an equal probability of being any number in the set.

random numbers A series of numbers in each of which the digit in each digit position has an equal probability of being any digit in the numeration system; a series of numbers selected by chance. See *pseudo random numbers.*

random processing The processing of data in a random file;

processing in which backing storage addresses are produced from values input to an algorithm. See *random file*.

random walk A statistical method of determining the range of possible results that can be obtained by performing a mathematical operation with random number inputs.

randomising algorithm (1)An algorithm that produces random numbers. (2)A hashing algorithm; an algorithm that generates, or generates and extracts, numbers that are random within certain limits (say, between the lowest and highest addresses of a storage location).

range (1)Also *extent*. All of the values between an upper limit and a lower limit; all of the values that a function or variable can take. (2)Of a loop, all of the instructions executed with each iteration. (3)A group of related computers (or other products) of a manufacturer; ('the ICL 2900 range'). See *new range*.

range independent A term applied to peripherals or software that can be used with two or more 'ranges' of a manufacturer's computers.

rank To arrange in order according to priority or importance.

raster (1)A coordinate grid of addressable points containing all possible positions on the screen of a cathode ray tube where elements of a display image can appear. (2)A scan line; ('rasters per character').

raster count The number of addressable points contained in a raster. See *raster; addressable point*.

raster display A display within a raster; a display generated by a raster scan.

raster grid The coordinates of a raster.

raster scan With respect to a graphics VDU; a term that denotes a line-by-line scan method similar to that used in the scan of a television set. The entire display image is held in random access memory with, typically, one word of memory for each addressable point (pixel) of the display surface. Each word controls the on-off condition of the cell and can also control brightness level and colour (when a colour CRT is used). This contrasts to the 'storage tube' (also 'calligraphic') method in which the terminal generates a display as vectors received from a computer. In addition to the necessary memory, raster scan graphics terminals commonly incorporate one or more microprocessors to provide such changes of the display as image rotation, zoom, panning, and scrolling without the need to interrupt computer processing. An alphanumeric VDU is 'raster scan' but uses a character generator for images. A raster

scan characteristic is 'jagging' which is the 'stair step' formation of diagonal and curved lines. See *vector scan*.

raster unit Increment size; the distance between adjacent addressable points in a raster.

rate Also, often, *frequency*. The number of occurrences of an event per unit time; ('bit rate'; 'pulse repetition rate'). There is no clear distinction in usage between 'rate' and 'frequency' though 'rate' is usually applied to sequences of lower speed. See *frequency*.

rated Tested and/or warranted for that capacity or capability; ('a line rated for 2400 Baud'; 'a power supply rated for continuous duty').

ratio The relationship between two values; the amount by which one value would have to be multiplied to make it equal to the other. If, for example, a system has four times as much magnetic tape storage as it has magnetic disc storage, the 'ratio' is four to one. A ratio is often indicated with a colon as in '4:1'.

rational number A number that can be obtained by dividing some other number by an integer other than zero. See *number*.

raw data Data as received on source documents; data on which no validation or organisational steps have been performed.

RBT *Remote Batch Terminal*.

RCA *Radio Corporation of America*. (Camden, N.J.)

RCV *ReCeiVe*.

read To convert data from a static form (holes punched in tape or cards; flux transitions on a magnetic disc track; set flip-flops of semiconductor memory) to a sequence of signals (electrical pulses or line transitions). The purpose is to 'write' the data to some other location, possibly in a different form. With one exception (core memory), all 'reads' in a computer system are non-destructive; they leave the data that is read in a condition in which it can be immediately read again. See *load; fetch; transfer; write; move*.

read-after-write A facility for detecting writing errors in some magnetic tape systems consisting of using a second head adjacent to the writing head to read data immediately after it is written and to compare it with the original data as held in a buffer.

read cycle A sequence of steps performed in order to read a unit of data.

read cycle time The minimum time between successive reads within a particular unit of (coordinate-addressable) storage.

read head (1)A term used to denote a 'read/write head' when it is in the read mode or when considered with respect to reading. See *head; write head; magnetisable surface recording.* (2)A separate head (or the elements of a dual-gap head) that perform a reading function but not a writing function.

read in Also, sometimes, *load.* To receive data in a storage location; particularly to receive data in main storage that has been read from backing storage; ('read in a block'). See *write out.*

read-mostly memory (RMM) Programmable memory (memory of a type that permits changing bit patterns) that is used to hold relatively permanent code or data; for example, arithmetic routines, a polling list, or the order code of a 'soft-centred' computer. The term may be applied to programmable read-only memory or to random access memory with special safeguards to prevent overwriting. See *PROM; read-only memory.*

read only An access restriction that prevents writing (to a particular location or volume). See *access mode.*

read-only memory (ROM) (1)Memory that can be read repeatedly but cannot be changed. Unless otherwise indicated, it is assumed to be a semiconductor memory that is programmed as a step in manufacture to meet the requirements of the user. The usual implementation is a device with memory and an addressing (select) circuit as shown. The figure is an elementary 2-bit

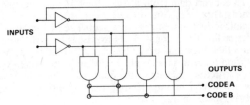

code converter. The memory is constructed with a link or diode at each intersection; these are selectively removed by etching during manufacture or by fusing (PROM). In MOS devices, transistors are formed only where there are to be connections. ROM's are used as storage (constants; instruction sequences) code converters, adders, and logic arrays. See *random access memory; PROM; programmable logic array.* (2)Random access memory that is prevented from being changed.

read-only storage (ROS) Read-only memory.

read out To read and transfer; ('read out to magnetic tape').

read-out A display of data in character form, typically, on the screen of a VDU.

read-out device A device capable of displaying data in character form as output from a computer; for example, a VDU, a group of light-emitting diodes, or a cathode ray tube in a microfilm recorder.

read path In a reader (OCR; MICR; OMR); a line in the path of document movement on which data on the document can be read.

read/write access mode An access mode that permits a (user) program to read and/or write data in an area of storage. See *access mode.*

read/write channel A channel (say, from a peripheral controller to a peripheral) that is used for both reading and writing (for both input and output).

read/write head A head (magnetisable surface recording) that is used for both reading and writing data. See *head.*

reader (1)A device that converts data from static form to electrical pulses or line transitions for transfer; for example, a punched card reader, a paper tape reader, or an optical mark reader. (The term is not applied to single devices, such as magnetic tape units, that perform both reading and writing operations.) (2)A device that enlarges microfilm for visual reference. See *COM; viewer.*

reader-copier A device that enlarges microfilm and makes paper copies of enlarged images.

reader-printer A reader-copier.

real (1)A term indicating that numeric values are represented by decimal digits, a decimal point (possibly assumed) and, optionally, a sign (+ or —). If no sign is included, it is assumed to be 'positive'. (2)Not conceptual or virtual; ('a real device'; 'real storage').

real address Also *actual address.* A term used in a virtual storage system to denote an address other than a virtual address. It may be used synonymously with 'hardware address' and applied to main (primary) storage only or it may be used to indicate either a hardware address or a 'physical address' in backing (secondary) storage. See *address; virtual storage addressing.*

real constant A string of decimal digits that includes a decimal point and, possibly, a sign (+ or —).

real device A device that is physically present. See *pseudo device.*

real drive In some systems; any magnetic disc unit other than a 'staging drive'. See *staging*.

real mode In a virtual storage system; the mode of execution of programs that are not organised for paging; execution in which fixed areas of primary storage must be allocated.

real number A number that can be represented in a fixed-radix numeration system. See *number*.

real partition An area of primary storage allocated to a program that must execute in real mode (that cannot be paged). See *real mode*.

real storage (1)Also *primary storage; main storage*. The main, internal, coordinate-addressable storage of a virtual storage system. (The term is used to differentiate such storage from 'virtual storage'.) See *virtual storage terms*. (2)A term sometimes applied to the total hardware-addressable (primary and secondary) storage of a virtual storage system.

real-time (1)A term applied to a data network in which a computer performs processing as initiated by operators at (remote) terminals and returns results in a short enough time (say, in less than three seconds) so that operators can perform tasks without sensed interruptions. Typically, such systems are used when customers are likely to be waiting for the processing to be performed; for example, in credit checking and airline seat reservation systems. See *on-line*. (2)A term applied to a system or process in which outputs reflect the current status of inputs or in which outputs follow inputs without a time lag; ('a real-time clock'; 'a sensor to provide real-time inputs'; 'a terminal that can perform real-time, local processing').

real-time clock In a computer; a clock (group of registers) that maintains the current year, month, day of the week, hour, minute, and second for purposes of display and/or logging events with respect to time.

real-time control By a computer; to provide continuous monitoring and control of a (chemical; manufacturing) process.

real-time inputs Inputs from sensors or monitoring devices that are used by a computer to provide real-time control of a process.

real-time operation A (computer) operation in which outputs/results are produced as soon as inputs are received and processed.

real-time output Computer output that is produced at times (or within time limits) to meet the requirements of a process (process control) or user (transaction processing).

real-time processing The processing of a computer in a real-time system. See *real-time*.

real-time system (RTS) A computer, communications links, and terminals or sensors that collectively perform real-time processing. Such a system is, typically, a transaction processing or process control system. See *real-time*.

realm Also *area*. A named subdivision of a data base to which records may be assigned without regard to their membership in sets. The purpose is to permit the grouping of records that have some device-related requirement or property. A temporary realm may be set up by a particular process to group records that will be referenced frequently during execution.

receive (1)To accept something (message; document; signal) that has been sent. (2)By data circuit terminating equipment; to detect line signals representing data and to perform such conversion functions as may be necessary for their use or interpretation. (3)By a terminal; to print or display incoming data.

receive and forward Store and forward.

receive interruption By a terminal; to interrupt a message being received in order to send a message.

receive-only (RO) A term that identifies a device that can receive but not transmit or a mode of operation in which sending is (temporarily) prevented.

receive-only typing reperforator See *ROTR*.

receiver In communications; a device or circuitry that converts input signals to speech (telephone) or to bits (modem).

receiver-transmitter Also *transceiver*. (1)Any device that can both transmit and receive; for example, a two-way radio or a modem. (2)An interface device in a microprocessor system that is used to selectively connect a microprocessor to inputs and outputs. See *UART; USART*.

receiving field Also *object field*. An instruction field that holds the address of a location to which data is to be moved or in which results are to be placed. See *source field*.

receiving perforator A paper tape punch that punches characters received on a communications link.

recirculating memory Also *bucket brigade memory*. A serial-access memory in which bits representing data travel in an endless path through such elements as shift registers, delay lines, and semiconductor materials. Examples include bubble, charge-coupled device, and delay line. See *serial access*.

recognition A machine operation of examining and interpreting data in some printed form. See *optical character recognition*.

recognition and control processor The main intelligence of an optical character reader.

recognition memory (REM) Of an optical character reader; a read-only memory that holds the bit-pattern representations of characters. Such memory is used in making comparisons with input representations of characters in order to identify them.

recompile (1) To perform a second or subsequent compilation using the same compiler. **(2)** To use another compiler to produce a different version of the object code (when a program is moved to a computer of a different type).

reconfiguration (1) The process of physically changing the functional units of a computer system; for example, to adapt it to a different type of processing. **(2)** The process of changing the peripheral devices available to the operating system (to meet the needs of a particular run). **(3)** A recovery procedure in which standby devices and/or interconnections are used to isolate a fault (and permit processing to continue).

reconnect (1) To connect after being disconnected; ('reconnect a printer'). **(2)** To make a different (wire or cable) connection; for example, in reconfiguration or to change the function of a device. See *strap*.

reconstitute (1) To reconstruct. **(2)** With respect to data that has been corrupted; to apply recovery procedures to obtain an accurate or usable version.

reconstruct Also *reconstitute* and, usually, *de-update*. To return a unit of code or data (typically, a file) to a previous state by reversing the effects of any changes that have been made to it.

record (rhymes with 'ford') With respect to data; to place it on or in a storage medium or device. Unless otherwise indicated, the term is assumed to apply to a magnetisable surface storage medium (magnetic disc, tape, or stripe). See *read; write*.

record A group of related data items considered as a unit for access and processing in a computer system. The term, typically, denotes a grouping of all the information an organisation requires about some entity; for example, an employee, a customer, a part, a vehicle, a purchase order, or an invoice. Depending upon the system and the file in which it is contained, a 'record' may also be a block of text to be printed, a single line entry of some list, or any of a variety of other items. Though the term normally denotes a group in bit-pattern representation on magnetic tape or disc, it is also applied to any physical input or intermediate form from which the storage form is obtained; for example, to a source document or punched card. A **logical record** is a record considered with respect to its content or use. A **physical record** is a unit of storage that holds a logical record, multiple logical records, or elements of a logical record. A physical record is an element of a file identified for access purposes by a **key** which is a value held in one of its fields (say, an employee number if the record contains details of one employee). If the records of a file are fixed-length (as would be the case with employee records), each logical record (details of one employee) is held in one fixed-length physical record. If a file consists of records that are (or can be) of different lengths, the records may be held individually as variable-length physical records. There are often access and overhead advantages in using fixed-length records and when these are used to hold variable-length logical records, each logical record may occupy only a part of a physical record or it may 'span' two or more physical records. The unit in which the operating system transfers records between backing storage and main storage is usually a **block** which is, typically, a fixed-length unit that corresponds to some portion of the length of a track on a magnetic disc unit. A block may consist of a single physical record or it may contain several physical records. The term 'record' is applied to either a 'logical record' or a 'physical record'; the one intended can be determined only from context. See *block; file; field; access; page; segment; entity record; relationship record*.

record block A block (magnetic disc) used to hold records.

record blocking The operation of writing two or more logical records to a single physical record. See *record spanning*.

record class Record type.

record count An element of a file header consisting of the number of records in the file.

record description In COBOL; the total set of data description entries associated with a particular logical record.

record format The arrangement of fields (and group fields) in a record.

record gap An interrecord gap.

record header Identifying or access-related data at the beginning of a record.

record key A value that uniquely identifies a record in a file. See *key (File organisation)*.

record layout Record format.

record length The number of characters or computer words in a (fixed-length) record.

record mode Recording mode.

record name A data name that identifies a logical record.

record number In some direct access files; a value that identifies the location of a record in a block or on a track. See *direct serial; key*.

record separator See *RS*.

record spanning The use of two or more physical records to hold a single logical record. See *record blocking*.

record type A classification of a record by storage-related attributes. A file may contain records of a single type (all of the same length and containing the same fields) or it may contain records of different types.

recorded Of speech or data; placed on some medium from which it can be retrieved.

recorded voice announcement (RVA) In a telephone system; a recorded voice of the type that gives the time of day or 'lines engaged'.

recorder A device used to produce computer output on microfilm. See *COM*.

recording (1)The operation of converting electric signals to a static form; unless otherwise indicated, the conversion is to flux reversals on a magnetisable surface medium (magnetic disc or tape). See *magnetisable surface recording*. (2)A static representation of electrical signals that can be 'read' to reproduce them; that which results from 'recording' (def. 1).

recording density The number of bits stored per unit area, volume, or length of track of a storage medium. Unless otherwise indicated, the term refers to the number of bits per inch of track of a magnetisable surface medium.

recording mode The (optional) method used in recording data on a magnetisable surface medium; for example, NRZI or PE.

recoverable error (1)A soft error; an error that is detected in one reading of data from a storage medium but is not detected in a subsequent reading. (2)An error that does not result in the loss of data. See *non-recoverable error*. (3)An error that can be resolved by a recovery procedure. (4)An error that does not result in the termination of execution of the program in which it is detected.

recovery (1)The operation of reversing the effects of an error; the operation of obtaining a correct version of data that has been corrupted. See *recovery procedure*. (2)The process of returning a system or functional unit to operable condition following a failure. (3)Of a circuit or device with two modes of operation; the process of returning to one mode after it has been in the other. See *recovery time*.

recovery procedure (1)Also *error control procedure*. A method used to resolve errors or (in some usages) to detect and resolve errors. Examples include requesting repetition of a message or block (ARQ) and forward error correction. (2)A recovery routine (system software). (3)Steps taken to return a computer system to full (or, possibly, limited) operation following a software crash or hardware failure. See *fault; reconfiguration*.

recovery routine A routine that is entered when an error occurs; typical functions include isolating the error, assessing its extent, performing retries and other steps to resolve the error, logging the conditions in which it occurred, and, when internal recovery attempts are unsuccessful, outputting an operator message giving relevant details.

recovery time Of an electronic circuit or device that has two modes of operation that use circuit elements in common (say, read-write or transmit-receive); the time required to resume one mode after having been in the other mode. With respect to modems, it is usually termed 'turnaround time'.

rectifier A circuit or device that converts alternating current to direct current by means of diodes (possibly valves/tubes) that limit current flow to one direction only. A **half-wave rectifier**

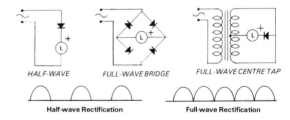

eliminates either the positive or the negative part of an A.C. input wave while a **full-wave rectifier** converts both parts of the A.C. wave to direct current. See *diode*.

recursive operation (1)An operation performed in several stages in which each stage (except the first) uses the output of the previous stage as input. Examples include exponentiation and finding factorials which are performed as repetitive steps of multiplication. (2)An operation performed to solve some relatively complex problem (say, finding a cube root) by making a guess, trying it, and using the result to modify the guess for a subsequent trial with modifications and trials continuing until an answer is obtained to the required degree of accuracy.

recursive process A recursive operation.

recursive routine (1) A routine that performs a recursive operation; a routine consisting of a loop in which the results of each iteration (except the last) are used as inputs to the next iteration. (2) A routine that calls itself when it has finished each execution (until interrupted) or which is an element of a 'round robin' group in which each calls the next in sequence with the last one in the sequence calling the first.

recursively defined sequence A series of terms in which each term (after the first) is determined by an operation performed with one or more of the preceding terms as inputs. (For example, a Fibonacci series.)

reduction The amount by which linear dimensions are reduced when a smaller copy is made of an image on film or microfilm. If, for example, an 8 in. × 12 in. original is reduced to 1 in. ×

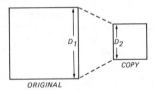

1¼ in., the reduction is 8:1. With respect to microfilm, this is indicated as '8X'. Low reduction (LR) is of less than 15X; medium reduction (MR) is from 16X to 30X; high reduction (HR) is from 31X to 60X; very high reduction (VHR) is from 61X to 90X; and ultra high reduction (UHR) is a reduction of greater than 90X. Microfilm recorders using cathode ray tubes are typically HR providing reductions of either 42X or 48X. The reduction is usually accomplished in two stages; the first is from 'printout size' to the display size of a small CRT (say, 3X) and the second is by camera lens (14X or 16X). The production of VHR or UHR microimages requires a further reduction that is, typically, a separate operation. See *COM; microfilm.*

redundancy (1) The condition in which bits or characters that have no data significance are added to a unit of data (character; block; message) for purposes of error detection (and recovery). Examples include parity bits and cyclic check characters. See *redundancy check.* (2) The percentage of the total length of a transferred unit of data (block; message) that consists of non data-significant bits and/or characters. (In communications, it includes address, routing, and other 'overhead' characters as well as any bits or characters that may be added for error control purposes.) (3) The condition in which a (computer) system incorporates duplicated functional units for backup purposes. See *parallel; fault; daisy chain.*

redundancy check A check of 'redundant' (error control) bits or characters to determine if they conform to some predesignated pattern and thus to indicate whether or not an error has occurred in the data to which they are attached. It is a check performed by receiving hardware upon such entities as parity bits, block check characters, and cyclic check characters. See *parity; polynomial code.*

redundancy check bit A parity bit.

redundancy check character A character added to a message or block for purposes of error detection; for example, a block check character or a cyclic check character.

reed relay Two electrical contacts on iron arms that are hermetically sealed in a small glass tube and opened and closed under the magnetic influence of an external coil. They provide

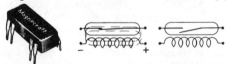

highly reliable operation with low noise and are widely used in telephone exchanges and in other switching applications. See *relay.*

reel (1) Also *spool.* The mechanical element upon which magnetic tape is wound. (2) A magnetic tape volume.

reenter (1) With respect to a sequence of instructions; to commence execution for a second or subsequent time without setting or initialising any values contained in the sequence. (2) By a called routine; to transfer control back to the calling routine at a 'reentry point'.

reenterable Reentrant.

reentrant Also *pure.* A term applied to a sequence of instructions (code; program; routine; subroutine) that contains no values that are changed during execution or that must be reset prior to execution. Such a sequence can be executed repeatedly by the same program or can be called by different programs. See *reusable; pure code; reenter.*

reentry point An entry point in a calling routine to which control is returned by a called routine. See *entry point; reenter.*

reference (1) By a program or process during execution; to output a label or address of a required unit of code or data (the referenced item) and thus to request the operating system to perform a fetch or access. The term may be applied only to internal calls and thus contrasts with 'call' which is an external call. In another usage, the term is applied only to instruction sequences with 'access' and 'fetch' applied to data; in this case, the term is synonymous with 'call'. **(2)** A term sometimes applied to relatively permanent units of required code or data; ('a reference file'). **(3)** That which is used for comparison or calibration; ('a reference voltage').

reference address A base address.

reference bit In some virtual storage systems; a bit (in a descriptor or other table entry) that is 'set' whenever the page or segment with which it is associated is either read or written to. See *change bit; use bit.*

reference edge Of a document that is to be read by machine (MICR; OMR); the edge from which measurements are made when setting up or adjusting the reader to set the read station(s) to the correct position(s) with respect to the data that is to be read.

reference level A level (voltage; sound) that is used for comparison or calibration purposes. See *relative transmission level.*

reference listing A final 'clean' source listing as retained in the documentation of a program.

reference voltage An accurate voltage as used for instrument calibration or for comparison purposes in an analogue computer.

reflected binary code Also *gray code; cyclic code.* A method of binary notation in which each valid binary 'number' differs from the previous one in a sequence in only one bit position. Such a code is often used in conjunction with electrical or optical sensors to convert analogue values (shaft rotation; voltage) to a digital form. The following is a comparison between a pure binary sequence and a reflected binary sequence:

Binary	*Reflected Binary*
0000	0000
0001	0001
0010	0011
0011	0010
0100	0110
0101	0111
0110	0101
0111	0100
1000	1100

refresh (1) To maintain a particular display on the screen of a cathode ray tube by repeated scans of the electron beam. It requires the presence of a 'refresh store' to hold the display image in raster or vector form and repeated access of the store to modulate the electron beam. **(2)** With respect to dynamic semiconductor memory; to provide repetitive electrical pulses at short intervals to 'refresh' the capacitive charge on gates where 1-bits have been written and, thus, to retain the data. See *dynamic memory.*

refresh interval (1) In dynamic semiconductor memory; the time between successive refresh pulses. **(2)** Scan period.

refresh rate Also *frame rate; regeneration rate.* The number of times per second that a display is rewritten (refreshed) on the screen of a cathode ray tube.

refresh store A section of memory or a memory module in which a display image is held in bit-pattern form and which is scanned as a step (or the only step) in modulating the electron beam to maintain the display image on the screen of a cathode ray tube. For a raster graphics device, the store contains a word for each screen addressable point; for an alphanumeric VDU, it holds data in characters (often ASCII). In the latter case, dot matrix characters are formed by addressing a 'character generator' which holds them as two-dimensional bit patterns. A refresh store may be incorporated in a VDU or held as a section of memory in a controlling device such as a terminal control unit. See *character generator; refresh; cathode ray tube.*

regeneration (1) The process of rewriting data to a storage location following a destructive read. See *core memory.* **(2)** The process of repeatedly rewriting a display onto the screen of a cathode ray tube. See *refresh.* **(3)** The process of amplifying and improving the wave form of signals in a communications circuit. See *repeater.* **(4)** Recovery; the process of obtaining a correct version of data that has been corrupted.

regeneration rate Refresh rate.

regenerative repeater A repeater in a (telegraph) data transmission system that receives weak and distorted signals and uses them to trigger circuitry that produces output signals of the original quality. See *repeater*.

region Also, sometimes, *area*. A term applied to a group of contiguous storage locations (main storage) that are allocated for a particular purpose; ('an operating system region'; 'a user program region').

register A storage location of standard length (typically, one computer word) with associated electronic circuitry to permit selected bits to be read and written or moved between bit positions. Registers are the essential elements of a control unit and arithmetic unit where they are used to hold parameters and other temporary values required during processing, to hold values with which arithmetic and logic operations are being performed, and for a variety of other purposes as required by the operating system as well as by user programs. A **general-purpose register** is a control unit register that is available for a variety of uses; for example, to hold a count, a modifier, a base address, a return address, a stack pointer, or one or more flags. An **instruction register** is a register that holds an instruction

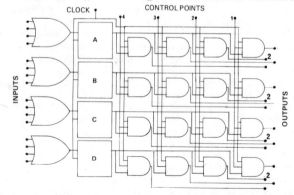

during decoding and execution and a **current address register** (also **program counter**) is a register that holds the address of the next instruction to be obeyed. General-purpose registers are often identified by their use in a particular run; for example, a 'base address register', an 'index register', or a 'modifier register'. A **shift register** is a register in which all bits can be moved left or right in increments of one bit position. An **accumulator** is an arithmetic-unit register with the circuitry of a full adder. A **stack** is a group of registers with circuitry to move all bits from one register to the same bit positions in an adjacent register. A **visible register** is a register that is read or written to by a user program and an **invisible register** is one that can be accessed only by the operating system. The figure shows the basic arrangement of four bit positions of a general-purpose register that can receive data from any of four other registers and transfer data to the same number of registers. The storage cells A, B, C, and D are flip-flops each of which has a clock input and an input from an OR gate; when the clock signal goes high, any 1-bits in the OR gates are loaded. On the output side. each flip-flop is connected to multiple AND gates. If, for example, Control Point 2 is set (high) then the contents of all register positions is sent to Destination 2 the next time the clock goes high. See *shift register; index register; microinstruction; control point; logic circuit; flip-flop*.

register and arithmetic logic unit (RALU) The grouped elements of a microprocessor in which arithmetic, logic, shift, and transfer operations are performed.

register length The number of bit positions (storage cells) in a register.

relation (1) A connection or dependency that one item has with respect to another; ('a relation between input and output'). **(2)** A group of related items as an element of a relational data base. In such a relation, related data items (for example, the complete identification of one part) constitutes a **tuple** and items of the same type (say, 'supplier' or 'price') are a **domain**.

relation character A symbol for a relational operator.

relation test A test performed when executing an instruction containing a relational operator.

relational associative processor An associative processor.

relational data base A data base in which information is held in the form of 'relations'. See *relation; data base*.

relational expression An expression containing a relational operator; an expression for testing the relation between two values.

relational operator An operator that specifies a comparison between two numeric values with a result that is either 'true' or 'false'. The following are the operators and examples of values of 'A' in relation to 'B' that will produce a 'true' result:

		A	B
EQ - EQUAL TO	=	10	10
NE - NOT EQUAL TO	≠	9/11	10
GT - GREATER THAN	>	11	10
GE - GREATER THAN OR EQUAL TO	≥	10/11	10
LT - LESS THAN	<	9	10
LE - LESS THAN OR EQUAL TO	≤	9/10	10

relational processor An associative processor.

relationship record A record that contains temporary or 'this time only' relationships; for example, customer numbers and their current order numbers.

relative address In a program or other sequence of instructions; a numeric value that identifies a location in which data will be placed and which is a displacement from a reference value or 'base address'. The address is adjusted to a common reference value when the sequence is linked, loaded, or incorporated in-line in another sequence.

relative data In a computer graphics program; display locations that are expressed as displacements from other coordinates rather than as origin-relative coordinates. See *absolute data*.

relative error An error expressed as a percentage of the true or correct value. See *absolute error*.

relative generation number A generation number of a file expressed in relation to the current generation which is '0'; the previous generation number is '—1' and the one before it is '—2'. See *generation*.

relative record file A direct access file in which records are loaded into fixed-length, numbered locations and accessed by location number rather than by key. See *self-indexed file*.

relative record number The number of a location in a relative record file.

relative redundancy The number of redundant bits or characters of a block or message expressed as a percentage of the data-significant bits or characters. See *redundancy*.

relative transmission level A measure of attenuation in a telephone line; the ratio of the test tone power in dB as measured at the transmitting equipment (the zero reference) and at some other point on the line. See *test tone*.

relay (1) To receive and to redirect or to retransmit; ('relay a message'). **(2)** An electrically operated switch. A small current in the control circuit passes through the coil creating a magnetic field that pulls the relay arm toward the coil thus operating the contacts and, in the illustration, connecting power to the load. Relays are used to 'amplify'; to permit a small coil current to

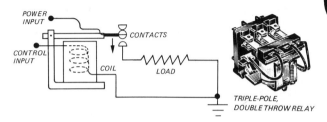

control a large load current. They are also used to facilitate remote operation of devices. Most relays are 'double throw'; operation can open and/or close a circuit. Many relays are 'multi-pole' in which a single coil current can control two or more circuits; the one illustrated on the right is 'triple pole double throw'. See *Strowger relay; reed relay*.

relay centre A message switching centre.

release (1) With respect to a facility (line; peripheral); to terminate use and make it available for reallocation. **(2)** With respect to a unit of proprietary software (operating system; application package); a particular (numbered) version.

reliability The attribute of a system or functional unit that relates to accuracy and consistency of performing operations and freedom from breakdowns. See *availability*.

relinquish To release or deallocate.

relocatable address An address that is intended to be changed by applying a constant; an address in a relocatable program.

relocatable program An object-code program that is designed to facilitate loading in different main-storage locations. The term may be applied to a program in a virtual storage system that is contained in pages/segments that can be placed as required by the operating system or, more usually, to a program in which all addresses are relative addresses.

relocatable sequence A sequence of instructions that can be placed in different main storage locations or incorporated in another sequence of instructions.

relocation and protection register In some systems; a register that holds the boundary addresses of two areas of main storage allocated to a program, one of which holds its code and the other its data. Each address generated during execution is checked against the register values to prevent attempts to execute data or to access unauthorised areas of storage. See *bound*.

relocation constant A value that is added to the relative addresses of a program to convert them to absolute addresses when a sequence of instructions is loaded or to new relative addresses when the sequence is incorporated in or linked with another sequence of instructions.

relocation dictionary The element of a load module or object module that identifies all addresses that must be adjusted for relocation. See *load module*.

relocation factor A relocation constant.

relocation interrupt A page fault.

reluctance Of iron, the resistance it has to becoming magnetised. See *magnet*.

REM (1)*REMark*. (Comment.) **(2)***REcognition Memory*.

remainder In division; that which is 'left over'; the non-integer part of a quotient. For example; the result of dividing 16 by 5 could be expressed as 3 with a 'remainder' of 1.

remedial maintenance Corrective maintenance.

remnance The magnetism that remains after the magnetising force has been removed. See *magnet*.

remnant amplitude Also *residual noise*. In magnetisable surface recording, the average value of the noise signal as measured when reading an erased track.

remote A term applied to a device or operation that is geographically separated from a computer but communicates with it. See *local; data network*.

remote access An access to a program or to data that is made or initiated from a remote terminal or computer.

remote batch entry The use of a remote terminal to submit data required for batch prouessing. See *remote batch processing; remote job entry*.

remote batch processing The use of a remote terminal in the performance of batch processing required at the location of the terminal. Programs and/or data may be keyed in by an operator or the terminal location may contain storage facilities (paper tape; punched card; magnetic disc) from which programs and/or data are read over the communications link to the computer. In most systems, results are returned via a printer at the terminal location though, in some systems, results may be returned by post. The term 'remote batch processing' usually indicates a system or procedure in which both programs and data are under control of the remote location and in which the computer centre performs a service for the location. The term **remote batch entry** may be applied to this system or to one in which the remote location provides data as required by the computer centre, with both programs and data held at the computer. See *remote job entry; batch processing; distributed processing*.

remote batch terminal (RBT) A terminal at a remote location that is used to send data (and programs) to a computer and which, usually, has facilities to receive the results of processing. See *remote batch processing*.

remote computing Distributed processing; computing in which inputs and/or outputs are carried by communications links.

remote device An item of data terminal equipment at a remote location; for example, a terminal control unit or a terminal.

remote file access In a data network; the facility or action by which an operator or program at one node loads, deletes, executes, or modifies a file held on a computer at another node.

remote job entry (RJE) **(1)**The operation of sending batch data from a remote location over a communications link for processing at a computer centre (using stored programs belonging to the remote location). **(2)**Remote batch entry.

remote power off A facility in which a character (or group) transmitted on a communications link causes electric power to a device (printer; logger) to be turned off. See *DC*.

remote program load See *teleload*.

remote spooling The transfer of data from a remote location to the peripheral storage of a computer under the control of a program run on the computer. The transfer is usually from a logger or a remote computer and, where PSTN lines are used, the connection may be made by modem equipment with automatic calling and answering facilities.

remote station A data station other than a master station; a satellite or tributary data station.

remote terminal A terminal (VDU; Teletype) at a remote location.

remote test In a data communications system; a test of lines and/or a remote site modem performed by an operator at the central site. See *analogue loop test; digital loop test*.

reorganise With respect to data or a data structure; to make a copy in a form that reduces access time and/or storage requirements. See *file reorganisation*.

repair To correct a hardware fault. See *maintenance*.

repair time The time required to correct a hardware fault and to return a device to full operability. See *mean time to repair*.

repeat-action key A key that, when held fully depressed, causes an action (spacing; line throw) to be repeated until the key is released.

repeat facility In a central processor; the facility to make two or more attempts to execute an instruction which does not produce accepted results.

repeatability The extent to which duplicate operations produce the same results; for example the coincidence of successively generated display images on a display device.

repeated selection sort See *selection sort*.

repeater (1)In a long communications cable; a device as installed at spaced intervals (say, every two or three miles) to amplify (and, possibly, reshape) signals. (2)A station in a microwave communications system that receives, amplifies, and retransmits signals.

repeater coil In a telephone system; a transformer with an equal number of primary and secondary turns used to transmit signals between two circuits while providing isolation between them.

repeater modem A modem that connects to another modem in order to interface two data communications circuits. See *onward link*.

repeating group A group of data items of identical format occupying adjacent storage locations.

reperforator A device (in a teletypewriter system) that receives messages by punching their characters in paper tape. See *typing reperforator; ROTR*.

reperforator-transmitter (RT) A device (in a teletypewriter system) combining a reperforator and an independent paper tape reader and transmitter. It is used for transforming the incoming speed to a different output speed and for holding messages awaiting retransmission.

repertoire The total of the entities or facilities available; ('an instruction repertoire'; 'a character repertoire').

repetition instruction An instruction that causes another instruction (or a group of instructions constituting a loop) to be executed an indicated number of times.

repetition rate The number of times an event occurs per unit time (usually one second). See *frequency; cycle time*.

repetitive addressing A method of addressing in which an instruction automatically performs its operation on or with the operand(s) used by the previous instruction.

replicate (1)To make a copy. (2)To parallel or duplex; to provide an additional functional unit or facility of the same characteristics.

reply (1)A message received in response to a message that has been sent. (2)To send a 'reply' (def. 1).

report A processing result in which data has been selected and presented in a way designed to provide information to a user; for example, on sales for a period or the status of work in progress.

report program Also *report generator*. A program designed to extract particular data from one or more input files and to manipulate it and format it to meet particular (user) requirements. See *report*.

report program generator (1)Any program (or, possibly, group of programs) designed to assist in the construction of report programs of some particular type. (2)(RPG) A common commercially oriented high-level language. See *RPG2*.

representation The method by which values are held in storage and manipulated; ('character representation'; 'binary representation').

representation system An established method by which values of a certain type are represented; ('a floating point representation system'; 'the binary representation system').

reproducer A device that makes copies; particularly a 'card reproducer'.

reprogram (1)With respect to a function; to write a new program or group of programs for its performance. (2)With respect to a (mini or micro) computer or other intelligent device; to change its function or method of operation by changing its program(s). (3)To construct a program to replace another program.(4)With respect to field-programmable semiconductor memory; to erase existing bit patterns and write new ones. See *PROM*.

reprogrammable Of a read-only memory device (integrated circuit); capable of having bit patterns erased and replaced. See *PROM*.

reroute (1)In data communications; to switch traffic to another circuit (say, because of failure of the first circuit). (2)To receive a message from one location and send it to another.

rerun To perform a processing run a second or subsequent time (because of a failure). See *restart*.

rerun point A checkpoint.

rescue dump A checkpoint dump; a dump of storage and register contents for use in reconstituting the execution environment of a program if made necessary by a failure. See *checkpoint*.

rescue point A restart point.

research and development (R&D) A department or activity concerned with developing new or improved products or finding new applications for existing products.

reserved Dedicated to a particular use or function; ('a reserved word in a programming language'; 'a reserved area of storage').

reserved field (1) In a record; a field that can only be used to hold a particular item of data; for example, the customer's name. (2) In an instruction in a fixed-format language; a location that can only be used to hold a particular item; for example, an operand.

reserved page A page that remains resident in main storage.

reserved volume A volume that normally remains mounted on its drive.

reserved word A word in a programming language with a meaning that is fixed by the rules of the language; it is usually prohibited in any other context.

reset (1) Also, in some contexts, *initialise*. To return values to their starting conditions; for example, to set a count to zero. (2) With respect to a circuit or all the circuits of a functional unit; to establish original or normal conditions (following a failure or error). (3) To change a 1-bit to a 0-bit. (4) An input to a flip-flop that changes Q̄ to 1 and Q to 0 independent of clock or other inputs. See *flip-flop; preset*.

reset button A button (switch) on a functional unit that, when pressed, establishes original or normal circuit conditions.

reset pulse A pulse used to establish original storage or circuit conditions.

resident (1) Of code or data; loaded in main storage. (2) Of a volume; mounted and accessible to the operating system.

resident control program A control segment.

resident set In a virtual storage system; all of a program's pages/segments that are in main storage at any one time. See *virtual storage system—processing units*.

resident supervisor In some systems; that portion of an operating system that must always be in main storage during processing.

resident volume A volume that is kept permanently mounted on its drive.

residual That which is left after all operations tending to eliminate it have been performed.

residual error A difference between an exact result of a mathematical operation and one produced by a particular method of calculation; for example, a difference between a value in a government tax table and the 'same' value as produced by a computer program. (The error commonly arises from cumulative rounding errors in repetitive operations.)

residual error ratio The ratio of the number of undetected or unresolved errors (in data transmission) to the number of units (characters; blocks) in which they occur.

residual noise See *remnant amplitude*.

residue check A redundancy (parity) check; particularly as performed on an operand.

resilience The capability of a system (or, possibly, a functional unit) to continue to perform a useful service following the failure of one or more of its elements. (The term usually implies the presence of standby circuits or facilities.) See *fault; graceful degradation*.

resistance (R) The limitation of flow of electric current caused by heating the conductors through which it passes. See *electricity; Ohm; dielectric*.

resistance element A device that presents only resistance (no inductance or capacitance) to the flow of electric current; for example, a heater, resistor, or light bulb.

resistor A device used to introduce resistance in an electrical or electronic circuit. Common applications include restriction of current flow to prevent overloading other components, biasing control circuits to hold them in their normal state (say, at +5 V.) in the absence of an input, and in voltage dividers. Resistors

are rated according to resistance in ohms, the tolerance (usually plus and minus 1%, 5%, or 10%) and the amount of power in watts which they can dissipate without overheating. Small discrete resistors (under one watt) are usually carbon or thin film and larger ones are of iron-alloy wire wound on a ceramic core. In integrated circuits, resistors may be either thin film or formed of seriesed transistors. See *thin film resistor*.

resistor-transistor logic (RTL) A circuit in which inputs through resistors determine the state of conduction of a transistor (or tube/valve) and, hence, the output. In the NOR circuit shown, if any of the inputs go high the associated transistor conducts

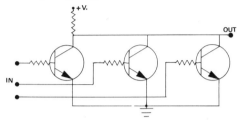

and OUT goes low; if all inputs are low, all transistors are off and the output is high. Inverters are commonly RTL and devices are available to perform all the other common logic functions. Such devices are inexpensive and fast though they provide limited fan-out and poor circuit isolation.

resolution (1)With respect to errors detected in data transfer or transmission; the process or act of correcting them or identifying them as uncorrectable. See *recovery*. (2)In computer graphics; the 'fineness' of detail that can be produced in an image. Highest resolution is usually obtained with vector scan systems rather than raster scan systems where the maximum resolution is determined by the raster count (the number of addressable points available to form an image)

resolver An element of an analogue computer that generates a particular function by 'resolving' two or more inputs (say, as voltages or shaft rotation).

resource (1)That which is allocated to a user or program in order to perform processing. The usual ones are peripheral devices, main storage space, and central processor time. (2)Any processing input that is chargeable to the user; for example, the 'resources' of definition 1 plus data preparation services, listing paper, and punched cards.

resource allocation The operating system activity of assigning resources to programs/jobs. Their assignment to meet current needs during processing is termed **dynamic resource allocation** and their assignment before a run begins is termed **static resource allocation**.

resource class the type of resource as distinguished for allocation purposes; the usual ones are 'files', 'main storage', and 'peripheral devices'.

resource deallocation The withdrawal of a resource from a program/job thus making it available for reallocation to another program/job.

resource management (1)The activity (by a group or individual) of allocating resources and accounting for their use. (2)The activity (by an operating system) of allocating processing resources to meet the needs of executing programs.

resource manager A term sometimes applied to a supervisory program that performs some function of allocating/controlling processing resources.

response (1)A reply or action taken following a request or the receipt of a message. (2)In data communications; a message from a computer to a terminal following some initiating message from the terminal. See *message pair*. (3)A circuit condition set by an initiating signal.

response duration In writing a bit to a storage cell; the time between generation of the write pulse and completion of the physical change (orientation of magnetic particles; change of flip-flop) in the storage cell.

response time In an interactive system; the time that elapses between an operator at a remote site terminal sending a message (pressing an 'enter' or 'return' key) and the receipt of the first character of the reply from the computer.

restart When the execution of a program has been terminated (by an error or failure); the recommencement of execution from some entry point (other than at the beginning of the program) after reconstructing the processing environment at that point (replacing contents of storage and registers) making use of data that has been dumped at that entry point used as a checkpoint during the previous attempted execution. A restart that is performed during a run may be termed an **automatic restart** and one in which the program (with entry point designated) is resubmitted after the run may be termed a **deferred restart**. See *rerun; checkpoint*.

restart condition A condition (flag status; peripheral allocation) that is retained (in a checkpoint dump) so that it can be reestablished if it is necessary to restart the program.

restart instruction (1)An instruction at which execution may be restarted; the first instruction following an entry point that is also a checkpoint. (2)The first instruction to be obeyed in a particular restart.

restore (1)To replace that which has been removed or deleted;

('restore electric power'; 'restore the contents of a register'). (2)With respect to the heads of a movable-head magnetic disc unit; to move them to their outermost position.

restricted Of data, locations, or volumes; not available for use or allocation without authorisation. See *access restriction; storage protection*.

restricted function An operating system function that cannot be initiated by a user program.

restricted instruction A priveleged instruction.

restricted-use volume A volume that can only be used for particular purposes (spooling; not as scratch file) or to which access restrictions apply.

result The product or output of an operation; for example, the 'answer' obtained by performing a calculation or a report produced by executing a computer program.

resultant (1)That which results; ('a resultant output'). (2)A vector sum; the total effect of two or more vectors. In the figure, OB is the 'resultant' of OA and OC; its end coordinates are determined by plotting OC from the end of OA, or the reverse.

results Printed or displayed data that is produced by executing a user program; the end product of a data processing operation. Unless otherwise indicated, the term denotes a printed output of a batch run.

retention period The length of time that data (usually a file) is retained in backing storage; the period after which it can be overwritten if the space is required for another purpose. See *generation*.

retrace time In a cathode ray tube; the time required for the electron beam to move to a position to start a new scan. The time required for it to move from the right-hand end of one scan line to the beginning (left-hand end) of the next scan line is the **horizontal retrace time** (also **fly-back time**) and the time required to move from the right-hand end of the lowest scan line of a display field to the left-hand end of the first (highest) scan line is the **vertical retrace time**. See *cathode ray tube*.

retrieval The operation of locating and obtaining a particular required item or group from storage holding a number of such items. See *information retrieval*.

retrieval code A code by which items can be identified for retrieval purposes; for example, a code used to locate microimages in a microfilm system.

retry A second or subsequent attempt to perform an operation when an error or failure has occurred preventing successful completion on a previous attempt. See *recovery procedure*.

retry-correctable A term sometimes applied to a soft error.

return (1)Also, often, *carriage return*. A key on a terminal keyboard that, when pressed, causes a connected program to read the current line buffer and take the appropriate action (pass an entered parameter to a subroutine; store or transmit the buffer contents), to clear the buffer (unless an error is detected), and to return the cursor or printing position to the beginning of the next line. See *newline*. (2)By a program; to produce a required parameter or value.

return address Also *link*. An address in a calling sequence to which a called sequence will return control.

return channel A channel on which messages are received.

return instruction In a called routine; an unconditional jump instruction that transfers control back to the calling routine.

return-to-reference Return-to-zero.

return-to-zero Signalling in which one of the possible line conditions is an absence of signal (zero voltage). See *dipole encoding; single-current signalling; NRZ*.

reusable Also, usually, *shareable*. A term applied to a unit of code (routine; page; segment) that is called or referenced by different programs (and, hence, is resident in main storage when any such programs are being executed).

reusable program A program that is loaded once and executed repeatedly to perform identical or similar operations for a particular job; if not reentrant, it includes provisions to return any instructions modified during execution to their original values after each performance.

reusable routine See *reusable program*.

reverse channel (1)A return channel. (2)A secondary channel that provides transmission in the direction opposite to that of the main channel. See *asymmetric duplex; secondary channel*.

reverse current Direct current that may flow in a circuit in the direction opposite to the normal or usual flow. It may cause malfunctions or errors and is commonly prevented by the use of diodes. See *blocking diode; wired OR*.

reverse Polish notation See *Polish notation*.

reversible counter A counter (register) that can be incremented and decremented.

reversible flexible disc A flexible disc on which data can be recorded on both sides. See *flexible disc*.

revision The process of making corrections or improvements (to software or manuals).

revision level Of a program in some systems; a number indicating its status with respect to the incorporation of changes. See *release*.

rewind To spool magnetic tape or paper tape from one reel to another so that, upon completion, it can be read from the beginning.

RF *Radio Frequency.*

RFI *Radio Frequency Interference.*

RFP *Request For Proposal.*

RI *Ring Indicator.*

ribbon Spoolable ink-impregnated fabric that is used to form characters by typewriters and other impact printers. See *scroll ribbon; tape ribbon; impact printer.*

ribbon cable Flat, plastic multiconductor cable in which the conductors lie parallel to each other and are insulated and supported by the plastic. It has an advantage over 'bundled cable'

in that terminations are easier to make (usually by an insulation displacement method) and it may also save space. See *bundled cable; insulation displacement.*

right angle An angle containing 90°.

right justified See *justify.*

right shift A movement of the contents of a register in increments (one bit, one character, or one digit position) to the right. See *shift register.*

rigid disc Also *hard disc.* A magnetic disc of metal (aluminium) as contrasted to a flexible disc (of Mylar). See *magnetic disc.*

ring file A chained file in which the last record has a pointer to the first.

ring indicator (RI) A signal from automatic answering equipment to a DTE indicating that it has detected an incoming call and gone off-hook. See *automatic answering.*

ring protection In some systems; a method of storage protection and access control accomplished by assigning programs numerical values that are checked against values in a system table to determine the validity of attempted accesses.

ring shift A circular shift.

ringback tone A signal that simulates a ringing telephone to notify a caller that a connection is being made.

ripple-carry adder A serial adder. See *adder.*

RIRO *Roll-In/Roll-Out.*

rise time The time from the beginning of sending a pulse until it reaches full voltage; the shorter the time the steeper the leading edge.

riser That part of certain lower-case characters (b; d; f; t) that extends above the height of a lower-case 'm'. See *descender.*

RJE *Remote Job Entry.*

RMM *Read-Mostly Memory.*

RMS *Root Mean Square.*

RMT *ReMoTe.*

RO (1)*Read Only.* (2)*Receive Only.*

robot A programmable (intelligent) device capable of performing physical operations involving three-dimensional movements.

robotics The design or construction of robots.

roll call See *polling.*

roll down A facility of a VDU that permits the operator to move a display downward in order to place display elements on the screen that were (apparently) hidden by the upper edge of the screen. See *roll up; scrolling.*

roll film Photographic film supplied on a 'roll' or spool (as contrasted to sheet film). See *COM; recorder.*

roll-in (1)In a virtual storage system; the operation of writing a page or segment to primary storage from secondary storage. See *roll-out; virtual storage transfers.* (2)To copy any unit of code or data into main storage from backing storage. See *load; overlay; roll-in/roll-out.* (3)Roll-on.

roll-in/roll-out (RIRO) Also *rollout/rollin.* The operation or facilities involved in deleting all or part of a program or its data from main storage, reallocating resources to perform higher priority processing, and reestablishing the program and its data when the higher priority processing is completed. It is often used in small mixed-mode systems where the deleted program/data is a batch job and the higher priority processing is that required to service a transaction.

roll-off Also, sometimes, *migration; roll-out.* The movement of data from fast-access storage (magnetic disc) to storage of lower access speed (magnetic tape).

roll-on Also, sometimes, *spooling; staging; radial transfer; roll-in.* The movement of data from storage of lower access speed (magnetic tape) to fast-access storage (magnetic disc).

roll-out **(1)** In a virtual storage system; the operation of deleting a page or segment from primary storage and writing it to secondary storage. See *roll-in; virtual storage transfers*. **(2)** To delete any unit of code or data from main storage and write it to backing storage. See *roll-in/roll-out*. **(3)** Roll-off

roll-to-roll duplicator A device to copy microfilm from one roll onto another. See *duplicator*.

roll up A facility of a VDU that permits the operator to move a display upward in order to place display elements on the screen that were (apparently) hidden by the lower edge of the screen. See *roll down; rack up; scrolling*.

rollback The operation of restoring a deleted program and its data to main storage in the state recorded at a checkpoint.

rollcall Roll call.

rollin Roll-in.

rollout Roll-out.

rollout/rollin Roll-in/roll-out.

rollover On a terminal or other keyboard device; the operator action of depressing two or more keys simultaneously or nearly simultaneously. See *n-key rollover*.

ROM *Read-Only Memory*.

root **(1)** With respect to a number; another number that, if multiplied by itself a designated number of times, will equal that first number. For example, the 'square root' of 144 is 12, the 'cube root' of 27 is 3 and the '4.5 root' of 2830 is 5.85. It is indicated by the symbol $\sqrt{\ }$ with a superscript indicating the root; for example, $^{4.5}\sqrt{2830}$ indicates that the 4.5 root is to be extracted from 2830. **(2)** Also *origin*. In a hierarchial structure; the entity of highest order or greatest privelege; for example, the 'head of department' in a departmental organisation chart. **(3)** In a hierarchial data structure; the 'owner' on the highest level; the entity that must be accessed first in order to access any other element of the structure.

root mean square (RMS) The common method of finding the mean value of a variable quantity (say, the voltage of a wave); it consists of squaring the input values, adding them, and extracting the square root of the total.

root segment A control segment.

ROS *Read-Only Storage*.

rotary dial On a conventional telephone; the rotatable element used to send a sequence of number pulses to a local telephone exchange to identify the station being called. See *impulse dialing; push-button telephone*.

rotary switch A switch with a handle that is turned to change the on-off status of one or more circuits. See *switch*.

rotate **(1)** On a graphics VDU; to turn a display image about some axis. **(2)** With respect to data in a shift register; to apply a circular shift. See *shift*.

rotating-belt printer An impact, shaped-character printer in which type slugs on type bars are carried by a belt that moves them past a printing position where they are selectively impacted against ribbon and paper by means of a hammer actuated by a solenoid.

rotating memory The memory of a mechanically rotated storage element (magnetic disc; magnetic drum). See *cyclic access; recirculating memory*.

rotational delay Latency; the time required for a location (magnetic disc; magnetic drum) to rotate to the position where it can be read or written.

rotational position sensing (RPS) A facility of a magnetic disc unit in combination with a peripheral controller in which the rotational position of the disc(s) is continuously monitored so that multiple transfers can be performed in the order that will produce minimum latency (rather than in the order the requests are received at the peripheral controller). For example; if a block has just passed the location of the read/write head when it is called for by the control unit, other transfers will be performed (if called for) during the time (say, 20 milliseconds) that it takes to rotate to the position where it can be read or written. The order in which transfers are to be made is determined by the location of the index and the displacements of the required locations from the index. See *latency; track-following servo; indexing*.

rotor The rotating element of a motor, servo, or similar device.

ROTR *Receive Only Typing Reperforator*. A receiving terminal in a teletypewriter system that prints incoming messages and also punches them on paper tape.

round With respect to a number (as output from a calculation); to reduce the number of digit positions by which it is represented by eliminating least-significant digits that are unnecessary for its intended use or that give a false impression of accuracy. Unless otherwise indicated, the term is synonymous with 'round off'. See *round down; round up; round off; rounding error*.

round down To drop one or more digits in least-significant position(s). For example, 15.63, 15.65, and 15.69 are all 'rounded' to 15.6. See *round*.

round off Also *round*. To drop one or more digits in least-significant position(s) and to adjust the least-significant of the retained digits, if necessary, so that its value is closest to that of the dropped digit(s). For example, 15.63 becomes 15.6, 15.69 becomes 15.7 and, by convention, a digit that is half the radix is rounded to the next higher digit so 15.65 also becomes 15.7. See *round*.

round off error A rounding error.

round-robin A term applied to a system in which a resource is allocated, or attention is given, in turn and in rotation to each of a number of claimants; for example, to a time division multiplexing system or a roll call polling system.

round up To drop one or more digits in least-significant position(s) and to add 1 to the least-significant of the retained digits. For example, 15.63, 15.65, and 15.69 are all 'rounded' to 15.7, See *round*.

rounding The process of shortening a number by deleting one or more digits in least-significant position(s). See *round*.

rounding error An error introduced by rounding; for example, a 'rounding error' of .03 is introduced if 15.63 is rounded to 15.6. See *residual error; truncation error*.

route (1) A path; a means for moving data or signals from one location to another, possibly via intermediate locations. **(2)** With respect to a message; to send it to or via a particular location or organisation; ('route it to the Leeds office'; 'route it via Birmingham').

routine (1) A sequence of instructions in the facilities of a computer system that can be independently loaded or called to perform some repetitive operation ('an operating-system routine'; 'a housekeeping routine') or an operation that is not specific to any user ('a library routine'; 'a mathematical routine'). A small routine that performs a repetitive operation is often termed a 'utility'. See *utility; subroutine*. **(2)** An independently loadable or callable sequence of instructions. In this sense, the term is synonymous with 'program' in most contexts. See *program*.

routing The operation of allocating lines, circuits, or intermediate destinations to telephone calls or to messages in a message switching system. See *route*.

routing code In some systems; hardware-interpretable digits attached to a message to control its routing.

routing indicator In a message header; a group of characters that identifies the final circuit, data station, or terminal through which the message will be routed for the addressee.

row (1) A linear, horizontal arrangement of items or of locations where items can be placed; for example, on a punched card. See *column; card row*. **(2)** A frame; a line of bit positions across magnetic tape or a line of punching positions across paper tape. **(3)** A vector; a one-dimensional array. See *array*.

row binary The use of punched card rows to hold (long) binary strings; each row of a standard (Hollerith) card can hold up to 80 binary digits. See *column binary*.

row pitch The centre-to-centre distance of adjacent rows (paper tape; edge-punched card).

RPG2 *Report Program Generator (2nd version)*. A high-level, commercially oriented programming language. It is somewhat easier to use than COBOL and is available for most minicomputers (and many mainframe computers).

RPL *Remote Program Load*.

RPQ *Request for Price Quotation*.

RPS *Rotational Position Sensing*.

RS *Record Separator*. A character used in data transmission, storage, or transfer to delimit two records (or other units of data).

RS-232C The EIA standard for serial data interfaces for connections up to 50 feet in length and for bit-serial data transmission at up to 20,000 bits per second. Signalling is NRZ with a 0-bit represented by a positive pulse between 3 V. and 25 V. and a 1-bit by a negative pulse in the same range. It has been adopted by CCITT in their Recommendations V.24 and V.28.

RS-422/3 A variation of the RS-232C interface that provides transmission at up to 10M bits per second over balanced lines up to 4,000 feet in length.

RT *Reperforator-Transmitter*.

RTC *Real-Time Clock*.

RTL *Resistor-Transistor Logic*.

RTS (1) *Ready To Send*. An interface signal from a DTE to a modem indicating that the DTE has data to send. See *modem interchanges*. **(2)** *Real-Time System*.

RTS-DCD simulation A facility for operating a switched carrier onward link via a constant carrier circuit between a central site modem and remote site modem. The purpose is to eliminate the need to raise and drop carrier in the 'main' circuit as DTE's in the onward link respond to polling messages. It, thus, permits the main circuit to be used for additional functions of communicating with multiple onward links and/or local DTE's at the remote site. When a DTE in the onward link responds to a polling message, it causes carrier to be sent to the repeater modem which passes RTS to the remote site modem. The remote site modem then sends a special Start Of Message (SOM) group to the central site modem which causes that modem to raise DCD to the central site DTE. After the completion of the transmission, the onward link DTE drops RTS causing its modem to drop carrier and when this is detected by the repeater modem, it drops RTS to the remote site modem. This modem then sends a 'DCD drop code' to the central site modem causing it to drop DCD to the central site DTE. See *onward link; DCD drop code.*

RTTY *Radio TeleTYpe.*

rubber banding In computer graphics; the movement of a common vertex of a set of lines without moving their other ends.

run (1)A single execution of a batch program; an execution with a particular set of input data. (2)The sequential execution of a group of programs or jobs; the execution of all the programs of a job queue. (3)Processing performed for the indicated purpose; ('an update run'; 'a spooling run'). (4)To execute or cause to be executed; ('run a program').

run duration (1)The elapsed time between the beginning of a run and its completion. (2)Running time.

run queue A job queue.

run stream A job stream.

run-time (1)The time when execution of a program or job commences or is scheduled to commence. (2)Running time.

run-time parameter Also *external program parameter.* A value that is required for the execution of a program and which is input before commencing the run.

run unit (1)A load module. (2)In some virtual storage systems; a named collection of the pages/segments required by a particular process.

running time Processing time; the time required to execute a particular program.

RVA *Recorded Voice Announcement.*

R/W *Read/Write.*

RX (Rx) A term used to indicate 'receive', 'receiver', or 'receive mode'. See *TX.*

RZ(NP) *Return-to-Zero (Non-Polarised).* See *non-polarised-return-to-zero.*

RZ(P) *Return-to-Zero (Polarised).* See *polarised-return-to-zero.*

S

S100 A common interconnecting bus for microprocessor systems; it contains a hundred pins and is designed particularly for systems using Intel 8080 and similar microprocessors.

SA (1)*Systems Analyst.* (2)*Systems Analysis.*

SAC *Store Access Control.*

sample and hold (S/H) A first step in making an analogue to digital conversion where high-speed digitising of analogue waves is performed; for example, in digital video and digital speech systems. It consists of charging a capacitor during each sample period (say, every 20 microseconds) and using the period between sampling to perform the A/D conversion.

sampling (1)The process of measuring a variable at timed intervals for purposes of control, analysis, or changing the form of representation. For an example, see *pulse amplitude modulation.* (2)The process of determining the characteristics of a group by determining the individual characteristics of a statistically significant percentage of its members.

satellite See *communications satellite; satellite computer.*

Satellite Business System (SBS) A large-scale communications and data base access system employing satellite communications links as proposed/operated by IBM, Communications Satellite Corp. and Aetna Life and Casualty Co.

satellite communications Communications by means of signals transmitted to and received from an orbiting satellite. In all current systems, the satellite is in a geosynchronous orbit (it remains stationary over a particular place on the equator) at a height of about 22,300 miles. The most widely used system is that provided by International Telecommunications Satellite Organisation (Intelsat) consisting of members from more than one hundred nations, most of which are governmental and private telephone organisations. Other systems include the Marisat group that handles ship-ship and ship-shore communications, the Canadian Telesat system for internal communications, the Western Union Westar system for television, data, and voice throughout the U.S., the RCA Satcom system which covers all states (including Alaska and Hawaii) and Puerto Rico, and the Comstar system operated by the Comsat General Corp. New systems include the Satellite Business System (SBS), the Xerox Telecommunications Network and

Advanced Communications Service. Internal communications systems using leased Intelsat facilities are in use or planned in Indonesia, Peru, Norway, Brazil, Nigeria, Algeria, and other countries. Nineteen European PTT's are cooperating to establish the Eutelsat system. Russia has an extensive system using Statsionar satellites. The current Intelsat satellites are the 4A and the 5. The 4A uses a 6 GHz. uplink and a 4 GHz. downlink and can provide 6000 simultaneous voice circuits. It uses focused east and west beams to provide extra power on the longest links, and a global beam that can be received throughout its area of coverage (about 120 degrees of longitude). The Intelsat 5 has an additional 14 GHz. uplink and 11 GHz. downlink and can provide from 12000 to 14000 simultaneous voice circuits. Communications with satellites is by earth stations that use steerable parabolic antennas of up to 90 Ft. in diameter. (Though the satellites are 'stationary', they have slightly irregular orbits due to variations in the earth's gravitational field.) Current systems derive circuits by frequency division multiplexing, in the same manner as used in most telephone systems. Future developments may include digital transmission and satellite-to-satellite message routing.

satellite computer (1) In a data network; a computer at a data station that can be linked with the main or central computer. **(2)**At a computer installation; a smaller computer that performs some operation or group of operations for the main computer; for example, a front-end processor or a data base processor.

SATCOM *SATellite COMmunications.*

saturation (1) With respect to a bipolar transistor; the condition in which the gate current equals or exceeds the value necessary to provide full emitter-collector conduction. A saturated transistor takes longer to turn off when gate current is removed than is the case with an unsaturated transistor (one in which the gate current is just sufficient to maintain the level of conduction). Hence, semiconductor circuits in which transistors are unsaturated (ECL; Schottky TTL) are faster than those in which it is difficult to prevent saturation (RTL; DTL; TTL). **(2)**In magnetisable surface recording, the condition in which magnetisable particles are essentially completely aligned; the condition in which an increased writing signal produces no increase in the signal obtained when reading. **(3)**With respect to a diode; the condition in which it is fully conducting; the condition in which circuit voltage exceeds its inherent forward voltage drop (usually about 1 V.).

save area (1) An area of main storage used to retain the contents of control unit and arithmetic unit registers. See *restart*. **(2)**In a virtual storage system; an area of primary storage used to hold pages/segments (say, those of the operating system) that cannot be deleted. See *locked down; partition; virtual storage transfers.*

SBC *Single-Board Computer.*

SBS *Satellite Business System.*

SC *SemiConductor.*

scalar Capable of being represented by a single number (as contrasted, for example, to a 'vector' which is represented by end coordinates). Examples of scalar quantities include weight, speed, and temperature.

scale (1) The size relationship between one entity or value and another. **(2)**To change values in order to bring them within some required range; for example, to change the dimensions of a drawing to make it smaller ('reduce its scale'). It is performed by multiplying or dividing by a constant (a 'scale factor').

scale factor A constant by which values are multiplied or divided in order to change scale.

scaling A term applied to the operation of reducing chip and element sizes in the manufacture of integrated circuits.

scan (1) In a cathode ray tube; to move the electron beam across the display area in closely spaced lines in order to place an image on the screen or to refresh it. See *raster; retrace time.* **(2)**With respect to a graphic image (OCR; facsimile); to pass a sensor or receptor across it in a sequence of closely spaced lines in order to detect differences in light transmission or reflectivity and, thus, to represent the image as a series of electrical signals for transmission. **(3)**With respect to a number of circuits (say, from each of a number of terminals); to connect them individually and in rotation to a single circuit. See *time division multiplexing.* **(4)**With respect to a group of bit positions or registers; to read them in continuing rotation in order to detect changes in contents; for example, to check for flags being set, for peripherals becoming free, or for a key pressed on a keyboard. **(5)**By a compiler or assembler; to examine source code for purposes of identifying elements, condensation, or ordering. See *lexical scan; arithmetic scan.*

scan frequency Scan rate.

scan head The movable element of a scanning device (OCR;

facsimile) that contains the sensor or receptor.

scan line One of the group of parallel lines that is followed by a scanning element (electron beam; scan head) across a display field (cathode ray tube) or graphic image (OCR; facsimile).

scan period The length of time taken to perform a scan; the time between successive presence of the scanning element at the same entity (scan line; circuit; bit position).

scan rate The number of scans performed per unit time (usually, per second).

scanner (1) A device that can examine a field (paper; film) in linear increments and output electrical signals to represent an image on the field for transmission and subsequent analysis, storage, or reproduction. **(2)** A device that can connect a single circuit in rotation to each of a number of other circuits (as in time division multiplexing). **(3)** A program of a compiler or assembler that examines source code to determine the significance of character groups and provides ordering and/or condensation. See *compiler*.

scatter (1) A dispersion around a central, correct, or normal value or position. **(2)** To place in non-contiguous storage locations.

scatter format An attribute of an overlay program that permits its sections to be loaded into non-contiguous locations in main storage.

scatter loading Loading in which segments of a program are placed in non-contiguous locations in main storage. See *block loading*.

scatter table An index to a sparse array.

scattered wind With magnetic tape; an uneven wind in which some strands protrude beyond others at the sides of the reel.

schedule (1) To determine the programs or jobs that will be executed in a particular run or during a particular period. **(2)** To preallocate resources to tasks.

scheduled maintenance Maintenance performed at predetermined times.

scheduler Also, in some systems, *dispatcher*. The elements of an operating system that initiate and terminate the execution of programs by maintaining a job queue and allocating resources to programs according to their priority and the availability of the resources.

scheduler proposed-queue A job queue.

scheduler waiting-queue A queue of jobs that are ready to run but are held for some reason (usually, awaiting release by the operator).

scheduling algorithm An algorithm used by the job scheduler to determine which program in the job queue to execute. It may take into consideration the priorities of the different programs, how long they have remained in the job queue, and the resources they require.

schema A description of the overall logical structure of a data base. In the CODASYL definition, it is a complete description (in Data Description Language) of all of the realms, set occurrences, record occurrences, and associated data items and data aggregates as they exist in a data base. See *data base; data description language; subschema; set; realm*.

Schottky diode A diode in which a doped silicon cathode is in direct contact with a metallic anode. It is characterised by a forward voltage drop of less than 0.5 V. though it has higher leakage current and poorer blocking characteristics than a conventional diode in which cathode and anode are opposite types of doped silicon.

Schottky transistor An NPN transistor that incorporates a Schottky diode between the base and collector, as indicated in Fig. 1. The purpose is to shunt excess base current into the

collector-emitter path and, thus, to prevent saturation of the base-emitter junction. Eliminating saturation reduces the ON-OFF transition time. The symbol is shown in Fig. 2.

Schottky TTL A type of TTL in which all transistors are 'Schottky'. It is characterised by propagation delay as low as 3 ns. and power dissipation of only about 2 mW. per gate. It is the storage and logic technology of many computers. See *Schottky transistor; transistor-transistor logic*.

scientific computer A computer with extensive hardware facilities for performing mathematical calculations at high speed and, usually, with a large library of mathematical and statistical routines. Input/output, backing storage, and text-handling facilities are often limited to those needed to input problems, control processing, and output results.

scientific language A programming language designed for writing programs to solve mathematical and statistical problems; the most common are ALGOL and FORTRAN. See *language*.

scissoring In a display on a graphics VDU; the removal of display elements that lie outside of a window. See *window*.

SCL *System Control Language*.

scope (1) The place from which a variable can be accessed; in set terminology, it is the total of its owners. **(2)** Of a variable (storage location identified in the program); the parts of the program in which it can be accessed. In a block-structured language, the scope extends to the end of the block in which it is declared and includes any inner blocks (unless it has been redeclared in an inner block). **(3)** An oscilloscope.

scramble pattern (1) A bit transformation as produced by a scrambler. **(2)** A random pattern as printed on a copy (say, of a multipart invoice) to make illegible any characters copied to the area of the pattern.

scrambler In a modem; circuitry that applies an algorithm to an input data stream to produce a different output data stream. The usual purpose is to ensure that there are enough line transitions in the output stream to enable the receiving modem to maintain synchronisation, regardless of the patterns of the input stream.

scratch (1) With respect to data (on a magnetisable surface medium); to erase it. **(2)** With respect to a label or file name; to delete it from system tables.

scratch file An area of a volume (magnetic disc; magnetic tape) allocated to a program as a work area.

scratchpad memory A module of high-speed, coordinate-addressable memory used as a system buffer or work area.

screen (1) That part of a display device (cathode ray tube; gas plasma panel; microfilm reader) on which a display can appear. See *cathode ray tube; display*. **(2)** All the items (lines of text; graphics) that are programmed to appear together on the screen of a VDU. **(3)** In an interactive system that operates by menu selection; a particular display considered with respect to its function or use by the operator; ('a mode select screen'; 'a menu screen'; 'an output screen').

screen-based A term sometimes applied to a small computer in which inputs are by keyboard and inputs and outputs are displayed on the screen of an (integral) cathode ray tube.

screen overlay A facility of a display-control program that permits an operator of a VDU to retain display images in one area of the screen while causing new images to appear in another area.

screen image A display image.

scroll ribbon The usual inked ribbon for a line printer; the standard size is 14 inches wide by 25 yards long. See *ribbon; tape ribbon*.

scrolling An operation or facility of a VDU in which display elements make a continuous bottom-to-top vertical movement across the screen (or a window) under control of the operator, with display lines appearing at the bottom edge and dropping off at the top. See *rack up; roll up; roll down; page turning*.

SDI *Selective Dissemination of Information*.

SDL *System Designers Limited*. (Camberley, Surrey)

SDLC *Synchronous Data Link Control*.

search An operation performed on a group of items to locate a particular item or all items with some common attribute or to verify that no items with a certain attribute are included in the group. It is commonly performed by a routine that loads the identifier of the required item(s) in one register and then successively loads identifiers of items in the group in another register and performs identity tests of the two items. It may or may not apply some algorithm to reduce the number of items that must be 'tested'. Typically, the identifiers are record keys (customer number; part number) and the 'group' is one or more files. If the items are in random order in storage, a **serial search** must be performed to read the identifiers one after the other (starting at one end of the storage) until a match is found or until all items have been read and tested. Where a search of this type is performed as a regular method of data retrieval, it is termed **content access** (also **associative access**). A **parallel search** is such a search in which the storage is divided into (equal-length) sections and items are tested in groups comprising one item from each section. When the items are in sequence according to the identifiers being searched (say, records searched by primary key in a sequential file), search time can be greatly reduced by using a **binary search** (also **dichotomising search; binary chop**) in which the key of the item that is physically nearest the centre of the storage area is tested first. If this identifier is a lower number than that of the item required, then the item is in the upper half and the lower half can be disregarded. The upper half is then divided at its midpoint and another identifier is tested which, again, causes half to be rejected. Division and testing are done on increasingly smaller areas of storage until the item is located. (A binary search will locate any item in 1000 by reading and testing 10 identifiers, as compared to an average of 500 for a serial search.) A **Fibonacci search** is similar to a binary search except that it makes an asymmetric division. Unless otherwise indicated, a search is performed to locate a single item or a contiguous group of items (or to verify that it is not present). A **sort** is a search to locate all items with a certain attribute where the items are distributed through the group. See *sort; identity; Fibonacci search*.

search cycle The loop performed to make a search; typically, it consists of reading an item, making an identity test with the item and another item, and outputting the result.

search key The identifier of the item for which the search is performed; the value with which other values are compared in making a search. See *search*.

search time (1) The time to locate an item in backing storage and read it into main storage. **(2)** The time taken to perform a 'search'; the time to locate a particular item or to determine that it is not present. **(3)** Access time; the time required to read the contents of a location across the device interface.

search word A word that holds a search key.

second-generation computer A computer employing discrete semiconductors and core memory. See *generation*.

second-level address An indirect address.

second-level storage (1) Also *secondary storage*. Storage with an access time between that of main storage and magnetic drum or fixed-head disc (say, with an access time between 5 microseconds and 20 milliseconds). The main technologies are bubble and CCD. **(2)** Backing storage.

second-source An arrangement by which a primary manufacturer (and patent holder) of a particular device (usually a semiconductor) provides rights and assistance to another manufacturer to enable it to produce an identical device. The second manufacturer is said to 'second-source' the device. The arrangement is made, at least partly, to ensure that OEM customers will not have their production disrupted in event the primary manufacturer becomes unable to supply the device.

second variable A logic operation with an output that is 'true' if the second of two inputs is 'true' and 'false' if it is 'false'. See *first variable; logic operation*.

secondary channel In data communications; a transmission channel with a narrow bandwidth that is derived from the main channel by a notch filter that introduces a 'guard band' of highly attenuated frequencies to split the channel. Such a channel can be used as a supervisory channel, for low-speed data that is independent of that on the main channel, or for telemetry. See *asymmetric duplex; supervisory channel*.

secondary coil In a transformer; the coil from which the output is taken. See *transformer*.

secondary console In a computer system with multiple consoles; any console other than the master console.

secondary destination Of a message; any destination other than the primary destination.

secondary entry point In a program; any entry point except at the beginning.

secondary function (1) Of a system or functional unit; a function other than the main (primary) function. **(2)** The function of a data station that responds to commands from the master station in accordance with the link protocol. See *primary function*.

secondary index (1) An index that is referenced via another index. **(2)** A secondary key.

secondary key Also *alternate key*. A key used to make a unique identification of a record where there are two or more records with the same primary key. See *key; auxiliary key; primary key*.

secondary key field In a record; a field that holds a secondary key (or a value that can be used as a secondary key).

secondary paging device A backing storage device (magnetic disc unit) that is available to hold pages/segments for transfer to and from primary storage when the primary paging device becomes overloaded. See *primary paging device*.

secondary space clearing An operation to zero-fill the space occupied by a file (magnetic disc; magnetic tape) when the file is deleted.

secondary station Also *tributary station*. In a data network; a data station that is capable of assuming the 'secondary function' but not the 'primary function' (a data station that responds to polling messages but does not initiate them).

secondary storage (1) In a virtual storage system; that part of backing storage (magnetic disc; magnetic tape) that holds code and data organised into pages and/or segments. In such a system, backing storage may be divided into 'secondary storage' and 'filestore' in which data is held in conventional file structures (for processing in non-virtual mode). In many virtual storage systems, backing storage is termed 'secondary storage' no matter how organised. When such storage is considered as hardware (in contrast to 'virtual storage'), it may be termed **physical storage**. See *storage; primary storage; backing storage; virtual storage terms.* (2)Auxiliary storage; any storage other than main storage. (3)Second-level storage; storage with an access time between that of main storage and magnetic disc.

section (1)A segment. (2)A named element of a COBOL program consisting of one or more paragraphs. (3)In computer graphics; to 'divide' a displayed object with an intersecting plane and display details of the intersection. (4)The details of the intersection produced (def. 3).

sector (1)In most magnetic disc systems; the smallest unit of any track that can be accessed directly by the hardware of the disc unit. (Finer accesses, say, of blocks or buckets, are made by reading headers.) When discussing the magnetic disc unit, the term usually denotes a 'pie-shaped' division of the disc surface(s) containing portions of all tracks; when discussing access, it denotes a portion of a single track. See *sectoring*. (2)To divide into 'sectors' (def. 1). (3)In some systems; a 'segment' or a 'block'.

sector counter In a magnetic disc unit; a register that is incremented by one as each sector mark is received (as each sector mark passes the sector transducer) and set to zero when the index mark is received (once each revolution). It, thus, always contains the number of the sector that is beneath the read/write heads.

sector mark A signal generated for access control purposes each time a sector mark passes the sector transducer (hard sectoring) or each time the 'missing clock' is detected (soft sectoring). See *sectoring; index mark.*

sector one-shot A sector pulse.

sector pulse Also *sector one-shot*. A pulse output from a sector transducer when a sector slot passes. See *sectoring.*

sector ring An element of a disc pack or the drive hub of a fixed disc in which sector slots are cut.

sector slot In a hard-sectored magnetic disc unit; a slot cut in a sector ring (that rotates with the discs) at the begining of each sector; it is detected by the sector transducer.

sector transducer An element of a magnetic disc unit that detects a flux or field discontinuity of the rotating sector ring when sector slot passes and generates a sector mark for access purposes. It is, typically, the same transducer that detects index slots and, when referred to in the latter function, it is termed an 'index transducer'. See *sectoring.*

sectored file A term sometimes applied to data (whether or not constituting a file) that is recorded on a sectored magnetic disc unit.

sectoring In a magnetic disc system; the division of disc surfaces (and, hence, of all tracks) into a number of equal-size portions (sectors) for access purposes. There are, typically, 12, 16, 24, or 32 sectors per surface and, hence, per track. With **hard sectoring** the division is determined by the number of **sector slots** which are gaps physically cut into a **sector ring** which rotates with the disc(s); in exchangeable disc systems, the sector ring is an element of the disc cartridge or pack and the number of slots is specified when ordering (24 slots is the most common). As the disc(s) rotate, a **sector transducer** detects a field or flux discontinuity as each slot passes and generates a **sector pulse** (also **sector one-shot**) which is used in a **sector counter** in the device to maintain the number of the sector that is under the read/write head(s).The contents of the sector counter are used to generate **sector marks** which, together with sector numbers, are transmitted to the host system (computer; peripheral controller) where they are used to control read and write operations. In some cases, more sectors are required than are provided by the sector slots and **pseudo sectoring** is employed; it consists of generating and transmitting a **pseudo sector mark** to the host system between each pair of sector marks, thus, effectively, doubling the number of sectors. In **soft sectoring** a special pattern (typically, two bytes long) is written at the beginning of each sector of each track during disc initialisation and the number of sectors is, thus, under the control of the initialisation program. The special pattern is formed by omitting (two) clock pulses and, for this reason, the method may be termed **missing-clock sectoring**. (It is usually an option available with a system that also includes facilities for hard sectoring.) In systems with track-following servo, index and sectoring information is normally recorded on the servo tracks. See *magnetic disc unit; sector; indexing; track-following servo; rotational position sensing.*

security A term applied to operations and checks made to prevent loss or corruption of data, to prevent unauthorised use of programs or access to data, and to prevent the presence of unauthorised persons in designated areas of a computer (or other) installation. See *integrity; privacy; privacy code; storage protection; access control; password.*

security code A privacy code.

seek In a movable-head magnetic disc unit; the operation of moving the read/write head(s) in order to read data from or write data to a different track. The mechanical movement is provided by a feedback-controlled servo system. When the new track address is received from the computer or device controller, it is compared with the current address to generate a 'difference address' with a sign that indicates the direction of movement. Most rigid disc units provide for multiple speed head movement with the highest speed reserved for long movements (say, more than 100 tracks). Flexible disc systems, and many 5¼ and 8 inch Winchester disc systems, use a stepping motor and begin each seek from the 'restore' (outermost track) position. In these devices, head movement is at a constant speed; typically at 6 ms. per track. A seek includes a head settling time of about 14 ms. and, in a flexible disc system, a head loading time of about 30 ms. In all systems, a seek is completed when the new track address (as recorded in the track header) is read and compared with the seek address as received from the computer or device controller. See *seek time; servo system; magnetic disc unit; latency*.

seek area A cylinder; all the tracks of a magnetic disc unit that can be read or written without repositioning the heads.

seek arm Also *access arm*. A movable member (part of a carriage) on which one or more read/write heads are mounted in a movable-head magnetic disc unit. See *magnetic disc unit; seek*.

seek command A cylinder address output from a host system (peripheral controller or I/O section of a computer) to a magnetic disc unit. See *seek*.

seek time Also *positioning time*. In a movable-head magnetic disc unit; the time required to reposition the heads to read or write a different track. It is usually expressed as an average time (the time required to move half the number of tracks on the disc surface). In a flexible-disc system, it also includes head loading and settling time. The table shows typical figures.

Type of unit	Seek Time	Track-to-Track
Standard, 14 in.	25-92 ms.	3-15 ms.
Winchester, 14 in.	25-65 ms.	3-15 ms.
Winchester, 8 in.	25-70 ms.	4-20 ms.
Flexible, 8 in.	160-300 ms.	50-70 ms.
Flexible, 5¼ in.	120-650 ms.	35-125 ms.

segment (1) A separately loadable sequence of instructions as part of an overlay program. See *overlay segment; control segment*. (2) In a virtual storage system; an individually accessible unit of code or data that is a standard (or the only) unit of secondary storage and transfer of code and data between secondary and primary storage. In most systems it is a **variable length segment** (also **logical segment**) that holds the code or data required by a program during a particular phase of its execution; a **shareable segment** can be used by more than one program. In a system that also uses 'pages' for storage and transfer; a short segment that is included with others in one page is a **paged segment**. Some paging systems provide for **fixed-length segments** which are units of storage and transfer consisting of a fixed number of pages that are not, necessarily, logically related. See *page; virtual storage allocation; virtual storage terms*. (3) A subdivision of a (linear) entity or group; ('a segment of a table'; 'a segment of paper tape'). (4) A sector; a division of the recording surface of a magnetic disc. (5) To divide into segments. (6) A component of an LED, LCD, or tungsten display; one of the 'bars' of a seven-segment display that can be illuminated (LED; tungsten) or darkened (LCD). See *segment decoder; seven-segment display*.

segment base The primary storage address of the first byte of a segment (a value held in a segment descriptor).

segment decoder A decoder and driver that inputs characters in bit-pattern form and outputs signals to the segment lights of characters (calculator; digital watch) to create the display. It operates in conjunction with a scan generator that provides the return electrical path from the segments. See *character generator; seven-segment display*.

segment descriptor In a segmented virtual storage system; an element of a segment table that holds access-related information about a particular segment. Typical contents include access mode and shareability, location in secondary storage, and, if loaded, its location in primary storage. If the segment is in primary storage, the descripor will also, typically, contain its bounds and an indication of frequency of use or when last used. See *descriptor*.

segment number A value by which a segment is known to the operating system; it, typically, consists of an identification of the segment table in which its descriptor is contained and the position of the descriptor in the table.

segment-relative address The address of a location within a

segment, taking the first location as zero. Added to the 'segment base', it produces the absolute address of the location.

segment table An operating system table containing segment descriptors, or all the descriptors of a particular group of segments. See *segment; page/segment table*.

segment table entry In some systems; a segment descriptor.

segment translation exception An interrupt condition caused by the inability to translate a virtual address to a physical address.

segmentation (1)The process of dividing a unit into segments. (2)A term sometimes applied to the operation of moving segments between secondary and primary storage; in this sense, it corresponds to 'paging' when the unit moved is a 'page'.

segmentation system A virtual storage system that employs segments.

segmented (1)Divided into segments; ('a segmented program'). (2)Of a virtual storage system; using segments as one of the standard units of storage and transfer (or the only unit).

select To chose one of several items or possibilities. See *deselect*.

selection (1)A method of operating a data network in which a data station with a message to send 'selects' (transmits the address) of the data station that is to receive it. The method requires the receiving equipment at each data station to have the facilities to recognise its station address (and to ignore others). It also requires a method of resolving contention. See *polling*. (2)The process of examining entities and placing them in groups according to common attributes; the process of determining which entities have specified attributes.

selection check A check made to ensure that an item located is the one required; for example, in a magnetic disc access, to read a track number from a track header and compare it with the track number output to the magnetic disc unit.

selection sort A method of placing items in sequential order according to value or key in which the items of a group are examined to locate the first item in the sequence and, when located, it is written to the new set (in a different location). This is repeated to locate the second item and then the third and this is continued until all items are in the new set. The number of items that must be read and tested in each pass can be reduced by using a **repeated selection sort** in which the original group is divided into sections. One item from each section (say, the lowest numbered) is then written to an intermediate set and when all items are in the intermediate set a selection sort is applied to it.

selective calling A method of operating a large data network (such as Telex) in which a data station with a message to send transmits a 'call directing code' or 'station selection code' which routes the call to the station that is to receive the message. (Switching is, typically, by means of relay equipment as used in a telephone system.)

selective dissemination of information (SDI) A service, as supplied by a library, in which individuals receive abstracts (or notices of receipt) of items (books; articles in periodicals) on topics in which they have expressed an interest.

selective dump A dump of the contents of specified registers or storage locations. See *dump*.

selective sequential Also *skip sequential*. An access method in which specific records or groups are read from an indexed sequential file (skipping those that are not required). When the access is to a sequential subset of the records, a keyed access is made to the first record and the others are read sequentially. See *indexed sequential file; sequential access*.

selective-serial update An update in situ.

self-check digit A digit with a property that can be used for validation purposes; for example, a digit that is invalid unless within a certain range.

self-checking code A code in which each valid instance must conform to a particular pattern, with the pattern inherent in the code rather than supplied or established externally; for example, an M-out-of-N code.

self-clocking A term applied to a method of magnetisable surface recording (FM; MFM) in which flux transitions representing clock pulses are introduced as integral parts of the data recording. When the data is read, these transitions are detected and used to establish and maintain synchronisation, thus making a clock track unnecessary.

self-indexed file A sequential file in which records are placed in fixed-length, numbered locations in which there is a direct relationship between key number and location number; for example, the location number could be determined by dividing the key by a constant. The algorithm is, typically, selected so that there is a one-to-one relationship between keys and locations so storage space is wasted wherever items are missing from the sequence. See *random file; relative record file*.

self-modifying instruction An instruction that is modified during execution. See *instruction modification*.

self-organising A term sometimes applied to a program that is capable of altering its function depending upon its inputs.

self-relative address An operand address that is a displacement from the address of the instruction in which it is contained.

semantic compatibility Of computers of different type or manufacture; the condition in which each can execute programs compiled for the other to produce the same results.

semantic error An error (detected during compilation) that consists of using the wrong operator or symbolic address.

semantics (1) The study of the meanings of words and the way these develop and change. It is concerned with definitions and not with how particular words are used in relation to others or how their use conforms to the rules of some language. See *syntax*. (1) The relationship between symbols and their meanings particularly, in the computer sense, between the symbols used in programming and their meaning (function) in the programming language being used or their consistency of meaning within a program. It is, for example, a 'semantic rule' that states that a particular symbolic address cannot be applied to different entities and that reserved words in a language cannot be used as data names.

semaphore (1) A flag; a bit or combination of bits that indicates that a particular event has occurred during processing. In some systems, a 'flag' is dealt with by software and a 'semaphore' by hardware. **(2)** In the concurrent processing of two interdependent programs; a control structure by which intermediate results are passed between programs. **(3)** In a multiprocessor system; a bit or combination of bits by which one processor indicates its status to others (or to the control processor); for example, a bit that is 'set' when one transfer is completed and another one can begin.

semiautomatic message switching Message switching in which an operator routes messages as indicated in their headers.

semiconductor An electronic device that depends for its operation on a controlled, unidirectional flow of electrons between two types of silicon or germanium. (Silicon is by far the most commonly used.) Pure silicon is a poor conductor of electric current because each atom has four electrons and four holes (places for electrons) in its outer or 'valence' ring and the atoms tend to lock tightly together with electrons of each atom filling holes in adjacent atoms. There are, thus, no available or 'free' electrons to conduct electric current. If the silicon is **doped** during processing with a small amount of material with five valence electrons (usually, phosphorus), free electrons become available to conduct current; silicon so treated is termed **N-type**. A battery is a source of electrons at its negative (—) terminal and has a need for electrons (is a source of 'holes') at its positive (+) terminal. In Figure 1, a battery is

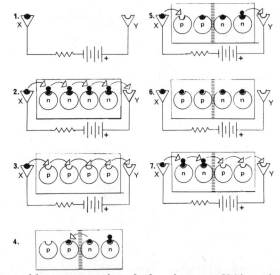

shown with a representation of a free electron at X (the end of a conductor from its negative terminal) and a 'hole' from the positive terminal at Y. If a piece of N-type silicon is placed between the conductors, as in Fig. 2, the electron at X bumps off one of the 'free' electrons in the doped silicon and it bumps off another in a continuing sequence until one reaches the other end of the silicon and 'jumps into' the hole at Y. As this is repeated millions of times per second, a current flows in the circuit. If, instead of phosphorus, the silicon is doped with boron or some other element with only three electrons in its valence ring, then an excess of holes is created; silicon so doped is termed **P-type**. Electric current can also be conducted by holes and such conduction is the distinguishing feature of semiconductors. In Fig. 3, a piece of P-type silicon is placed between the conductors, and an electron at X jumps into a hole in the silicon and then jumps from hole to hole until it reaches Y and, again, a current flows in the circuit. (In both types of conduction mentioned, the surplus of electrons at X tends to 'throw off' electrons and the deficit at Y attracts them thus creating a 'field' that causes the transfer.) If a piece of pure silicon is doped on one side to create N-type and on the other side to create P-type, a **junction** is formed where the two types meet, as shown in Fig. 4. Along a thin plane through the junction, the holes in the P-type silicon attract and 'capture' free electrons from the N-type silicon thus forming a **depletion layer** in which there are no **carriers** (holes or free electrons). If a battery is connected with polarity as shown in Fig. 5, this depletion layer prevents a current flow because electrons from X jump in and fill holes in the P-type silicon while free electrons in the N-type jump out to Y. Note that the effect has been to broaden the depletion layer; within limits, the greater the external voltage applied to the junction, the greater the resistance to current flow. This broadening of the depletion layer is shown in Fig. 6. If the silicon is reversed so that it is connected as shown in Fig. 7, electrons from X jump into the adjacent N-type silicon and bump off electrons which tend to jump into the depletion layer at the same time that Y is attracting electrons from the layer. The depletion layer is thus eliminated as a barrier to current flow, as long as the battery is connected with this polarity. A semiconductor, such as described, that limits current flow to only one direction is a **diode** which is a common element of electronic circuits. All semiconductors rely upon depletion layers to control conduction, though not all use junctions as described. A circuit or device that uses semiconductors is often termed **solid state**. See *diode; transistor; field effect transistor; integrated circuit*.

semiconductor device An electronic component containing one or more semiconductors and appropriate terminals for wiring it into a circuit. Common devices include integrated circuits, diodes, and transistors. See *semiconductor; element; package*.

semiconductor memory Memory in which each storage cell consists of one or more semiconductors. The basic types are **read-only memory** (ROM) in which a bit is permanently written in each storage cell and **random access memory** (RAM) in which cell contents can be changed rapidly by an electrical pulse. The term also includes certain 'serial access' types such as CCD and BEAMOS; unless otherwise indicated, the term denotes a **coordinate-addressable** memory in which storage cells are arranged in a matrix with connecting 'row' and 'column' conductors by which they are selected for reading (and writing, in the case of RAM). See *random access memory; read-only memory; coordinate-addressable storage*.

send With respect to signals or a message; to move from one location to another (say, by telegraph or telephone facilities).

send-only (SO) A term applied to an item of equipment in a communications system that can send messages/signals but not receive them. See *receive-only*.

sending field A source field.

sense To detect a particular physical condition or change in physical condition (magnetic particle orientation; light transmission through paper) and output an electrical signal that can be used to identify it.

sense amplifier A circuit used to amplify the signals produced in the coil of a read/write head when reading data recorded on a magnetisable surface medium.

sensing station In a card reader, optical mark reader, or similar device; the position of a sensor (read head; photodiode) in relation to the reference edge of the data carrier.

sensitive (1) Capable of responding to a small change in some physical condition; ('a sensitive photodiode'; 'a sensitive transducer'). (2) Critical of adjustment or lacking tolerance for variations in operating conditions; ('a sensitive circuit'). (3) Responsive to the indicated input or condition; ('a light-sensitive diode'; 'a program-sensitive fault').

sensor A device that detects and/or measures some physical condition and outputs an analogue indication. Examples include a thermocouple and a strain gauge.

sensor-based A term applied to a computer with inputs that are mainly or exclusively from 'sensors' (as in a process control application).

sentinal (1) A flag. (2) Also *tape mark*. In some magnetic tape systems; a short block that identifies the data that precedes it or follows it. It is used in searching to eliminate the need to read the entire contents of headers.

separating character In a code; a character that is used as a delimiter.

separator A delimiter; a character that separates units of data in storage or transmission; ('a file separator'; 'a field separator').

septet A unit consisting of seven elements.

sequence (1) A group of items arranged in numerical order in which the items are themselves numbers, the items contain numbers as identifiers (keys), or for which numbers are derived by the quantification of some attribute. See *order; collating sequence*. (2)To place items in a 'sequence' (def. 1). (3)A string; a group in which items are arranged one following the other; ('a bit sequence'; 'a sequence of random numbers'). (4)A set of procedural steps that are taken one following another; ('a calling sequence'; 'a compiling sequence').

sequence by merge To sequence by repeated splitting and merging (while applying some algorithm that improves the sequencing with each performance).

sequence control program A system program that performs some function in determining the order in which programs are to be executed. See *scheduler*.

sequence control register (1)A register used by a sequence control program. (2)A current address register.

sequence control statement In a source program; a statement that specifies a branch and, possibly, the conditions for branching; a statement that specifies a conditional or unconditional branch.

sequenced frames See *standard data link control*.

sequencer A command interpreter.

sequencing The operation of placing items in a sequence.

sequencing key A sort key.

sequential Arranged or occurring in sequence.

sequential access (1)An access in which an operating system presents records to an application program in order according to the numeric values of their keys. In this sense, the term is used without regard to the organisation of the file or the steps taken to locate and sequence the records. (2)A serial access of a sequential file; an access in which records are presented for processing in the order in which they are stored, which is also their order by key. See *serial access; selective sequential*. (3)An access made to write one or more records to a storage medium in a sequence according to numeric values of keys.

sequential access storage Serial access storage.

sequential batch processing Batch processing in which the programs of a run are executed in the sequence in which they are input.

sequential circuit A circuit that performs some operation (multiplication; exponentiation) in a 'sequence' of steps, with the output of one step used as input to the next. See *iteration*.

sequential data set See *sequential file*.

sequential file A file in which records are held in physical locations in storage (magnetic disc; magnetic tape) in order according to the numeric values of their keys. See *sequential access; indexed sequential file; serial file*.

sequential operation An operation performed in a sequence of steps, each of which must be completed before the next in sequence is begun.

sequential processing (1)Sequential batch processing. (2)The processing of records in sequence according to the numeric values of their keys. See *sequential access; serial processing*.

sequential search A search performed to locate one or more records in a sequential file. See *search*.

sequential storage Serial storage; the storage of a serial access device.

serial In a string; following one after another in space or time. See *sequence; series*.

serial access (1)An access in which an operating system presents records to an application program in the order in which they are held on their storage medium. See *sequential access*. (2)An access made to write one or more records to a storage location following any records that are already in the location. (3)An access to any particular item of data that is held with other items of data on a serial access device; an access in which the access time depends upon the number of other items of data that must be read, checked, or counted before the required one appears at the location where it can be read.

serial access device A device in which the access of a particular data item involves the reading, checking, or counting of other data items on the storage medium. The term is applied to a magnetic tape unit or a paper tape punch or reader and may also be applied to a 'recirculating' memory device such as CCD or bubble. See *cyclic access*.

serial access medium A storage medium (magnetic tape; paper tape) that only supports serial access.

serial adder An adder that adds digits in one digit position at a time. See *adder; parallel adder*.

serial addition Binary addition in which the digits are added in one digit position at a time, beginning at the rightmost digit position, and in which any carries are performed before adding the digits in the next digit position. See *adder; parallel addition*.

serial computer A term sometimes applied to a 'conventional' computer with a single control unit and arithmetic unit to differentiate it from a parallel computer. See *parallel computer*.

serial file (1) A file in which records are stored one following the other on the storage medium without regard to key sequence. See *sequential file*. (2) A file of any organisation on a serial access medium.

serial interface An interface (as between a DTE and a modem) through which data can only pass in bit-serial form. See *bit serial; bit parallel*.

serial number (1) An integer denoting the position of an item in a series. (2) A number and, possibly, letters placed on an item by its manufacturer (say, on a nameplate) to provide identification for such purposes as performing maintenance and supplying replacement parts.

serial operation (1) An operation performed with serial inputs. (2) A sequential operation.

serial printer A character printer; a printer that prints characters one after the other in the sequence in which they appear in a line. The printing is usually from left to right though some printers also have the facility to print lines starting at the right. See *printer*.

serial processing (1) Processing in which each unit to be processed passes through the same set of processing facilities. See *parallel processing*. (2) The processing of records in the order in which they are held in their storage medium. See *serial; sequential processing*.

serial transfer (1) A synchronous transfer; a transfer that interrupts instruction execution. (2) A bit-serial transfer.

serialiser A device that converts data from bit parallel to bit serial form. See *deserialiser; UART; USART*.

series (Ordering) (1) Also *sequence*. Events or items that occur one following the other; ('a series of messages'; 'a series of errors'). (2) Also *string; one-dimensional array*. A group of entities in contiguous positions; ('a series of records'; 'a series of numbers'). The term 'series' does not preclude logical ordering but where it exists, the term 'sequence' is preferable. See *sequence*. (3) A term often applied to those products of a manufacturer that have a basic structure in common; ('the IBM 4300 series').

series (Electrical) A term applied to a circuit in which two or more load items ('R' in the figures) are connected in a 'chain' between the terminals that supply voltage. In the first figure two load items (say, light bulbs) are connected in 'series' to a 220 V. supply. If they have the same resistance, they divide the voltage equally and each receives 110 V. The second figure shows a **parallel** circuit in which each load item is connected to the terminals and thus receives 220 V.

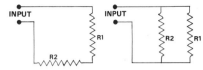

server In queue terminology, a facility or unit that is capable of providing the service for which the queue is formed.

service program A utility or a housekeeping program.

service routine A utility (often one that deals with interrupts).

servo A feedback controlled electromechanical device that provides the movement in a servo system. See *servo system*.

servo head In a magnetic disc unit with track-following servo; a read head that follows tracks on a disc servo surface and outputs signals that indicate whether it is centred between tracks and, if not, the direction the servo mechanism must move the heads to correct. See *track-following servo*.

servo surface In a magnetic disc unit with track-following servo; a disc surface on which servo tracks are recorded. See *track-following servo*.

servo system A system that provides accurate mechanical movement and is controlled, at least partly, by feedback from sensors that monitor the movement or its effects. In computer systems, the most common application is in positioning the read/write heads in magnetic disc units. The movement of the heads may be made by a **linear actuator** as indicated in Fig. 1

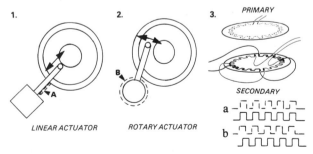

or by a **rotary actuator** as indicated in Fig. 2. An actuator of either type is operationally similar to a direct current motor. The other essential element of the system is a **position transducer** which is attached to the base and carriage in the location 'A' (Fig. 1) or 'B' (Fig. 2). The transducer is, in effect, a transformer with clock pulses applied to the primary (the transmitter) on the carriage and with track indication obtained from the secondary (the receiver) attached to the fixed deck of the drive. The transducer elements for a rotary actuator are shown in Fig. 3. When the two are precisely aligned, as indicated in 3a, the linkage is maximum and full pulses are output from the secondary. A small movement of the carriage changes the relative positions to 3b where no current is induced in the secondary. Maximum output of the secondary coincides with the centreline of a track on the magnetic discs; the 'pulses' produced as the carriage moves are counted by an electronic circuit to locate the new track. When the heads are on the track, any falling off of the output of the secondary indicates a 'wander' from the centreline and causes the circuitry to output a pulse to the actuator to cause it to move the heads back to the centre of the track; this operation is termed **electronic detenting**. Another, and somewhat more precise, method of control is provided by track-following servo. See *track-following servo; magnetic disc unit*.

servo track On a magnetic disc in a unit with track-following servo; a track with a recorded pattern that, when read by a servo head, indicates whether or not the heads are positioned correctly. See *track-following servo*.

session (1)The time during which an operator at an interactive terminal is in communications with the computer; the time between log on and log off. (2)The time during which programs or devices are in communications with each other.

set (1)A group of entities of the same class or type that are intended to be used in sequences or combinations to perform some function; ('a character set'; 'an instruction set'). See *group; subset*. (2)A named collection of related records consisting of an owner and some or all of its members. See *net*. (3)To place a device in a specified condition (by means of controls or adjustments); ('set screen brightness'; 'set a scan rate'). (4)To establish a particular value or condition; ('set a counter to 20'; 'set space characters in all positions'). See *reset*. (5)To write a 1-bit in a particular location; ('set a flag'; 'set a core'). (6)To put into a form acceptable for printing; ('set type'; 'set an instruction manual').

set up (1)To establish a system; to select and arrange elements to accomplish some function; ('set up a data network'). (2)To place a functional unit in initial operation; ('set up a printer').

settle Of a device or circuit; to reach a stable state after change or disruption.

setup Also, sometimes, *architecture*. The arrangement or function of a system; ('a batch setup').

seven-segment display The common 'figure-8' display of calculators, digital watches, petrol pumps, and many other devices. The segments are selectively activated to produce decimal digits and/or a limited alphabetic set. See *calculator; segment decoder*.

sexadecimal Hexadecimal; with a radix of 16.

sextet Six contiguous bits or bit positions.

S/H *Sample and Hold*.

shadow memory Memory that has the same range of addresses as some other memory and which can be accessed by means of a 'shift' or 'escape' facility.

shannon The binary unit of information content equal to the decision content of a set of two mutually exclusive events expressed as a logarithm to base 2. For example, the decision content of a character set of eight characters is equal to 3 shannons and that of a 3-character set is 1.58 shannons. See *hartley*.

shaped character printer A printer that prints the characters of some standard type font (from type slugs), as contrasted to one that prints dot-matrix characters. Examples include a typewriter, a chain printer, and a barrel printer.

shareable Of a unit of code or data (file; page; segment) in a multiprogramming system; available to two or more concurrent programs. See *local; global; public*.

shared file In a multiprocessor system; direct access storage that can be accessed by two or more processors.

shared logic system A system in which a single intelligent device performs certain functions for associated unintelligent devices. Examples include a system in which a terminal control unit holds video buffers and performs line interface functions for unintelligent VDU terminals and a word processing system in which a central control unit performs memory accesses and formatting functions for a number of operator work stations.

sheet feed A term applied to a page printer or other printer in which the input is separate sheets of paper, as contrasted to one that uses paper in the form of a web (continuous roll) or fanfold stack.

sheet film Photographic film that is supplied in flat pack rather than on a roll.

sheet-to-roll duplicator A device for making multiple copies of single microforms. See *duplicator*.

sheet-to-sheet duplicator A device for making individual copies of microforms. See *duplicator*.

shelves A term sometimes applied to registers or storage locations that permit data items to be added and removed at both ends. See *stack*.

shift (1) With respect to bits in a register; to move them to the left or right in increments of one bit position at a time. An **arithmetic shift** is one in which provision is made for retaining a sign bit and, usually, to raise an interrupt if a (leftward) shift would cause truncation of significant digits; it has the effect of multiplying (leftward) or dividing (rightward) by the radix; for example, moving a binary number one bit position to the left has the effect of multiplying it by two. A **logic shift** is a shift of an item for which the register holds no sign bit or a shift in which no provision is made to retain a sign bit. A **cyclic shift** is a shift in which items that 'fall off' at one end of the register are written back in at the other end of the register. **(2)** With respect to characters (letters or numbers) in their bit-pattern form (in the computer storage code); to move them in increments of one character (say, eight bit positions) to the left or right in a computer word or in a multiword unit of storage. Such shifts are made in text editing, for example, when adding new words in a displayed line or when centering lines in a print field. **(3)** In a keyboard device; to change the relationship between the keys and the characters they cause to be printed, displayed, or transmitted. For example, in a typewriter, a 'shift' changes the key functions to cause upper-case letters and special symbols to be printed. The term 'shift' is commonly used if the change includes going to upper-case letters. When the change is made to extend the range of a code or to provide the keys with additional functions (say, to permit the 8-key to be used to clear margins), the term 'code shift', 'code extension' or 'escape' is used. See *code extension; figures shift; letters shift; locking*. **(4)** A change in position or value; for example, a frequency change in 'frequency shift keying' or a 'bit shift' in magnetisable surface recording. **(5)** A period of computer operation considered with respect to staff assignment or work scheduling.

shift character In a data transmission code or system protocol; a bit pattern that causes receiving hardware to change the interpretation of one or more of the bit patterns that follow it, particularly one that causes a change from 'letters' to 'figures' (or the reverse). See *escape; code extension character; shift in; shift out*.

shift in In a data communications system in which bit-pattern characters have primary and secondary graphic (or control) interpretations; to change from the secondary interpretation to the primary. See *SI; shift out*.

shift key On a keyboard; a key that can be used to change the characters produced by other keys (from upper to lower case or the reverse). See *shift; escape key*.

shift out In a data communications system in which bit-pattern characters have primary and secondary graphic (or control) interpretations; to change from the primary interpretation to the secondary; for example, from 'letters' to 'figures'. See *SO; shift in*.

shift register A string of storage cells with the necessary circuitry to permit reading, writing, and moving all bits to the left or

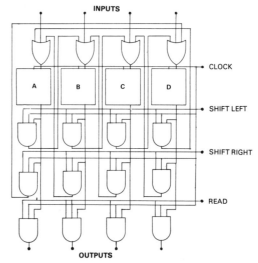

right in increments of one bit position (storage cell). In the figure, A, B, C, and D are storage cells (transistor flip-flops).

Each time the clock pulse goes high, whatever bits are present at the OR gates are 'set'. A high placed on the SHIFT RIGHT control point will cause each bit to be 'shifted' to the adjacent storage cell on the right when the clock pulse goes high. Similarly, a high on SHIFT LEFT causes a movement of bits to the left and a high on READ causes the bits to be output. Shift registers are used in arithmetic units to perform multiplication and division and in I/O circuits to perform bit-serial/bit-parallel conversion. They are also used as timers and frequency converters; if a 1-bit and three 0-bits are loaded in a four-bit register as shown, and either the SHIFT LEFT or SHIFT RIGHT control point is held high, a single output will be at a frequency equal to one-quarter of the clock frequency.

shoe In a fixed-head magnetic disc unit; a support and positioning element for a read/write head.

short circuit Also *short*. In an electrical or electronic device; an accidental (and often destructive) contact between circuit elements with different voltages; a sudden drop in resistance.

short-form A term applied to the shorter of two possible representations of numeric values for computer computation. See *floating point*.

shuttlecock A thimble; a rotatable type font functionally similar to a daisy wheel.

SI (1)*Systeme International* d'Unites. (The international metric system.) **(2)***Shift In.* A control character indicating to receiving hardware that the characters that follow it are to be given their primary interpretations. See *shift in; SO.* **(3)**(Si) *SIlicon.*

SID *Swift Interface Device.*

side effect A result produced by a routine or procedure in addition to the one required for a particular processing operation; if, for example, the sine of an angle is required and the called procedure returns both the sine and cosine, the cosine is a 'side effect'.

side circuit In a four-wire circuit from which a phantom circuit is derived; either of the 'main' circuits (a forward channel or a return channel).

sideband Either the upper or lower component of a carrier wave.

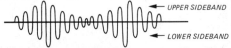
← UPPER SIDEBAND
← LOWER SIDEBAND

Since all of the transmitted information (effect of modulation) is carried by both sidebands, the suppression of one sideband is a basic step of receiving in a carrier system. In radio telephony (above 25 mHz.) the carrier is suppressed and only one sideband (usually the lower) is transmitted. The technique doubles the possible number of channels (as compared with AM) for a given bandwidth. See *carrier wave; modulation.*

sifting sort An exchange sort.

sight check In determining whether the punching pattern on two punched cards or sections of paper tape is identical; a check made by holding them up to light to see if all holes are aligned.

sign A symbol, character, or group that is associated with a number to indicate whether it is positive or negative; in mathematical notation it is conventionally a '+' to indicate 'positive' and a '—' to indicate 'negative'. A place where a sign can be placed is a **sign position**; a number with a sign may be termed a **signed number** and one without a sign an **unsigned number**. A number without a sign is assumed to be positive. See *number; sign code.*

sign bit In a register that holds a numeric value in a computational format (binary; floating point); a bit in the most significant bit position (the storage cell at the left end of the register) indicating the sign of the value; it is, conventionally, a 0-bit to indicate 'positive' and a 1-bit to indicate 'negative'. See *sign code; floating point.*

sign character (1)A graphic character associated with a number to indicate its sign; either a '+' or a '—'. **(2)**In a code; a bit pattern that may precede the bit patterns that encode a number to indicate the sign of the number; for example, 0101101 to indicate 'negative' in ASCII.

sign code A bit or bit pattern that indicates the sign of a number with which it is associated. Though the term is used to include a 'sign bit' associated with a number in a computational format, unless otherwise indicated, a 'sign code' refers to a combination associated with a number in some internal-storage code (EBCDIC) or transmission code (ASCII). In a transmission code, a sign code is, typically, a separate character transmitted before the characters of the number to which it applies; for example, in ASCII the character 0101101 indicates 'negative' and 0101011 indicates 'positive'. Similarly, in punched card and paper tape codes, the sign code is a separate character preceding a numeric value. (In some punched card systems, the sign is indicated by an overpunch.) In any representation in which a sign code is optional (in most graphic and code systems), the absence of a sign code indicates a positive number. When decimal digits are in binary coded decimal (BCD) with two digits per byte, the first (most significant) byte is used to hold the sign code; conventionally, 00 indicates 'positive', 01 indicates 'normally positive', 11 indicates 'negative' and 10 indicates 'normally negative'. In EBCDIC, the sign can be provided as a separate character, as with transmission codes with, for example, —34 being represented in three bytes by (hexadecimal) 60 F3 F4. However, when an item has been declared to be numeric, it is more common to indicate sign by a **sign quartet** which is substituted for the F (1111) as the 'zone quartet' of the least-significant digit. In this method, C (1100) indicates 'positive' and D (1101) indicates 'negative'. The —34 of the previous example would, then, encode as F3 D4 in two bytes. Again, absence of sign indicates 'positive' so +34 could be represented by either F3 F4 or, if declared numeric, by F3 C4. In packed decimal, the same sign quartets are used as in EBCDIC but they are held as the least-significant quartet of the number; for example, +34 is represented as 34 or 03 4C, —34 as 03 4D, and 834 as either 08 34 or 83 4C. (The form in which a sign is included may be termed **signed packed decimal**.)

sign digit In binary; a sign bit.

sign field In a register in which arithmetic operations are performed; a one-bit field (usually, the most significant bit position) where a sign bit is placed.

sign position The place immediately to the left of a number where a sign (+ or —) can be placed. See *sign field*.

sign quartet A four-digit sign code. See *sign code*.

sign test An instruction that tests if a numeric value is less than, equal to, or greater than zero and outputs a 'true' or 'false'.

signal (1) A particular line condition (voltage; carrier wave frequency), or a change of line condition, that has data or control significance. It is that which is passed between two locations to represent data, to indicate status, or to affect the receipt or interpretation of data. See *line condition; data transmission*. (2) To send a 'signal' (def.1)

signal converter A device or circuit that changes the electrical characteristics of signals (polarity and/or voltage).

signal distance See *Hamming distance*.

signal regeneration The process of forming a signal of correct characteristics and transmitting it in response to the receipt of an attenuated/distorted incoming signal. See *repeater*.

signal shaping Also *signal transformation*. The process of changing the shape (steepening the leading edge; clipping the top) of a signal before transmitting it.

signal strength See *power level*.

signal-to-noise ratio (S/N) The amount by which a signal exceeds the circuit noise on a line on which it is transmitted. See *noise*.

signal transformation Signal shaping.

signalling rate See *data signalling rate*.

signed field A sign field containing a sign code. See *sign field*.

signed number A number with a 'sign'; a number with a graphic or bit-pattern indication of whether it is positive or negative. See *sign*.

signed packed decimal Packed decimal in which the last quartet of the last byte consists of a sign code. See *sign code*.

significance Weight; positional value.

significant digits Those digits of a number that are essential to its correct use or interpretation; those digits that must be retained when a number that is output from one operation is to be used as input to another. In a positional representation system, those digits with the highest positional values (weights) in a number (those at the left end) are termed **most significant digits** and those with low positional values (at the right end) are termed **least significant digits**. See *round; truncate*.

significant event In an event-driven (interrupt-driven) system; a change in processing conditions that indicates a change in system status; for example, the arrival of a transaction in a TP system, an input or output request by an executing program, the completion of an input or output, or a task exit.

silicon (Si) An abundant element that occurs in sand and rock; in a refined form, it is the main constituent of glass and the wafers used to form semiconductors. The term is also used with the meaning of 'semiconductor integrated circuit'; ('software being replaced by silicon'; 'control functions now on silicon').

silicon dioxide (SiO_2) Glass (in microelectronics usage).

silicon foundary A business or operation of manufacturing integrated circuits to perform customer-specified functions or to meet particular customer specifications.

silicon gate An MOS technology in which the gate is embedded polycrystalline silicon. See *MOS*.

silicon nitride (Si_3N_4) A silicon compound that is capable of retaining a static electric charge. It is used as a gate element of some MOS transistors and as the 'programmable' substance of MNOS devices. See *MOS; MNOS*.

silicon-on-sapphire (SOS) A construction technique for MOS semiconductors in which the active silicon layers are built up epitaxially on an inert (synthetic sapphire) substrate. By ensuring short, thin conducting paths in the silicon, the technique provides somewhat higher speed than 'monolithic' devices.

silicon valley A term sometimes applied to the area around Palo Alto and Sunnyvale (south of San Francisco) where there is extensive manufacture and development of semiconductors.

silver halide film See *microfilm*.

SIMD *Single Instruction Multiple Data stream.* A type of parallel computer with multiple memories and an arithmetic

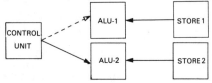

logic unit for each memory. A single control unit allocates instruction execution according to the memory that holds the required operands. See *SISD; MIMD; MISD*.

simple interrupt An interrupt in a system in which there is a single interrupt condition. See *interrupt*.

simple name In a qualified name; the identifier of the item at the lowest hierarchial level; for example, the 'CULIB' in the qualified filename 'SYS/FOR/CULIB'.

simple stack (1)A single-purpose stack. (2)A push-down stack. See *stack*.

simplex A term applied to a circuit or method of working in

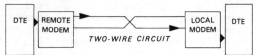

which data is transmitted in only one preassigned direction. See *duplex; half-duplex*.

simplex circuit A (two-wire) circuit that provides one-way communications; for example, in telemetry. See *circuit; channel; duplex*.

simplex communications One-way communications.

simplex mode A method of operating a (duplex) circuit for one-way communications.

simplex transmission Transmission in one preassigned direction only on a data link.

simulate To use a set of facilities or procedures in such a way that, for some purpose, they duplicate another set of facilities or procedures; ('simulate another computer'; 'simulate a network interface'; 'simulate a failure').

simulation (1)Also, often, *modeling*. The use of a computer and special programs to form an analogue of some system (molecule; chemical process; airfoil; railway system) so that it can be tested with different inputs and under different conditions. (2)The use of programming techniques to duplicate the operation of one computing system on another computing system. See *emulation*.

simulator A device (possibly a program) that, for some purpose, can duplicate a system or another device; ('a modem simulator').

simultaneous Also, sometimes, *parallel; synchronous.* Occurring at the same instant of time or during the same time interval. The term implies separate (possibly duplicate) facilities; for example, when applied to programs, 'simultaneous execution' would indicate execution by different processors or computers. (As contrasted to 'concurrent' which could indicate the interleaved use of a single set of facilities.) See *concurrent; parallel*.

simultaneous computer A parallel computer.

simultaneous operation An operation performed in steps in which two or more steps are performed at the same time.

simultaneous processing The processing of two computers or of a parallel computer.

simultaneous transmission With respect to a duplex circuit; the transmission of messages in both directions at the same time. See *channel; circuit; duplex*.

sine Of an acute angle in a right triangle; the relation between the length of the opposite side and the hypotenuse. For example, in the triangle shown, Sine ϕ = BC/AB. Sines are obtained from **sine tables** which are entered with the value of the angle in degrees, for example, if 36° its 'sine' is 0.5878.

sine wave A wave whose instantaneous displacement from an average value is proportional to the sine of the angle subtended by a rotating vector at that instant. If the 'rotating vector' is plotted with the centre of rotation on the line of 'average value', then the height of the wave (displacement from average value) is equal to the length of the vector times the sine of the angle, and this is equal to the vertical distance from the end of the vector to the line of average value. In the figure, at time T0, the end of the vector lies on the line of average value and, thus, the wave has no displacement from it. As the vector rotates to position T1, the wave rises (in the plot at the right)

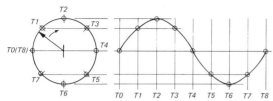

and this continues until it reaches a maximum value at T2 where the height of the wave is equal to the length of the vector. As the vector continues to rotate, it falls to T3 (at which the height is the same as at T1) and then to 'zero crossing' at T4. Further rotation brings it to a maximum negative value at T6 and then, as one rotation is completed, back to zero at T8. The sine wave is the wave inherently produced by a rotating alternator (as supplies the power mains) and is the basic component of the complex waves that carry speech and data by radio and telephone. See *alternating current; carrier wave; square wave; frequency; cycle.*

single-address instruction A one-address instruction; an instruction that specifies a unary operation.

single-board computer A minicomputer or microcomputer in which all logic, timing, internal memory, and external interfaces are incorporated on a single printed circuit board.

single-current signalling Unipolar signalling.

single-length register A register with a length of a computer word in the system in which it is used.

single operation Half-duplex operation.

single precision The use of a single computer word to hold a numeric value in a computation. See *precision.*

single-precision floating point See *floating point.*

single-shot A one-shot.

single-step operation A method of computer operation in which instructions are translated into source code one at a time, executed, and the result displayed (listed). It is the mode provided by an interpreter. See *interpreter.*

single-stream batch processing Batch processing in which one job is completed before the next is begun. See *multistreaming.*

single threading A method of handling transactions in a small transaction processing system in which all steps in handling and replying to one transaction are completed before beginning to deal with another. See *multithreading; pipelining.*

single-user access An access classification of a volume that contains only code or data belonging to a particular user.

single-wire line A (direct current) electrical transmission line that uses earth as the other conductor to complete the circuit.

sink A term applied to something that 'receives'. For example, in a semiconductor device, a 'heat sink' is a metallic element (part of the mounting) that receives internally generated heat and dissipates it and a place where a message or data is received may be termed a 'message sink' or a 'data sink'.

SIO *Serial Input/Output.*

SiO$_2$ Silicon dioxide. (In its natural state it is 'silica' and in processed form it is 'glass'.)

SISD *Single Instruction Single Data Stream.* A term applied to a conventional computer in which a single arithmetic logic unit

operates with a single stream of 'instructions' (operators) from the control unit and a single stream of data (operands) from memory. See *SIMD; MIMD; MISD.*

site A term often applied to a place where a particular type of computer is installed; ('a Burroughs 3700 site').

six-bit byte A character or sextet; a six-bit unit of storage and transfer.

size error An error condition (possibly resulting in truncation of significant digits) resulting from attempting to store a numeric result in a location (word; register) that is too small to hold it. See *bound; truncation.*

sizing A study of a computer system in relation to its tasks and expected performance with a view of optimising the use of existing facilities or making cost effective additions to the hardware and/or software.

skeleton A sequence of programming instructions designed to meet the needs of different users for a particular type of program; it is customised for a particular application by making appropriate additions and deletions and, possibly, combining with other skeletons. See *generator.*

skew (1) Of a data carrier (punched card; paper tape), a turning about the normal path of movement through a punch or reader causing it to jam or, possibly, to be punched or read incorrectly. (2)A change in timing or phase of signals during transmission.

skip (1)Of locations or data items on a data medium; to pass over without reading or writing; ('skip records'; 'skip blocks'). (2) By a printer; to leave one or more printing positions blank; ('skip lines'; 'skip characters').

skip sequential access Selective sequential access.

slack bytes Byte-length fillers (zeros; space characters) inserted in data items to provide synchronisation (alignment on word boundaries).

slack storage Storage that is left unused.

slave (1)A term applied to a device that can perform some operation on command but cannot initiate an action or control other devices. (2)A term sometimes applied to a device that cannot 'stand alone'; for example, to a VDU terminal that does not contain a video buffer.

slave mode The processing mode in which application programs are being executed. See *master mode*.

slave station A tributary data station; a data station other than the master station.

slave store Also, in some systems, *cache*. A unit of fast storage in a control unit used as a processing buffer to hold code and data that is transferred in relatively large blocks (say, 64 words) from main storage. Its purpose is to increase processing speed by reducing main storage accesses. See *cache; scratchpad*.

slew (1)A throw; a movement of paper through a printer. (2)A rapid change of voltage or some other circuit parameter; ('an operational amplifier with a slew rate of 200 volts per microsecond').

slice (1)A thin wafer of crystalline silicon that is cut into 'chips' in manufacturing semiconductors. See *chip; semiconductor*. (2)A term sometimes applied to a portion of a sideband between two amplitude limits. (3)A portion of a larger unit. See *time slice; bit slice*.

slider The part of a magnetic disc read/write head consisting of a ceramic wafer, the underside of which is contoured to form the air bearing surface. It supports the read/write and erase structures (epoxy cemented in a central slot) and is mounted to an access arm through gimbals. See *head*.

slit scanner In a graphic recognition system; an element that analyses a character or other image along paths or 'slits' that dissect the image. See *scanner; magnetic ink character recognition*.

sliver In some systems, a 32-word section of memory.

slot (1)An element of a cage; the space and guides to hold a single, replaceable printed circuit board. (2)A storage space of the correct size to hold a unit of data; ('a page slot'; 'a record slot'). (3)A time slot.

slow device Also *slow peripheral*. A term applied to any storage or input/output device with a slower data transfer rate than magnetic tape (say, slower than about 800 characters per second). Examples include card and paper tape readers and punches, printers, and document readers.

SLSI *Super Large Scale Integration*. A term applied to an integrated circuit with more than about 100,000 gates per chip. See *VLSI*.

slug A piece of metal with one or more characters embossed on it as used for printing in a shaped-character printer. See *type bar; impact printer; train printer*.

SM *Storage Module*.

small business system A computer with a main storage capacity of from about 16K to 64K bytes that is intended for business use and is often supplied with software for business applications such as stock control and payroll. It is, typically, a minicomputer. See *minicomputer; visible record computer*.

small scale integration (SSI) A term applied to integrated circuit devices with less than about ten gates per chip.

smart Intelligent; with programmable memory.

SMD *Storage Module Drive*.

smoke test The connection of electric power to a new or repaired functional unit.

smooth To reduce fluctuations, for example, in a power supply.

smoothing algorithm An algorithm intended to distribute records as evenly as possible in the address space of a random file. See *random file; hashing algorithm*.

SNA *Systems Network Architecture*.

snapshot dump A dump of designated locations made during the execution of a program. See *dump*.

snapshot program A trace program that performs snapshot dumps. See *trace program*.

sneak current In a telephone circuit; a leakage current from some other (power or control) circuit; it is too weak to cause immediate damage but can produce harmful heating effects over a period of time.

SNOBOL *StriNg-Oriented symBOlic Language.* A programming language used in the compilation and generation of symbolic equations.

SNR *Signal to Noise Ratio.*

SO (1)*Shift Out.* (2)*Send Only.* (3)*Serial Output.*

socket A female connector.

soft centred A term applied to a computer in which the instruction set and microcode are in random access memory and are loaded in the same manner as an operating system.

soft copy A term sometimes applied to data that is displayed on a VDU screen rather than printed. See *hard copy.*

soft error An error that is detected on one reading or transfer of data but which 'disappears' and is not detected on a subsequent reading or transfer.

soft keys In a VDU keyboard or word-processing station; keys that can be programmed with functions to meet specific user needs.

soft-sectored Of a magnetic disc system; with sectors established by information recorded during disc initialisation. See *missing clock; sectoring; hard-sectored.*

software (1)Any meaningful arrangement of bit patterns stored and manipulated within a computer system. In this broadest definition, the term contrasts with 'hardware' and includes both programs (system as well as user) and data. (2)The user programs and system programs of a computer system; all of the programs required to perform the processing tasks of the system. (3)A program or group of programs to accomplish a particular function; ('interrupt software'; 'transaction processing software'). (4)The operating system and associated programs for a particular computer; ('VAX-11 software').

software development (1)Software engineering. (2)The development of programs for a particular computer or application.

software engineering Also *software development.* The profession or activity of designing, coding, and testing major system software.

software error (1)An interrupt-causing condition that results when attempting to execute an invalid instruction sequence or a valid instruction sequence with invalid data; any error condition not resulting from a hardware failure or malfunction. (2)An error in supervisory or system software.

software failure An error in supervisory software that interrupts processing (and may require reloading the operating system).

software house A company that specialises in writing, adapting, and testing software for computer users.

software stack A stack implemented in main storage. See *stack.*

SOH *Start Of Heading.* A control character that indicates that the message heading begins with the following character.

solid state A term applied to a device or circuit that uses semiconductors rather than alternative elements such as relays or vacuum tubes. (The term is sometimes used to include ferrite core as well as semiconductor technology.)

solid-state computer A computer that uses no vacuum tubes.

solid state relay (SSR) A relay that accomplishes its switching function with transistors or thyristors instead of movable contacts.

solid-stroke character A shaped character.

SOM *Start Of Message.* (1)In some systems; a character in a poll response that precedes the address(es) of any data stations other than the master station that are to receive a following message. Its use permits a tributary station to communicate directly with one or more other tributary stations. (2)A character used in some constant-carrier, point-to-point systems to indicate that a message from a switched-carrier onward link is to follow. See *RTS-DCD simulation.*

son (1)A term sometimes applied to the current version of a file. See *generation.* (2)A term sometimes used in place of 'member'. See *tree.*

sonic delay line An acoustic delay line.

sort To arrange entities according to some predefined criteria. The term may be applied to an arrangement by class or type (say, customers by sales territory), to sequencing (say, customers by customer number or alphabetically by name), or to combinations (customers alphabetically by name for each sales territory). See *collate; merge; insertion sort; merge sort; internal sort; external sort; exchange sort.*

sort generator A program that can be used to produce a variety of sort programs to meet specific user requirements.

sort key (1)In a sort of items into groups; a value (attribute) that, if present in an item or characteristic of it, results in its being placed in a particular group. (2)Also *sequencing key.* The identifier of the sequence that is to be used in sorting items into some sequence; it is usually 'numeric' or 'alphabetical'.

sort needle See *edge-notched card.*

sort pass One examination by a sort program of all the items of a group that remain unsorted with attendant movement of one or more items from the unsorted group to a sorted or intermediate group.

sort program A program that tests items of data according to some criteria and allocates them to groups or to a sequence in accordance with the results of the test.

SOS *Silicon On Sapphire.*

sounder A telegraph receiving apparatus consisting of an electromagnet that attracts an armature against a metallic stop when a pulse is received and releases it to contact another metallic stop when it ends. An operator interprets the clicks and intervals as the dots and dashes of Morse code.

source (1)An original or input form; ('source code'; 'source documents'). (2)In source code or consisting of source code; ('source listing'; 'a source library'). (3)Suitable for producing source code; ('a source language'). (4)A place from which data is read; ('an operand source'). (5)A data source; a place where a data transmission originates. See *data sink*. (6)In a field effect transistor; the area from which electrons flow. See *field effect transistor; drain*.

source code (1)A source language. (2)Also *coding*. The form of a program or other sequence of instructions as produced by a programmer in a source language. The term is applied to code written on a coding sheet, keyed in at a terminal, or punched in cards or paper tape. (3)Instructions in a source language that are held in computer storage in their character format (in the storage code of the computer). By this definition, the term includes 'source code' (def. 2) as input to storage, a compiler output version as for 'source listing', and sequences held in a source library. See *language; compiler*.

source computer The make and model computer on which a particular program is to be compiled. See *object computer*.

source converter A program that converts object code to a source code form for listing purposes.

source data Data as received at a computer department from users, say, on source documents or entered via a terminal.

source data card A punched card on which data is typed or marked for subsequent punching onto the card.

source-destination file A single file (unit of magnetic disc or magnetic tape storage) that holds the input data for a job and to which the results are written.

source document A document (invoice; purchase order; inventory) containing source data as received by a data control department.

source field Also *sending field*. A field in a source-language instruction that holds the address of an operand that is to be read or moved or a literal that is to be moved; for example, in MOVE ZETA-1 TO WAL-PM-3, the ZETA-1 occupies the 'source field'.

source file (1)A library file of programs/routines in source-language form. (2)A file that holds the input data for a particular run. See *destination file; source-destination file*.

source instruction An instruction in its source-code form. See *source code*.

source language A programming language; a language in which statements can be written in a form acceptable to a particular compiler or assembler.

source library A library in which programs/routines are held in their source-language form.

source listing A listing in source code as output by a compiler.

source machine A source computer.

source module A program module in source code.

source module library A source library.

source program A program in source code; a program before compilation. See *program; source code*.

source recording The placement of data in machine readable form; for example, on punched cards, paper tape, or magnetic disc or tape (from a terminal input).

source statement A statement in its source-code form. See *source code*.

SP *SPace*. The 'space character'; a bit pattern in some code that, when received, causes a printer or display device to advance the printing/display position one character space.

space (1)A storage location of the correct size for a particular unit; ('a record space'; 'a character space'). (2)A delimiter in printed or displayed text; a portion of a line one character position in length (usually, the length of the letter 'n') in which no character is printed or displayed. (3)A bit-pattern character that, when received by a printer or display device, causes the insertion of a 'space' (def. 2). (4)In telegraph communications; the line condition when no 'mark' is being transmitted. (5)A term sometimes used synonymously with '0-bit', particularly in a communications or hardware-related sense. (6)To insert one or more 'spaces' in text.

space character The SP character.

space hold A continuous line condition that is the same as that which represents a 'space' (0-bit) in data transmission. See *mark hold*.

space suppression The operation of eliminating unnecessary spaces from data as transmitted, printed, or displayed.

space-to-mark transition In telegraphy; a change of line condition from that which represents a space to that which represents a mark. See *mark; space*.

spacefill To place the bit pattern of the space character in contiguous character positions in storage thus overwriting characters that may have been in these positions and causing blank space to appear in data that is read from the storage and printed or displayed.

span (1)Also *range*. The difference between the highest and the lowest values that a quantity or function can take. (2)To cross storage boundaries, as a 'spanned record'.

spanned record A (long) logical record that is held in two or more physical records. See *record*.

sparse With gaps or omissions; without all places being filled.

sparse addressing (1)The distribution of the instructions of a program through a larger address space than they require in order to leave spaces for possible additions or changes. See *virtual storage addressing*. (2)The declaration of storage locations or structures that will not be used in a particular (initial) version of a program. (3)The declaration of storage locations larger than known to be required (in order to allow space for items of varying and unknown lengths).

sparse array (1)An array with a declared size greater than initially required. (2)An array in which space is allocated only as variables are explicitly defined and without any preallocation of total space.

special character In a character set; a character other than a letter, a digit, or a space character; for example, any of the characters : . ; , * / $! ( ) £ or ?.

special-purpose computer A computer other than a general-purpose computer; a computer designed to operate with a restricted class of applications.

specific (1)Individual (and not of the general class or type); ('a specific value'; 'a specific location'). (2)Also, sometimes, *dedicated*. Intended for a particular use; for example, an assembly language is 'specific' to a particular model or range of computers, a programmed integrated circuit may be 'customer specific' and a device that can do only one thing may be termed 'function specific'.

specific address An absolute address.

specific coding Absolute coding.

specific volume request By a program; a request for one or more volumes identified by serial number.

specification A description of function and design features of that which exists or is to be produced; ('a program specification'; 'an interface specification'; 'a language specification').

spectral response Of a light-sensitive device (photodiode; phototransistor); its output as a function of the wavelength (colour) of the light it receives.

speech In a telephone system; a term applied to any non-data transmission that makes use of voice-grade lines.

speech and duplex The division of a voice-grade channel into a speech channel and two slow-speed data channels.

speech channel A voice-grade channel.

speech chip An integrated circuit that holds speech in digital form and can be used to reproduce it; for example, in a teaching device.

speed-power product Also *power delay product*. A measure of the efficiency of a semiconductor logic gate consisting of its propagation delay in nanoseconds times its power dissipation in milliwatts; the unit is 'picojoules'. Typically a very fast gate (such as TTL) has a large power dissipation and it is a major design goal to obtain a low speed-power product and, thus, a fast circuit that requires little power. High-speed TTL may have a speed-power product of up to 150 pj. while I^2L may have a speed-power product of less than 1 pj.

spinwriter A printing element functionally similar to a daisy wheel except that the slugs and typebars are held in the form of a cylinder rather than a wheel.

spool (1)To use an intermediate storage (magnetic disc) when making a data transfer between high-speed storage (usually main storage) and a device that operates at a lower speed. See *spooling*. (2)An element on which paper tape is wound.

spool file Space on magnetic disc that is used as intermediate storage for data that is being transferred between main storage and magnetic tape or between main storage and some slow-speed device (printer; card reader or punch). See *spooling*.

spooling The operation of using a fast peripheral device (magnetic disc) as a 'buffer' for data transferred between main storage and magnetic tape or between main storage and such slow-speed devices as printers, document readers, paper tape punches and readers, and card punches and readers. It is performed to avoid the inefficient use of processing facilities that would result from making such transfers in 'real time'. The volume that is used as the intermediate storage (buffer) is termed a **spool file**. The process of writing data from a slow device to a spool file is termed **input spooling** and the process of 'dumping' data to a spool file from main storage is termed **output spooling**. Where input spooling is employed, it is usually done as a background job or during periods of low system demand. Output spooling of data for printers is usually an autonomous operation performed concurrently with normal processing. The term **remote spooling** may be applied to the operation of reading data into computer storage from a remote location. See *staging; radial transfer; migration*.

spot carbon Transferrable pigment (carbon) as applied to selected locations on the reverse of a form in order to provide a transfer of data in certain fields to another (interleaved) form and to prevent a transfer from other fields.

spot punch A hand punch.

sprocket feed Also *pin feed*. A term applied to a printer mechanism that moves paper (continuous stationery) by means of a sprocket or tractor with pins that engage pre-punched holes at the edges of the paper. See *tractor; friction feed*.

sprocket holes Also *feed holes*. Holes punched in paper that are engaged by a 'sprocket' (toothed wheel) or 'tractor' (toothed belt or chain) to move it through a device such as a punch or printer. When 'feed holes' and 'sprocket holes' are differentiated, 'feed holes' are in paper tape or an edge-punched card and 'sprocket holes' are at the edges of stationery as used by a printer.

sprocket track A feed track.

sputtering A method of deposition used in the manufacture of integrated circuits and similar devices; it consists of using an electric discharge in a low-pressure gas to produce positive ions that bombard a cathode of the material to be deposited thus 'knocking off' negatively charged particles that are attracted to the positively charged 'workpiece'.

SPX *SimPleX*.

square wave A wave with a form (as seen on an oscilloscope) that is square or rectangular; a wave with a steep leading and trailing edge and of nearly constant amplitude.

squelch To stop sending or generating; for example, a modem may 'squelch' the carrier wave to end a data transmission.

SSI *Small Scale Integration*.
SSR *Solid State Relay*.
ST *System Table*.

stable (1) Requiring few if any changes or corrections; ('a stable process'; 'stable programs'). **(2)** Of an electronic circuit or device; capable of maintaining an operating condition without change or fluctuations.

stable state Of a trigger circuit; in one of the operating conditions that it is capable of maintaining; not in a state of transition.

stack A data structure (group of registers or contiguous main storage locations) in which data items (operands; return addresses) can be added or removed at one end only. A **push-down stack** (also **classic stack**) is one in which the addition of an item (a **push**) causes all items in the stack to move down one position and the removal of an item (a **pop**) causes all items to move up one position. It is an inherently LIFO structure and only the top item(s) can be accessed. Push-down stacks may be incorporated in control units to provide a flexible storage space close to the arithmetic unit and thus to reduce the need for transfers to and from main storage. They are used to hold operands and partial results of arithmetic operations and are particularly suited to handling expressions in reverse Polish notation where operators are held in one stack and operands in another. They are also used to hold and 'keep track of' return addresses when executing called routines and they are particularly valuable when several levels of return addresses are being held when executing nested routines. A somewhat more complex stack (in a large computer) is often termed a **procedural stack**. Such a stack is of variable size and is defined by its highest and lowest addresses. If the lowest-numbered address is fixed, it is a **frame pointer** and if variable may be termed a **bottom-of-stack pointer**. The highest-numbered location is indicated by a movable **top-of-stack pointer** (TOS). When a single stack is used for data or addresses belonging to more than one executing program, a **local name base register** holds the address of the first location belonging to each program. By changing the top-of-stack pointer, any location in the stack can be made the 'top' and, thus, operations can be performed on or with any items in the stack. A stack consisting of dedicated registers and circuitry is termed a **hardware stack** and one that is organised by program and uses main storage locations is a **software stack**; unless otherwise indicated, the term 'stack' denotes a 'hardware stack'. A single-purpose stack (say, one used only for return addresses or to provide 'key rollover' in a keyboard device) may be termed a **simple stack** and a multipurpose stack or a linked set of simple stacks may be termed a **complex stack**.

stack computer A computer with hardware stack facilities.

stack pointer The address of a location in a stack. See *stack*.

stacked job processing A method of organising batch processing in which job definitions (typically on punched cards) are grouped (stacked) so that the system can initiate and run jobs in sequence with little if any involvement by the operator.

stacker (1)An element or accessory of a line printer that receives (and stacks) printout. (2)An element of a card reader or punch that receives and 'stacks' the cards as output. (3)In a digital cassette system that handles multiple cassettes; a device that removes one cassette from the read/write position and loads another.

stage (1)A phase; a time when particular events occur; ('a data preparation stage'; 'an execution stage'). (2)To move data from slow-access backing storage to magnetic disc in anticipation of its being required in processing. See *staging*.

staging The movement of code or data from a slower backing storage device to a faster, direct access, device that is made in anticipation of its being required by an active program. The movement is typically from mass storage (cartridge; cassette) or magnetic tape to magnetic disc; it may be under the control of the central processor or of a separate storage management minicomputer. By eliminating device-related considerations during processing, it can, effectively, extend one-level storage to include all backing storage. The movement of data before the run time of the program that will require it is termed **anticipatory staging** and movement initiated by instructions in an executing program is termed **demand staging**. See *spooling; radial transfer; one-level storage*.

staging drive A magnetic disc unit that is used to hold data received from slower devices in a staging system. See *staging*.

staging pack A magnetic disc pack initialised for use as the data medium on a staging drive.

stand-alone (1)Capable of functioning independently; not requiring the support of other systems or devices; ('a stand-alone computer'; 'used for stand-alone computing as well as for RJE'). (2)Of a program or job; running by itself; not multiprogrammed.

standard deviation The usual measure of the dispersion of values (of the way they vary from some average value). It is basic to the statistical analysis of such things as the ages of individuals in a population and frequency of transactions in a transaction processing system. It is obtained as follows (referring to the example): 1. Find the average of the values being considered; (obtain the total and divide by the number of values). 2. Find the differences between the individual values and this average value. 3. Square each of the differences found in Step 2. 4. Add the squares found in Step. 3. 5. Divide this sum by the number of values (the same figure as used in Step 1). The resulting figure is the **variance**. 6. Take the square root of the variance found in Step 5.

Example: Find the standard deviation of 9, 6, 7, 3, 7, and 4.

1. Add the numbers: $9 + 6 + 7 + 3 + 7 + 4 = 36$
Since there are six numbers, divide by 6: $36/6 = 6$

2. Find the differences between the individual values and 6: $9—6 = 3, 6—6 = 0, 7—6 = 1, 3—6 = —3, 7—6 = 1, 4—6 = —2$

3. Square these values: $3^2 = 9, 0^2 = 0, 1^2 = 1, 3^2 = 9, 1^2 = 1, —2^2 = 4$

4. Add these squares: $9 + 0 + 1 + 9 + 1 + 4 = 24$

5. Divide by the mean (found in Step 1): $24/6 = 4$
(This is the 'variance'.)

6. Find the square root of the variance: $\sqrt{4} = 2$, which is the standard deviation.

(The figures of the example are chosen to make the standard deviation come out 'even'; in practice, this would not often be the case.) See *normal distribution*.

standard file organisation A file organisation for which computer manufacturers provide access and organisational software; the usual ones are 'serial', 'sequential', 'random', and 'indexed sequential'.

standard form Normalised form (floating point representation). See *normalisation*.

standard peripherals A term sometimes applied to those peripherals that are common components of general-purpose computer installations; they include the basic peripherals plus magnetic disc units. See *basic peripherals*.

standardisation (1)The process, by manufacturers, of accepting certain designs and conventions and incorporating them in their products in order to provide a common user interface and/or interchangeability between the products of different manufacturers. (2)Normalisation (def. 2).

standby (1)The condition in which a functional unit is ready to operate and is waiting for inputs. (2)A term applied to a system or facility that is available to perform a function in event of a failure; ('a standby power supply'; 'a standby circuit'). See *backup*. (3)A low-voltage condition used with static RAM to reduce power dissipation when inactive (when not being read or written).

standing-on-nines A method of speeding carry operations in decimal addition; if a carry is to a digit position holding a 9, the 9 is set to 0 and the carry digit is added to the digit in the next higher digit position. The steps are as shown:

```
    Conventional        Standing on Nines
        197                    197
      +   6                  +   6
      -----                  -----
         13                   +103
      + 10                     203
      -----
        203
```

star A method of connecting 'satellite' units (peripherals; data stations) to a central unit in which each has a separate circuit to the central unit. See *loop; daisy chain*.

star network A data network in which the remote stations are connected radially (via individual circuits) to the master station. See *multipoint; loop network*.

start bit A start element.

start element In asynchronous data transmission; a 0-bit that indicates to receiving hardware that the following bits are those of a character. See *stop element; start-stop transmission*.

start of heading (SOH) A transmission control character indicating that the characters following constitute the message heading.

start of message (SOM) (1)In some multipoint systems; a character or group that can be sent by a polled data station to indicate that groups that follow are the addresses of one or more tributary data stations that can receive the poll response. Its use permits direct communication between tributary data stations. (2)A character or group used in some point-to-point systems to indicate to the other station that a (switched carrier) message follows. See *RTS-DCD simulation*.

start of text (STX) A transmission control character that terminates a message heading and indicates that the characters following constitute the text or 'body' of the message.

start restriction A restriction that prevents the execution of a job in a particular run.

start signal (1)A pulse that is used to initiate some operation. (2)A start element.

start-stop transmission Data transmission in which a character is preceded by a **start element** and followed by a **stop element**. The start element is commonly a single 0-bit which is also a **start bit**. The stop element is commonly a single 1-bit which is a **stop bit**. Slow speed (110 bps.) systems use stop elements of two 1-bits. The bits of the start and stop elements are sent without separation from character bits. Continuous 1-bits are transmitted when no character is being sent and the appearance of a 0-bit indicates to receiving equipment that a character has started. Receiving equipment is programmed with the length of characters in the code being used (say, 7-bit ASCII) and it uses this to separate the character bits from the 'framing bits'. Start-stop transmission can be either anisochronous or asynchronous; unless otherwise indicated, 'asynchronous' is assumed. In asynchronous start-stop transmission, bits and characters are commonly sent with fixed timing (say, at 1200 bits per second) and receiving equipment incorporates a 'retime buffer' to provide adjustment for minor differences between the transmitter and receiver clocks. See *synchronous; asynchronous transmission; anisochronous transmission*.

starter operating system An operating system (as supplied to a new computer installation) containing the minimum elements required for system generation.

startup (1)The operation of placing a new computer system or subsystem in the state in which it can perform its intended tasks. (2)Either a 'cold boot' or a 'warm boot'; the performance of those operations and checks necessary to place a computer in the state in which it can execute user programs. See *cold boot; warm boot; restart*.

STAT MUX *STATistical MUltipleXor*.

state of the art (1)A term used to indicate the current status of a developing technology; for example, memory with an access time of less than 20 nanoseconds might be said to be 'beyond the state of the art'. (2)A term sometimes used to indicate that a

state table (1) A state transition table. **(2)** In a system that can assume a number of different 'states'; a table that shows the resulting action or change of state for each possible input. For example, a device driver (hardware or software) could have states 'receive ready', 'receive not ready', 'timed out', and 'recovering from time out' and the table would show what is to occur for each state when each input 'data in', 'reset', and 'timer out' is received. Typically, each table entry is the address of the first instruction of a subroutine that is to be executed. The table can be used to design a complex program and may be directly implemented by a matrix in storage.

state transition table Also *state table*. The equivalent of a 'truth table' for a multiple-gate circuit device such as a data selector, multiplexor, or logic array. It gives the output(s) for each combination of its inputs. (When the device has memory, it gives the output(s) for each relevant combination of present and previous inputs.)

statement In a high-level programming language or a job control language; a brief description of one or more operations that are to be performed during processing. (The term 'processing' is used here to include not only the execution of instructions in a user program but also such ancillary and system functions as initialisation, allocating storage and devices, formatting, and inputting and outputting code and data.) In its use with respect to a high-level language, a 'statement' is equivalent to an 'instruction' in a low-level language; the terms are sometimes used synonymously. See *instruction; job control statement.*

statement of requirements A specification of a data processing operation as produced by a systems analyst. It, typically, gives the purpose of the operation, describes the input data and its method of acquisition, indicates the processing resources that can be allocated, identifies constraints and interfaces with other operations, and describes the results that are to be produced.

static (1) Not occurring or performed during the time a program is being executed; ('static allocation'; 'a static dump'). **(2)** Not moving or rotating; ('static memory'; 'a static inverter'). **(3)** Interference on a communications channel.

static allocation The allocation of processing resources (devices; main storage locations) to a program at run time rather than during execution. See *dynamic allocation.*

static buffering The allocation of buffer storage of a fixed size as contrasted to **dynamic buffering** in which buffer space is expanded and contracted according to requirements for it.

static dump A dump that is not initiated by an executing user program; a dump made at a particular point in processing or at the end of a run. See *dump.*

static electricity Electricity that does not flow in a circuit; electricity that is created by friction and accumulates as a static charge of electrons (as in a capacitor). In computer systems, it may occur when magnetic tape is searched or rewound at high speed in a low-humidity environment (less than about 40% relative humidity). It may cause tape to adhere to elements of the drive causing skew or erratic feed, it may attract dust with resultant secondary effects, and, in extreme cases, it can cause discharges that corrupt data. (The problems are seldom encountered when using modern, low-resistance magnetic tape in a normal, air conditioned, computer environment where the relative humidity is in the 50-60% range.)

static linking Linking (to form load modules) that is completed before beginning execution of the program to which the modules belong.

static memory (1) Memory in which each bit is held in a transistor flip-flop (two transistors). Such memory needs no refreshing but is volatile (data is erased when electric power is turned off). Unless otherwise indicated, the term by this definition denotes an MOS memory rather than a bipolar form. See *dynamic memory; random access memory.* **(2)** A term sometimes applied to non-volatile memory; for example, to core, ROM, photodigital, or bubble. **(3)** A term that is sometimes applied to any 'non-moving memory' (to any form other than cyclic or recirculating).

static RAM Static random access memory.

static random access memory (1) An MOS memory that requires no refreshing; a random access memory in which each bit is held in a transistor flip-flop. **(2)** Random access memory (either MOS or bipolar) that incorporates a battery standby system (on the same circuit board) to prevent loss of memory contents when the regular power supply is interrupted.

static resource allocation See *static allocation.*

static set The total of the pages/segments that can be accessed by a program. See *dynamic set; virtual storage system—processing units.*

static storage Static memory.

static variable A variable (storage location) that is allocated to a program at run time and remains allocated throughout execution.

staticiser A term that has been applied to the circuitry (possibly a separate device) that performs write operations to coordinate-addressable memory; a unit that converts 'moving' electrical signals to 'static' bits in storage cells. See *dynamiciser*.

station (1) A term often used in preference to 'local terminal' to denote an operator-interface device that is part of (or directly connected to) a computer system; ('an operating station'; 'a direct data entry station'; 'an order entry station'). See *terminal; multi-access computing*. (2) A location where some operation is performed; ('a read station in a card reader'). (3) A telephone circuit interface device on a customer's premises (a telephone or a modem). (4) A data station; a place where data enters and/or leaves a network.

station code An identifier of a particular data station in a data network.

station selection code A code used to 'select' a data station to receive a message. See *selective calling*.

stationery Paper used to produce computer output on a (line) printer. Most printer paper is **continuous stationery** which is provided in fan-fold packs (typically, of 1000 pages) with perforations on the fold lines for separating the pages. Such paper is often **multipart stationery** with which up to six copies can be made with a single printing; it may be **one-time carbon** with interleaved carbon paper or **carbonless copy** in which copies are made by chemical transfer. This type of stationery is **edge punched** with sprocket holes with one-half inch spacing along each edge; it is available in widths of 4 inches to about 20 inches with 14-inch (between sprocket tracks) the 'industry standard'. Other forms of stationery include A4 sheets as used in typewriters and page printers, rolls from which paper is friction fed through Teletypes and similar devices, and various specially treated papers (usually in rolls) as used in thermal and electrosensitive printers. Paper of less than about four-inch width is usually termed 'paper tape'. See *printer; web; form; paper tape; plotter*.

statistical collection file In some systems; a journal to which the operating system writes statistics relating to event occurrences and resource utilisation.

statistical data recorder An operating system facility that logs the cumulative error status of an input/output device.

statistical equalizer In a modem; amplitude and/or phase compensating elements to provide a correction required for average (as 'statistically' determined) PSTN lines. See *equalization*.

statistical multiplexing A term applied to time division multiplexing in which scanning is limited to those devices that have messages to send or receive at a particular time. It is used to improve circuit utilisation by eliminating time slots that would otherwise be allocated to inactive devices. Such a system may also modify scanning in accordance with priorities. See *time division multiplexing*.

statistics The science of assembling, classifying, and analysing data obtained by counting the occurrences of events or conditions. In relation to computing, statistical analysis is used to provide answers (or best estimates) when such questions as these are asked: 'If an average of 10 transactions are handled per minute, during what percentage of the time will the system be required to handle more than 30 per minute?' 'What effect would the purchase of 64K of additional main storage have on throughput?' 'What are the chances of two magnetic disc units being down at the same time?'

stator The stationary element of a motor, servo, or similar device.

status The condition a device or operation is in at a particular time; ('operable status'; 'receive status').

status block A location a task can use to receive a completion status for a command (an error/completion code) during synchronous execution.

status word A word (in a system table) that holds the status of a particular peripheral device.

STC *Storage Technology Corporation*. (Louisville, Colorado)

step-by-step operation Single-step operation.

step-by-step switching Switching (as in a dialed telephone system) in which a hierarchial group of switches such as Strowger relays or crossbar relays are operated in a controlled sequence with each dialed digit making a switching selection at one hierarchial level. The dialing of a complete telephone number makes selections on as many levels as there are digits in the number.

step-by-step system A communications system that uses step-by-step switching.

step number A number that identifies a line in a program in some languages/systems.

step restart A restart from the beginning of a job step; it may be automatic or deferred. See *restart*.

stepping motor A pulse-actuated electromechanical device with a rotor that turns one rotational increment (say, 20°) with each pulse; the term may be applied to a device that also converts the rotation to linear movement, as in a flexible disc system.

stepping switch A rotary switch driven by a stepping motor.

STD *Subscriber Trunk Dialing.*

stochastic Involving chance or probability.

stochastic computer A digital computer that incorporates probability operations by manipulating random numbers.

stock Merchandise held for sale or distribution, say in a warehouse or on the shelves of a store.

stop bit A stop element or one of the bits of a stop element.

stop code A bit pattern that, when read by a device, causes some operation to stop; for example, a 'read stop code' that causes a paper tape reader to stop.

stop element One or two 1-bits used as a character delimiter in start-stop transmission. See *start-stop transmission.*

stop instruction (1) A stop-run instruction. (2) A halt instruction.

stop signal (1) A pulse used to stop some operation. (2) A one-bit stop element.

storage Also, often, *store; memory.* A medium or device that can receive, retain, and output bit patterns representing data. It is an ordered group of cells or small locations in some medium (such as magnetic tape) in each of which a physical change can be made to take place by means of an electrical pulse (sometimes secondarily via light or a magnetic field) and which can retain the condition and 'report' it when queried. The most common forms of storage are **coordinate-addressable storage** (semiconductor; core) in which the physical changes are made directly by the electrical pulses and **magnetisable surface recording** in which the pulses create magnetic fields that produce the physical changes. Other forms, of less frequent use, are 'beam-accessed' and 'recirculating' in both of which the physical changes are made secondarily. To **write** data is to send it as encoded patterns of electrical pulses to a storage medium or device. To **read** data is to determine the physical conditions (which transistor of a flip-flop is conducting; direction of magnetisation of a core or surface particles) and to convert it into electrical pulses. In all common forms of storage, the cells or locations can take either of two physical conditions, one of which is defined as 'holding a 1-bit' and the other of which is defined as 'holding a 0-bit'. The terms 'storage' and 'store' are often used interchangeably as nouns though there is an increasing preference (and international acceptance) for 'storage' in most contexts; ('main storage'; 'backing storage'; 'virtual storage'; 'mass storage'). The term 'store' is applied mainly to the older and traditional forms ('main store'; 'core store') rather than to later forms ('semiconductor storage'). With respect to 'storage' and 'memory', the term 'storage' is usually applied to units and media that are in common use in computer systems ('disc storage; magnetic tape storage') while 'memory' is applied to newer and experimental types ('bubble memory'; 'holographic memory'). The term 'memory' is also well-established when the form of access is being considered; ('read-only memory'; 'random access memory') and it is often preferred to 'storage' with respect to the facilities of a minicomputer or microprocessor. See *read; write; access; coordinate-addressable storage; magnetisable surface recording; core memory; semiconductor memory.*

storage allocation The (operating system) function of assigning storage locations to user programs or to system functions. Unless otherwise indicated, 'main storage' is assumed. See *dynamic allocation; static allocation.*

storage battery A battery that can be recharged. See *battery.*

storage block (1) A block (unit of storage and transfer). (2) A group of contiguous words of main storage. (3) In some systems a fixed-size (say, 2K-byte) unit of main storage.

storage capacity The amount of data that can be held by a unit of storage (main storage; volume; device). Unless otherwise indicated, it is usually understood to be in 'words' of the length used in the computer with which the storage is associated. (Other common units are 'bytes' and 'characters'.) See *packing density.*

storage cell (1) A discrete unit of storage that is capable of holding one bit; for example, a core, a diode in a diode matrix, or a transistor flip-flop in semiconductor storage. (2) The amount of a storage medium that can hold one bit; for example, a 'storage cell' (def. 1) or the amount of a magnetic-disc track that is capable of holding a bit in a particular method of encoding.

storage code Also *internal storage code.* The code in which data in character form is held and manipulated within a computer system. The most common are EBCDIC and ASCII with EBCDIC most common for larger 'mainframe' computers and ASCII favoured for minicomputers, microcomputers, and intelligent devices in communications systems in which ASCII is the line code. Numeric data is commonly entered and stored as decimal digits in the storage code with conversion to a computational format made when it is to be used in arithmetic operations. (The conversion is often transparent to the user program.) Magnetic tape and disc units, printers, and local terminals usually operate with the storage code of the computer with which they are associated. Punched card and paper tape devices commonly use their own codes (Hollerith; BCD) with conversion to the storage code performed by an interface device. Conversion between storage code and a line code (ASCII) is usually required when a mainframe computer interfaces with a data network. See *code*.

storage compacting See *compaction*.

storage cycle Also *memory cycle*. The sequence of events that takes place between successive main storage accesses (of single-word locations) performed to fetch operands or store results. When main storage is core memory, it includes regeneration of contents of the location following a (destructive) read.

storage cycle time The minimum time between successive (read) accesses of a unit of coordinate-addressable storage.

storage density Packing density; the number of bits that can be held in some standard unit of storage.

storage device (1)A functional unit in a computer system that is capable of receiving, retaining, and outputting data. Though the term is sometimes used to include coordinate-addressable units (main storage; cache; slave), it usually denotes a peripheral such as a magnetic disc or tape unit. (2)An integrated circuit consisting of memory as contrasted, possibly, to a processor or interface device.

storage element A storage cell or, possibly, a component of a storage cell such as one of the transistors in a flip-flop.

storage fragmentation See *fragmentation*.

storage hierarchy An ordering of storage units according to their access times. The following are some available units arranged in such a hierarchy:

Microcode storage	Drum or fixed-head disc
Control unit stacks and registers	Movable-head disc
Slave store or cache	Magnetic tape
Main storage	Mass (retrievable cartridge)
Bulk (directly accessible core)	Paper tape
Second-level (bubble; CCD)	Punched cards

storage image (1)Also, often, *core image*. The contents of an area of main storage at a particular time (as revealed by dumping and listing). (2)With respect to a program; the main storage locations occupied by its code and data.

storage interface device A functional unit in a computer system that performs backing storage accesses for a central processor. The term may be applied to an intelligent device or an unintelligent device and includes units variously identified as peripheral controllers, device controllers, data channels, store access controllers, input/output controllers, store control units, and interface computers. See *peripheral controller*.

storage interference In a system with shared storage; the condition in which two processors or storage interface devices attempt to access the same storage locations at the same time.

storage interleaving The operation of a multiple data stream computer (SIMD; MIMD) in which successive instructions obtain their operands from different storage modules.

storage key A storage protection key. See *storage protection*.

storage location An addressable position (main storage; magnetic disc; magnetic tape) where data can be held.

storage medium (1)A substance or processed combination of substances in which bits can be represented as detectable, physical states. Examples include ferric oxide (as formed into 'cores' or deposited as a surface coating), semiconductor junctions, photographic emulsions, and orthoferrite materials. (2)Computer storage as identified by its physical form (core; semiconductor; magnetisable surface; thin film). (3)A particular type of storage as considered for access purposes (main storage; magnetic disc; magnetic tape).

storage module (1)A separate section of coordinate-addressable storage. (2)A data module.

storage module drive (SMD) A data module drive.

storage overlap The condition in which the code and/or data of a program is divided among storage modules (say, in an SIMD computer).

storage peripheral A storage device; a peripheral that can store data (magnetic disc unit; magnetic tape unit).

storage protection The steps and procedures used to prevent corruption of data and/or the unauthorised access of data. Insofar as it is an operating system function, it is concerned with preventing executing programs from accessing locations other than those that they are intended to access during particular phases of processing. The simplest form of protection is

datum and limit in which each address as produced by instruction decoding is checked to determine that it is not greater than the highest-numbered location in an authorised area of storage (the limit) nor less than the lowest-numbered location (the datum). A program may be allocated two or more non-contiguous areas of storage, in which case, the datums and limits of all are checked. An attempt to access outside of an authorised location is a **bound violation** and causes an unconditional jump to an error routine. Datum and limit protection is commonly used in both single programming and multiprogramming systems. Another form of protection (used in multiprogramming systems) is **lock and key**. In this system, main storage is divided into equal-size blocks, each of which is given a value termed a **storage protection key**. Each program in the system is given an 'indicator number' and, when the program is active, this number is held in a system table together with all the 'keys' that identify locations it is authorised to access; the keys may be dynamically changed to reflect the authorisation at different phases of processing. As the program executes, its decoded addresses are associated with the relevant keys and these are checked against those held in the table for the program. Another system, often used in virtual storage systems, employs **access control levels** which are numbers (say from 1 to 15) that are assigned to each page and segment in the system. Typically, the lowest numbers are allocated to pages/segments that hold elements of the operating system, low numbers are given to utilities and other system routines, intermediate numbers are given to library routines and other shareable pages/segments, and the highest numbers are assigned to pages/segments that hold the code and data of user programs. Each program is given an **access control number** (again, say, from 1 to 15) that identifies its processing requirement/entitlement at each phase of processing; when active, these are held in an **access control register**. As a program executes, the access control levels of the pages/segments it references are checked against its current access control number and an error condition is indicated if the access control level is lower than the number. In some systems, a **protection ring** is an 'access control level'; there are other variations in terms between systems. The term 'storage protection' also includes the prevention of unauthorised or accidental overwriting of data on backing storage media. See *access mode; access right; password; protection ring; write protect*.

storage protection key See *storage protection*.
storage reconfiguration See *reconfiguration*.
storage region A partition or a storage location.
storage register (1) A (single word) main storage location. **(2)** A register.
storage stack (1) A software stack; a stack configured in main storage. **(2)** A pushdown stack.
storage tube (1) A cathode ray tube as used in some computer graphics terminals. In addition to the elements of a conventional CRT, it has a wide-angle, low-energy electron beam produced by a 'flood gun' and a conducting grid that is interposed in the electron beam paths adjacent to the screen phosphors. Prior to writing a display, the grid is made negative and when the display is written with the main electron beam, this places a positive charge on the grid wherever the beam impinges the screen phosphors. The positive charge allows the beam from the flood gun to reach the phosphors in these locations and, thus, to maintain the display when no longer refreshed by the main beam. The display persists for several minutes; it is of relatively low intensity. **(2)** A Williams tube; the storage element of an electrostatic memory.
storage unit (1) A storage device or module. **(2)** The unit in which data is held in storage (bit; character; word; byte).
store (1) To place data in storage; to write data to a storage medium. **(2)** To retain data in storage. **(3)** A term sometimes used synonymously with 'storage' (as a noun). See *storage*.
store access controller In some systems; an intelligent functional unit that handles data transfers via multiple peripheral controllers. See *storage interface device; peripheral controller; data channel*.
store and forward A method of operating a data network in which one or more intermediate stations receive message units from senders and reroute them to addressees. The operation may include message consolidation. Systems that are 'store and forward' include torn-tape and some message switching systems. See *message switching; torn tape system*.
store control unit In some systems; an intelligent device that acts as an interface computer for main storage, handling multiplexed transfers to and from the central (or 'order code') processor as well as peripheral devices.
stored-program computer A term once applied to a computer in which programs were held in storage for use as required (rather than input with the data).

STR *STRobe*.

straddle erase Track trimming (magnetic disc recording) in which the erase head gap 'straddles' the gap of the read/write structure. See *head; track trimming; tunnel erase*.

straight-line code Also *in-line code*. An instruction sequence that contains no loops; wherever repetitive operations are to be performed the entire required instruction sequence is included 'in line'. See *unwind*.

straight-line coding The process of writing straight-line code.

strand In rolled magnetic tape; one turn of tape as seen 'edgewise' when looking at the side of the reel. See *scattered wind*.

strap (1) A short connector (often moulded into a plastic 'cap') that is used to make a removable connection between two terminals (often pins on a printed circuit board). The purpose is to permit selecting or setting some operating parameter; for example, a fallback data rate or a clock source for transmitter timing. **(2)** To select or set by means of a 'strap'; ('strap for 2400 bits per second'; 'strap RTS constant high').

strapping option A capability or operating characteristic of a functional unit that can be enabled or disabled depending upon which terminals are connected by 'straps'.

strapping table A table (in an operating or maintenance manual) that lists the strapping options and gives the straps and the strap positions by which they can be selected.

stratified language A language that (because of lack of facilities or flexibility) cannot be used as its own metalanguage; all usual programming languages are 'stratified'. See *unstratified language*.

stream (1) A flow of operators or operands during processing (in a multiprocessor system); either a data stream or an instruction stream. **(2)** In mixed-mode processing; one of the types of processing for which input and scheduling facilities are provided; ('a batch stream'; 'a multi-access stream'). **(3)** The continuous movement of bit patterns around the loop of a loop network. **(4)** A job queue for jobs of a particular priority in a multiprogramming system. See *multistreaming*. **(5)** In data transfers; the data moved on a channel in a single read or write operation. **(6)** By a remote site modem in a multipoint system; to transmit continuously (to maintain carrier high), thus disrupting communications with other data stations. (It is a fault condition.) See *anti-stream timer*.

stream access Serial access.

stream computing See *pipeline; dataflow processor*.

streamer A magnetic tape unit designed specifically to support a fixed-disc (Winchester) magnetic disc system by holding files and transferring them rapidly to and from disc as required. The unit, typically, uses one-half inch tape recorded at 1600 characters per inch and incorporates a microprocessor to calculate the tape diameter on each reel and to control reel speeds accordingly to maintain constant tape tension.

streaming (1) The transmission mode of a loop network. **(2)** A fault condition of a modem in which it transmits continuously.

string (1) A sequence or series; a number of items or events that follow one after the other in time; ('a string of 1-bits'; 'a string of clock pulses'; 'a string of errors'). **(2)** A linear group of items in contiguous positions; ('a character string'; 'a string of digits'; 'an alphanumeric string'). **(3)** A concatenated set; a group of items (in non-contiguous locations) joined by pointers. **(4)** A sequence; a group of items (say, records) in order by their keys. **(5)** To concatenate; to join items to form a 'string'. **(6)** Also *list; row; vector; one-dimensional array*. A number of items (or locations) in linear arrangement in contiguous storage positions.

string descriptor See *descriptor*.

string handling The operations or facilities involved in forming and manipulating strings; for example, counting, numbering, sorting, merging, inserting, deleting, appending, concatenating, and deconcatenating. When used in the sense of computer capability, the term is synonymous with 'character handling'.

strip ribbon Narrow, inked ribbon (usually one-half inch wide) as used in most typewriters and some printers. See *ribbon; scroll ribbon*.

strobe Pulses applied in a high-speed sequence to a group of contiguous locations; for example, in reading data from coordinate-addressable storage where the pulses test the status (1-bit or 0-bit) of storage cells and send the results as pulses on a circuit.

stroke (1) A vector; a line produced by a display writer. **(2)** A keystroke; a depression of a key on a keyboard.

stroke generator An element of a computer graphics device that produces a vector for display or plotting.

Strowger relay A telephone exchange switching unit with a rotating and sliding armature and contacts that can connect any of ten input circuits to any of ten output circuits. A number of relays operate in a hierarchial arrangement in making a dialed call with each dialed digit making a selection at one level. (They are generally considered to be obsolete but they continue in use in the U.K. and certain other countries.) See *relay; crossbar; reed relay.*

structure (1) The elements and the way they are organised; ('the structure of a program'; 'the structure of a language'; 'the structure of a data network'). **(2)**A data structure; a group of items (or locations) organised for access purposes. **(3)**To select elements and combine them in a particular way; ('structure a program'; 'structure a computer system'). **(4)**An assembly identified by function; ('a straddle erase structure').

structure diagram See *structured programming.*

structured file A file of standard (commonly supported) organisation. See *standard file organisation; unstructured file.*

structured program A program produced by structured programming. Typically, it is a hierarchy of modules each of which has a single entry and exit point and through which control is passed in downward sequence without unconditional branches to higher levels of the structure. See *structured programming.*

structured programming A programming method intended to produce efficient programs with economy of programming effort; it is particularly suited for work with large or complex applications where the best way to proceed may not be evident when the task is begun. Essentially, it consists of representing the problem as a combination of **structure diagrams** corresponding to 'sequence', 'iteration' and 'selection', each of which is the basis for a single module of code. The method (ideally) results in successive refinements of an outline program during which errors and ambiguities are revealed and resolved and the most efficient form of the final coding becomes evident. Structured programming is intended to force the emphasis to be placed upon the logical requirements of the problem and to discourage trial and error and individualistic techniques that often result in programs that are wasteful of programming effort, slow in execution, and difficult to maintain. (Decision tables may be used as an aid in structuring individual modules; flowcharts are avoided.) See *structured program.*

structured variable A term sometimes applied to a variable of two or more dimensions (to one that is accessed by name and multiple subscripts).

stunt box In a teletypewriter or similar device; the elements that recognise control characters and control non-printing functions such as carriage return, bell, and tabulate.

STX *Start of TeXt.*

stylus (1) An element of a computer graphics device that can be moved by hand to identify or manipulate coordinate data; for example, a light pen. **(2)**In a matrix printer; an element of the print head that contacts the paper to produce dots that form dot matrix characters. In an impact matrix printer, it may also be termed a 'needle' or a 'wire' and in an electrosensitive printer or thermal matrix printer, an 'electrode'.

stylus printer An impact or thermal matrix printer.

SUB (1)*SUBroutine.* **(2)***SUBstitute.* The substitute character.

suballocated file A file that occupies part of a unit of magnetic disc storage that has already been allocated; it may contain one or more additional files. See *unique file.*

suballocation With respect to a resource (buffer; magnetic disc storage) that has already been allocated to one entity or for one use; the further allocation of part of it to another entity or for another use. The term is particularly applied to such allocation of an extent (area of magnetic disc storage) wherein a global extent is divided among two or more files.

subblock A portion of a message ending with the ETB character.

subcatalogue A part of another catalogue; particularly one held in a different storage location.

subchannel A part of a channel that can be used independently; for example, to handle a single input or output of data in a channel that can handle paralleled movements of data.

subfile In some systems; a library routine.

subgroup Two or more elements from a larger group that are considered as an entity for some purpose.

subject data base A data base that is structured to meet the 'real world' needs of an organisation, as contrasted to an **application data base** that is structured according to processing-related requirements.

subloop (1)A loop that is executed within another loop. **(2)**In a telephone system; a loop that terminates at a device that is itself connected to a loop (usually, a 'local loop'); for example, a circuit to an internal telephone that is terminated at a private branch exchange.

subminute Less than a minute; a term applied to a facsimile system that can transmit a page (A4) in less than a minute.

subordinate task A task other than the main task. The term is usually applied to a peripheral transfer (or, possibly, staging) that is performed concurrently with instruction execution.

subprogram A labeled module of a program that is intended to be executed more than one time during the execution of the program. It is assumed to be specific to the program and to be compiled with the program (as contrasted to a 'subroutine'). Such a subprogram may be termed an **internal subprogram** and where this term is used an **external subprogram** is a 'subroutine' (a separately compiled sequence). A subprogram is assumed to be referenced by its label during execution; an **in-line subprogram** is one that is copied into the main sequence of instructions wherever it is required. See *subroutine*.

subroutine A short sequence of instructions written to accomplish a particular operation (a validation; calculating VAT; formatting an invoice; finding factorials) that is available (usually on a library tape) to be included in or to be called by different programs. There is no precise difference between a subroutine and a routine, though a 'routine' is assumed to be longer and, possibly, less-frequently required. A **system subroutine** is one supplied with an operating system and a **user subroutine** is one written by an application programmer. A subroutine, as defined, may be termed an **external subroutine** and where this term is used, an **internal subroutine** is a 'subprogram' (a sequence compiled with the program in which it is used). An **open subroutine** (also **in-line subroutine**) is one that is copied into a program wherever it is required and a **closed subroutine** is one that is present as a single copy that is referenced by label wherever required. See *routine; subprogram; call*.

subschema A subset of a schema that specifies those facilities of a data base that can be accessed by a particular application program or group of programs. It is, in effect, a masked version of the schema. See *data base; schema*.

subscriber A person or organisation that receives and pays for a communications service from a PTT or common carrier.

subscriber loop A local loop.

subscriber trunk dialing (STD) A facility of a telephone system by which subscribers can make dialed calls to numbers outside their local service area.

subscript (1) That which is printed or written in a lower (inferior) position; for example, the '2' in SiO_2. **(2)** Also, sometimes, *index*. A value that identifies a particular location in a table or array; it is often indicated by parentheses in source code; for example, ADD DAILY-OUT (3) TO WEEKLY-OUT. See *index; array*.

subset (1) A group of items from a set; ('a character subset'; 'a subset of a computer's resources'). **(2)** A term applied to a form of a programming language with fewer facilities or more restrictions than provided by the full language specification.

subsetting The formation of subsets.

substitute character (SUB) A control character that may be inserted in a message in place of an invalid character (say one with a parity failure) or one that cannot be represented by the sending and/or receiving device.

substitution error An error in which an incorrect item is selected; for example, in optical character recognition, the encoding of an 'O' from reading a 'C'.

substrate The base or supporting structure; that on which something else is formed. The term is applied to the silicon chip on which an integrated circuit is formed and a flexible disc could be described in such terms as 'a magnetisable coating on a Mylar substrate'.

substring A division of a string (usually for purposes of storing or manipulation). See *string*.

subsystem A secondary or subordinate system, usually capable of operating independently of, or asynchronously with, a controlling system.

subsystem controller In a data network; a device that performs line interfacing and control functions for those elements of a system at a particular data station; for example, a terminal control unit.

subtracter A device that performs subtraction; a device that produces an output that represents the difference between two input values. See *adder*.

subtrahend See *minuend*.

subvoice-grade Also *telegraph-grade*. A designation of a narrow-band channel (240-300 Hz.) that is suitable for telegraph and low-speed data transmission (up to about 150 bits per second) but not for speech or data at higher speeds. Such channels may be leased from a PTT or common carrier (subvoice-grade lines) or derived from voice-grade channels with modem notch filters. See *voice-grade; telegraph*.

suffix That which comes after something else; in telephone usage, it denotes one or more digits (say, the number of an internal extension) that are dialed after a call is completed to subscriber's equipment.

suite A term sometimes applied to a group of items that are used together to accomplish some operation; for example, a 'program suite'.

sum (1) A total; the result of an addition. **(2)** To perform addition.

summary A report giving the important facts or significant figures but omitting details and/or calculations.

summation check A check using a control total; the performance of addition on values at a particular stage of handling or processing and comparing the total with the total of the same values obtained at an earlier stage. See *check digit; control total*.

super large scale integration See *SLSI*.

supergroup See *group*.

superposed circuit In a telephone link in which there are two wire or cable circuits; an additional channel (two-wire circuit) obtained by means of transformers that enable each of the other circuits to act as a single wire in the new circuit.

superscript That which is printed or written in an upper (superior) position; for example, the '2' in '16^2'. See *subscript*.

supervisor Also, in some systems, *executive*. A set of interrelated programs provided by a computer manufacturer to perform recurring operations required in the execution of user programs. The operations performed vary with the system but generally they relate to scheduling programs for execution, performing inputs and outputs, initialisation of values prior to processing, monitoring processing and detecting and reporting abnormal conditions, and communicating with an operator via the console. There is no clear distinction between a supervisor or executive and an operating system and, in some systems, a supervisor is a set of programs that is part of the operating system. Generally, the software that 'manages' a large system and has the capability to handle multiprogramming is termed an 'operating system' and the more limited software required to handle a small batch system is termed a 'supervisor' or 'executive'. See *operating system; system software*.

supervisor call A jump to a supervisory routine made by an instruction in an executing user program. It is usually made to perform an input, an output, a dump, or a communication with an operator. See *call*.

supervisor call instruction (SVC) An instruction in a user program that makes a supervisor call.

supervisor call interrupt An interrupt resulting from decoding a supervisor call instruction.

supervisor state Also *supervisory mode*. The processing state in which the instructions of system software are executed.

supervisory A term applied to that which performs a control or scheduling function.

supervisory channel Also *backward channel*. In a data communications system; a channel of narrower bandwidth than the main channel that is used to carry acknowledgements and other supervisory messages. Such a channel is a 'subvoice-grade channel'. A system that uses such a channel is termed **asymmetric duplex**.

supervisory console The operator's console; the main console in a multi-console system.

supervisory message A short message relating to operation of the data link on which it is sent. It is, typically, a single character (say, ACK or NAK) plus those characters required for error detection. It may be sent as an ordinary return message in either a full duplex or half-duplex system; in an asymmetric duplex system, it is sent on the 'supervisory channel'.

supervisory mode Supervisor state.

supervisory program (1) A supervisory routine. **(2)** A supervisor; all of the routines that control processing (or perform certain processing operations) considered as a single program.

supervisory routine Also, in some systems, *executive routine*. A routine that is part of an operating system or supervisor; a routine that performs some operation required to execute user programs or to maintain the facilities of a computer system. See *supervisor; operating system; supervisory software*.

supervisory signals Signals used to monitor or control the operation of peripherals or line interface devices.

supervisory software (1) Supervisory routines considered as a class or group. **(2)** Those supervisory routines that comprise the supervisor, executive, or operating system of a particular computer or range of computers. See *software; system software; utility; supervisory routine; supervisor; operating system*.

support (1) A term used in various contexts to indicate the presence of a capability or necessary facilities; ('an operating system that supports multiprogramming'; 'a circuit that supports two-way communications'; 'a computer that supports COBOL'; 'a file that supports indexed access'). **(2)** By a manufacturer or supplier; to assist a user of their hardware/software to keep it in good operating condition.

support control program A limited operating system with facilities to run certain test and diagnostic programs.

suppress(1) Also, often, *disable*. To prevent from occurring or to nullify; ('suppress interrupts'; 'suppress DCD'). **(2)** To reduce or limit; ('suppress noise'; 'suppress transients').

suppression See *suppress; zero suppression*.

surge arrestor A small gas-filled tube with two electrodes, one which is connected to ground and the other to the circuit that is to be protected from high-voltage pulses. The gas ionizes at a predetermined voltage, thus shunting pulses to ground.

suspend With respect to a program; to temporarily discontinue execution while retaining storage and register contents to permit restoring it when conditions of system loading or resource availability permit. See *restart; checkpoint; roll-in roll-out*.

SVC *SuperVisor Call instruction*.

SW (1) *SWitch*. **(2)** *(S/W) SoftWare*.

swap (1) To interchange two items or the contents of two areas of storage. **(2)** To move a page/segment between primary and secondary storage; to either 'swap-in' or 'swap-out'.

swap-in Also *roll-in* and, in a paging system, *page in*. To move a page or segment from secondary storage to primary storage. See *virtual storage transfers*.

swap-out Also *roll-out* and, in a paging system, *page out*. To delete a page or segment from primary storage and write it to secondary storage. See *virtual storage transfers*.

swappable (1) Preemptible. **(2)** A term applied to a page or segment (containing system software) that can be deleted.

swapping Also, in a paging system, *paging*. In a virtual storage system; the process of bringing pages/segments from secondary storage to primary storage as required to meet the needs of executing tasks. See *virtual storage transfers*.

swapping set The pages/segments (of system software as well as user programs) that are available to a program during execution in a virtual storage system.

SWIFT *Society for Worldwide Interbank Financial Telecommunication*. A group responsible for an electronic, interbank funds transfer system encompassing more than 1000 banks in 20 countries and handling about 250,000 transactions per day.

SWIFT interface device An approved on-line terminal for use in the SWIFT system.

swim In computer graphics; an undesired movement of display elements about their normal positions.

switch (1) With respect to a storage cell; to change its contents from a 1-bit to a 0-bit or the reverse. **(2)** A basic logic circuit; a circuit that performs an AND, NAND, OR, or NOT operation. See *logic operation*. **(3)** A switch cell; a storage cell that can be individually accessed. **(4)** A conditional branch instruction. **(5)** A switchpoint. **(6)** A switch value. **(7)** A manually operated device containing contacts that are used to open and close one or more electrical circuits. **(8)** To operate a 'switch' (def. 7); ('switch off the computer'). **(9)** To change or exchange; ('switch lines'; 'switch disc packs').

switch cell A one-bit storage location that can be individually accessed. See *flag*.

switch core A core used as a switch cell.

switch element (1) In some systems; a character that indicates a user option; for example, a '/'. **(2)** A switching element.

switch hook The actuator and the switch that is operated when a telephone handset is lifted from the cradle.

switch indicator A flag; a bit that indicates the setting of a 'switch' (storage cell).

switch instruction (1) A conditional branch instruction; an instruction that holds a switch value and specifies its use in testing an item of data. **(2)** An instruction that tests whether or not a particular switch is set; an instruction that checks the status of a flag.

switch status test A test to determine if a switch (storage cell) holds a 1-bit or a 0-bit; a test performed by a switch instruction.

switch train The sequencing of switching elements (relay contacts) that are closed to establish a circuit between a calling telephone and a called telephone.

switch value Also *switch*. A value (parameter) that controls branching at a particular branchpoint and that is bound before the branchpoint is reached during execution. It is one of the inputs to a logic operation that determines which instruction sequence is followed from the branchpoint. For example, in the statement IF AGE-IN GREATER THAN 50 PRINT "PENSION B", the 50 is a 'switch value'. A switch value can also be the specified value of a flag that is to cause a jump as in IF SWITCHON-1 GO TO ERROR-3. See *conditional branch instruction; jump*.

switched carrier In data communications; a carrier wave that is not transmitted continuously. The term usually identifies a

multipoint polling system in which constant carrier is transmitted from the central site to the remote sites on one channel of a four-wire circuit with carrier in the other channel raised only when remote sites reply to polling messages. The term is sometimes applied to 'dial-up' or to include both dial-up and polling. See *multipoint; constant carrier*.

switched communications Communications via a switched (PSTN) line.

switched connection In a telephone system; a connection established by dialing or operator routing.

switched data network (1) A multipoint network; a data network that uses polling. **(2)** A data network that uses dialed PSTN lines. **(3)** A network that uses message or circuit switching.

switched line Also, usually, *dialed line*. A communications link that is established between two locations by selectively closing switching elements (relay contacts). See *leased line; public switched telephone network*.

switched network (1) A public switched telephone network (PSTN); the facilities of a telephone system that provide dialed and/or operator-routed connections (as contrasted to the facilities that provide leased lines). **(2)** A switched data network.

switched network backup Dial backup; the facilities of modem-associated equipment (line access unit; data access arrangement) that provide for changing data transmission from a leased line to a dialed (PSTN) line. See *automatic answering*.

switching (1) The process of changing from one thing to another. **(2)** The process of routing communications between points. See *line switching; message switching; packet switching*.

switching centre (1) A message or packet switching centre. **(2)** A telephone exchange. **(3)** A line control centre.

switching element A device that provides for selectively opening and closing one or more electrical circuits; for example, a switch or a transistor.

switching function (1) The function of a switching element. **(2)** A function in which inputs and outputs can have only a finite number of values; if the finite number is '2', it is a 'logic function'.

switching pad An attenuator that is automatically cut in and out of a (telephone) circuit depending upon conditions.

switching variable A variable that can take only a finite number of values or states; if it can take only two values or states (representable by 'true' and 'false' or '1' and '0'), it is a 'logic variable'.

switchpoint Also *switch; branchpoint*. A place during the execution of a program where control can be transferred from one sequence of instructions to another. See *branchpoint*.

syllable (1) In source coding; a part of a word or name that has individual significance; for example, the SWITCH and the ON in the COBOL condition name SWITCHON. **(2)** With respect to an instruction; a term sometimes used synonymously with 'field' ('an operator syllable'; 'a value call syllable').

symbol (1) A character that represents an entity, an operation, or a concept in accordance with some convention or rule, for example, a '£' to represent 'Pounds', a '×' to indicate that a multiplication operation is to be performed, or a '⚓' on a chart to indicate an anchorage. The term **special symbol** may be applied to such a symbol to differentiate it from a letter (possibly a digit) used as a symbol; for example a 'Z' to indicate 'impedance' or a 'k' to denote 'thousands'. A symbol other than a letter or digit that is part of a character set is termed a **special character**. An alphabetic symbol that is the first letter of the word it represents ('R' for 'resistance') is also an 'abbreviation'. **(2)** A character group that, for some purpose or in some context, has a meaning other than that by which it may be defined in a language. Examples include a data name GROSSPAY and an airline station address LAX for 'Los Angeles'. See *mnemonic; symbolic address*.

symbolic address A name in source coding as assigned by a programmer to a storage location that the program will use during execution. It is converted to a relative or virtual address by a compiler and to an absolute address when the program is loaded. See *address; data name*.

symbolic addressing In programming; the identification of storage locations by 'symbolic addresses' (rather than by relative addresses or absolute addresses which are numbers). See *absolute addressing*.

symbolic coding Programming in a symbolic language.

symbolic file A file name that identifies a group of files; the one required for a particular execution of a program (in transaction processing) is indicated by a further input from the terminal operator.

symbolic generation name A file name that uniquely identifies a file of a particular generation (as contrasted to the usual identification of a file by name and the generation by number).

symbolic I/O assignment A name assigned by a programmer to an input/output device that will be used by his program during execution.

symbolic language A programming language in which operations are identified by 'symbols' (typically, mnemonic words), and which provides for the use of symbolic addresses. Virtually all modern high-level and low-level languages are 'symbolic'.

symbolic logic A system for solving non-numerical problems by using a set of unambiguous symbols to represent logical conditions and relationships. See *logic; Boolean algebra*.

symbolic parameter A formal parameter; a symbol that will be replaced by a numeric value prior to the execution of the instruction in which it is contained.

symmetric channel (1) A channel that is 'binary symmetric'. See *binary symmetric*. **(2)** In a duplex circuit; a channel that has the same speed and characteristics as the other channel. See *asymmetric duplex*.

symmetric circuit A full-duplex circuit with the capability to transfer data at the same speed in both directions (on both channels). See *asymmetric duplex*.

symmetric processors In a multiprocessor system; processors with identical characteristics.

SYN (pronounced 'sin') *SYNchronising; SYNchronous*. **(1)** A transmission control character that is used to establish synchronisation between sending and receiving equipment on a binary synchronous communications link. In many systems, the master station sends a repeating sequence of the characters during periods when no messages are being sent and, when used in this way, it may be termed a **synchronous idle character**. **(2)** SYNC.

SYNC (pronounced 'sink') *SYNChronising*. An identifier of that which is used to establish synchronisation; ('a sync pulse'; 'a sync pattern').

sync bits Framing bits.

sync pulses Synchronisation pulses.

SYNCH *SYNCHronising*. See *SYNC*.

synchronisation (1) The condition in which two or more operations are performed with common timing. **(2)** The process of adjusting event timing of a system or functional unit so that events occur in time frames established by another system or functional unit. **(3)** The process of aligning numeric data in computational format to the correct (word or half-word) boundary for performing arithmetic operations.

synchronisation pulses Also *sync pulses*. Pulses sent from one system or functional unit to another for purposes of establishing, checking, or adjusting event timing.

synchronise (1) To adjust event timing so that events in two or more systems or functional units occur with common timing. **(2)** To place or move numeric data in storage so that it is aligned at an access-significant boundary. See *justify; synchronised*.

synchronised (1) Of events or operations; occurring with common timing. See *synchronisation*. **(2)** Of numeric data in a computational format (fixed-point binary; floating point); placed in a storage location so that it occupies successive bit positions to the left of an access-significant boundary (it is, thus, right justified). Usually, the access-significant boundary is that of a word and an item aligned to it is said to be **word synchronised**. Short items may sometimes be 'half-word synchronised. When considering items other than numeric data in computational format, the term 'aligned' or 'justified' is usually used instead of 'synchronised'.

synchronous (1) A term applied to a system or operation in which events occur in a sequence of fixed time frames; ('a binary synchronous communications system'; 'a bit synchronous transfer'). **(2)** Of a data transfer for an executing program; requiring the suspension of instruction execution for the time that it is being accomplished. See *autonomous; asynchronous*. **(3)** With respect to events that occur without common timing; a term sometimes used to indicate that the completion of one event initiates the next.

synchronous computer A computer in which data transfers and manipulations are performed in sequences controlled by clock pulses. (All digital computers are 'synchronous'.)

synchronous data link control (SDLC) A discipline for managing binary synchronous data communications systems using duplex or half-duplex transmission, leased or dialed lines, and in point-to-point, multipoint, or loop configurations. It provides for the use of **frames** in structuring messages, with each frame beginning and ending with a **flag** which is the character 01111110; consecutive frames are separated by a single flag. Receiving hardware searches incoming data to locate flags; in addition to their function as frame delimiters, they are used to establish, check, and adjust synchronisation. The system is code transparent and in order to prevent some encoded character from duplicating a flag, a 0-bit is automatically inserted after any sequence of five 1-bits in an operation that is termed 'bit stuffing'. Receiving hardware deletes a 0-bit following five 1-bits before transferring data to the receive buffer and, thus, restores it to the original form. A frame is the unit of data transfer and it is divided into multiple fields. An **address field** follows the opening flag; it is an 8-bit byte with the first bit a 0-bit if it is the only address byte and a 1-bit if there is a second address byte. The address field is followed by a **control field** which contains an I if the frame constitutes an information transfer, an S if it contains a supervisory message and a U-A if it is used for some other purpose. The next field is the **information field** which may contain a **logical control field** as its first element when such a field is required for some user purpose. (A logical control field is not included in the HDLC specification, which is otherwise the same as SDLC with respect to frame format.) The remainder of the information field contains the 'message'; it can be in any code from 5-level to 8-level and the length of the characters in this field can be set to any number of bits from 5 to 8. Receiving hardware always outputs 'characters' of 8 bits and if a shorter character length is used in the information field the unused bit positions are set to zero. The information field is followed by a **frame check sequence field** which holds a 'cyclic check character' in 16 bit positions. This field is followed by the closing flag. A frame can be aborted by sending from 8 to 16 consecutive 1-bits (without inserting any 0-bits). When the transmitter is not transmitting a frame (when it is in the 'out of frame' condition'), it sends continuous flags (**time fill**) or continuous 1-bits (**mark idle**). SDLC systems use the CCITT V.24 interface. See *high-level data link control; packet switching.*

synchronous data network A data network that uses binary synchronous communications; a network in which a timing reference is essential to the correct interpretation of bit patterns.

synchronous execution Execution in which each instruction (except the first) can only execute when the action specified by the previous instruction has been completed.

synchronous idle The condition in which a continuous stream of synchronising information is sent on a data link during times when no messages are being sent. See *mark idle; time fill.*

synchronous idle character See *SYN.*

synchronous operation An operation in which correct performance depends upon the timing of events.

synchronous receiver-transmitter Also *synchronous transceiver.* An interface device that is capable of receiving and transmitting synchronous bit-serial data. The term usually denotes a single integrated circuit in a microprocessor system. See *USART.*

synchronous transceiver A synchronous receiver-transmitter.

synchronous transfer In a time-interleaved multiprogramming system; a peripheral transfer that does not overlap instruction execution. Such a transfer takes place during the time slices allocated to the program for which it is performed and, thus, no instructions are executed during the period. See *cycle stealing; asynchronous transfer.*

synonym (1) A word that, in some context, has the same meaning as another word; it is a 'synonym' of the other word. **(2)** With respect to magnetic disc files; a term sometimes applied to a record with the same key as another record (usually produced by a hashing algorithm). **(3)** An alias; a second name by which a compiler recognises an item of data or storage location.

syntactic compatibility The condition in which two programming languages have a common syntax.

syntactical error An error in syntax as detected during compilation.

syntax (1) In a language; the rules or practice governing the placement of words of different types (nouns; verbs; adjectives) in relation to each other in sentences. **(2)** In a programming language; the rules for forming valid instructions (or statements/commands). See *semantics.*

synthesizer A device that holds the bit-pattern representations of analogue waves (speech; drum beats) and performs the necessary digital to analogue conversion to produce the sound.

SYSGEN *SYStem GENeration.*

system (1) A group of complementary elements organised to 'work together' to perform an operation or to perform various operations of the same type; ('a computer system'; 'a magnetic disc system'; 'a servo system'). **(2)** A method or technique; ('a data base system'; 'an encoding system'; 'a validation system'). **(3)** Pertaining to the control and management of processing functions; ('system software'; 'a system routine'; 'a system disc').

system activity An activity performed by an operating system, particularly one that is logged for report or analysis purposes; for example, processor utilisation, paging, and the use of devices and input/output channels.

system administrator A person who is responsibile for the activities of users of a computer system.

system analysis Systems analysis.

system availability The time during which a (computer) system is available for use. See *availability*.

system console A master console; the main operating station of a multi-console computer. See *console*.

system control area Those tracks of a magnetic disc volume that are accessible only to the operating system; they are used to hold data relating to the contents and access of the volume. See *file directory*.

system control language (SCL) A language supplied by a computer manufacturer and used to control processing; it consists of the 'job control language' and (where considered a separate entity), an 'operator control language'. See *job control language; operator control language*.

system crash A complete failure of an operating system caused by an attempt to execute an illegal instruction (or another error condition) that occurs in conjunction with a failure of built-in protective mechanisms. It usually results in the loss of some or all of the contents of main storage. Recovery consists of reloading the operating system and reestablishing programs from their checkpoints. See *checkpoint*.

system data Data held and used by an operating system to control processing operations; for example, the contents of a configuration table or a mapping table. See *data; user data*.

system definition (1) The process of defining a new computer system and selecting its components. **(2)** System generation.

system design The process of determining the elements of an application system and their organisation in order to meet the objectives given in a 'statement of requirements'. It, typically, includes an analysis of input data and its method of collection and handling, design of forms, determining methods of maintaining and updating data, estimating costs of both operation and implementation, and determining the form and method of dissemination of results. The output of the system design function is usually a **system specification** that provides the basis for program and file design. See *systems analysis; statement of requirements*.

system designer A person (systems analyst) who performs system design work.

system device (1) The peripheral device on which the operating system is stored and from which it is loaded into main storage during startup. **(2)** A device used in the management of processing and which is not accessed by user programs; for example, a magnetic disc unit used to hold system software or for spooling or paging.

system disc A magnetic disc used for some system function. See *system device*.

system documentation Documentation relating to system software or to other facilities of a computer system. See *documentation*.

system effective data rate In a computer system with (cartridge) mass storage; the amount of data transferred between the staging drives and main storage per second (usually the average for one hour).

system error An error (wherever occurring) that affects the processing capability of a computer system. See *error; system crash*.

system error message A message to the operator giving details of a system error.

system file (1) A file accessible only by the operating system. **(2)** A global file; a file available to all user programs.

system flowchart (1) A flowchart indicating the flow of data to be provided for by an application system. It, typically, includes clerical and distribution and collection operations as well as computer operations.

system generation (SYSGEN) The selection, adaption, and tuning of an operating system to meet the requirements of a particular hardware configuration and data processing work load.

system input control The system software functions relating to managing inputs; where used, the term would include such functions as validation, spooling, scheduling, and loading.

system input device A device (magnetic disc unit) that holds jobs in an input stream.

system instrumentation file In some systems; a journal used to record system activities and events. See *system monitor; instrumentation*.

system integrity The condition of a system with respect to its protection against potentially damaging/disruptive external influences.

system key A storage-protection key used to protect system code or data from unauthorised access by non-system programs. See *storage protection*.

system library The backing storage volume(s) that hold the operating system and/or other units of system software. See *system device*.

system loader A loader for an operating system.

system lock In some virtual storage systems; the condition in which no pages can be loaded except those of the paging supervisory software.

system log A journal to which a record of events that occur during processing is written.

system macro definition A macro definition that defines a macro in a job control language (or, possibly, supervisory routines).

system manager A person in overall charge of a computer installation.

system monitor Supervisory software used to detect the occurrence of system events as may be required by users, user programs, or for purposes of analysis. It writes the data collected to a journal (sometimes a system or user instrumentation file).

system name A name by which a peripheral device is known to the operating system.

system output device A device assigned to receive the output from several jobs (as contrasted, possibly, to a device allocated to a particular job).

system overhead That part of the resources of a computer system used to perform functions other than compiling, testing, modifying, and executing user programs.

system parameter (1) That which may constrain or limit the work or performance of a computer system; for example, the size of main storage. **(2)** A default parameter supplied by an operating system. **(3)** An objective that is to be met in the design of a new system.

system productivity The amount of work that a system can perform in a particular time as compared to the amount it was designed and structured to perform.

system program A unit of system software; a program other than an application program. See *system routine*.

system programmer A programmer who works on operating systems, compilers, or other system software. See *programmer*.

system residence volume (1) A volume that holds the nucleus of the operating system and high-level catalogue indexes. **(2)** Any volume that must be permanently on-line during processing.

system resource A resource; that which can be allocated to serve a processing function in a computer system.

system restart (1) A restart following a system crash. **(2)** A warm boot.

system routine A sequence of instructions that is a unit of supervisory or system software. The term usually includes library routines and subroutines (which may be user written). When 'system routine' and 'system program' are differentiated, a system routine is usually a utility while a system program is a sequence of instructions that returns a result or one that is a major element of an operating system; thus, a 'fetch routine' and a 'monitor program'.

system segment (1) A segment that holds a system routine. **(2)** A public segment; a segment available to all programs.

system shutdown The time during which processing activities are being terminated (say, at the end of the last shift of the day). Typically, it is a period in which no new jobs can be submitted nor execution begun on further jobs in the job queue.

system slowdown In a transaction processing system; the condition (when input buffers are nearly full) in which the acceptance of additional transactions is restricted while processing and output 'catches up'.

system software (1) Also, often, *software*. Those programs (or sequences of instructions by other names) that are available in a computer system to perform processing (or related activities) that are not specific to the needs of a particular user. See *application; software; application program*. **(2)** Those system routines that are available in a computer system that are not part of the operating system. See *supervisory software*. **(3)** System routines considered as a class or type.

system specification See *system design*.

system standard format A storage format that is standard for files in a particular computer system.

system table A table accessible only by the operating system; a table used to hold system data.

system task (1) An active unit of system software. **(2)** A function performed by system software.

system update Modifications to an operating system that do not constitute complete system generation.

system utility device A peripheral (magnetic disc unit) that is used to hold scratch files for different jobs.

system utility program A utility.

system volume A volume on a system device; a volume that contains the operating system or elements of it.

systems analysis The job or operation of determining how best to implement particular user applications on particular computer systems. It, typically, consists of forming a precise statement of the problem and what is to be accomplished, listing desired attributes of the system, determining the method of implementation that is most effective with respect to performance and cost, and preparing a feasibility study. If the decision is made to proceed with the implementation, a 'statement of requirements' is prepared for use in the system design stage. (System design may or may not be considered part of systems analysis.) See *feasibility study; system design; statement of requirements.*

systems analyst A person who is trained and employed to perform systems analysis and/or system design.

systems network architecture (SNA) *IBM definition:* The total description of the logical structure, formats, protocols, and operational sequences for transmitting information units through the communication system. Communication system functions are separated into three discrete areas: the application layer, the function management layer, and the transmission subsystem layer. The structure of SNA allows the ultimate origins and destinations of information—that is, the end users— to be independent of, and unaffected by, the specific communication-system services and facilities used for information exchange.

T

T *Tera-.*
T-carrier system A long-distance PCM system (in the U.S.). See *pulse code modulation.*
TAB *TABulate.*
table Also, sometimes, *array; list; flat file; relation.* A structure consisting of (or with places for) like items of data that are accessed by referencing their locations in the structure. The structure is assumed to be either one-dimensional or two-dimensional and to occupy (or consist of) contiguous storage locations. See *variable; array; matrix; subscript; relation.*
table element A single item in a table or a place for such an item.
table fragmentation The condition in which so much main storage space is occupied by address-transformation and other system tables that the amount available to meet the processing requirements of user programs is materially reduced. See *fragmentation.*
table lookup (1) An access of a location in a table, catalogue, or index, for example, as a step in address modification. **(2)** A manual operation of finding a value (say, a logarithm) in a table.
table lookup instruction An instruction that initiates a table lookup.
tabulate (1) To move the printing position of a printer or the cursor of a VDU to a preset position to the right along the same line (horizontal tabulate) or to a lower line position (vertical tabulate). Unless otherwise indicated, 'horizontal' is understood. See HT; VT. **(2)** To organise items into tables.
tabulation character See *HT; VT.*
tabulator (1) A tabulator key. **(2)** An office machine that reads accounting-related figures from a data carrier (punched cards; paper tape), performs arithmetic and formatting operations, and prints tables, totals, and subtotals.
tabulator key (TAB) A key on a typewriter or terminal keyboard that, when pressed, causes the printing or display position to move to a preset position along the current line. (If not preset, it is often defaulted to movements in eight-space increments.)
tag (1) A bit or bits (usually in a header) that indicate some condition with respect to the data or storage location with which they are associated; for example; 'not validated' or 'track defective'. **(2)** In a magnetic disc file; an address of an overflowed record as held in its home location. **(3)** To identify an item with a 'tag' (def. 1). **(4)** A term sometimes used synonymously with 'record key'.
tag file A file consisting of record keys sorted into some order for access purposes; it may be the result of a 'tag sort'.
tag sort A sort of keyed items in two steps in the first of which the keys are sorted according to some criteria and in the second of which the actual items (usually records) are written to a storage location in their new order.
take off (1) To read and copy; ('take off totals from invoices'). **(2)** By a read/write head in some magnetic disc systems; to rise from the surface of an accelerating disc. See *head; land; fly.*
tally (1) A non-positional numeration system in which a single line (pen stroke; scratch mark on wood) represents a '1' with, often, a diagonal line as in ⁄⁄⁄⁄ closing a group of five. **(2)** To count or add; ('tally the items of an invoice'). **(3)** A count or total.
tandem Consisting of two (presumably identical) items; ('tandem processors').
tap (1) In a multi-voltage transformer; a terminal that connects to the secondary winding at the correct place to produce one of the voltages. **(2)** A shoulder tap.

tape Either magnetic tape or paper tape; unless otherwise indicated, 'magnetic' is usually understood.

tape bin An open-topped box that is sometimes used to receive paper tape as it comes out of a reader or punch.

tape cartridge A self-contained magnetic tape volume that is unit-mountable on its drive. See *digital cassette; data cartridge; magnetic tape*.

tape cassette See *digital cassette*.

tape code A code by which data is represented on tape; unless otherwise indicated, it is a 'paper tape code' rather than a 'magnetic tape code'.

tape comparator A paper tape validation device that compares two separately punched lengths of paper tape and indicates any differences in punching patterns.

tape deck (1) The part of a magnetic tape unit that is presented to the user; the part containing the reels and tape path. See *tape drive*. **(2)** A magnetic tape unit.

tape drive (1) The motor, capstans, and related devices that move magnetic tape through a magnetic tape unit. See *tape deck*. **(2)** A magnetic tape unit.

tape feed (1) The elements that move paper tape through a punch or reader. **(2)** To advance paper tape (without data punching).

tape file A magnetic tape file.

tape operating system (TOS) An operating system (for IBM System/360 computers) that is held on magnetic tape. See *disc operating system*.

tape punch A paper tape punch.

tape reader A paper tape reader.

tape relay A term sometimes applied to a torn tape system.

tape reproducer A device that makes a copy of punched paper tape; a device that reads hole patterns in one paper tape and punches them in another.

tape-resident A term applied to code or data that is held on magnetic tape; ('a tape-resident operating system').

tape ring (1) Also *tape spool*. A flangeless, plastic (sometimes cardboard) ring on which paper tape is wound, as supplied by the manufacturer. **(2)** A write-permit ring for a magnetic tape volume.

tape row A frame; a position where a hole pattern encoding a character is punched (or can be punched) in paper tape.

tape sort A sort in which the sorted set is written to magnetic tape.

tape spool A tape ring; a ring on which paper tape is supplied.

tape spooler A tape winder.

tape station A magnetic tape unit.

tape storage Magnetic tape storage.

tape-to-card A term applied to the equipment or operation involved in reading data from magnetic tape (sometimes paper tape) and punching it in punched cards.

tape transport (1) A magnetic tape drive (tape-moving mechanism). **(2)** A magnetic tape unit.

tape transport mechanism A magnetic tape drive (tape-moving mechanism).

tape unit A magnetic tape unit.

tape winder Also *tape spooler*. A device or mechanism that rewinds paper tape after reading or punching. Unless otherwise indicated, the term usually denotes a hand-cranked device for bench mounting.

target computer Also *image computer*. In emulation; the computer that is emulated. See *emulation; host computer*.

target language Also *object language*. The language to which a translation is made.

target machine A target computer.

target program The program that is intended to result from coding or from translation. If it is in object code (as contrasted to another programming language or to an intermediate language), it is an 'object program'.

tariff The published charge for a particular service provided by a common carrier.

task (1) A logical unit of work as performed by a computer. In this sense, the term may be applied to a major function of a system (preparing a payroll; order entry), to an operation (data capture; input/output), or to some step of processing (sorting; updating). See *application; job*. **(2)** Also *job*. A processing unit consisting of one or more application programs and associated data for a particular run. **(3)** In a multiprogramming system; the basic unit to which resources are allocated. See *subtask; multitasking*. **(4)** A user task; a loaded user program.

task control block (TCB) A block that holds execution-related information about a task.

task identification The characters by which a scheduled or executing task is known to the operating system.

task input queue An input queue.

task management The functions of an operating system relating to scheduling tasks and allocating resources during execution.

task queue An input queue; a queue of task control blocks.

tasking See *multitasking*.
TCAM *TeleCommunications Access Method*.
TCB *Task Control Block*.
TCU (1)*Terminal Control Unit*. (2)*Transmission Control Unit*.
TD (1)*Transmitter-Distributor*. (2)*Transmit Data*.
TDG *Test Data Generator*.
TDM *Time Division Multiplexing*.
TDMA *Time Division Multiple Access*.
TDS *Transaction-Driven System*.
teaching machine A computer-based device (usually a video terminal) by which a student can interact with an instructional program.
TEDS Twin Exchangeable Disc Storage.
tele-autograph A system for transmitting handwriting over communications links by which movement of a pen at the sending station is converted to signals that control two-dimensional movement of a stylus at a receiving station.
telecomms *TELECOMMunicationS*.
telecommunication access method (TCAM) Software used to control transfers between a computer and on-line terminals (in an IBM system).
telecommunication control unit A transmission control unit.
telecommunication link A communications link provided by the lines and facilities of a telecommunication system.
telecommunication network (1)The lines and facilities of a PTT or common carrier. (2)A data network.
telecommunications system (1)A common carrier or PTT system; a set of facilities and procedures that provides a user-to-user communications service between geographically separated locations. See *public switched telephone network*. (2)A system (computer; telemetry) that uses telecommunications facilities.
telecommunications A term applied to the organisation and facilities that provide a user-to-user communications service between geographically separated locations. The term encompasses telephone, telegraph, radio, and satellite-based systems; unless otherwise indicated, 'telephone' is usually assumed.
Telecoms British Post Office Telecommunications.
telegraph Data communications at less than about 200 words per minute. The term is used to include: 1.A teletypewriter common carrier system (TWX; Telex) that provides start-stop transmission on subvoice-grade lines at speeds up to about 150 bits per second. 2.A user-specific data transmission system with any type of equipment that makes use of leased subvoice-grade lines. 3.A data transmission system in which characters are sent by Morse code. Such a system may make use of radio (radio telegraphy) or of land lines; unless otherwise indicated, 'land line' is understood. Lines are, typically, open-wire and transmission is by direct current with the ON-OFF condition controlled by a hand-operated key. 4.A baseband (direct current) teletypewriter system in which a voltage of one polarity represents a 1-bit (mark) and of the other a 0-bit (space).
telegraph code A code used to send data by telegraph. The internationally recognised codes are IA-2 for teletypewriter systems and Morse for hand-keying (dot-dash) systems.
telegraph-grade See *subvoice-grade*.
telegraph key A hand-operated, spring-loaded switch mechanism used for sending the dots and dashes of Morse code.
telegraphy Pertaining to telegraph systems. See *telegraph*.
teleload Also *remote program load; down-line load*. The use of a communications link from a mainframe computer to load the operating system or other system software of a remote computer or other intelligent device. The method is used where the remote device is unattended or without backing storage.
telemetering The use of communications links to carry the outputs of sensors or counters to a computer or other location where they can be recorded or analysed. It is used, for example, in monitoring flow in pipelines, levels of tanks and reservoirs, and in-flight performance of missles.
telemetry Pertaining to telemetering systems. See *telemetering*.
telephone The common line interface (and, usually, circuit-routing) device for station-to-station transmission of speech.
telephone call A speech interchange between two stations made via telephones and the facilities of a telephone system. (The term 'call' may be applied to the transmission of either speech or data while 'telephone call' usually denotes speech.)
telephone company The usual term for a telephone common carrier in the U.S. and other countries where telephone systems are operated by private 'companies'. See *public switched telephone network; Post, Telephone, and Telegraph Authority*.
telephone exchange (1)A set of lines and switching facilities that provides a telephone service to a particular city or area; it includes one or more 'telephone exchanges' by definition 2. (2)Also, in the U.S., *office*. A set of circuit interconnection facilities (and also, usually, monitoring, metering, amplification, and circuit-balancing facilities) used to provide a

telephone service for users in a particular area. (3)A subscriber-operated facility (PBX; PABX) for routing telephone calls.

telephone system An organisation of lines, switching facilities, interface equipment, and procedures that provides a station-to-station communication service within a particular country or geographical area.

telephony Pertaining to telephone systems. (In some contexts, the term excludes the facilities or role of data handling.)

teleprocessing Data processing in which elements of the total function are performed at geographically separated locations that are joined by communications links. The term assumes that the communications links are those of a telephone system.

telesoftware (TSW) Software distributed by viewdata.

teletex A word processor network designed to provide letter-quality (upper and lower case; formatted) communications between subscribers. Special terminals provide automatic routing and store-and-forward facilities and links are dialed PSTN lines or a packet switching system.

teletext A system for broadcasting text material (subtitles; traffic reports; train schedules) in conjunction with broadcast television. Text characters and formatting information are transmitted during beam flyback time and are decoded by special circuitry in the receiving set. Systems include the British Ceefax and Oracle and the French Antiope. See *videotex; viewdata*.

Teletype A product of the Teletype Corporation (Skokie, Ill.). Though the company manufactures a variety of communications products, unless otherwise indicated, the term

usually denotes a KSR teletypewriter. See *teletypewriter; glass teletype; ASR; KSR; KTR; RT; ROTR; TD*.

teletypewriter A keyboard printer (often similar in appearance to a typewriter) with a serial interface that is intended for asynchronous communications (usually, both sending and receiving) in a telegraph system. Interface options are usually available to permit their use as local terminals and as remote terminals in data networks using telephone lines. The term is sometimes used synonymously with 'Teletype'. See *Teletype*.

teletypewriter exchange service (TWX) A dial-up teletypewriter service provided by Western Union in the U.S. and Canada. Equipment for 5-level (Murray) or 7-level (ASCII) codes can be connected. Transmission speeds are up to 150 bits per second.

teletypewriter switching system A message switching system in which the terminals are teletypewriters.

telewriter A sending and receiving device used in a teleautograph system.

TELEX A world-wide, dial-up (and operator routed) teletypewriter service provided by Western Union. Only equipment for 5-level (IA-2) code can be connected. Transmission is at 50 bps.

teller work station A term sometimes applied to a user terminal in a banking system.

temporary disc A unit of magnetic disc storage (a cylinder or group of tracks) allocated to a job for the duration of a run.

temporary error A soft error; an error that 'clears' on retry.

temporary file A scratch file; a file (unit of backing storage) that can be overwritten after the end of a run.

temporary run file A temporary file.

temporary storage (1)Working storage. (2)Storage for data that is being moved or is waiting for attention; for example, the storage of a buffer or of an exchange in a message switching system.

tens complement The radix complement in the decimal system. See *radix complement*.

tentative module A compiler module that may contain unresolved symbols or references.

tentative segment A tentative module.

tera- (T) A combining form meaning 'trillion' (10^{12}).

terabit storage A term sometimes used synonymously with 'mass storage'; storage with a capacity of more than 10^{12} bits.

term (1)A pronounceable speech unit (word, word group, acronym; character) that has significance as a unit in some context. See *symbol*. (2)An element of an arithmetic or logic expression; the smallest unit to which a value can be assigned.

terminal (1)A device by which an operator can communicate with a computer. Common examples are VDU's and Teletypes. Unless otherwise indicated, it is a 'remote terminal' rather than a local terminal or operator console. In some systems, the term is synonymous with 'station' or 'work station'. See remote terminal; local terminal; audio response terminal; online; multi-access computing. (2)A data source and/or data sink; a point in a data network where data can enter or leave the system. See *data terminal equipment*. (3)Also *connector*. An element soldered or crimped to the end of a conductor to facilitate its connection to other circuit elements; for example, to a 'terminal' (def. 4). (4)A post, screw, or stud used to make an electrical connection. See *strap; terminal strip*.

terminal address An identifier of a particular terminal in a data network, or of a particular terminal at a multi-terminal data station; a character or group of characters by which a message can be routed to a terminal or identified as originating from a terminal. See *address (Communications); interchange address*.

terminal board An element of a functional unit that contains terminals (screws; studs) by which 'strapping options' can be selected by interconnection and/or by which internal circuits can be connected to external circuits.

terminal component A term sometimes applied to an input section or an output section of a terminal that can perform both functions.

terminal connector A connector; an element that is used to join conductors.

terminal control unit (TCU) Also, depending upon the system, *interface computer; multiplexor; line sharing adapter; concentrator*. An intelligent device (often a minicomputer) that performs line interfacing functions (and, often, other functions) for a group of terminals at a multi-terminal data station. Typical functions include responding to polling messages, routing messages to and from the communications link and the various terminals, buffering incoming and outgoing messages, performing modem interchange functions, multiplexing, and performing error detection and recovery functions. If unintelligent CRT terminals are connected, it also holds the video buffers. See *data network; interface computer*.

terminal entry The use of a terminal in data entry.

terminal equipment See *data terminal equipment*.

terminal I/O wait The condition in which a program is unable to continue executing until an input is received from a terminal.

terminal job The processing and interchanges performed by a computer in dealing with a request or inputs from a terminal.

terminal monitor program A transaction processing monitor.

terminal operator A person employed and/or authorised to use a terminal to send messages to and receive messages from a computer.

terminal repeater The end repeater in a trunk line. See *repeater*.

terminal session A session; the time during which a terminal operator is in communications with a computer.

terminal strip A device of phenolic or similar insulating material containing screws to which wires or terminals can be attached for interconnecting circuits. See *terminal; terminal board*.

terminal symbol A terminator.

terminal user A terminal operator.

terminal voltage The voltage as measured at the input terminals of a device; it is usually understood to be a line or power supply voltage rather than a signal or control voltage.

terminate (1)Also, sometimes, *suspend; abend*. To stop some operation; it is usually understood to be a stop before normal completion; ('terminate execution'; 'terminate a run'). (2)With respect to a line or cable; to connect resistors of calculated value between the conductors at the ends of the line or cable to adjust the line impedance to its designed value and, thus, to reduce or eliminate echoes. Termination is usually required on any cable that carries data.

termination (1)The act of discontinuing an operation. (2)The process of selecting and connecting resistors to 'terminate' a line or cable. (3)A terminator.

terminator (1)Also *terminal symbol*. A flowcharting symbol used to indicate the end of a program or sequence of operations. With respect to a program, it is represented by an 'exit instruction' when coded. (2)A device containing resistors that is intended to be plugged into a device (say, a magnetic disc unit) to 'terminate' its connecting cable. See *terminate*.

termiprinter A printer intended to be used as a stand-alone, receive-only terminal or in conjunction with one or more VDU's to provide a hard-copy facility. It is, typically, an impact character printer. See *printer*.

ternary (1)Pertaining to systems in which three possible states or values can be represented; for example, to a system of data transmission in which an absence of signal, a positive signal, and a negative signal all have data significance. (2)Pertaining to a numeration system with a radix of 3.

TES *Time-Encoded Speech*.

test (1) With respect to a program; to run it with selected data in order to reveal any errors and to ensure that it produces the results intended. (2) With respect to equipment and circuits; to provide controlled inputs and to observe the results/reaction in order to confirm operability or to locate a fault.

test bed Special routines and data written to facilitate testing a particular type of program.

test board Also, sometimes, *patch panel*. A switchboard device for use in conjunction with test equipment to select telephone circuits that are to be tested.

test data A set of special input data that is designed to test a particular program or group of programs. Typically, it causes a program to follow each of its possible execution paths in order to reveal any errors that may be present and, thus, to permit their correction before live running. The term is also applied to the data used with a benchmark program. See *benchmark*.

test data generator (TDG) A program that can be used to produce a variety of different types of test data for use in program testing.

test equipment Devices used to test the operation of other equipment and to locate faults. Examples include a voltmeter, a signal generator, and an oscilloscope.

test lead One of (usually two) flexible insulated wires that can be used to connect test equipment to a circuit during testing. See *test probe*.

test panel See *engineering test panel*.

test point (TP) A post, terminal, or metalised pad (often on a printed circuit board) where an electrical input to test equipment can be obtained for fault isolation.

test probe A hand-held termination of a test lead with an exposed conductor 'tip' that can be used to obtain an electrical input to test equipment.

test program A program that is run when a particular type of hardware fault is detected in order to establish the circumstances that cause it and, thus, to aid in diagnosis. See *program-sensitive fault; diagnostic test program*.

test tone In the testing of telephone circuits; a standard tone (1 mW. at 1000 Hz.) that can be sent on a circuit to locate trouble or serve as a reference for adjustment.

testing envelope One or more programs that can simulate the operational environment in which a program or module will be used. Its purpose is to aid the development and testing of programs for applications in which the actual environment (transaction processing; process control) cannot be used during the development stage.

TEX *TEleX*.

text (1) Data in character (graphic) form as printed or displayed. (2) Data that is to be displayed or printed as held in character (bit pattern) form in storage. (3) In data communications; the part of a message that has significance outside the data link; it is commonly the part between an STX and an ETX character. See *heading*.

text editor (1) A program used in the management and structuring of data in character format. Depending upon the system and purpose, it may perform error detection, formatting, unpacking, deletion of unwanted items, and zero suppression. (2) In a word processing system; a program that performs such functions as locating particular words or groups, making deletions, and entering additions. See *compose-edit processor*.

text origination In word processing; the operation of entering copy into the system (by use of a terminal keyboard).

text preparation In word processing; the operations of revising, correcting, and formatting text material.

text processing Text editing. See *text editor*.

thermal Involving heat or accomplished by heating.

thermal coupling The facilities or characteristics of heat transfer; for example, from a power transistor to its heat sink or from the heat sink to the surrounding air.

thermal matrix printer Also, often, *thermal printer; electrothermal printer*. A printer with a print head containing electrically heated styli that are selectively pressed against special heat-sensitive paper to form dot matrix characters as the head moves along a line to be printed. The paper darkens

```
GHIJKLMNOPQRSTUVWXYZ[\]^_`abcdefghijkl
FGHIJKLMNOPQRSTUVWXYZ[\]^_`abcdefghijk
```

where it is heated. Such printers are relatively inexpensive and are quiet in operation; typical speeds are from about 15 to about 80 characters per second. See *dot matrix; matrix printer*.

thermionic Operating, at least partially, by thermal effect. For example, a vacuum tube is a 'thermionic device' because its operation depends upon electron emissions from a heated filament in the cathode.

thermographic paper Paper that is chemically treated to darken where heat is applied; the paper of a thermal printer.

thick oxide A common MOS technology in which a metal gate is separated from the source-drain channel by a fairly thick (one-tenth of a micron) layer of silicon dioxide. See *MOS*.

thimble A type font similar to a daisy wheel but in the form of a 'thimble' (small cup). See *daisy wheel*.

thin film memory A memory system in which bits are held as the direction of magnetisation of areas with a 'thin film' of magnetisable material. In the planar system illustrated, the storage cells are spots of ferric oxide A deposited onto a glass substrate B. To write a 1-bit to a cell such as C, currents as indicated by the arrows are sent through conductors X_2 and Y_2 and the resultant magnetic field magnetises the spot of ferric oxide as shown by the solid arrow. To read, a stronger current is sent in the opposite direction through Y_2 only and this rotates the magnetisation as shown by the dotted arrow. This rotation induces a small voltage in X_2 which is now the

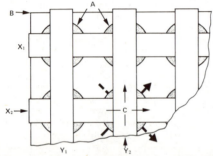

read wire. As with core memory, the read operation is destructive and the contents of locations must be regenerated after reading. Packing densities of planar systems are about 2000 bits per square inch and access times are about 5 μs. (The term 'thin film memory' also includes 'plated wire'.) The technology was at one time pursued as a possible low-cost substitute for core memory, but many problems were encountered in both manufacture and operation. See *plated wire memory; core memory*. **f1**

thin-film resistor The common resistor of integrated circuits; it consists of a thin deposited film of resistive material (silicon-chromium) that is trimmed (often by laser) to the length and width required to produce a particular resistance. The tech-

nology is also used to make discrete, single-value resistors and resistor networks as dedicated integrated circuits. The latter may incorporate multiple resistors of the same value or they may provide tapped paths of various lengths and widths (as shown) to permit selecting different values at the pins.

third-generation computer A computer of 1970+ technology; a computer that uses semiconductors in integrated circuits for both data storage and data manipulation. See *generation*.

third normal form (3NF) In some data bases; a final form for data. See *normalisation*.

thrashing In a virtual storage system; the condition in which throughput is significantly reduced because a high percentage of system resources are devoted to paging rather than to program execution. It can result from faulty scheduling which creates too many active processes or a discard method that deletes pages/segments from working sets thus causing virtual storage interrupts whenever a process attempts to execute.

thread In some transaction processing systems; a path an incoming transaction takes through the various system routines ('beads') that are used in queueing, validation, interpretation, processing, editing, and outputting a reply. See *multithreading; single threading; bead*.

three-address instruction An instruction containing three address fields, two of which are usually understood to be for operands and the third for storing the result.

three-bit byte A triplet.

three-input adder A full adder.

three-plus-one address instruction A three-address instruction that, in addition, contains the address of the next instruction.

threshold (1) A level at which something becomes evident or detectable; for example, signals in the presence of noise. (2) A multiple-input logic operation with an output that is 'true' if more than N inputs are 'true' and false if less than N inputs are true or if they are equally divided, where N is a preset value termed the **threshold condition**. See *majority operation*. (3) A threshold condition or a threshold value.

threshold condition A value that determines the result of a threshold logic operation. See *threshold; threshold value*.

threshold function A switching function with an output that is 'true' if the total of its input values exceeds a preset **threshold value**. The inputs are assumed to be non-Boolean (they may have any values) and they may be individually weighted. For example, if the inputs have values of 2, 4, and 27 which are, respectively, weighted by multipliers 3, 6, and 2, then a total is obtained as: (2 × 3) + (4 × 8) + (2 × 27) = 92. If the threshold value is, say, 30, 46, or 91, the output is 'true' and if it is 92 or higher, it is 'false'. See *threshold*.

threshold switching See *ovonic memory*.

threshold value A value that determines the result of a threshold function. See *threshold function; threshold condition*.

throughput (1) The amount of work performed per unit time; for example, instructions executed per second or transactions handled per hour. **(2)** With respect to a functional unit in a data communications system; the amount of data that it passes per unit time. See *data rate*.

throw (1) Also *slew*. To move continuous stationary through a printer without printing; the term usually denotes a movement of more than one line space. See *feed*. **(2)** The amount by which the paper is moved; ('a ten-line throw').

thyristor A semiconductor device that is placed in a conducting state by applying a positive pulse to the gate and remains in the conducting state until the anode-cathode current is removed. (In A.C. circuits, the 'removal' usually occurs at the position in each cycle where the voltage goes negative.) The device

illustrated is a high-power (100 Amp.) type as used in power supplies; the small terminal connects to the gate, the larger one adjacent to it is the anode terminal, and the screw base connects to the cathode.

TI *Texas Instruments*. (Houston, Texas)

tie-breaking A term applied to a method or operation of resolving contention (the condition in which a single resource is claimed simultaneously by two or more entities).

tie line A leased line.

tie trunk A telephone circuit connecting two branch exchanges.

time base A repeating sequence of accurately spaced pulses of specified interval available in a computer or other functional unit to control the occurrence or synchronisation of events. A time base is, typically, produced by a **time base generator** that counts clock pulses in shift registers and outputs a pulse whenever a particular register is full. See *clock*.

time delay circuit A circuit with an output that lags the input(s). It is usually a monostable trigger circuit in which the change of state depends on the time taken to charge or discharge a capacitor. In the circuit shown, a high input on 'A' causes capacitor C1 to receive a charge through resistor R1 to a voltage at which transistor T1 turns ON. This drops the collector voltage which is applied through C2 to the base of T2 causing it to turn OFF and, thus, placing high on output 'O'. Capacitor C2 then charges through R2 and when a certain level is reached, T2 turns ON again, dropping 'O'. The amount of delay depends upon the values of R1 and C1 and the length of the high output pulse depends upon the values of R2 and C2.

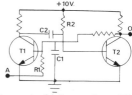

time division multiple access (TDMA) A method of operating a (large) data network in which each (active) user is assigned a (one-character) time slice for transmission on a shared channel. User equipment monitors a continuous data stream on the other channel to intercept messages for its station and to maintain synchronisation for transmissions.

time division multiplexing (TDM) A method of multiplexing in which the use of a single channel for the transfer or transmission of data is allocated in turn and in rotation for a short period of time (a **time slice**) to each of several sending or

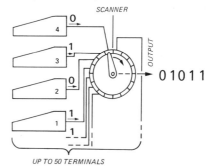

receiving units. From the view of a user (say, a terminal operator) or of a user program, it, typically, causes the channel to appear to be allocated exclusively for their transfers. It is accomplished by an electronic scanner (represented in the illustration as a mechanical device) that has a scan rate such that a specific, synchronised, unit of data is sent or received in each time slice. A **bit-interleaved** system is one in which the unit of data is the 'bit'; in a **character interleaved** system the unit of data is the number of bits required to represent a character in the code being used. Multiplexed peripheral transfer systems may be **byte interleaved, word interleaved,** or **block interleaved.** In its simplest form, time division multiplexing is accomplished by allocating time slices to all connected receiving/sending units whether or not they are actually involved in a data transfer. In **statistical multiplexing** time slices are only allocated to devices that are actually sending or receiving. See *multiplexing; frequency division multiplexing; pulse amplitude modulation; pulse code modulation; statistical multiplexing.*

time fill In some systems (SDLC; HDLC); the transmission of a continuous sequence of flags when there are no frames to be transmitted. See *mark idle; synchronous idle.*

time frame In data transfer or transmission; a unit of time in which an item of data (often, a character) can be sent and which can be recognised by receiving hardware. The term may be applied to time units in either synchronous or asynchronous transfers. See *start-stop; binary synchronous communications.*

time interleaving The allocation of a resource in turn for a fixed, short time to each of two or more entities (terminals; executing programs) that require it. See *interleave; multiprogramming; time division multiplexing.*

time-of-day clock (TOD) A time base and read-only memory program to maintain the current year, date, hour, minute, and second for purposes of validation, logging events, and accounting for the use of computer resources.

time-out (1) To cause a timer to run out to signal the end of a period (the maximum time) in which an event can occur; ('time-out keyboard inputs'). **(2)** An interrupt condition that occurs at the expiration of an allocated time for an event occurrence, without the event having occurred. For example, a 'polling time-out' occurs when a remote station fails to respond to its polling message within a specified time (causing the next station on the polling list to be polled). **(3)** The amount of time allocated; ('a three-second time-out').

time register A register that constitutes a timer or is an element of a timer.

time scale With respect to simulation (traffic flow; industrial process); the time taken to simulate a sequence of events by computer program in relation to the time they would actually take in the simulated operation.

time scale factor Time scale expressed as a ratio.

time sharing (1) A multiprogramming (usually event-driven) computer system that provides for multiple users to control execution of their programs and to input data and receive results at remote terminals. **(2)** Also *time slicing; time interleaving.* A term applied to a system in which resources are allocated in 'time slices' in rotation or in accordance with some algorithm, as, for example, in multiprogramming or time division multiplexing.

time-sharing bureau A bureau that provides a contract multi-access computing service, typically leasing terminals to users and charging for the number of hours per month that a user's terminal is connected plus an additional charge for use of storage media and other resources.

time-sharing language A programming language (BASIC; JOSS) that is intended for use in multi-access systems.

time slice (1) A short period in which a resource is allocated to a claimant, as in time division multiplexing or multiprogramming. See *time sharing.* **(2)** In some systems, a period of time allocated by an operating system to process a particular program.

time slicing Time interleaving.

timer A device or circuit that provides time signals at regular, specified intervals for purposes of controlling a sequence of events or synchronising events in separate operations. In a computer or related device, it consists of one or more registers that count clock pulses and output a signal (pulse) when a particular register is full. See *clock; time base.*

timing pulse An output of a timer; a circuit transition used for timing purposes. See *timer.*

timing signal A timing pulse.

TOD *Time-Of-Day (clock).*

toggle A flip-flop; a bistable circuit.

toggle switch A switch with a handle that can be moved to an 'up', 'down', and (possibly) 'centre' position to set the conduction path between its terminals.

token The smallest meaningful representation of a concept in a language. It is a character group or construction that loses its meaning (or assumes some other meaning) if divided; for example, 'John D. Smith', 'greater than' and 'work in progress'.

toll In a telephone system; a charge for making a call outside of the caller's local service area.

toll centre The telephone exchange facilities that handle calls to and from locations outside of a particular local service area.

toll-free number (1) A number within the caller's local service area. **(2)** An Enterprise number.

tone dialing Pushbutton dialing.

top-of-form The first line that is printed on a form or on a page of continuous stationary; with respect to continuous stationary, it is often four line spaces below the perforation line.

top-of-stack The upper bound of a stack; the highest numbered location. See *stack*.

top-of-stack pointer (TOS) The address of the highest numbered location in a stack. See *stack*.

torn tape switching A message switching system in which exchanges receive incoming messages on perforators (paper tape punches) from which operators 'tear' the tape and manually transfer it to reader-transmitters for onward routing. It has been largely (or completely) superseded by faster and less labour intensive systems. See *store and forward; message switching; packet switching*.

torodial coil A coil wound on a magnetic flux path in the form of a 'torus'; it is a common form of inductor for use in electronic circuits.

torus A ring; a round solid with a hole in the centre. It is the form of a ferrite core and of a common inductor.

TOS (1) *Top Of Stack pointer*. **(2)** *Tape Operating System*.

Touchtone A trademark of the Bell Telephone Co. applied to their multifrequency signalling equipment and services. See *multifrequency signalling; pushbutton dialing*.

tournament sort A repeated selection sort in which each subset consists of two items. See *selection sort*.

TP (1) *Transaction Processing*. **(2)** *Test Point*.

TPI (tpi.) *Tracks Per Inch*.

TPS *Transaction Processing System*.

trace (1) Also, sometimes, *log*. A record of a series of events made as they occur. **(2)** A listing of the instructions of a sequence in the order in which they were executed in a particular run. **(3)** The lines or pattern produced by an oscilloscope.

trace facility A capability to output individual instructions and their results as the instructions are executed.

trace program A program used to monitor the execution of another program by logging each instruction as it is executed, together with the results produced.

trace table A set of (main storage) locations to which trace information is written by a trace program.

tracing routine A trace program.

track (1) A thin (.003 in.) path on a magnetisable surface medium (magnetic disc, tape, card, or drum) where data has been written or where data can be written. The surface is homogeneous and the location of 'tracks' depends upon the locations at which read/write heads are installed or at which they can be positioned in relation to the recording surface. (Unless otherwise indicated, the term denotes such a path on a magnetic disc.) See *head; magnetisable surface recording; magnetic disc unit*. **(2)** Also *level*. On paper tape; one of the lines parallel to the edges along which data holes are punched or along which they can be punched.

track address A value by which a particular track (on magnetic disc) can be accessed. It, typically, consists of the disc number, the number of the read/write head, and the track or cylinder number.

track ball A control ball.

track density On a magnetic disc; the number of tracks per inch (measured along a radius) of the recording surface. Densities in flexible disc systems are, typically, 48 tracks per inch (TPI), and in rigid disc systems, from 100 to 400 TPI with 200 TPI the 'standard' for exchangeable disc systems. Fixed-head disc systems, typically, have from 25 to 100 TPI. See *magnetic disc unit*.

track flag In many magnetic disc systems; the contents of a one-byte location in the home address space (header) of a track that indicates whether it is usable or defective and, if usable, whether a normal-use track or an alternate. See *initialise (Magnetic disc)*.

track-following servo A method of head positioning in a magnetic disc unit in which the position of the carriage (and, hence, of all read/write heads) is controlled by means of a special (non-data recording) **servo head** that follows prerecorded **servo tracks** on a **servo surface** which occupies a disc surface or part of a surface. The heads are moved to read or write tracks on a particular cylinder by means of a servo unit and track-counting circuitry, as in other magnetic disc units.

When the other heads are positioned at a particular cylinder, the servo head is midway between two servo tracks; the head is designed to read signals from both tracks simultaneously. Odd numbered servo tracks are recorded with one repeating bit pattern and even numbered tracks are recorded with another pattern; they are recorded so that they 'interleave' during reading. Circuitry then compares the reading amplitude of the two patterns. If the pattern recorded on the odd-numbered track increases in amplitude while the one from the even-numbered track decreases, this indicates that the servo head (and all other heads) have moved toward the odd-numbered track and this activates a feedback circuit that causes the servo mechanism to move the carriage so that the servo head is once again centred between the tracks and reading both with the same amplitude. The reverse movement is applied if the signals from the even-numbered track are of greater amplitude than those from the odd-numbered track. Many magnetic disc units employing track-following servo have two read/write heads per data surface and, in this case, only half of a disc surface is required for servo tracks and the servo head; the remaining half of the surface is often used for data that is read and written by fixed heads. The servo surface is bounded on the inside and outside by **guard bands**; the tracks of the inner band are recorded with the pattern for odd-numbered tracks and, when read, cause the heads to move away from the spindle. Similarly, the outer guard band is recorded with the pattern for even-numbered tracks that have the effect of moving the heads back toward the spindle. The servo tracks are also, typically, recorded with special bit patterns required for sectoring and for synchronisation. Because of minor variations in head positioning between drives, tracks may not align precisely when discs are read on a drive other than the one on which they were recorded; an adjustment is provided in the amplitude comparison circuitry to bias the head position towards one servo track or the other when required to improve reading. See *servo; magnetic disc unit; head; seek.*

track hold A facility that prevents two programs from attempting to access the same track simultaneously.

track index A second-level index of an indexed sequential file. See *indexed sequential file.*

track number The number by which a magnetic disc track is identified for access purposes. Track 000 is at the outer edge of the recording surface and the highest numbered track is the one closest to the spindle. In the usual system in which there are multiple disc surfaces and multiple heads, the 'track number' is also the 'cylinder number'. See *cylinder; track address.*

track overflow The facility or condition in which data (a variable length record) that overflows from one track is written to the first available position in another track.

track pitch The centre-to-centre distance between adjacent tracks (on magnetic disc).

track trimming In magnetic disc recording; the operation of removing excess magnetisation pattern at the sides of tracks as they are recorded in order to permit design for closer track spacing and prevent interference with the magnetisation patterns of adjacent tracks. The operation is performed by **track-trimming heads** (also **erase heads**) that are incorporated in the structure of the read/write head with gaps that 'follow behind' the main gap where reading and writing are performed. In **straddle erase** the heads remove the excess pattern by writing a continuous pattern at right angles to the track; in **tunnel erase** the heads, effectively, write a narrow 'zero pattern' alongside the track. A representative figure for track width (and, hence, of the pattern left unaffected) is .003 in. Track trimming with tunnel erase is used in flexible disc systems. Straddle erase is used in most modern rigid disc systems. See *head; erase; magnetisable surface recording.*

track-trimming head Also *erase head.* A write-only head used to remove excess magnetisation pattern from the sides of tracks in magnetic disc recording. See *track trimming.*

track width In magnetic disc recording; the width of the path in which magnetisable surface particles have data-significant orientations as produced by writing data to a track. The width is, typically, .013 in. for flexible discs, .003-.005 in. for rigid discs, and as low as .0018 in. in Winchester systems.

tracking In display computer graphics; the process of following a display writer (say, a light pen) as it is moved on the display surface.

tracking symbol An aiming symbol.

tracks per inch (TPI) The usual unit for expressing track density. See *track density.*

tractor In many line printers; a short, continuous belt or chain with 'teeth' that engage the sprocket holes of continuous stationery to move the paper through the machine. See *throw; feed; barrel printer.*

traffic In data communications; messages considered with respect to routing or utilisation of communications facilities; ('route traffic for Manchester via...'; '...during hours of peak traffic').

trailer card Also *detail card*. A punched card that follows other cards in a pack and contains information relating to them.

trailer label A unit of housekeeping and control data as written at the end of a (magnetic tape) file or volume.

trailer record The final record in a file. See *trailer card; batch trailer.*

trailing blanks Also *trailing spaces*. Spaces to the right of the last character displayed in a line on a VDU screen. In some systems, when a short line is entered the trailing blanks are encoded as space characters in the video buffer while other systems can begin a new line in the buffer wherever the previous one ended, thus providing **trailing blank truncation.**

trailing edge The last edge of a punched card to enter a punch or reader.

trailing end The end of a segment of paper tape that is last to enter a reader.

trailing spaces See *trailing blanks*.

trailing zeros In a numeric string; zeros to the right of the least significant non-zero digit. See *leading zeros*.

train (1) A sequence; a group of items or events that occur one following the other; ('a pulse train'; 'a train printer'). **(2)** A chain; a particular connection of items arranged to perform some operation; for example, the lines and equipment that are 'joined' to complete a telephone call.

train printer An impact line printer in which the characters of a type font are embossed on slugs that move horizontally in an endless 'train' which passes along the line being printed. The slugs move along a track with each slug pushing the one ahead; the slugs have teeth that engage in the teeth of a drive sprocket at one end of the train and an idler sprocket at the other. The track must always be full; in most printers the slugs and track are replaceable as a unit and the assembly is termed a **cartridge** (also **chain module**). Typically, each of the slugs contains four characters and there are either 72 or 96 slugs in the cartridge. Considering the 72-slug cartridge, common arrangements are six repeating 48-character fonts, three 96-character fonts, or four 64-character fonts. (When using 64-character fonts, eight blank slugs are included in the train.) Printing speed depends upon both the sprocket speed and the number of times the font is repeated in the cartridge; typical speeds are 640 or 880 lpm. with a 96-character font, 1020 or 1200 lpm. with a 64-character font, and 1240 or 1960 lpm. with a 48-character font. Printing is accomplished in much the same way as with barrel printers; hammers synchronised by electronic circuitry strike the ribbon

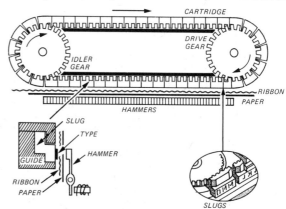

and paper against characters as they pass along the line. Typically, the bit-pattern for each character is cleared from the buffer as the character is printed and a new line begins whenever the buffer is empty. A train printer experiences somewhat higher wear of moving parts than a barrel printer but has an advantage of being able to accomodate a larger font and allowing for the font to be changed or customised to meet particular requirements. The illustration shows the basic mechanism and it is followed by a sample of printout from a train printer. See *printer; impact printer; chain printer; band printer.*

training sequence Also *learning sequence*. A special sequence sent by one modem to another prior to the commencement of a data transfer. The sequence commonly consists of phase reversals and/or 1-bits and is intended to permit the receiving modem to obtain synchronisation/equalization in the shortest possible time. It is the usual first element of a poll response by a remote site modem in a multipoint, binary synchronous system. Depending upon the protocol and type of modems, sequences can be from about 20 milliseconds in length to about 250 milliseconds. See *synchronisation; equalization; answerback; new sync*.

TRAN *TRANsmit*.

transaction (1)In an on-line system; an interchange between a terminal operator and a computer, including the processing performed by the computer. The interchange may involve a single message pair or multiple messages in one or both directions. See *on-line; transaction processing; multiphase transaction*. (2)A term sometimes used synonymously with 'enquiry' ('an incoming transaction'). (3)A term sometimes used in place of 'job' or 'job step' in relation to batch processing or remote job entry. (4)In a business sense, a single instance of obtaining and paying for goods or services. There is some 'overlap' between the term by this definition and by that of definition 1 in that many operator-computer interchanges (order entry; airline seat reservation) initiate or confirm 'transactions'. (5)In some systems; a record that causes the amendment, creation, or deletion of a record in a master file.

transaction-driven A term applied to a mixed-mode computer system in which the arrival of a transaction (message from a terminal) causes the interruption of other (batch) processing and the reallocation of resources as necessary to deal with the transaction. See *transaction processing*.

transaction file (1)Also *transaction journal* and, in some systems, *transaction data set*. A designated area of (magnetic disc) backing storage to which all terminal interchanges are copied. It is, typically, a source for updating files and may be used for charging and/or statistical analysis. (2)Also *detail file; amendments file*. A file to which data is written that will be used to update other files (whether the data arises via terminal interchanges or otherwise). (3)An area of (magnetic disc) storage used to pass data between programs or jobs.

transaction journal A transaction file.

transaction processing (TP) Processing in which the programs to be executed are selected from a (remote) terminal which also supplies some or all of the input parameters, and in which results are returned to the terminal upon completion of processing. Such processing is 'on-line' and it is also, usually, 'real-time'. See *on-line; real-time; enquiry; transaction; conversational*.

transaction processing monitor (TP monitor) A program or group of programs that perform the interrupt and scheduling functions required in a transaction-driven system. It may also perform communications interface and/or journalising functions.

transaction processor A computer that is dedicated to handling 'transaction processing' or, possibly, a subset of computer resources that are allocated to this processing mode.

transaction record A transaction (def. 5).

transceiver (1)An interfacing circuit or device that can both transmit and receive; for example, a telephone, a two-way radio, or a computer circuit that handles transfers to and from main storage. (2)A term sometimes applied to a terminal with facilities for both sending and receiving messages. See *ASR; KSR*.

transcendental number See *number*.

transcribe Also, usually, *copy*. To read data in one location and write it to another, possibly with a concurrent change of medium or method of representation. The term can be applied to a variety of manual and programmed operations but, unless otherwise indicated, it usually denotes the operation of reading source documents and punching data in cards or paper tape.

transcription A copy; that which has been transcribed.

transducer A device or element that is capable of detecting some physical condition and representing it by an electric current and/or receiving an electric current and representing its characteristics as changes in a physical condition. In relation to computers, the term is applied to a read/write head, to a detector of sector marks in a magnetic disc system, and to electronic/sonic pulse converters of delay line memory.

transfer (1)Also, often, *move*. To read data in one location and to write it to another location on a different medium or device. In some contexts, the term 'move' is preferred when considering the data as a logical entity and 'transfer' when only its physical form is considered; ('move a file'; 'transfer a block'). The term 'transfer' usually denotes a change of location within a computer installation ('a data transfer'; 'a peripheral transfer'), while 'transmit' denotes a change in which a communications link is used. See *transmission; move; copy; read; write; transcribe*. (2)With respect to control of the central processor; to deallocate it from one sequence of instructions and allocate it to another.

transfer control To discontinue executing the instructions of one sequence and to commence executing those of another sequence.

transfer instruction A branch instruction.

transfer interpreter A device that reads the bit patterns from one punched card and prints the corresponding characters on another card. See *interpreter*.

transfer rate See *data transfer rate*.

transfer time (1)The time that elapses between the reading of a bit from a source location and its writing to a destination location. It is a measure of the speed of electronics and circuits. (2)The time that elapses between the commencement of reading a unit of data (block; page; word; byte) in one location and the completion of writing it to another location.

transfer unit A unit in which data is transferred, or can be transferred, within a computer system. Between backing storage and main storage, it is usually a 'block' or 'bucket' or, in a virtual storage system, a 'page' or 'segment'. Between main storage and a control or arithmetic unit, it is usually a 'word'. Within a communications system, the common units are blocks and characters.

transform (1)To change the form of data in such a way that the original could be reconstructed by a reversal of the operation; for example, to make a code change or to change numeric data from decimal to binary. (2)To make a new entity by combining elements of other entities.

transformer An electromagnetic device that is used to change the voltage of alternating current. It consists of a **core** of steel laminations A on which two coils are wound, a **primary coil** B connected to the input and a **secondary coil** C to which the output can be connected. The input and output voltages are in direct ratio of the number of turns (once around

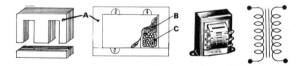

the laminations) of the primary and secondary coils; for example, if the input is 230 V. and the primary coil has 1000 turns, then 115 V. would be output by a secondary coil of 500 turns and 460 V. by one of 2000 turns. A transformer that is designed to raise voltage may be termed a **step-up transformer** and one that is designed to drop voltage, a **step-down transformer**. A transformer can produce multiple output voltages by means of **taps** which are multiple external connections to the secondary coil, with voltages proportional to the number of turns between one end of the coil and each tap. For example, a transformer with a 230 V. input, a primary coil of 1000 turns, and a secondary coil of 500 turns would have an output of 57.5 V. from a 'centre tap' at turn 250 and 11.5 V. from a tap at turn 50. Power supplies usually obtain their D.C. voltages by rectifying different outputs from a tapped secondary coil. A transformer that has only a single tapped coil is termed an **autotransformer**. An **isolation transformer** is one that is used primarily to separate two circuits; typically, such a transformer has the same number of turns in the primary and secondary coils and, thus, an output voltage which is the same as the input.

transient (1)Not always present or required; ('a transient routine'). (2)Occurring at random and unpredictable intervals; ('a circuit transient'; 'a transient error'). (3)In process of change from one mode or condition to another; ('a transient state'). (4)Also *circuit transient*. An unpredictable short-duration change in circuit condition; a pulse or increase in circuit noise. An example is 'impulse noise' in a communications circuit. See *noise*.

transient area An area of main storage available to system routines on an as-required basis.

transient error A soft error; an error that clears on retry.

transient library A library set up for a particular job and overwritten when the run is completed.

transient routine A unit of system software with a usage that is too low to justify keeping it continuously in main storage; when active, such a routine is held in the 'transient area'.

transient state The condition of changing from one condition or mode of operation to another; for example, of a modem changing from receiving to transmitting or a flip-flop changing from one stable condition to the other.

transient supervisor The elements of an operating system that manage storage and access of a transient area.

transistor A common semiconductor switch or amplifier. Though the term includes 'field effect transistors', unless otherwise indicated, it usually denotes a **bipolar transistor** in which conduction is controlled by a gate current. A bipolar transistor is a 'sandwich' of N-type and P-type silicon or germanium; silicon is by far the most common. If the outer layers are P-type and the inner layer is N-type, it is a **PNP**

transistor and if the outer layers are N-type and the inner is P-type, it is an **NPN transistor**. Because the speed of electron travel is somewhat higher in N-type silicon than it is in P-type, NPN transistors are preferred in most computer and control applications; power transistors are often PNP. An NPN transistor in a simple switching circuit is shown in Fig. 1

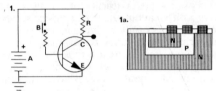

and the basic construction is shown in Fig. 1a. As connected in the circuit of Fig. 1, the **collector** goes to positive (+) (in this case, it receives positive voltage from battery A through the 'load' R), the **emitter** connects to negative, and control is by selectively applying a positive voltage to the **base**. As shown, the transistor is off (it is not conducting) and, hence, no current flows through R. If switch B is closed, positive is applied to the base through the resistor and a small current flows through the emitter to negative. This has the effect of turning the transistor on (placing it in a conducting state) which 'drops' the voltage at the collector to very nearly that of the emitter. With the collector at substantially negative voltage, a current then flows through R. A very low current through the base-emitter (say, a few milliamps) is sufficient to turn on a fairly large current (say, a few amps) through the collector-emitter. The ratio of the two currents is the **gain** of the transistor. The layers and electrons of an unconnected NPN transistor are represented in Fig. 2. As described in the *semiconductor* entry,

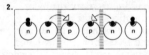

'holes' in the thin, inner P-type layer capture electrons from the adjacent N-type layers to form a 'depletion layer' along the junctions between the two types of silicon. In Fig. 3, the transistor is shown in the circuit of Fig. 1. With switch B open, no current flows in the circuit because the depletion layer prevents free electrons at N (the negative connection to the emitter) from reaching P (the positive connection to the collector). Fig. 4 shows the circuit at the instant that switch B is closed. The base is now positive and this draws the 'captured' electrons out of the P-type layer as indicated by the arrows. This frees some holes in the layer, as shown in Fig. 5, thus breaking down the depletion layer. Electrons from N then enter the N-type layer of the emitter and move through it by bumping

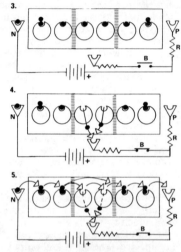

off electrons which jump across the junction into holes in the base; because the barrier is broken, some jump straight across the thin P-type layer into the N-type layer of the collector. Of the electrons that enter holes in the P-type layer, some move into the base circuit, as shown by the dotted arrow, while others jump from hole to hole to reach the collector layer. Once in the collector layer, they move through it by bumping off electrons, in the same manner as they moved through the emitter layer. As they jump out of the collector layer and reach the area of electron deficit at P, a current flows through the circuit. The amount of current that can flow depends upon the current in the base circuit; if this is very low (if the resistor in series with switch B has a high value), then only a few holes are 'opened' in the P-type layer and the depletion layer remains largely intact, thus allowing only a small current flow between the emitter and the collector. All transistor applications in digital computers are 'switching', meaning that base resistor values are selected to support full emitter-collector current flow when transistors are turned on. In radios, telephone equipment, and other analogue devices, varying signals (effectively varying base resistance) are applied to the base in order to use the transistor as an amplifier.

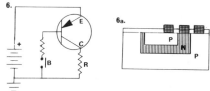

Fig. 6 shows a PNP transistor in a switching circuit similar to that of Fig. 1 and the basic construction is shown in Fig. 6a. The operation of a PNP transistor is illustrated in Fig. 7; when the switch B is closed, the base connection supplies

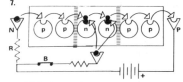

free electrons which jump into the N-type base layer as indicated by the arrows. A current can then flow as electrons from N move from hole to hole in the P-type collector layer, then by jumping through and bumping off electrons in the N-type base, arriving at the positive connection P after jumping from hole to hole through the P-type emitter layer. In modern computer storage and control circuits, transistors are usually incorporated into integrated circuits together with other circuit elements. A **discrete transistor** is a single transistor contained in

a separate 'package'; Fig. 8 shows transistors in three of the commonly available packages. See *semiconductor; field effect transistor; semiconductor memory.*

transistor-transistor logic (TTL) A common semiconductor memory and logic circuit characterised by high speed and low power dissipation. Figure 1 is of a basic NAND gate. When either input is low, transistor T2 is ON (its base is high and one or both emitters low) so collector C is low. Collector C of T2 connects to the base of T1 and when it is low, T1 is OFF and the output is high. When both inputs are high, T2 'floats' high

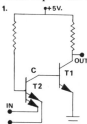

causing collector C to be high and this is applied to the base of T1 turning it ON and dropping the output to low. (Transistor T2 can have a single emitter or more than the two emitters shown.) Figure 2 is a basic TTL flip-flop such as constitutes a

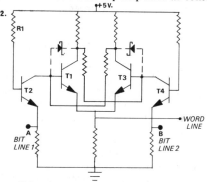

single storage cell in memory. If T1 is ON (assumed to be the condition in which the cell holds a 1-bit), its collector is low and this is applied to the gate of T3, causing T3 to be off, so its collector is high and this is applied to the base of T1, keeping it ON. This high is also placed on the collector of T2 causing it to float high which raises Bit Line 1 and this is sensed as a high at Point A in the coder-decoder. To write a 0-bit to the cell, Point A is dropped to low which drops the collector of T2, dropping the base of T1 and turning it OFF which raises its collector which is applied as a high to the base of T3 turning it on. This also raises the collector and emitter of T4 which raises Bit Line 2 causing Point B to be high which is sensed as a 0-bit. One disadvantage of TTL is that transistors T1 and T3 tend to 'saturate' when they are ON which increases the time required to change. This saturation can be prevented by installing Schottky diodes as shown with dotted connections. Such memory is termed 'Schottky TTL'. (The actual implementation in an integrated circuit is somewhat more complex than the cell shown in Figure 2.) Power dissipation ranges from about 20 mW. per gate (40 mW. per memory cell) for high-speed devices and as low as 2 mW. for low-power Schottky. Propagation delays are from 30 ns. for low-power devices to 3 ns. for the fastest Schottky devices.

transistorised Containing transistors; with switching and/or amplification functions performed by transistors (rather than by valves/tubes, relays, magnetic cores, or other elements).

transition A change from one condition or state to another; for example, a 'flux transition' or a 'line transition'.

translate (1)With respect to a program or other sequence of instructions; to change the language or code in which it is represented. Unless otherwise indicated, the term denotes a compiler or assembler operation of changing source code in a particular programming language into object code suitable for a particular computer. (2)To perform a code conversion; for example, to change data from Hollerith code representation to EBCDIC. (3)In display graphics; to move a display image to another part of the screen. (4)In a telephone system; to allocate circuits or groups of circuits to a multiplexed channel. See *group; multiplexing.*

translating program A translator.

translation specification exception An interrupt condition in which a virtual address cannot be converted to a physical address (because the address is invalid or there is an error in a page/segment table).

translation tables Page/segment tables.

translator (1)A computer program used in translating source code in one programming language to source code in another language. (2)A unit of telephone exchange equipment that allocates circuits to a multiplexed group. See *group.*

transliteration (1)Code conversion; a change of the bit patterns used to represent the characters of a set. (2)A change in the representation of characters. (3)An erroneous substitution of one bit or character for another.

transmission (1)The operation of sending data over a communications link between geographically separated locations. See *transfer.* (2)A single instance of sending a block or message on a communications link.

transmission block character The ETB character.

transmission code A line code.

transmission control The implementation of a link protocol.

transmission control character See *control character.*

transmission control unit (TCU) An unintelligent communications interface device that performs operations under the control of an operating system.

transmission extension A send-only extension in an internal (company) telephone facility; a non-ringable extension.

transmission header See *header.*

transmission interface See *communications interface.*

transmission interrupt Also *reverse break.* When a terminal is transmitting a message; to interrupt the transmission in order to send a high-priority message to the terminal.

transmission level See *relative transmission level.*

transmission limit In a multipoint communications system; the maximum permitted duration of transmission for a particular data station in one session.

transmission line See *line (Communications).*

transmission mode The method of transmission used on a link; for example, 'start-stop' or 'binary synchronous'.

transmission speed (1)The number of characters, blocks, or other units of data transmitted on a communications link per unit time. (2)Data rate; the number of bits transmitted per second. (3)Propagation speed.

transmit To send data from one location for reception at one or more other locations. See *transmission; transfer.*

transmit clock The clock from which the transmitter of a modem obtains timing. In most cases, the transmit clock is a free-running (not externally synchronised) clock in the transmitter. If a remote site modem slaves to the transmit clock of the central site modem, it uses the clock derived from the receive data stream (often 'receive baud clock') as the transmit clock. If the transmitter uses an **external transmit clock**, it slaves to transmit signal element timing received via the DTE interface (typically, from a modem in an onward link).

transmitter A device that can generate and propagate signals representing data or speech. See *receiver*.

transmitter-distributer (TD) In a teletypewriter system; a device (or section of a device) that can read data from punched paper tape and transmit it as signals on a line. See *ASR*.

transmitter-receiver A transceiver.

transmitter start code (TSC) In some teletypewriter systems; a character sequence that is sent from a master station to a tributary station to cause a transmitter-distributer to send any messages it may be holding on paper tape or to indicate to an operator that a message may be sent from the keyboard.

transparent (1) A term applied to any processing steps that are performed by an operating system, compiler, or other system software without a need for them to be programmed or considered by a programmer. (2) A term applied to functional units and facilities of a communications system that are not evident to a user. (3) A term used with respect to data communications systems to indicate that link control is effectively insulated from the text portion of messages and, hence, that bit patterns of control characters can occur (accidentally or with other significance) in the information part without any risk of their being interpreted as control characters by receiving hardware. Such a system may be said to be **code transparent** and, when operating in this way, to be in **transparent mode**. Examples of 'transparent' systems include those using SNA, SDLC, and HDLC protocols. Transparency is, typically, provided by using recognised delimiters to frame the information part of messages or by preceding each control character with a special (DLE) character.

transparent text mode A mode of binary synchronous communications in which receiving hardware only interprets bit patterns as control characters when they are immediately preceded by the DLE character.

transport (1) A tape transport; a magnetic tape unit or the part of such a unit that moves the tape. (2) The part of a punched card reader or punch that carries and moves the cards.

transportable A term sometimes used synonymously with 'portable'; ('transportable software').

transposition (1) The operation of exchanging the positions of two adjacent items; for example, to change 'SE' to 'ES'. (2) The operation of reconnecting telephone circuits that are carried by open wires so that particular wires are elements of different circuits. It may be done in an attempt to reduce noise or induced signals.

transverse redundancy check (TRC) A horizontal parity check. See *parity*.

trap An unprogrammed conditional jump; a jump that occurs when a monitor routine detects a particular processing condition (seek failure; bound violation; parity error). The jump is, typically, to some interrupt routine with provision made to hold the address from which the jump was made so that control can be returned to that point. See *interrupt*.

trap condition An interrupt event.

trap door A term sometimes applied to a weak point in the security of a computer system; for example, to an engineering test panel that could be used to access data to which access restrictions apply.

TRC *Transverse Redundancy Check*.

tree (1) A term applied to a hierarchial structure of entities; for example, to a company organisation chart or a geneology. (2) A hierarchial net; a multilevel data structure. It consists of a number of entities in 'from top down' relationships and a specification of the orders in which they can be accessed. The entity of highest position (the entity that must be accessed first in order to access any other entity in the structure) is the **root** (also **origin**). Though in somewhat inconsistent analogy with 'tree', it is commonly at the top in a diagram. The other entities

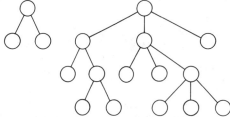

of the structure are **owners** and **members**; they are connected for access purposes by **pointers** which may also be termed **links, connectors,** or **relationships.** An owner is an entity on one level that contains at least one pointer to an entity on a lower level; a member is an entity that is pointed to. Owners on one level are, typically, members with respect to a higher level. The defining characteristic of a 'tree' is that each member can have only one owner but an owner can have any number of members. A member that is not also an owner is termed a **leaf**. An owner has sometimes been termed a **father** or **parent** and a member a

son or **child**; similarly, entities on the same level have been termed **brothers** or **twins**. A sequence of entities and pointers that can be followed during execution is an **access path**. Most computer data structures are 'trees' and data base structures that are not inherently hierarchial usually contain trees. In the usual example, a file as identified for access is a 'root' and its records are 'members'. On the next level, the records are 'owners' with respect to their fields which are, again, 'members'. See *net; access path;*. (3)Also *tree diagram*. A graphic representation of a tree structure or of a sequence in which operations can be performed. It may be used to define or describe a 'tree' (def. 1 or 2) or to identify operations and their possible sequences of performance. In the latter case, a tree can, for example, be used to represent the sequence in which segments of an overlay program will be mapped onto main storage or the sequence in which tests are to be performed in trouble shooting an item of equipment.

tree diagram A graphic representation of a hierarchial structure or sequence. See *tree*.

tree name A qualified name; a name that defines an access path.

tree search A search performed to locate an item of data in a hierarchial structure.

tree structure An arrangement of entities in the form of a tree. See *tree*.

triad A group containing three entities.

tribit ('try-bit') Three bits treated as a unit; for example, three bits transmitted in one Baud in a data communications system using phase shift modulation. See *dibit; quadbit*.

tributary station Also *slave station; secondary station* and, often, *data station*. In a data network; a station other than the master station. See *data network; secondary station*.

trigger (1)A trigger circuit. (2)By one device or circuit; to initiate an action or operation by another device or circuit, particularly to initiate it by means of a single pulse. (3)With respect to a sequence of instructions (say, an interrupt routine); to cause its immediate execution. See *trap; interrupt*.

trigger circuit A circuit with more than one stable state in which a transition from one stable state to another is initiated by a single pulse. Unless otherwise indicated, the term denotes a bistable circuit (flip-flop).

trimmer A small potentiometer (often for printed circuit board mounting) that is used for circuit balancing or fine adjustment.

trimode Having three modes or uses; ('a terminal with six trimode control keys').

triple-length register Three registers that, for some purpose, can be used as a single register.

triple precision In floating point arithmetic; the use of three computer words to represent numeric values.

triple register A triple-length register.

triplet Three entities; particularly three contiguous bits or bit positions.

tristate Capable of assuming three different physical states. The term is commonly applied to an interface device in a microprocessor system that makes a connection to a multipurpose bus. Such a device can send and receive 1-bits and 0-bits and, when inactive, assume a high-impedance state that disconnects it from the bus (while transfers are taking place between other devices).

tristate buffer A buffer that holds 0-bits and 1-bits (as any other buffer) and which is in a high-resistance 'off' state when no data is being transferred to or from it. Such buffers are commonly used in microprocessor systems where multiplexed transfers to and from different locations are made on the same 'party line' bus.

trouble shooting A term applied to operations performed to locate and correct faults in electronic equipment. Typically, it is performed by making a sequence of observations and tests ('Cursor displayed?'; 'Voltage on Pin 23?') as recommended by the equipment manufacturer, to systematically eliminate possible faults and thus to identify the particular item that must be replaced or adjusted. See *maintenance; fault*.

true (1)One of the two possible logic conditions; in computer operations it is, typically, represented by a 1-bit. See *logic operation; false*. (2)Of a two-condition circuit; carrying whatever voltage the system designer has designated as 'true'; in many systems, it is +5 V. Typically, 'true' enables and 'false' is neutral or inhibits.

true complement The radix complement.

truncate (1)To remove leading or trailing digits from a number without regard to the effect upon the remaining digits. See *round*. (2)With respect to a string of any type; to shorten it by removing elements from one end. The term may be applied to a programmed operation or to an accidental removal caused by attempting to write a data item to a location that is too short to hold it. (3)With respect to a run or execution of a particular program; to halt it before normal completion (say, when only intermediate results are required). See *abort; suspend*.

truncation error An error in numeric data introduced by truncation. See *rounding error*.

trunk (1) In a telephone system; a multiple-circuit connection between two exchanges; it is often a coaxial cable. **(2)** Also, sometimes, *highway; bus*. A major data transfer path within a computer installation.

trunk circuit A trunk.

trunk exchange The elements of a telephone exchange that perform the interconnection of trunks.

trunk group Trunks of the same physical characteristics that interconnect two exchanges and make use of the same multiplexing equipment.

trunk hunting In a telephone system; the process of routing a (long-distance) call in which the most direct trunk route between exchanges is tried first and, if it is busy, the successive attempts to locate an available route through other points.

trunk line A circuit carried by a trunk in a telephone system.

trusted A term applied to a program to indicate that it has been thoroughly tested and debugged and can be relied upon not to corrupt other code or data.

truth Also *truth value*. Either of the two possible input or output states of a logic operation; the condition of being either 'true' or 'false' or, in computer representation, a 1-bit or a 0-bit.

truth table Also *operation table*. A table that gives the output of a logic operation for each possible combination of inputs. The following are truth tables for AND, OR, and NAND logic operations. The AND table, for example, states that the output

A	B	X
0	0	0
0	1	0
1	0	0
1	1	1

A	B	X
0	0	0
0	1	1
1	0	1
1	1	1

A	B	X
0	0	1
0	1	1
1	0	1
1	1	0

is 'true' (a 1-bit) if and only if both inputs are 'true'. See *logic operation; state transition table*.

TSC *Transmitter Start Code*.

TSS *TimeSharing System*.

TSW *TeleSoftWare*.

TTL *Transistor-Transistor Logic*.

TTL compatible A term applied to an MOS device that can interface directly with bipolar TTL devices. A problem can arise because a standard 'thick oxide' MOS device has a threshold voltage in excess of 4.0 V. which is too high to assure reliable operation on the nominally 5 V. outputs of TTL (and other bipolar) devices. The term usually denotes a nitride 'enhancement' or silicon gate device with a 2.2–3 V. threshold.

TTY *TeleTYpe*.

tube See *electron tube; cathode ray tube*.

tungsten An identifier of a display (as on a petrol pump) that uses seven-segment incandescent (tungsten-filament) lights.

tuning The process of optimising the performance of an operating system with respect to a particular workload and hardware configuration; the process of adjusting system variables to obtain maximum performance from a computer.

tunnel erase See *head; track trimming*.

tuple In a data base; an element of a relation consisting of an identifier of an entity and its attributes. A relation may be described by the number of its tuples, and the general case is an 'n-tuple relation'. See *relation*.

turing machine A mathematical model of a computer or other intelligent device in which computer-like functions are represented by changes of internal state that control the reading, writing, and movement of tape.

turnaround (1) The process of changing direction. **(2)** By a modem; to change from receiving mode to transmitting (or the reverse).

turnaround time (1) The time that elapses between the submission of a job for processing (either on-line or as a batch) and the receipt of results. When the term is applied to the handling of an enquiry in an on-line system, it includes the time taken to print or display the reply. See *response time*. **(2)** See *modem turnaround time*.

turnkey A term applied to a contract or operation in which the supplier designs and installs and tests a (computer) system and delivers it to the purchaser in fully operable condition.

tutorial display At a terminal in an on-line system; a display that guides and prompts the terminal operator to assist him/her to make a valid enquiry or data entry. See *menu operation*.

twin Also *brother*. In a hierarchial structure; an entity on the same level as another entity. See *tree*.

twin exchangeable disc storage (TEDS) Storage on a magnetic disc unit with two drives. See *magnetic disc unit*.

twin transistor logic Transistor-transistor logic.

twisted pair In a telephone system; two wires constituting a two-wire circuit as contained in an insulated cable. See *quad*.

twix A term applied to a message sent or received in the TWX system.

two-address instruction An instruction that contains two addresses (usually assumed to be two operand addresses for a dyadic operation).

two-bit byte A doublet.

two-input adder A half adder.

two-level addressing Indirect addressing in which there are two levels of indirection (two table lookups). See *indirection*.

two-level storage The usual storage of a computer system consisting of main storage (first-level) and backing storage (second-level). See *one-level storage*.

two-out-of-five code A form of binary coded decimal in which each decimal digit is represented by a binary quintet which, to be valid, must contain two 1-bits and three 0-bits. The usual weights (positional values) are 6-3-2-1-0. A 5 would, thus be represented as 01100 and an 8 as 10100. The exception is '0' which is represented as 00110. See *M-out-of-N code*.

two-plus-one address instruction A two-address instruction that, in addition, contains the address of the next instruction to be executed.

two-way alternate communications The communications of a half-duplex system.

two-way communications The communications of a full-duplex or half-duplex system.

two-way simultaneous communications The communications of a full-duplex system.

two-wire circuit The usual circuit of a local loop as provided for a telephone or for use as a dial-up data circuit. Depending upon the telephone system and the modems used, it can, typically, support full-duplex operation at up to 1200 bps., half-duplex operation at up to 4800 bps., or asymmetric duplex operation with a message channel at up to 4800 bps. and a return channel at up to 150 bps. See *four-wire circuit*.

TWX *TeletypeWriter eXchange service.*

TX (Tx) A term used to indicate 'transmit', 'transmitter' or 'transmit mode'. See *RX*.

typamatic key A repeat-action key.

type (Classification) An attribute or set of attributes by which entities are allocated to a group. Entities that are of the 'same type' have common attributes that are considered significant for some purpose.

type (Manual operation) **(1)** To print using a typewriter; ('type a letter'). **(2)** To make an entry via a terminal with a (QWERTY or AZERTY) keyboard; ('type an enquiry').

type (Printing) Embossed, metallic, shaped characters as used in printing in most impact printers. See *printer; slug; font*.

type bar Also *print bar*. An element of a typewriter or belt printer consisting of a 'bar' with a type slug at the end; it is movable to strike the slug against ribbon and paper.

type basket The assembly of a typewriter or similar device that consists of the type bars and their cradle and pivots; with respect to some devices, the term denotes an element that can be changed to change type fonts.

type channel The element of a train printer along which the type slugs move. See *train printer*.

type drum The rotating, printing element of a barrel printer. See *barrel printer*.

type element (1) A single embossed character of a particular font. **(2)** A golfball; the spherical printing element of a golfball typewriter or printer.

type face A named style of type, usually of specified size; for example, '11-point Univers medium'.

type font A set of characters of the same size and style in type, photographic, or other reproducible form.

type fount A type font.

type wheel A daisy wheel.

typewriter A manually operated impact character printer; the common mechanisms are 'type bar' and 'golfball'.

typing reperforator A reperforator that prints graphic characters on paper tape as their bit patterns are punched.

U

UART *Universal Asynchronous Receiver Transmitter*. Also, in some systems, *Asynchronous Communications Interface Adapter*. An integrated circuit device that performs interfacing functions between a bit-parallel bus and a bit-serial asynchronous device such as a modem or peripheral. Typical functions include bit-parallel/bit-serial conversion with necessary buffering, parity generation and checking, and synchronisation of transfers. See *USART*.

UC (u.c.; uc.) *Upper Case*.

UCI *User Class Identifier*.

UHR *Ultra High Reduction*.

ULA *Uncommitted Logic Array.*

ULC (u.l.c.; ulc.) *Upper and Lower Case.*

ultrafiche A term applied to microfiche in which a reduction of greater than 90X is used. See *microfiche; reduction; COM.*

ultrasonic memory A memory incorporating an acoustic delay line. See *delay line memory.*

ultraviolet (UV) Radiation of short wavelength (2500-3000 Angstroms) at the end of the visible spectrum. It is used to erase certain types of reprogrammable memory. See *FAMOS.*

unallocate To deallocate.

unary Also *monadic.* Consisting of a single entity or performed with a single operand.

unary operator A monadic operator; an operator that specifies an operation on or with a single operand.

unattended operation Operation that does not require the presence of an operator. The term is often applied to the operation or facilities of a data station that permit it to receive incoming messages and/or to transmit (punched tape) outgoing messages under the control of another data station.

unbalanced (1) With respect to electronic circuitry in which the outputs of one section provide the inputs to another; configured or adjusted in such a way that the outputs do not meet the requirements for inputs. **(2)** Not efficiently using a particular set of resources; ('an unbalanced workload').

unbiased partitioning Partitioning in which an area of storage is divided into equal parts or in which each program is allocated the same amount. See *partitioning.*

unblanked In dot matrix printing or display; a term applied to a square or rectangular 'character' formed by placing dots in all positions; it may, for example, be used in place of a character in which a parity error has occurred.

unblock See *deblock.*

unbundle Also, sometimes, *unpack.* By a computer manufacturer; to begin charging separately for software (or, possibly, services) that had previously been included in the price of the computer.

uncommitted (1) Unallocated. **(2)** Available for different uses or to perform different functions.

uncommitted logic array (ULA) A logic array (AND and OR matrices) that can be programmed (as a final stage of manufacture) to meet specific requirements. See *programmable logic array.*

unconditional branch An unconditional jump.

unconditional branch instruction An unconditional jump instruction.

unconditional control transfer An unconditional jump.

unconditional control transfer instruction An unconditional jump instruction.

unconditional jump Also *unconditional branch; unconditional control transfer.* **(1)** A transfer of control from one sequence of instructions to another that always takes place when a particular instruction in the first sequence is executed. It is usually a transfer to or from a subroutine or utility. See *branch; jump.* **(2)** A jump; either an 'unconditional jump' (def. 1) or a transfer of control with initiation external to the program being executed; for example, a transfer to an interrupt routine initiated by a monitor routine.

unconditional jump instruction Also *unconditional branch instruction; unconditional control transfer instruction.* An instruction that specifies an unconditional jump (def. 1); an instruction that specifies a transfer of control to an entry point in another sequence of instructions.

unconditional transfer An unconditional jump.

unconditioned line In a telephone system; a line that has not been balanced to improve transmission characteristics. See *conditioning.*

uncorrectable error An error that results in loss of data. See *error; hard error; correctable error.*

undefined Not specified or not known to an operating system. For example, an 'undefined record' is a record of unspecified or unknown length.

underflow (1) Also *arithmetic underflow.* In an arithmetic operation; the condition in which the result is too small to be represented by the method in use; for example, the condition in which a 16-bit word is designated to hold a number in which the first significant digit occurs in the twentieth bit position. **(2)** The condition in which a data item contains less than a specified number of digits or characters. **(3)** An attempt to read an item from an empty stack.

underpunch A digit punch; a punch other than a zone punch.

undisturbed With respect to core memory; a term applied to a core that holds a 1-bit with magnetisation that has not been weakened by repetitive reading of other cores on the same word or bit line. See *core memory.*

unformatted capacity The capacity of a magnetic disc (usually in bits) without allowance for headers, sector marks, guard bands, etc.; the capacity if data was written to completely fill all tracks.

unformatted disc A magnetic disc to which no access-related information has been written. See *initialise (Magnetic disc)*.

unformatted display A display in which data can be placed on all lines; a display without any protected fields.

unices Versions of the Unix operating system.

unidirectional (1) Of a printer; capable of printing only when the printing element (print head; golfball) is moving from left to right along a line. See *bidirectional.* **(2)**Of a data bus; used for data transfers in only one direction. See *bidirectional*.

unintelligent Also *dumb*. A term applied to a terminal (possibly to another device) that has no self-contained memory. See *intelligent*.

uninterruptable power supply (UPS) A power supply that contains a battery and means for transferring a load from the regular (mains) source to the battery in such a way that the power source appears to be unchanged to the load.

unipolar (1) With respect to a transistor; with conduction all through the same type (N-type or P-type) silicon; it is the conduction mode of a field effect transistor. See *field effect transistor; bipolar transistor*. **(2)**With respect to circuit operation; using either positive or negative pulses but not both; with all information carried by voltages of the same polarity.

unipolar signalling Data transmission in which there are only two line conditions, one of which is 'neutral' (0 V.) and the other of which is positive (or negative, depending upon the system). A mark could, for example, be represented by +10 V. and a space by 0 V.

uniprocessing The processing (execution of user programs) performed by a uniprocessor.

uniprocessor A term sometimes applied to a computer with only one processor for executing program instructions. (Other processors may be present for handling data transfers or performing other functions.)

unit address A number by which a peripheral device is known to the operating system.

unit multiplexing Multiplexing in which units (bits; bytes) are interleaved for transmission; time division multiplexing as contrasted to frequency division multiplexing.

unit record processor In some systems; the microprogrammed facilities for performing autonomous transfers.

unit separator (US) A character used in data transfer, storage, or transmission to delimit units of data.

unit string A string in which only a single entity is present.

universal asynchronous receiver transmitter See *UART*.

universal character set A feature of a printer or display device with a user-programmable character generator. Such a device can be programmed to print/display the characters of any alphabet (Roman; Arabic; Kanji).

universal product code (UPC) A standard bar code for marking products to identify the product and container size to point-of-sale equipment. See *bar code; point-of-sale*.

universal set A set that includes all the elements that have significance for a particular purpose or field of study.

universal synchronous/asynchronous receiver transmitter See *USART*.

Unix A real-time operating system developed by Bell Laboratories and licensed for use on many 16-bit minicomputers and microcomputers.

unload (1) With respect to a read/write head in a movable head, rigid disc, magnetic disc unit; to retract it from read/write proximity to the disc surface. See *load; fly*. **(2)**With respect to a work-performing system (processing; communications; electrical); to remove some or all of the work.

unloaded With respect to a unit of code or data; not written to main storage.

unmapped system A computer system in which the location of each unit of code and data in main storage must be specified by the operator or user program; a system without supervisory hardware/software for storage management.

unpack (1) To expand packed data to its original form. See *pack*. **(2)**With respect to numeric values in packed decimal; to change them to a representation in which each digit is held in a separate byte. See *packed decimal*. **(3)**Also, sometimes, *unbundle*. To charge separately for items that were previously included in a one-price package.

unpacked decimal The use of one byte per digit to represent decimal values. See *packed decimal*.

unpacked microinstruction See *microinstruction*.

unpaged segment A segment held as the only segment in a page. See *segment*.

unprintable character A character that has no agreed, discrete, graphic representation; for example, the control character DLE, FS, or CR. See *character; printable character*.

unprotected field On the screen of a display device; a field in which an operator can enter, modify, or delete data by means of keys/controls on the keyboard. See *protected field*.

unrecoverable error An uncorrectable error; an error that results in loss or corruption of code or data. The term is applied to an error that cannot be resolved by the normal hardware/software recovery facilities without interrupting processing. The lost or corrupted code/data is normally reinstated from a checkpoint dump, a backup file, or by reloading. See *high-level recovery*.

unsaturated (1)With respect to a diode; not fully conducting. (2)With respect to a bipolar transistor; with no excess gate current; with only sufficient gate-emitter current to sustain the emitter-collector current that is required in the circuit. See *Schottky transistor*.

unshift With respect to a typewriter or similar printer; to change from printing capital letters to printing lower-case letters. See *shift*.

unsigned number A number in which no + or — has been placed in the sign position. (It is assumed to be 'positive'). See *sign*.

unspanned Of a record (or other unit); not crossing a block boundary; contained in a single block. See *spanned*.

unstable (1)Of a system or software; still being modified or improved. (2)Of an electronic circuit or device; of varying or unpredictable operation; subject to random changes in electrical characteristics. (3)See *unstable state*.

unstable state Of a trigger circuit; in process of changing from one stable state to another, or returning to its only stable state.

unstratified language A language that can be used as its own metalanguage; a natural language. See *stratified language*.

unstring To deconcatenate.

unstructured file A file that does not provide for the access of individual data items; for example, a spool file, a scratch file, or a journal file. See *structured file*.

unwind (1)To state (print out) all the instructions of a loop in the sequence they are executed. (2)To convert a loop to repetitive sequences of in-line instructions.

up channel A return channel. See *channel*.

up-line dump In a data network; an action that may be taken by a computer without its own backing storage to save storage and register contents (say, at the beginning of a power fail) by sending them to a computer at another node that has the facilities to hold them.

up time The time during which a system or functional unit is capable of normal operation. See *down time*.

UPC *Universal Product Code.*
UPC-E *Universal Product Code (Europe).*

update (1)With respect to a master file; to create a new generation by incorporating changes to reflect the current status of its data. The operation, typically, consists of deleting obsolete records, adding new records, and incorporating new versions of records in which there have been changes of data. A customer file may, for example, be updated by deleting the records of inactive customers, adding records for new customers, and replacing existing records with new versions when details such as address or credit limits have changed. See *generation*. (2)With respect to instructions, operating manuals, parts lists, and the like; to make changes and corrections to reflect the current status of the hardware or software to which they apply.

update by copy A method of updating a sequential file by merging it with an amendments file and writing the resultant version to a different storage device than the one used to hold the pre-updated file. It is performed sequentially with the key of each record in the file being updated checked against the keys of the amendments file to locate matches and keys not included in the sequence. Where no match is found, the record is copied to the new location. Where a match is found, the record in the amendments file is written to the new location. If a record in the amendments file has a key that is not represented in the file being updated, it is written to the new location in its correct sequence. Update by copy has the advantage of retaining the pre-updated version, of being able to accomodate variable length records, and providing for easy insertion of 'missing' records without the need to leave unused space for them. See *update in situ*.

update by overlay Update in situ.

update file An amendments file; a file that holds changed versions of existing records of a master file and/or new records that are to be included during updating.

update generation (1)Generation; the location of a particular version of a master file in a sequence each of which is formed by updating the previous version. (2)The process of creating a new version of a master file. It includes retaining a copy of the old version and, usually, of the amendments file.

update in situ Also *update by overlay*. To update a master file by overwriting changed records with their new versions from an amendments file. It is not suitable for updating files with variable length records or when new records must be added, unless considerable unused space is left to accomodate them. It has the disadvantage of requiring a copy to be made before the update begins, in order to retain the previous version. It is used mainly for updating low hit-rate disc files and, in transaction processing systems, it is often done as the changes occur. See *update by copy.*

update notes Additions or changes to an instruction manual, parts list, etc. as supplied to users by a manufacturer.

update period The time between scheduled updates of a file or the time during which update material for a file has accumulated.

update program A program that performs updating.

update run A run performed to update a master file by incorporating changes/additions from an amendments file.

upgrade (1) Also *enhance*. With respect to a computer system; to add new hardware and/or software to improve performance or extend capability. **(2)**By a manufacturer; to improve performance/capability of a product. **(3)**That which is provided by upgrading; ('an upgrade for System 32').

uplink The path on which transmissions are sent from an earth station to a communications satellite; the usual frequency (Intelsat 4A) is 6 GHz. See *downlink; satellite communications.*

upper and lower case (u.l.c.; ulc.) With respect to printed or displayed data; consisting of small letters as well as capital letters. See *upper case; lower case.*

upper bound The highest numbered location in an area of (main) storage.

upper case (1)A printing term applied to the capital letters of a font. See *lower case.* **(2)**With respect to computer printers and display devices; a term that denotes the representation of character data by capital letters, digits, and symbols (and without lower-case letters). See *upper and lower case.*

upper curtate The (three) rows at the top of a punched card. See *curtate.*

UPS *Uninterruptable Power Supply.*

upshift Also, often, *shift.* To change a printer to print upper case letters (and various symbols) instead of lower-case. See *shift; downshift.*

uptime Up time.

upward compatible Also, often, *forward compatible.* A term applied to user programs (and, perhaps, system software) for one range of computers that can be run (with little if any alteration) on larger (possibly, later model) computers produced by the same manufacturer.

US *Unit Separator.*

usage bits Access bits.

USART *Universal Synchronous/Asynchronous Receiver Transmitter.* An integrated circuit interface device to provide serial-parallel data conversion between a microprocessor (or larger computer) and a modem and which can handle both synchronous and asynchronous transfers. Some devices provide a wider range of functions including clocking of synchronous transfers, sending and receiving modem interchange signals, and echoplex checking for asynchronous transfers. The device may also provide hardware implementation of a network protocol by performing such functions as adding control characters to outgoing messages and deleting them from incoming messages. See *UART; USRT.*

USASCII See *ASCII.*

USASI *Unites States of America Standards Institute.* The former name of the American National Standards Institute.

use bit A change bit; a flag that indicates whether or not a page/segment has been written to while in primary storage. See *change bit.*

user (1) With respect to a particular computer installation; a person or organisation for which it performs processing. **(2)**With respect to the products of a particular manufacturer or software house; an organisation (possibly an individual) that owns them or leases them. **(3)**Also *controller.* With respect to particular programs and data in a computer system; an individual or organisation with access rights to it. **(4)**With respect to a unit of data (file; data base); a program that accesses it.

user account Records kept for purposes of charging a particular user for services/materials supplied.

user address space That part of main storage available to user programs.

user area (1) User address space. **(2)**A main storage partition allocated to a particular user program.

user attribute file A file containing information with respect to all authorised users of a computer system; for example, name, account number, password, authorised individuals, and files/volumes to which access is allowed.

user catalogue (1)A user attribute file. **(2)**A catalogue of the files/volumes that belong to a particular user.

user console A console dedicated to a user for a particular purpose. See *user terminal*.

user data (1) Data as received (by data control) from a user or from users. (2) Data in computer storage that belongs to a particular user.

user-defined With function or meaning specified by a user; ('a user-defined key'; 'a user-defined macro').

user department A department of a company (or other organisation) for which a computer department performs processing.

user disc A magnetic disc that can be accessed by user programs.

user exit A place in a system program where control can be transferred to a user exit routine.

user exit routine A user supplied routine to perform specified functions on exiting.

user friendly A term applied to terminal-type computer equipment that is easy to operate and has good error recovery facilities.

user group An organisation of the owners and operators of a particular type (manufacturer's model or series) of computer, or, within such a group, members with a particular operating system or other major software; ('an ICL 2900 user group'; 'the George 3 User Group'). Such groups are usually organised on regional or national basis; their purpose is to interchange information related to use and maintenance and to make mutually agreed recommendations to the manufacturer.

user identification A character group that uniquely identifies a particular user (individual; organisation) to an operating system of a computer for purposes of determining access rights and resource entitlement and for accounting. See *password*.

user input area On the screen of a display terminal; a location in which data keyed in by the operator appears.

user memory In some virtual storage systems; a term applied to that part of primary storage available to hold pages/segments for user programs.

user mode The mode in which a central processor is executing instructions of a user program and is prevented from executing instructions of system programs.

user profile The attributes of a particular user; for example, access rights, file ownership, and resources that can be allocated.

user program A program owned by a particular user of a computer system. The term is synonymous with 'application program' except that the emphasis is upon control and access rights rather than on the function it performs. See *application; program*.

user program area (1) User address space. (2) An area of main storage (partition) allocated to user programs.

user's set In a telephone system; a circuit-terminating device (telephone or modem) on a user's premises.

user subroutine A subroutine written by a user. See *subroutine*.

user task (1) A task consisting of one or more user programs. (2) A loaded user program.

user terminal A terminal on a user's premises; a terminal by which a user (stockbroker; travel agent; subscriber to timesharing services) can communicate with a computer system.

user-written A term applied to (system) software that is written by the user of a computer (rather than supplied by a manufacturer or software house).

USRT *Universal Synchronous Receiver Transmitter.* An integrated circuit device designed to perform series-parallel conversion and timing of synchronous bit-serial data in a microprocessor system. (It may also perform other functions.) See *UART; USART*.

utility A unit of system software that performs some operation that is frequently required during execution; for example, initialisation, printing, copying a file, or performing a call or interrupt. A particular utility is usually termed a 'routine' and identified by function, for example, a 'call routine' or a 'print routine'. Many utilities are also 'housekeeping routines'. See *housekeeping*.

utility program A utility. While 'utility' usually denotes a short and frequently used sequence, 'utility program' may be applied to a longer or less-frequently used sequence; for example, to one that performs a sort or merge or a diagnostic function.

UV *UltraViolet.*

UV-erasable A term applied to a memory device in which ultraviolet light is used to dissipate gate charges and, thus, to 'erase' stored data. See *PROM; FAMOS*.

V

V (V.) *Volts; Voltage.*

V-format A term applied to a file in which the records are of variable length and in which each record header holds a length indicator; they may be blocked in which case each block header also holds a length indicator.

V-mode records Records of variable length.

V response In a teletypewriter system; a terminal response to a polling message or address selection.

V.3 A CCITT Recommendation that defines International Alphabet No. 5 and national variations.

V.4 A CCITT Recommendation that specifies the representation of binary 1 and 0, the use of parity bits, and start/stop elements.

V.21 A CCITT Recommendation concerning 200 bit per second asynchronous modems.

V.22 A CCITT Recommendation concerning 600 and 1200 bit per second synchronous and asynchronous modems for 2-wire circuits, including full-duplex modems operating on frequency-separated channels.

V.23 A CCITT Recommendation concerning 600 and 1200 bit per second synchronous and asynchronous modems for 2-wire and 4-wire circuits.

V.24 A CCITT Recommendation relating to the interface between a modem (DCE) and a computer or terminal (DTE). It assigns numbers to the circuits of the interface and identifies the data, control, and clock signals that they carry.

V.25 A CCITT Recommendation relating to automatic calling and answering equipment and procedures for use in 2-wire, dial-up systems.

V.26 A CCITT Recommendation relating to 2400 bit per second synchronous modems for 4-wire circuits.

V.27 A CCITT Recommendation relating to 4800 bit per second synchronous modems. V.27 *bis* relates to modems for 2-wire and 4-wire leased circuits and V.27 *ter* relates to modems for dial-up 2-wire circuits.

V.28 A CCITT Recommendation concerning the electrical characteristics of the signals of a V.24 interface.

V.30 A CCITT Recommendation relating to 50-110 bit per second modems that operate by FSK on 2-wire circuits.

V.35 A CCITT Recommendation relating to 48,000 bit per second modems for use on wideband 4-wire circuits.

V.54 A CCITT Recommendation relating to loop testing of modems and inter-modem circuits.

VAC *Voltage (Alternating Current).*

vacuum tube See *electron tube.*

valence A term used when indicating the number of electrons in the outermost orbital sphere of an atom; it can be from 0 to 8 depending upon the element (helium—0; hydrogen—1; silicon—4). It determines the ways in which an atom can combine with other atoms to form molecules.

valid A term indicating conformance to standards or criteria; for example, 'valid data' is data that has been checked for errors (and corrected if necessary) and a 'valid reference' is a reference that correctly identifies a storage location in an area to which a program has access rights. See *invalid; legal.*

validate To perform validation.

validation (1) Also *data vet.* A programmed operation of checking operator input to ensure that entered data conforms to certain standards. Typically, checks are made to ensure that items are of correct length for their fields, if patterns are conformed to (say, that the first two characters of a part number are letters), if alphabetic characters are included in fields that are supposed to be numeric (and the reverse), if numeric values fall within certain limits, if dates are correct, and if there is an entry for each required field (say, to ensure that the customer number is included). See *verification.* **(2)**Also *program validation.* An operation performed to ensure that a new or changed program is error-free and capable of performing its intended function.

validity check (1)A check to determine if a particular bit-pattern character is a 'valid' character in the code in which it is used. **(2)**One of the checks performed during validation; a check to determine if a particular item of data has certain attributes.

value A non-specific term for a (short) individually accessible item; ('a flag value of '1'; 'print the value FAILURE').

value-added network A network with nodes that perform computing functions (format/protocol conversion) as well as message routing functions.

value call syllable An address syllable; a part of an instruction that contains an operand.

valve An electron tube.

variable (Location or structure) A unit of storage with specified attributes that is declared for purposes of holding specific data or parameters that may change during execution or between executions of a program. A variable may, for example, be a word, a string, an array, or a stack. A variable of two or more dimensions is a **structured variable**. A **local variable** is one that can only be referenced within the block in which it is declared and a **global variable** is available throughout a program.

variable (Logic operation) A monadic operation with an output that is 'true' if the input is 'true' and an output that is 'false' if the input is 'false'.

variable (Mathematics) A quantity that can assume any of a given set of values. When in a mathematical expression, such a quantity may be termed an **independent variable** as distinguished from a **dependent variable** which is a quantity with a value that depends upon the value of one or more independent variables. For example, in the expression 'z = 3xy', the 'x' and 'y' are independent variables and the 'z' is a dependent variable. (Whether a variable is dependent or independent depends on how the expression is structured; if the example is in the form 'y = z/3x', the 'y' becomes the dependent variable.) See *constant*.

variable (Ordinary usage) That which can change or can be changed; that which does not have a fixed form or value.

variable declaration In programming; a declaration that establishes the size, structure, and data type of a variable. See *variable (Location or structure)*.

variable-length block A block with a length that can be established by a programmer.

variable-length record A record with a length that depends upon its contents. See *fixed-length record*.

variable-length segment The usual segment of a virtual storage system. See *segment*.

variable microcode timing In some systems; a facility for changing the speed of microcode execution depending upon the operation being performed.

variable partitioning Multiprogramming storage allocation in which the operating system changes partitions during execution in order to meet the varying needs of active programs.

variable-point representation The representation of a quantity by a number in which a special character (say, a decimal point) can be inserted to indicate the location of the radix point. See *numeration system*.

variable-word computer A computer with the facilities for storing and manipulating words of different lengths.

VCS *Video Computer System*.

VDC *Voltage (Direct Current)*.

VDE *Voice Data Entry*.

VDU *Visual Display Unit*.

vector (1)A row; a one-dimensional array. (2)In mathematics and computer graphics; a directed line segment; a line segment defined by the coordinates of its ends or by the coordinates of its origin, its direction, and its length. (3)A stream; a continuous movement of operators or operands from storage to a processing unit. See *stream*. (4)Of a quantity; requiring two numbers for its representation. See *scalar*.

vector computer An array computer.

vector scan Also *calligraphic*. A computer graphics technique in which a display is formed of vectors that are, typically, used in conjunction with routines in ROM to produce curves and characters. Programming consists of supplying the vector coordinates that the electron beam will follow in generating and refreshing the display. The system provides good brightness and linearity but requires continuous availability of large, high-speed RAM and there can be flicker problems due to long refresh cycles. See *raster scan; storage tube*.

vectored interrupt An interrupt that identifies the cause. See *interrupt*.

Venn diagram A method of representing logic relationships in which a rectangular field identifies the environment and either one or two circles represent the specific conditions. The following are some examples:

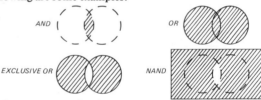

verb In a programming language, a reserved word that is available for use as an operator; for example, AND, READ, NEGATE, and DO.

verge-punched card An edge-punched card.

verification (1)The operation of determining if a condition that is supposed to exist does, in fact, exist. (2)With respect to data that is to be entered into computer storage; the process of checking manual operations in an attempt to ensure that they have been performed correctly. The term usually denotes an operation in which the steps of punching punched cards or paper tape are repeated by another operator and comparing the two copies (or machine-held electronic representations) to determine if they are identical. Validation is commonly used in place of verification when the data entry is by means of keying from a terminal. See *validation; card verifier; data preparation; verifier.*

verifier A machine used in (punched card or paper tape) verification; a machine in which source data is entered a second time (by a different operator) in order to detect errors as revealed by differences in the two versions.

verify To determine whether an operation has been performed correctly. See *verification.*

version number A generation number.

vertical feed With respect to a card reader or punch; designed for cards to enter with a short edge first. See *horizontal feed.*

vertical format unit (VFU) An element of a printer that can be programmed to provide combinations of paper throws as required for different printing operations. See *paper tape loop.*

vertical microinstruction See *microinstruction.*

vertical MOS See *VMOS.*

vertical parity Parity as applied to a message or block rather than to an individual character. See *parity.*

vertical redundancy check A longitudinal redundancy check.

vertical tabulate To move paper through a printer in order to bring a preset, lower position to the place where it can be printed. It is, typically, an operation controlled by a paper tape loop or vertical format unit. See *tabulate; throw.*

vertical tabulate character See *VT.*

very large scale integration See *VLSI.*

vesicular film See *microfilm.*

vet See *vetting.*

vetting Also *vet; data vet.* To check data to determine if it is accurate and complete; a term sometimes used synonymously with 'validation'. See *validation.*

VFC *Voltage to Frequency Converter.*

VFU *Vertical Format Unit.*

VGU *Video Generation Unit.*

VHR *Very High Reduction.*

via In microelectronic devices; an opening through an internal insulating layer. See *ovonic memory.*

video (1) A term applied to the techniques or equipment involved in presenting data or other images on the screens of cathode ray tubes. **(2)** A term applied to the picture-producing elements of a television or other cathode ray tube display device.

video buffer A section of random-access memory that holds the bit-pattern characters of the data that is displayed. It is scanned to refresh the display with the output of the scan going to a 'character generator' that holds the actual two-dimensional forms of the characters as they appear on the screen.

video collect A feature of an optical character reader that causes an uninterpretable character to be displayed on a cathode ray tube for examination and resolution by an operator.

video computer system (VCS) A microprocessor computer system with a primary function of supporting a video display. The term usually denotes an amusement machine ('Space Invaders') or a games attachment for a television set.

video generation unit (VGU) An intelligent CRT controller (for a raster-scan graphics VDU).

videotex (1) A television-based information system; either teletext or viewdata. **(2)** Viewdata.

view mode In a printer in which the print head blocks the operator's view of the characters as they are printed; the mode in which the print head moves to a margin position to permit the operator to see the characters. When characters are entered via a keyboard, the movement usually takes place automatically when no keystrokes have been made for a certain period (say, a quarter of a second).

viewdata Also, sometimes, *videotex.* A system by which essentially text material is transmitted 'on demand' from a computer to a subscriber's special (or adapted) television receiver. In a public system (British Prestel; French Teletel; Canadian Teledon; Japanese Captain), the television set is used for regular broadcast reception and when the user requires a viewdata service he dials (automatically) the nearest computer of the system on local telephone lines; this sends a code to identify the user. Selection uses a hierarcy of menus displayed on the screen; identification of the required item is made by pressing keys on a numeric pad, each of which sends a unique signal to the computer. When the required page (stock market quotations; flight schedule; race results) is located and displayed, the dialed line can be released and the display will be retained on the screen. The system allows responses from the user to the 'information provider' (an organisation that provides digitised text for the system). For example, a user who wants to purchase an item offered by a store can identify the item in a 'response frame' by number and, possibly, add a credit card number. (The system forwards the request as computer printout.) The system may also offer a 'gateway' facility by which a user can connect directly to the computer of the information provider. When in viewdata mode, all text and display-control information is sent on the telephone line at the established rate for the system (1200, 2400, or 4800 bits per second). Responses are asynchronous at low speed (75 bps.). Private viewdata systems (using public telephone lines) can be implemented, for example, to provide a stock check and order entry system.

viewer A hand-held light source and magnifier for use in reading microfilm. See *reader*.

virgin A term applied to a data recording medium that has never had data written to it; for example, new magnetic tape may be termed 'virgin tape'.

virtual A term used in various ways to indicate that the actual physical implementation (storage; peripheral device; communications circuit) is different than that perceived by a user or user program.

virtual address In a virtual storage system; an address in the form in which it occurs in source coding or in object code; an address that has not yet been mapped onto real (hardware-identifiable) storage. It is the equivalent of a 'presumptive address' in a non-virtual storage system. See *real address; virtual storage addressing*.

virtual auxiliary memory Secondary storage.

virtual card reader A magnetic-tape simulation of a card reader.

virtual circuit In a packet switching system; the notional circuit that is set up between a sender and receiver by means of routing information included with a packet. See *packet switching*.

virtual computer A term sometimes applied to a computer that uses virtual storage.

virtual connection A virtual circuit.

virtual console A terminal that is temporarily used as a system console (for diagnostic or trouble-shooting purposes).

virtual console spooling The journalisation of console-operating system interchanges.

virtual device A programming identification of a peripheral device that is not an identification of any specific device.

virtual disc In some systems; a part of a magnetic disc or of a disc pack that is treated by an operating system as if it was a separate disc.

virtual drive A direct access device that does not actually exist but which is implemented by staging from mass storage.

virtual file (1) A file that is a masked version of a larger file. **(2)** A file that appears to be a single file but is actually two or more linked files.

virtual image In computer graphics; a term used to denote a complete image (as held in storage) of which only a part can be displayed at any one time.

virtual machine (VM) **(1)** A subset of the resources (system software; storage; peripherals) of a computer system that is available to a particular executing program or job in a virtual storage system. Its purpose is to provide an executing environment resembling that of a separate computer, as seen from the view of application programs. A single computer would, typically, have several or many virtual machines active at the same time; the fact that they interleave execution and share resources is not apparent to programs and need not be considered by programmers. **(2)** A functional simulation of a particular computer and its associated devices. **(3)** In some systems; a subset of computer resources used to perform a particular type of processing (batch; transaction processing). **(4)** A term sometimes applied to a computer that uses virtual storage.

virtual memory Virtual storage.

virtual partition A virtual storage partition.

virtual peripheral Also *virtual device*. **(1)** A peripheral as identified in a program where the operating system makes the actual selection. **(2)** A peripheral used to hold spool files.

virtual storage (1) Also *apparent storage; one-level storage*. The total range of addresses used, or that are available for use, in programming a computer that is organised so that there is no direct relationship between locations specified in programs and locations actually available in storage hardware. Such storage is 'one-level' because the programmer need not differentiate between that which will be in main storage and that which will be in backing storage during particular phases of execution. **(2)** The total primary and secondary storage available in a virtual storage system. In some systems, the range of virtual addresses is limited to the range of hardware addresses; in such a system, the term indicates only that the storage is 'one-level'. **(3)** The range of virtual addresses used by, or available to, an application program, system program, or virtual machine. In this sense, it is a subset of 'virtual storage' (def. 1). **(4)** The range of hardware addresses used by, or available to, a program during execution in a virtual storage system.

virtual storage addressing The location of code and data in a virtual storage system. During compilation, a symbolic address in source coding is converted into a numerical value in the address space of the program and these are further 'gathered' into pages and/or segments organised according to the time in which they will be required during execution. The term **virtual address** may be applied to either a symbolic address that is to be so converted or to the numerical value; unless otherwise indicated, 'numerical value' is understood. During execution, virtual addresses produced by instructions during decoding are converted to addresses in particular pages/segments by means of references to page/segment tables made by the operating system. When a page or segment is in primary (main) storage, its addresses are termed **real addresses** (also **actual addresses**) and these terms are synonymous with 'hardware address' in a non-virtual storage system. An address in a page or segment that is not in primary storage is termed a **physical address**. The process of converting virtual addresses to real or physical addresses is termed **mapping**. See *addressing*.

virtual storage allocation The allocation of space for code and data in a virtual storage system. Depending upon the system, the common (or only) unit of storage and transfer may be the variable-length **segment** or the fixed-length **page**; many systems use both. A system that uses pages is termed a **paged system** (also **paging system**) and one that uses segments only may be termed a **segmentation system**. In systems in which both pages and segments are used, access may be performed for both pages and segments but the page (often of 512 or 1024 bytes) is usually the only unit of storage and transfer between secondary and primary storage. In such a system, two or more short segments may be contained in a single page and long segments may be divided into multiple pages; a divided segment is termed a **paged segment**. A unit of storage of the correct length to hold a page is termed a **page slot** or a **page frame**; though the terms are applied to both primary and secondary storage, 'primary storage' is understood unless otherwise indicated. Because pages are fixed-length (some systems provide for two or three fixed lengths), the code or data will not always fill them; **internal fragmentation** is the condition in which significant primary storage space is wasted in partially filled pages. In a paged system, a new page from secondary storage is placed in any available page slot in primary storage. In a segmentation system, an 'allocation algorithm' is used to place segments in primary storage with as economical use of space as possible. The condition in which significant primary storage space is wasted in inter-segment spaces that are too small to allocate is termed **external fragmentation** (also **checkerboarding**). See *allocation algorithm; discard policy; page; segment*.

virtual storage interrupt (VSI) Also, in a paged system, *page fault*. An interrupt in the execution of a program caused by its referencing a page or segment that is not in primary storage. Following the VSI, system routines locate the required page/segment in secondary storage, locate a place for it in primary storage, read it into primary storage, and adjust table entries to indicate its new location. When a VSI occurs, instruction execution is commonly passed to another program. See *virtual storage transfers; discard; thrashing; VSI rate; VSI trace*.

virtual storage management Those functions of an operating system that relate to locating and moving pages/segments, keeping track of their locations, and making efficient use of storage space.

virtual storage partition Also *virtual partition*. An area of primary storage dynamically allocated to a particular process. See *virtual storage partitioning*.

virtual storage partitioning The process of allocating primary storage space to the pages/segments required by the various active programs. Small and relatively simple systems may use **fixed partitioning** in which each program is restricted to the amount of space allocated at run time. If **unbiased partitioning** is used, each program receives the same amount of space and if **biased partitioning** is used, programs of different size are allocated different amounts of space. Most virtual storage systems use **variable partitioning** in which the operating system dynamically allocates space to meet the changing requirements of the various active programs during execution. Variable partitioning may be 'Class V1' in which space is allocated according to priority, with high-priority programs given relatively unlimited space, often at the expense of programs of lower priority. In systems that use 'Class V2' partitioning, each page/segment that is brought in from secondary storage to meet the needs of a program is placed in the top of a FIFO list and, if necessary, a page/segment (possibly from the resident set of another program) is discarded from the bottom of the list. A more sophisticated method is termed 'Class W'; in this method, the operating system uses an algorithm or combination of algorithms to attempt to identify pages/segments that constitute the working sets of the various programs in order to discard those that are no longer needed. See *discard policy; virtual storage system—processing units*.

virtual storage system A multiprogramming computer system in which units of code and data are dynamically allocated main storage space to meet the changing needs of executing programs. Essentially it is a system in which the hardware and operating system incorporate facilities that eliminate (or, in any case, greatly reduce) the need for programmers to consider the limitations of main storage when designing and writing programs. In such a system, code and data for a program are written separately to pages and/or segments that are brought into main (primary) storage as and when required during processing and are deleted when no longer needed. With respect to the code, such a system effectively provides automatic overlaying. Besides simplifying programming and improving primary storage utilisation, such systems also provide data and device independence and, usually, sophisticated methods of sharing and protecting code and data.

virtual storage system—processing units A **set** (used in this sense mainly in compound terms) is the group of pages/segments needed by a program during execution. The group includes pages/segments of code as well as of data and those that are shared with other programs and/or are units of system software as well as those that are used only by the particular program. All of the pages/segments that can be referenced by a program constitute its **static set**; those that it will reference in a particular run are termed its **dynamic set**. During any phase of execution, some of the pages/segments of the dynamic set will be in primary storage, and this constitutes the program's **resident set**. The resident set includes the **active set** (also **locality set**) of pages/segments that are being actively referenced during that phase of execution and, usually, ones with which the program has finished and those that are yet to be required. The term 'locality set' may also be applied to those pages/segments that the operating system has identified by algorithm as being required by a program during a particular phase of processing. The term **working set** may be used synonymously with 'active set' or 'locality set'. See *discard policy; working set*.

virtual storage terms In virtual storage systems; the fast, random-access storage is usually termed **primary storage** rather than 'main storage' and that which is held on magnetic discs, tape, or other external devices is usually termed **secondary storage** rather than 'backing storage'. Many virtual storage systems continue to execute programs in which code and data are not organised into pages or segments and, in this case, that part of 'backing storage' used to hold their code and data is often termed **filestore**. A program with elements in primary storage is often termed a **process**; the term is applied to executing sequences that would otherwise be identified as 'system programs' as well as 'user programs'. A **virtual machine** is a subset of computer resources (both hardware and software) that is available to a particular process. The term **process image** is applied to the total pages/segments available to a virtual machine; it corresponds to the 'dynamic set' of the process. When primary storage is considered from the programming viewpoint, it is often termed **real storage** and it, thus, contrasts with 'virtual storage'. The term 'real storage' may also be used synonymously with **actual storage** as well as **physical storage** to denote any hardware storage (primary or secondary) and to differentiate such storage from 'virtual storage'. The term 'physical storage' may also be used synonymously with 'secondary storage'. In addition to other 'virtual storage' entries, see *discard policy; storage; page; segment; swap; roll-in; roll-out; fragmentation*.

virtual storage transfers When a process references a location in a page or segment that is not in primary storage, a **virtual storage interrupt** (VSI) occurs; in a paged system, it is usually termed a **page fault**. Control is transferred to a system routine that locates the required page/segment in secondary storage and writes a copy of it to a location in primary storage in an operation that is termed a **roll-in, swap-in** or, in a paged system, a **page-in**. It is placed in 'allocatable space' which, in a paged system, is termed a **page frame** or **page slot**. When a page/segment in primary storage is overwritten, it is said to be **deleted** or **discarded**. If any change has been made to the page/segment while in primary storage, it is written out to secondary storage where it overwrites the previous version held in the location before the primary storage copy is overwritten. The operation of writing it to backing storage is termed a **roll-out, swap-out** or, in a paged system, a **page-out**. The term **paging** is applied to the general process of transferring pages/segments between primary and secondary storage.

visible (1) In a graphic (printed or displayed) representation rather than as a bit pattern. **(2)** Evident to a programmer or a user program; not transparent; ('a visible register'; 'a visible operation').

visible record computer (VRC) Also, sometimes, *electronic accounting machine*. A small computer with limited user programmability that is intended to perform standard accounting functions for small-business users. A characteristic of such a computer is that it makes entries directly on standard documents (invoices; ledger cards; stock record cards) rather than using a separate printer. Typically, the document is placed in the machine and relevant data is filled in partly from memory and partly by operator keyboarding. It performs standard computations and holds repeating operations and reusable data in a memory of from a few hundred bytes to upwards of about 64K bytes. A visible record computer without provision for writing data magnetically to ledger cards may be termed an **accounting computer** while one with this capability is often termed a **magnetic ledger computer**. Ledger cards for use with a magnetic ledger computer have one or more 'magnetic stripes' on the reverse side; these can be read and written in the same manner as magnetic tape. As the card is loaded, it passes through a read station and the data from the stripe(s) is read into memory. As new data is keyed in (and entered on the front of the card), the data in memory is updated and the new version is written back to the stripe(s) as the card leaves the machine. See *small business system*.

visual display unit (VDU) Also *CRT terminal*. A display device with keyboard as used by an operator to communicate with a computer. As an operator types a message or text on the keyboard, the characters are displayed on the screen. When data has been checked for accuracy, it is transmitted to the computer by

pressing an 'enter key' (often, 'carriage return'). This also clears the line buffer and moves the cursor to the beginning of the following line. Typically, a program performs validation and provides prompts to assist the operator. Responses from the connected program are returned to the VDU and displayed, often in a protected field. An 'intelligent VDU' is one that incorporates a memory to hold the bit pattern representations of the displayed characters (a video buffer) and a character generator which is another section of memory that holds the actual dot-matrix form of each displayable character. An 'unintelligent VDU' is one in which these elements are held in the computer or in a device such as a terminal control unit. An intelligent VDU may also have the facilities to perform editing and formatting functions. Most VDU's are interactive; they can both send and receive. One without a keyboard that can only receive is termed a 'monitor' or 'passive VDU'. Standard line lengths are 80 and 132 characters and most can display either 12 or 24 lines at a time. Common interfaces are V.24 and current loop. See *video; cathode ray tube; graphics VDU; display; raster; scan; monitor*.

visual record computer A visible record computer.

VLSI *Very Large Scale Integration*. An identifier of an integrated circuit with more than about 1000 gates per chip. See *LSI; MSI; SSI; SLSI*.

VM (1) *Virtual Memory*. **(2)** *Virtual Machine*.

VMOS *V-groove Metal Oxide Silicon*. A term applied to a planar transistor technology in which a groove is incised in the area between source and drain and gate metalisation is extended through the groove. The purpose is to lengthen the effective electron path (without increasing the size of the device) and to extend the area of gate control in order to increase current-carrying capacity and operating voltage. See *field effect transistor*.

voice-actuated device A voice-operated device.

voice adapter A piece of equipment associated with a modem to permit selectively switching a leased telephone line between data and voice communications.

voice coil A linear motor; a device that converts an electrical input into linear movement. See *seek*.

voice data entry (VDE) The facilities or operation involved in converting the human voice directly into a form suitable for computer input. The operation, typically, consists of the person speaking the required vocabulary one word at a time into the control unit which digitises the words and assigns their relevant encoded characters (say, in ASCII). When data is to be entered, the spoken words are digitised in real time and compared with those held in storage to find the correct match or 'best fit'. The data in character format may then be entered directly or displayed for the speaker's verification prior to entry. The input of 'training' words permits the system to adapt to different accents; each user begins an entry with a number that identifies his file of stored words. Applications have included the receipt of telephoned orders from salesmen and data entry and control by operators in environments where the use of a keyboard would be difficult or impossible.

voice-data terminal A terminal with facilities for both voice and data communications; for example, a pushbutton telephone used in multifrequency signalling or, possibly, a terminal-modem combination in which the modem has an associated telephone and facilities to change from voice to data.

voice-frequency telegraph A telegraph system that uses the voice-grade lines of a telephone system. By use of frequency division multiplexing, up to 20 telegraph channels can be derived from a single voice-grade channel.

voice-grade A term applied to a telephone line with sufficient bandwidth to carry speech (about 3000 Hz.). See *group; subvoice-grade.*

voice-operated device In a telephone system; a device (echo suppressor; compandor) with operation initiated or controlled by the presence or level of signals representing voice or data.

voice recognition A machine facility or operation involved in recognising spoken words and converting them to a form that can be used for storage and manipulation.

voice response terminal An audio response terminal.

voice unit (VU) A unit of measurement of signal level on a telephone line relative to 0 VU which corresponds to the level produced by a 1 millivolt sine wave into a 600 ohm resistive load. Acceptable levels are about —10 VU to —50 VU.

void In optical character recognition; a place in a character where ink should be present but is not.

volatile (1)Subject to frequent or unpredictable change. (2)A term applied to a memory that requires a continuous electrical input in order to retain stored data (data is lost if the electric power is interrupted). Though the term usually denotes a semiconductor type, it can also be applied to CCD and delay line. See *static; dynamic.*

volatility protection The provision of a standby power source (battery) to prevent loss of data when the power supply to volatile storage is interrupted.

volt (V.) The standard unit of electromotive force; it is that difference of potential (energy level of electrons) that will cause a current of one ampere to flow through a resistance of one ohm. See *electricity.*

voltage (V.) The number of 'volts' that are applied or measured at some point in an electrical circuit, or at which a particular circuit or device is intended to operate.

voltage to frequency converter (VFC) An electronic device (usually an integrated circuit) that performs periodic sampling of an input voltage and produces pulses of a frequency proportional to the voltage. When the output is sent to a counter that counts pulses for a measured period, it performs analogue to digital conversion.

volume A physical unit of (magnetisable-surface) backing storage; for example, a reel of magnetic tape, a disc pack, a data module, or a digital cassette. The term may also be applied to a drum or fixed disc; it is not usually applied to a magnetic card or other magnetic-stripe medium.

volume serial number (VSN) A number by which a particular volume is identified for access and storage.

volume table of contents (VTOC) Also, often, *file index.* On a magnetic disc volume; a table that contains access-related data on all files on the volume.

von Neuman machine A computer constructed according to the proposals made by John von Neuman in a 1946 paper entitled *Preliminary Discussion of the Logical Design of an Electronic Computing Instrument.* Such a machine became the standard general-purpose computer; it is characterised by the use of stored programs, separation of code and data in storage, an automatically incremented program counter, and provision for modifying instructions during execution.

VRC *Visible Record Computer.*

VS *Virtual Storage.*

VSI *Virtual Storage Interrupt.*

VSI rate The number of virtual storage interrupts that occur per unit time or, possibly, per specified number of instructions executed. See *virtual storage interrupt; thrashing.*

VSN *Volume Serial Number.*

VT *Vertical Tabulate.* A format effector that actuates a vertical format unit (or other device) to cause a printer to make a paper throw to a preset, lower position.

VTOC *Volume Table Of Contents.*

VU *Voice Unit.*

W

W (1)*Write.* (2)(W.) *Watts.*

WADS *Wide Area Data Service.* In the U.S.; a service of AT&T that permits subscribers to make unlimited dial-up use of telegraph-grade circuits within a particular geographical area for a fixed monthly fee. See *WATS.*

wafer A thin, polished piece of silicon, say 0.01 in. thick and 2 in. in diameter, that is the input material for the manufacture of semiconductors. It is the unit on which photolithography and etching are performed to produce a number of smaller units that, when sliced from the wafer, are termed 'chips'. See *chip; semiconductor.*

waiting line A queue.

waiting list A list of the items in a queue.

waiting mode Waiting state.

waiting state (1) Of an active program in a multiprogramming system; the condition in which its instructions are not being executed (because the instructions of another program are being executed). **(2)**The condition of a functional unit that is in the operating state but without inputs.

waiting time (1) The time (or percentage of total time) when a program or functional unit is in the 'waiting state'. **(2)**The time that elapses between the initiation of an operation and the beginning of its performance. **(3)**Latency.

wand A hand-held detector (magnetic transducer; light source and photodiode) as used at point-of-sale terminals to read bar codes or magnetic stripes for computer input.

warm (1) Of an electronic circuit or device; at normal operating temperature. **(2)**Of a computer; with some or all system software present in main storage. (Used in compound terms.)

warm boot A term applied to the steps necessary to place a computer in fully operational status; it, typically, consists of loading the operating system. See *cold boot.*

warm restart An automatic restart. See *restart.*

WATS *Wide Area Telephone Service.* In the U.S.; a service of AT&T that permits subscribers to make an unlimited number of telephone calls within a particular geographical area for a fixed monthly fee. See *WADS.*

watt (W.) The standard unit of measuring and expressing the use of electricity; the measure of electrical power. It is equal to volts multiplied by amps; for example, a load of 2 amps in a 200 volt circuit consumes 200 watts.

wave A repeated variation in voltage, sound, light, or other physical condition that is capable of transferring energy between two points. See *sine wave; carrier wave; modulation; sideband.*

waveform The shape of a wave as traced by an oscilloscope or plotted; a visible representation of its different conditions.

WCS *Writeable Control Storage.*

web Printing paper (sometimes paper tape) supplied in a continuous roll.

weight Also *positional value.* In obtaining the total value of a number or digit string; a value by which a particular digit is multiplied depending upon its position in the number or string. For example, in the decimal number 346, the 3 has a weight of 100, the 4 a weight of 10 and the 6 a weight of 1. In a positional representation system (decimal; binary), weights of digits in adjacent positions differ by the amount of the radix of the system. In some systems (for example, in calculating check digits), the weights are arbitrary and not necessarily progressive between digit positions. The first digit of a 3-digit string might, for example, have a weight of 3, the second of 9 and the third of 6. See *numeration system; check digit.*

weighting A value by which a digit is to be multiplied.

weighting factor Also, sometimes, *scale factor.* A constant used as a multiplier to bring numeric data into some particular range.

wet cell See *battery.*

wideband See *broadband; band; multiplexing.*

whetstone A unit of computer throughput.

white noise Noise without a distinctive frequency pattern. See *noise.*

wideband Also *broadband.* **(1)**A continuous range of frequencies that is large enough to be divided into multiple, narrower bands for some purpose. See *band.* **(2)**A teleuommunications channel, typically, 48 kHz. wide, that is leased to a user to provide high-speed (48-56 bits per second) data communications. See *group.*

Winchester technology A term (taken from the name of an IBM project) that denotes a type of magnetic disc unit. Such a unit has one or more fixed discs, heads that land and take off on the disc surface, track-following servo, and a special enclosure and air filtering system to keep out dust. See *magnetic disc unit.*

window (1)A period that has time significance for the occurrence of some event or a period in which an event must occur if it is to be considered significant. For example, in a virtual storage system, a period (possibly number of instructions) in which a particular page or segment must be referenced in order for it to be retained as a member of an active set. **(2)**In computer graphics, an area around which a frame has been placed by keyboard control, typically, to select part of a display image for enlargement. See *scissoring; zoom.*

windowing In computer graphics; the operation or facility involved in using 'windows' or the act of placing a window around a particular portion of a display image.

wire (1) A non-rigid electrical conductor, typically, of copper with an insulating coating. (2) To electrically join components with 'wires', as in constructing an electronic device. (3) A needle or stylus; a dot-forming element of a matrix printer. (4) A telegram. (5) To send by telegram.

wire printer A matrix printer.

wire storage Plated wire memory.

wire wrap A common method of making wire connections in the manufacture of electrical and electronic equipment. The method involves using a special tool to form stripped solid-conductor wire (the end of a wire to be connected) into a coil and pressing the coil over a sharp-edged pin terminal.

wired (1) With direct electrical connection (say, by a wire or printed circuit board conductor). (2) Hardwired; performed by electronic circuits rather than by software.

wired OR A term applied to an OR circuit in which inputs are directly connected to the output without reverse current protection on the input lines. Such a circuit is shown on the left

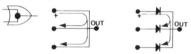

while that on the right is the more usual OR circuit with fan-in diodes to prevent a voltage on one input line from travelling back along the others (as indicated by the small arrowheads).

word (1) Also *computer word*. A fixed number of bits (commonly 16, 24, or 32) that the computer has hardware facilities to transfer and manipulate as a unit within storage and the central processor. For example, a computer with a 32-bit word has main storage locations and registers that are 32 bits in length and has data buses to transfer 32 bits at a time in parallel. The length of the word is the basic design parameter of most computers. The term may be applied to a physical storage location or to a unit of code or data that occupies such a location. See *byte*. (2) A character string that has significance as a unit in some (programming or natural) language.

word boundary In coordinate-addressable storage; the location of the beginning or end of a 'word'; a location to which a bit pattern held in a 'word' must be aligned. See *justify; aligned; synchronised*.

word-count word A word in a record header that contains a count of the words in the record.

word length The number of bits (possibly bytes or characters) in a 'word'.

word machine A term sometimes applied to a computer in which the word is the only unit for which hardware transfer and manipulation facilities are provided. (Such a machine, typically, has poor performance when required to handle characters or bytes individually.) See *byte machine; character-oriented machine*.

word-organised A term applied to a computer or to a unit of coordinate-addressable storage in which the 'word' is the standard (or only) addressable unit.

word processing The use of intelligent devices to assist in the preparation of typewritten or short-run printed documents. Typically, a **word processor** is an electric typewriter with a memory that stores text input via the keyboard and that has programs in read-only memory to assist the operator in locating and recalling particular items and in making insertions and deletions. It may also have facilities for margin justification and/or for typing the same letter with individual addressing. In many systems, a VDU is provided to display copy input via the keyboard so that the operator can check it and make any corrections before it is typed or placed in memory. There are many variations in facilities and equipment; in some, the equipment is free-standing and used by a single operator while, in others, central intelligence and printing facilities support a number of operator work stations. Word processing facilities may also be provided by software packages for minicomputers.

word synchronised With bit patterns aligned to word boundaries. See *synchronised*.

word time The time required for bit-serial transfer of a word.

word wrap-around A text editing facility for input at a VDU; if an operator enters a word that crosses a set margin (or would extend beyond maximum line length for the device), the part that would otherwise be truncated is deleted and the entire word is written to the following line. For example:

    This is a line as entered and as 'corrected' to illustrate
    word wrap-around.

    This is a line as entered and as 'corrected' to
    illustrate word wrap-around.

work area A unit of main storage that is allocated to a program for such purposes as buffering, holding partial results, and assembling outputs.

work file (1) A scratch file; a unit of magnetic disc or magnetic tape storage allocated to a program or job for the duration of a run. **(2)** An intermediate file used to hold data between phases of a sort.

work queue A job queue.

work station A VDU terminal at which a certain type of (business-related) work is performed; for example, order entry or invoicing. Unless otherwise indicated, it is assumed to be a local terminal rather than a remote terminal.

work unit A number of executed instructions that is standard for some evaluation or comparison purpose.

work volume A volume that is used for work files.

working area A work area.

working set In a virtual storage system; the pages/segments that contain all the code and data required by a process during a particular phase of execution. See *virtual storage system—processing units; working set policy*.

working set policy A method of managing the real storage of a virtual storage system by which the operating system uses one or more algorithms to attempt to determine which of the pages/segments in primary storage are still required by some process and which can be deleted or, when all are required, which can be deleted without degrading processing or interrupting processing of high priority. A system in which a working set policy is used may be termed 'Class W'. See *discard policy; virtual storage partitioning*.

working space Space available to a program in a work area or work file.

working storage A work area and/or a work file.

workstation A work station.

WP (1) *Word Processing.* **(2)** *Write Permit.*

WPM (wpm.) *Words Per Minute.*

WPR *Write Permit Ring.*

wrap-around A facility of a full-screen text editor that will accept any input that exceeds set column width or device line length and write the part that would otherwise be truncated to the next line. Unless the editor also has 'word wrap-around', words at the ends of lines will be randomly broken. See *word wrap-around*.

write (1) To place data in a particular type or location of computer storage; ('write a file to disc'; 'write a word to a buffer'; 'write a block to main storage') **(2)** To cause a data-significant change to a storage medium; ('write a sequence to PROM'; 'write a bit pattern to a track'). **(3)** To produce source coding; ('write a program'; 'write a compiler').

write cycle A sequence of steps performed to write data.

write cycle time The minimum time interval between two successive write operations. (Particularly where read cycles and write cycles are of different length.)

write enable A signal that must be 'true' before a write operation (to magnetic disc or tape) can be performed.

write-enable ring A write-permit ring.

write head An electromagnetic element used to record data on a magnetisable surface medium. See *head*.

write inhibit A term applied to a signal or device that prevents writing. See *write enable; file protect*.

write mode Of a circuit or device; the condition in which writing is being performed or in which it can be performed.

write operation The process of placing a unit of data in storage.

write out With respect to data in main storage; to copy it to backing storage. See *read in*.

write-permit ring Also *write-enable ring; protection ring; file-protect ring*. A plastic ring that must be in place on the hub of a magnetic tape reel before it can be written to or erased.

write-protect A term applied to a circuit, device, or procedure that prevents data from being accidentally overwritten. See *file protect*.

writeable control store (WCS) Microcode storage that can be written to by a user, thus permitting a computer to be customised for most efficient handling of a particular type of work.

X

X With respect to microfilm; an indicator of the amount of reduction. See *reduction*.

X.3 A CCITT Recommendation concerning the packet assembly/disassembly (PAD) facilities of a packet switching network.

X.25 A CCITT Recommendation relating to the interface between a packet switching network and a packet-mode DTE (a computer). It describes the interface on three levels: Level 1 deals with the circuit interface between a DTE and a DCE; it is currently the same as that of CCITT V.24. Level 2 deals with the 'frames' in which packets are sent. It defines the beginning and ending flags, an error-detection frame check sequence (FCS) and the method of sequencing frames. Level 3 deals with the 'packet-level' interface. It covers setting up and clearing virtual circuits, error conditions and interrupts, and packet sequencing.

X.28 A CCITT Recommendation relating to the interface between the PAD facilities of a packet switching network and a start-stop (asynchronous) terminal.

X.29 A CCITT Recommendation relating to the interface between the PAD facilities of a packet switching network and a packet-mode DTE.

xerographic printer An electrostatic printer.

XOR *eXclusive OR*.

XS3 *eXcesS-3*.

Xtal Crystal.

XY plotter A flatbed plotter; a plotter in which the stylus is controlled in two dimensions of movement.

Y

yield In the manufacture of semiconductor devices; the percentage of good devices produced of a particular kind or in a batch in relation to the number of chips on which processing was begun.

Z

Z The symbol for 'impedance'.

Z80 A common (Zilog) 8-bit microprocessor.

Z8001 A Zilog 16-bit microprocessor.

zener diode A diode that is designed to conduct current in the reverse direction when a voltage over a certain value is applied in that direction. They are used for pulse trimming, transient suppression, and voltage regulation in circuits such as the one illustrated. In this circuit, the 50 V. zener diode keeps the voltage across the neon light at a constant 50 V. though the supply voltage fluctuates between 60 V. and 100 V.

zero (1) The binary or decimal digit represented by '0'; it indicates the absence of a numeric value in a digit position or a 'false' input or result of a logic operation. **(2)** To zeroise.

zero-address instruction An instruction that contains no address part; an instruction that does not identify an operand.

zero bit (0-bit) A storage and transfer unit that represents 'binary 0'. See *binary; space; one bit*.

zero-constant A logic operation with an output that is zero ('false') for every input. See *one-constant*.

zero crossing The point in a circuit transition when the voltage passes through zero; the point at which the voltage changes from positive to negative or the reverse.

zero deletion See *zero insertion*.

zero fill Zerofill.

zero insertion Bit stuffing; the operation of inserting 0-bits in strings of 1-bits to prevent any groups in the user data stream from being interpreted as flags (or, possibly, control characters). See *bit stuffing*.

zero insertion force (ZIF) A designation of a socket for DIL integrated circuit devices in which a cam action is incorporated to permit a device to be inserted or removed without applying pressure to the in-line pins. (The socket solders to a printed circuit board.)

zero-level address A literal.

zero suppression The editing operation of eliminating zeros that have no significance from numbers before they are displayed or printed; for example, to change 001.95000 to 1.95. The term may also be applied to an operation in which another character is substituted for some or all non-significant zeros; for example, to one in which 001.95000 is changed to **1.95. See *truncation; cheque protection*.

zero-suppression character A character that may be substituted for suppressed zeros; for example, a 'Z', a 'Y', or an '*'.

zerofill Also, sometimes, *pad; zeroise*. To write the bit pattern for 'zero' (in the code used in the system) in all or part of the character positions in a storage location in order to delete other bit patterns. See *characterfill; pad*.

zeroise (1) Also, often, *erase*. To write 0-bits in all bit positions of a storage location, thus overwriting any 1-bits that may have been held in the location. **(2)** To zerofill; to overwrite data with zero characters. **(3)** With respect to a counter; to set it so that the zero digit appears in all digit positions. **(4)** With respect to a voltmeter or similar device; to adjust it (mechanically or by changing circuit values) so that it indicates 'zero' in absence of input or with a certain specified input.

ZIF *Zero Insertion Force.*

zone (1) A term applied to a range of locations with collective significance for some purpose. **(2)** Also *frequency zone.* In some magnetic disc systems; a group of adjacent tracks that have the same storage capacity; a band in which the surface is divided to allow for the fact that tracks nearer the spindle are shorter than those near the periphery.

zone punch With respect to a punched card; a punch in row 11, 12, or 0. See *digit punch.*

zone quartet The most significant (leftmost) quartet in an 8-bit byte.

zoned decimal External decimal.

zoom In computer graphics; to change the size of all or part of the elements of a display; unless otherwise indicated, enlargement is assumed. See *window.*

HEXADECIMAL – DECIMAL – OCTAL CONVERSIONS

	0	1	2	3	4	5	6	7	8	9	A	B	C	D	E	F
000 -	0000 0000	0001 0001	0002 0002	0003 0003	0004 0004	0005 0005	0006 0006	0007 0007	0008 0010	0009 0011	0010 0012	0011 0013	0012 0014	0013 0015	0014 0016	0015 0017
001 -	0016 0020	0017 0021	0018 0022	0019 0023	0020 0024	0021 0025	0022 0026	0023 0027	0024 0030	0025 0031	0026 0032	0027 0033	0028 0034	0029 0035	0030 0036	0031 0037
002 -	0032 0040	0033 0041	0034 0042	0035 0043	0036 0044	0037 0045	0038 0046	0039 0047	0040 0050	0041 0051	0042 0052	0043 0053	0044 0054	0045 0055	0046 0056	0047 0057
003 -	0048 0060	0049 0061	0050 0062	0051 0063	0052 0064	0053 0065	0054 0066	0055 0067	0056 0070	0057 0071	0058 0072	0059 0073	0060 0074	0061 0075	0062 0076	0063 0077
004 -	0064 0100	0065 0101	0066 0102	0067 0103	0068 0104	0069 0105	0070 0106	0071 0107	0072 0110	0073 0111	0074 0112	0075 0113	0076 0114	0077 0115	0078 0116	0079 0117
005 -	0080 0120	0081 0121	0082 0122	0083 0123	0084 0124	0085 0125	0086 0126	0087 0127	0088 0130	0089 0131	0090 0132	0091 0133	0092 0134	0093 0135	0094 0136	0095 0137
006 -	0096 0140	0097 0141	0098 0142	0099 0143	0100 0144	0101 0145	0102 0146	0103 0147	0104 0150	0105 0151	0106 0152	0107 0153	0108 0154	0109 0155	0110 0156	0111 0157
007 -	0112 0160	0113 0161	0114 0162	0115 0163	0116 0164	0117 0165	0118 0166	0119 0167	0120 0170	0121 0171	0122 0172	0123 0173	0124 0174	0125 0175	0126 0176	0127 0177
008 -	0128 0200	0129 0201	0130 0202	0131 0203	0132 0204	0133 0205	0134 0206	0135 0207	0136 0210	0137 0211	0138 0212	0139 0213	0140 0214	0141 0215	0142 0216	0143 0217
009 -	0144 0220	0145 0221	0146 0222	0147 0223	0148 0224	0149 0225	0150 0226	0151 0227	0152 0230	0153 0231	0154 0232	0155 0233	0156 0234	0157 0235	0158 0236	0159 0237
00A -	0160 0240	0161 0241	0162 0242	0163 0243	0164 0244	0165 0245	0166 0246	0167 0247	0168 0250	0169 0251	0170 0252	0171 0253	0172 0254	0173 0255	0114 0256	0115 0257
00B -	0176 0260	0177 0261	0178 0262	0179 0263	0180 0264	0181 0265	0182 0266	0183 0267	0184 0270	0185 0271	0186 0272	0187 0273	0188 0274	0189 0275	0190 0276	0191 0277
00C -	0192 0300	0193 0301	0194 0302	0195 0303	0196 0304	0197 0305	0198 0306	0199 0307	0200 0310	0201 0311	0202 0312	0203 0313	0204 0314	0205 0315	0206 0316	0207 0317
00D -	0208 0320	0209 0321	0210 0322	0211 0323	0212 0324	0213 0325	0214 0326	0215 0327	0216 0330	0217 0331	0218 0332	0219 0333	0220 0334	0221 0335	0222 0336	0223 0337
00E -	0224 0340	0225 0341	0226 0342	0227 0343	0228 0344	0229 0345	0230 0346	0231 0347	0232 0350	0233 0351	0234 0352	0235 0353	0236 0354	0237 0355	0238 0356	0239 0357
00F -	0240 0360	0241 0361	0242 0362	0243 0363	0244 0364	0245 0365	0246 0366	0247 0367	0248 0370	0249 0371	0250 0372	0251 0373	0252 0374	0253 0375	0254 0376	0255 0377
010 -	0256 0400	0257 0401	0258 0402	0259 0403	0260 0404	0261 0405	0262 0406	0263 0407	0264 0410	0265 0411	0266 0412	0267 0413	0268 0414	0269 0415	0270 0416	0271 0417
011 -	0272 0420	0273 0421	0274 0422	0275 0423	0276 0424	0277 0425	0278 0426	0279 0427	0280 0430	0281 0431	0282 0432	0283 0433	0284 0434	0285 0435	0286 0436	0287 0437
012 -	0288 0440	0289 0441	0290 0442	0291 0443	0292 0444	0293 0445	0294 0446	0295 0447	0296 0450	0297 0451	0298 0452	0299 0453	0300 0454	0301 0455	0302 0456	0303 0457
013 -	0304 0460	0305 0461	0306 0462	0307 0463	0308 0464	0309 0465	0310 0466	0311 0467	0312 0470	0313 0471	0314 0472	0315 0473	0316 0474	0317 0475	0318 0476	0319 0477
014 -	0320 0500	0321 0501	0322 0502	0323 0503	0324 0504	0325 0505	0326 0506	0327 0507	0328 0510	0329 0511	0330 0512	0331 0513	0332 0514	0333 0515	0334 0516	0335 0517
015 -	0336 0520	0337 0521	0338 0522	0339 0523	0340 0524	0341 0525	0342 0526	0343 0527	0344 0530	0345 0531	0346 0532	0347 0533	0348 0534	0349 0535	0350 0536	0351 0537
016 -	0352 0540	0353 0541	0354 0542	0355 0543	0356 0544	0357 0545	0358 0546	0359 0547	0360 0550	0361 0551	0362 0552	0363 0553	0364 0554	0365 0555	0366 0556	0367 0557
017 -	0368 0560	0369 0561	0370 0562	0371 0563	0372 0564	0373 0565	0374 0566	0375 0567	0376 0570	0377 0571	0378 0572	0379 0573	0380 0574	0381 0575	0382 0576	0383 0577
018 -	0384 0600	0385 0601	0386 0602	0387 0603	0388 0604	0389 0605	0390 0606	0391 0607	0392 0610	0393 0611	0394 0612	0395 0613	0396 0614	0397 0615	0398 0616	0399 0617
019 -	0400 0620	0401 0621	0402 0622	0403 0623	0404 0624	0405 0625	0406 0626	0407 0627	0408 0630	0409 0631	0410 0632	0411 0633	0412 0634	0413 0635	0414 0636	0415 0637
01A -	0416 0640	0417 0641	0418 0642	0419 0643	0420 0644	0421 0645	0422 0646	0423 0647	0424 0650	0425 0651	0426 0652	0427 0653	0428 0654	0429 0655	0430 0656	0431 0657
01B -	0432 0660	0433 0661	0434 0662	0435 0663	0436 0664	0437 0665	0438 0666	0439 0667	0440 0670	0441 0671	0442 0672	0443 0673	0444 0674	0445 0675	0446 0676	0447 0677
01C -	0448 0700	0449 0701	0450 0702	0451 0703	0452 0704	0453 0705	0454 0706	0455 0707	0456 0710	0457 0711	0458 0712	0459 0713	0460 0714	0461 0715	0462 0716	0463 0717
01D -	0464 0720	0465 0721	0466 0722	0467 0723	0468 0724	0469 0725	0470 0726	0471 0727	0472 0730	0473 0731	0474 0732	0475 0733	0476 0734	0477 0735	0478 0736	0479 0737
01E -	0480 0740	0481 0741	0482 0742	0483 0743	0484 0744	0485 0745	0486 0746	0487 0747	0488 0750	0489 0751	0490 0752	0491 0753	0492 0754	0493 0755	0494 0756	0495 0757
01F -	0496 0760	0497 0761	0498 0762	0499 0763	0500 0764	0501 0765	0502 0766	0503 0767	0504 0770	0505 0771	0506 0772	0507 0773	0508 0774	0509 0775	0510 0776	0511 0777
020 -	0512 1000	0513 1001	0514 1002	0515 1003	0516 1004	0517 1005	0518 1006	0519 1007	0520 1010	0521 1011	0522 1012	0523 1013	0524 1014	0525 1015	0526 1016	0527 1017
021 -	0528 1020	0529 1021	0530 1022	0531 1023	0532 1024	0533 1025	0534 1026	0535 1027	0536 1030	0537 1031	0538 1032	0539 1033	0540 1034	0541 1035	0542 1036	0543 1037
022 -	0544 1040	0545 1041	0546 1042	0547 1043	0548 1044	0549 1045	0550 1046	0551 1047	0552 1050	0553 1051	0554 1052	0555 1053	0556 1054	0557 1055	0558 1056	0559 1057
023 -	0560 1060	0561 1061	0562 1062	0563 1063	0564 1064	0565 1065	0566 1066	0567 1067	0568 1070	0569 1071	0570 1072	0571 1073	0572 1074	0573 1075	0574 1076	0575 1077
024 -	0576 1100	0577 1101	0578 1102	0579 1103	0580 1104	0581 1105	0582 1106	0583 1107	0584 1110	0585 1111	0586 1112	0587 1113	0588 1114	0589 1115	0590 1116	0591 1117
025 -	0592 1120	0593 1121	0594 1122	0595 1123	0596 1124	0597 1125	0598 1126	0599 1127	0600 1130	0601 1131	0602 1132	0603 1133	0604 1134	0605 1135	0606 1136	0607 1137
026 -	0608 1140	0609 1141	0610 1142	0611 1143	0612 1144	0613 1145	0614 1146	0615 1147	0616 1150	0617 1151	0618 1152	0619 1153	0620 1154	0621 1155	0622 1156	0623 1157
027 -	0624 1160	0625 1161	0626 1162	0627 1163	0628 1164	0629 1165	0630 1166	0631 1167	0632 1170	0633 1171	0634 1172	0635 1173	0636 1174	0637 1175	0638 1176	0639 1177
028 -	0640 1200	0641 1201	0642 1202	0643 1203	0644 1204	0645 1205	0646 1206	0647 1207	0648 1210	0649 1211	0650 1212	0651 1213	0652 1214	0653 1215	0654 1216	0655 1217
029 -	0656 1220	0657 1221	0658 1222	0659 1223	0660 1224	0661 1225	0662 1226	0663 1227	0664 1230	0665 1231	0666 1232	0667 1233	0668 1234	0669 1235	0670 1236	0671 1237
02A -	0672 1240	0673 1241	0674 1242	0675 1243	0676 1244	0677 1245	0678 1246	0679 1247	0680 1250	0681 1251	0682 1252	0683 1253	0684 1254	0685 1255	0686 1256	0687 1257
02B -	0688 1260	0689 1261	0690 1262	0691 1263	0692 1264	0693 1265	0694 1266	0695 1267	0696 1270	0697 1271	0698 1272	0699 1273	0700 1274	0701 1275	0702 1276	0703 1277
02C -	0704 1300	0705 1301	0706 1302	0707 1303	0708 1304	0709 1305	0710 1306	0711 1307	0712 1310	0713 1311	0714 1312	0715 1313	0716 1314	0717 1315	0718 1316	0719 1317
02D -	0720 1320	0721 1321	0722 1322	0723 1323	0724 1324	0725 1325	0726 1326	0727 1327	0728 1330	0729 1331	0730 1332	0731 1333	0732 1334	0733 1335	0734 1336	0735 1337
02E -	0736 1340	0737 1341	0738 1342	0739 1343	0740 1344	0741 1345	0742 1346	0743 1347	0744 1350	0745 1351	0746 1352	0747 1353	0748 1354	0749 1355	0750 1356	0751 1357
02F -	0752 1360	0753 1361	0754 1362	0755 1363	0756 1364	0757 1365	0758 1366	0759 1367	0760 1370	0761 1371	0762 1372	0763 1373	0764 1374	0765 1375	0766 1376	0767 1377
030 -	0768 1400	0769 1401	0770 1402	0771 1403	0772 1404	0773 1405	0774 1406	0775 1407	0776 1410	0777 1411	0778 1412	0779 1413	0780 1414	0781 1415	0782 1416	0783 1417
031 -	0784 1420	0785 1421	0786 1422	0787 1423	0788 1424	0789 1425	0790 1426	0791 1427	0792 1430	0793 1431	0794 1432	0795 1433	0796 1434	0797 1435	0798 1436	0799 1437
032 -	0800 1440	0801 1441	0802 1442	0803 1443	0804 1444	0805 1445	0806 1446	0807 1447	0808 1450	0809 1451	0810 1452	0811 1453	0812 1454	0813 1455	0814 1456	0815 1457
033 -	0816 1460	0817 1461	0818 1462	0819 1463	0820 1464	0821 1465	0822 1466	0823 1467	0824 1470	0825 1471	0826 1472	0827 1473	0828 1474	0829 1475	0830 1476	0831 1477
034 -	0832 1500	0833 1501	0834 1502	0835 1503	0836 1504	0837 1505	0838 1506	0839 1507	0840 1510	0841 1511	0842 1512	0843 1513	0844 1514	0845 1515	0846 1516	0847 1517
035 -	0848 1520	0849 1521	0850 1522	0851 1523	0852 1524	0853 1525	0854 1526	0855 1527	0856 1530	0857 1531	0858 1532	0859 1533	0860 1534	0861 1535	0862 1536	0863 1537
036 -	0864 1540	0865 1541	0866 1542	0867 1543	0868 1544	0869 1545	0870 1546	0871 1547	0872 1550	0873 1551	0874 1552	0875 1553	0876 1554	0877 1555	0878 1556	0879 1557
037 -	0880 1560	0881 1561	0882 1562	0883 1563	0884 1564	0885 1565	0886 1566	0887 1567	0888 1570	0889 1571	0890 1572	0891 1573	0892 1574	0893 1575	0894 1576	0895 1577
038 -	0896 1600	0897 1601	0898 1602	0899 1603	0900 1604	0901 1605	0902 1606	0903 1607	0904 1610	0905 1611	0906 1612	0907 1613	0908 1614	0909 1615	0910 1616	0911 1617
039 -	0912 1620	0913 1621	0914 1622	0915 1623	0916 1624	0917 1625	0918 1626	0919 1627	0920 1630	0921 1631	0922 1632	0923 1633	0924 1634	0925 1635	0926 1636	0927 1637
03A -	0928 1640	0929 1641	0930 1642	0931 1643	0932 1644	0933 1645	0934 1646	0935 1647	0936 1650	0937 1651	0938 1652	0939 1653	0940 1654	0941 1655	0942 1656	0943 1657
03B -	0944 1660	0945 1661	0946 1662	0947 1663	0948 1664	0949 1665	0950 1666	0951 1667	0952 1670	0953 1671	0954 1672	0955 1673	0956 1674	0957 1675	0958 1676	0959 1677
03C -	0960 1700	0961 1701	0962 1702	0963 1703	0964 1704	0965 1705	0966 1706	0967 1707	0968 1710	0969 1711	0970 1712	0971 1713	0972 1714	0973 1715	0974 1716	0975 1717
03D -	0976 1720	0977 1721	0978 1722	0979 1723	0980 1724	0981 1725	0982 1726	0983 1727	0984 1730	0985 1731	0986 1732	0987 1733	0988 1734	0989 1735	0990 1736	0991 1737
03E -	0992 1740	0993 1741	0994 1742	0995 1743	0996 1744	0997 1745	0998 1746	0999 1747	1000 1750	1001 1751	1002 1752	1003 1753	1004 1754	1005 1755	1006 1756	1007 1757
03F -	1008 1760	1009 1761	1010 1762	1011 1763	1012 1764	1013 1765	1014 1766	1015 1767	1016 1770	1017 1771	1018 1772	1019 1773	1020 1774	1021 1775	1022 1776	1023 1777

HEXADECIMAL – DECIMAL – OCTAL CONVERSIONS

	0	1	2	3	4	5	6	7	8	9	A	B	C	D	E	F
040 –	1024 2000	1025 2001	1026 2002	1027 2003	1028 2004	1029 2005	1030 2006	1031 2007	1032 2010	1033 2011	1034 2012	1035 2013	1036 2014	1037 2015	1038 2016	1039 2017
041 –	1040 2020	1041 2021	1042 2022	1043 2023	1044 2024	1045 2025	1046 2026	1047 2027	1048 2030	1049 2031	1050 2032	1051 2033	1052 2034	1053 2035	1054 2036	1055 2037
042 –	1056 2040	1057 2041	1058 2042	1059 2043	1060 2044	1061 2045	1062 2046	1063 2047	1064 2050	1065 2051	1066 2052	1067 2053	1068 2054	1069 2055	1070 2056	1071 2057
043 –	1072 2060	1073 2061	1074 2062	1075 2063	1076 2064	1077 2065	1078 2066	1079 2067	1080 2070	1081 2071	1082 2072	1083 2073	1084 2074	1085 2075	1086 2076	1087 2077
044 –	1088 2100	1089 2101	1090 2102	1091 2103	1092 2104	1093 2105	1094 2106	1095 2107	1096 2110	1097 2111	1098 2112	1099 2113	1100 2114	1101 2115	1102 2116	1103 2117
045 –	1104 2120	1105 2121	1106 2122	1107 2123	1108 2124	1109 2125	1110 2126	1111 2127	1112 2130	1113 2131	1114 2132	1115 2133	1116 2134	1117 2135	1118 2136	1119 2137
046 –	1120 2140	1121 2141	1122 2142	1123 2143	1124 2144	1125 2145	1126 2146	1127 2147	1128 2150	1129 2151	1130 2152	1131 2153	1132 2154	1133 2155	1134 2156	1135 2157
047 –	1136 2160	1137 2161	1138 2162	1139 2163	1140 2164	1141 2165	1142 2166	1143 2167	1144 2170	1145 2171	1146 2172	1147 2173	1148 2174	1149 2175	1150 2176	1151 2177
048 –	1152 2200	1153 2201	1154 2202	1155 2203	1156 2204	1157 2205	1158 2206	1159 2207	1160 2210	1161 2211	1162 2212	1163 2213	1164 2214	1165 2215	1166 2216	1167 2217
049 –	1168 2220	1169 2221	1170 2222	1171 2223	1172 2224	1173 2225	1174 2226	1175 2227	1176 2230	1177 2231	1178 2232	1179 2233	1180 2234	1181 2235	1182 2236	1183 2232
04A –	1184 2240	1185 2241	1186 2242	1187 2243	1188 2244	1189 2245	1190 2246	1191 2247	1192 2250	1193 2251	1194 2252	1195 2253	1196 2254	1197 2255	1198 2256	1199 2257
04B –	1200 2260	1201 2261	1202 2262	1203 2263	1204 2264	1205 2265	1206 2266	1207 2267	1208 2270	1209 2271	1210 2272	1211 2273	1212 2274	1213 2275	1214 2276	1215 2277
04C –	1216 2300	1217 2301	1218 2302	1219 2303	1220 2304	1221 2305	1222 2306	1223 2307	1224 2310	1225 2311	1226 2312	1227 2313	1228 2314	1229 2315	1230 2316	1231 2317
04D –	1232 2320	1233 2321	1234 2322	1235 2323	1236 2324	1237 2325	1238 2326	1239 2327	1240 2330	1241 2331	1242 2332	1243 2333	1244 2334	1245 2335	1246 2336	1247 2337
04E –	1248 2340	1249 2341	1250 2342	1251 2343	1252 2344	1253 2345	1254 2346	1255 2347	1256 2350	1257 2351	1258 2352	1259 2353	1260 2354	1261 2355	1262 2356	1263 2357
04F –	1264 2360	1265 2361	1266 2362	1267 2363	1268 2364	1269 2365	1270 2366	1271 2367	1272 2370	1273 2371	1274 2372	1275 2373	1276 2374	1277 2375	1278 2376	1279 2377
050 –	1280 2400	1281 2401	1282 2402	1283 2403	1284 2404	1285 2405	1286 2406	1287 2407	1288 2410	1289 2411	1290 2412	1291 2413	1292 2414	1293 2415	1294 2416	1295 2417
051 –	1296 2420	1297 2421	1298 2422	1299 2423	1300 2424	1301 2425	1302 2426	1303 2427	1304 2430	1305 2431	1306 2432	1307 2433	1308 2434	1309 2435	1310 2436	1311 2437
052 –	1312 2440	1313 2441	1314 2442	1315 2443	1316 2444	1317 2445	1318 2446	1319 2447	1320 2450	1321 2451	1322 2452	1323 2453	1324 2454	1325 2455	1326 2456	1327 2457
053 –	1328 2460	1329 2461	1330 2462	1331 2463	1332 2464	1333 2465	1334 2466	1335 2467	1336 2470	1337 2471	1338 2472	1339 2473	1340 2474	1341 2475	1342 2476	1343 2477
054 –	1344 2500	1345 2501	1346 2502	1347 2503	1348 2504	1349 2505	1350 2506	1351 2507	1352 2510	1353 2511	1354 2512	1355 2513	1356 2514	1357 2515	1358 2516	1359 2517
055 –	1360 2520	1361 2521	1362 2522	1363 2523	1364 2524	1365 2525	1366 2526	1367 2527	1368 2530	1369 2531	1370 2532	1371 2533	1372 2534	1373 2535	1374 2536	1375 2537
056 –	1376 2540	1377 2541	1378 2542	1379 2543	1380 2544	1381 2545	1382 2546	1383 2547	1384 2550	1385 2551	1386 2552	1387 2553	1388 2554	1389 2555	1390 2556	1391 2557
057 –	1392 2560	1393 2561	1394 2562	1395 2563	1396 2564	1397 2565	1398 2566	1399 2567	1400 2570	1401 2571	1402 2572	1403 2573	1404 2574	1405 2575	1406 2576	1407 2577
058 –	1408 2600	1409 2601	1410 2602	1411 2603	1412 2604	1413 2605	1414 2606	1415 2607	1416 2610	1417 2611	1418 2612	1419 2613	1420 2614	1421 2615	1422 2616	1423 2617
059 –	1424 2620	1425 2621	1426 2622	1427 2623	1428 2624	1429 2625	1430 2626	1431 2627	1432 2630	1433 2631	1434 2632	1435 2633	1436 2634	1437 2635	1438 2636	1439 2637
05A –	1440 2640	1441 2641	1442 2642	1443 2643	1444 2644	1445 2645	1446 2646	1447 2647	1448 2650	1449 2651	1450 2652	1451 2653	1452 2654	1453 2655	1454 2656	1455 2657
05B –	1456 2660	1457 2661	1458 2662	1459 2663	1460 2664	1461 2665	1462 2666	1463 2667	1464 2670	1465 2671	1466 2672	1467 2673	1468 2674	1469 2675	1470 2676	1471 2677
05C –	1472 2700	1473 2701	1474 2702	1475 2703	1476 2704	1477 2705	1478 2706	1479 2707	1480 2710	1481 2711	1482 2712	1483 2713	1484 2714	1485 2715	1486 2716	1487 2717
05D –	1488 2720	1489 2721	1490 2722	1491 2723	1492 2724	1493 2725	1494 2726	1495 2727	1496 2730	1497 2731	1498 2732	1499 2733	1500 2734	1501 2735	1502 2736	1503 2737
05E –	1504 2740	1505 2741	1506 2742	1507 2743	1508 2744	1509 2745	1510 2746	1511 2747	1512 2750	1513 2751	1514 2752	1515 2753	1516 2754	1517 2755	1518 2756	1519 2757
05F –	1520 2760	1521 2761	1522 2762	1523 2763	1524 2764	1525 2765	1526 2766	1527 2767	1528 2770	1529 2771	1530 2772	1531 2773	1532 2774	1533 2775	1534 2776	1535 2777
060 –	1536 3000	1537 3001	1538 3002	1539 3003	1540 3004	1541 3005	1542 3006	1543 3007	1544 3010	1545 3011	1546 3012	1547 3013	1548 3014	1549 3015	1550 3016	1551 3017
061 –	1552 3020	1553 3021	1554 3022	1555 3023	1556 3024	1557 3025	1558 3026	1559 3027	1560 3030	1561 3031	1562 3032	1563 3033	1564 3034	1565 3035	1566 3036	1567 3037
062 –	1568 3040	1569 3041	1570 3042	1571 3043	1572 3044	1573 3045	1574 3046	1575 3047	1576 3050	1577 3051	1578 3052	1579 3053	1580 3054	1581 3055	1582 3056	1583 3057
063 –	1584 3060	1585 3061	1586 3062	1587 3063	1588 3064	1589 3065	1590 3066	1591 3067	1592 3070	1593 3071	1594 3072	1595 3073	1596 3074	1597 3075	1598 3076	1599 3077
064 –	1600 3100	1601 3101	1602 3102	1603 3103	1604 3104	1605 3105	1606 3106	1607 3107	1608 3110	1609 3111	1610 3112	1611 3113	1612 3114	1613 3115	1614 3116	1615 3117
065 –	1616 3120	1617 3121	1618 3122	1619 3123	1620 3124	1621 3125	1622 3126	1623 3127	1624 3130	1625 3131	1626 3132	1627 3133	1628 3134	1629 3135	1630 3136	1631 3137
066 –	1632 3140	1633 3141	1634 3142	1635 3143	1636 3144	1637 3145	1638 3146	1639 3147	1640 3150	1641 3151	1642 3152	1643 3153	1644 3154	1645 3155	1646 3156	1647 3157
067 –	1648 3160	1649 3161	1650 3162	1651 3163	1652 3164	1653 3165	1654 3166	1655 3167	1656 3170	1657 3171	1658 3172	1659 3173	1660 3174	1661 3175	1662 3176	1663 3177
068 –	1664 3200	1665 3201	1666 3202	1667 3203	1668 3204	1669 3205	1670 3206	1671 3207	1672 3210	1673 3211	1674 3212	1675 3213	1676 3214	1677 3215	1678 3216	1679 3217
069 –	1680 3220	1681 3221	1682 3222	1683 3223	1684 3224	1685 3225	1686 3226	1687 3227	1688 3230	1689 3231	1690 3232	1691 3233	1692 3234	1693 3235	1694 3236	1695 3237
06A –	1696 3240	1697 3241	1698 3242	1699 3243	1700 3244	1701 3245	1702 3246	1703 3247	1704 3250	1705 3251	1706 3252	1707 3253	1708 3254	1709 3255	1710 3256	1711 3257
06B –	1712 3260	1713 3261	1714 3262	1715 3263	1716 3264	1717 3265	1718 3266	1719 3267	1720 3270	1721 3271	1722 3272	1723 3273	1724 3274	1725 3275	1726 3276	1727 3277
06C –	1728 3300	1729 3301	1730 3302	1731 3303	1732 3304	1733 3305	1734 3306	1735 3307	1736 3310	1737 3311	1738 3312	1739 3313	1740 3314	1741 3315	1742 3316	1743 3317
06D –	1744 3320	1745 3321	1746 3322	1747 3323	1748 3324	1749 3325	1750 3326	1751 3327	1752 3330	1753 3331	1754 3332	1755 3333	1756 3334	1757 3335	1758 3336	1759 3337
06E –	1760 3340	1761 3341	1762 3342	1763 3343	1764 3344	1765 3345	1766 3346	1767 3347	1768 3350	1769 3351	1770 3352	1771 3353	1772 3354	1773 3355	1774 3356	1775 3357
06F –	1776 3360	1777 3361	1778 3362	1779 3363	1780 3364	1781 3365	1782 3366	1783 3367	1784 3370	1785 3371	1786 3372	1787 3373	1788 3374	1789 3375	1790 3376	1791 3377
070 –	1792 3400	1793 3401	1794 3402	1795 3403	1796 3404	1797 3405	1798 3406	1799 3407	1800 3410	1801 3411	1802 3412	1803 3413	1804 3414	1805 3415	1806 3416	1807 3417
071 –	1808 3420	1809 3421	1810 3422	1811 3423	1812 3424	1813 3425	1814 3426	1815 3427	1816 3430	1817 3431	1818 3432	1819 3433	1820 3434	1821 3435	1822 3436	1823 3437
072 –	1824 3440	1825 3441	1826 3442	1827 3443	1828 3444	1829 3445	1830 3446	1831 3447	1832 3450	1833 3451	1834 3452	1835 3453	1836 3454	1837 3455	1838 3456	1839 3457
073 –	1840 3460	1841 3461	1842 3462	1843 3463	1844 3464	1845 3465	1846 3466	1847 3467	1848 3470	1849 3471	1850 3472	1851 3473	1852 3474	1853 3475	1854 3476	1855 3477
074 –	1856 3500	1857 3501	1858 3502	1859 3503	1860 3504	1861 3505	1862 3506	1863 3507	1864 3510	1865 3511	1866 3512	1867 3513	1868 3514	1869 3515	1870 3516	1871 3517
075 –	1872 3520	1873 3521	1874 3522	1875 3523	1876 3524	1877 3525	1878 3526	1879 3527	1880 3530	1881 3531	1882 3532	1883 3533	1884 3534	1885 3535	1886 3536	1887 3537
076 –	1888 3540	1889 3541	1890 3542	1891 3543	1892 3544	1893 3545	1894 3546	1895 3547	1896 3550	1897 3551	1898 3552	1899 3553	1900 3554	1901 3555	1902 3556	1903 3557
077 –	1904 3560	1905 3561	1906 3562	1907 3563	1908 3564	1909 3565	1910 3566	1911 3567	1912 3570	1913 3571	1914 3572	1915 3573	1916 3574	1917 3575	1918 3576	1919 3577
078 –	1920 3600	1921 3601	1922 3602	1923 3603	1924 3604	1925 3605	1926 3606	1927 3607	1928 3610	1929 3611	1930 3612	1931 3613	1932 3614	1933 3615	1934 3616	1935 3617
079 –	1936 3620	1937 3621	1938 3622	1939 3623	1940 3624	1941 3625	1942 3626	1943 3627	1944 3630	1945 3631	1946 3632	1947 3633	1948 3634	1949 3635	1950 3636	1951 3637
07A –	1952 3640	1953 3641	1954 3642	1955 3643	1956 3644	1957 3645	1958 3646	1959 3647	1960 3650	1961 3651	1962 3652	1963 3653	1964 3654	1965 3655	1966 3656	1967 3657
07B –	1968 3660	1969 3661	1970 3662	1971 3663	1972 3664	1973 3665	1974 3666	1975 3667	1976 3670	1977 3671	1978 3672	1979 3673	1980 3674	1981 3675	1982 3676	1983 3677
07C –	1984 3700	1985 3701	1986 3702	1987 3703	1988 3704	1989 3705	1990 3706	1991 3707	1992 3710	1993 3711	1994 3712	1995 3713	1996 3714	1997 3715	1998 3716	1999 3717
07D –	2000 3720	2001 3721	2002 3722	2003 3723	2004 3724	2005 3725	2006 3726	2007 3727	2008 3730	2009 3731	2010 3732	2011 3733	2012 3734	2013 3735	2014 3736	2015 3737
07E –	2016 3740	2017 3741	2018 3742	2019 3743	2020 3744	2021 3745	2022 3746	2023 3747	2024 3750	2025 3751	2026 3752	2027 3753	2028 3754	2029 3755	2030 3756	2031 3757
07F –	2032 3760	2033 3761	2034 3762	2035 3763	2036 3764	2037 3765	2038 3766	2039 3767	2040 3770	2041 3771	2042 3772	2043 3773	2044 3774	2045 3775	2046 3776	2047 3777

HEXADECIMAL – DECIMAL – OCTAL CONVERSIONS

	0	1	2	3	4	5	6	7	8	9	A	B	C	D	E	F
080 –	2048 4000	2049 4001	2050 4002	2051 4003	2052 4004	2053 4005	2054 4006	2055 4007	2056 4010	2057 4011	2058 4012	2059 4013	2060 4014	2061 4015	2062 4016	2063 4017
081 –	2064 4020	2065 4021	2066 4022	2067 4023	2068 4024	2069 4025	2070 4026	2071 4027	2072 4030	2073 4031	2074 4032	2075 4033	2076 4034	2077 4035	2078 4036	2079 4037
082 –	2080 4040	2081 4041	2082 4042	2083 4043	2084 4044	2085 4045	2086 4046	2087 4047	2088 4050	2089 4051	2090 4052	2091 4053	2092 4054	2093 4055	2094 4056	2095 4057
083 –	2096 4060	2097 4061	2098 4062	2099 4063	2100 4064	2101 4065	2102 4066	2103 4067	2104 4070	2105 4071	2106 4072	2107 4073	2108 4074	2109 4075	2110 4076	2111 4077
084 –	2112 4100	2113 4101	2114 4102	2115 4103	2116 4104	2117 4105	2118 4106	2119 4107	2120 4110	2121 4111	2122 4112	2123 4113	2124 4114	2125 4115	2126 4116	2127 4117
085 –	2128 4120	2129 4121	2130 4122	2131 4123	2132 4124	2133 4125	2134 4126	2135 4127	2136 4130	2137 4131	2138 4132	2139 4133	2140 4134	2141 4135	2142 4136	2143 4137
086 –	2144 4140	2145 4141	2146 4142	2147 4143	2148 4144	2149 4145	2150 4146	2151 4147	2152 4150	2153 4151	2154 4152	2155 4153	2156 4154	2157 4155	2158 4156	2159 4157
087 –	2160 4160	2161 4161	2162 4162	2163 4163	2164 4164	2165 4165	2166 4166	2167 4167	2168 4170	2169 4171	2170 4172	2171 4173	2172 4174	2173 4175	2174 4176	2175 4177
088 –	2176 4200	2177 4201	2178 4202	2179 4203	2180 4204	2181 4205	2182 4206	2183 4207	2184 4210	2185 4211	2186 4212	2187 4213	2188 4214	2189 4215	2190 4216	2191 4217
089 –	2192 4220	2193 4221	2194 4222	2195 4223	2196 4224	2197 4225	2198 4226	2199 4227	2200 4230	2201 4231	2202 4232	2203 4233	2204 4234	2205 4235	2206 4236	2207 4237
08A –	2208 4240	2209 4241	2210 4242	2211 4243	2212 4244	2213 4245	2214 4246	2215 4247	2216 4250	2217 4251	2218 4252	2219 4253	2220 4254	2221 4255	2222 4256	2223 4257
08B –	2224 4260	2225 4261	2226 4262	2227 4263	2228 4264	2229 4265	2230 4266	2231 4267	2232 4270	2233 4271	2234 4272	2235 4273	2236 4274	2237 4275	2238 4276	2239 4277
08C –	2240 4300	2241 4301	2242 4302	2243 4303	2244 4304	2245 4305	2246 4306	2247 4307	2248 4310	2249 4311	2250 4312	2251 4313	2252 4314	2253 4315	2254 4316	2255 4317
08D –	2256 4320	2257 4321	2258 4322	2259 4323	2260 4324	2261 4325	2262 4326	2263 4327	2264 4330	2265 4331	2266 4332	2267 4333	2268 4334	2269 4335	2270 4336	2271 4337
08E –	2272 4340	2273 4341	2274 4342	2275 4343	2276 4344	2277 4345	2278 4346	2279 4347	2280 4350	2281 4351	2282 4352	2283 4353	2284 4354	2285 4355	2286 4356	2287 4357
08F –	2288 4360	2289 4361	2290 4362	2291 4363	2292 4364	2293 4365	2294 4366	2295 4367	2296 4370	2297 4371	2298 4372	2299 4373	2300 4374	2301 4375	2302 4376	2303 4377
090 –	2304 4400	2305 4401	2306 4402	2307 4403	2308 4404	2309 4405	2310 4406	2311 4407	2312 4410	2313 4411	2314 4412	2315 4413	2316 4414	2317 4415	2318 4416	2319 4417
091 –	2320 4420	2321 4421	2322 4422	2323 4423	2324 4424	2325 4425	2326 4426	2327 4427	2328 4430	2329 4431	2330 4432	2331 4433	2332 4434	2333 4435	2334 4436	2335 4437
092 –	2336 4440	2337 4441	2338 4442	2339 4443	2340 4444	2341 4445	2342 4446	2343 4447	2344 4450	2345 4451	2346 4452	2347 4453	2348 4454	2349 4455	2350 4456	2351 4457
093 –	2352 4460	2353 4461	2354 4462	2355 4463	2356 4464	2357 4465	2358 4466	2359 4467	2360 4470	2361 4471	2362 4472	2363 4473	2364 4474	2365 4475	2366 4476	2367 4477
094 –	2368 4500	2369 4501	2370 4502	2371 4503	2372 4504	2373 4505	2374 4506	2375 4507	2376 4510	2377 4511	2378 4512	2379 4513	2380 4514	2381 4515	2382 4516	2383 4517
095 –	2384 4520	2385 4521	2386 4522	2387 4523	2388 4524	2389 4525	2390 4526	2391 4527	2392 4530	2393 4531	2394 4532	2395 4533	2396 4534	2397 4535	2398 4536	2399 4537
096 –	2400 4540	2401 4541	2402 4542	2403 4543	2404 4544	2405 4545	2406 4546	2407 4547	2408 4550	2409 4551	2410 4552	2411 4553	2412 4554	2413 4555	2414 4556	2415 4557
097 –	2416 4560	2417 4561	2418 4562	2419 4563	2420 4564	2421 4565	2422 4566	2423 4567	2424 4570	2425 4571	2426 4572	2427 4573	2428 4574	2429 4575	2430 4576	2431 4577
098 –	2432 4600	2433 4601	2434 4602	2435 4603	2436 4604	2437 4605	2438 4606	2439 4607	2440 4610	2441 4611	2442 4612	2443 4613	2444 4614	2445 4615	2446 4616	2447 4617
099 –	2448 4620	2449 4621	2450 4622	2451 4623	2452 4624	2453 4625	2454 4626	2455 4627	2456 4630	2457 4631	2458 4632	2459 4633	2460 4634	2461 4635	2462 4636	2463 4637
09A –	2464 4640	2465 4641	2466 4642	2467 4643	2468 4644	2469 4645	2470 4646	2471 4647	2472 4650	2473 4651	2474 4652	2475 4653	2476 4654	2477 4655	2478 4656	2479 4657
09B –	2480 4660	2481 4661	2482 4662	2483 4663	2484 4664	2485 4665	2486 4666	2487 4667	2488 4670	2489 4671	2490 4672	2491 4673	2492 4674	2493 4675	2494 4676	2495 4677
09C –	2496 4700	2497 4701	2498 4702	2499 4703	2500 4704	2501 4705	2502 4706	2503 4707	2504 4710	2505 4711	2506 4712	2507 4713	2508 4714	2509 4715	2510 4716	2511 4717
09D –	2512 4720	2513 4721	2514 4722	2515 4723	2516 4724	2517 4725	2518 4726	2519 4727	2520 4730	2521 4731	2522 4732	2523 4733	2524 4734	2525 4735	2526 4736	2527 4737
09E –	2528 4740	2529 4741	2530 4742	2531 4743	2532 4744	2533 4745	2534 4746	2535 4747	2536 4750	2537 4751	2538 4752	2539 4753	2540 4754	2541 4755	2542 4756	2543 4757
09F –	2544 4760	2545 4761	2546 4762	2547 4763	2548 4764	2549 4765	2550 4766	2551 4767	2552 4770	2553 4771	2554 4772	2555 4773	2556 4774	2557 4775	2558 4776	2559 4777
0A0 –	2560 5000	2561 5001	2562 5002	2563 5003	2564 5004	2565 5005	2566 5006	2567 5007	2568 5010	2569 5011	2570 5012	2571 5013	2572 5014	2573 5015	2574 5016	2575 5017
0A1 –	2576 5020	2577 5021	2578 5022	2579 5023	2580 5024	2581 5025	2582 5026	2583 5027	2584 5030	2585 5031	2586 5032	2587 5033	2588 5034	2589 5035	2590 5036	2591 5037
0A2 –	2592 5040	2593 5041	2594 5042	2595 5043	2596 5044	2597 5045	2598 5046	2599 5047	2600 5050	2601 5051	2602 5052	2603 5053	2604 5054	2605 5055	2606 5056	2607 5057
0A3 –	2608 5061	2609 5061	2610 5062	2611 5063	2612 5064	2613 5065	2614 5066	2615 5067	2616 5070	2617 5071	2618 5072	2619 5073	2620 5074	2621 5075	2622 5076	2623 5077
0A4 –	2624 5100	2625 5101	2626 5102	2627 5103	2628 5104	2629 5105	2630 5106	2631 5107	2632 5110	2633 5111	2634 5112	2635 5113	2636 5114	2637 5115	2638 5116	2639 5117
0A5 –	2640 5120	2641 5121	2642 5122	2643 5123	2644 5124	2645 5125	2646 5126	2647 5127	2648 5130	2649 5131	2650 5132	2651 5133	2652 5134	2653 5135	2654 5136	2655 5137
0A6 –	2656 5140	2657 5141	2658 5142	2659 5143	2660 5144	2661 5145	2662 5146	2663 5147	2664 5150	2665 5151	2666 5152	2667 5153	2668 5154	2669 5155	2670 5156	2671 5157
0A7 –	2672 5160	2673 5161	2674 5162	2675 5163	2676 5164	2677 5165	2678 5166	2679 5167	2680 5170	2681 5171	2682 5172	2683 5173	2684 5174	2685 5175	2686 5176	2687 5177
0A8 –	2688 5200	2689 5201	2690 5202	2691 5203	2692 5204	2693 5205	2694 5206	2695 5207	2696 5210	2697 5211	2698 5212	2699 5213	2700 5214	2701 5215	2702 5216	2703 5217
0A9 –	2704 5220	2705 5221	2706 5222	2707 5223	2708 5224	2709 5225	2710 5226	2711 5227	2712 5230	2713 5231	2714 5232	2715 5233	2716 5234	2717 5235	2718 5236	2719 5237
0AA –	2720 5240	2721 5241	2722 5242	2723 5243	2724 5244	2725 5245	2726 5246	2727 5247	2728 5250	2729 5251	2730 5252	2731 5253	2732 5254	2733 5255	2734 5256	2735 5257
0AB –	2736 5260	2737 5261	2738 5262	2739 5263	2740 5264	2741 5265	2742 5266	2743 5267	2744 5270	2745 5271	2746 5272	2747 5273	2748 5274	2749 5275	2750 5276	2751 5277
0AC –	2752 5300	2753 5301	2754 5302	2755 5303	2756 5304	2757 5305	2758 5306	2759 5307	2760 5310	2761 5311	2762 5312	2763 5313	2764 5314	2765 5315	2766 5316	2767 5317
0AD –	2768 5320	2769 5321	2770 5322	2771 5323	2772 5324	2773 5325	2774 5326	2775 5327	2776 5330	2777 5331	2778 5332	2779 5333	2780 5334	2781 5335	2782 5336	2783 5337
0AE –	2784 5340	2785 5341	2786 5342	2787 5343	2788 5344	2789 5345	2790 5346	2791 5347	2792 5350	2793 5351	2794 5352	2795 5353	2796 5354	2797 5355	2798 5356	2799 5357
0AF –	2800 5360	2801 5361	2802 5362	2803 5363	2804 5364	2805 5365	2806 5366	2807 5367	2808 5370	2809 5371	2810 5372	2811 5373	2812 5374	2813 5375	2814 5376	2815 5377
0B0 –	2816 5400	2817 5401	2818 5402	2819 5403	2820 5404	2821 5405	2822 5406	2823 5407	2824 5410	2825 5411	2826 5412	2827 5413	2828 5414	2829 5415	2830 5416	2831 5417
0B1 –	2832 5420	2833 5421	2834 5422	2835 5423	2836 5424	2837 5425	2838 5426	2839 5427	2840 5430	2841 5431	2842 5432	2843 5433	2844 5434	2845 5435	2846 5436	2847 5437
0B2 –	2848 5440	2849 5441	2850 5442	2851 5443	2852 5444	2853 5445	2854 5446	2855 5447	2856 5450	2857 5451	2858 5452	2859 5453	2860 5454	2861 5455	2862 5456	2863 5457
0B3 –	2864 5460	2865 5461	2866 5462	2867 5463	2868 5464	2869 5465	2870 5466	2871 5467	2872 5470	2873 5471	2874 5472	2875 5473	2876 5474	2877 5475	2878 5476	2879 5477
0B4 –	2880 5500	2881 5501	2882 5502	2883 5503	2884 5504	2885 5505	2886 5506	2887 5507	2888 5510	2889 5511	2890 5512	2891 5513	2892 5514	2893 5515	2894 5516	2895 5517
0B5 –	2896 5520	2897 5521	2898 5522	2899 5523	2900 5524	2901 5525	2902 5526	2903 5527	2904 5530	2905 5531	2906 5532	2907 5533	2908 5534	2909 5535	2910 5536	2911 5537
0B6 –	2912 5540	2913 5541	2914 5542	2915 5543	2916 5544	2917 5545	2918 5546	2919 5547	2920 5550	2921 5551	2922 5552	2923 5553	2924 5554	2925 5555	2926 5556	2927 5557
0B7 –	2928 5560	2929 5561	2930 5562	2931 5563	2932 5564	2933 5565	2934 5566	2935 5567	2936 5570	2937 5571	2938 5572	2939 5573	2940 5574	2941 5575	2942 5576	2943 5577
0B8 –	2944 5600	2945 5601	2946 5602	2947 5603	2948 5604	2949 5605	2950 5606	2951 5607	2952 5610	2953 5611	2954 5612	2955 5613	2956 5614	2957 5615	2958 5616	2959 5617
0B9 –	2960 5620	2961 5621	2962 5622	2963 5623	2964 5624	2965 5625	2966 5626	2967 5627	2968 5630	2969 5631	2970 5632	2971 5633	2972 5634	2973 5635	2974 5636	2975 5637
0BA –	2976 5640	2977 5641	2978 5642	2979 5643	2980 5644	2981 5645	2982 5646	2983 5647	2984 5650	2985 5651	2986 5652	2987 5653	2988 5654	2989 5655	2990 5656	2991 5657
0BB –	2992 5660	2993 5661	2994 5662	2995 5663	2996 5664	2997 5665	2998 5666	2999 5667	3000 5670	3001 5671	3002 5672	3003 5673	3004 5674	3005 5675	3006 5676	3007 5677
0BC –	3008 5700	3009 5701	3010 5702	3011 5703	3012 5704	3013 5705	3014 5706	3015 5707	3016 5710	3017 5711	3018 5712	3019 5713	3020 5714	3021 5715	3022 5716	3023 5717
0BD –	3024 5720	3025 5721	3026 5722	3027 5723	3028 5724	3029 5725	3030 5726	3031 5727	3032 5730	3033 5731	3034 5732	3035 5733	3036 5734	3037 5735	3038 5736	3039 5737
0BE –	3040 5740	3041 5741	3042 5742	3043 5743	3044 5744	3045 5745	3046 5746	3047 5747	3048 5750	3049 5751	3050 5752	3051 5753	3052 5754	3053 5755	3054 5756	3055 5757
0BF –	3056 5760	3057 5761	3058 5762	3059 5763	3060 5764	3061 5765	3062 5766	3063 5767	3064 5770	3065 5771	3066 5772	3067 5773	3068 5774	3069 5775	3070 5776	3071 5777

HEXADECIMAL – DECIMAL – OCTAL CONVERSIONS

	0	1	2	3	4	5	6	7	8	9	A	B	C	D	E	F
0C0 -	3072 6000	3073 6001	3074 6002	3075 6003	3076 6004	3077 6005	3078 6006	3079 6007	3080 6010	3081 6011	3082 6012	3083 6013	3084 6014	3085 6015	3086 6016	3087 6017
0C1 -	3088 6020	3089 6021	3090 6022	3091 6023	3092 6024	3093 6025	3094 6026	3095 6027	3096 6030	3097 6031	3098 6032	3099 6033	3100 6034	3101 6035	3102 6036	3103 6037
0C2 -	3104 6040	3105 6041	3106 6042	3107 6043	3108 6044	3109 6045	3110 6046	3111 6047	3112 6050	3113 6051	3114 6052	3115 6053	3116 6054	3117 6055	3118 6056	3119 6057
0C3 -	3120 6060	3121 6061	3122 6062	3123 6063	3124 6064	3125 6065	3126 6066	3127 6067	3128 6070	3129 6071	3130 6072	3131 6073	3132 6074	3133 6075	3134 6076	3135 6077
0C4 -	3136 6100	3137 6101	3138 6102	3139 6103	3140 6104	3141 6105	3142 6106	3143 6107	3144 6110	3145 6111	3146 6112	3147 6113	3148 6114	3149 6115	3150 6116	3151 6117
0C5 -	3152 6120	3153 6121	3154 6122	3155 6123	3156 6124	3157 6125	3158 6126	3159 6127	3160 6130	3161 6131	3162 6132	3163 6133	3164 6134	3165 6135	3166 6136	3167 6137
0C6 -	3168 6140	3169 6141	3170 6142	3171 6143	3172 6144	3173 6145	3174 6146	3175 6147	3176 6150	3177 6151	3178 6152	3179 6153	3180 6154	3181 6155	3182 6156	3183 6157
0C7 -	3184 6160	3185 6161	3186 6162	3187 6163	3188 6164	3189 6165	3190 6166	3191 6167	3192 6170	3193 6171	3194 6172	3195 6173	3196 6174	3197 6175	3198 6176	3199 6177
0C8 -	3200 6200	3201 6201	3202 6202	3203 6203	3204 6204	3205 6205	3206 6206	3207 6207	3208 6210	3209 6211	3210 6212	3211 6213	3212 6214	3213 6215	3214 6216	3215 6217
0C9 -	3216 6220	3217 6221	3218 6222	3219 6223	3220 6224	3221 6225	3222 6226	3223 6227	3224 6230	3225 6231	3226 6232	3227 6233	3228 6234	3229 6235	3230 6236	3231 6237
0CA -	3232 6240	3233 6241	3234 6242	3235 6243	3236 6244	3237 6245	3238 6246	3239 6247	3240 6250	3241 6251	3242 6252	3243 6253	3244 6254	3245 6255	3246 6256	3247 6257
0CB -	3248 6260	3249 6261	3250 6262	3251 6263	3252 6264	3253 6265	3254 6266	3255 6267	3256 6270	3257 6271	3258 6272	3259 6273	3260 6274	3261 6275	3262 6276	3263 6277
0CC -	3264 6300	3265 6301	3266 6302	3267 6303	3268 6304	3269 6305	3270 6306	3271 6307	3272 6310	3273 6311	3274 6312	3275 6313	3276 6314	3277 6315	3278 6316	3279 6317
0CD -	3280 6320	3281 6321	3282 6322	3283 6323	3284 6324	3285 6325	3286 6326	3287 6327	3288 6330	3289 6331	3290 6332	3291 6333	3292 6334	3293 6335	3294 6336	3295 6337
0CE -	3296 6340	3297 6341	3298 6342	3299 6343	3300 6344	3301 6345	3302 6346	3303 6347	3304 6350	3305 6351	3306 6352	3307 6353	3308 6354	3309 6355	3310 6356	3311 6357
0CF -	3312 6360	3313 6361	3314 6362	3315 6363	3316 6364	3317 6365	3318 6366	3319 6367	3320 6370	3321 6371	3322 6372	3323 6373	3324 6374	1325 6375	3326 6376	3327 6377
0D0 -	3328 6400	3329 6401	3330 6402	3331 6403	3332 6404	3333 6405	3334 6406	3335 6407	3336 6410	3337 6411	3338 6412	3339 6413	3340 6414	3341 6415	3342 6416	3343 6417
0D1 -	3344 6420	3345 6421	3346 6422	3347 6423	3348 6424	3349 6425	3350 6426	3351 6427	3352 6430	3353 6431	3354 6432	3355 6433	3356 6434	3357 6435	3358 6436	3359 6437
0D2 -	3360 6440	3361 6441	3362 6442	3363 6443	3364 6444	3365 6445	3366 6446	3367 6447	3368 6450	3369 6451	3370 6452	3371 6453	3372 6454	3373 6455	3374 6456	3375 6457
0D3 -	3376 6460	3377 6461	3378 6462	3379 6463	3380 6464	3381 6465	3382 6466	3383 6467	3384 6470	3385 6471	3386 6472	3387 6473	3388 6474	3389 6475	3390 6476	3391 6477
0D4 -	3392 6500	3393 6501	3394 6502	3395 6503	3396 6504	3397 6505	3398 6506	3399 6507	3400 6510	3401 6511	3402 6512	3403 6513	3404 6514	3405 6515	3406 6516	3407 6517
0D5 -	3408 6520	3409 6521	3410 6522	3411 6523	3412 6524	3413 6525	3414 6526	3415 6527	3416 6530	3417 6531	3418 6532	3419 6533	3420 6534	3421 6535	3422 6536	3423 6537
0D6 -	3424 6540	3425 6541	3426 6542	3427 6543	3428 6544	3429 6545	3430 6546	3431 6547	3432 6550	3433 6551	3434 6552	3435 6553	3436 6554	3437 6555	3438 6556	3439 6557
0D7 -	3440 6560	3441 6561	3442 6562	3443 6563	3444 6564	3445 6565	3446 6566	3447 6567	3448 6570	3449 6571	3450 6572	3451 6573	3452 6574	3453 6575	3454 6576	3455 6577
0D8 -	3456 6600	3457 6601	3458 6602	3459 6603	3460 6604	3461 6605	3462 6606	3463 6607	3464 6610	3465 6611	3466 6612	3467 6613	3468 6614	3469 6615	3470 6616	3471 6617
0D9 -	3472 6620	3473 6621	3474 6622	3475 6623	3476 6624	3477 6625	3478 6626	3479 6627	3480 6630	3481 6631	3482 6632	3483 6633	3484 6634	3485 6635	3486 6636	3487 6637
0DA -	3488 6640	3489 6641	3490 6642	3491 6643	3492 6644	3493 6645	3494 6646	3495 6647	3496 6650	3497 6651	3498 6652	3499 6653	3500 6654	3501 6655	3502 6656	3503 6657
0DB -	3504 6660	3505 6661	3506 6662	3507 6663	3508 6664	3509 6665	3510 6666	3511 6667	3512 6670	3513 6671	3514 6672	3515 6673	3516 6674	3517 6675	3518 6676	3519 6677
0DC -	3520 6700	3521 6701	3522 6702	3523 6703	3524 6704	3525 6705	3526 6706	3527 6707	3528 6710	3529 6711	3530 6712	3531 6713	3532 6714	3533 6715	3534 6716	3535 6717
0DD -	3536 6720	3537 6721	3538 6722	3539 6723	3540 6724	3541 6725	3542 6726	3543 6727	3544 6730	3545 6731	3546 6732	3547 6733	3548 6734	3549 6735	3550 6736	3551 6737
0DE -	3552 6740	3553 6741	3554 6742	3555 6743	3556 6744	3557 6745	3558 6746	3559 6747	3560 6750	3561 6751	3562 6752	3563 6753	3564 6754	3565 6755	3566 6756	3567 6757
0DF -	3568 6760	3569 6761	3570 6762	3571 6763	3572 6764	3573 6765	3574 6766	3575 6767	3576 6770	3577 6771	3578 6772	3579 6773	3580 6774	3581 6775	3582 6776	3583 6777
0E0 -	3584 7000	3585 7001	3586 7002	3587 7003	3588 7004	3589 7005	3590 7006	3591 7007	3592 7010	3593 7011	3594 7012	3595 7013	3596 7014	3597 7015	3598 7016	3599 7017
0E1 -	3600 7020	3601 7021	3602 7022	3603 7023	3604 7024	3605 7025	3606 7026	3607 7027	3608 7030	3609 7031	3610 7032	3611 7033	3612 7034	3613 7035	3614 7036	3615 7037
0E2 -	3616 7040	3617 7041	3618 7042	3619 7043	3620 7044	3621 7045	3622 7046	3623 7047	3624 7050	3625 7051	3626 7052	3627 7053	3628 7054	3629 7055	3630 7056	3631 7057
0E3 -	3632 7060	3633 7061	3634 7062	3635 7063	3636 7064	3637 7065	3638 7066	3639 7067	3640 7070	3641 7071	3642 7072	3643 7073	3644 7074	3645 7075	3646 7076	3647 7077
0E4 -	3648 7100	3649 7101	3650 7102	3651 7103	3652 7104	3653 7105	3654 7106	3655 7107	3656 7110	3657 7111	3658 7112	3659 7113	3660 7114	3661 7115	3662 7116	3663 7117
0E5 -	3664 7120	3665 7121	3666 7122	3667 7123	3668 7124	3669 7125	3670 7126	3671 7127	3672 7130	3673 7131	3674 7132	3675 7133	3676 7134	3677 7135	3678 7136	3679 7137
0E6 -	3680 7140	3681 7141	3682 7142	3683 7143	3684 7144	3685 7145	3686 7146	3687 7147	3688 7150	3689 7151	3690 7152	3691 7153	3692 7154	3693 7155	3694 7156	3695 7157
0E7 -	3696 7160	3697 7161	3698 7162	3699 7163	3700 7164	3701 7165	3702 7166	3703 7167	3704 7170	3705 7171	3706 7172	3707 7173	3708 7174	3709 7175	3710 7176	3711 7177
0E8 -	3712 7200	3713 7201	3714 7202	3715 7203	3716 7204	3717 7205	3718 7206	3719 7207	3720 7210	3721 7211	3722 7212	3723 7213	3724 7214	3725 7215	3726 7216	3727 7217
0E9 -	3728 7220	3729 7221	3730 7222	3731 7223	3732 7224	3733 7225	3734 7226	3735 7227	3736 7230	3737 7231	3738 7232	3739 7233	3740 7234	3741 7235	3742 7236	3743 7237
0EA -	3744 7240	3745 7241	3746 7242	3747 7243	3748 7244	3749 7245	3750 7246	3751 7247	3752 7250	3753 7251	3754 7252	3755 7253	3756 7254	3757 7255	3758 7256	3759 7257
0EB -	3760 7260	3761 7261	3762 7262	3763 7263	3764 7264	3765 7265	3766 7266	3767 7267	3768 7270	3769 7271	3770 7272	3771 7273	3772 7274	3773 7275	3774 7276	3775 7277
0EC -	3776 7300	3777 7301	3778 7302	3779 7303	3780 7304	3781 7305	3782 7306	3783 7307	3784 7310	3785 7311	3786 7312	3787 7313	3788 7314	3789 7315	3790 7316	3791 7317
0ED -	3792 7320	3793 7321	3794 7322	3795 7323	3796 7324	3797 7325	3798 7326	3799 7327	3800 7330	3801 7331	3802 7332	3803 7333	3804 7334	3805 7335	3806 7336	3807 7337
0EE -	3808 7340	3809 7341	3810 7342	3811 7343	3812 7344	3813 7345	3814 7346	3815 7347	3816 7350	3817 7351	3818 7352	3819 7353	3820 7354	3821 7355	3822 7356	3823 7357
0EF -	3824 7360	3825 7361	3826 7362	3827 7363	3828 7364	3829 7365	3830 7366	3831 7367	3832 7370	3833 7371	3834 7372	3835 7373	3836 7374	3837 7375	3838 7376	3839 7377
0F0 -	3840 7400	3841 7401	3842 7402	3843 7403	3844 7404	3845 7405	3846 7406	3847 7407	3848 7410	3849 7411	3850 7412	3851 7413	3852 7414	3853 7415	3854 7416	3855 7417
0F1 -	3856 7420	3857 7421	3858 7422	3859 7423	3860 7424	3861 7425	3862 7426	3863 7427	3864 7430	3865 7431	3866 7432	3867 7433	3868 7434	3869 7435	3870 7436	3871 7437
0F2 -	3872 7440	3873 7441	3874 7442	3875 7443	3876 7444	3877 7445	3878 7446	3879 7447	3880 7450	3881 7451	3882 7452	3883 7453	3884 7454	3885 7455	3886 7456	3887 7457
0F3 -	3888 7460	3889 7461	3890 7462	3891 7463	3892 7464	3893 7465	3894 7466	3895 7467	3896 7470	3897 7471	3898 7472	3899 7473	3900 7474	3901 7475	3902 7476	3903 7477
0F4 -	3904 7500	3905 7501	3906 7502	3907 7503	-3908 7504	-3909 7505	3910 7506	3911 7507	3912 7510	3913 7511	3914 7512	3915 7513	3916 7514	3917 7515	3918 7516	3919 7517
0F5 -	3920 7520	3921 7521	3922 7522	3923 7523	3924 7524	3925 7525	3926 7526	3927 7527	3928 7530	3929 7531	3930 7532	3931 7533	3932 7534	3933 7535	3934 7536	3935 7537
0F6 -	3936 7540	3937 7541	3938 7542	3939 7543	3940 7544	3941 7545	3942 7546	3943 7547	3944 7550	3945 7551	3946 7552	3947 7553	3948 7554	3949 7555	3950 7556	3951 7557
0F7 -	3952 7560	3953 7561	3954 7562	3955 7563	3956 7564	3957 7565	3958 7566	3959 7567	3960 7570	3961 7571	3962 7572	3963 7573	3964 7574	3965 7575	3966 7576	3967 7577
0F8 -	3968 7600	3969 7601	3970 7602	3971 7603	3972 7604	3973 7605	3974 7606	3975 7607	3976 7610	3977 7611	3978 7612	3979 7613	3980 7614	3981 7615	3982 7616	3983 7617
0F9 -	3984 7620	3985 7621	3986 7622	3987 7623	3988 7624	3989 7625	3990 7626	3991 7627	3992 7630	3993 7631	3994 7632	3995 7633	3996 7634	3997 7635	3998 7636	3999 7637
0FA -	4000 7640	4001 7641	4002 7642	4003 7643	4004 7644	4005 7645	4006 7646	4007 7647	4008 7650	4009 7651	4010 7652	4011 7653	4012 7654	4013 7655	4014 7656	4015 7657
0FB -	4016 7660	4017 7661	4018 7662	4019 7663	4020 7664	4021 7665	4022 7666	4023 7667	4024 7670	4025 7671	4026 7672	4027 7673	4028 7674	4029 7675	4030 7676	4031 7677
0FC -	4032 7700	4033 7701	4034 7702	4035 7703	4036 7704	4037 7705	4038 7706	4039 7707	4040 7710	4041 7711	4042 7712	4043 7713	4044 7714	4045 7715	4046 7716	4047 7717
0FD -	4048 7720	4049 7721	4050 7722	4051 7723	4052 7724	4053 7725	4054 7726	4055 7727	4056 7730	4057 7731	4058 7732	4059 7733	4060 7734	4061 7735	4062 7736	4063 7737
0FE -	4064 7740	4065 7741	4066 7742	4067 7743	4068 7744	4069 7745	4070 7746	4071 7747	4072 7750	4073 7751	4074 7752	4075 7753	4076 7754	4077 7755	4078 7756	4079 7757
0FF -	4080 7760	4081 7761	4082 7762	4083 7763	4084 7764	4085 7765	4086 7766	4087 7767	4088 7770	4089 7771	4090 7772	4091 7773	4092 7774	4093 7775	4094 7776	4095 7777